A BIOGRAPHICAL DICTIONARY
OF RAILWAY ENGINEERS

A BIOGRAPHICAL DICTIONARY
OF RAILWAY ENGINEERS

JOHN MARSHALL

DAVID & CHARLES
Newton Abbot   London   North Pomfret (Vt)   Vancouver

British Library Cataloguing in Publication Data

Marshall, John, b.1922 (May)
   Biographical dictionary of railway engineers.
   1. Railroad engineering – Biography
   I. Title
625.1'0092'2   TF139

ISBN 0–7153–7489–3

Library of Congress Catalog Card Number: 77–85011

Set by Trade Linotype Limited   Railway Terrace   Birmingham B7 5NG
and printed in Great Britain
by Biddles Limited   Guildford   Surrey
for David & Charles (Publishers) Limited
Brunel House   Newton Abbot   Devon

Published in the United States of America
by David & Charles Inc.
North Pomfret   Vermont 05053   USA

Published in Canada
by Douglas David & Charles Limited
1875 Welch Street   North Vancouver   BC

INTRODUCTION

This book is intended as a work of reference for the railway historian. To this end it includes an index of railways with which anyone working on the history of a particular railway can quickly locate the various engineers and others concerned with its construction and operation. There are numerous cross references. To pack the maximum information into the available space abbreviations are used extensively. These are listed, and it should be found that they offer little hindrance to the reader. Standard abbreviations of States in the USA are not listed. Place names not in Great Britain are either obvious, eg Vienna, or their location is given.

The book provides a quick reference to dates and places of birth and death and age at death, sources and further information. Many obscure and even unknown persons are included if they made important, progressive contributions to railway development. Important North American and European engineers are included because their work often had a universal influence.

The word 'engineer' derives from the Latin *ingenium* meaning 'skill', and the Old French *engigneor* and is closely related to 'ingenious'. The *Oxford English Dictionary* gives the meaning 'one who contrives, designs or invents, an author, designer'. The word 'engine' derives from the same sources and means primarily 'a device'.

This is the reason for the inclusion of some of the more important railway promoters and managers, because they 'engineered' railway schemes on which civil—that is, not military —engineers subsequently worked. In this respect Edward Pease (qv) was as much an 'engineer' of the Stockton & Darlington Railway as was George Stephenson.

Despite seven years of research there are some inevitable omissions. One important early locomotive engineer, John Gray, has defeated all efforts to find his dates and places of birth and death. For many others only the years have been found. The following names are omitted because of insufficient information: BREDIN, E. C.; BROTAN, Johann; CHALMERS, Walter; CUMMING, Christopher; FLAMME, Jean Baptiste; GOOCH, William Frederick; GREULICH, Karl; HAMMEL, Anton; HALL, Joseph; MELLING, John; OWEN, William George; PATERSON, W. A.; ROSS, A. P.; SHEPHERD, John; TAYLEUR, Charles; TODD, Charles.

The editor of *The Railway Magazine* has kindly consented to publish additional details which come to light from time to time, and if users of the *Dictionary* find they can fill gaps I shall be grateful for the information via the publishers.

Principal sources have been the proceedings of the Institutions of Civil, Mechanical and Locomotive Engineers; *The Engineer*; *Engineering*; *The Railway Gazette*; *The Locomotive*; *Dictionary of National Biography*; Boase, *Dictionary of English Biography*; *Dictionary of American Biography*, and various other foreign biographical dictionaries; Röll, *Enzyklopädie Eisenbahnwesens*; *The Times* and *The New York Times*; and also personal contact with descendents. Because of the enormous expense involved the General Register Office, Somerset House, has been little used. At best it can supply only a date, and there is no guarantee of that.

I must record my gratitude to the staffs of Manchester Public Library, Manchester University Library, and the Library of the National Railway Museum, York, and of libraries around Britain, USA, Canada and various European countries who have answered my enquiries. Mr John H. White Jr at the Smithsonian Institution, Washington, has provided some valuable information. The list of individuals who have helped is too long to include, but to all of them I extend my grateful thanks.
Bolton.   J.M.

ABBREVIATIONS USED IN
THE DICTIONARY

amalg	amalgamat/ion/ed
app	appoint/ed/ment
assoc	associat/ed/ion
asst	assistant
b	born
BA	British Association
B & O	Baltimore & Ohio RR
bd	board
BOT	Board of Trade
BR	British Rail/ways
bro	brother
C	century
CLC	Cheshire Lines Committee
CME	Chief Mechanical Engineer
CNR	Canadian National Railways
Coll	College
comm	committee
conj	conjunction
const	construct/ed/ion
CPR	Canadian Pacific Railway
CR	Caledonian Railway
C & W	carriage & wagon
cyl	cylinder
d	died, death
DAB	*Dictionary of American Biography*
dep	deputy
dept	department
dir	director
dist	district
div	division/al
DNB	*Dictionary of National Biography*
dr	daughter
drg	drawing
Ed	educated
ELR	East Lancashire Railway
emp	employ/ed/ment
eng	engineer
engg	engineering
Engg	*Engineering* (periodical)
f	father
FRGS	Fellow of the Royal Geographical Society

FRS	Fellow of the Royal Society
ft	foot/feet
g	gauge
G & SWR	Glasgow & South Western Railway
GB	Great Britain
GCR	Great Central Railway
GEC	General Electric Company
GER	Great Eastern Railway
GIPR	Great Indian Peninsula Railway
GJR	Grand Junction Railway
g mgr	general manager
GNR	Great Northern Railway
GN of S	Great North of Scotland Railway
GS & WR	Great Southern & Western Railway, Ireland
GTP	Grand Trunk Pacific Railway
GTR	Grand Trunk Railway, Canada
Gr Sch	Grammar School
GWR	Great Western Railway
H & BR	Hull & Barnsley Railway
hp	horse power
h p	high pressure
hq	headquarters
i/c	inside cylinders
ICE	Institution of Civil Engineers
ILE	Institution of Locomotive Engineers
IME	Institution of Mechanical Engineers
insp	inspector
Inst T	Institute of Transport
jn	junction
jt	joint
LBSCR	London, Brighton & South Coast Railway
LC & DR	London, Chatham & Dover Railway

LD & ECR	Lancashire, Derbyshire & East Coast Railway	pw	permanent way
LMS	London, Midland & Scottish Railway	R	railway
		rbg	rebuilding
LNER	London & North Eastern Railway	rbt	rebuilt
		RCH	Railway Clearing House
LNWR	London & North Western Railway	RCTS	Railway Correspondence & Travel Society
loco	locomotive	R Eng	*The Railway Engineer*
l p	low pressure	rep	representative
LSWR	London & South Western Railway	REs	Royal Engineers
		res eng	resident engineer
Lt R	Light Railway	ret	retire/d/ment
LT & SR	London, Tilbury & Southend Railway	RG	*Railway Gazette*
		RM	*The Railway Magazine*
LYR	Lancashire & Yorkshire Railway	Röll	Röll, Viktor, *Enzyklopädie Eisenbahnwesens*, Vienna
		RR	Railroad
m	married		
m	(after figures) metre	S Bz	*Schweizerische Bauzeitung*
M	member	Sch	School
M & CR	Maryport & Carlisle Railway	SE & CR	South Eastern & Chatham Railway
M & GN	Midland & Great Northern Joint Railway		
		sec	secretary
Met R	Metropolitan Railway	SER	South Eastern Railway
Met Dist R	Metropolitan District Railway	SLS	Stephenson Locomotive Society
mfr	manufacture/r	Soc	Society
mg	managing	SP	Southern Pacific Railroad
mg dir	managing director	SR	Southern Railway
MOT	Ministry of Transport	stn	station
MR	Midland Railway	supt	superintendent
MS & L	Manchester, Sheffield & Lincolnshire Railway		
		The Eng	*The Engineer*
NBR	North British Railway	Univ	University
NCC	Northern Counties Railway		
NER	North Eastern Railway	vdt	viaduct
NRM	National Railway Museum, York		
		wks	works
NSR	North Staffordshire Railway	wks mgr	works manager
NYT	*New York Times*	WW1	World War 1
		WW2	World War 2
o/c	outside cylinder/s		
op	opened	yd	yard
		yr	year
parl	parliamentary		
Prof	Professor	ZVDI	Zeitschrift des Vereines deutscher Ingenieure
PRR	Pennsylvania Railroad		
pub	published		

ABT, Roman

b Bünzen, Canton Aargau, Switzerland, 17.7.1850; d Lucerne 1.5.1933 aged 82. Swiss loco eng and inventor of the Abt system of rack Rs. Ed Federal Polytechnic, Zurich, 1869–72. 1872–5 trained in engg at the Swiss Central R wks at Olten under N. Riggenbach (qv). 1875–9 eng and wks mgr at the International Company for Mountain Rs at Aarau. 1879–81 chief eng in the Swiss R Dept, Berne. 1881–5 chief eng of the waterworks contractors of C. Zschokke & Terrier in Paris. While in France he invented, and patented in 1882, his rackrail system for which he became famous, using two or three toothed plates mounted side by side. In the double rack the tooth on one plate is opposite a gap in the other, and in the triple rack opposite half a gap in the next. By this system at least one tooth is in engagement all the time. It was first applied in 1884 on the mixed rack and adhesion Harz R from Blankenburg to Tanne in Braunschweig (Brunswick), with 11 rack sections. Soon afterwards he was granted the highest award by the Society of German Engs for the most ingenious device of the time. From 1885 he worked on his own, and 1887 moved to Lucerne where, 12 yrs later, he established a private local history museum. In 1890 his system was used on the metre-gauge Visp-Zermatt R; in 1891 on the standardgauge Erzberg R in Austria. By 1914 66 Rs including 12 in Switzerland and 14 in overseas countries had been equipped with Abt racks. In 1920–9 a further 6 sections were built making a world total of 72, totalling 1053 miles (1695km) to gauges of 600–1676mm (1ft 11½in–5ft 6in) and gradients up to 255°/oo (1 in 3.9). Abt was responsible for many of the projects as well as locos and rolling stock. On 10.7.1911 he was awarded hon Dr of Engg at Hanover Tech High Sch. For many yrs he was a member of Lucerne council. In 1892 he was a member of the bd of the St Gotthard R and in 1903 president until 1909 when it was taken over by the Swiss Federal R. He was deeply interested in cultural activities and in 1896–1906 was president of the Society of Arts in Lucerne. In 1904 he was a member of the Federal Arts Commission; 1905 president of the Swiss Confederation of Arts.
S.Bz V 102 1.7.1933 pp 11–12; Hefti, Walter. *Zahnradbahnen der Welt*, Basle 1971 pp 16–17

ADAMS, John Henry

b London 10.9.1860; d Congleton, Cheshire, 7.11.1915 aged 55. Loco supt, NSR. Third son of William A. (qv). Ed Brighton Gr Sch, and Thanet Coll, Margate, and privately in Brussels. 1877 apprenticed under his f at Stratford, GER, London. When his f became loco eng LSWR in 1878 he transferred to Nine Elms wks, London. On completion of his training he served as a fireman for 9 months and was later driver of goods and passenger trains for 15 months on the LSWR. He then spent a year with Tannett, Walker & Co, Leeds, to gain experience in hydraulic engg. From 7.1887 to 9.1898 he was loco C & W supt of the Donna Teresa Christina R, Brazil. In 1.1899 he became asst mgr of the SE & CR wks at Ashford, Kent. In 3.1902 he was app loco C & W supt, NSR, at Stoke on Trent, where he remained until his death. His colleague J. A. Hookham (qv) followed him from Ashford to become wks mgr at Stoke. A. introduced many improvements in the loco and wagon stock, and also introduced the madder lake livery for NSR locos. He fitted all tender axle-box bearings with a 3/16in (4mm) lining of white-metal and a lubricating pad in the bottom of the axle-box. He also introduced the 4-wheel bogie on engines and coaches, and from 1903 onwards he built all his new engines and nearly all his new coaches in the Stoke wks, after reorganising the wks and equipping them with up-to-date appliances and tools. Locos introduced by A. at Stoke included the L class 0–6–2T, 1903; M class 0–4–4T, 1907; H class 0–6–0, 1909; G class 4–4–0, 1910; K class 4–4–2T, 1911, and C class 0–6–4T, 1914. Elected MIME 1902.
Proc IME 1.1916 p 121; 'Manifold', *The North Staffordshire Railway*, 1952; Christiansen, R. and Miller, R. W., *The North Staffordshire Railway*, 1971

ADAMS, William

b Limehouse, London, 15.10.1823; d

Putney, London, 7.8.1904 aged 80.
Loco eng, N. London R, GER and
LSWR. Son of John Samuel A., res eng
of the E & W India Docks Co. Ed
privately at Margate. At 17 apprenticed
to Miller & Ravenhill, engs and millwrights, with whom he remained afterwards to work on marine engines at
Blackwall. About 1845 he went to Philip
Taylor & Co, first at Marseilles, then at
Genoa, again on marine engine work.
He then spent 4 yrs in the Sardinian
navy as eng. In Genoa he m. Isabella
Park, on 13.9.1852, and they had 10
children, the last in 1875. Returned to
England 1853 and was app loco supt, N.
London R, at Bow wks, which he had
then just helped to erect. For the NLR
he designed an i/c 4–4–0T with outside-
frame bogie. In 1865 he introduced his
famous loco bogie which became universally used. In 1868 he brought out his
o/c 4–4–0T. In 8.1873 he was app loco
supt of the GER at Stratford wks,
London. Here his o/c 4–4–0 of 1876–7
was not a great success, but he introduced the 2–6–0 or 'Mogul' type into
Britain. The engines were completed by
M. Bromley (qv) after A. had left.
Following the forced resignation of W.
G. Beattie (qv) on the LSWR, A. was
app his successor as loco supt at Nine
Elms, London, on 17.1.1878. Here he
achieved great success with his various
classes of o/c 4–4–0. The first of the
famous express 4–4–0s appeared in 1880.
Other outstanding designs were his 0–6–0
goods, 0–6–0, 4–4–2 and 0–4–4 tanks,
and the 'Jubilee' 0–4–2 passenger engines.
His engines had large bearing surfaces;
their simple design and robust construc-
tion enabled them to give long service.
Many lasted well into BR days, some
into the 1960s. A 4–4–0 is preserved at
York, a 4–4–2T on the Bluebell R.
Sussex, an 02 class 0–4–4T in the Isle of
Wight. A. was both MICE and MIME.
He ret 31.7.1895 and went to live at
Putney. He was an active musician and
had a wide circle of friends.
The Eng V 98 8.1904 p 164; *Engg* V 78
8.1904 p. 210; Min Proc ICE V 158
1903–4 p 426; Ellis, Hamilton. *Twenty
Locomotive Men*, 1958; Bradley, D. L.
Locos of the LSWR (RCTS) 1967

ADAMS, William Alexander

b Quintero, nr Valparaiso, Chile,
26.8.1821; d Gams, Herefordshire,
31.1.1896 aged 74.
Son of William Bridges A. (qv) who
had gone to South America for health
reasons. In 1826 moved to London
where, in 1836, A. began his training
in the carriage wks of his f and uncle
in Drury Lane. In 1837 he built a model
oscillating-cylinder engine. In 1843 his
f and uncle opened the Fairfield wks,
Bow, and A. was taken into partnership
in the building of road and rail carriages.
In 1846 he became mgr to Fox Henderson & Co, London Wks, Birmingham,
and later that year entered into partnership with George Allcock. In 1850 the
partnership was dissolved and he began
on his own account. He had become
MIME in 1848 and presented papers on
R carriage and wagon springs (Proc IME
1.1850 p 19; 4.1850 p 14) and on R
carrying stock (Proc IME 1.1851 p 10;
1852 p 206). In 1851 he started the
letting of R wagons on the purchase–
lease plan. In 1853 he took a leading
part in establishing the Midland Wagon
Wks at Rotherham, later moved to Birmingham. 1862 became dir of the
Birmingham Joint Stock Bank. 1863 A.
and his partner Henry Griffith sold their
business to the Midland Wagon Co in
which he retained his seat on the bd of
dirs. He also became a dir of Muntz's
Metal Co. 1873–4 he travelled extensively in the USA and formed the Union
Rolling Stock Co in USA for the purchase–lease of R wagons. A. was a JP
for Herefordshire and was a keen sports-
man. Elected MICE 1865.
Proc IME 1.1896 pp 91–2

ADAMS, William Bridges

b Madeley, Staffordshire, (?).(?).1797; d
Broadstairs, Kent, 23.7.1872 aged 75.
Loco eng and mfr; inventor of the steam
railcar. Son of a carriage builder, but
bad health forced him to seek recovery
in Chile where he remained until 1837.
While there he decided to take up R
engg and in 1838 he applied his inventive
talents to the production of a rail brake
which gripped the sides of the rail but
which could not be applied on the track
of the time. In 1843 he opened the Fair-

field Wks at Bow, London (later Bryant & May's match factory). His first product was a light hand-propelled inspection car for James Samuel (qv) on the Eastern Counties R. From this he developed his first steam railcar, the *Express*, which was tested on the ECR. It was followed by another, the *Fairfield*, for the Bristol & Exeter R, with a saloon coach seating 58 passengers. His next railcar, the *Enfield*, built for the Enfield branch of the ECR in 1849, had a separate 2–2–0 loco. In 5.1847 A. took out a patent for a rail fish plate. His most important invention to be applied to locos was the radial axlebox, first applied to a 2–4–2T built by Cross & Co, St Helens, for the St Helens R in 1863. It was A. who, in 1850, suggested the idea for the Crystal Palace which was developed by Paxton. A. was a prolific journalist, contributing to numerous papers, and was author of *English Pleasure Carriages* 1837; *Railways and Permanent Way* 1854; and *Roads and Rails* 1862. He was m 3 times: his first wife, Sarah (Flower), 1805–48, was a writer of hymns and poems. His dress was as unconventional as everything else about him and, detesting buttons, he devised a variety of devices for holding his clothing together. *Engg* V 14 26.7.1872 pp 63–4; *The Eng* V 34 26.7.72 p 52; *The Locomotive* 6. and 7. 1943 pp 80–2, 104–6; Ellis, Hamilton, *Twenty Locomotive Men* 1958 p 3

ADIE, Alexander James

b Edinburgh 16.12.1808; d nr Linlithgow 3.4.1879 aged 70.

Civil eng on Bolton & Preston and Edinburgh & Glasgow Rs. Son of Alexander A., mathematical instrument maker and optician. Ed Edinburgh High Sch and Univ. Apprenticed to James Jardine, civil eng, whom he afterwards assisted on various works. 1837 became res eng on Bolton & Preston R under J. U. Rastrick (qv), completing this in 1841. Notable masonry work included the famous 'flying arches' at Chorley and a skew bridge over the Lancaster Canal. During this period he gave valuable papers to the ICE on skew bridges and other aspects of his work. He made several important experiments on the expansion of stone by heat. He then

moved to Glasgow where he took charge of some colliery Rs, and on 19.3.1847 was app civil eng and mgr of the Edinburgh & Glasgow R. Resigned 2. 1863 when the E & G bd decided to have a res eng. Interested in horticulture and the fine arts. Became a member of the Royal Society of Edinburgh 1846. Details from Scottish Record Office (Henderson Collection GD.76/457)

ADDISON, John

b Liverpool 12.4.1820; d Maryport, Cumbria, 22.3.1903 aged 82.

Civil eng, later mgr, M & CR. In 10.1836 articled to Stephen Robinson of Hartlepool. Became res eng on Clarence & Hartlepool Jn R. He then spent a year at the Hartlepool Engg Wks to learn mech engg. 1839–40 he lectured on surveying, levelling and mech drg at Durham Univ. 1842 entered office of John and Benjamin Green, Newcastle. In 3.1844 A. was app to the staff of Locke & Errington, then engs of the Lancaster & Carlisle R and the CR. He continued with Locke and Errington on surveys of the Shrewsbury & Stafford, Shrewsbury & Wolverhampton, Hayton & Warrington and other lines. During the parliamentary contest between the CR and the G & SWR in 1845 A. was sent by the CR to survey a line through the Dalveen Pass connecting Thornhill on the G & SW with Elvanfoot on the CR with a view to combining the routes, but his report was hostile and the CR obtained its Act. A. was then app res eng on the S div of the CR on which he superintended construction of the first 30 miles. He also surveyed several other CR projects, including the Dumfries branch. In 12.1857 A. became mgr of the Maryport & Carlisle R, remaining there for 27 yrs until he ret at 64 on 1.3.1884 when he became a dir of the M & C. Became MICE 1.2.1859.

Min Proc ICE V 152 1902–3 p 315

AGNEW, William Alexander

b Newton Stewart, Wigtownshire, 9.11.1874; d Sutton, Surrey, 16.3.1958 aged 83.

Mech eng, London underground Rs. Ed Douglas Academy, Edinburgh, and Glasgow. After private tuition in electrical technology he was apprenticed in elec engg with King, Brown & Co, Edinburgh, continuing his studies at Heriot Watt Coll. Later engaged on power plant installation and on the original hydro-electric plant at Foyers on Loch Ness, as well as on an early experimental electric traction project for Glasgow Corpn in 1898. In 1900 employed in designing and building electric dynamos. 1901 joined staff of Glasgow Corpn Tramways Dept at the time of the electrification and was emp as emergency eng and staff instructor. His experience enabled him to write *The Electric Tramcar Handbook for Motormen, Inspectors and Depot Workers* which ran to many editions. Moved to London 1904 as rolling stock supt on the Metropolitan District R, then being electrified. He supervised the training of staff during the electrification and helped to prepare the first rule book for electric train working. In 1907 became mech eng to the District R Co, his jurisdiction being extended in 1912 to the London Electric Rs and in 1913 to the Central London R and the City & S London R. In 1921 he was app mech eng (Rs) to the Underground Electric Rs of London Ltd; this position became CME (Rs) in 1928. He continued at this post after the formation of the London Passenger Transport Bd in 7.1933 until he ret in 2.1935. On his retirement he wrote another book *Electric Trains*, designed to appeal more to the practical than to the tech man, but this book was not as popular as his earlier work. He was MIME, M Inst T and M Inst Psychology, but he gave most of his time and energy to the ILE, to which he was elected M in 1930 and president 1931–2. *RG* 21.3.1958; *Journal* ILE V 48 1958–9 p 150

AHRONS, Ernest Leopold

b Bradford 12.2.1866; d Nottingham 30.3.1926 aged 60.
Loco eng and writer. Ed Bradford Gr Sch, and Yorkshire Coll, Leeds, and at Hanover. 1885–8 pupil at Swindon, GWR. 1888–90 in Swindon drg office, and inspector of materials. 1890 chief draughtsman to Fleming, MacFarlane & Co, Middleton; then in the drg office of Beyer Peacock & Co, Manchester. 1892 app to the Ecole Khédiviale d'Arts

et Metiers, Boulac, Cairo, as eng and mgr of the govt workshops. Resigned in 1898 because of ill health and became eng in charge of the general dept of Henry Simon Ltd, Manchester. 1902–17 held various positions and during WW1 was trade officer at the Dept of Overseas Trade (Development and Intelligence) which he resigned in 1919. He made many contributions to *The Engineer*. Published works by A. include: *The development of British Locomotive design* 1914; *Repairing locomotives* 1920; *The Steam Railway Locomotive* 1920; *Lubrication of locomotives* 1921; *Steam engine valves and valve gears* 1921; *Steam locomotive construction and maintenance* 1921; *The British Steam Railway Locomotive 1825–1925* 1927; *Locomotive and train working in the latter part of the nineteenth century* 6 Vols 1951–4. A. was a founder member of the ILE, March 1911. IME 1898
Journal ILE V 16 1926 p 406; Proc IME 5.1926 p 631; *The Eng* V 141 4.1926 p 416

AIRD, Sir John

b London 3.12.1883; d Beaconsfield, Bucks, 6.1.1911 aged 77.
Civil eng and contractor. Only child of John A. (1800–76), for 20 yrs supt of the Phoenix Gas Co's station at Greenwich, and who started a contracting business in 1848, laying many gas and water mains in London. A. was ed privately at Greenwich and Southgate, London. At 18 he joined his f's business which became John Aird & Son. They removed the Crystal Palace, erected in Hyde Park by A's f for the 1851 Exhibition, and re-erected it at Sydenham. They then undertook gas and water contracts in London, Amsterdam, Copenhagen, Berlin, Moscow and elsewhere in Russia, France, Italy and Brazil. In 1860 the firm became Lucas & Aird. In 1876, on the d of his f, A. became chief partner. In 1895 the firm became John Aird & Co. During this period it carried out much R and dock work, including extensions of the Metropolitan District and St John's Wood lines in London, Royal Albert and Tilbury docks and E & W India docks extension, London, and the West Highland R in Scotland. The firm also completed the Manchester Ship

Canal. A's greatest work was the damming of the Nile, 1898–1902. Other dock works followed. He became AICE in 1859 and member of the Iron & Steel Institute 1887. In 1900 he became the first mayor of Paddington (see Armstrong, John). Created baronet 5.3.1901. On 6.9.1855 he m Sarah Smith (d 4.4.1909). They had 2 sons and 7 drs. *Engg* V 91 13.1.1911 (portrait); Min Proc ICE V 184 1910–11 p 351

ALCOCK, Edgar

b Macclesfield (?).(?).1877; d Leeds 2.3.1951 aged c 74.
Mgr and chairman of Hunslet Engine Co Ltd, Leeds. Apprenticed at Horwich LYR wks 1892–5, then at general engg shops in Lancashire and Cheshire. Returned to the LYR in 1898 as outdoor asst to the CME, Aspinall (qv). His first job was the erection of coal hoists at Goole, followed by similar work at Fleetwood and Manchester. In 1899 Hoy (qv), then CME, asked A. to investigate tyre failures on the 2–4–2Ts. A's next work was the supervision of the electro-pneumatic signalling installation at Bolton in 1904, the first of its kind in Britain. Soon after Hoy became mg dir of Beyer Peacock, Manchester, in 1904 A. was app asst wks mgr there. During this period the Garratt loco design was developed. In 1.1912 A. was app wks mgr at Hunslet Engine Co Ltd. In 1917 he became a dir while retaining his position as wks mgr. A. then became mg dir; the firm was expanded and larger locos were built, such as 5ft 6in (1.676m) gauge 0–8–0s of 130 tons for India and the world's largest 0–8–0T for the Yangste train ferry in China. From 1930 the firm began building diesel locos to which A. gave great encouragement. On the d of Alec Campbell in 3.1941 A. became chairman and retained joint mg directorship with John Alcock. Under his supervision the famous 'Austerity' 0–6–0ST was produced during WW2. Many are still at work on preserved steam Rs in Britain. For his work in WW2 he received the OBE.
The Locomotive 4.1951 pp 58–9 (portrait)

ALLAN, Alexander

b Montrose, Scotland, (?).(?).1809; d Scarborough, Yorks, 2.6.1891 aged 82.

Loco eng, LNWR. Apprenticed to Gibb at Lochside nr Montrose. 1832 joined Robert Stephenson & Co at Newcastle where he saw the development of the 'Patentee' type 2–2–2. 1843 moved to Liverpool to work with George Forrester at the Vauxhall Foundry where he worked on the *Swiftsure* for the Liverpool & Manchester R. This engine had outside cylinders secured in double framing. In 2.1840 A. became wks mgr and asst supt of the Grand Jn R at Edge Hill, Liverpool, under Buddicom (qv). Trouble with crank axles on the i/c 2–2–0 and 2–2–2 types led to the introduction of an o/c design based on the Forrester *Swiftsure*. In 1843 the GJR wks were transferred to Crewe under Francis Trevithick (qv). In 9.1853 A. left Crewe to become loco supt on the Scottish Central R. In Scotland he took out several patents, chief being his straight-link valve gear in 1854. When the SCR amalgamated with the Caledonian R in 1865 A. became mgr of the Worcester Engine Wks until 1872 when he injured his back in an accident. He then ret to Scarborough. Elected MIME 1847, the year of the formation of the Institution.
Proc IME 1856 p 70 (valve gear); 1891 p 289; *The Locomotive* 2.1941 pp 31–6; *The Eng* V 71 6.1891 p 471

ALLCARD, William

b London 30.6.1809; d Rouen, France, 5.8.1861 aged 52.
Loco eng associated with Buddicom (qv). Member of a quaker family. At an early age apprenticed at Robert Stephenson & Co, Newcastle. He worked in the drg office, and also helped on the Leeds & Selby and Newcastle & Carlisle projects. 1826 transferred to Liverpool and took charge of preliminary work on Chat Moss on the Liverpool & Manchester R, and then on the Bolton & Leigh R. Early in 1828 app res eng of the middle portion of the L & M including Sankey vdt. At the opening he drove the *Comet* loco. He then took charge of the Liverpool end of the line and began the tunnel down to Lime Street station. Early in 1834 he was app res eng to the Birmingham-Stafford section of the Grand Jn R until the line opened in 7.1837 when he was awarded the maintenance contract. He also contracted for the

Lancaster & Preston Jn R, opened 26.6.1840, and for p w for the Sheffield & Manchester R, completed 12.1845. In 1841, when J. Locke (qv) began the Paris & Rouen R, A. with Buddicom, Thomas Brassey, and William Mackenzie (qqv) contracted for the supply of locos and rolling stock and established large works at Rouen. Here they both built and operated engines and trains, on the Paris & Rouen, Rouen & Havre, Dieppe, Paris & Caen and the Cherbourg Rs, from their openings until 1861. Although A. took no active part in operations after 1847 he remained a partner until his d. Elected MICE 1858. Min Proc ICE V 21 1861–2 pp 550–1

ALLEN, Horatio

b Schenectady, NY, USA, 10.5.1802; d Montrose, NJ, 1.1.1890 aged 87. American loco pioneer and civil eng. His f, Dr Benjamin A. was prof of mathematics and natural philosophy at Union Coll, NY, 1800–9. A. entered Columbia Coll in 1821 and graduated in 1823 with high honours in maths. After starting in law, he changed to engg and began with the Delaware & Hudson Canal Co under Judge Wright, the eng. 1824 app res eng of the Delaware & Susquehanna Canal and in 1825 res eng of the summit level of the Delaware & Hudson Canal under John B. Jervis (qv). Early in 1826 A. visited England to study the Stephenson loco and was app by the Delaware & Hudson Co to purchase rails in England for 16 miles (25.75km) of line from the company's mines in the Lackawanna Valley to the Lackawaxen, a tributary of the Delaware, and also for 4 locos to be built according to his specifications. At Liverpool A. met George Stephenson, then eng of the Liverpool & Manchester R, whom he consulted about his plans. One loco was ordered from Robert Stephenson & Co, Newcastle, and 3 from Foster, Rastrick & Co of Stourbridge. It was one of these, the *Stourbridge Lion*, which was the first loco to run in America. The locos arrived in NY in winter 1828–9 and were tested off the ground. It was not until 8.1829 that they were taken to the R. This began at Honesdale, Pa, ran about 600yd (550m) straight, then crossed the Lackawaxen

Creek on a curve of 750yd (686m) radius. A. drove the engine himself, but it proved too heavy and was withdrawn without going into traffic. In 1829 A. was app chief eng of the S Carolina RR, from Charleston SC to Augusta Ga, the first long R in USA. In 1832 the world's first articulated loco, a 2–2–0 + 0–2–2, was built to his design by the West Point Foundry, New York, for use on the SCR. In 1834 he m Mary Moncrief Simmons of Charleston and in 1835 they travelled abroad for 2 yrs. In 1837 A. was app principal asst eng of the Croton Aqueduct Dept and on completion of the aqueduct in 1842 he was chosen as one of the bd of water commissioners. At the same time he was consulting eng for the New York & Erie RR. In 1844 he became a member of Stillman, Allen & Co, proprietors of the Novelty Ironworks, building engines for steamships. His last official position was consulting eng of the Brooklyn Bridge. In 1870 he ret from active life and built a house at Montrose, NJ, where he settled down to a life of study and invention. He was credited with the invention of the bogie coach and an improved expansion valve gear for locos. President of the American Society of Civil Engineers 1872. Survived by a widow, 3 drs and a son.
The Eng V 69 24.1.1890; *Engg* V 49 3.1.1890 p 11; *DAB* V 1 p 193

ALLOTT, Charles Sneath

b Lincoln 17.5.1842; d Manchester 27.2.1907 aged 64. Civil eng and bridge builder. Pupil of L. H. Moorsom on Ringwood—Christchurch R, Hants. 1862 joined staff of Fairbairn Engg Co, Manchester, and remained there until liquidation of the co in 1875 when he was asst mgr. In this period he had charge of works including roofs of Albert Hall, and Liverpool Street station in London and bridges on the Intercolonial R, Canada. 1875 began on his own and built the iron vdt and bridges on the CLC between Manchester Central station and Cornbrook. He reported on all the LYR iron under-bridges and afterwards prepared drawings for strengthening many of them. Designed many new bridges for the LYR and other Rs. In 1897 he took his son Henry N. Allott into partnership under the name of C. S. Allott & Son. MIME 1891; also MICE and member of Liverpool Engg Soc and the Manchester Lit & Phil Soc.

Proc IME 3.1907 pp 379–80

ALLPORT, Sir James Joseph

b Birmingham 27.2.1811; d St Pancras, London, 25.4.1892 aged 81

Mgr, MS & L, MR. Son of William A., mfr of small arms. Ed in Belgium. In 1839 at age 28 he began in the service of the Birmingham & Derby R as agent and rep for traffic at Hampton, the jn with the London & Birmingham R. In 1843 he rose to become mgr of the B & D, steering the company through the fierce competition which ended in 4.1844 with its amalg with the Midland Counties and North Midland Rs to form the Midland R under George Hudson (qv) as chairman. Hudson made A. mgr of the Newcastle & Darlington R (later York, Newcastle & Berwick). In 1850 A. became mgr of the MS & L until 1853 when he returned to the MR as mgr. In his 27 yrs with the MR, except for a short break from 1858–60 as mgr of Palmer's Shipbuilding Co, Jarrow, he guided its growth from a local line into a major trunk R system extending from London to Carlisle. Under A. the MR was the first R to run 3rd class carriages on all trains, from 1872, and was the first line to abolish 2nd class carriages. The MR bought about 40 000 wagons used on its lines from former owners. He established standards of comfort and efficiency which placed the MR in the front rank of British Rs. At his ret in 1880 he was presented with a sum of £10 000 in token of the gratitude of the shareholders, and at the same time he was made a dir of the company. In 1883, he was sent to USA to report on the NYC, Pennsylvania and B & O RRs. He was knighted in 4.1884. From 1853–80 he was lieut-col in the Eng & R Volunteer Staff Corps. He was JP for the county and borough of Derby. Assoc MICE. His wife, dr of John Gold of Birmingham, d 1886 after a m life of 54 yrs. He d in the Midland Grand Hotel at St Pancras from acute inflamation of the lungs.

The Times 26.4.1892 p 6; *The R Eng*

5.1892 p 133; *The Eng* V 83 29.4.1892 p 365; Min Proc ICE V 114 1892–3 pp 390–6; Williams, F. S. *The Midland R* 1878; Dow, George, *Great Central* V 1 1959

ARMSTRONG, George

b Bewcastle, Cumberland, 5.4.1822; d Wolverhampton 11.7.1901 aged 79.

N div loco supt, GWR. Youngest son of Thomas A. (1785–1844) and bro of Joseph A. senior (qv). In 1824 the family returned to England from Canada and settled at Newburn on Tyne, Northumberland. At age 14 George began work at Walbottle Colly under Robert Hawthorn (qv), following his bro Joseph. After 4½ yrs, in 1840, he went with Joseph to the Hull & Selby R at Hull where he worked under John Gray (qv), loco supt, subsequently moving to Brighton with Joseph when Gray became loco supt on the London–Brighton R in 1845. After a short time he went to France where he worked as engine driver on the Northern R. In 1848, during the unsettled period of the second revolution, he returned to England and obtained employment as engine driver on the Shrewsbury & Chester R, so rejoining Joseph, and soon becoming loco foreman. In 1854 the S & C and the Shrewsbury & Birmingham R were taken over by the GWR and A. became a GWR employee. In 1860 he was associated with William Dean (qv) in taking over jointly with the LNWR the locos of the Birkenhead, Lancashire & Cheshire Jn R. When Joseph A. was app loco supt of the GWR at Swindon in 1864 George succeeded him as N Div loco supt at Wolverhampton, with William Dean as asst and wks mgr at Stafford Road wks. At Wolverhampton he was responsible for the maintenance of a great variety of locomotives from the Shrewsbury & Chester; Shrewsbury & Birmingham; Birkenhead–Chester; Oxford, Worcester & Wolverhampton; Newport, Abergavenny & Hereford, and Shrewsbury & Hereford Rs, and GWR engines designed by Gooch at Swindon and by Joseph A. at Wolverhampton. Under George A. in 1864–6 9 2–4–0Ts and 8 0–6–0Ts and in 1866 12 2–4–0 tender engines were built at Wolverhampton. Next came 60 0–6–0STs and nearly 100 0-4-2Ts, a type which was to remain a GWR standard for the next 90 years. In 1868 Dean was moved to Swindon to become chief asst loco supt under Joseph. A., thereby achieving superior status to George A. When Dean became GWR loco supt in 1877 George A. remained in charge at Wolverhampton. He refused to take orders from Dean, saying 'I only give orders not take them', and so Wolverhampton remained an empire on its own with its own distinctive loco livery. Dean wisely left Wolverhampton alone for the next 20 yrs. George A. ruled at Wolverhampton for 33 yrs during which 626 engines were built and 513 were rebuilt. In 1864-97 the number employed there rose from 750 to 1500 and in the N Div as a whole from 1650 to 4230. In 1897, at age 75, he ret. He maintained his contact with the wks until on a very hot Thursday, 11.7.1901, he collapsed and died at the Wolverhampton flower show. A. was not married, and although he did not share the religious enthusiasm of his bro Joseph, he was a staunch member of the Methodist church. MIME 1866.

Holcroft, Herbert. *The Armstrongs of the Great Western* 1953; Proc IME 12.1901 p 1283

ARMSTRONG, John, MVO

b Chester 27.8.1851; d Acton, London, 28.2.1931 aged 79.
GWR loco & carr supt, Paddington, London. Second son of Joseph A. senior (qv). Ed Tettenhall Coll, Wolverhampton, until aged 16. 1867 entered Swindon Wks, GWR, as pupil under his f, later moving into the drg office. 1878 app by William Dean (qv), successor to Joseph A., as asst div loco supt, Swindon Div. 1882 promoted to div loco supt, Paddington Div, remaining there until his ret in 1916, after over 50 yrs service. During this period he had charge of royal trains in 3 reigns. Responsible for much work on the new loco depot at Old Oak Common from 1902 when the depot at Westbourne Park had to be closed to enable the Paddington improvements to be completed. After Paddington became a borough in 1900 A. was its first alderman (see Aird, Sir John, first mayor). His engg knowledge was of great service to the council. Like

his f and bros, a staunch supporter of the Methodist Church. At Swindon he m Caroline James of Newlyn, Cornwall, d 1925. They had 1 son and 3 drs.

Holcroft, Herbert. *The Armstrongs of the Great Western* 1953; *The Locomotive* 10.1916 p 213, 3.1931 p 105

ARMSTRONG, Joseph (senior)

b Bewcastle, Cumberland, 21.9.1816; d Matlock 5.6.1877 aged 60.
GWR loco eng. 4th son of Thomas A. (1785-1844), and bro of George A. (qv). His family emigrated to Canada in 1817 but returned in 1824 to settle at Newburn on Tyne, Northumberland. Joseph was ed at Bruce's Sch, Newcastle, where Robert Stephenson had been. Early contact with locos aroused an interest in mech engg and on leaving school he started at Walbottle Colly, near his home, under Robert Hawthorn, chief eng, f of Robert and William Hawthorn (qqv), founders of the loco firm in Newcastle. Became friendly with George Stephenson and Timothy Hackworth (qv) who was eng at Walbottle Colly until he went to the Stockton & Darlington R in 1825. In 1836 A. went to the Liverpool & Manchester R as an engine driver under Edward Woods (qv), loco supt. In 1840 moved with his bro George to the Hull & Selby R as a driver under John Gray (qv), later becoming foreman of the sheds and shops at Hull under Thomas Cabrey. In 1845, when Gray became loco supt of the London-Brighton R, A. with his bro George went to the Brighton wks. In 1847, after Gray had left Brighton to be succeeded by J. C. Craven (qv), A. left to become asst loco supt on the Shrewsbury & Chester R under Edward Jeffreys at the wks at Saltney nr Chester. Shortly afterwards Jeffreys left to become loco supt of the Shrewsbury & Hereford R and A. succeeded him as loco supt of the S & C. When the Shrewsbury & Birmingham R opened in 1849 it was operated as one R with the S & C and in 1853 A. was transferred to the newly opened shops at Wolverhampton. In 1854 the whole system to Chester was amalgamated with the GWR, forming a standard-gauge division. A. became loco supt of the whole N Div of the GWR with hq at Stafford

Road, Wolverhampton, and responsible only to Daniel Gooch at Swindon. Before leaving Chester A. m Sarah Burdon. They had 5 sons and 4 drs. At Wolverhampton his total loco stock numbered 56, in various stages of dilapidation. During his 10 yrs there A. added many new designs, all of which are described in detail in *The Locos of the GWR*, pub in 12 parts by the RCTS. In 1864 Gooch resigned as loco supt as also did J. Gibson, C & W supt. A. was app to both positions at Swindon, thus becoming the first loco C & W supt on the GWR. The stock of 7ft gauge locos then numbered over 400. A. at once set about improving working conditions. Few new broad-gauge locos were built under A., but he established the Swindon C & W wks and from then on almost all GW rolling stock for broad and standard gauge was built at Swindon. From about 1874, when James Holden (qv) was transferred from Saltney to become the first C & W wks mgr, new coaches were built as 'convertibles', looking towards the end of the broad gauge. In 1868 A. sent for William Dean (qv), then wks mgr at Wolverhampton, to become chief asst at Swindon. The most famous locos built under A. were the standard-gauge 0–6–0 'standard goods' with double frames (1866); 2–4–0s (1868) and 2–4–0Ts (1868). In 1873 he introduced his large 2–2–2, the first being No 55 *Queen*. In his 13 yrs at Swindon about 600 new engines were built. 1872–4 saw the extension of the additional standard-gauge rails through Swindon to Bristol and Weymouth and much of the West. In 1876 the Bristol & Exeter, South Devon, and two Rs in Cornwall were taken over by the GWR and repairs transferred from Newton Abbot to Swindon. The following year A. rebuilt one of the famous 9ft (2.743m) 4–2–4Ts of the B & E into an 8ft (2.438m) 4–2–2. On 10.4.1877 he was elected MICE. By now he was in control of nearly 13 000 employees, and the strain began to affect him. After earnest appeals from his family and friends he decided to have a rest, but on his journey to Scotland he died at Matlock leaving a widow, 4 sons and 3 drs. A. was active in social work in Swindon, was president of the mechanics institute for 13 yrs and chairman of the

New Town Local Bd for 9 yrs. He was a local preacher in the Wesleyan Methodist Church which in 1869 acquired the building, formerly a hostel for GWR workers, which in 1962 became the Great Western Railway Museum.

Holcroft, Herbert. *The Armstrongs of the Great Western* 1953; Proc IME 1.1878 pp 9–10; Min Proc ICE V 49 1877 p 255; *Engg* V 23 6.1877 p 447; *The Eng* V 43 6.1877 p 109

ARMSTRONG, Joseph (junior)

b Wolverhampton 14.8.1856;
d Wolverhampton 1.1.1888 aged 31.
GWR eng. Third surviving son of Joseph A. (sen) (qv), then loco supt, Wolverhampton. Ed Tettenhall Coll, Wolverhampton, and later became a pupil under his f at Swindon wks. Showed outstanding mechanical ability and was noted for his sound and original ideas. William Dean (qv), loco supt in succession to Joseph A. (sen), entrusted him with the design of the standard GWR vacuum brake, bringing to his assistance another young GWR eng, G. J. Churchward (qv). On the completion of this Dean promoted him to the position of asst div loco supt, Swindon Div. In Summer 1885 he was promoted to Wolverhampton as asst div supt, N Div and wks mgr at Stafford Road wks under his uncle George A. (qv). Here he continued to produce designs for various loco parts. At 00.30 on 1.1.1888 he was walking beside the line at Wolverhampton when he was run over by a goods train and instantly killed.

Holcroft, Herbert. *The Armstrongs of the Great Western* 1953; Proc IME 2 1888 p 153

ARROL, Sir William

b Houston, Renfrewshire, 15.2.1839;
d Ayr 20.2.1913 aged 74.
Civil engg contractor and bridge builder. Son of Thomas A., cotton spinner. At age 14 he started work with a blacksmith at Paisley. After several years as journeyman smith he obtained employment in 1863 with Blackmoor & Gordon of Port Glasgow. By age 29 he had saved £85, half of which he spent on a boiler and engine, and in 1868 started a small wks of his own nr Glasgow. This prospered and in 1871 he began the Dalmarnock

wks. He had added bridge building to his work and his first contract was on the CR Hamilton branch, inc a multi-span bridge over the Clyde at Bothwell. The CR then entrusted him with the first portion of the bridge over the Clyde at Glasgow in 1875. Two yrs earlier A. had undertaken construction of a R suspension bridge over the Forth to designs by T. Bouch (qv). Work began but, after the Tay Bridge collapse on 28.12.1879, the project was stopped and a new cantilever design was produced by John Fowler and Benjamin Baker (qqv) for which A. was again given the contract. In the meantime he constructed the NBR bridge over the South Esk on the Arbroath–Montrose line, gaining experience which became useful when he built the second Tay Bridge, designed by W. H. Barlow (qv). This was begun in 1882 and completed in 1887; the longest R bridge in Europe. The Forth Bridge was begun in 1882 and completed in 1890. For his work A. was knighted by Queen Victoria. While engaged on the Forth Bridge. A. was also busy with the steelwork for the Tower Bridge, London. Besides these A. constructed the Red-heugh Bridge, Newcastle, 3 bridges over the Nile at Cairo, the Queen Alexandra Bridge, Sunderland (1909), the Scherzer lifting bridge at Barrow, and the second section of the Clyde bridge into Central station, Glasgow.

The Eng V 115 28.2.1913 pp 230–1 (portrait); *Engg* V 95 21.2.1913 pp 268–70 (portrait); Proc IME 2.1913 p 323

ASHBURY, Thomas

b Davyhulme, nr Manchester, 9.2.1836; d Manchester 11.9.1920 aged 84.
G mgr of Ashbury Carriage Co, Openshaw, Manchester. MIME 1873, also MICE.
Proc IME 5.1921 p 535

ASPINALL, Sir John Audley Frederick

b Liverpool 25.8.1851; d Woking 19.1.1937 aged 85.
Eng and g mgr LYR. Ed Beaumont Coll, Berks, 1863–8. In 12.1868 began as a pupil of John Ramsbottom (qv) at Crewe, LNWR. When Ramsbottom ret in 1871 A. continued under F. W. Webb (qv). A fellow pupil was H. A. Ivatt (qv), later loco supt GNR, and they

became lifelong friends. During 1871 A. spent a period as loco fireman. In 1872 he was sent to USA to study R and steel making developments, and on his return he was made asst mgr of the Crewe steel wks. On 2.9.1874 he m Gertrude Schräder of Liverpool. In 3.1875 he became wks mgr and asst loco supt under Alexander McDonnell (qv) on the Great Southern & Western R at Inchicore, Dublin. While in this position he improved the automatic vacuum brake. In 1882 McDonnell resigned to become loco supt of the NER at Gateshead, and on 1.11.1882 A. succeeded him as loco supt GS & W. At the same time Ivatt, then supt of the Cork div, became wks mgr at Inchicore. A. designed a large express 4–4–0 and a 0–4–4T for local work. In 1886 Barton Wright (qv), loco supt LYR, resigned and A. was app to succeed him, as CME, on 14.7.1886. Wright, with Ramsbottom, had largely laid out the new loco wks at Horwich nr Bolton and A's first job was to complete and fit out the wks. Loco repairs began there in 1887, and on 20.2.1889 the first new loco emerged, 2–4–2T No 1008. Large numbers of this type were built, until 1911. Next came an 0–6–0 goods engine, built in large numbers from 1889 to 1918 to the same basic design. His 7ft 3in (2.210m) 4–4–0 appeared in 1891. Next came 2 classes of shunting tanks, the 0–4–0 'pug' in 1891 and an o/c 0–6–0T in 1897. His last 2 designs were much larger, for expanding traffic demands. His i/c 4–4–2 was the largest British express engine when it came out on 22.2.1899, with 7ft 3in (2.210m) wheels, and for its time, an enormous high-pitched boiler. For heavy goods traffic a large i/c 0–8–0 appeared in April 1900. From 1890 A. rebuilt 230 of the 280 Barton Wright 0–6–0s into saddle tanks. By standardising components A. reduced the stock of spares. Following LNWR practice he adopted Joy valve gear as standard and this continued for almost all the LYR designs. On 31.5.1899 the LYR bd took the unprecedented step of appointing the CME as g mgr, a tribute to A's universal ability. In this position he was instrumental in developing the LYR shipping services until the co possessed more ships than any other British R. He also developed the Yorkshire coal traffic by securing running powers over the Dearne Valley R and by negotiating the LYR's share in the S Yorkshire Jt R. He made the bold decision to electrify the Liverpool–Southport section, one of the first main-line electrification projects in Britain, completed in 1904. It was extended to Ormskirk in 1913, and its success led to further electrification between Manchester and Bury in 1916. For his work at Horwich in WW1 A. was knighted in 1917. He took a keen interest in the education of young engineers, particularly at the Horwich Mechanics Institute which he founded in 1888. In 1902 app Associate Prof of R Engg at Liverpool Univ. 1908–15 Chairman of the Faculty of Engg. 1909 president IME. 5.11.1918 elected president ICE. Ret 27.1.1919, but continued as an LYR dir. He contributed numerous papers at meetings of the IME and ICE. In 11.1936 he was awarded the James Watt International Medal by the IME to mark the James Watt bi-centenary. So A. achieved the highest honour of all in engg, but shortly before he was due to receive the medal he died, in his 86th year. His later years were saddened by the death of his wife on 13.3.1921, and of his only son, J.B.A., in 6.1932. He was survived by 2 drs.

Bulleid, H. A. V. *The Aspinall Era* 1967; *The Eng* V 163 29.1.1937 p 109; and *Engg* V 143 29.1.1937 p 116 (portraits); *Journal* ICE V 5 1936-7 p 795; Proc IME V 135 1937 p 539; Marshall, John. *The Lancashire & Yorkshire R* V 2 1970, V 3 1972

ASTON, William

b Ironbridge, Shropshire, (?).(?).1829;
d. Oswestry, Shropshire, 25.2.1901 aged 71.
Cambrian Rs loco eng. After apprenticeship at Sharp Stewart, Manchester, worked under Ramsbottom (qv) at Crewe, LNWR. 1865 became draughtsman on the Cambrian Rs at Oswestry under Alexander Walker, loco supt, whom he succeeded in 4.1879. Officially app loco supt 1.9.1882 for a trial period until ratified 1.6.1884. He began by removing the names from the Camb Rs locos, completed 1892. He adopted the Camb Rs loco livery of 'invisible green',

a greenish black. In 4.1888 the locos of the Mid Wales R were taken into Camb stock making a total of 58 of many types by various mfrs. The engines, inc those built to A's specifications, worked well, and he designed some good rolling stock, but the dirs were not satisfied with the running of Oswestry wks. In 1898 V. Raven (qv) of the NER was asked to report which led to the bd deciding, on 21.12.1898, to ask for A's resignation from 25.3.1899. He was succeeded by H. E. Jones.

Christiansen, R., and Miller, R. W. *The Cambrian Rs* V 1 1967, V 2 1968; *The R Eng* 6.1901 pp 161–2

BAGNALL, William Gordon

b Cliff Hall, Tamworth, Staffs, 19.1.1852;
d Stafford 19.7.1907 aged 55.
Loco mfr. Ed privately. Began in banking. After 2 yrs entered wks of John Bagnall & Sons of W. Bromwich, eventually becoming a dir. At age 22 in 1876 he removed to Stafford and began at Massey & Hill's small millwright's business employing about 30 men. He then established his own wks for the mfr of small locos and general engg work. He soon realised the need for specialisation in loco work and supply of other material for narrow gauge light Rs. An example of his success in this was the light R at Spezia Harbour, one of many designed and carried out entirely by B. At his d in 1907 the Castle Engine Wks, Stafford, emp about 300 men in high-class loco and R const. B. was for many yrs a member of both Stafford Town and Staffs County councils.

The Locomotive 15.8.1907 p 144 (portrait); *The Eng* V 104 26.7.1907 p 84

BAIN, David

b Isauld, Caithness, (?).(?).1855;
d Derby 18.9.1933 aged 78.
C & W eng. NER and MR. 1875-9 apprenticed with Neilson & Co, Glasgow. 1883 joined the NER as draughtsman at Gateshead under T. W. Worsdell (qv) and in 1887 became wks mgr in the C & W wks, York, taking full charge in 1890 when he became C & W supt. Active in the design of sleeping cars for the East Coast Route, and in 1895

produced the composite semi-corridor coach built in large numbers for the NER until about 1905. On 1.1.1903 he became C & W supt, MR Derby. Here his first carriages were magnificently furnished sleeping and dining cars, followed in 1904 by 3rd class dining cars. In 1908 he designed the rolling stock for the Lancaster–Morecambe–Heysham electric trains. In 1912 he produced the MR royal saloon for King George V and Queen Mary. Soon after his app to Derby he introduced electric lighting on trains. Other carriages produced under B. were family sleeping carriages and invalid carriages. At Derby he designed one of the largest C & W lifting shops in the world, remodelled the sawmill and introduced electric power throughout the C & W wks. During WW1 he served on the staff of the Dir Gen of Munitions Supply and was awarded the CBE. He ret 1919.
Engg V 136 13.10.1933 p 421; *Proc IME* V 125 1933 p 781; *The Locomotive* 10.1933 p 314; Barnes, G. G. *The Midland Main Line* 1969; Ellis, Hamilton. *The Midland Railway* 1953, *Nineteenth Century Railway Carriages* 1949

BAIRD, Matthew

b nr Londonderry, Ireland, 1817; d Philadelphia, USA, 19.5.1877 aged 60.
American loco eng. Son of coppersmith who moved to Philadelphia in 1821. Left school at 15 and after 2 yrs as an asst to a prof of chemistry began as apprentice in the copper and sheet iron wks of the New Castle (Del) Mfg Co, 1834. 1836 became supt of Newcastle & Frenchtown RR shops. In 6.1838 app foreman of sheet iron and boiler dept of Baldwin Loco Wks, Philadelphia, until 1850. After working in a marble business with his bro John, in 1854 he bought an interest in the Baldwin Wks, the firm becoming known as M. W. Baldwin & Co. On Baldwin's d, 7.9.1866, B. became sole proprietor. In 1867 reorganised the firm, taking as partners George Burnham and Charles T. Parry, changing the name to 'The Baldwin Locomotive Works, M. Baird & Co, proprietors'. In 4.1873 he ret, closing out his interest for $1 660 000. 1866 assumed control of a jewellery business formerly run by his son, conducting this

until his d. He was 3 times m. Associated with the first spark arrester, invented by Richard French in 1842, and was credited with the first use of a firebrick arch in the firebox in 1854.
DAB; White, John H. jr. *American Locomotives, an engineering history 1830–80* 1968

BAKER, Sir Benjamin

b Keyford, Frome, Somerset, 31.3.1840; d Pangbourne, Berks, 19.5.1907 aged 67.
Civil eng, designer of the Forth Bridge. Ed Cheltenham Gr Sch. 1856–60 apprenticed to H. H. Price at Neath Abbey Ironworks, Wales. 1860 went to London as asst to W. Wilson on const of Grosvenor Road R bridge over the Thames, and Victoria station. 1861 joined the staff of (Sir) John Fowler (qv) and became his partner in 1875. From 1861 was engaged with Fowler on the Metropolitan (Inner Circle) line in London, and the St John's Wood extension. In 1869 became Fowler's chief asst on the const of the District R from Westminster to the City. With Fowler, B. was consulting eng for the first of the London tube Rs, the City & S London, opened in 1890, and with J. H. Greathead (qv) they were joint engs for the Central London tube, opened in 1900. In the const of this B. put into effect a scheme he had suggested 25 yrs earlier of making the line rise in entering a station and dip on leaving it to reduce braking and starting power. Fowler and B. undertook many overseas works including Rs in Australia and S Africa. In England B. was responsible for docks at Avonmouth and Hull, in association with Sir James Wolfe Barry (qv). In 1877 B. designed the wrought iron cylinder used to transport Cleopatra's Needle from Egypt to London arriving, after being lost at sea, in 1879. From 1869 b was engaged with Fowler on the Nile dams in Egypt. Following the Tay Bridge disaster in 12.1879 (see T. Bouch) B. designed the great cantilever bridge to span the Firth of Forth. The Forth Bridge was begun in 1883 and opened on 4.3.1890. In the same year B. was knighted. (See also W. Arrol and B. Baker). Elected AICE 1867, member 1877, FRS 1890. Also MIME.
Proc IME 5.1907 pp 533–9; *Min Proc*

ICE V 170 1906–7 p 377; *Engg* V 83
24.5.1907; *The Eng* V 103 24.5.1907
p 524; *The Forth Bridge* in *Engg* V 49
28.2.1890 (portrait); Rolt, L. T. C. *Great
Engineers* 1962

BAKER, William

b (?) 19.5.1817; d (?) 20.12.1878 aged 61.
Chief eng, LNWR. 1834–9 articled to
George Watson Buck, eng, then engaged
on the London & Birmingham R
between London and Tring. In 10.1837
B. went with Buck to work on the Manchester & Birmingham R, completed in
1842. Later he became eng of the MSJ
& AR, at the same time being engaged
on the Shrewsbury & Birmingham and
Shropshire Union Rs, opened 1849. B.
was then app eng of the Stour Valley R,
Birmingham–Wolverhampton, and while
there, in 1852, he was app by the
LNWR as eng of the S Div to succeed
R. B. Dockray. On the d of R. Stephenson in 1859 B. was app chief eng of the
LNWR. Works carried out under his
supervision included the Runcorn Bridge;
stations at London, Liverpool, Man-
chester, Birmingham, Preston, Bolton,
Crewe, Warrington and Stafford; widen-
ing works, and many miles of new lines.
In addition he acted as consulting eng
to the W London Extn R, 1859–63; N
London R, 1863–6; and was eng to
various Rs built jointly with the LNWR.
In Ireland he was responsible for the
const of the Dundalk, Newry &
Greenore and N Wall Extn Rs. Elected
MICE 7.3.1848.
Min Proc ICE V 55 1878–9 pp 315–17;
The Eng V 46 27.12.1878 p 462

BALDRY, James Danford

b London (?).(?).1816; d Hyères, France,
10.2.1900 aged 83.
Articled to Edward Lomax and later
entered service of Joseph Cubitt (qv).
1848–52 asst eng on const and maintenance of E Lincs R. 1853 joined staff of
(Sir) John Fowler (qv), engaged on const
of Oxford, Worcester & Wolverhampton
R. 1855–81 he worked with Fowler,
taking charge of many large engg works
including the Severn Valley R, Craven
Arms–Much Wenlock R, Coalbrookdale
line, and the Isle of Wight R. In 1881
he became a partner of Fowler and
Benjamin Baker (qv). Became MICE

5.12.1865.
Min Proc ICE V 143 1900–1 p 309;
Engg V 69 23.2.1900

BALDWIN, Matthias William

b Elizabethtown, NJ, USA, 10.11.1795;
d Philadelphia, Pa, 7.9.1866 aged 70.
American loco eng and mfr. Youngest
of 5 children of William B., carriage
builder, who d when B. was 4. His fortune was lost by executors and he was
ed through the efforts of his mother.
Apprenticed to Woolworth Bros, mfg
jewellers of Philadelphia. At age 24 he
set up as a jeweller, but abandoned this
after 6 yrs and entered a partnership
with David Mason making tools, then
hydraulic presses, printing machinery,
and in 1827 built a 6 hp stationary
engine and the firm began building
engines for sale. On 25.4.1831 he exhibited in Peale's Museum a dummy loco
and 2 cars, a development of an English
model. In 1832 he const his first loco,
named *Old Ironsides*, for the Philadelphia & Germantown RR. It was built
partly of iron and partly of wood,
weighed 6 tons and pulled 30 tons at
28 mph. It remained in service for over
20 yrs. His 2nd loco, the 4–2–0 *E. L.
Miller*, completed in 1834 for the South
Carolina RR, was a great advance and
introduced features which became standard American practice. During the next
10 yrs he const many stationary engines
and 10 more locos of improving designs,
after which he specialised in loco mfr.
In 1838 he introduced standardisation
using templates and gauges and by 1840
he was using metallic packing for glands.
His first European loco was built for
Austria in 1841. Horizontal cylinders in
identical castings including half the
smokebox saddle were introduced in
1858. In 1854 Matthew Baird (qv) bought
an interest in the Baldwin wks and continued as a partner until B's d in 1866
by which time the firm had built over
1500 locos and was producing 120 a
year. Also in 1866 the 2–8–0 type was
introduced, becoming the most numerous in America. Besides loco mfr, B.
was a noted philanthropist and worked
for 35 yrs as a Sunday school supt. In
1827 he m Sarah C. Baldwin, a remote
relation. In 1835 he founded a school
for coloured children. For many years he

was a county and city prison inspector. He was a lover of music and art, a total abstainer, and was noted for his shrewd and concise speech and his positive decisions. The original Baldwin wks of 1836 was in the heart of Philadelphia. By 1906 it covered 19 acres (7.69ha) and was producing 1000 locos a year. A new wks was then opened at Eddystone, Pa, about 12 miles from Philadelphia. The Philadelphia plant was closed down in 1928. The Eddystone site grew to cover 500 acres (202ha). In 1950 Baldwin Loco Wks acquired control of the Lima–Hamilton Corporation and the new organisation became known as the Baldwin–Lima–Hamilton Corporation. The last Baldwin steam engine was built for India in 1955 bringing the total to about 75 000.

Westing, F. H. (ed) *The Locomotives that Baldwin built* 1966; DAB; White, John H. Jr *American Locomotives, an engineering history 1830–80* 1968

BALDWIN, John

b Bolton, Lancs, 8.3.1824; d Southend on Sea 14.7.1891 aged 77.
Civil eng. Ed at Bury. 1843 apprenticed to Kaye & Sons, engs and millwrights, Bury. 1848 began his career as R eng, becoming asst eng and agent on Oxford–Birmingham, GWR, with Peto & Betts (qqv) 1848–53. 1854 took charge of const of LBSCR Wandsworth–Crystal Palace (op 1.12.1856) and Wimbledon–Croydon (op 22.10.1855) lines as contractor's eng and agent. 1858 Peto & Betts entrusted him with a portion of the LCDR E Kent line, op 3.12.1860. He then took a hand in the Herne Hill–Beckenham section of the LCDR (op 1.7.1863) inc Sydenham Tunnel 1 mile 440 yd (2011m), for which he adopted a circular section which he proved was best suited to London clay (see Min Proc ICE V 49 1876–7 p 232). 1863 began the LCDR Nunhead–Crystal Palace High Level line (op 1.8.1865), and in 1864 the Nunhead–Blackheath Hill (Greenwich) line (op 1.9.1871). However, following the fire at Crystal Palace, Christmas 1866, he left Peto & Betts and was engaged under Edwin Clarke on its restoration. 1867–70 in charge of S. Dock works of E & W India Docks, London. 1870 prepared an exhaustive report on the Channel Tunnel with estimates for

Brassey and Wythes, advocating running a preliminary heading from end to end. It was abandoned on the outbreak of the Franco–German war. 1871–5 engaged by Wythes on const of Sharpness docks on the Severn. Elected MICE 2.12.1878. Min Proc ICE V 107 1891–2 p 416

BALL, Sir James Benjamin

b 9.3.1867; d Forest Row, Sussex, 16.9.1920 aged 53.
Chief eng GCR and LBSCR. In 1884 articled to Joseph Hall. 1890 joined staff of GNR as asst to Richard Johnson (qv). 1895 engaged under Elliott Cooper on const of LD & ECR and in 1899 became chief eng until the R was absorbed into the GCR on 1.1.1907. He then became head of new works dept, GCR, and was engaged on many const jobs inc the Ardwick and Hyde Jn widenings nr Manchester, the new C & W Wks at Dukinfield, Wath gravity shunting yard, Torside–Woodhead widening on Manchester–Sheffield line, opening out of Bridghouses tunnel and rearrangement of Sheffield station, new avoiding line at Doncaster, and other works. At Immingham Dock he was responsible for hydraulic equipment and for laying out about 160 miles of track, ferro-concrete bridges and gantries, granary, etc. In 1906 he was president of the P W Inst, being largely concerned in its incorporation. On 1.1.1912 he became chief eng, GCR. In 2.1917, on the ret of Sir Charles Morgan (qv), chief eng LBSCR, B. was app his successor. 1917 app controller of timber supplies. 1918 knighted. MICE 1902, MIME 1914. Twice m and was survived by 3 drs by his first wife and a son by his second.
The Eng V 130 24.9.1920 p 305; *Engg* V 110 24.9.1920 p 414 (portrait); Dow, George. *Great Central* V 3 1965

BALLARD, Stephen

b Malvern Link, Worcs, 5.4.1801; d Colwall, Herefordshire, 14.11.1890 aged 89.
Civil eng on MR. Trained as builder and civil eng, becoming mgr and later eng of the Hereford & Gloucester Canal, carrying out extns between Ledbury and Hereford. B. was then app res eng by Walker & Burges of the Middle Level Main Drain from the Ouse to the

Sixteen Foot River at Upwell. A chance meeting with Thomas Brassey (qv) on Cambridge station led to his app on the const of the GNR Biggleswade–Peterborough (op 7.8.1850) where his experience of fen country was valuable. After a brief visit to India he undertook const of 2 sections of the Dutch Rhenish R, Utrecht–Rotterdam and Arnheim–Prussian frontier, for Brassey. On the former section his fen experience was again valuable. He next built the Worcester–Hereford R (op 1860–1) inc the tunnels at Colwall (1567yd, 1433m) and Ledbury (1323yd, 1210m). This was followed by the Ashchurch–Evesham, 1862, and the Evesham–Redditch, 1864. His last undertaking was the MR extn from Bedford to London, begun 1865 and op 1.10.1868 (see W. H. Barlow). He then ret to live at Colwall. Elected MICE 17.2.1846.
Min Proc ICE V 104 1890–1 p 288

BANDERALI, David

b Paris 18.1.1836; d Paris 30.3.1890 aged 54.
Chief asst eng, Northern R, France. Graduated in engg at Ecole Polytechnique and Ecole des Mines. 1859 joined Northern R as insp of traction dept, Amiens. 1873 app chief asst eng at Paris, until his d. He advocated introd of vacuum brake which was fitted to all vehicles of NR in 1876. He strongly favoured bogies on locos and rolling stock. Also closely associated in France with creation of Chemins de Fer Economiques, the narrow-gauge feeder lines to the main line. Many of the engines and carriages were designed according to his ideas. His ready command of English and his capacity for making friends made him well liked in Britain and USA. Became MIME 1879.
Proc IME 1.1890 p 171; *Engg* V 49 11.4.1890

BANISTER, Frederick Dale

b London 15.3.1823; d Forest Row, Sussex 22.12.1897 aged 74.
Civil eng, LBSCR. Ed Preston Gr Sch. At 15 articled to John J. Myres of Preston for 6 yrs. 1844 engaged by C. E. Cawley (qv) on laying out part of the ELR. 1846 moved to Brighton and entered service of LBSCR under Robert

Jacomb-Hood. 1847 placed in charge of branch from New Cross to Deptford and the dock there. After a period of private practice at Brighton from 1849, in 1860 he succeeded Jacomb-Hood as chief res eng of the LBSCR and for the next 35 yrs undertook many heavy and costly works inc the S London extn to London Bridge involving a 1½ mile (2.4km) viaduct, rebuilding London Bridge and Brighton stations, and the const of the Newhaven–Seaford, Sutton & Epsom Downs, Tunbridge Wells–Eastbourne, Chichester–Midhurst, Croydon, Oxted, East Grinstead and Tunbridge Wells lines, the Portsmouth extn and the Ryde Pier R. In 1878 he prepared plans for Newhaven Harbour and later carried out the work. He also carried out various widening and rebuilding works. Ret 1.1896. Elected MICE 13.3.1866.
Min Proc ICE V 131 1897–8 p 359

BARLOW, Peter

b Norwich (?).10.1776; d London 1.3.1862 aged 85.
Scientist and eng. Early interest in scientific matters. After teaching maths and writing scientific articles, he experimented in electricity and magnetism. 1801 app to Royal Military Academy, Woolwich. About 1830 became interested in Rs and in the testing of various rail sections and determining the effects of gradients and curves. In 1836 he was app one of the Royal Commissioners for determining the best system of Rs for Ireland, the report being presented to Parliament in 1838. In 1839 he prepared a similar report on the best routes to Scotland and Wales and the most convenient port for traffic to Ireland. In 1842 he was engaged in an enquiry into the general merits of the atmospheric system and in 1845 he was appointed one of the Gauge Commissioners in which work he was associated with Sir Frederick Smith and Prof Airy. In 1847, being then 71 yrs old, he ret from his duties at the Royal Military Academy. He was the f of William Henry and Peter William B. (qqv).
Min Proc ICE V 22 1862–3 pp 615–18

BARLOW, Peter William, FRS

b Woolwich 1.2.1809; d Notting Hill, London, 19.5.1885 aged 76.

Eldest son of Prof Peter Barlow (qv) and bro of William Henry (qv). After ed at private schools decided on civil eng career. 1826 became pupil of Henry Robinson Palmer and worked on Liverpool & Birmingham Canal and the New London docks. 1836 engaged by Sir William Cubitt (qv) as res eng on the central div of the London–Dover R, later SER. Subsequently became res eng of the whole line. 1844 became chief eng. Built the North Kent (op 30.7.1849), Tunbridge–Hastings (op 1851–2) and many other extensions. In 1842–5 built the Tunbridge Wells branch (op. 20.9. 1845) before the Act was obtained. Resigned 10.7.1851 following dissatisfaction with his C.I. sleepers. He const the Londonderry–Enniskillen, and Londonderry–Coleraine lines in Ireland, and the Newtown–Oswestry in Shropshire. In 1858 B. investigated the const of long-span bridges in great detail, especially concerning the stiffening of suspension bridges, demonstrating his theories on large models. In this connection he visited Niagara gorge in 1855 to study the road/rail suspension bridge by Roebling (qv). On his return he was app eng for a suspension bridge over the Thames at Lambeth. The sinking of the cylinders for the piers of this bridge gave B. the idea for using similar cylinders horizontally for boring tunnels under rivers in suitable rock. To prove his idea he bored a tunnel under the Thames near the Tower. The Tower Subway, opened in 1870, was the first tube R tunnel in the world. It later became a footway, and now carries a water main. B. was author of several scientific papers. Became FRS 1854. Elected MICE 1827. *The Eng* V 59 29.5.1885 p 422; Min Proc ICE V 81 1884–5 pp 321–3; DNB V 12 Supplement p 126

BARLOW, William Henry

b Woolwich, London, 10.5.1812;
d Greenwich, London 12.11.1902 aged 90. Civil eng. Younger son of Peter B. (qv) and bro of Peter William B. (qv). Trained at Woolwich dockyard and London docks. In 1832 he was sent by Maudslay & Field to Constantinople where he spent 6 yrs erecting machinery and buildings for the mfr of ordnance for the Turkish govt. On his return to England in 1838, became asst eng on Manchester & Birmingham R and in 1842 res eng on Midland Counties R. 1844 res eng on N Midland and the other lines which in 1844 were amalgamated to form the Midland R of which B. became chief eng at Derby. 1857 moved to London. Between 1844 and 1886 took out several patents relating to p w including, in 1849, the saddleback form of rail which bore his name and which was much used on the GWR. 1862–9 carried out the MR extn from Bedford to London inc St Pancras station with the largest roof span (240ft, 100ft high, 73m, 30m) in Britain. In 1860 B. and Hawkshaw (qv) completed Brunel's Clifton suspension bridge near Bristol. 1868 app to committee to study use of steel in structures. In 1874 he took into partnership his second son Crawford and his asst C. B. Baker. He was a member of the court of inquiry into the Tay Bridge disaster of 1879 and was consultant for the design of the replacement bridge, built 1882–7. Elected MICE 1.4.1845 and was president 1879–80, also MIME, and FRS 6.6.1850. He m Selina Crawford, dr of W. Caffin and they had 4 sons and 2 drs.
Min Proc ICE V 151 1902–3 pp 388–400

BARRY, Sir John Wolfe—
See WOLFE-BARRY

BARTON WRIGHT, William

b Murton House nr North Shields, Northumb, 13.11.1828; d St Leonards-on-Sea, Sussex, 7.5.1915 aged 86.
Loco eng, Madras R and LYR. Son of William Clark Wright, and grandson of John W of Wallsend Hall. (John W's dr Elizabeth Clark W m George Hawks whose mother was sister of Anna Longridge, mother of T.L., Viret and Daniel Gooch qqv). BW's mother was dr of Joshua Parr of Liverpool who m Althea, dr of George Barton of Manchester. (The Parrs were merchants in Liverpool from 1700 and the Bartons were merchants in Manchester from 1772.) In 1839 the BWs moved to Bayswater, London, where BW's f d in 1844. In 1845, at age 17, BW began a 6 yr apprenticeship at Swindon, GWR, under Daniel Gooch, being emp in the erecting shop, then as draughtsman and lastly as

asst to the wks mgr, Archibald Sturrock (qv). In 1851 he was placed in charge of the GWR loco depot at Paddington, London. In 10.1854 he was app the first loco C & W supt on the Madras R, India, where he arrived in 3.1855. His salary was £700 pa. In 1858, while on leave in England, he m, at Paddington parish church, Janet, dr of William Forlonge. BW's engagement in Madras was renewed, at a salary of £1000, in 1859. The locos supplied to the Madras R were mainly 2–4–0 passenger, 0–4–2 mixed traffic and 0–6–0 gds, specified and ordered by John Hawkshaw (qv) who was consulting eng for the R. On 11.1. 1859 BW was elected AICE; MICE 7.12.1869; MIME 6.1878. In 1875 the LYR decided to combine its loco depts under one head and in Oct app BW as loco supt at the Miles Platting wks, Manchester, possibly through the influence of Hawkshaw who was also consulting eng, and formerly chief eng, of the LYR. In 10½ yrs BW renewed almost the entire LYR loco stock, mainly with 5 well tried designs from reliable builders; a 6ft (1.829m) 4–4–0 (Sharp Stewart), 0–6–0 gds (identical to a Kitson design on the Taff Vale R), 0–4–4T and 0–6–2T passenger and 0–6–2T gds, also Kitson. These incorporated many standard interchangeable components. He also rbt several earlier engines. So well were the engines designed and built that one of the 0–6–0s, rbt as a saddle tank, was the last LYR engine and oldest BR engine in service when withdrawn in 9.1964 after 87 yrs. BW was responsible for the establishment and layout of the new LYR loco wks at Horwich nr Bolton in 1885-6, in conj with John Ramsbottom (qv). In 6.1886, at age 57, he resigned to give more time to private practice as an eng in London. He became a dir of the Balmadies Estates Co Ltd and of the Assam Rs & Trading Co Ltd in India until 1892 in which year his wife d in London. He then ret, and resigned from the IME in 12.1892, and moved to an ancestral home in Dover. He resigned from the ICE on 9.1.1906. In 1907 he moved to St Leonards where he spent his last years. He was survived by 3 sons and 2 drs.
R Times 18.12.1875 p 1191; *The R Eng* 7.1886 p 201; Marshall, John, The

Lancashire & Yorkshire R V 2 1970, V 3 1972; Family records

BASSETT-LOWKE, Wenman Joseph
b Northampton 27.12.1877;
d Northampton 21.10.1953 aged 75.
Designer and builder of model locos and ships. Son of T. J. Lowke, eng at Northampton to whom BL was apprenticed. Deciding to set up on his own account as a model eng, he adopted his mother's maiden name of Bassett and began trading with a German mfr in Nuremburg. His first catalogue was issued in 1899. Soon he began building larger models culminating in 15in (381mm) gauge engines weighing several tons, in collaboration with Henry Greenly (qv). BL 15in gauge engines were supplied for pleasure lines at Blackpool, Southport, Rhyl and elsewhere. He built the 4–4–2 *Sans Pareil* (1912) and 4–6–2 *Colossus* (1914) which ran on the Ravenglass & Eskdale R from 1915 to 1926 and 1927. Became MILE 1911.
The Model Engineer V 109 12.11.1953 p 584; Engg V 176 6.11.1933 p 607; *Journal* ILE V 44 1954 p 448

BAYLEY, Joseph Petter
b Horsehay, Shropshire, (?).(?).1889;
d Gibraltar 24.4.1931 aged 42.
Designer of GKN steel sleeper and other p w material. Apprenticed at Horsehay Bridge & Engg Wks, later becoming wks mgr. 1921 app g mgr of Cwmbran Wks, Monmouthshire, of Guest, Keen & Nettlefold until his d. Patented GKN composite steel & iron sleeper, used on British and foreign Rs, and other ideas on p w. Became AIME 1922.
Proc IME V 120 6.1931 p 739; *The Eng* V 151 1.5.1931 p 491

BAYLISS, John
b Birmingham 30.3.1826; d Ryde, Isle of Wight, 4.12.1900 aged 74.
R contractor. 1844 articled to Charles Henry Capper, Birmingham. 1846–9 emp as contr's agent under W. McCormick on Walton Tunnel, Liverpool, and at Bradford on the LYR. In 1847 while on the LYR Mirfield–Bradford line he met William Eckersley, res eng. In 1851-2 B. and Eckersley built the section of the Londonderry & Enniskillen R between Strabane and Newton Stewart. 1853–6

engaged under Robert Rawlinson on water and sewage works. 1862–70 B. and Eckersley built the MR between Dove Holes tunnel and New Mills, the Bath–Mangotsfield and Mansfield–Southwell lines, part of the Chesterfield–Sheffield line, Yate–Thornbury branch and other MR extns, and the LNWR Huddersfield–Kirkburton branch. In 1870 the firm was awarded the contract for the Carlisle end of the Settle & Carlisle R, but shortly afterwards the partnership was dissolved and B. carried it out himself.

Min Proc ICE V 143 1900–1 p 338

BEAMES, Major Hewitt Pearson Montague, CBE

b near Dublin 9.5.1875; d Crewe 5.3.1948 aged 72.

LNWR loco eng. Ed Corrig Sch, Kingstown, Dublin; Dover Coll; Crawley's Military Academy, Dublin. Apprenticed under F. W. Webb (qv) at Crewe, LNWR. 1899 became jnr asst wks mgr, Crewe. Served in S Africa during Boer War, returning 1901 to become asst to outdoor supt, LNWR, Crewe, taking over supervision of pumping, lifting and conveying machinery and the R's dredging and dock plant. In 1909 he became personal asst to C. J. Bowen-Cooke (qv) who was app CME that year. In this position B was responsible for design and const of a loco coaling plant. In 1914 he was posted to command the 110th Company (Railway) of the REs in France, but in 1916 returned to Crewe as chief asst to the wks mgr in charge of munitions mfr and locos for war service. 6.1919 app dep CME and on 1.12.1920 succeeded Cooke as CME of the LNWR. He remained in charge at Crewe after the amalgamation with the LYR on 1.1.1922, although he became subordinate to George Hughes (qv) at Horwich. In 1921 he designed the 0–8–4T of which 30 were built in 1923 for goods and pass work on the 1 in 34 gradients on the Abergavenny–Brynmawr–Merthyr line. By now the LNWR was part of the LMS, but B. continued at Crewe under Hughes, in 1923–4 producing his redesigned 'Prince' 4–6–0 with outside Walschaert's valve gear, eliminating the perforated main rod of the Joy gear. Four were rebuilt and one was built new

by William Beardmore & Co Ltd. From 1925–7 B. supervised the complete reorganisation of Crewe wks, introducing the conveyor-belt system for the first time in a European loco wks. In 1.1931 he was app dep CME, LMS Derby, under H. Fowler (qv) until his ret 30.9.1934. B. was MIME, MICE and for several yrs was vice president of the ILE. At his d in Crewe in 1948 he was chairman of Cheshire County Council.

Proc IME V 160 1949 p 263; *The Eng* V 185 12.3.1948 p 259; *Journal* ILE V 37 1947 p 548

BEATTIE, Joseph Hamilton (and William George)

b Ireland 12.5.1808; d London 18.10.1871 aged 63.

Loco eng LSWR. Son of George B., architect in N Ireland. Apprenticed under his f and was for several yrs in the same business. 1835 went to England and worked under Joseph Locke (qv) as asst eng on the GJR, and in 1837 on the London & Southampton R, later LSWR, on which he was in charge of much of the const and p w. Later he took charge of C & W stock. On 1.7.1850 he became loco supt in succession to J. V. Gooch (qv). His first patent, in 1840, included a device for temporarily increasing the weight on loco driving wheels when required, also improvements in buffers, brakes, couplings and other details. Numerous other patents followed, including feed-water-heating apparatus and a firebox for burning coal, oil axleboxes for engines and carriages, and sprinkler pipes for putting out fires in buildings. In 1863–4 he designed the new workshops at Nine Elms, London. For many yrs locos of his design were built by Beyer Peacock & Co Manchester, and the improved appearance of the engines was the influence of Charles Beyer (qv). Became MIME 1848; elected MICE 1.12.1857. He died in office and was succeeded by his son **William George BEATTIE** who joined the LSWR as a draughtsman in the loco C & W dept at Nine Elms in 1862. In 1869 he was app supt of hydraulic machinery. As a loco supt he was a failure. His one design, an o/c 4–4–0, was not successful and he was forced to resign in 1878. He d on 28.5.1918, at Belsize Park, London.

Min Proc ICE V 33 1871–2 pp 204–6; Proc IME 1872 p 15; Bradley, D. L. *Locos of the LSWR* (RCTS) Part 1 1965; Ellis, Hamilton. *Twenty Locomotive Men* 1958; *LSWR Magazine* 7.1918 p 94

BEATTY, Sir Edward Wentworth, GBE

b Thorold, Ontario, 16.10.1877; d Montreal 23.3.1943 aged 65.

President CPR. Son of Henry B. from Ireland, founder of the Beatty Line of steamships on the Great Lakes. Curiously, the elder B. declined to join a syndicate formed by James J. Hill (qv) to build the R of which his son later became president. Ed Upper Canada Coll; Toronto Univ (BA 1898); Osgoode Hall Law Sch. 1901 called to the Bar and after a short spell in private law practice he was app asst in the law dept of the CPR. In 1905 he became asst solicitor and in 1910 gen solicitor. In 1914 he was made chief counsel and vice president and in 1918 on the ret of Lord Shaughnessy he became the first Canadian born president. He guided the CPR through its period of greatest prosperity from 1925–9 and through the depressions which followed when many R companies went bankrupt. He controlled about 100 000 employees and 20 000 miles (32 187km) of R and a fleet of steamers. During his presidency the CPR spent millions of dollars improving its vast property, two huge enterprises being the Royal York Hotel in Toronto built at a cost of $17 mil, and the launching of the 43 000 ton liner *Empress of Britain* in 1931. In 1935 he was created GBE. At the beginning of WW2 B. was app Canadian rep of the British Ministry of Shipping. He was also associated with the New Brunswick R Co, the Northern Alberta Rs, the Toronto Terminals Co and the Toronto, Hamilton & Buffalo R Co. He also served as vice president of Canadian Airways and a dir of the Consolidated Mining & Smelting Co. He took great interest in social and educational work and did much for Queens Univ, Kingston, Ont, and the McGill Univ, Montreal, both of which he served as chancellor. Ill health forced his ret in 1942.

New York Times 24.3.1943 p 23 (portrait); *The Eng* V 175 2.4.1943 p 261;

RG 2.4.1943 pp 351, 363 (portrait)

BEHN-ESCHENBURG, Hans

b Switzerland 10.1.1864; d nr Zurich 18.5.1938 aged 74.

Swiss electrical eng and pioneer of high-voltage ac R electrification; mg dir Maschinenfabrik Oerlikon (MFO). Studied under H. F. Weber. 1892 entered MFO which was being reorganised under Emil Huber-Stockar (qv). Engaged in development of transformers and traction machinery. Became chief elec eng 1897. Introduced 3-phase induction motor 1902. 1904 introduced a practical single-phase traction motor used on Seebach-Wettingen and later, in 1913, on the Rhaetian R, Lötschberg and other Swiss main lines. 1911 succeeded Huber-Stockar on the mgt and in 1913 became mg dir.

S Bz V 92 20.10.1928 p 193; V 112 31.12.1938 p 327

BELL, Theodor

b Lucerne 8.3.1840; d Lucerne 17.1.1933 aged 92.

Son of the founder of Maschinenfabrik Bell & Co, Kriens, Switzerland. Ed Tech High Sch, Karlsruhe. Entered Bell wks. Specialised in bridges, ropeways and water turbines. Responsible for design and const of many large iron and steel R bridges throughout Europe.

S Bz V 101 25.3.1933 p 148

BELPAIRE, Alfred Jules

b Ostend, Belgium, 26.9.1820; d Schaerbeck 27.1.1893 aged 73.

Loco eng and designer of the B firebox. At age 17 gained entrance to the Central Sch of Arts & Mfrs, Paris, and gained engg diploma in 1840. In that year the Belgian State Rs entrusted him with charge of the loco repair shops at Malines where his contemporary E Walschaert (qv) began work. Shortly afterwards he had both legs broken in a R accident between Brussels and Malines, but, despite this, in 1850 B. was app dir of the rolling stock dept, Brussels. From 1835–53 the Belgian State Rs used a mixture of coke, briquettes and coal, and fuel costs were high, and the quality of Belgian coal was poor. To achieve greater efficiency from the fuel, in 1860 he produced his famous firebox which, in its round form, was tested on a 2-4-0, No 1. In 1864 he abandoned the round form of firebox and adopted the square form which greatly facilitated the use of vertical and horizontal stays which were the principal feature in which it differed from the older fireboxes, this was used on all Belgian State Rs locos from 1864-84. At the end of 1884 B introduced new and important details, greatly increasing the length and width of the grate which extended over the wheels and frames and, on some express engines on the Luxembourg line, reached an area of 73.8 sq ft (6.79m²). B. also invented a combined reversing lever and screw. In 1878 he invented the 'Belpaire Steam Carriage', the precursor of the steam rail-motor, and large numbers were built for Belgium, Holland, Italy, Sweden and Norway. B. also designed many locos. He presided over the International R Congress at Moscow in 1892. As administrative president he achieved the highest position on the Belgian State Rs.

Engg V 55 3.2.1893 p 137; *The Locomotive* 15.9.1932 pp 314-16

BENER, Gustav

b Chur, Switzerland, 17.7.1873; d Chur 25.1.1846 aged 72.
Swiss civil eng. Qualified 1897 and worked under Fritz Hennings (qv) on the Rhine Valley line, Reichenau-Ilanz (1900-3) and Filisur-Bergün (1903) sections of the Rhaetian R. Later worked on planning and const of Filisur-Wiesen (1906-9) and Bever-Schuls (1910-13) sections, both involving immense works. In 1911-14 he undertook what was to be his most outstanding work, the planning and building of the Chur-Arosa R on which he remained as chief eng and mgr. This included two of the greatest concrete R bridges in Switzerland. In autumn 1919 he was app mgr of the Rhaetian R at Chur. In the next few yrs he rebuilt the entire economic structure of the R. Adopted the then revolutionary principle of making himself available to any staff member or worker on the R every week. B. was responsible after WW1 for negotiating a loan of 8 million francs from the Federal and Cantonal authorities for the complete electrification of the Rh R

network and for the purchase of 15 C-C electric locos. He was instrumental in the completion of the Furka-Oberalp R in 1926 following its suspension in 1914. Ret 1936 after 40 yrs intensive R service. Studer, Hans. in *S.Bz* V 127 2.2.1946 p 61; Marshall, John. *Metre gauge railways in South and East Switzerland* 1974

BENGOUGH, Cyril Francis

b (?) (?).(?).1864; d Tewkesbury, Glos, 22.7.1931 aged c 67.
Chief eng, NER. Ed Marlborough Coll and in engg at Univ Coll, Bristol. 1885 became articled pupil of Messent, eng to River Tyne Commissioners. 1890 app res eng on const of NER Anfield Plain and Team Valley branches under T. E. Harrison (qv). 1899 took charge of Bishop Auckland dist. 1906 dist eng Newcastle. 1909 NER S Div eng, York. 1912 took charge of maintenance of entire NER lines as well as new works on S Div. On 1.1.1915 app chief eng until his ret on 31.12.1924.

BENNETT, Alfred Rosling

b Islington, London, 1850; d Matlock, Derbyshire, 24.5.1928 aged 78.
Elec eng with special interest in telephony and Rs. R writer. Ed private sch; later Belle Vue Academy, Greenwich. Originally intended taking up R engg at Bow Wks, NLR, but instead accepted app with Indian Govt Telegraph Dept, and visited Baluchistan, Mesopotamia and Turkey. Received special mention from Indian Govt for proficiency in submarine cable and land line testing. 1873 returned to England and became electrician to the Highton Battery Co. In 1877 he set up the first telephone line in England. Later carried out experiments resulting in the invention of the caustic alkali and iron battery, patented in 1881. 1880 app engg supt in E London Dist of United Telephone Co. 1881 patented a telephone transformer. 1883 entered service of National Telephone Co as eng for Scotland and Ireland, later becoming mgr for Scotland and N W England. B. was responsible for the installation of the first incandescent lamp in Scotland in 1882. Supervised the first electric lighting installation in a coal mine, at Earnock nr Hamilton, with special airtight switches. 1880 organised

the R annexe of the International Electrical & Engg Exhib in Edinburgh. 1895 designed the telephone system for Guernsey and later in Jersey, and was eng to the municipal systems of Glasgow, Tunbridge Wells, Portsmouth, Brighton and Hull, all except the last later taken over by the Post Office. B. was keenly interested in loco engg and in 1911 was vice president of the ILE. His pub works include: *The Telephone Systems of the Continent of Europe*, 1895; *Historic Locomotives* 1906; *The first Railway in London* (The London & Greenwich) 1912; *London and Londoners in the 1850s and 60s* 1924; *The History of the States of Guernsey telephone system 1895–1925* 1926; and *Chronicles of Boulton's Siding* 1927. In 1904 he pub *Proposals for London improvements* revealing considerable artistic and architectural ability. A man of remarkable energy, great sincerity and charm, always ready to acknowledge merit in others.
The Locomotive 6.1928 p 177, 7.1928 pp 235–6; *Journal* ILE V 18 1928 p 448

BERKELEY, James John

b Holloway, London, 21.10.1819; d Sydenham, Kent, 25.8.1862 aged 42.
Eng on Indian Rs. Completed ed at King's Coll, London. Worked under G. P. Bidder (qv) 1836–9 and then began pupilage under Robert Stephenson. Worked on Northampton–Peterborough, Trent Valley, Churnet Valley lines and the NSR. 1850 went to Bombay to become chief res eng on the GIPR. He was first concerned in constructing 33 miles of experimental line from Bombay to Callian. He then engineered the lines up the Bhore Ghat and the Thal Ghat, beginning surveys in 1852. On 16.4.1853 the first 20 miles (32km) from Bombay to Thana were opened, the first Indian R. In 1856 the North Eastern line up the Thal Ghat was sanctioned, to complete the GIP system as projected by B., totalling 1237 miles (1991km). B. suffered severely from the Indian climate, and in 1861 was forced to return to England where he d after a lingering illness.
Min Proc ICE V 22 1862 pp 618–24

BEST, Stephen Charles

b (?) 27.6.1831; d London 24.9.1891 aged

60.
Articled in 1847 to an architect and civil eng, W. Millson, for 3 yrs. 1853 went to Paris where he worked with Gandell Frères on plans and designs for Rs in France and Italy. Later emp on const of Bourg–Mâcon branch of the Lyons & Geneva R. Returned to England 1855 and, after a period on municipal works, in 1859 became res eng on LCDR under William Mills and was placed in charge of const of the Dover section inc 4 tunnels. Later took charge of maintenance of 50 miles of p w. 1864 made parliamentary surveys for a branch from the LCDR to Walmer and Deal. 1865 app chief eng for Crampton (qv) on const of E & W Jn R, Towcester–Stratford on Avon, 33 miles. 1883, for Lucas & Aird, he took charge of const of the Hull section of the H & BR, with several tunnels and heavy earthworks, opened in 1885. From then until his d he practised as a consulting eng at Westminster. Became MICE 7.1.1879.
Min Proc ICE V 109 1891–2 p 392

BETTS, Edward Ladd

b Sandown, Kent, 5.6.1815; d Assoan, Egypt, 21.1.1872 aged 56.
R contractor. Began under his f building Bell Rock lighthouse near Beaumaris, N Wales. At age 18 had sole responsibility for const of Dutton vdt, GJR, under Joseph Locke (qv). Later engaged on MR Rugby–Leicester, then SER Reigate–Dover under W. Cubitt (qv). Later under Robert Stephenson he carried out the first contract on the Chester & Holyhead R; then the N Wales Mineral R; Chester–Wrexham; Chester–Mold and the whole of the line through Anglesey. Shortly after completion of this B. entered into partnership with S. M. Peto (qv) with whom he built the GNR loop line Peterborough–Gainsborough and the MS & L from there to Retford and the GNR to Doncaster, opened 1848–9. Other Rs built by Peto & B. included GWR Oxford–Birmingham, and Oxford–Worcester & Wolverhampton R. In Russia they built the Dunaburg & Witepsk R, and in Argentina the Buenos Ayres Great Southern. During the Crimean war Peto & B. built the Balaclava R. In conjunction with Brassey (qv) Peto & B. built many diffi-

cult works in Britain and abroad, inc the Grand Trunk R, Canada, with the great tubular bridge over the St Lawrence at Montreal; Elizabeth R, Austria; Lyons & Avignon R, France; Jutland & N & S Sleswig Rs, Denmark; London Tilbury & Southend R; Hereford, Ross & Gloucester R; and the Victoria and Thames graving docks, London. Peto & B. & Crampton (qv) built the whole of the LCDR inc 2 bridges over the Thames. In 1843 B. m the youngest dr of William Peto. Elected AICE 26.6.1849. 1851–2 chairman ECR. B. was magistrate and dep lieutenant for Kent; 1858 high sheriff for Kent. In 1871 he visited Egypt to try to restore his failing health, but he d there. He was buried at Aylesford, Kent, his home for many years.
Engg V 13 8.3.1872 p 157; Min Proc ICE V 36 1872–3 pp 285–8

BEYER, Charles Frederick

b Plauen, Saxony, 14.5.1813;
d Llantisilio, Wales, 2.6.1876 aged 63.
Loco eng & mfr. Son of a weaver and at first apprenticed to a weaver. However, Carl B. excelled as a draughtsman and artist, so he was released from his apprenticeship and sent to Dresden Polytechnic. He struggled through his training in a state of great poverty. After 4 yrs B. went to Hanbold's machine shop at Chemnitz for 2 yrs. He then received a state grant £45 to visit England and to report on mechanical improvements in the spinning of cotton. At Manchester he met Richard Roberts of Sharp, Roberts & Co. Roberts, inventor of the self-acting spinning mule, greatly influenced B. After returning to Dresden he soon went back to Manchester. After some difficulty he started as a junior draughtsman with Sharp, Roberts & Co in 1834. In 1837 they began the mfr of locos in which Richard Roberts had been interested since 1832. It was B. who helped to establish the firm's reputation for sound engines. The famous 'Sharp Standard' 2–2–2 passenger and 0–4–2 goods engines were designed by B. Roberts ret in 1843 and B. is believed to have done all the loco designing for Sharp Bros as the firm became known. In 1844 Friedrich August II, King of Saxony, visited Sharp Bros during a tour in England and his pleasure at

finding an ex subject in charge of loco design may have influenced ordering of Sharp engines for Saxony shortly afterwards. The bell-mouthed brass dome cover was copied by Borsig (qv) of Berlin and Hartmann of Chemnitz. B. and Richard Hartmann were close friends from 1832. In 1853 C. P. Stewart (qv) joined the firm which then became Sharp, Stewart & Co. Shortly afterwards B. left to form a partnership with Richard Peacock (qv), then loco supt MS & L, and they founded the famous firm of Beyer Peacock & Co, Manchester. They bought 12 acres (4.86ha) beside the MS & L at Gorton and the works was begun on 14.3.1854. The first loco appeared on 31.7.1855, the first GWR standard-gauge engine, designed by Daniel Gooch (qv). Among notable B. designs produced by BP were 2–2–2s for the Edinburgh & Glasgow R, some of which ran for 52 yrs. B. was one of the first engs to explode the theory of a low centre of gravity for a loco. Perhaps the most famous B. design was the o/c 4–4–0T with leading Bissell truck for the Metropolitan R, originating in a 2–4–0 tender design for the Tudela & Bilbao R in 1862. A tank version for 3ft 6in (1.067m) gauge for Norway followed in 1866 and was modified to the Isle of Man 3ft (0.914m) gauge in 1873. The Bissell truck was not a complete success and subsequent engines of this type were designed with Adams bogies. During the 1860s and 70s B's friendship with the Beatties (qv) resulted in a large number of heavy goods engines of almost pure B. design for the LSWR, all 0–6–0s. The best of the B. express engines were built for the Dutch State Rs in the 1860s and 70s. Another famous design was the inside-frame 2–2–2 class for the Swedish State Rs. After unsuccessfully courting Sharp's dr B. remained a bachelor for the rest of his life, but was able to enjoy only a short retirement at Llantisilio. B. was the founder of the IME, in 1847 in his house in Manchester, and George Stephenson was elected president while B., J. E. McConnell (qv) of the LNWR and Joseph Miller (qv) were the first vice presidents. In 1861 B. invited Hermann Ludwig Lange (qv) to join the firm and on the ret of B. Lange became chief eng. Beyer Peacock closed down

in 1966. A history of the firm is pub by the North Western Museum of Science & Industry, Manchester, which houses all the BP records, drawings and photographs.
Engg V 21 16.6.1876 p 505; *Proc IME* 1.1877 p 16; *The Eng* V 41 9. 6.1876 p 439; *The Locomotive* 11.1937 pp 351–5; *Min Proc ICE* V 47 1876–7 p 290

BIDDER, George Parker

b Moreton Hampstead, Devon 14.6.1806; d Dartmouth, Devon, 28.9.1878 aged 72.
Civil eng and mathematician. Son of a stone mason. Ed at village sch, and at early age showed great powers of mental calculation. 1819 attended classes at Edinburgh Univ, obtaining a prize for higher maths in 1822. 1824 left Edinburgh and worked on the Ordnance Survey, but in 1825 left to work with Henry Robinson Palmer, civil eng, on London docks and several R and canal surveys. About 1829 he was emp by Walker & Burges on the laying of the granite tramway in Commercial Road, Limehouse, London, which was used until removed in 1871. 1834 invited by Robert Stephenson to work on the London & Birmingham R. 1835–6 asst to George Stephenson in Parliamentary work where his powers of rapid calculation made him a formidable opponent to rival schemes, especially the lines between London and Brighton and from Manchester through the Potteries to Rugby. 1837 worked with Robert Stephenson on the const of the Blackwall R and in the application of the rope system by which it was first worked. With Robert Stephenson he was responsible for the installation of the electric telegraph on 16 miles of the London & Birmingham R and on the Blackwall R in 1840. B. was one of the first to see the great advantage of the telegraph in R operation. With George Stephenson, B. advised on the laying out of the Belgian R system. He was responsible for a large portion of the GER and designed the swing bridge over the Wensum at Norwich. With Robert Stephenson B. built the first R in Norway, Christiania–Eidsvold, about 40 miles. Also chief eng of the Royal Danish R. B's greatest work was the Victoria dock system, London. He also

worked for the Metropolitan Water Bd. He was interested in the Indian R system and was consulting eng, from 1862, to the Scind R Co, the Indus Steam Flotilla and the Punjab R Co, all associated. It was largely B. who established the Indian gauge of 5ft 6in (1.676m) and he successfully opposed the Indian govt which wanted a break of gauge. He also opposed the atmospheric system of propulsion. He was engaged in most of the great R contests in Parliament. He was a dir of the GER; became MICE 1835 and member of the council in 1847 and president 1860–1.
Min Proc ICE V 57 1878–9 pp 294–309; *The Eng* V 46 27.9.1878 p 228

BIGGS, Sir Albert Ashley

b (?) 7.12.1872; d Devon 12.5.1938 aged 65.
Eng on Indian Rs. Received scientific training at Univ Coll, Bristol, while a pupil under Stothert & Pitt of Bath. 1895 became asst to H. F. Donaldson, chief eng of the London & India Docks Jt Committee. 1897 asst eng Southern Mahratta R, India. His outstanding work led to his being 'lent' to the Indian govt in 1902 as executive eng, Madras Presidency Famine Feeder Lines. In 1909 the Portuguese govt requisitioned his services as res eng, Marmugao Harbour extn works. In 1915 he became dep chief eng, Madras & Southern Mahratta R, into which the Southern Mahratta R had been merged, and soon afterwards became chief eng. In 1925 he became agent of the R. In 1927–8 he was president of the Indian R Conference Assoc. He was knighted on ret in 1928. Twice m, having 1 son and 1 dr by the first.
Journal ICE V 10 1938–9 p 126

BILLINGTON, John Robert

b Freckleton, Lancashire, 18.4.1873; d Horwich 22.3.1925 aged nearly 52.
Loco eng and draughtsman, LYR and LMS, Horwich. Ed Kirkham Gr Sch. Spent 9 months with Thomas Riley, contr on the widening of the Preston–Blackpool line. In 1889 began apprenticeship at Horwich wks, LYR, under John Aspinall (qv), and in 1894 was transferred to the drg office. He was a brilliant scholar and achieved several

examination honours at Horwich Mechanics Institute, inc Whitworth Exhibition 1897, County Council Exhibition, and 1st Class Hons in Engg. In 1897, in addition to his ordinary duties, he was app teacher at the Inst where he had a valuable influence on many younger engs. 1901 took charge of testing dept. On 29.6.1904 he was app gas mgr, remaining in that position until 1912 when he returned to the drg office. On ret of Z. Tatlow in 6.1913 he became chief draughtsman and worked with George Hughes on the redesigning of the LYR 4-cyl 4–6–0. B. was also largely responsible for the design of the standard LMS 2–6–0, the 'Crab', one of the finest loco designs on the LMS. He was an enthusiast for all scientific pursuits, and was a pioneer among early motorists in Lancashire. His untimely death robbed loco engg of a valuable member. He was MIME, MILE and AICE.

The Eng V 139 27.3.1925 p 360; *Journal ILE* V 15 1925 p 376; Proc IME 7.1925 p 1069; Marshall, John. *The Lancashire & Yorkshire R* V 2 pp 223–4

BILLINTON, Col Lawson Boskovsky

b Brighton (?).(?).1882; d Brighton 19.11.1954 aged 72.
Loco eng, LBSCR. Son of R.J.B. (qv). Ed Tonbridge Sch. After a course in mech eng entered LBSCR wks at Brighton as pupil under his f and was afterwards app draughtsman and then inspector. Supervised const of LBSCR bogie steel wagons at Glasgow. Took charge of experiments with oil fuel for locos and of trials of LBSCR express engines. In 2.1907 became asst dist loco supt, New Cross, and later chief supt there. At end of 1911 app loco eng to succeed D. E. Marsh (qv) from 1.1.1912. In 1917 he was commissioned in REs and sent on a mission to Roumania. His loco designs were of pleasing appearance and gave good service. They included the E2 class 0–6–0T, 1912; K class 2–6–0, 1913, on which he introduced his top feed arrangement; and the L class 4–6–4T, 1914. He ret at end of 1922, at the grouping, when only 40. For details of his locos see Bradley, D. L. *The Locos of the LBSCR* (RCTS) Part 3 1974.

RG V 101 26.11.1954 p 607 (portrait)

BILLINTON, Robert John

b Wakefield 5.4.1845; d Brighton 7.11.1904 aged 59.
Loco C & W Supt, LBSCR. Son of a R contractor. In 9.1859 apprenticed to William Fairbairn & Sons, Manchester, who had been building R locos since 1839 but who ended this work in 1862. In 3.1863 B. moved to Simpson & Co of Pimlico, London, from where, after a short time, he returned north to work with S. Witham at Calderdale Ironworks, Wakefield. From 6.1865 to 6.1866 he worked with Roland Child, mining and civil eng, Wakefield. He then became asst wks mgr to Munro, Walker & Eaton, Sheffield, where he was responsible for the design and erection of locos, stationary machinery and engines for ships. In 5.1870 he was app asst to William Stroudley (qv) at the Brighton wks of the LBSCR, taking charge of design and const of locos and rolling stock. 1874 app asst to S. W. Johnson (qv), loco supt of the MR at Derby, becoming chief draughtsman. On the d of Stroudley on 20.12.1889 B. was recommended as his successor and on 13.1.1890 he was app loco C & W and marine supt, LBSCR. After 16 yrs at Derby B. had become steeped in the MR tradition of small locos and light trains and he at first adopted this policy at Brighton, introducing small 4–4–0s and 0–6–0s less powerful than existing Stroudley 0–4–2s and 0–6–0s and it was not until 1899 that he built more powerful engines. His first design was the D class 0–4–4T of which 36 were built from 1892–6, followed by the 55 C2 class 0–6–0s from 1893–1902. In 1894 he introduced the 0–6–2 radial tank, class E3, and in 1895 the B2 4–4–0s. Next came the 75 0–6–2Ts class E4, 1897–1903. In 1899–1902 he brought out 33 more powerful 4–4–0s of class B4. His last locos were the E5 and E6 0–6–2Ts, 1902–4. Altogether 282 engines were built to his designs at Brighton, though the 12 E6 tanks were completed after his d in 1904. Many of his locos were greatly improved by the fitting of larger boilers under his successor D. E. Marsh (qv). B. was responsible for the introduction of lavatory carriages on the LBSCR, steel carriage underframes, and the construction of a

new carriage, paint and trimming shop at Preston Park, Brighton, the considerable enlargement of the boiler shop, the building of a new steel carriage underframe shop, the lengthening of the erecting shop and the building of a new wheel and press shop, a new smith's shop, turning and machine shops. During his regime the number of engine drivers increased by 40 per cent. A total of 8377 wagons and 1839 carriages were built. Carriages were built with higher pitched roofs and ran on 6 wheels or bogies. Four-wheeled carriages were replaced and gas and electric lighting was installed in all the stock. Although MIME from 1888, MICE from 1899, the Iron & Steel Institute and the Institute of Naval Architects, he took little part in their meetings and was almost unknown outside the LBSCR. He was a man of kindly and genial disposition and was well liked by those under him.

Min Proc ICE V 162 1904–5 p 412; Proc IME 2.1905 p 149; *The Eng* V 98 11.11. 1904 p 478; *Engg* V 78 11.11.1904 p 658; Bradley, D. L. *The Locos of the LBSCR* (RCTS) Part 2 1972; Burtt, Cyril. *Locos of the LBSCR 1839–1903* 1903; Maskelyne, J. N. *Locos of the LBSCR 1903–1923* 1928; Burtt, F. *LBSCR Locos* 1946

BIRKINSHAW, John Cass

b Bedlington, Co Durham, (?).(?).1811; d (?).3.1867 aged 55.

Civil eng on Rs in NE and S England. Son of John B., principal agent of Bedlington Ironworks and who patented the malleable iron fish-bellied rail on 23.10. 1820. When Robert Stephenson returned from S America B. became his first articled pupil. B's first app was as res eng on the Leicester & Swannington R, opened 1832–3. He also worked with Thomas Cabry on the const of the Canterbury & Whitsable R, opened 4.5.1830. In 1834 he was app asst eng on the London & Birmingham R at Camden under Robert Stephenson, the works inc Primrose Hill tunnel. In 1837 he took charge of the works of the Birmingham & Derby Jn R from Derby to Hampton. On completion of the Birmingham station and the Tame Valley line in 1842 B. resigned. In 1844–5 he was app jt eng with Robert Stephenson to the York–Scarborough line. In

1845 he made surveys for the Seamer–Bridlington and Hull–Bridlington lines. He also carried out the Harrogate–Church Fenton line, inc Crimple vdt and tunnel. He was eng of the Rillington Jn–Pickering, York–Beverley, Malton & Driffield and, in conjunction with T. E. Harrison (qv), the Thirsk & Malton lines. B. then moved to London and prepared plans for the Ware & Hertford and Luton & Hertford Rs, the LSWR Lymington branch, and for lines in the Isle of Wight. Became MICE 2.3.1847.

Min Proc ICE V 31 1870–1 pp 202–7

BISSELL, Levi

b (?) c 1800; d New York City 5.8.1873 aged 73.

Widely known for his leading truck for locos. On 11.10.1841, while at Newark, NJ, he obtained a US patent (2307) for an 'air spring' for loco suspension, but apart from experimental use on a passenger car it was not applied. During the 1850s B. was critical of the 4-wheeled centrally-pivoted loco truck which caused many derailments. He extended the truck frame and pivot rearwards so permitting the axles to remain nearly parallel to the radius of the curve. He also devised a system of centring on the truck using inclined planes of 1 in 11. This truck was first tested on the Central RR of New Jersey a few months before it was patented (US patent 17913, 4.8.1857). The B. safety truck was taken up by the Rogers Loco Wks which equipped many engines with it. In 1857, at the suggestion of Zerah Colburn (qv), B. devised a 2-wheeled truck which he patented in 1858. It was first used in 1859 on a 'Stephenson long boiler' type 2–4–2 designed by Robert Sinclair (qv) for Belgium and tested on the Eastern Counties R, England. It was used on some similar 2–4–2s built by Sinclair for the GER in 1864. This 'pony truck' was tested in USA later in 1859 and became widely used on freight engines. The widest application of the 4-wheel truck in England was on the 4–4–0Ts built from 1864 by Beyer Peacock & Co, Manchester, for the Met and Met District Rs, based on some engines built earlier by them to a design by Thomas Hunt for the Tudela & Bilbao R, Spain. No personal information about B. can be found.

White, John H. Jr, *American Locos, an engg history 1830–80* 1968; Ahrons, E. L. *The British Steam R Loco 1825–1925* 1925, 1961

BLACK, William

b Airdrie, Lanarkshire, Scotland 9.2.1823; d Newcastle upon Tyne 11.7.1905 aged 82.
Loco mfr; co-founder of Black, Hawthorn & Co. Began commercial career with the Jarrow Alkali Co. Later started an iron foundry at Fatfield, Co Durham, and then took over the North Eastern Foundry at South Shields which he greatly enlarged. In conjunction with H. T. Morton and others and Thomas Hawthorn (qv) he founded the firm of Black, Hawthorn & Co, Gateshead, producing locos and gen engg. B. also founded the St Bede Chemical Wks, Jarrow, later part of United Alkali Co. Also one of the promoters of the North Eastern Marine Engg Wks, Sunderland and Wallsend. B. was member of Inst of Shipbuilders & Engs; MIME, and of other societies. He was a keen yachtsman. He was not m. B. was magistrate for S Shields and Gateshead.
The Eng V 100 14.7.1905 p 42; *Evening Chronicle* (Newcastle) 13.7.1905

BLACKBURNE, John George

b London 4.6.1815; d Oldham 30.9.1871 aged 56.
Civil eng. Ed at Worksop, Notts. On 31.5.1828 he was articled to William Dunn, a land and mining surveyor in Oldham. On 5.6.1835 B. became Dunn's partner until Dunn d on 27.6.1840. During the 'R Mania', 1844–6, he was emp under Hawkshaw (qv) in surveying the Oldham Alliance system of Rs which, however, was only completed about 20 yrs later by the LYR. In 1858 he laid out the Oldham, Ashton & Guide Bridge R and supervised const, taking charge of the Hyde–Marple line at the same time. In 1859 he laid out the Marple, New Mills & Hayfield line and the Stockport & Woodley R, later acting as eng of both. They inc large vdts at Park Bridge, Marple and Goyt Cliff. In 1862 B. took his son John William into partnership. His other works consisted largely of reservoirs and waterworks. Elected MICE 1855.
Min Proc ICE V 33 1871–2 pp 206–9

BLAKE, Rustat

b (?) 16.5.1871; d London 14.4.1940 aged 69.
Civil eng. Ed at Haileybury and Cambridge Univ and trained in engg under Sir John Wolfe Barry (qv) and H. M. Brunel. Remained with Barry & Partners and was engaged in R const in Britain and India. 1911–18 was personal asst and later chief asst to Barry and was responsible for all the firm's work on the Bengal–Nagpur R. He was also jt consulting eng for the S Punjab R until its liquidation. In 1918 he became a partner in the firm of Sir John Wolfe Barry, Lyster & Partners. In 1920 B. was app civil engg member of the Royal Commission on the Uniform Gauge for the Commonwealth of Australia. He was active in engg right up to his d. In 1911 he m Maud Wallace of Moffat.
Journal ICE V 14 1940 p 599

BLENKINSOP, John

b Leeds 1783; d Leeds 22.1.1831 aged 48.
A pioneer of the steam loco. Became principal agent of the Brandling family who owned the Middleton collieries near Leeds. In conjunction with Matthew Murray (qv) he obtained a patent on 10.4.1811 for a steam loco propelled by a toothed wheel engaging in a rack on one of the rails. The engine had 2 cyls driving cranks set at right angles. It was first tried on 24.6.1812. (*Leeds Mercury* 27.6 and 18.7.1812). B's engine was the first commercially successful engine on any R. Four locos were built and they continued at work for over 20 years. A set of wheels from one of these can be seen at the National R Museum, York.
Leeds Mercury 29.1.1831; Smiles, Samuel. *Lives of the Engineers* V3, 1862

BLOOD, Aretas

b Weatherfield, Vermont, USA (?).(?).1816; d (?) (?).(?).1897 aged about 81.
Supt Manchester Loco Wks. At age 17 apprenticed as blacksmith. Learned machining and then spent 7 yrs in Locks & Canals Co machine shop, Lowell, Mass. About 1849 became job hand at Essex Machine Shop, Lawrence, Mass,

producing small parts for locos. By 1853 he was able to purchase a share in the new Manchester Loco Wks. Until 1857 the wks, under O. W. Bayley, built locos which were too light. B. then took over and developed a heavier machine, later becoming principal owner of the wks. In 1872 added the fire engine business of Bayley's old firm of Amoskeag Mfg Co to the MLW. The MLW built nearly 1800 locos by 1901 when it was absorbed into ALCO.
White, John H. Jr. *American Locos, an engg history 1830–80* 1968

BLOTNITZKI, Leopold

b (?) 15.11.1817; d Berne 23.6.1879 aged 61.
Swiss eng and insp. Worked under Etzel (qv) on the Württemburg State R and went to Switzerland in 1852. After a short period on the Swiss Central R he became Canton eng in Geneva in 1853, building the Rhone and Mont Blanc bridges and also the Rs from Geneva to Versoix and Carouge. In 1855 he surveyed the Lausanne–Freiburg–Berne R project and in 1856 was entrusted with the mgt of R const in Freiburg. For several years he was engaged on other projects, but returned to R work with the Bödeli and Brünig (1888) Rs. From 1873 he became the first technical inspector of the Swiss R Dept and was responsible for the first Swiss signalling regulations, from 7.9.1874.
Röll V2 p 623

BLYTH, Benjamin Hall

b Edinburgh 14.7.1819; d N Berwick 21.8.1866 aged 47.
In 1834 became pupil of T. Grainger and J. Miller, civil engs (qqv). In 1841 he was app res eng on the Kilmarnock branch of the Glasgow & Ayrshire R (later G & SWR). During 1844–6 he rose to become principal asst in Miller's office, laying out lines from Kilmarnock to Carlisle, part of the NBR and the Direct Northern from London to York. In early 1850 he began on his own account, his first work being the Slamannan–Bo'ness branch of the Monkland R. 1852 app eng in chief to the GN of S and in 1854 was joined by his brother Edward as partner. He was connected as adviser and engineer to the CR, GNS, G & SW, Monklands, Scottish Central, Perth & Dundee, Portpatrick and other lines. At an early age his health began to decline from overwork. Became MICE 1851.
Min Proc ICE V 26 1866–7 p 556

BODMER, John George

b Zurich 6.12.1786; d Zurich 29.5.1864 aged 79.
Mech eng of German and Huguenot descent, christened Johann Georg. Was intended for merchant's office, but went into engg and in 1799–1800 was apprenticed to a millwright named Mesmer at Hauptweil nr Zurich. Later he established a small workshop at Küsnacht nr Zurich where his inventive genius was soon displayed. Besides general millwright work he produced guns and projectiles. 1806 went into partnership with Baron d'Eichthal at St Blaise, Baden, Germany, to establish a cotton mill. B. designed most of the machinery. He returned to Switzerland in 1821 and was occupied with textile machinery. Early in 1828 went to England for the second time, having in 1816 failed to interest the British govt in his new cannon, and lived in Manchester where he tried to establish his inventions in Textile machinery. He then moved to Bolton where he was concerned with his machinery. After a further spell in Switzerland from 1828 he returned to England in 1833 and appointed Sharp, Roberts & Co as makers of his cotton machinery. In 1834 he again settled in Bolton and at the Union Foundry of Rothwell & Co he designed his famous mechanical stoker. He also invented a double-piston balanced steam engine, patented in 1834, primarily intended for R locos. He built his first loco in 1842. In 1844 he took out a patent for a loco incorporating rocking grate, corrugated firebox and a new link motion. In 1845 he supplied 2 2–2–2s to the Brighton and SER Jt Comm. The SER engine did little work but the Brighton engine ran until rebuilt in 12.1858. In 1844 he invented and set up a rolling mill to produce steel tyres for loco and carriage wheels at P. R. Jackson's rolling mill, Salford. There is strong evidence that J. J. Meyer's expansion valve (France 1842) and A. K. Rider's valve (USA 1869) were both

invented by B. He also designed a centre-corridor R carriage giving passage from one car to the next, which was developed in USA. B's last British patent, for R carriages and p w was taken out by Charles Fox (qv) on his behalf. Elected MICE 15.2.1835. From 1846–8 he lived in London. He then lived in Vienna until 1860 when he returned to Zurich where he died 4 yrs later.

Min Proc ICE V 28 1868–9 pp 573–608; *The Locomotive* 15.2.1911 pp 43–4; 15.1. 1909 p 10; 15.3.1909 p 56; 15.6.1909 p 110; 15.3.1910 p 58; 15.11.1910 p 247

BOOTH, Henry

b Liverpool 4.4.1788; d Liverpool 28.3.1869 aged 81.
Mech eng; secretary & treasurer of Liverpool & Manchester R. Eldest son of Thomas B., corn merchant. Began as a corn merchant, later on his own account. On 27.8.1812 he m the eldest dr of Abraham Crompton. His f was a member of the committee formed in 1822 to promote the Liverpool & Manchester R and Henry B. acted as secretary in which position he is stated to have written the original draft prospectus and to have prepared numerous reports. On the incorporation of the L & M Co by the Act of 5.5.1826 he became secretary and treasurer, or chief executive officer. He had great mechanical ingenuity and was associated with George and Robert Stephenson in entering the *Rocket* in the Rainhill trials. It was B. who suggested the multi-tubular boiler. He also devised the screw coupling, later developed on the L & M by Nathaniel Worsdell (qv), spring buffers, and a method of lubricating R carriage axles. In 6.1830 he pub his *Account of the Liverpool & Manchester R*. In 1831 a second edn appeared, and also it was pub in Philadelphia with James Walker's *Report* and Robert Stephenson's and Joseph Locke's *Observations*. On the formation of the LNWR on 16.7.1846 B. became the joint secretary responsible for the N section until his ret in 1859. He was elected to the bd in 10.1848 and continued as dir until 18.5.1859.

Lee, Charles E. Introd to *Account of the Liverpool & Manchester R* by B

BORRIES, August von (see VON BORRIES)

BORSIG, Albert

b Berlin 7.3.1829; d Berlin 10.4.1878 aged 49.
German loco eng. Son of August B. (qv), founder of the Borsig Loco Wks, whom he succeeded as mgr in 1854. In 1856–8 he enlarged the Berlin wks and in 1859–60 established blast furnaces at the Moabit ironworks to further the supply of material. Loco const reached 150–160 a year. 1860–70 he established rolling mills in Westphalia and Schlesien, transferring the rolling mills from Moabit and using the space for mfr of boilers and loco erection. The 500th loco was built in 1854 and the 3000th in 1873. By this time B. employed 1800 in the loco erecting shops, 700 at Moabit, and 3000 at Oberschlesien.

Röll V 2 p 672; *Engg* V 25 10.5.1878 p 373

BORSIG, Johann Carl Friedrich August

b Breslau 25.6.1804; d Berlin 7.7.1854 aged 50.
Founder of one of the most important German loco wks. Ed Breslau tech sch and at Royal Industrial Institute, Berlin. Trained in mech eng at F. G. Egells, Berlin. In 1837 B. established a wks in Berlin employing c 50 persons. By 1847, in which year 67 locos and tenders were built, it had expanded to 1200 employees. By mid 1851 over 330 locos had been built. Also in 1847 he established an ironworks at Moabit near Berlin for production of good quality rails, until then only obtainable from England. This came into production in 1850, so freeing German Rs from the British monopoly. In 1854 B. opened a colliery in Biscupitz in Oberschlesien.

Röll V 2 p 672; *The Locomotive* 15.10. 1929 p 327

BOSSHARD, Eugen

b Bauma, Switzerland, 31.10.1873; d Bad Ragaz, Switzerland, 21.8.1942 aged 68.
Swiss civil eng. Studied at Federal Polytechnic, Zurich, 1892–6, obtaining diploma of building eng. He first worked on Berne tramways and on const of the Berne–Muri–Worb R. 1899 became a

leading eng in the firm of Albert Buss & Co, Basle, in which he gained vast experience in R building, roads, bridges, drainage works, etc. B. was responsible for the rebuilding of Basle station. One of his most outstanding works was the metre-gauge Bernina R, St Moritz–Tirano, the highest R over the Alps, begun in 1906 and opened throughout in 1910. In 1921 became chief eng to City of Zurich, being concerned in the development of the town tramways and in R works in the district. Largely responsible for the main station in Zurich. S.Bz 28.11.1942 pp 261–2; V 59 1912 p 73 et seq article by B. on the Bernina R; Marshall, John. *Metre gauge Rs in S and E Switzerland* 1974

BOUCH, Sir Thomas

b Thursby, Cumberland, 22.2.1822; d Moffat, Dumfries-shire, 30.10.1880 aged 58.
Civil eng, bridge builder. Third son of William B., sea captain. Ed locally and at Carlisle under Joseph Hannah. In 1840 he entered a mech engg business in Liverpool, but soon left and was engaged by Larmer, a civil eng on the Lancaster & Carlisle R, under Locke and Errington (qqv). In 11.1844 B. went to Leeds, and then obtained employment for 4 yrs on the Stockton & Darlington R under John Dixon. In 1.1849 B. left Darlington to become mgr and eng of the Edinburgh & Northern R, later the Edinburgh, Perth & Dundee which became part of the NBR. The breaks at the estuaries of the Forth and Tay led him to devise wagon ferries, for which he designed the loading and unloading arrangements, in 1851. Shortly afterwards B. left to engage in gen engg. He was responsible for surveys and plans for the Darlington & Barnard Castle (S & D) 20 miles (32km); South Durham & Lancashire Union (S & D) 50 miles (80km); Eden Valley (S & D) 22 miles (35km); Cockermouth, Keswick & Penrith 31 miles (50km); Sevenoaks & Maidstone (SER) 20 miles (32km); Peebles (NBR) 21 miles (34km); Kinross-shire (NBR) 10½ miles (17km); Leven, Fife (NBR) 6 miles (10km); Leslie (NBR) 5 miles (8km); St Andrews (NBR) 5 miles (8km); Crieff Jn (CR) 9 miles (14km); Coatbridge 8 miles (13km); Edinburgh, Loanhead & Roslin (NBR) 6 miles (10km); Leadburn, Linton & Dolphinton (NBR) 10 miles (16km); Penicuick (NBR) 6¼ miles (10km); Arbroath–Montrose (NBR) 16 miles (26km); Newport, Fife (NBR) 6 miles (10km); Tay Bridge, tunnel and connecting lines (NBR) 8 miles (13km); and Edinburgh Suburban R (NBR) 8 miles (13km). He built some remarkable bridges including the Barnard Castle vdt, Deepdale and Belah vdts on the S Durham & Lancashire Union R, Bilston Burn bridge on the Edinburgh, Loanhead & Roslin line, a bridge over the Esk at Montrose and the Hownes Gill vdt at Consett. His greatest work was the Tay bridge, a single-line structure nearly 2 miles long with 85 spans, completed on 22.9.1877. In 6.1879 Queen Victoria crossed it and knighted B. on 26.6.1879. But there were serious faults in the bridge design and const. In a violent storm on the evening of 28.12.1879 the centre spans blew down while a train was crossing. Over 70 people were drowned and there were no survivors. The shock of this undermined B's health and hastened his d. Many flaws in B's designs and work arose from a desire to carry out the work as cheaply as possible. This often led to his work being improved or redone by other engs, leading in the end to greater expense than would have been incurred by a sounder basic design. He acquired a poor reputation for inattention to work in progress and lack of concern for the consequences. It was largely these that were responsible for the Tay Bridge disaster. In 7.1853 B. m Margaret Ada Nelson who survived him with one son and 2 drs. He became AICE on 3.12.1850 and member on 11.5.1858, MIME 1859. He was bro of William B. (qv), loco eng on the S & D.
Proc IME 1881 p 1; 1883 p 27; Min Proc ICE V 63 1880–1 pp 301–8; *The Eng* V 50 5.11.1880 pp 347–8; *Engg* V 30 5.11.1880 p 409; Thomas, John, *The Tay Bridge Disaster* 1972; *North British Railway* V 1 1969

BOUCH, William

b (?) (?).(?).1813; d Weymouth 19.1.1876 aged 62.
Loco eng, Stockton & Darlington R. Elder bro of Thomas B. (qv). Appren-

ticed at Robert Stephenson & Co, Newcastle upon Tyne, afterwards going to Russia as chief eng on a ship in the Russian navy. In 1840 he returned to England and was app loco supt of the Stockton & Darlington R. His best known engines were the 1001 class 0–6–0s, a development of the Stephenson 'long-boiler' type, of which No 1275 is preserved at Darlington. His two o/c 4–4–0s of 1860, among the first of their type in Britain, had large side-window cabs for working over the Stainmore line. His later 4–4–0s with 30in (762mm) stroke and 13in (330mm) diam piston valves were a failure. After the amalg of the S & D and NER in 1863 B. remained in command at Shildon until his ret in 1875. The responsibility then passed to Edward Fletcher (qv). B. was also joint eng with Hawksley of the Weardale & Shildon District Water Works and of Consett Water Works. Became MIME 1858.
Proc IME 1.1877 p 17; *The Eng* 28.1. 1876 p 63; Nock, O. S., *Locos of the NER* 1954

BOULTON, Isaac Watt

b Stockport (?).(?).1823; d Ashton-under-Lyne 20.6.1899 aged 76.
Loco eng; proprietor of the famous 'siding'. Son of John B. and a relative of Matthew Boulton, financier of James Watt. His f removed to Ashton-u-L in 1830 and later ran a service of canal packet boats. B. was ed at Ashton and Macclesfield and in 1841 began an apprenticeship at the wks of the Sheffield, Ashton & Manchester R near Hyde, under Richard Peacock (qv), loco supt. In 1849 he built a steam road coach which ran a service between Ashton and Manchester. Next the NSR asked him to provide a steamboat service on Rudyard Lake near Leek, which went into operation in 1850. In 1854 he joined the loco dept of the MS & L (successors to the SA & M) at Gorton, Manchester, until 1856 when he started on his own as an eng at Ashton, building and repairing engines and machinery and small locos. He built many road steamers throughout his life. In 1858–9 he bought 3 Bury 2–2–0 locos and began a business in hiring locos out for various jobs. In the 1860s he purchased more and in

1864 the MS & L built a siding to serve his works, off the Oldham line. A workshop was built beside it and here he conducted a business in rebuilding second hand locos and hiring them to contractors. A series of misfortunes began with a fire in 1879 and the loss of his eldest son Thomas in a shipwreck in 1880. He designed a water-tube boiler and built several engines with it, but maintenance was difficult and business declined until by 1894 there was almost none left. Alfred Rosling Bennett left a brilliantly written account of the work in *The Chronicle of Boulton's Siding*, 1927 and 1971.
The Eng V 87 23.6.1899 p 620

BOUSQUET, Gaston du.
(see DU BOUSQUET)

BOVERI, Walter

b Bamberg, Bavaria, 21.2.1865; d Baden, Switzerland, 28.10.1924 aged 59.
Elec and mech eng. Trained in Nuremberg. At age 19 joined Maschinenfabrik Oerlikon nr Zurich where he worked under C. E. L. Brown (qv) on mfr of electrical machinery. He later took over mgt of the erecting dept, and supervised the devt of the dc motor. 1888 supervised erection and installation of the first power transmission line from Kriegstellen to Solothurn. 1891 joined C. E. L. Brown to found the famous Swiss firm of Brown, Boveri & Co, Baden (BBC). At first Boveri was engaged in designing and erecting various electrical installations. Growth of the firm was rapid. In 1895 he founded 'Motor A-G' in Baden to finance electrical works. There followed a series of important electrical installations, power stations, etc, between 1896 and 1917. Later during this period the firm made increasing amounts of material for R electrification. In 1923 'Motor A-G' amalg with 'Columbus A-G' concerned with S American interests. From 1911 B. was president of BBC and related interests, and a member of the commission on electrification of the Swiss Federal Rs. In 1916 he received a doctorate from Zurich Technical High School.
S Bz V 84 13.12.1924 pp 292–3

BRADSHAW, George

b Salford, nr Manchester, 29.7.1801;
d Christiania, Norway, 6.9.1853 aged 52.
Founder of B's R Guide. Son of poor
parents. Left sch at 14 and was apprenticed to Thomas Tonbridge, a Manchester engraver. At age 19 he joined
the Soc of Friends (Quakers). 1820 set
up as engraver in Belfast but returned to
Manchester in 1822 and began engrav-
ing maps. In 1830 he produced the first
of his maps of canals and inland navigation. In 1831 he took on William Blacklock as apprentice. A letterpress printing
dept was opened in 1835. In 1838
Blacklock became a partner and the firm
became Bradshaw & Blacklock, at 27
Brown St, Manchester, in 1839. On
16.5.1839 he m Martha, dr of William
Darbyshire of Stretton nr Warrington.
B's famous R timetable first appeared
in 1839. In 1840 it became *B's R Com-
panion* with maps, price one shilling (5p)
and in 12.1841 *B's Monthly R Guide*.
Other publications included *B's Conti-
nental R Guide*, 1847–1939, and *B's
General R Directory & Shareholders'
Guide* 1849–1923. B. d of Asiatic cholera
while on a visit to Norway and he was
survived by his only son. The last B.
timetable was No 1521, pub in 6.1961.
Blacklock's Printing wks, successor to
B. & Blacklock, closed in 1971.
Min Proc ICE V 13 1854 pp 145–9;
Manchester Guardian 17.9.1853 p 7;
Smith, G. Royde, *The History of
Bradshaw* 1939

BRAITHWAITE, John

b London 19.3.1797; d London
25.9.1870 aged 73.
3rd son of John B., constructor of the
earliest diving bell. Trained in mech eng
under his f. On the d of his f in 1818 B.
and his bro Francis carried on the
business. After the d of Francis in 1823
B. continued alone, building high-
pressure steam engines. In 1827 he was
introduced to G and R Stephenson and
at the same time became acquainted
with Capt John Ericsson (qv). In 1829 B.
and Ericsson built a loco, the *Novelty*,
which they entered in the Rainhill trials
on the Liverpool & Manchester R. It
was the first loco to run a mile in under
a minute (56sec). At this time B. built

his first steam fire engine. In 1834 he
worked with C. B. Vignoles (qv) on the
laying out of the Eastern Counties R,
adopting a gauge of 5ft (1.524m). On the
advice of R. Stephenson it was later
converted to standard g. B. was joint
founder with J. C. Robertson of *The
Railway Times* in 1837. In 1844 and
1846 B surveyed Rs in France. Elected
MICE 13.2.1838.
Min Proc ICE V 31 1870–1 pp 207–11

BRANDRETH, Thomas Shaw

b Cheshire 24.7.1788; d Worthing
27.5.1873 aged 84.
Mathematician, classical scholar and
barrister-at-law. Ed Eton and Trinity
Coll, Cambridge, graduating BA in 1810
and MA 1813. His scientific interests
stimulated a friendship with G. Stephenson and he was one of the original
directors of the Liverpool & Manchester
R, taking an active part in the survey,
especially across Chat Moss. A 10mph
(16km/h) speed limit led him to design
and build the 'Cycloped', a machine
propelled by a horse walking on a moving platform. It could move at 15mph
(24km/h). However, although not used
on the L & M it was used on some Rs
in Italy and USA.
DNB V 2 p 1133

BRANDT, John

b Lancaster, Pennsylvania, (?).(?).1785;
d Lancaster (?).(?).1860 aged c 75.
Famous for his pioneer 4-4-0. Asst eng
on Philadelphia & Columbia RR. 1832–
9 chief eng Philadelphia, Germantown &
Norristown RR. He then joined the
Erie RR. In 1851 he was supt of the
newly formed New Jersey Loco &
Machine Co, Paterson, NJ. About 1854–
5 he left to establish a loco wks in
Lancaster.
White, John H. Jr. *American locomo-
tives, an engineering history 1830–80*;
Sinclair, Angus, *Development of the
Locomotive Engine* 1907, 1970

BRASSEY, Thomas

b Buerton, Cheshire, 7.11.1805;
d St Leonard's on Sea 8.12.1870 aged 65.
Civil eng and contractor. Son of John B.
of Bulkeley, Cheshire. Ed at Chester.
At 16 articled to a surveyor named
Lawton at Chester with whom he later

went into partnership. In 1831 he m Maria Harrison of Birkenhead, and soon took charge of the entire business of Lawton & Brassey. In 1835 Joseph Locke (qv), eng of the GJR, awarded B. the contract for 10 miles (16km) of line, following his building of Penkridge vdt. B. next undertook large contracts for Locke on the London & Southampton R, employing c 3000 men, and at the same time, also for Locke, for portions of the Chester–Crewe (1838–40), Sheffield–Manchester (1838–45) and Glasgow–Greenock (1838–41) Rs. In 1840 some of the directors of the LSWR and some French capitalists formed a co to build the Paris & Rouen R. B. in partnership with Mackenzie (qv) secured the contract. In 1843–8 B. and Mackenzie contracted for the Havre & Rouen and 5 other French Rs, and B. also undertook, in whole or in part, 3 lines in Scotland and 2 in England and Wales. At this time B. employed 75 000 men, his payments for labour were £15 000–£20 000 weekly and the capital involved was c £36 million. Among these works were the CR, and Welwyn vdt on the GNR (1850). In 1851 B. began works in Shropshire, Somerset and Inverness-shire. In 1852 he undertook the Sambre & Meuse R, Belgium, the Dutch Rhenish R, the Barcelona & Mataro R and the Maria Antonia R in Italy. In partnership with M. Peto (qv) and Edward Betts (qv) he built the Grand Trunk R in Canada (1852–5) and between 1853–7 built 6 more Rs in France, 6 in Italy, the Bilbao & Miranda R, Spain, besides contracts in Norway, Sweden, Denmark, Switzerland, and the Fell R over Mont Cenis Pass (1868), and extensive contracts in Turkey and Austria. He built a great part of the East Indian R, hundreds of miles of R in Australia, the first Rs in S America; and one of his last undertakings was a contract for docks at Callao, Peru, which had to be carried out by his executors. Barrow docks (1863) and Runcorn vdt (1865) were among his most important works. His total R contracts 1848–61 amounted to 2374 miles (3871km) at a cost of £28 million. B. was a man of absolute reliability and integrity. When the Barentin vdt on the Paris & Rouen R collapsed in 1846, although it was not his fault,

he rebuilt it at his expense. He always completed his contracts to time. He treated his employees with scrupulous honesty and fairness. He had outstanding ability to delegate work to others, and for selecting the right men for the job. He was never elated by prosperity and remained a simple man to the end. Became AICE 13.1.1852.
Min Proc ICE V 33 1871–2 pp 246–51; *The Eng* V 30 12.1870 p 406; Walker, Charles, *Thomas Brassey, Railway Builder* 1969; Helps, Sir Arthur, *The Life and Labours of Mr Brassey* 1872, 1969

BREWER, John Williams
b Llanelly 26.3.1841; d Cardiff 26.8.1894 aged 53.
Civil eng, Taff Vale R. 1856–9 worked in loco dept of Rumney R under his f who was then mgr. He was then articled to David Jones, eng of the RR. In 6.1861 B. was app asst to John Williams, eng of new works on the TVR. In 1870 he took an office in Cardiff where until 1880 he practised as a civil and mining eng, during which period he const several branch Rs. From 1880 to his d B. was permanently with the TVR, first on mining surveys. On the d of Williams in 1887 B. became surveyor and asst eng, and on the ret of H. O. Fisher in 1891 he became chief eng. He prepared parliamentary plans for the Cowbridge & Aberthaw R which he built with Fisher. Became AICE 12.5.1891.
Min Proc ICE V 119 1894–5 p 402

BRIDEL, Gustav
b Biel 26.10.1827; d Bern 3.12.1884 aged 57.
Swiss eng. Ed Central School of Arts and Mfrs, Paris. App insp of rolling stock materials of the Eastern R, France. 1855 supervised const of Palace of Industry, Paris. He then founded an institution for R const in Yverdon and designed most of the R bridges in western Switzerland. 1873 app chief eng of the Jura–Bern–Lucerne R and supervised const of the line from Biel to Delsberg–Delle and Basel. In 1878 he was entrusted with the examination of the plans for the St Gotthard R of which he supervised estimates and entire const.
Röll V 2 p 748

BRIDGEMAN, Henry Orlando

b Blymhill, Shropshire, 26.1.1825;
d London 14.6.1879 aged 54.
Civil eng. Son of Rev H.E.B. Ed
privately, then 3 yrs at Coll for Civil
Engs, Putney. Then entered office of
Charles Liddell and became asst eng on
the Syston–Peterborough R. 1848–50
emp under John Fowler (qv) as res eng
on Leverton–Lincoln extn of the MS
& L including Torksey bridge over the
Trent, an early tubular bridge. He was
then engaged on parliamentary work and
surveys for Oxford–Brentford, Worcester–Hereford, London–Mid Kent and the
Chipping Norton branch; and the
Rheims–Douai R in France. 1852–6 he
was acting eng under G. P. Bidder (qv)
and Fowler on the London, Tilbury &
Southend R. He was then sent by
Fowler to Algeria for the survey of
Philipville & Constantine R. On return
to England he took charge of const of
the Severn Valley R under Fowler,
1858–62. His remaining years were spent
assisting Bidder and investigating foreign
R projects. Became AICE 1849, MICE
1855.
Min Proc ICE V 58 1878–9 p 339

BRIGGS, James CBE

b (?) 24.8.1855; d Derby 2.2.1933
aged 77.
Chief eng, MR. Ed Castle Donington
Gr Sch, Leics. Served 3 yrs under
Gilbert Murray. Joined MR 3.1872.
1880–90 chief asst to Frederick Campion,
S div eng. In 8.1890 became div eng,
S div; 10.1897 asst eng for maintenance;
7.1917 asst eng. 12.1904–6.1905 acted
temporarily as chief maintenance eng,
and as chief eng from 11.1915–4.1916.
Became chief eng 10.1917 following ret
of W. B. Worthington (qv). He continued as chief eng following formation
of the LMS until his ret in 6.1923.
Elected MICE 1881. Awarded CBE for
services in World War 1.
The Eng V 155 10.2.1933 p 141; *Engg*
V 135 17.2.1933 p 197

BROMLEY, Massey MA

b Wolverhampton (?).(?).1846;
d Penistone 16.7.1884 aged 37.
Loco supt, GER. Son of Rev. T.B.,
vicar of St Mary's, Leamington. Ed

Leamington Coll and Brasenose Coll,
Oxford, where he graduated MA in
1872. In 2.1869 he went to Stratford
wks, GER, London, as a pupil of S. W.
Johnson (qv), loco supt, and passed
through the shops, running shed and
drwg office. During 1872–3 he was sent
as insp of the building of locos for the
GER at Avonside Engine Wks, Bristol.
1873 app running shed foreman at Stratford. He devised improvements in lathes
for facing and turning tyres etc. In 1874
he became wks mgr under William
Adams (qv) and on the app of Adams
to the LSWR in 1878 B was app loco
supt. His first engines were the 15 2–6–0s
designed under Adams, the first of their
type in Great Britain. B's first design
was the 7ft 6in (2.286m) o/c 4–2–2,
similar in layout to the GNR 8ft
(2.438m) singles; 20 were built by Dübs
and Kitson in 1879–82. In 1879–83 60
0–4–4Ts were built, similar to those of
Johnson and Adams. In 1880 he introduced the standard GER 0–6–0 shunting
tank, later built in large numbers. His
last design was an 0–6–0 with raised
footplating and side-window cab. Ten
were built by Kitson in 1882. In 8.1881
B. resigned and was succeeded in 1.1882
by T. W. Worsdell (qv). In 6.1882 he
joined John C. Wilson in business in
Westminster. On 16.7.1884, while returning from Manchester, he was one of the
24 passengers killed in the derailment at
Bullhouse nr Penistone following a
broken crank axle on the loco. It was
partly this accident which led to the
suicide of Charles Sacré (qv). B was
elected MICE 1874, MIME 1877.
The Eng V 58 1.8.1884 p 130; *Engg*
25.7.1884 p 94; Proc IME 1884 p 400;
Min Proc ICE V 82 1884–5 p 382

BROTAN, Johann

b (?) (?).(?).1843;
d (?) (?).(?).1923 aged c 80.
Austrian loco eng. Between 1868 and
1912 he held several posts in boiler and
R wks in Austria and Hungary. He was
inventor of a water-tube firebox, about
1870, and of the most successful semi
water-tube boiler, first used in 1902. He
is believed to have died in 1923, but
trace of him was lost in the disorganisa-
tion after World War 1.

BROWN, Charles

b Uxbridge, Middlesex, 30.6.1827;
d Basle, Switzerland, 6.10.1905 aged 78.
Founder of the Swiss Loco & Machine Wks (SLM), Winterthur. Apprenticed at Maudslay & Field, London. Before the end of his 7 yr apprenticeship he left to start his own workshop. In 1851 a relative of Sulzer at Winterthur invited him to start building steam engines at the Sulzer wks. In 1871 he left Sulzer and started his own firm which became SLM, coming into full operation on 1.7.1873. The first engines built were 4 rack locos, Nos 7–10, for the Rigi R, opened in 1871. He was interested in the development of the Swiss electrical engg industry and in the late 1880s he joined the Oerlikon Machine Wks (MFO). In 1885 he established an armaments factory at Naples. In 1890 he ret and practised as a consulting eng at Basle. His son Charles Eugene (qv) was one of the founders of Brown Boveri & Co (BBC).
The Eng V 100 20.10.1905 p 384; S Bz 14.10.1905 p 203

BROWN, Charles Eugene Lancelot

b Winterthur, Switzerland, 17.6.1863;
d Lugano 2.5.1924 aged 60
Elec eng. Son of Charles B. (qv). At an early age he went to the Oerlikon Machine Wks (MFO) nr Zurich where at age 23 he took over mgt of the electrical dept. He started the building of powerful generators, then among the world's largest. In 1889 he turned to ac and developed the first single-phase generators and motors. With Dolivo-Dobrowolski (qv) he developed multiphase traction. After several yrs B. resigned from MFO and with W. Boveri (qv) he founded the firm of Brown Boveri & Co (BBC). From 1900 they built steam turbines following patents by Parsons. B. continued to manage the firm until he ret to Lugano in 1911. BBC have built vast quantities of electrical equipment for all purposes for Rs throughout the world.
S Bz V 83 31.5.1924 pp 257–9

BROWN, Charles John CBE

b Bannockburn, Scotland, 28.1.1872;
d Guildford 17.11.1939 aged 67

Civil eng. Ed Edinburgh Univ and Heriot-Watt Coll, Edinburgh 1888–93. From 1889–93 he was a pupil of J. B. Young of the eng's dept, NBR. 1893–8 he received further training from James Bell, chief eng, NBR. He then became asst eng, NBR, until 1909, supervising many major works. In 1909 he was app chief eng until on 1.10.1911 he succeeded Alexander Ross (qv) as chief eng GNR. After the grouping in 1923 B. took charge of the eng dept of the former GCR and in 1925 of the former GER, thus becoming responsible for the whole of the S area of the LNER. In 1901 he m Alice Milridge of Edinburgh and they had 2 drs. He ret in 1.1937, and was succeeded by R. J. M. Inglis (qv).
Journal ICE V 14 1940 p 245

BROWN, Harold

b Maryport (?) (?).(?).1882;
d (?) (?).(?).(?) aged (?).
Chief eng, Maryport & Carlisle R. Ed Higher Grade Sch, Maryport. Entered eng's office of the M & C at end of 1897 as pupil. Later became asst to Cartmell whom he succeeded as chief eng in 1915. Obtained external BSc (London) (engg) 1913. AICE 1.1916. Also F of PW Inst.

BROWN, William Henry

b Little Britain, Pa, USA, 29.2.1836;
d Belfast 25.6.1910 aged 74.
Chief civil eng, Pennsylvania RR (PRR). His parents were Quakers of limited means. Ed Central High Sch, Philadelphia, later teaching himself engg and surveying. On 15.10.1863 he m Sarah A. Rimmel in Pittsburgh. During the Civil War he served as an eng. In 1864 he entered the service of the PRR with which he remained for 40 yrs, for the last 25 of which he was chief eng. His major work was the Broad Street terminal and station, Philadelphia, 1891–6, with a vast train shed with a roof span of 300ft (91.44m), the world's largest. B. was a great believer in stone bridges in preference to steel. Among his important bridges is one across the Susquehanna 5 miles (8km) W of Harrisburg, 3680ft (1122m). Other important works included rebuilding Jersey City station 4 times; a bridge across the Hackensack River; the elevated line through Newark, New Brunswick, and Elizabeth; Dela-

ware River bridge and RR; a new line from Philadelphia to Harrisburg; 2 new stations in Harrisburg and the low-grade line through the Allegheny mts at Gallitzen, Pa, 1874. He ret 1.3.1906. DAB V 3 p 159; Burgess, George H., and Kennedy, Miles C., *Centennial History of the Pennsylvania RR Co* 1949

BRUCE, Sir George Barclay

b Newcastle upon Tyne 1.10.1821; d London 25.8.1908 aged 86.
Civil eng largely concerned with Indian Rs. Son of John B., founder of the Percy Street Academy, Newcastle, where Robert Stephenson was a pupil and where B. was also ed. In 1836–41 he served a 5 yr apprenticeship at Robert Stephenson & Co. After 2 yrs experience on the Darlington–Newcastle line (op 18.6.1844) he spent a period as res eng on the Northampton–Peterborough line (op 31.5.1845). In 1845 he was app by R. Stephenson and T. E. Harrison (qv) as res eng of the Royal Border Bridge between Tweedmouth and Berwick, op by Queen Victoria on 29.8.1850. For his account of it in Min Proc ICE V 10, 1851, p 219, B. was awarded the Telford Medal. While engaged on the Alston branch of the Newcastle & Carlisle R he was called to India where he became involved in R const. He worked on the Calcutta section of the E Indian R until 1853, then as chief eng of the Madras R on which he laid out about 500 miles (805km) with native labour, until 1856 when ill health compelled him to return to England. From 1856 he was established as a consulting eng in Westminster, from 1888 in partnership with Robert White. For 50 yrs he was consulting eng to the metre g S Indian R and from 1894 to the 5ft 6in (1.676m) g GIPR and Indian Midland R. Other Rs laid out by B. included the Kettering–Thrapston–Huntingdon (MR 1866); Peterborough–Wisbech–Sutton (M & GN 1.8.1866); Whitehaven, Cleator & Egremont, and Stonehouse–Nailsworth (MR 4.2.1867). In Europe he built the Tilsit–Intersburg, E Prussian and Berlin–Gorlitz lines. In 1873–6 he built works for the shipment of ore from the Rio Tinto copper mines at Huelva, Spain. He also carried out eng work on the E Argentine R, Buenos Aires Grand

National Tramways, and on the Beira R in S Africa. B. became MICE in 1850 and was president in 1887 and in 1888 when he was knighted. Became MIME 1874. He was deeply interested in the Presbyterian Church. In 1849 he m Helen Norah Simpson; they had 1 son and 4 drs.
Min Proc ICE V 174 1907–8 p 369; *The Eng* V 106 8.1908 p 215; Proc IME 7.1908 pp 785–6

BRUFF, Peter Schuyler

b (?) 23.7.1812; d Ipswich 24.2.1900 aged 87.
Civil eng in E Anglia. Gained engg experience under Joseph Locke (qv). On formation of the Eastern Union R in 1845 B. became responsible for const of the direct Colchester–Ipswich line (op 15.6.1846). It was continued to Bury St Edmunds (24.12.1846) and Norwich (1849). B. acted as eng and mgr to the Eastern Union R until 1.1.1854 when it was taken over by the Eastern Counties R and continued on the ECR until he resigned in 1857. He was succeeded by Robert Sinclair (qv). B. planned and built branches to Woodbridge (1.6.1859), Harwich (15.8.1854), Hadleigh (21.8.1847), Thetford (1845), Tivetshall (1849), the Tendring Hundred line from Walton-on-the-Naze to Colchester (1867), the Norwich–Spalding line (1.4.1867) and the branch to Clacton on Sea (4.7.1882). Besides R engg, B. established the Harwich water supply. He was eng to the Harwich Harbour Conservancy Bd, building a breakwater in 1865, making possible the establishment of Parkeston Quay. He built gas and water works at Walton on the Naze, and the pier and Royal Hotel at Clacton. At Ipswich he was eng for drainage work and later for tramways. Elected MICE 8.4.1856. Pub *Treatise on engg field work; practical land surveying for Rs* 1838.
Min Proc ICE V 141 1899–1900 pp 339–41

BRUNEL, Henry Marc

b London (?).(?).1842; d Westminster 7.10.1903 aged 61.
Civil eng; 2nd son of I.K.B. (qv) and contributor with his brother Dr Isambard B. (d 1902) to the *Life of I. K. Brunel* pub in 1870. Ed Harrow and King's Coll

London, afterwards serving a premium apprenticeship at the Armstrong wks at Elswick. From here he became a pupil of John Hawkshaw (qv) and was engaged in surveys for the Channel Tunnel. He later assisted Hawkshaw in an examination of the Caledonian R. He was asst eng in the const of Penarth dock and Albert dock, Hull. Various projects followed, and in 1878 he entered into partnership with John Wolfe Barry (qv) and was concerned with the const of Barry dock, St Paul's station, London, and the Blackfriars R bridge over the Thames, the Tower Bridge, and the cantilever bridge at Connel Ferry near Oban, Scotland. He was a man of rigid principles and high sense of purpose, and with a whimsical sense of humour. In 1901 he had a slight stroke and a few months later a burst blood vessel in the brain from which he never fully recovered. He was a MICE (1877) and MIME, and a member of the Institute of Naval Architects.

The Eng V 96 16.10.1903 p 379; *Engg* V 76 16.10.1903 p 531; Min Proc ICE V 155 1903-4 pp 427-8; Proc IME 12.1903 pp 916-17

BRUNEL, Isambard Kingdom

b Portsmouth 9.4.1806; d London 15.9.1859 aged 53.
Civil eng, GWR. Son of Sir Marc I. Brunel (qv). Ed at private schools and Coll of Henri Quatre, Paris. In 1823 began training as eng under his f and assisted in building the Thames tunnel between Wapping and Rotherhythe, in which he was later app res eng. Excessive work in bad conditions, and lack of rest, damaged his health. In 1829 and 1831 he prepared a design for the Clifton suspension bridge at Bristol and was app eng, beginning work in 1836. Work had to be suspended because of lack of funds and the bridge had to be finished in 1860 by W. H. Barlow and John Hawkshaw (qqv). B. was app eng to Bristol docks and in 1831 designed the Monkwearmouth dock and later docks at Plymouth, Briton Ferry, Brentford and Milford Haven. In 3.1833 he was app eng to the Great Western R, laying out a magnificent line from London to Bristol with a gauge of 7ft (2.134m) and a tunnel at Box 1 mile 1452yd (2.937km)

long. The main line was opened throughout in 1841. On extensions into S Wales and Cornwall he built the great bridges at Chepstow (1851-2) and Saltash (1859) in which the deck was suspended from chains and the whole structure braced by great iron tubes above. As a R eng B's imagination sometimes exceeded his practical sense. Locos built to his specification were failures; in 1844 he used atmospheric propulsion on the S Devon R, again a failure. His 7ft gauge was too late to establish itself against the standard gauge, though it lasted until 1892. Any possible advantages for steam loco design were never exploited. For diesel and electric traction it would have had no advantages and its expense would be unjustified. A feature of B's Rs in Devon and Cornwall was the timber viaducts, mostly on stone piers. They were well designed and gave good service for many years. B. also achieved fame as a designer and builder of large steamships. His first, the *Great Western* was, when new in 1838, the largest ship afloat, and it made the Atlantic crossing to America in 15 days. For the *Great Britain* (1845) he adopted the screw propellor. His greatest ship, the *Great Eastern*, incorporated many novel features which later became standard practice. It was begun in 1853, but the anxieties and accidents during its const and trials broke his health and led to his early d. The ship was later used for laying the first Atlantic cables (see **D. Gooch**). In 7.1836 he m Mary Horsley of Kensington. She survived him with 2 sons and a dr.

Min Proc ICE V 19 1859 p 169; *The Eng* V 8 9.1859 p 219; V 208 1959 p 225; Brunel, Isambard, *Life* 1870; Rolt L. T. C., *I. K. Brunel* 1957

BRUNEL, Sir Marc Isambard

b Hacqueville nr Gisors, Normandy, 25.4.1769; d London 12.12.1849 aged 80.
Eng of the Thames tunnel. After a career in the French navy he went to N America in 1793 where he carried out surveys, one for a canal from the River Hudson to Lake Champlain. He then became chief eng of New York. Having devised machinery for making pulley blocks for ropes he sailed to England in 1799 and in 1803 obtained a contract to

erect his machinery at Portsmouth. He also established sawmills at Battersea and Woolwich. In 1814 his Battersea saw-mills were nearly destroyed by fire. His financial affairs declined and in 1821 he was imprisoned for debt. In 1818 he had proposed a Thames tunnel on the line of that begun by Richard Trevithick (qv) between Wapping and Rotherhythe. A company was formed in 1824 and boring began at Rotherhythe on 16.2. 1825. B. designed and built a shield from which excavation could proceed on the whole tunnel face. His son I.K.B. (qv) became res eng. After numerous delays the tunnel was completed in 1842. The twin bores were used by pedestrians only. In 1869–70 under the direction of John Hawkshaw (qv) the tunnel was incor-porated in the E London R. In 1799 B. m Sophia Kingdom and on 9.4.1806 their son Isambard Kingdom was b.
Min Proc ICE V 10 1850 p 78

BRUNLEES, Sir James

b Kelso, Scotland, 5.1.1816;
d Wimbledon 2.6.1892 aged 76.
One of the most outstanding civil engs of his time. His f was gardener and steward to the Duke of Roxburgh. Left school at 12 when his f put him to gardening and farming under Innes, agent to the Duke of Roxburgh, to become a landscape gardener. He met Alexander Adie (qv) who frequently visited Innes on road surveys and with whom B. learned surveying. In 1838 B. was engaged by Adie as asst on the Bolton & Preston R. He later worked under Locke and Errington on the CR from Beattock to Carstairs, Glasgow and Edinburgh. On its completion in 1844 he became acting eng under Hawk-shaw (qv) on the LYR until 1850 when he was app eng for 36 miles (58km) of the Londonderry & Coleraine R in N Ireland. In 1851 app eng on Ulverston & Lancaster R, responsible for building vdts across the Kent and Leven estuaries. One of his most difficult assignments in 1851 was the Sao Paulo R in Brazil, carrying the line up an escarpment through trackless jungle by the famous cable inclines. It had been surveyed by D. M. Fox. In 1865, with J. B. Fell (qv), B. was eng of the Mont Cenis R, op 15.6.1868, on which the Fell centre rail

was used. The R was closed in 1871 when the Mont Cenis tunnel was opened. Other Rs for which B. was eng were the Solway Junction R, 1865–9, with the Solway vdt 5790ft (1765m) long, and the Saltburn Extension R in Yorkshire, op 1.6.1872, with a vdt over Skelton Beck about 150ft (46m) high. With Charles Douglas Fox (qv) he was eng of the Mersey R, op 1.2.1886 with the 3820yd (3493m) tunnel of which 1300yd (1188m) was under the river. On its completion B. and Fox were knighted. They were also jt engs of the Southport & Cheshire Lines Extn, West Lancashire and Liver-pool, Southport & Preston Jn Rs. He also built docks, and the piers at Southport and Southend. In conjunction with John Hawkshaw (qv) B. was eng to the original Channel Tunnel Co from its incorporation in 1872 to 1886 when it ceased operations as a separate com-pany. In 8.1845 B. m Elizabeth, dr of James Kirkham of Bolton, and they had 2 sons and 1 dr. His wife d in 1888. B. was president of the ICE 1882–3.
Min Proc ICE V 111 1892–3 p 367; Proc IME 1892 p 223

BRUNTON, William

b Lochwinnoch, Ayrshire, 26.5.1777;
d Camborne, Cornwall, 5.10.1851 aged 74.
Civil and mech eng. Son of a watch and clock maker at Dalkeith. Received his mech training under his grandfather who was a colliery viewer. In 1790 began work in the fitting shop at New Lanark Mills, a branch of Arkwright's mill at Cromford. In 1796 he transferred to Boulton & Watt at Soho, Birmingham, becoming foreman and supt of engine mfr, working closely with James Watt. Left Soho in 1808 to work under William Jessop (qv) at Butterley wks where he established the mfr of engines. On 30.10.1810 he m Anne Elizabeth Button. His work here brought him in contact with John Rennie, Telford and other engs. Doubting the ability of a loco engine to grip the rails on anything but level track, on 22.5.1813 he patented a loco propelled by a pair of legs. An example was built at Butterley for Newbottle colliery nr Newcastle where it worked all through 1814. In 1815 it was fitted with a new boiler and while

this was being tried, on 31.7.1815, it exploded, killing 5, fatally injuring 9 and maiming 43 others. B. left Butterley in 1815 and became partner in and mech eng of Eagle Foundry, Birmingham. 1825 moved to London and practised as a civil eng. 1835 became partner in Cwm Avon tin wks where he erected copper smelting furnaces and rolling mills. 1838 became connected with Maesteg wks and a brewery at Neath which failed and lost him his fortune. In 1845 his wife d at Neath. As a mech eng B. was mainly connected with marine work.
Wood, Nicholas, *Treatise on Rail-Roads* 1838; Min Proc ICE V 11 1852 pp 95–9; Charlton, L. G., *The first Loco Engs* 1974

BUCK, George Watson

b Stoke Holy Cross, Norfolk, 9.4.1789; d Ramsey, Isle of Man, 9.3.1854 aged nearly 65.
Civil eng. Son of quaker parents. Ed Friends' Sch, Ackworth, Yorkshire. First emp under John Rennie (senior) on E London water works. 1818 settled at Welshpool and became eng of Montgomeryshire canal for 14 yrs. About 1834 his friend Robert Stephenson (qv) entrusted him with const of the London & Birmingham R between Camden Town and Tring. On this section he built his first oblique bridge. 1838 app chief eng of Manchester & Birmingham R in conjunction with R. Stephenson. Here the principal work was the Stockport vdt. In 1839 he pub *A practical and theoretical essay on oblique bridges*. 1840 went to Germany to take charge of const of R from Altona to Kiel but was forced by illness to retire before its completion. On return to England he soon resumed duties on the M & B which he completed in 1842. In 1846, after a period of strenuous work his health broke down and he was forced to retire to the Isle of Man where he spent his time correcting his published works and writing essays. He d from scarlatina, his wife and dr dying of it less than 2 weeks later. His son J.H.W.B. (qv) became eng on LNWR. Elected MICE 1821.
Min Proc ICE V 14, 1854–5, pp 128–30

BUCK, Joseph Haywood Watson

b Manchester 22.11.1839; d Crewe 9.7.1898 aged 58.
Son of George Watson B. (qv). LNWR civil eng. Ed King William's Coll, Castletown, Isle of Man. In 1856 he began in the LBSCR eng's office in London, and later in the office of Sir Charles Fox (qv). In 1860 became pupil of William Baker (qv), chief eng LNWR who had earlier been a pupil of B's f. In 1863 took charge of const of Eccles–Tyldesley–Wigan (op 1.9.1864) and the Kirkburton branch (op 7.10.1867), LNWR. B. was then engaged as res eng on const of the second single line tunnel at Standedge, op 1871. He was then moved to Watford as res eng on widening works between London and King's Langley, 28 miles (45km), including Colne vdt and new tunnels at Watford and Primrose Hill. 1877–8 he built 11 miles of line between Northampton and Rugby, op 1.12.1881. He next built the Stalybridge–Diggle loop, op 1.12.1885. After a short spell at Stockport he was app div eng, Crewe, where he remained until 3.1898 when failing health forced him to resign, after 38 yrs on the LNWR. Elected MICE 2.2.1869.
Min Proc ICE V 134 1897–8 p 402

BUDDICOM, William Barber

b Liverpool 1.7.1816; d Mold, Flintshire, 4.8.1887 aged 71.
Loco and civil eng and R contractor. Second son of Rev Robert Peddie B. of St George's, Everton; later principal of St Bees Coll. After leaving school in 1831 B. began a 5 yr apprenticeship with Mather, Dixon & Co of Liverpool. In 1836 he was app res eng of the Liverpool–Newton Bridge portion of the Liverpool & Manchester R under Edward Woods, responsible for the pw, bridges, tunnels, stations, the winding engines for the Wapping and Lime Street tunnels at Edge Hill and for the replacement of the original 35lb/yd (17.8kg/m) rails by 75lb (37.2kg/m). 1838 became res eng of Glasgow, Paisley & Greenock R under Locke and Errington (qqv). On 3.6.1840, at age 24, app loco supt of Grand Junction R (Birmingham–Warrington). Here he introduced a system of premiums for engine drivers for

economy in fuel and oil, thereby reducing working expenses. In 1840 it was decided to transfer the main works from Edge Hill to Crewe, then a small wayside station at the junction of the lines to Chester and Manchester, then under const. B. prepared plans and an estimate of £71 000–£72 000. Frequent crank axle failures in the Bury engines then in use led to the introduction by B. of what became known as the 'Crewe' type engine, with outside cylinders supported in an outside framing. It was developed later by B. in France and by his successors at Crewe and was also used on the Caledonian and Highland Rs. Also in 1841 the contractors Brassey & Mackenzie (qqv) had undertaken const of the Paris & Rouen R and the supply of rolling stock. Locke (qv), the eng, decided the latter would cost less if built in France, and he arranged that B. should go to Rouen to take charge of the works. B. resigned from the GJR and formed a company with the name Allcard, Buddicom & Co. (William Allcard (qv) had at the time the p w contract on the GJR.) They began operations in an old millwright's shop at Les Chartreux, a suburb of Rouen, while extensive works were being built at Sotteville nearby. From the opening of the line in 1842 the firm entered into a contract for working it. The arrangement was extended to the Hâvre & Rouen line when it opened in 1843, the Fécamp, the Mantes & Caen, and the Caen & Cherbourg lines, a total of 390 miles (628km), and it continued in force until 1860. Further shops were built at Sotteville in 1845 when the wks at Chartreux were abandoned. The firm supplied engines and rolling stock for the Orleans & Tours and Boulogne & Amiens Rs, the nucleus of the Nord system. In 1849, having contracted to supply rolling stock and fixed machinery to the Southern R of France, the firm erected a branch wks at La Bastide nr Bordeaux. In the revolution in 2.1846 B. was in some danger but the firm survived and was able to continue to work the Rs. In the unsettled period in 1848, thanks to B's untiring energy, the Paris & Rouen R was the only line running into Paris that did not fall into the hands of the 'Clubists'. In 1851 Allcard left the

firm which then became Buddicom & Co employing between 1500 and 2000 men at the Sotteville wks. In 1854, with Parent & Shaecken, the Belgian contractors, and Brassey (Parent, Brassey & Buddicom) a contract was made with the Lyons & Geneva R Co for the const of the Bellgarde tunnel on that line, over 4000m long. In 1860 B. ended his contract for working the French Rs and joined with Brassey and Charles Jones for the const and stocking of the Maremma R, completed in 1865. Also in 1860 he and Brassey undertook the doubling of the Rouen–Dieppe line. In 1863 Parent, Brassey & Buddicom contracted for the const of a portion of the Southern R in Italy. Following the deaths of Parent and Brassey in 1870 B. gave up engg. He became MICE on 3.6.1845, MIME 1874, a member of the Society of Civil Engs in France, a JP and high sheriff of the county of Flint. In 1847 he was awarded the Cross of the Legion of Honour from King Louis Philippe for services to the National Institution of France.

Engg V 44 12.8.1887 p 70; Min Proc ICE V 91 1887–8 pp 412–21; Proc IME 8.1887 pp 466–7; *Journal of the Flintshire Historical Society* V 25 1971–2 pp 132–52

BULLEID, Oliver Vaughan Snell

b Invercargill, New Zealand, 19.9.1882; d Malta 25.4.1970 aged 87.
CME Southern R, England, and Coras Iompair Eireann (Ireland). In 1901 began apprenticeship at GNR wks, Doncaster, under H. A. Ivatt (qv). In 1908 left to join the French Westinghouse Co and soon had enough money to m Ivatt's youngest dr Marjorie, then aged 19, on 18.11.1908. He acted as mech and elec eng for the BOT at the international trade exhibitions at Brussels in 1910 and Turin in 1911. In 12.1912 he returned to the GNR at Doncaster as personal asst to H. N. Gresley (qv) who had succeeded Ivatt as CME. B. became the 'ideas man' behind many of Gresley's designs. In 1937, at the age of 54, B. was app CME of the SR in succession to Maunsell (qv). Here his inventive capacities had full freedom. His first loco designs were revolutionary. The Q1 class 0–6–0 of 1941–2 incorporated many novel fea-

tures, but it was the 'Merchant Navy' class 3-cyl 4-6-2 with its thermic syphons, enclosed chain-driven valve gear, boxpok wheels and numerous other features which was the most extraordinary. The first appeared in 2.1941 and the 30th, last, in 4.1949. A lighter version, the 'West Country' class, appeared in 6.1945 for working W of Exeter. The engines were swift and powerful, but suffered from slipping and most were rebuilt with Walschaert gear in 1957-61. He also produced 3 electric locos, 2 diesel electrics, an electric train with seats at two levels, and his last SR design, the C–C type 'Leader' steam loco, the most revolutionary of all. It was barely completed before nationalisation of BR terminated B's career as CME and the numerous snags could not be overcome. The result was an expensive failure. In 1949 he moved to Dublin and became CME of the CIE. Here he continued his experimental designs, producing a turf-burning steam loco which, although it worked well, was soon superseded by diesel-electrics. To the end B. never lost his faith in steam power. He ret in 1958 and went to live in Malta. He was MIME, MILE.
The Times 28.4.1970; Day-Lewis, Sean, *Bulleid, last giant of steam* 1964; Allen, Cecil J. and Townroe, S. C., *The Bulleid Pacifics* 1951; Allen, Cecil J., *British Pacific Locomotives* 1962; Reed, Brian, *Loco Profile Merchant Navy Pacifics* 1972

BURLEIGH, Benjamin

b Oxford 24.5.1820; d London 25.4.1876 aged c 56.
Civil eng and architect. Learned surveying at an early age and about 1840 was engaged by Col Landmann and John Braithwaite (qv) on drawings for bridges and other works on the Eastern Counties R. In 1845-9 he was emp on the E Lincs R under James Hodges. From 1849 he was res eng on the GNR London–Peterborough line under Joseph Cubitt (qv), building many important works. On completion of this project he took office in Westminster and practised as an eng and took out several patents. In 1862-3 he designed and carried out the Bristol Port R from Clifton to Avonmouth, and under John Hawkshaw

superintended const of the E London R through Marc Brunel's Thames tunnel. In 1873 he was app architect to the NER and was one of the architects of York station, completed in 1877 after his d. Became AICE 1.2.1853.
Min Proc ICE V 47 1876-7 p 301

BURTT, George Frank

b Greenwich 22.3.1871; d Brighton (?) 22.8.1949 aged 78.
Loco draughtsman, Brighton, and author. Ed Colfes Gr Sch, Lewisham, and W Kent Gr Sch. On 28.1.1887 he began as apprentice at New Cross wks, LBSCR, under Stroudley (qv). In 1892 transferred to drwg office, Brighton, where he remained until he ret in 1932. He is best known for his history of LBSCR locos, 1839-1903, which first appeared as a series of articles in *Moore's Monthly Magazine* and the *Locomotive Magazine*, and pub in book form as *The Locos of the LBSCR 1839-1903* in 1903. The loco supt R. J. Billinton (qv) forbade disclosure of authorship. It was one of the first comprehensive loco histories. B. was one of the founders of the Stephenson Loco Soc in 1909 and of the ILE of which he was secretary and treasurer 1911-22. He also pub: *Cross Channel and coastal paddle steamers* 1934; *LBSCR Locos 1870-1927* 1946; *SE & CR Locos 1874-1923* 1947; *LSWR Locos 1873-1922* 1948; *Steamers of the Thames and Medway* 1949.
Journal ILE V 39 1949 p 386; *The Locomotive* 9.1949 p 143; SLSJ 10.1949 p 209

BURY, Edward

b Salford, nr Manchester, 22.10.1794; d Scarborough 25.11.1858 aged 64.
Designer and mfr of locos and machinery at Liverpool. Ed at Chester where he displayed an interest in machinery and skill in making models. Details of his training as eng have not been found, but before 1829 he established the wks of Bury & Co in Liverpool for the mfr of machinery. His first loco was begun in 1829. He also produced some 'improved' engines for steamboats working on the River Rhone. Following the opening of the Liverpool & Manchester R in 1830 B. devoted himself to the mfr of locos and in 1838 became responsible for the

loco dept of the London & Birmingham R. He established the bar frame type of const which became standard N American practice while other British designers adopted the plate frame. All his early engines were four-wheel designs, either 2–2–0 or 0–4–0, with the 'D' pattern firebox, with domed top, behind the rear axle. It was the difficulty of extending the bar frame behind the firebox to provide for a rear axle which, on standard gauge, restricted the firebox width and ultimately brought about the discontinuance of the Bury design. He resigned from the London & Birmingham in 1846 and was succeeded at Wolverton by McConnell (qv), and in 1847 took up mgt of the loco dept of the GNR at Boston until he resigned in 1850 to be succeeded by Sturrock (qv). Throughout this period he remained head of Bury, Curtis & Kennedy at the Clarence Foundry, Liverpool, James Kennedy (qv) being his former wks mgr. Following the mfr of some plate-framed 2–2–2s for the LYR, for which he probably under-priced the contract, the firm closed down in 1850. He moved to Windermere and then to Scarborough where he d. Elected FRS 1.2.1844, his claim being founded on improvements he had effected in loco design.
Proc of Royal Society V 10 p 12 (1860); DNB V 3

BURY, Oliver Robert Hawke

b London 3.11.1861; d London 21.3.1946 aged 84.
Civil eng and R mgr. In 1.1879 articled to W. Adams (qv) as pupil on LSWR. In 1881 he went to Hunter & English, engs, where he worked on Hunter's floating crane and on the const of a distillery. He then became asst eng on the Coleford & Monmouth R. In 10. 1884 he was app res eng on the Great Western R of Brazil under Alison Janson, becoming also loco supt in 1885. He held both posts until 1.1891 and acted as chief asst to Jason Rigby during const of the line from Nazareth to Timbauba. In 1.1891 he succeeded Rigby as chief eng of the R. B. had an extensive knowledge of R administration in Britain and S America where he held various posts including chief eng of the GW of Brazil, g mgr and chief eng of the Entre Rios R; g mgr of the Buenos Aires & Rosario R, later part of the Central Argentine R. In 1902 B. returned to England and became g mgr of the GNR. In 1912 he resigned to become a GNR director. At the grouping, 1923, he was elected to the board of the LNER where he remained until he ret in 12.1945. After his return to England he retained an active interest in S American undertakings and from 1913–37 was chairman of the Leopoldina R; also for many years chairman of the São Paulo (Brazil) R Co Ltd, and chairman and mg dir of the Peruvian Corporation Ltd until 10.1945. During 1923–45, while a director of the LNER, he served on 4 committees, was chairman of the works committee and a member of the S Area local bd. He was also a member of the CLC for many years, and held a seat on the Forth Bridge R Co. The scope of his directorate was not confined to R undertakings; he was once chairman of the London Electric Supply Corpn Ltd, and the London Power Co Ltd and was on the bd of the City & International Trust Ltd and the Provident Mutual Life Assurance Association. B. was elected MICE 27.2.1894.
Journal ICE V 26 1946 p 542

BUTLER, John

b Bowling nr Bradford, 25.4.1822;
d Farsley, Yorks, 17.10.1884 aged 62.
Mfr of R ironwork. Elder son of Joseph B. In 7.1828 his f moved to Stanningley nr Leeds and in partnership with several others established an iron foundry. After a few years they began making R plant and engg equipment. B. was trained in the foundry. In 1838 the business was taken over and carried on by Joseph B. alone and with his son John they began the mfr of iron R bridges, first making those for the Leeds & Selby R. They later built the cast iron bridge which carried the ELR over the Ribble at Preston, and many other similar spans. They also supplied the ironwork for York station (op 27.6.1877), and many other large structures. The development and prosperity of Stanningley ironworks was largely due to John B. and later his sons. At the time of his d the wks employed 800–1000 men. B. became MIME 1859.
Proc IME 1.1885 p 71

BUTTERWORTH, Sir Alexander Kaye

b Henbury Court, Gloucestershire,
4.12.1854; d London 23.1.1946 aged 91.
G mgr, NER. Ed Marlborough Coll;
London Univ. Grad LLB 1877. Barrister
of Inner Temple 1878–83. Entered solicitor's dept, GWR, 1883. Was active in
R Rates Inquiry 1889–90. Clerk to
Bedfordshire County Council 1890–1.
1891 app solicitor to NER until 2.3.1906
when he succeeded George S. Gibb (qv)
as g mgr NER. Under his administration
the NER brought into use the Riverside
Quay at Hull for the jt NER/LYR
steamer service to Zeebrugge, 1907; new
excursion platforms at Scarborough,
1908; he negotiated the NER interests
in the S Yks Jt R, the Axholme Jt R
and the High Level Wear Bridge,
Sunderland, 1909; the Shildon–Newport
electrification and the NER/HBR Jt
Dock at Hull, 1914. In 1913 he was
chairman of the G Mgrs' Conference of
the RCH. He was knighted 1.1.1914.
Member of R Executive Committee, and
of R Advisory Committee associated
with the Min of T. Served on Civil
Service Arbitration Bd 1917–20, 1921–2.
His last task before ret in 1921 was the
NER/HBR amalg. In 1884 he m Julia
Wigan who d 1911. Their only child,
George Kaye B., was the composer, b
1885, killed in WW1 in 1916. In 1916 B.
m Dorothea Mavor Ionides.
The Times 24.1.1946 p 7

CALTHROP, Everard Richard

b (?) (?).(?).1857; d Maida Hill,
London, 30.3.1927 aged 70.
Eng of light and narrow gauge Rs, and
inventor of life-saving appliances for
aircraft. Ed Uppingham Gr Sch. Began
engg career in the wks of Robert
Stephenson & Co but, preferring R
work, became apprenticed at Crewe,
LNWR, in 1874. In 1879 he joined the
GWR and was shortly afterwards inspector of stores and materials and asst mgr
of the C & W wks. 1882 app loco insp
on GIPR, and it was then that he first
considered the provision of light Rs as
feeders to the main lines. He received
special permission from his directors to
become chairman of an Indian co
formed for that purpose. In 1887 he pub

a pamphlet on *A System of standard
details as applied to the const of rolling
stock on Rs in India*. This resulted in
the appointment by the Indian govt of
a R committee which reported strongly
in favour of uniformity, and the movement for standardisation later extended
widely. He left the GIPR in 1889 and
surveyed and reported on several lt R
projects later carried out in India. In
1895 he obtained a special concession for
the 2ft 6in (762mm) g Barsi Lt R (op
1897) and its success showed the advantages of his system. In 1892 he began a
consulting practice in England and of
the many lt Rs which he planned the
2ft 6in (762mm) g Leek & Manifold
Valley Lt R in Staffordshire was an
English example. It was op 27.6.1904
and was first R to use his system of
transporter wagons, narrow gauge
wagons which could carry standard
gauge wagons. In 1916 C. studied life-
saving appliances for aircraft and established the firm of E. R. Calthrop's Aerial
Patents, striving for a law which would
demand that every person flying should
be equipped with a parachute. Became
MIME and MICE in 1900. He was also
a breeder of Arab horses and author of
The Horse as Comrade and Friend, 1920.
Proc IME 12.1927 p 1087; *Engg* V 123
8.4.1927 p 420; *The Eng* V 143 1.4.1927
p 354; 'Manifold', *The Leek & Manifold
Lt R* 1955; W. J. K. Davies, *Lt Rs* 1964

CAMERON, John

b Wigtownshire (?).(?).(?);
d (?) 17.3.1938 aged (?).
Loco supt, TVR. Ed at Inverness.
Apprenticed to Stroudley at Brighton
becoming foreman in the C & W shops
and later rolling stock insp. He then
became insp of rolling stock, LSWR,
until 1885 when he moved to Cardiff as
wks mgr, TVR. App chief asst to loco
supt Hurry Riches (qv) 1894, and
became loco supt from 1911 until he ret
in 1922. In 1912 he designed the 'A'
class 0–6–2T of which 58 were built
1914–22.
RG 25.3.1938 p 603; *The Locomotive*
4.1938 p 117; *Locos of GWR* Part 10
(RCTS 1966) pp K187–91

CAMPBELL, Henry R.

b (?) c1810; d (?) c1870.

Originator of the American 4-4-0. Asst eng on Philadelphia & Columbia RR; chief eng Philadelphia, Germantown & Norristown RR 1832-9. Built and patented the first 4-4-0 1837. It had inside cyls and outside frames. Chief eng Vermont Central c 1848-55.
White, John H. Jr, *American Locos, an Engg History 1830-80* 1968; Reed, Brian, *Loco Profile 4. The American type 4-4-0*; Sinclair, Angus, *The development of the loco engine* 1907, 1970

CAMPBELL, James

b Greenock 19.6.1838; d Leeds 12.10.1905 aged 67.
Loco mfr; mgr of Hunslet Engine Co. Son of Alexander C., mgr of the R Foundry, Leeds, from 1851. Apprenticed to his f. 1858 entered service of E Indian R at Howrah wks. 1862 returned to England and became mgr of Hunslet Engine Co, Leeds, on the establishment of that firm in 1864. 1875 acquired the wks in partnership with his bro after whose d in 1889 he carried on the business in association with his sons. In 1902 the concern became a limited liability co of which C. became chairman and mg dir until his d. Became MICE and MIME in 1869. He took a great interest in the establishment of the Yorkshire Coll, later Leeds Univ, of which he was elected a governor, and member of committees of engg, science and arts.
Proc IME 12.1905 p 1047; *The Eng* V 100, 20.10.1905, p 384 (portrait)

CAPROTTI, Arturo

b Cremona 22.3.1881; d Milan 9.2.1938 aged 58.
Inventor of the Caprotti valve gear. Trained at the Royal Tech Inst, Cremona. Spent 2 yrs at the Univ of Pavia, then graduated as industrial mech eng in Turin Royal Polytechnic Coll (1899-1904). After 2 yrs in the shops of the Florence Motor Car Co, then 2 yrs as consulting eng experimenting on a reversing petrol engine, and another yr on designing a turbo-electric loco, he carried out research on the application of poppet valves to R locos and took out his first Italian patent in 1916. It was first applied in 1920 on a 2-6-0 goods engine of the Italian State Rs.

Afterwards he devoted himself to the development and improvement of his valve gear which was applied to locos in many countries. Its first application in Britain was on LNWR 'Claughton' 4-6-0 No 5908 in 1926, resulting in a coal economy of 20.76 per cent. Elected MILE 1924, MIME 1929.
RG 18.2.1938 p 317; *Journal* ILE V 28 1938 p 129; *The Locomotive* 2. 1938 p 63; Proc IME V 138 1938 p 152.

CARMICHAEL, David

b Dundee (?).(?).1818; d Dundee 5.4.1895 aged 77.
Mech eng; co-founder of James Carmichael & Co, builders of the first R loco in Scotland in 1833. This was a 0-2-4 for the Dundee & Newtyle R, 4ft 6in (1.372m) gauge and was the first British loco to have a bogie. C. was the 3rd son of Charles C. whose valve gear with single fixed eccentric was introduced in 1818. C. was apprenticed at his f's wks and then moved to Bristol as a draughtsman and later to the govt dockyard at Woolwich. Returned to Dundee in 1849 to join his cousin George C. at Ward Foundry, Dundee. The firm became a limited liability co in 1893.
The Eng V 79 10.5.1895 p 398.

CAWLEY, Charles Edward

b Middleton, nr Manchester, 7.2.1812; d nr Manchester 3.4.1877 aged 65.
Civil eng, ELR. Son of Samuel C., colliery owner, Middleton. Ed Middleton Gr Sch where he excelled in maths and mechanical studies. Assisted his f on Hopwood estates, gaining experience in colliery working. In 1837, during const of the Manchester & Leeds R which passed through the Hopwood estates, he was app by George Stehenson and T. L. Gooch (qqv) to supervise const of several miles at the Manchester end. On completion of this C. went into private practice as eng in Manchester until 1845 when he was app chief eng of the Manchester, Bury & Rossendale R, later East Lancashire R, serving Bury, Rossendale, Accrington, Blackburn, Preston, Burnley and Colne. On completion of these lines in 1849 he returned to private practice and was engaged in various R and water works. 1868 elected MP for Salford, and again in the next election.

The BOT app him as umpire, arbitrator and valuer under the Rs and Lands Clauses Consolidation Acts. Elected MICE 30.6.1846.
Min Proc ICE V 50 1876–7 p 175; *Engg* V 23 6.4.1877 p 266; Marshall, John, *The Lancashire & Yorkshire R* V 1 1969

CHALMERS, Robert James

b Brighton (?).(?).1874; d Ipswich, Queensland, Australia, 31.7.1940 aged 66.
CME Queensland Govt Rs. Brother of Walter C. (qv) of the NBR. Ed Allan Glen's Tech Coll, Glasgow. 1889 apprenticed at Cowlairs Wks, NBR. 1894 entered drg office. 1895–1901 worked as loco draughtsman in various R and private loco wks. In 1901 went to Australia and until 1904 worked on loco and rolling stock design at the Ipswich wks of Queensland Govt Rs. He then went to India as asst loco supt NWR and later C & W supt, Lahore. Returned to Queensland 1911 as leading draughtsman at Ipswich wks. 1920 app asst wks mgr and chief draughtsman. He was responsible for introducing the C17 class 4–8–0 loco on the 3ft 6in (1.067m) gauge QGR. 1925 app CME of QGR until he ret in 2.1940. Became MIME 1921.
Proc IME V 145 1941 p 234

CHALMERS, Walter

b (?) (?).(?).(?);
d (?) (?).(?).(?) aged (?).
CME, NBR. Son of Robert C. of the NBR. Apprenticed at Cowlairs, Glasgow, wks, NBR. After passing through all depts and the drwg office he became insp of new materials and was emp in purchase of rolling stock. On 11.1.1906 he succeeded his f as chief draughtsman. On 1.1.1920 he succeeded W. P. Reid (qv) as loco supt, the office of loco running supt being taken by John Grassick.

CHAN TIEN-YU (TIEN YOW JEME)

b Kwangtung, China, (?)(?).1861;
d (?) (?).12.1919 aged 58.
First Chinese R eng: founder member of Chinese Inst of Engs. In 1873, with 30 other young Chinese boys, he was sent to USA. Ed New Haven High Sch,

Con. 1878 to Sheffield Scientific Sch, Yale Univ. Graduated in R Eng 1881, head of his class in maths. Returned to China and spent 7 yrs in the navy. 1888 obtained employment on the Tientsin R. 1902 app chief eng for the 29 mile (47km) Peking-Hsiling line, quickly completed. 1905–9 chief eng Peking–Kalgan R to the Mongolian frontier. Tremendous obstacles had to be overcome by reversals and the 1252yd (1145m) Paterling tunnel. Standard gauge was adopted and so became established in China. The R was op 24.9.1909, the first built entirely by Chinese. From 1909 he worked on the Hankow-Szechuan R, but after many delays only the Wuchang–Changsha section was opened, in 9.1918, before his d.
China Reconstructs V 4 No 7 1955 pp 26–9

CHAPELON, Andre

b St Paul en Cornillon, Loire, France, 26.10.1892.
French loco eng. His enthusiasm for steam locos developed at an early age. After achieving distinction in maths and science he served as an officer of heavy artillery in WW1. 1919–21 completed his ed at the Ecole Centrale, Paris, and graduated as Ingenieur des Arts et Manufactures. His first app was on the PLM as a probationer in the rolling stock and motive power section under Etienne Tribolet at Lyon–Mouche depot. However, seeing little hope of promotion he left loco work in 1924 and joined the Société Industrielle des Telephones, soon becoming asst mgr. On 12.1.1925 he was back on the R in the research and development section of the Paris Orléans R. In conjunction with Kylälä, a Finnish eng who had designed a steam and gas exhaust device in 1919, C. designed a new exhaust system which he named the Kylchap, in 1926, producing an adequate draught with minimum back pressure. This was applied to the 4500 and 3500 class compound Pacifics and the 3591 class simple Pacifics and other P0 locos and the results were highly encouraging. By redesigning and enlarging steam passages he reduced throttling losses. The first rebuild, No 3566, emerged from Tours wks in 11.1929 and was an outstanding success. Until then C's ideas

had been regarded with scepticism; with this success faith in his principles was established. His next success was the rebuilding of one of the 4500 class Pacifics, No 4521, as a 4–8–0, completed in 8.1932. Its performance excelled that of the rebuilt Pacific 3566, and 11 more were rebuilt, renumbered 4701–12 and later 240 701–12. In 1936 he began a new 6-cyl 4–12–0 rebuilt from a P0 6000 class 2–10–0. It had 2 hp cyls inside between the 2nd and 3rd coupled axles and 4 lp cyls in line in front. The hp cyls drove the 4th coupled axle, the outside lp cyls the 3rd and the inside lp cyls the 2nd. His greatest achievement was the 3-cyl compound 4–8–4 No 242 A.1 rebuilt in 1942–6 from 4–8–2 3-cyl simple No 241.101. It is fair to describe it as the greatest steam loco ever built. It could maintain continuous 4000 hp at the tender drawbar at 44–62mph (70–100km/h) and 3800 hp at 74mph (120km/h). The triple Kylchap exhaust resulted in a high steaming rate at all speeds. The hp cyls had Trick valves with double admission and the lp cyls had Willoteaux valves with double admission and double exhaust. At 62.4mph (100km/h) and developing a drawbar hp of 4000 coal consumption was 2.64lb/hr (1.197kg/h) and water 14.3lb/hp/hr (6.486kg/hp/h). For a Stanier Pacific on BR at 60mph (96.6km/h) developing 825dbhp the amounts were 3.03lb/hr (1.375kg/h) and 25lb/hp/hr (11.34kg/hp/h). The failure to preserve 242 A.1 was one of the greatest tragedies in R loco history; it was scrapped in 1960. Many honours were awarded to C.: in 7.1934 he was app Chevalier of the Legion of Honour and in the same year was awarded the Plumey Prize of the Academie des Sciences and the Gold Medal of the Société d'Encouragement pour l'Industrie Nationale. Various other medals and awards followed. In 1938 he pub his great book *La Locomotive á Vapeur* (revised edn 1952). C's principles influenced other steam loco engs throughout the world, particularly Gresley on the LNER in England, and engs in Brazil and Argentina.
Rogers, Col H. C. B., *Chapelon, Genius of French Steam*, 1972; Cox, E. S., *World Steam in the Twentieth Century* 1969; Vuillet, Gérard, *R Reminiscences*

of three Continents 1968; SLS *Journal* 7/9/11.1970; Livesey, E. H. 'Andre Chapelon and the steam loco', *The Eng* V 200 1955 p 140

CHURCHWARD, George Jackson
b Stoke Gabriel, Devon, 31.1.1857; d Swindon 19.12.1933 aged 76.
Loco eng, GWR. At age 16 articled to John Wright, loco supt of the S Devon R, Newton Abbot. This became GWR in 1876 when C. was transferred to Swindon, working in the drwg office under Joseph Armstrong (qv) who d in 1877 and was succeeded by William Dean (qv). C. then became insp of materials and, in 1882, asst mgr of the C & W wks, becoming mgr in 1885. Became asst loco wks mgr 1895 and mgr 1896 for one year, being then app chief asst to Dean. In this position he clearly gained the confidence of his chief who, with failing mental powers, gave C. increasing freedom to experiment with new boiler designs incorporating a high Belpaire firebox which appeared on most of the later Dean engines including the 'City' class 4–4–0 and the 'Aberdare' 2–6–0. Thus the transition from Dean's to C's superintendency was so smooth that when Dean retired in 5.1902 and C. became CME there was no abrupt change of policy. In fact C's first 4–6–0, named *William Dean*, appeared in 2.1902 while Dean was still CME. It was the forerunner of the famous 'Saints' and later the 'Halls' and 'Granges'. Like Aspinall on the LYR, C. adopted a system of standard components such as boilers, cylinders etc, combinations of which could be worked into a wide range of different locos. Greatly impressed by the De Glehn compound 4–4–2s in France, in 1903 C. persuaded the GWR to buy one of these for trials. Two more were bought in 1905. For comparison C. designed a 4-cyl simple 4–4–2 which could later be rebuilt into a 4–6–0, the forerunner of the 'Star' class. From the French engines C. adopted the high steam pressure of 225psi and the generous bearing surfaces, while from current American practice he adopted the front-end arrangement with long-travel valves, the tapered boiler, cylindrical smokebox and, in his 2-cyl designs, the combined cylinder casting and half

smokebox saddle. In many of these 2-cyl engines he adopted a stroke of 30in (762mm), much longer than was common in British practice. Another innovation was his 'Swindon' pattern superheater designed at a time when the merits of superheating were still doubted on other Rs. His design of deep narrow piston ring avoided the steam leakage which detracted from the performance of many of his contemporaries' engines. In 2.1908 he produced his greatest loco, No 111 *The Great Bear*, the first British Pacific. Unfortunately its use was restricted by the chief civil eng to the London–Bristol main line and so it remained the sole example of its type. With the help of his subordinates C. designed the standard GWR unit engine shed, many of which were erected all over the GWR. Numerous accounts of C's locos make it unnecessary to list or describe them here. He ret in 12.1921, but remained in close contact with work at Swindon and it was while crossing the main line on one of his almost daily visits that he was struck and instantly killed by 4–6–0 No 4085 *Berkeley Castle* on the 08.55 Fishguard express at about 10.25 on the misty morning of 19.12.1933.

The Eng V 156 29.12.1933 p 647 (portrait); *Engg* V 136 29.12.1933 p 717; Proc IME V 125 1933 p 783; Holcroft, H., *Great Western Locomotive Practice 1837–1947* 1957; RCTS *The Locos of the GWR* in 12 parts 1951–74; Rogers, H. C. B., *G. J. Churchward* 1975; Ellis, Hamilton, *Twenty Locomotive Men* 1958; Tuplin, W. A., *Great Western Saints and Sinners* 1971

CLAPEYRON, Benoit Paul Emile

b Paris (?).(?).1799; d (?) (?).(?).1864 aged c 65.
Chief projector of the Paris–St Germaine R. He was concerned with the mfr of locos for gradients of 1 in 200 and had these built at Sharp, Roberts, Manchester, in 1836. He then projected the Northern R and was app eng. He shared in the const of the Southern R, the Bordeaux–Cette and Bordeaux–Bayonne lines. He was the first French eng to build several large iron bridges, over the Seine at Asnières, the Lot and Tarn rivers, and he established principles of construction, and stress diagrams.

Röll V 2 p 817

CLARK, Daniel Kinnear

b Edinburgh 17.7.1822; d London 22.1.1896 aged 73.
Civil and mech eng and author. Apprenticed to Thomas Edington & Son, Phoenix Ironworks, Glasgow. After further experience in another wks and on the NBR he set up in practice as a consulting eng in London in 1851. In 10.1853 app loco supt, GN of S, at Kittybrewster, Aberdeen. For the opening, to Huntley, 12 2–4–0s of C's design were built by William Fairbairn & Sons, Manchester. A condition of C's contract was that he should live in Aberdeen, but this he refused to do so, in 3.1855, he had to resign and was succeeded by J. F. Ruthven. He patented a smoke preventing device which was used on many GNS locos. In 1855 he pub *Railway Machinery* in 2 vols, then the most comprehensive book on the subject. It was followed by: *R Locos*, 2 vols 1856, 1860; *Manual of rules for mechanical engineers* 1877, 1884; *Tramways and their construction and working*, 2 vols 1878, 1881; *The steam engine*, 2 vols 1893. Became MIME 1854, MICE 27.1.1863.

Proc IME 1.1896 pp 92–4; Min Proc ICE V 124 1896 pp 409–13; Valance, H. A., *The Great North of Scotland R* 1965; Harvey, Sir Malcolm Barclay, *A history of the Great North of Scotland R*

CLARK, Edwin Kitson, Lieut Col

b Grantchester nr Cambridge 18.4.1866; d Leeds 15.4.1943 aged 87.
Loco eng and mfr. Son of Dr E.C.C., Regius Prof of Civil Law, Cambridge. Ed Sutton Vallence, Shrewsbury, and Trinity Coll, Cambridge, where he gained a first class classics tripos in 1887. With this degree he proceeded, in 1888, to the Airedale Foundry of Kitson & Co, loco mfr, Leeds, as apprentice, becoming successively foreman, wks mgr, partner, director and chairman. He was engaged in design and mfr of numerous locos for home and abroad including the Kitson-Meyer articulated type and the experimental Kitson-Still steam/diesel loco. He worked for Kitsons for over 50 yrs. In 1897 he m Georgina, dr of George Parker Bidder QC and grand dr of

George Parker Bidder (qv). C. was MICE, MIME (1903), MILE. President ICE 1921–2; IME 1931–2. Pub *Kitsons of Leeds 1837–1937* 1938.
Journal ICE V 20 1943 p 202; Proc IME V 151 1944 p 99

CLARK, George Thomas

b London 26.5.1809; d Tal-y-garn, nr Llantrisant, Wales, 31.1.1898 aged 86.
Civil eng, historian and archaeologist. Eldest son of George C., chaplain to the Royal Military Asylum, Chelsea. Ed Charterhouse. After training as eng he was entrusted by Brunel with const of 2 divs of the GWR, the main works being Paddington station and bridges at Basildon and Moulsford. During this period he compiled the first official guide to the GWR, pub in 1839 without his name and dedicated to Brunel. In 1846 he pub a more detailed account: *The history and description of the GWR*, again anonymous, in connection with a series of prints by J. C. Bourne. About 1843 C. went to India and reported on prospects for the first R in India, Bombay to Tannah, later GIPR, and also on the feasibility of extn through the Western Ghats. He was offered the post of chief eng but preferred to return to England where he exerted himself in the improvement of public health work and sanitation. In 1852 he became trustee of Dowlais estate and ironworks. One of the first ironmasters to assist Henry Bessemer perfect his process for making malleable iron direct from ore. Experiments at Dowlais resulted in the first rails ever to be rolled without the intervention of a puddling furnace. The difficulty of finding adequate British ore of suitable quality led him, in conjunction with the Consett Iron Co and Krupp of Essen, to acquire an extensive tract of iron ore deposits near Bilbao in Spain. He also purchased large coal measures in Glamorganshire. To avoid transport, in 1888–91 he established furnaces and mills by the sea at Cardiff. Under C. Dowlais became a great training school for engs and mgrs. On the formation of the British Iron Trade Association in 1876 C. was elected its first president. He was sheriff in Glamorganshire in 1868. As an archaeologist C. achieved great renown and was recognised as the leading authority on mediaeval fortifications for half a century. He was also an authority on heraldry and genealogy. C. m Ann Price, second dr of Henry Lewis of Greenmeadow nr Cardiff, on 3.4.1850. She d on 6.4.1885 leaving a son, Godfrey Lewis C. and a dr.
Western Mail (Cardiff) 2.2.1898; *Merthyr Express* 5.2.1898; *Journal* of the Iron & Steel Institute 1898/1 p 313; DNB

CLARKE, John

b Allendale, Northumb, 6.2.1825; d Leeds 8.2.1890 aged 65.
Senior partner in Hudswell, Clarke & Co, loco mfrs, Hunslet, Leeds. Apprenticed at Hawthorn's Forth Banks wks, Newcastle. 1847 went to Leeds and entered the Airedale Foundry of Kitson, Thompson & Hewitson. 1851 app mgr. 1860 began business on his own account in partnership with W. S. Hudswell, establishing the Foundry in Jack Lane, Hunslet. He was active until the day before his d. Became MIME 1865.
Proc IME 1.1890 p 171; *Engg* V 49 21.2.1890 p 197

CLARKE, Seymour

b Streatham, Surrey (?).(?).1814; d Walthamstow, Essex, 15.3.1876 aged c 62.
Civil eng and g mgr GNR. About 1834 he began in the office of I. K. Brunel (qv) working on designs for Monkwearmouth docks, Clifton and Hungerford bridges and the GWR. On the opening of the GWR between London and Maidenhead on 4 June 1838 C. was app supt of the London div. In 10.1837 he was sent to N England and to Belgium to study methods of R working. In 1840 he was placed in charge of the GWR from London to Swindon. He gave evidence on R gauges in 1846. In 5.1850 C. was app g mgr of the GNR which was shortly afterwards, on 7.8.1850, opened from Peterborough to London. C. was highly successful in developing traffic. In 1867 he was app member of a Royal Commission to examine Irish Rs. In 9.1870, following a severe illness, he had to resign from the GNR. By 1874 his health appeared restored and he accepted office of vice president of the Great Western R of Canada. He was also dep

chairman of the Banbury & Cheltenham R. Became AICE 5.12.1865.
Min Proc ICE V 44 1875–6 p 225

CLIFFORD, Charles

b (?) (?).(?).(?);
d (?) 5.9.1927 aged 84.
Loco supt, GNR Ireland. Began R career as apprentice at the wks of the Dublin & Wicklow R. In 1861 joined the Irish NWR at Dundalk; 1866 loco foreman at Bundoran; 1869 dist loco supt, Derry. Later returned to Dundalk to become chief loco supt of Irish NWR. On amalg to form the Great Northern of Ireland on 28.6.1877 C. went to Dublin as dist loco supt. 1891 again returned to Dundalk as wks mgr. 1895 promoted to loco supt GNR. Under C. the Dundalk wks were greatly enlarged and better equipped to build and repair locos. Became MIME 1897.
Proc IME 5.1928 p 507

COEY, Robert

b Belfast (?).(?).1851; d Harrogate 24.8.1934 aged 83.
Loco supt GS & WR. After obtaining a B.Eng degree at Queen's Coll, Belfast, in 1876, he began as a draughtsman at the wks of the GS & WR at Inchicore, Dublin, and rose to become chief draughtsman in 1880. He next became asst loco supt and wks mgr and in 1896, when H. A. Ivatt (qv) left to join the GNR at Doncaster, C. succeeded to the position of loco supt. He ret in 7.1911 and was succeeded by R. E. L. Maunsell (qv).
RG 31.8.1934 p 353; The Locomotive 10.1934 p 287; The Eng V 158 7.9.1934 p 325

COLBURN, Zerah

b Saragota Springs, New York, (?).(?).1833; d Belmont, Mass, 25.4.1870 aged 37.
1847 employed as clerk in a textile mill at Lowell, Mass, and later that year as clerk on Concord RR. 1848–51 draughtsman with John Souther (qv) at Boston. In 1851 he pub The Locomotive Engine. C. then became mechanical editor of the American RR Journal. In 1854 he founded the RR Advocate. 1854–8 served as consulting eng for the New Jersey Loco & Machine Co. 1858

became editor of The Engineer, London, and in 1866 founded Engineering. Also pub: Loco Engg and the Mechanism of Rs, 2 vols 1872. Elected MIME 1864. Committed suicide at Belmont, Mass.
Proc IME 1871 p 15; Engg V 9 20.5.1870 p 361; White, John H. Jr The American Locomotive, an engineering history 1830–80 1968; Min Proc ICE V 31 1870–1 pp 212–17

COLE, Francis J.

b (?), England (?).(?).1856;
d Pasadena, Cal, 11.1.1923 aged 65.
Loco eng. After working on the West Shore and B & O RRs he moved to the Rogers Loco Wks at Paterson, NJ. From 1902 he worked with ALCO and made tremendous contributions to the development of loco design. In 1904 he introduced a 4-cyl balanced compound design which he developed, later with Walschaert valve gear, over several years. In 1910 ALCO completed their 50 000th loco, an experimental 4-6-2 numbered 50 000, designed by C., using numerous advanced features such as vanadium steel cylinders, wheel centres and rods. Steam pipes were taken outside the smokebox to the steam chests, another innovation which became standard practice. It had the greatest superheating surface of any American loco up to that time, 897sq ft (83.33m^2). In 1914 he pub his Locomotive Ratios, presenting evaporative tables for boiler tubes and flues together with a constant evaporative rate for the firebox, which were not superseded until 1933, and which established his international reputation.
New York Times 12.1.1923 p 15; Sinclair, Angus, Development of the Loco Engine, 1970 edn; Bruce, A. W., The steam loco in America 1952

COLLETT, Charles Benjamin, OBE

b (?) (?).(?).1871; d London 23.8.1952 aged 81.
GWR loco eng. Ed Merchant Taylors and City & Guilds Eng Coll, S Kensington. Began as pupil to Joshua Field of Maudslay, Sons & Field Ltd, London, marine engs, 1887–93, and in 1893 entered the GWR as draughtsman at Swindon. His outstanding ability soon led to promotion: 1898 asst to chief draughtsman, 1900 tech insp in Swindon

wks, 6.1900 asst wks mgr, 12.1912 wks mgr, 5.1919 dep CME. In 1.1.1922 he succeeded Churchward (qv) as CME. During his period of office Swindon exerted considerable influence on British loco practice. C. continued in the tradition of Churchward. His 'Castle' class 4-6-0 was a direct development of the 'Star'. It became one of the most outstanding British express locos. In 1927 it was followed by the 'King' class, the most powerful 4-6-0 in Britain. Like Churchward C. urged the necessity for only a few standard types of engines to suit traffic requirements and he began an extensive standardisation programme. In 1921 the co's stock included 17 types comprising 52 classes of engines. By 1941 there were 13 types of 37 classes. This reduced running costs and expedited overhauls. An important part of this work was C's insistence upon absolute accuracy in boiler dimensions to make standard boilers interchangeable. C. was also interested in C & W design and was responsible for notable improvements in restaurant cars, sleeping cars, etc. A new profile developed by C. in 1937 enabled the stock to be used for cross-country working on other co's lines. C. played an important part in the installation of the GWR automatic train control and was a member of the second special committee set up by the Min of T in 1927 under the chairmanship of Sir John Pringle to consider the introduction of a standard system of automatic train control for the whole country. The GWR system was unanimously considered most satisfactory for adoption on British Rs. C. always showed consideration and interest in conditions of work and the problems of the men under him and was much respected, though he was a very retiring person, devoted to his wife. They had no children. His work during WWI earned him the OBE. He was MIME from 1920-41 and MICE 1922-41 when he retired from R service at the age of 70.

Engg 5.9.1952 p 308; *The Eng* V 194 29.8.1952 pp 289-90; RCTS *Locos of the GWR* Parts 3-11

COLLINSON, Arthur

b Halifax (?).(?).1871; d York 9.1.1947 aged 76.

NER eng. Son of Emily C. (b 1843, dr of Nathaniel Worsdell qv), and Thomas C., J.P., coal merchant of Halifax. Ed Quaker sch, Ackworth nr Pontefract, 1883-6, and Bootham, York, 1886-9. His relationship to the Worsdells led to a career on the NER beginning as a pupil of T. W. Worsdell (qv) and Wilson Worsdell (qv) at Gateshead, 1889-93. 1894-7 chief insp of materials to which was added, 1897-1900, the duty of chief boiler insp. 1900-3 mgr of York loco wks, formerly the York & N Midland R shops (and later the Queen Street R Museum). 1903-5 asst to Vincent Raven (qv) who was then asst loco supt. In 1905 he left the NER to become mgr of the Metropolitan District R, but returned in 1908 as dist supt, NER, Middlesbrough. In 6.1912 app asst g supt, York, responsible for train working and wagon supply. His duties later included new works and signalling. Awarded OBE 1.1920. Ret 26.11.1935.

Family records. NER minutes

CONNER, Benjamin

b Glasgow (?).(?).1813; d Glasgow 3.2.1876 aged 62.

Loco supt CR. Apprenticed to James Gray of Glasgow. Introduced to loco eng at Murdoch, Aitken & Co, Glasgow. Later with Stark & Fulton and then John M. Rowan. He also worked in Manchester and Liverpool. Returning to Scotland he became connected with W. M. Neilson (qv) at Hyde Park Street wks, Glasgow, as under mgr and mgr for about 10 yrs. Spent some time in Robert Napier's wks at Lancefield and became familiar with marine engg, also sailing to and from Spain as marine eng. For several yrs he was mgr for Smith & Roger until his app as loco supt, CR, in 1856. In 1858 he introduced his 6ft 2in (1.880m) 2-4-0 in which he adopted the 'Crewe' type framing of W. B. Buddicom (qv). These and similar engines were built for the CR until 1877. The 'Crewe' type framing was also used in his 12 famous 8ft (2.438m) 2-2-2s built 1859-75. Three more were exported to Egypt (see illus, *The Eng* 1.12.1922 p 580 and *The Locomotive* 10.10.1903). In 1867 he introduced his 7ft 2in (2.184m) 2-4-0 for expresses, and later a similar 6ft 8in (2.032m) version. In 1874-7 his 39 'long-boiler' o/c 0–6–0s were built for heavy goods work. In 1870–1 he experimented with steel fireboxes, but with little success. He remained in office until his d. *Engg* V 21 11.2.1876 p 117, 18.2.1876 pp 135–6

CONRAD, Frederik Willem

b Spaarnwoude nr Haarlem, Holland, 15.2.1800; d Munich 1.2.1870 aged 70.
Dutch R and hydraulic eng. Son of Frederik Willem C., insp gen of bdgs and roads, Holland. In 1814 began a course of study in engg at Delft. At 17 entered the dept of bdg and roads, passing through the ranks until in 1866 he was made insp gen. In 1822 he undertook const of a dock at Hellevoetsluis. 1824–5 built the Zederik canal between the Leck at Vianen and the Merwede at Gorcum. Important river works followed. In 3.1839 his career as R eng began when he was app by the govt as chief eng of the R Co of Holland and at once took in hand const of the Amsterdam–Rotterdam R which had been begun in 1838. For crossing the marshy ground he laid embankments on a mattress of stakes and wattles. He had to const numerous opening bridges over canals. In 1844 he presented an account of its history and const to the ICE for which he was awarded a Walker Premium (Min Proc ICE V 3 1844 pp 173–96). The account includes 25 detailed drawings of bridges, etc. The R was opened throughout on 6.12.1843. In 1847 he described the bridge over the Poldevaart (Min Proc ICE V 6 1847 pp 149–57) on the same R. His account of the Katwyk canal (Min Proc ICE V 2 1842 pp 172–6) earned him a Telford Medal. He was elected MICE 7.3.1843. He became chief eng of bdgs and roads in 1852. In 1855 he became M of the international committee to report on the practicability of a canal through the Isthmus of Suez. C. was elected president. In 1856 he became M of the supervising committee for const of a new dock at Nieuwediep. He reported and advised on R works in the province of Zeeland in 1866. In 10.1868 he went to Egypt, to the opening of the Suez Canal. On his way home he d shortly after arriving at Munich.
Min Proc ICE V 33 1871–2 pp 209–13; *Nieuw Nederlandsch biografisch Woor-*denbock V 3 cols 314–20

COOK, Thomas

b Melbourne, Derbyshire, 22.11.1808; d Leicester 18.7.1892 aged 83.
Founder of the famous firm of travel agents. Began as an asst gardener, then apprenticed to a wood turner and later worked for a printer at Loughborough who pub books for the Baptists. C's interest led him to become a bible reader and missionary in 1828. His interest in the temperance movement led to his arranging the first R excursion, on the Midland Counties R from Leicester to Loughborough, on 5.7.1841. Its success led to further excursions. C. moved to Leicester where he continued to print and pub books, in addition to organising excursions to ever more distant places. His son John Mason Cook (1834–99) became his first partner in 1864 and in 1865 they moved the office to London. The first tours to the USA followed in 1866. In 1872 TC made a tour round the world to prepare the way for tourists. *Cook's Continental Timetable* first appeared in 3.1873. JMC became sole mgr from 1878 after which Thomas withdrew with oncoming blindness. Under JMC the co expanded greatly. He established the issue of through tickets over Continental Rs and international hotel bookings. In 1884 the British govt entrusted him with the conveyance of the Gordon Relief Expedition to Khartum. He also organised the pilgrimages of Muslims from India to Mecca. From 1948 control of Thomas Cook & Son passed to the British Transport Commission and its successors until 26.5.1972 when it was sold for £22 500 000 to a consortium led by the Midland Bank.
The Times 6.3.1899; *Blackwood's Magazine* 8.1899; DNB Supplement

COOKE, Charles John Bowen, CBE

b Orton Longueville, Huntingdonshire, 11.1.1859; d Falmouth, Cornwall, 18.10.1920 aged 61.
LNWR loco eng. Son of rector of Orton Longueville. Ed privately and at Cheltenham Coll, King's Coll, London for 1 yr, and at Tech High Sch, Neuwied, Rhineland, Germany for 1 yr. 1875 began as pupil of F. W. Webb (qv) at

Crewe, LNWR, and remained with that co until his d. 1880 app asst supt in loco running dept, LNWR S div, under A. L. Mumford at Rugby. 1899–1903 when Webb ret C. was asst running supt of the S div based at Crewe under George Whale (qv). When Whale became CME in 1903 C. became supt of the S div running dept. On the ret of Whale in 2.1909 C. was app CME. Most of his designs closely followed those established by Whale but with improvements such as Schmidt superheaters, piston valves, larger cylinders and Belpaire fireboxes. His greatest departure from established LNWR principles was the 4-cyl 'Claughton' 4–6–0 of 1913 which, because of various shortcomings in the design (see Cox, E. S., *Locomotive Panorama* Vol 1, 1965, p 79) never achieved the distinction of the GWR 'Stars'. C's most outstanding express loco was the 'George the Fifth' class 4–4–0 of 1910 developed from Whale's 'Precurser' type. Other locos produced during his period as CME were the 'Prince of Wales' class 4–6–0 (1911), developed from Whale's 'Experiment' class, a 4–6–2T (1911), 0–8–2T for goods (1911) and 0–8–0 goods (1912). For his part in the mfr of war supplies at Crewe in WW1 C. was made a CBE in 1918. He was MICE and MIME (1912), JP and county councillor for Cheshire and a major in the Eng & R Staff Corps. Pub *British Locos, their history, construction and modern development* 1893, and *Some recent developments in loco practice*, 1902.
Eng V 130 22.10.1920 p 397 (portrait); *Engg* V 110 22.10.1920 p 54 (portrait); Proc IME 5.1921 pp 538–9

COOKE, Sir William Fothergill
(see FOTHERGILL-COOKE)

COOPER, Peter
b New York 12.2.1791; d New York 4.4.1883 aged 92.
Inventor, builder of the first American loco, philanthropist. No formal ed. At 18 apprenticed for 5 yrs to John Woodward, New York coach builder. After experience in various businesses he bought a glue factory which he ran with success. In 1828, with two partners, he erected the Canton Ironworks at Balti-more. In 1829 he built *Tom Thumb* for the Baltimore & Ohio RR, the first steam loco to be built in America (apart from the experimental machine built in 1825 by John Stevens (qv)). It was tested on 25.8.1830 from Baltimore to Ellicott's Mills and back. In 1836 he sold the property to the B & O for stock at $45 a share which he soon sold for $230. He now expanded his interests until they included a wire works at Trenton, NJ, blast furnaces at Pittsburgh, Pa, a rolling mill and a glue factory in New York, foundries at Ringwood, NJ, and Durham, Pa, and iron mines in NJ. In 1854 he rolled the first structural iron for fireproof buildings in the USA. C. was responsible for the success of the New York, Newfoundland & London Telegraph Co of which he was president for 20 yrs. He also became president of the North American Telegraph Co. As a philanthropist he was an early advocate of paid police and fire depts, sanitary water services and public schools. In 1857–9 he founded the Cooper Institute in New York for the advancement of science and art. On 18.12.1813 he m Sarah Bedell (d 1869) at Hampstead.
DAB V 4 pp 409–10

CORAY, Richard
b Trins, Graubünden, Switzerland, 30.7.1869; d Wiesen Graubünden, 3.10.1946 aged 77.
Swiss bridge eng. Trained as eng in the Tech Sch, Winterthur, nr Zurich, 1889–92. Later worked on the Breitenburg–Rongellen rope incline in the Viamala and on the scaffolding for the iron bridge over the Versamertobel. From early 1900s C. carried out centring and scaffolding for an increasing number of important bridges, first in Graubünden then elsewhere. Major projects included the Solis and Wiesen bridges on the Rhaetian R, Gründjetobel and Langwies bridges on the Chur–Arosa R, Sitter bridge near St Gallen on the Bodensee–Toggenburg R, Perolles and Zalmringer bridges in Canton Fryburg and the slender centring of the Salginatobel bridge near Landquart on which his sons cooperated with the great Swiss eng and pioneer of concrete arches, Robert Maillart (1872–1940). Abroad he carried out notable work in Jugoslavia.

His advice was sought by engs in all kinds of problems and was always highly valued.

S Bz V 128 19.10.1946 p 211; Marshall, John, *Metre gauge Rs in S and E Switzerland* 1974

COTTRELL, Stephen Butler

b London, (?).(?).1865;
d Liverpool, 5.3.1933 aged 67.
Chief eng, Liverpool Overhead R. 1882 apprenticed to R. E. Wilson and later to Sir Douglas Fox (qv) and Francis Fox. During the latter period C. was asst eng on the const of the Scarborough–Whitby R, NER (op 1885). He later became res eng on various contracts carried out by the firm. 1889–92 res eng Liverpool Overhead R of which, in 1892, he became chief eng, resigning from this position in 1909. He was frequently engaged as consultant on electric traction schemes and gave evidence before many Parliamentary committees. President of Liverpool Engg Soc 1906–7. MICE, MIME 1896.

Proc IME V 124 6.1933 pp 772–3; Box, C. E., *The Liverpool Overhead R 1893–1956* 1959

COULTHARD, William

b Stamfordham, Northumberland, (?).5.1797; d London 19.3.1863 aged 65.
Eldest son of Walter C., contractor and mason, under whom he began his career. 1824 engaged by John Green as asst on the suspension bridge over the Tyne at Scotswood, the stone bridge over the Tees at Blackwell near Darlington, Free Schools at North Shields, and other works. In 1834 he rebuilt the stone bridge over the Esk at Whitby. His son Hiram Craven, named after the R contractor, was b at Whitby in 1836. C's R career began in 1835 as res eng under Vignoles (qv) on the N Union R between Preston and Wigan, remaining with the co until 1846. He was also responsible for the branch down to the Ribble at Preston, 1845–6. He then became a R contractor and was responsible for the following works on the NWR (later MR) with dates of opening: Lancaster–Morecambe (12.6.1848); Skipton–Ingleton (30.7.1849); Lancaster–Wennington (17.11.1849); Wennington–Clapham (1.6.1850); Morecambe harbour and pier

(1851–2). In conjunction with his son he built the LNWR Ingleton–Low Gill (24.8.1861) and Morecambe–Hest Bank (16.10.1864). Joined ICE 6.1849 and always took a lively interest in its progress.

Min Proc ICE V 23 1863 p 506

COWAN, William

b Edinburgh (?).(?).1823;
d Aberdeen (?).3.1898 aged 75.
Loco supt, Gt N of Scotland R. 1839 entered loco dept, Arbroath & Forfar R. Later went to Edinburgh & Glasgow R and GNR. In 9.1854 joined loco dept GN of S, becoming wks mgr at Kittybrewster, Aberdeen, in 1855 and loco supt in 1857. He ret at 60 in 10.1883, having equipped the R with a stud of robust engines some of which ran until the 1920s. One of his o/c 4-4-0s of 1866, No 45, took part in the R Centenary celebration at Darlington in 1925.

Vallance, H. A., *The Great North of Scotland R* 1965

CRAMPTON, Thomas Russell

b Broadstairs, Kent 6.8.1816;
d Westminster 19.4.1888 aged 71.
Civil eng, and one of the most original loco engs of his time. Ed in a private academy. Began as engg pupil of John Hague, then 1839–44 under Marc Brunel, later with Daniel Gooch (qv) with whom he designed some of the early GWR locos, the 'Firefly' class. He began work on his famous 'single driver' design, with driving axle behind the firebox, in 1842 while still working with Gooch, and took out a patent in 1843. The design made possible a large boiler with a low centre of gravity, then thought desirable. In 1844 he left Gooch to work with Rennie (qv). The first two C. engines were built for Belgium in 1845. There followed two for the LNWR and one for the Dundee & Perth R in 1848. The greatest 'Crampton' for a British R was the LNWR 6-2-0 *Liverpool* in 1848. 320 engines were built to C's patent, mostly in France, Germany and Belgium. They were good runners but suffered from lack of adhesion. As a civil eng C. was partly responsible for the London, Chatham & Dover R and wholly responsible for the Swanley Jn–Sevenoaks, Faversham–Herne Bay and

Strood–Dover lines, and several Rs in eastern Europe and Asia Minor. C. designed other more conventional engines. He became interested in the Channel tunnel project and invented a boring machine which pulverised the chalk and mixed it with water to sluice it out over the shaft. He was also responsible for laying the world's first international submarine cable, across the Strait of Dover. He was a founder member of the IME in 1847. Elected AICE 3.3.1846 and MICE 7.3.1854.
Min Proc ICE V 94 1887–8 p 295; Proc IME 7.1888 pp 437–9; *The Locomotive* 3.1940 pp 67–70; Ellis, Hamilton, *Twenty Locomotive Men* 1958

CRAVEN, John Chester

b Leeds 11.9.1813; d Brighton 27.6.1887 aged 73.
Loco supt, LBSCR. Apprenticed first to Robert Stephenson & Co, Newcastle, and from 1827 at Fenton, Murray & Jackson, Leeds, loco builders. At age 19 he m Jane Jefferson, a quaker girl of Beverley, Yorkshire. His ability was such that in 1832 he was placed in charge of an order for locos for the Liverpool & Manchester R. During the strike of 1837 he left FMJ and worked for a while at the Sun Foundry, Leeds, before moving to London to spend a year at Maudslay & Co. He then returned to Leeds to work for Todd, Kitson & Laird and then with Shepherd & Todd at the R Foundry (afterwards E. B. Wilson & Co) where he was wks mgr for 3 yrs working with David Joy (qv) and John Gray (qv). On 9.11.1842 C. was app loco foreman at Miles Platting, Manchester, on the Manchester & Leeds R under James Fenton (qv). Fenton was a partner in Fenton, Murray & Jackson where C. formerly worked and which closed down in 1843. C. continued after Fenton's resignation in 1.1845 and became outdoor supt under William Jenkins (qv). While on the M & L C. demonstrated that locos could pull trains up the 1 in 47 incline from Manchester Victoria Station to Miles Platting without assistance of the winding engine. In 5.1845 he left to become loco eng of the Eastern Counties R at Stratford, London. Little is known of his work here. In 12.1847 he took up his principal app, as loco

C & W supt on the LBSCR at Brighton. Under C. the wks were greatly enlarged and loco building became possible at Brighton for the first time. He opposed standardisation, producing a new type for every duty so that the LBSCR loco stock became a collection of 'one-off jobs' of extraordinary variety. When ultimately pressed to reduce the number of types he stubbornly refused and in 11.1869 he resigned, leaving on 31.1.1870. His successor, Stroudley (qv), had to sort out the mess. Following his resignation he was frequently called upon for advice on all branches of engg, from locos to graving docks and canal locks. He took a great interest during his last years in the preservation of old Kent and Sussex windmills and in the drainage of Romney Marsh. He became a Brighton councillor in 1871 and was elected alderman 1881. C. was a man of formidable temper but of outstanding ability in the handling of large numbers of men, by whom he was feared and respected.
Engg V 44 15.7.1887 p 71; Ellis, Hamilton, *Twenty Locomotive Men* 1953; Min Proc ICE V 90 1886–7 p 420; Bradley, D. L., *Locos of the LBSCR* V 1 RCTS 1969; Burtt, G. F. *Locos of the LBSCR* (pub anonymously by Loco Pub Co) 1903

CROSBIE DAWSON, George James

b Liverpool (?).(?).1841;
d Stoke on Trent 14.6.1914 aged c 73.
Civil eng, LNWR, NSR. Pupil of Robison Wright of Westminster. Later joined engg staff of LNWR, serving 21 yrs with that co. 1883–6 was chief asst eng, LYR. 1886 app chief eng NSR where he remained until his d. He relaid nearly all the pw and carried out considerable improvements and extensions. Elected MICE 27.3.1872.
Min Proc ICE V 197 1914 p 331; Christiansen, R. and Miller, R. W. *The North Staffordshire R* 1971

CROSS, James

b Uddingston, nr Glasgow, 22.2.1829;
d Llangollen, Wales, 15.10.1894 aged 65.
Civil eng. Trained under Alexander Adie (qv). 1854 app eng to St Helens Canal & R Co. He remained there until 1864 when the co was purchased by the LNWR. In 3.1865, on the d of John

Hutchinson, one of the founders of Widnes, C became mg trustee and supt of the estate including West Bank Dock and important chemical wks. He remained in this connection until his d. In 1864 he rented the wks of the former St Helens R and began mfr of locos and was later joined by Arthur Sinclair, former wks mgr of the St Helens R, and the firm became James Cross & Co, Sutton Engine Works. In 1863 C. built the first 2-4-2T, with W. Bridges Adams' radial axle-boxes at each end, for the St Helens R. In 1865 C. built the first double-boiler Fairlie loco with 2 power bogies, *Progress*, for the Neath & Brecon R. A second, smaller, Fairlie named *Mountaineer* was delivered to the Anglesey Central R in 1866. In 1866-7 the firm built 30 i/c 2-4-0s for the E India R. Loco building ended about 1869 and shortly afterwards the shops were taken over by the LNWR. James Cross & Co merged with Edward Burrows. C. took an active interest in the affairs of Widnes and was chairman of the local bd 1875-82. Elected MIME and MICE 1865. C. built the joint MS & L and MR line from Widnes to Hough Green, opened in 1879.

Min Proc ICE V 109 1894-5 p 390; Proc IME 1894 p 464; Ahrons, E. L. *The British Steam R Loco 1825-1925* 1927; Abbott; Rowland A. S. *The Fairlie Locomotive* 1970

CROSSLEY, John Sydney

b Loughborough, Leics, 25.12.1812; d Barrow on Soar, Leics, 10.6.1879 aged 66.

Civil eng, Midland R. Orphaned at age 2 and placed under guardianship of a Leicester architect named Staveley by whom he was articled at an early age to the son Edward Staveley, eng of Leicester Navigation Co. In 1832, when Edward Staveley went to USA, C. was app eng in his place, continuing in this position and later as director until his d. Began R work in 1832-3 when engaged under W. A. Provis on parliamentary surveys for the Leicester & Swannington R. In 1835 employed under Vignoles (qv) on parliamentary work for the Midland Counties R. 1835 on surveys for the S Midland R (Leicester-Blisworth and Stamford). 1846 on parliamentary work

for the MR extn to the Leicester & Swannington R under Charles Liddell, chief eng, and later on the Ashby-Coalville and Coalville-Leicester lines (op 1.8.1849), and stations from Burton to Leicester, until 1851 when he was engaged under Hawksley for Leicester Waterworks Co. In 9.1852 C. began surveys for the MR Leicester-Hitchin branch but the intensity of the work led to a paralytic stroke on 30.11.1852 in Liddell's office. By 9.1853 he had recovered sufficiently to be app res eng under Liddell on the Leicester-Hitchin line, op 15.4.1857. C. then became MR res eng and in 1858 was app chief eng. In addition to routine maintenance work C. carried out parliamentary work and supervised const of about 225 miles (362km) of new R including the Erewash Valley extn from Pye Bridge to Clay Cross with Clay Cross tunnel, 1 mile 26yd (1633m), op 1.5.1862; Cudworth-Barnsley, including the lofty iron Barnsley vdt, op 28.6.1869; the Wirksworth branch, op 1.10.1867; Derby-Melbourne-Breedon-Ashby,   1868-9; Mangotsfield-Bath, op 1869; Thornbury branch, op 2.9.1872; Stenson-Weston on Trent,   3.11.1873;   Mansfield-Worksop, 1.6.1875; Ambergate-Pye Bridge, 1.5. 1875; Radford-Trowel, 1.5.1875; Trent-Leicester widening; Shipley-Guiseley, 4.12.1876; and, greatest of all, the Settle-Carlisle line, 72¼ miles (116km) through some of the most difficult country in England, op 1.5.1876, with numerous tunnels and viaducts. His wife Agnes laid the last stone in the 130ft (39.62m) high Smardale vdt, the highest on the line, in 6.1875. He was joint eng of Otley-Ilkley; Ashby-Nuneaton; CLC lines and the Furness extn. He resigned as chief eng in 4.1875, before completion of the Carlisle line, but was retained as joint consulting eng. He was also joint consulting eng on the Leeds & Liverpool canal. Elected MICE 1859. Also F Geological Soc and M Soc of Arts.

Min Proc ICE V 58 1878-9 pp 341-3; Baughan, P. E., *North of Leeds* 1966; Barnes, E. G., *The Midland Main Line* 1969; Ellis, Hamilton, *The Midland R* 1953

CROUCH, John Peachey

b Yorkshire c 1875;

d (?) (?).(?).1937 aged c 62.
CME Central Argentine R. Received
early scientific training at Leeds Univ
and at Univ Coll, Liverpool. Apprenticed
at Horwich Wks, LYR, 1893. 24.4.1901
app asst mgr at Newton Heath C & W
wks; 26.6.1901 supt outdoor loco dept.
1909 asst mech eng; 3.1910 pass supt,
LYR. Left in 10.1910 to become CME,
Central Argentine R, until 1920. Became
MIME 1910.
R Eng 12.1910 p 375; Marshall, John,
The Lancashire & Yorkshire R V 2
1970

CUBITT, Benjamin

b Dilham, Norfolk (?).(?).1795;
d London 12.1.1848 aged 53.
Loco eng, GNR. Son of Joseph C. and
bro of William C. (qv) to whom he was
apprenticed as millwright. Later became
foreman of wks of John Penn at Greenwich. His next appointment was in
charge of the engine and machinery
wks of Fenton, Murray & Jackson,
Leeds, remaining there for nearly 10 yrs.
He then moved to the same position at
the wks of Peter Rothwell (qv) at Bolton
in 1833 after Benjamin Hick (qv) had
left the concern. After 10 yrs he left to
take charge of the loco dept of the
Croydon, Brighton and Dover Rs, of
the last of which his bro William was
chief eng. Following the separation of
the 3 companies he was app loco supt of
the newly formed GNR on 3.11.1846
until his d in office. He ordered carriages
for the E Lincs R and the GNR from
Walter Williams of London. From Sharp,
Roberts & Co, Manchester, he ordered
50 2–2–2s and from R & W Hawthorn,
Newcastle, 20 2–2–2s and 15 0–4–2s.
Elected MICE 1843.
Min Proc ICE V 8 1849 p 10; Brown,
F. A. S., *Great Northern R Loco Engs*
V 1 1966

CUBITT, Joseph

b Horning, Norfolk, 24.11.1811;
d London 7.12.1872 aged 61.
Civil eng GNR, SER and other Rs.
Only son of Sir William C. (qv). Apprenticed at Fenton, Murray & Jackson,
Leeds, where his uncle Benjamin C. (qv)
was eng. After 2 yrs he went to assist
his f on the SER until 1846 when he
became chief eng, GNR, again under

his f. On the ret of his f in 1855 he
became consulting eng, GNR. Other
works included the SER Ashford–
Canterbury–Ramsgate and Margate line,
completed 1846; the LCDR from 1853;
Oswestry & Newtown R completed 1860;
Rhymney R 1857–8; Weymouth pier;
and the Carmarthen & Cardigan R 1860–
4. He was consulting eng to many other
projects including from 1860 the extn
of the LCDR over Blackfriars Bridge
into London, op 6.11.1869. Elected
MICE 21.1.1840.
Min Proc ICE V 39 1874–5 pp 248–51

CUBITT, Lewis

b Norfolk (?).(?).1799;
d (?) (?).(?).1883 aged c 84.
Youngest son of Jonathan C.; nephew
of Sir William C. (qv), brother of Thomas
(1788–1855) and William (1791–1863).
Pupil of H. E. Kendall. In 1842 he designed the frontage of the Bricklayers
Arms station, SER, London, op 1.5.
1844. He is best remembered as architect of Kings Cross station, GNR,
London, and the goods warehouse, 1851–
2, and of the Great Northern Hotel,
Kings Cross, 1854.
Jackson, Alan A. *London's Termini* 1969

CUBITT, Sir William

b Dilham, Norfolk, (?).(?).1785;
d Clapham Common, London,
13.10.1861 aged 76.
Son of Joseph C., miller, of Bacton Wood
near Dilham. Became millwright at
Horning, Norfolk. Invented and patented
self-regulating windmill sails 1807. Employed by Ransome & Son of Ipswich,
agricultural implement makers, 1812–21,
and was a partner 1821–6. In 1817 he
invented the treadmill, at once adopted
in the main British gaols. 1826–58 practised as civil eng in London. Designed
the Oxford canal improvements and the
Birmingham & Liverpool Junction (now
Shropshire Union) canal. 1836–46 built
the SER. The biggest operation was
blasting down the face of Round Down
Cliff with one charge of 18 000lb (8165kg)
of gunpowder exploded electrically on
26.1.1843. The work included Shakes-
peare Cliff tunnel, 1387yd (1268m). On
23.9.1844 he was app consulting eng to
the GNR following the resignation of
Locke (qv), until his ret in 1855. He

superintended const of the Crystal Palace for the Great Exhibition of 1851, for which he was knighted at Windsor Castle on 23.10.1851. He built 2 large floating landing stages on the Mersey at Liverpool and the iron bridge across the Medway at Rochester. Elected MICE 1823; member of council 1831; vice president 1836; president 1850–2; FRS 1.4.1830.

Min Proc ICE V 21 1862 pp 554–8; *The Eng* V 12 18.10.1861 p 230; ILN V 2 1843 pp 76–7; Williams, F. S., *Our Iron Roads* 2nd edn 1883 pp 123–6

CUDWORTH, James I'Anson

b Darlington 12.1.1817; d Reigate, Surrey, 22.10.1899 aged 82

Loco eng, SER. Son of William C., grocer and druggist, and Mary (I'Anson), both Quakers. Bro of William (qv). Pupil at Robert Stephenson & Co, Newcastle. Later took charge of the loco wks of the Great N of England R at Darlington. On 22.5.1845 he was app loco supt of the SER where he was in charge of the wks at Bricklayers Arms, London. When these wks became inadequate he planned the new wks at Ashford, Kent, in 1847. So well did he do this that his advice was sought in 1859 when the Stockton & Darlington was laying out its new wks at Darlington. On 17.5.1848 C. m Priscilla Poulter (1827–1910) at the Dover Friends' Meeting House. There were no children. C. was noted for several improvements to locos: his 7ft (2.143m) long sloping firebox made to consume the smoke. His inclined double grates were adapted to hundreds of locos because they burned cheap quality fuel with less smoke. Unfortunately it was a difficult firebox to maintain and it was abandoned soon after C's resignation. He provided the SER with some sound locos, among the best known of which were his outside-frame 0–6–0 standard goods (1856); various 2–4–0s; 7ft (2.134m) 2–2–2 'Mail' engines (1861); 0–4–2 well tanks (1863–4, 1867–9); 0–4–4 well tanks (1866). In 1875, unknown to C., the chairman of the SER, Sir Edward Watkin, approached John Ramsbottom (qv) of the LNWR about larger express engines which C. was unwilling to introduce. Ramsbottom and C. produced an inside frame 2–4–0

design, the 'Ironclads', of which 20 were built in 1876. However, on 14.9.1876 C. tended his resignation. He was noted for his fairness in his dealings with men and he was greatly respected. The Cs moved to Reigate about 1879.

The Eng V 88 10.11.1899 p 479; *Dictionary of Quaker Biography*; Bradley, D. L., *The Locos of the SER* (RCTS) 1963

CUDWORTH, William

b Darlington 7.7.1815; d Saltburn, Yorkshire 4.6.1906 aged nearly 91.

Eng of Stockton & Darlington R. Bro of James (qv). Apprenticed to a Sunderland shipbuilder and later began a business as a shipbuilder in the then new town of Middlesbrough. In 1840 he entered the service of the Stockton & Darlington R under John Harris. In 1850 during the development of the Cleveland iron mining he was app eng for the const of the Middlesbrough & Guisborough R op 11.11.1853. 1857–8 he was engaged on the const of the Hownes Gill vdt nr Consett. He then succeeded John Dixon as eng of the S & D, retaining this position in the Darlington district after amalg with the NER in 1863. He carried out large marshalling yards at Shildon and Newport and new passenger and goods stations. In 1869 he enlarged Middlesbrough dock. In 1883, after the d of his wife, he ret and devoted himself to classical literature. Elected MICE 1.5.1860.

Min Proc ICE V 166 1905–6 p 381

CUDWORTH, William John

b Darlington 4.5.1849;
d York 31.12.1909 aged 60.

Civil eng, NER. Son of William C. (qv). As a member of the Soc of Friends (Quakers) he was ed at Stramongate Sch, Kendal, and at Bootham, York. In 1865 he began as a pupil of his f on the Stockton & Darlington R. From 1870–4 he studied architecture in the office of George Somers Clarke in London. He then returned to R engg and until 1891 was chief asst under his f and Joseph Cabry on the central div of the NER. On 1.9.1880 he m Margaret Thistlethwaite at Birkenhead. In 1891 he succeeded Cabry as eng of this div and in

1899 when, on the ret of Harold Copperthwaite from the S div, the NER was divided into 2 instead of 3 divs, C. was app chief eng of the enlarged S div at York. During his term of office automatic signalling was installed between Alne and Thirsk and a new signal box at York containing the largest number of manual levers in Britain. C. was also responsible for the extensions of Hartlepool docks and of the Wear Valley R, the coast line from Hartlepool to Seaham, the Isle of Axholme Jt R including the swing bridge at Crowle, and the Selby–Goole line. In 1908 he spent several months in Canada and USA studying modern R engg. Ret 10.1909 because of ill health C. was greatly concerned in social work at York, and was noted as a temperance advocate.

Min Proc ICE V 180 1909–10 p 342; *The Eng* V 109 1.1910 p 12; *Dictionary of Quaker Biography*.

DAGLISH, Robert (Sen)

b Northumberland 21.12.1777;
d Orrell, Lancashire, 28.12.1865 aged 88.
In 1804 he settled at Wigan as eng to Lord Balcarrs, becoming mgr of the Haigh Foundry and Brock Mill Forge. He then became mgr of the Orrell colliery nr Wigan and built a R to it. On this he introduced the steam loco of John Blenkinsop (qv) and Matthew Murray (qv) of Leeds, using a rack drive. By arrangement he built the loco in 1812–13. It was known as the *Yorkshire Horse*. In 1825 D. projected and surveyed the Bolton & Leigh R. In 1834 he won a prize of £100 for a rail design for the London & Birmingham R. As an eng his advice was sought by colliery proprietors in Lancashire, Cheshire and N Wales and by many British R companies, and by the New York & Haarlem R. He was one of the projectors of and partner in the St Helens Foundry, later managed by his son and grandson. Became MICE 30.3.1830.

Min Proc ICE V 26 1866–7 pp 561–3

DAGLISH, Robert (Jr)

b Wigan (?).(?).1809;
d London 6.5.1883 aged c 74.
3rd son of Robert D. (qv). Apprenticed

at Rothwell, Hick & Co, Bolton. 1830 joined Lee, Watson & Co, iron founders at St Helens which, in 1832, built an engine and machinery for working the inclines on the St Helens & Runcorn Gap R. In 1837–8 D. contracted for erection of engines, boilers and machinery for glass mfr at Birmingham and St Helens. About 1839 D., with John Smith, undertook to work the traffic on the St Helens & Runcorn Gap R and continued to do this until 1848, maintaining locos and rolling stock at Sutton shed at St Helens Jn. In 1845 D. erected his first cotton mill engines at Wigan. In 1846 he contracted for bridges on the Liverpool & Bury line of the LYR, including two large iron lattice girder bridges near Bolton, the first of their type. In 1849 Robert Daglish Jr & Co built the iron bridges for the Tithebarn Street extn of the LYR at Liverpool. In 1850 D. with McCormick built the Preston extn of the ELR including a large iron bridge over the Ribble. From 1851 D. conducted the foundry business alone until 1869 when he took his nephew George H. Daglish into partnership. This continued until his d. D. supplied many waterworks pumping engines, for St Helens, Newark, Southport, Wirral, Bristol, Hodbarrow mines, Widnes and Warrington. In 1852 he erected the coal drops at the LNWR docks at Garston on the Mersey. Became MIME 19.7.1848; MICE 1874. He was a dir of the St Helens Canal & R Co from 1854–64 and of the LYR from 1876–83.

Min Proc ICE V 74 1882–3 p 283

DAVIES, John Vipond

b Swansea, South Wales, 13.10.1862;
d Flushing, Long Island, New York, 4.10.1939 aged 77.
Civil eng with international reputation. Ed Wesleyan Coll, Taunton, and London Univ. In Wales he was engaged in coal mining and steel mfr until 1889. He then went to New York and worked on the Long Island RR. Later he was app chief asst eng of the tunnel under the East River for the East River Gas Co. He was one of the board of engs responsible for the const of the Moffat tunnel in Colorado, 6 miles 373 yd (9.997km) long, op 27.2.1928. He was also in charge of design and const of the West

Virginia Short Line and the Kanawha and Pocahontas RRs and was concerned with the Huey P. Long bridge over the Mississippi at New Orleans, the world's longest R bridge, completed 1935. He also designed and built the 4 tunnels under the Hudson River for the Hudson & Manhattan RR and planned the Pennsylvania RR tunnel under the Hudson and East Rivers. He also designed and supervised the building of the Paris Metro tunnel under the Seine and across the Place de la Concorde. In 1895 he m Ruth Ramsey of Pottsville, Penn, who d 1931. They had 1 son and 2 drs.
Journal ICE V 13 1939 p 353.

DEAN, William

b London 9.1.1840; d Folkestone 24.9.1905 aged 65.
GWR loco eng. Ed Haberdashers' Company's Sch. In 10.1855 entered the GWR wks at Wolverhampton where he was apprenticed under Joseph Armstrong (qv), then loco supt on the N Div of the GWR, later becoming chief asst to Armstrong. In 1864 Armstrong moved to Swindon as chief loco C & W supt, GWR, leaving D. to manage the Wolverhampton wks where 850 men were employed. In 6.1888 D. also was moved to Swindon and was app chief asst supt. On the d of Armstrong in 1877 D. was app to succeed him as loco C & W supt. Under D. Swindon wks grew considerably. He equipped the GWR with a stud of strong, simple and efficient engines of which the most notable were the 'standard goods' 0-6-0, the 7ft 8½in (2.349m) singles, the 'Badminton' and 'Duke' class 4-4-0s. Towards the end of his career his mental powers began to fail and he gave increasing freedom to his chief asst, G. J. Churchward (qv), who was able to develop his new domeless Belpaire boiler on the Dean engines so that when D. ret in 5.1902 the transition to the Churchward era was a smooth one. D. took a great interest in the volunteer regiment at Swindon in which he held the rank of major. He was also JP for Wiltshire. He became MIME in 1868 and was also MICE.
The Eng V 100 29.9.1905 p 316 (portrait); Proc IME 12.1905 p 1051; Min Proc ICE V 165 1905–6 p 354; Ellis, Hamilton, *Twenty Locomotive Men*

1958; Holcroft, Herbert, *An Outline of GW Loco Practice 1837–1947* 1957; *The Locos of the GWR* (RCTS) parts 1, 4, 5, 6, 7

DEANE, Henry MA

b Clapham London, 26.3.1847;
d Malvern, Victoria, Australia, 12.3.1924 aged nearly 77.
Civil eng on Australian Rs. At age 15 entered Queen's Coll, Galway, and later King's Coll, London. 1867 began as pupil of T. Marr Johnson, working on portions of the Metropolitan R, London. 1869 app to Waring Bros, contractors on the East Hungarian R. Worked on the Grosswardein–Klausenburg line and on the Medias–Hermannstadt section. Then moved to Danube Steam Nav Co at Altofen wks nr Budapest for 3½ yrs as principal asst to chief eng and g mgr. 1875 returned to England to work under Benjamin Baker (qv). 1877 to Manila on sugar plant. He then went to Australia, landing at Sydney, NSW, in 1.1880 and was engaged as R surveyor on the GN Mallet Creek–Ourimbah line. Early 1881 app dist eng on Gunnedah–Narrabri extn. 1882–4 in charge of const of Homebush–Hawkesbury River R. Then transferred to Sydney, engaged on plans for proposed City R extn, later as asst eng on R surveys, and from 7.1886 as inspecting eng following the d of W. B. Wade. In 6.1889 app acting eng in chief for Rs, soon becoming eng in chief. 1894 commissioned by govt to visit USA and Europe to investigate light R and tramway const. 1899 took over all tramway const in Sydney. Visited USA and Europe again in 1904 to report on engg matters. Returned 6.1906 and became consulting eng in Sydney. Responsible for const of 32 miles of difficult R for Commonwealth Oil Corpn, from Clarence on the GWR of NSW to Newnes in the Wolgan valley, a climb of 1850ft (564m). 1909–13 member of various commissions. 1911 app consulting eng to Commonwealth Govt on survey for transcontinental R Kalgoorlie–Port Augusta. 1912 became eng in chief on Commonwealth Rs. Ret 1914. Became MICE 1886. He was twice m and left a widow, 3 sons and 3 drs.
Min Proc ICE V 218 1923–4 pp 507–9

De BERGUE, Charles

b Kensington, London, (?).(?).1807;
d Kensington, 10.4.1873 aged 65.
Bridge builder. Showed interest in engg
as a boy, inventing machinery for
making reeds for looms. His family
moved to Paris where his f opened an
engg wks. 1836 returned to England and
invented several valuable machine tools.
Established engg wks at Manchester and
Cardiff building bridges, his designs
aiming at a combination of strength with
lightness. He invented a new system of
iron pw, used in Spain, also R buffers, a
moulding table, and various machine
tools including a machine for making
rivets. (See Proc IME 1861 p 212)
Became MIME 1857.
Proc IME 1874 p 18; Min Proc ICE V
38 1873–4 p 309

DEELEY, Richard Mountford

b Chester 24.10.1855; d Isleworth,
19.6.1944 aged 89
Loco supt, MR. Ed Chester Cathedral
Gr Sch. 1873 entered wks of Hydraulic
Engg Co, Chester, as pupil of Edward
B. Ellington, mg dir. 1874 sent to work
with Brotherhood & Hardingham, London, on a 3-cyl hydraulic engine. 1875
left to serve pupilage under S. W.
Johnson (qv) at the MR wks at Derby.
1880 app chief of testing dept. 1893 app
inspector of locos. 1899 given supervision of all electrical plant on MR. 1902
mgr of loco wks. 1904 succeeded Johnson
as loco supt and mech eng until he ret
in 1909. D. developed the Johnson 4–4–0
compound into a powerful and economical machine and also developed a
number of other Johnson designs of
4–4–0 and 0–6–0. In his 990 class 2-cyl
4–4–0 he used a 'scissors' type valve gear.
He collaborated with Leonard Archbutt,
MR chief chemist, in design and const
of a water softening plant. Became
MIME 1890 and MICE 1906. Pub
Lubrication and Lubricants 1900/07/12/
27; *A Manual of the principles of
Meteorology* 1935; and *A Geneological
History of Montfortsur–Risle and Deeley
of Halesowen* 1941.
Engg V 158 7.7.1944 p 14; Proc IME V
152 1945 p 336; *RM* 9/10.1944 p 265;
RG 30.6.1944 p 671

DEES, James

b Meldon nr Morpeth, Northumb,
(?).3.1815; d nr Bellingham 19.9.1875
aged 60.
Civil eng, Cumbria Rs. Began business
as builder and contractor and worked on
the R bridge over the Tees at Croft,
designed by Henry Welch. 1845 went to
Cumberland as asst res eng on Whitehaven & Furness Jn R after which he
became eng to the co and also to
Whitehaven Jn R. 1851 built R tunnel
under Whitehaven. 1853 app eng to wet
dock at Maryport and to Whitehaven,
Cleator & Egremont R. His connection
with a haematite ore mine proved so
lucrative that he ret after a few yrs.
Became MICE 7.2.1854.
Min Proc ICE V 43 1875–6 p 297

DE GLEHN, Alfred George

b Sydenham, Kent, (?).(?).1848;
d Mulhouse, Alsace, 8.6.1936 aged 88.
One of the pioneers of steam loco compounding. He was the son of Robert von
Glehn who settled in England from the
Baltic provinces. Alfred von Glehn later
settled in France where he changed his
name to de Glehn, eventually becoming
tech head of the Société Alcacienne,
Belfort, and in this capacity was responsible for design and const of the first
4-cyl compound loco, No 701, for the
Northern R of France in 1866, 4 yrs
after Webb's first 3-cyl compound
Experiment had been built at Crewe.
In the de G. compound the 2 h p cyls
outside drove the rear driving wheels
and the 2 l p cyls inside drove the forward axle. In 1890 the Nord ordered
2 more incorporating improvements made
in collaboration with Gaston du Bousquet
(qv), chief eng of the Nord. These were
so successful that in 1903 the GWR of
England ordered a similar engine built
at Belfort and erected at Swindon, and
2 others slightly larger 2 yrs later. The
de G.–du B. compound system achieved
its maximum size in the great Pacifics
built in 1928 for India on a gauge of
5ft 6in (1.68m). Elsewhere its development was restricted by limitations
imposed on the size of the l p cyls by the
standard gauge.
The Locomotive 15.7.1936 p 232; *RG*
12.6.1936

DENDY MARSHALL, Chapman Frederick

b (?) (?).(?).1873; d Wonersh nr Guildford 14.6.1945 aged 72.

R technician and historian. Ed Hurstpierpoint and Trinity Coll, Cambridge. Called to the Bar at the Inner Temple in 1898 but did not practise. In WW1 he was technical examiner at the Munitions Inventions Dept. He contributed numerous articles on technical and historical matters to various journals. Although his method of writing R history, and occasionally his accuracy, have been criticised, he was one of the first to establish a high standard in this branch of writing. On the practical side he evolved a method of loco compounding which was applied to LNWR 4–6–0 No 1361 *Prospero* (see *The Locomotive* V 21 p 219). Elected MILE 1916. He was a founder of the Newcomen Society of which he was president in 1934–5. He also wrote a history of the Post Office. His works on R history include: *First hundred R engines* 1928; *Centenary History of the Liverpool & Manchester R* 1930; *History of the Southern R* 1936; *History of British Rs down to the year 1830* 1938; *Early British Locomotives* 1939; *History of R Locos down to the year 1831* 1953.

The Locomotive 7.1945 p 109; *Journal ILE* V 35 1945 p 259

DIESEL, Dr Rudolph

b Paris (?).3.1858; d North Sea 29–30.9.1913 aged 55.

Son of German parents. Ed in Paris. When war broke out in 1870 his parents moved to England, sending D. to school in Augsburg. He then entered Munich Tech Coll where he graduated in 1879 and became asst to Prof von Linde. After a short time in practical work at Sulzer Bros wks, Winterthur, he was app mgr of the Paris wks for the mfr of von Linde refrigerating machinery. From his student days he was engrossed with the idea of a prime mover with a much higher thermal efficiency than the steam engine. He designed an engine which he described in 1893 in his book *Theorie und Konstruktion eines rationellen Wärmemotors*. An English translation was pub in 1894. He was financed by Krupp and the Augsburg–Nuremburg Co for the construction of an engine to his design. The first diesel engine, a vertical stationary type, was built in 1893. It was not a success. His second, built immediately afterwards, while still not successful, proved his theories. His third, the first reliable diesel, was built by the Augsburg Co in 1897. It was a 4-stroke engine developing 18 hp. Other engines followed, each embodying improvements. A large number of British, Continental and American firms took up the patents and many were built and used all over the world before D. d. By 1912 D. had established a successful 2-stroke engine, but it was not as economical as the 4-stroke. The first marine diesel engine was built in France in 1903. Its first application to rail traction was in a Sulzer–Diesel loco completed at Winterthur in 1913 and supplied to the Central R Dept of the Prusso–Hessian State R, Berlin in 3.1913. On trials it ran at speeds up to 60mph (97km/h). (See *Engg* V 96 5.9.1913 p 317) D. is believed to have refused to allow his engine to be used for war purposes. On the night of 29.9.1913 he was on a steamer to Harwich to visit wks at Ipswich. He was last seen about 22.00, but at Harwich the following morning he had disappeared.

Engg V 96 3.10.1913 pp 465–6 (portrait)

DIXON, Edward

b Cockfield, County Durham, 13.6.1809; d Wandsworth, London, 18.11.1877 aged 68.

Civil eng. Son of John D., colliery proprietor. Ed Ackworth Sch, nr Pontefract. Began engg career on Liverpool & Manchester R under his bro John (qv) on the crossing of Chat Moss. Later he worked under Robert Stephenson on London & Birmingham R and under Locke (qqv) on London & Southampton R. Returning to R. Stephenson he worked on surveys for Rs in Buckinghamshire and Warwickshire. He then superintended const of Leamington–Coventry, op 9.12.1844; Rugby–Leamington R, op 1.3.1851; Bletchley–Oxford op 1850–1; and Nuneaton–Coventry op 12.9.1850. After serving as acting res eng of the London–Birmingham section for a period he moved to Southampton where he was elected president of the

Chamber of Commerce and a JP. He was a founder of the Union Steamship Co. He ret in 10.1873. Elected MICE 1.2.1842.

Min Proc ICE V 54 1877–8 pp 280–1

DIXON, John

b Cockfield, Northumberland, (?).(?).1796; d Darlington 10.10.1865 aged 68.

One of the earliest R civil engs. Began as a bank clerk under Jonathan Backhouse, one of the promoters of the Stockton & Darlington R on which D. later became a clerk. In 1821 he took up surveying with George Stephenson. After completion of the S & D in 1825 he went to the Canterbury & Whitstable R, begun in 12.1825. In 1827, before completion of this, he went to the Liverpool & Manchester R and surveyed the line across Chat Moss. On the opening of the L & M he was put in charge of locos. In 1845 he returned to Darlington where he became a consulting eng.

Jeans, J. S. *Jubilee Memorial of the R System* 1875; Warren, J. G. H. *A Century of Loco Building at Robert Stephenson & Co 1823–1923* 1923, 1970

DIXON, John

b Newcastle upon Tyne (?).(?).1835; d East Croydon 28.1.1891 aged 56.

Civil eng. Eldest son of Jeremiah D. and nephew of John D. (qv) of the S & DR. Ed Dr Bruce's Sch, Newcastle. Apprenticed at Robert Stephenson & Co. Became eng at Consett Ironworks, later going into business on his own and restarting the old ironworks at Bedlington. This was unsuccessful so he moved to London where he began a successful career as eng and contractor. Among his R works was the first experimental R in China from Shanghai to Woosung, about 20 miles (32km), a 2ft 6in (762mm) gauge line opened in 1876 (see Rapier). The Chinese, however, were suspicious of it and in 10.1877 they uprooted it and dumped it in Formosa. D. built the Custom House piers at Lisbon and 60 miles (96.5km) of R. His most famous achievement was the transporting of Cleopatra's Needle from Alexandria to London (see Baker, Sir B.).

Engg V 51 6.2.1891 pp 168–9

DODDS, Isaac

b Hewarth, Co Durham, 9.7.1801; d (?) 1.11.1882 aged 81.

Loco and civil eng. In 1814 became pupil of his uncle Ralph D., colliery viewer at Killingworth who, with George Stephenson, built a loco. On the formation of Robert Stephenson & Co at Newcastle D. went there as a pupil. On completion of his pupilage he began a works at Felling, Co Durham. In 1832 he became eng at Horsley Ironworks, Staffordshire, and began mfr of locos. In 1833 he designed the *Star* for the Liverpool & Manchester R. D. became interested in working inclines with locos instead of ropes, and built the *Monarch* which worked the incline near St. Helens on the L & M. About 1841 he went with his bro in law John Stephenson to the N Midland R on which he became loco supt and built the first loco turntable to work on a smooth outer ring. He introduced spring buffers and a number of other devices. In 1845 he worked with Stephenson, Mackenzie & Brassey on the Lancaster & Carlisle and Caledonian Rs. He was responsible for several wrought iron girder bridges on the CR and Scottish Central in 1846–8. Late in 1850 D. took his eldest son T.W.D. (qv) into partnership and re-formed the Holmes Engine & R Wks, Rotherham, where he introduced steeled rails and where much R equipment was made. The wks closed about 1867. Became AICE 30.4.1839.

Min Proc ICE V 75 1832–3 pp 308–14

DODDS, Thomas Weatherburn

b Hewarth, County Durham, 2.5.1826; d Sheffield 6.9.1899 aged 73.

Civil eng, mfr, inventor, and loco supt NSR. Son of Isaac D. (qv). Pupil of Sir James Falshaw (qv), then engaged on R works in the Midlands. In 1845 went to Glasgow with his uncle John Stephenson of Stephenson, Mackenzie & Brassey, and assisted in building the Lancaster & Carlisle R and CR. Late in 1850 D. was taken into partnership with his f with whom he opened the Holmes Engine & R Wks at Rotherham. Here they mfd steeled rails and other plant for Rs at home and abroad. They designed and built the rolling stock of the Santander & Alar R, Spain, and in conjunction with

Alfred Jee (qv) built part of the line. In the early 1860s they erected converting furnaces at Pittsburg for Andrew Carnegie. D. took out many patents for inventions and took a leading role in the promotion of steel for rails, boilers, ship plates and artillery. They claimed to have built the first loco turntable to work on a smooth outer ring, to have introduced various self-acting switches (points), and to have led in the replacement by spring buffers of the old leather ones stuffed with horsehair. D. was one of the first to make a success of burning coal instead of coke in locos. The depression of 1866 forced closure of the wks and in 1870 D. accepted the position of eng and loco supt on the NSR and as eng to the Trent & Mersey Nav. In 1882 he went to Transvaal for 6 months, reporting on R works. 1884 app g mgr of Santa Fé Colonial Rs. Returned to England 1887. 1892 sent to S America to investigate costs on the Buenos Aires & Pacific R of which he eventually became g mgr, with a seat on the bd. In 1896 he was forced by ill health to retire. Elected MICE 1873.
Min Proc ICE V 139 1899–1900 pp 351–2; *The Eng* V 88 15.9.1899 p 266; 'Manifold' *The N Staffordshire R* 1952; Christiansen, R. and Miller, R. W., *The N Staffordshire R* 1971

DODGE, Grenville Mellen

b Danvers, Mass, USA 12.4.1831;
d Council Bluffs, 3.1.1916 aged 84.
Civil eng, politician. Ed Durham academy, NH, and Norwich Univ, Vt. After graduating as eng in 1851 began as eng on Illinois Central RR in 1.1852. Met Peter A. Dey who took D. as chief asst on surveys for the Mississippi & Missouri RR, Davenport to Iowa City, 1853. From there D. and his party pushed on westwards and reached the Missouri near Council Bluffs on 22.11. 1853. Here he made his permanent home. 1855–61 he was engaged in R building in Iowa and in business in Council Bluffs. Served in Civil War in the Iowa Regt. In 1.1866 became chief eng on Union Pacific RR on which the first grading had been done in autumn 1864 and on which the last spike was driven at its connection with the Central Pacific on 10.5.1869. In one year 568 miles (913km)

of line were located, built and equipped. In 1.1870 he resigned and became chief eng of the Texas & Pacific R in 1871. On its failure in 1873 he joined Jay Gould (qv) in R development in the south west, assisting in building nearly 9000 miles (14 484km) of line including Denver, Texas & Fort Worth, and Denver, Texas & Gulf RRs. With Sir William Van Horne (qv) he organised the Cuba RR Co and in 1903 completed the line from Santa Clara to Santiago. D's surveys totalled about 60 000 miles (96 516km). In 1866 he was elected to Congress. He m Anne Browne on 29.5.1854.
DAB V 5 pp 347–8; *Trains* 6.1948 p 36; Griswold, Wesley S., *A work of giants* 1963

DOLIVO-DOBROWOLSKI M.

b St Petersburg (?).(?).1862;
d Heidelberg, Germany, 15.11.1919 aged 58.
Pioneer of 3-phase ac. Studied in Darmstadt, Germany, 1881–4. Joined Allgemeine Elektrizitäts-Gesellschaft, Berlin, in 1884 and pioneered work on multi-phase ac. Invented the term 'Drehstrom' (revolving current) for 3-phase ac in 1888. Most of the basic principles of 3-phase ac technique were developed by him. Spent most of his life with AEG, finally as a tech dir.
S Bz V 75 28.2.1920 p 105

DORNING, Elias

b (Bury?) 25.1.1819;
d Manchester 18.7.1896 aged 77.
Civil eng. 1836 articled to William Benson, Bury, for 5 yrs. 1841–3 res eng Bury waterworks. Then began private practice in Manchester as civil and mining eng, surveyor and land agent, making extensive parliamentary surveys and valuations of properties for R works. Associated with Thomas Bouch (qv) in the purchase of land for LNWR Eccles-Tyldesley–Wigan line, and they were jt engs for the Lancashire Union Rs. D. also carried out similar work for the CLC and Wirral Rs. Acted as surveyor for the LYR until that co app a permanent surveyor, and in 1884 was responsible for securing the land for Horwich loco wks. Again he acted for the LYR in the purchase of land for the

Pendleton–Hindley line, also in 1884. As consulting eng D. acted for the Earls of Derby, Sefton and Wilton, and many other landowners in the north. He was standing arbitrator for the Corpn of Manchester for which he purchased 25 miles (40km) of land for the Thirlmere pipeline. D. was frequently engaged by other Lancashire corpns and was also a witness in engg and compensation cases involving large public and private interests. He had been sitting 3 days as arbiter in a land-purchase case for the Liverpool, St Helens & S Lancashire R Co when he was taken ill, and he d at his home in Pendlebury nr Manchester. Min Proc ICE V 126 1895–6 p 395; Marshall, John, *The Lancashire & Yorkshire R* V 2 1970, also article on '*The Lancashire Union Rs*' in *RM* 4/5/6.1970.

DREDGE, James

b Bath 29.7.1840; d Pinner, Mddx, 15.8.1906 aged 66.
Civil eng and journalist. Ed Bath Gr Sch. 1858–61 in office of D. K. Clark (qv); 1862 entered office of Sir John Fowler (qv) with whom he worked several yrs on the Metropolitan District R. Then turned to journalism and wrote for *Engg* from its start in 1.1866 (founded by Zerah Colburn, qv, on his ret from editorship of *The Eng* in 1865). On the d of Colburn in 1870 D. and the sub-editor W. H. Maw became jt editors and proprietors. D. continued until disabled by paralysis in 5.1903. Pub *History of the Pennsylvania RR* 1879. Responsible for many loco illustrations in *Engg* and was author of the 779 page *Record of the Transportation Exhibits at the World's Columbia Exposition* 1903. Elected MIME 1874 and MICE 4.2.1896.
The Eng V 102 24.8.1906 p 194; *Engg* V 82 24.8.1906 pp 241–2; Min Proc ICE V 166 1906 p 382; Proc IME 7.1906 pp 635–7

DRIPPS, Isaac L.

b Belfast 14.4.1810; d Altoona Pa USA 28.12.1892 aged 82.
Inventor and loco eng. While he was a child his parents emigrated to Philadelphia, Pa. Ed Philadelphia city schools. At 16 apprenticed to Thomas Holloway, then the largest builder of steamboat machinery in Philadelphia.

In 1830 the co formed a subsidiary, the Camden & Amboy RR Co in NJ, and ordered a loco from Robert Stephenson & Co. In 1831 it arrived in Philadelphia in parts which D. transported to Bordentown where he erected it, although he had never seen a loco. It was named *John Bull*. In 1832–3 he added a leading pony truck and pilot (cowcatcher). He drove it on its trial trip on 12.11.1831. He stayed on the C & A 22 yrs, at first in charge of loco building in Hoboken shops (see Robert L. Stevens). Introduced the bonnet spark arrestor in 1833 and the first 8-wheeled freight loco in 1834–8. He became supt of machinery, responsible also for the company's steamboats. Later he became supt of motive power and machinery. 1853 became partner in Trenton Loco & Machine Wks, Trenton, NJ. Here he designed and built a wide-tread-wheeled loco for running on different gauges. 1859, after closure of the firm, he was app supt of motive power and machinery, Pittsburgh, Fort Wayne & Chicago RR, and moved with his family to Fort Wayne, Ind. During the next 10 yrs he completely rebuilt the mech dept, making the shops the most modern in USA. On 1.4.1870 he became supt of motive power and machinery at the Altoona shops of the Pennsylvania RR. Here he undertook const of the most extensive R shops in USA. Failing health forced him to resign on 31.3.1872, but he continued to serve the PRR as consultant until 1878 when he had to retire. He invented numerous mechanisms, tools, etc, for locos, freight and passenger cars and steamboats, but never patented any. In 1830 he m at Bordentown, NJ, and was survived by his son William.
DAB V 5 p 458; Sinclair, Angus, *Development of the Loco Engine* 1907; White, John H. Jr *American Locos, an engg history 1830–80* 1968

DRUMMOND, Dugald

b Ardrossan, Ayrshire, 1.1.1840; d Surbiton, Surrey, 8.11.1912 aged 72.
Loco eng, NBR, CR, LSWR. His f was a p w insp, later on the Caledonian & Dumbartonshire Jn R (Bowling–Balloch) on which P. Stirling (qv) was for a time loco supt. Apprenticed with Forrest & Barr of Glasgow. He spent some time

on the Bowling–Balloch line; 2 yrs with Peto, Brassey & Betts at Birkenhead; in 1862 in the Cowlairs, Glasgow, wks of the Edinburgh & Glasgow R, under S. W. Johnson (qv) and then at the HR wks at Inverness under W. Stroudley (qv). In 1866 D. became wks mgr at Inverness. When Stroudley went to Brighton in 1869 D. was in charge at Inverness until D. Jones (qv) arrived in 2.1870. D. then followed Stroudley to Brighton where he was greatly influenced by Stroudley's design work. 1875 app loco supt NBR following the dismissal of Thomas Wheatley (qv). Here his first locos closely followed Stroudley's designs. However, for the Waverley route, Carlisle–Edinburgh, he designed a new type of 4–4–0, the 'Abbotsford' type built in 1876–8, which became a classic type on the NBR, CR, HR and LSWR. Examples were still running in the 1960s. In 1882, after making himself rich, non too honestly, at the NBR's expense, D. moved to the neighbouring St Rollox wks of the CR and continued his famous 4–4–0 designs which were later developed still further by his successors Lambie, McIntosh and W. Pickersgill (qqv). Also, both on the NBR and CR, he established an 0–4–4T design which was continued, in an enlarged form, by his successors. His own M7 type (see later) lasted well into the 1960s. In 1890 he resigned and went to Queensland, Australia, and established an engg wks, but soon returned to Glasgow where he founded the Glasgow Engg Co, building industrial locos. On 1.8.1895 he was app mech eng on the LSWR at Nine Elms, London. His title became CME in 1.1905. He was later responsible for the reorganising of the loco wks and the layout of the new wks at Eastleigh, opened in 1909. In addition to continuing his well developed 0–4–4T, 4–4–0 and 0–6–0 types he carried out experiments with an uncoupled 4–4–0, or 4–2–2–0, and with water tubes across fireboxes, feedwater heaters and spark arrestors. He distrusted superheaters. While he produced some outstanding successes such as the T9 4–4–0s and M7 0–4–4Ts, his 4–6–0 designs were dismal failures. Only one type achieved moderate success, the T14, and then only when rebuilt by Urie and Maunsell (qqv). He was a for-

midable, ferocious man who spared no-one the lash of his tongue and his strong language when he was aroused. In the end he was a victim of his own obstinacy. He neglected a badly scalded leg and feet which led to gangrine, amputation and death. He became MIME 1886; also MICE.

Engg V 94 11.1912 p 685; *The Eng* V 114 11.1912 p 523; Min Proc ICE V 195 1914 pp 371–2; Proc IME 12.1912 pp 1163–5; Ellis, Hamilton, *Twenty Locomotive Men* 1958; Bradley, D. L., *Locos of the LSWR* Part 2 (RCTS) 1967

DRUMMOND, Peter

b Polmont, Stirlingshire, 13.8.1850; d Kilmarnock 30.6.1918 aged 67.
Scottish loco eng, son of a NBR p w insp and younger bro of Dugald D. (qv). While he was still a child his family moved to Maryhill nr Glasgow where he received his general and tech ed. Apprenticed at Forrest & Barr, general engs and millwrights, Glasgow. 1871 began work on the LBSCR at Brighton wks where his bro was also working under Stroudley (qv). In 1875 followed his bro to the NBR at Cowlairs, Glasgow. When Dugald moved to the CR wks at St Rollox Peter followed him there and in 1882 was app asst loco eng and wks mgr. In this capacity he rearranged and reorganised the wks and also superintended the building of the famous McIntosh 'Dunalastair' 4–4–0s. In 1896 D. was app loco C & W supt of the Highland R at Inverness. Here he found the shops needed complete overhaul and rearrangement, as had St Rollox, and this he carried out. He designed the large, medium and small snow ploughs used on the HR and later adopted on other Rs. His first engines were the 20 'Ben' type 4–4–0s (1808–1906), similar to Dugald's '290' class on the LSWR. They were followed by the 12 'Barney' 0–6–0s (1900–7). His most famous HR engines were the 'Castle' class 4–6–0s, a development of the well known Jones 'Big goods' 4–6–0, for passenger trains. Ten were built in 1900–2 and 9 in 1910–11, 1913 and 1917; in addition another 50 in 1911 for the French State Rs. In 1908–9 a further 6 4–4–0s were ordered with larger boilers, the 'Big Bens', and in 1909–12 he brought out 8 0–6–4Ts

for banking on the heavy grades of the HR main line. In 1912 he was app loco C & W supt of the G & SWR at Kilmarnock. Here he decided to adopt a 'big engine' policy, introducing his 15 huge 0–6–0s in 1913. They were heavy on coal, sluggish and unpopular. He also ordered 6 similar 4–4–0s. In 1914 a further 6 4–4–0s with superheaters were such an improvement that he decided to apply the superheater to the 0–6–0 but the extra weight required another pair of wheels in front and they appeared as 2–6–0s of which 11 were built in 1915. Last came 18 0–6–2Ts for heavy mineral traffic, 1915–17. Peter D's engines closely resembled his brother's in many details, but he did not use Dugald's built-up crank axle. He took a keen interest in the education of his men and in their improvement classes. Became MIME 1898.
Proc IME 10.1918 p 450; Engg 5.7.1918 p 10; SLS pub The Highland R Co 1855–1955 1955; SLS pub The Glasgow & South Western R 1950; Smith, D. L. Locos of the G & SWR 1976

DU BOUSQUET, Gaston

b Paris 20.8.1839; d Paris 24.3.1910 aged 70.
French loco eng associated with development of compounding. On leaving the State Sch of Engg, Paris, in 1862, he began his career on the Northern R of France where he spent the whole of his working life. 1883 became div loco supt at Lille; 1889 chief loco supt, and 1890 chief eng of rolling stock and motive power. Worked with de Glehn (qv) on the first 4-cyl compound of 1886 and on the later 4–4–0, 4–4–2, 4–6–0 and 4–6–2 designs. 1894 elected president of the French Soc of Civil Engs. 1901 introduced a class of successful 4–6–0 tandem compound tank engines on the Ceinture R. For freight traffic, in 1905, he introduced his famous 0–6–2 + 2–6–0 articulated compound tank engine with two driving bogies supporting a frame which carried the boiler, tanks, cab, buffing and draw gear. The cylinders were at the centre, h p on the rear unit. It was a development of the Wiener Neustadt loco built for the Semmering trials of 1851. Others were built for China in 1906 and Spain in 1911. Latterly he conducted experiments with water-tube fireboxes and at the time of his death he was working on a 4–6–4 express engine which he did not see completed. For 14 yrs he was an officer of the Legion of Honour.
Le Genie Civil 9.4.1910 p 450; The Locomotive 4.1910; The Eng V 109 1.4.1910 p 330; Wiener, Lionel, Articulated Locomotives 1930, 1970 p 233

DÜBS, Henry

b Guntersblum, Hesse Darmstadt, Germany, 10.3.1816; d Glasgow 24.4.1876 aged 60.
Loco mfr. At 14 apprenticed at a small fitting and turning shop at Mainz. 1834 entered the machine wks of Reuleux & Co, Aix-la-Chapelle, becoming shop mgr at 21. 1839 visited England to see engg wks at London and Manchester, where he spent a period in the drg office of Sharp, Roberts Ltd. 1842 became wks mgr at Vulcan Foundry nr Warrington. After a brief connection with Beyer Peacock, Manchester, 1857–8, he went to Glasgow and became a partner of W. M. Neilson (qv) with whom he laid out the Hyde Park Loco Wks at Springburn, the first loco factory of importance in Scotland. In 1863 he began plans for a loco wks of his own in Glasgow and in 1865 he opened the Glasgow Loco Wks. 1874 became mg dir of the Steel Co of Scotland at Newton nr Glasgow. He was one of the founder members of the IME in 1847. Dübs & Co was amalg with Neilson, Reid & Co and Sharp, Stewart & Co Ltd to form the North British Loco Co in 1903.
Engg 5.5.1876 p 366; Proc IME 1.1877 p 18; Beyer Peacock Quarterly 10.1930 pp 52–3

EDDY, Wilson

b Chelsea, Vermont, (?).(?).1813; d (?) (?).(?).1898 aged c 85.
Loco eng, Western RR, USA. 1832 began as machinist at the Locks & Canals Co machine shop, Lowell, Mass. 1840 became foreman of Western RR loco repair shops, Springfield, Mass. 1850 app master mechanic of Western RR. His first loco was built in 1851, the 4–4–0 Addison Gilmore for fast passenger work. E. developed large fireboxes,

and large diameter domeless boilers. About 135 engines were built to his standard design, the last in 1881 a year after his ret. By then his design was becoming obsolete, but his engines were fine runners.

White, John H. Jr *American Locos, an engg history 1830-80* 1968

EDMONDSON, Thomas

b Lancaster, 30.6.1792; d Manchester, 22.6.1851 aged 59.

Originator of the standard card R ticket. Son of quaker parents, John and Jane E. of whose 12 children only 5 reached maturity, Joseph, Thomas and George and 2 drs. Thomas displayed inventive and practical skill early and was apprenticed to a cabinet maker, becoming journeyman with the firm of Waring & Gillow, Lancaster, where he invented improvements in cabinet making tools and designs. Later, after a brief but unsuccessful business career, he went into partnership in a firm of furniture mfrs at Carlisle. This became bankrupt, though in time E paid all his creditors. His son John Beeby E. was b at Carlisle on 22.6.1831. In 1836 he obtained employment as a clerk on the Newcastle & Carlisle R at Milton, later Brampton, station, about 14 miles from Carlisle. In 1837 he invented a machine for printing R tickets on cards 57.5 x 30.5mm (2¼ x 1¹⁄₁₆in), and a press for stamping dates on the tickets. Almost identical date presses and other E. equipment are still in use today. The N & C, however, was not interested in his inventions, so he applied to the Manchester & Leeds R and was app at Manchester. His system was soon adopted for use throughout the country and elsewhere in the world. E. patented his inventions and charged Rs 10 shillings (50p) a mile per year for their use, so a R 100 miles long paid £50 a year. He was always generous with the proceeds. His system avoided the time consuming labour of writing out individual tickets for passengers. After his d the firm was managed by his eldest bro Joseph at Manchester until it was taken over by the son J.B.E. who d in 1887. Branches were later opened in London, Glasgow and Dublin, operated by E's grandsons.

DNB V 6 p 396; *RM* 11.1897 p 401;

12.1912 p 792; Edmondson, John B., *The early history of the R Ticket* 1968 (from *English Mechanic and World of Science* No 697 2.8.1878 pp 524-6)

EIFFEL, Alexandre Gustave

b Dijon, France, 15.12.1832; d Paris, 28.12.1923 aged 91.

Civil eng, best remembered for his great Paris tower of 1887-9, and designer of many outstanding bridges still in use on French Rs. Ed at Dijon and the Lycée Ste Barbe, and the Central School of Arts & Crafts, Paris, where he studied civil engg until 1855. Became a member of the Société des Ingénieurs Civils de France in 1857. After experience in designing the great iron bridge over the Garonne in Bordeaux in 1858, and bridges on the Poitiers-Limoges R in 1867-8, he developed his principle of const in wrought iron and cast iron which he employed in the great viaducts at Sioule and Neuvial on the Orléans R in 1868-9. Other important iron vdts were the Tagus bridge on the Caceres R in Spain (1880), 1024ft (312m) long; the Vianna bridge on the Minho R, Portugal, 2414ft (736m) long, on 9 masonry piers; and the Tardes vdt in Central France on the Montluçon-Eygurande line (1883), 820ft (250m) long and 240ft (73m) high. His iron arched R bridges included the Douro bridge at Porto, Portugal (1875) 525ft (160m) long and 200ft (61m) high; the Garabit vdt, Sud R, France (1882) 1850ft (564m) long with a main span of 541ft (165m), 400ft (122m) high. By 1887 his R bridges alone accounted for 38 000 tons of iron and steelwork. He received many honours, was an hon MIME and of similar institutions in USA, Belgium, Holland, Russia, Spain.

Engg V 117 4.1.1924 p 19; Proc IME 12.1923 pp 1171-2

ELLIOTT-COOPER, Sir Robert, KCB, VD

b Leeds 26.1.1845; d Knapwood, Surrey, 16.2.1942 aged 97.

Ed Leeds Gr Sch. Pupil of John Fraser (qv), serving as res eng on Rs in Yorkshire, 1864-74. In 1874 went to India to inspect eng works. Returned in 5.1875. In 6.1876 began in private practice in Westminster. During his long career he was responsible for design and const of

numerous R and engg works in many parts of the world. Consulting eng of Regents Canal & Dock Co, and in 1908–16 for Rs in Nigeria and Gold Coast Colonies. In 1919 awarded KCB for war services. 1911–28 chairman of commission of the Engg Standards Assoc on steel bridges. 1912 app member of advisory bd of Science Museum, London. 1914 member of India Office Committee for appointments in Public Works Dept and state Rs. Married 1878; 3 sons and 3 drs.
Journal ICE V 20 1941–2

ELLSON, George, CBE

b Ripley, Derbyshire, 2.6.1875;
d Seaford, Sussex, 29.9.1949 aged 74.
Chief eng, SR. Ed Ripley Coll. Apprenticed at Butterley Co, in shops and drg office, and studied at Nottingham Univ Coll. 1896 app draughtsman to E. C. & J. Keay Ltd and was put in charge of several contracts. In 1898 to engg dept, SE & CR. 1906 app res eng. E. was responsible for several important works, including demolition of old Charing Cross station roof and building the new, and strengthening Charing Cross and Canon Street R bridges. He then became chief asst to the chief eng. 1920 app res eng in charge of maintenance on entire SE & CR system. On amalg in 1923 he became dep chief eng, SR, and in 1927 succeeded A. W. Szlumper (qv) as chief eng until he ret in 2.1944. Received several Telford Premiums for papers to the ICE and a Telford Gold Medal in 1921. E. was a fellow and past president (1928) of the P W Inst. Also MICE. Responsible for a vast electrification programme including Brighton, Worthing, Bognor and Portsmouth and many suburban lines. Other works included various bridges, and the train ferry dock at Dover for the Dover–Dunkerque ferry inaugurated in 1936. He introduced welding for building up worn crossings and experimented with long welded rails, especially in tunnels. Awarded CBE in 1942.
RG 7.10.1949 p 428 (portrait); *The Eng* V 188 7.10.1949 p 405

ENGERTH, Wilhelm Freiherr von

b Pless, Prussian Schlesien, 26.5.1814;
d Leesdorf nr Baden 4.9.1884 aged 70.

Chief eng, Austrian Southern R. On completion of primary ed went to Vienna to study architecture but changed to mech engg which he studied at Vienna Polytechnic. In 1840 he became asst lecturer and in 1843 Prof of Machinery at Graz. Here he became interested in the problem of designing a suitable loco for the Semmering R, then under const (see Ghega). A competition was arranged and in 1850 he began designing a loco which he patented in 1852. It was named *Engerth*. The frames were in two portions, the rear enclosing the firebox. The cyls drove the coupled wheels of the front unit which were geared to those of the rear unit which also acted as the tender. 'Engerth System' locos were also built for Switzerland and France (French patent 10.3.1854). In 1850 he was app tech dir in the Ministry of Communications. 1863–5 served as mech eng on the governing body of the Austrian Bd of Trade. 1855 became tech dir of the Austrian R Administration in Vienna and later became general dir. E. served on the panel of judges at the Great Exhibition in London in 1851. His loco was exhibited at the Paris Exhibition in 1855. 1865–8 he produced elaborate designs for control of the Danube and in 1872 his project for control of the Danube Canal was carried out. In 1873 he was in charge of the building for the Great Exhibition in Vienna. In 1874 he was app to the Austrian House of Lords and was later elevated to the Barony. E. was an active writer on technical matters, on const of mountain locos, boiler testing, etc.
Röll V 3 p 1424; Wiener, Lionel *Articulated Locos* 1930, 1970 pp 247–51

ENNIS, Dr Joseph Burroughs

b Wortendyke, NJ, USA, (?).(?).1879;
d Paterson, NJ, 22.9.1955 aged 76.
Senior vice president of ALCO. Son of William C. and Kate Burroughs Ennis. Began work in 1895 as a draughtsman with Rogers Loco Co. In 1899–1900 he worked on general loco design for the Schenectady (NY) Loco Wks. 1900–1 he worked again at the Rogers plant and later transferred to the Cook Loco Wks in Paterson, NJ, both facilities of ALCO which was formed in 1901. E. handled loco design and calculation specification

for ALCO from 1902–6. He progressed from asst mech eng to design eng in 1908 and CME in 1912. Became vice president of engg 1917. He was senior vice president from 1941 until he ret in 1947. He continued as a dir of the company until he ret in 1953. He directed design of locos including 4–8–2, 4–6–2, 4–6–4 and 2–8–8–4 types. In 1944 he won the Henderson Medal of the Franklin Institute for his work in steam and diesel loco eng. Awarded hon Dr Engg from Clarkson Coll of Tech 1945. Was president of the Steam Loco Research Institute and a trustee of the Nathan Mfg Co of New York. Elected MILE 1947.
Journal ILE V 45 1955 p 594; *New York Times* 23.9.1955 p 26

ERICSSON, John

b Vermland, Sweden, 31.7.1803;
d New York, 8.3.1889 aged 85.
Inventor and mech eng. His f was a mine owner and inspector. After some engg training and a spell in the army and navy he went to London in 1826 and concentrated his efforts to produce an engine which would use heat more economically than the steam engine. In 1828 he designed a steam fire engine with a 12in (304.8mm) diam cylinder and a boiler provided with forced draught. It was built by John Braithwaite (qv). In 1829 he designed a loco, named *Novelty*, which was built by Braithwaite and entered in the Rainhill trials on the Liverpool & Manchester R. But for an unfortunate breakdown the loco would have come close to winning the prize. It was the first engine to run a mile in under a minute. On 13.7.1836 he took out a patent for the screw propellor and built a screw vessel in 1837. Failing to stimulate interest in his work in Britain, and having received an order for a screw ship from USA he went there in 1839. Here he produced a whole series of inventions, but nothing more concerning Rs.
DAB V 6 p 171; *Engg* 15.3.1889 pp 258–9

ERRINGTON, John Edward

b Hull 29.12.1806; d London 4.7.1862 aged 55.
Civil eng, associated with Locke (qv). Received engg training on public works in Ireland, then worked on R surveys in England under Padley. He was then engaged by J. U. Rastrick (qv) on preparation of plans for the Grand Junction R on which he met Joseph Locke. Under Locke E became res eng on the GJR. He then took charge of the Glasgow, Paisley & Greenock R (op 3.1841) and Greenock Harbour works. His principal work began with his association with Locke as jt eng of the Lancaster & Carlisle R (op throughout 17.12.1846) and later the Caledonian R. He also built the Clydesdale Jn R (op 1.6.1849), Scottish Central (op to Perth 23.5.1848) Scottish Midland Jn, Perth–Forfar (op 2.8.1848), Aberdeen R (later Scottish North Eastern, then Caledonian, op 1848). In 1856 he began work on the Yeovil–Exeter section of the LSWR (op 18.7.1860) which he completed shortly before his d. Became MICE 22.1.1839.
Min Proc ICE V 22 1862–3 pp 626–9; *The Eng* V 14 7.1862 p 22; *The Times* 7.7.1862 p 6; DNB V 6 p 817

ETZEL, Karl von

b Heilbronn in Württemberg, 6.1.1812;
d (?) 2.5.1865 aged 53.
Civil eng on central European Rs. Ed Stuttgart and Blaubeuern. 1835 went to Paris and then to Cologne to study architecture. 1836 went as architect to the Paris–St Germaine R under Clapeyron (qv), building the Seine bridge. In winter 1836–7 he visited England to study R const, returning to become eng of the Versailles R. 1838 returned to Württemberg and in 1839 to Vienna where he undertook various building projects. In 1843 he became chief of building works in the service of Württemberg State and he directed const of the Plochingen–Stuttgart–Heilbronn R. In 1848 he went to Vienna where he directed a machine works. He then undertook const of the Bietigheim–Bruchsal R and in 1852 the Swiss Central R, including the great Sill bridge at St Gallen and the Aare bridges at Olten and Bern, the old Hauenstein tunnel and other works. He then moved to Vienna as dir of the Franz Josef Orient R Co, and after its amalg with the Austrian Southern R as eng of the entire system. He supervised const of the Ofen–Pragerhof, Alba–Uj–Szöny, Steinberg–

Sissek, Agram–Karlstadt, Marburg–Villach, Ödenburg–Kanizsa Rs and most of the bridges and stations on the Vienna–Trieste line. His last and greatest work was the Brenner R, opened 24.8.1867.
Röll V 3 p 1485

FAIRBAIRN, Sir William

b Kelso, Roxburghshire, 19.2.1789;
d Farnham, Surrey, 18.8.1874 aged 85.
Manchester loco builder, general eng, bridge designer and builder. Son of a farm labourer and later farm mgr. Little formal ed. Late in 1803 the family moved to a farm near Newcastle upon Tyne belonging to Percy main colliery. F. worked at the colliery and on 24.3.1804 was apprenticed to John Robinson, a millwright, while he continued studies in literature and mathematics, becoming a member of Shields library where he met George Stephenson (qv). They became lifelong friends. In March 1811 he obtained employment as millwright at Newcastle, but in December he joined a fellow worker named Hogg and they sailed to London and managed to obtain employment in various engg work. He then spent a period in Dublin and in 1813 moved to Manchester which was to be his permanent home. At Bedlington on 16.6.1816 he m Dorothy Mar of Kelso. In 1817 he formed a partnership with John Lillie, a former fellow worker, and they set up an engg works in High Street, Manchester. In 1818 they moved to an old building in Mather Street, Ancoats, and in 1824 they established a new works in Canal Street, with a steam engine to drive machinery. In that year F. successfully erected two water mills at Zurich. By 1830 F. and Lillie had made about £40 000 and their wks employed about 300 men. In 1830 F. became MICE. He then began experiments in the const of iron boats, resulting in a light iron packet boat, *Lord Dundas*, which operated between Glasgow and Edinburgh along the Forth & Clyde canal. In 1832 F. bought out Lillie and traded simply as William Fairbairn. He was joined by his son Thomas in 1841 and by his son William Andrew in 1846, the firm then becoming William Fairbairn & Sons. From 1832

they built stationary steam engines and boilers. He also founded an association for the prevention of boiler explosions. He built iron ships, in sections, in Manchester, but in 1835 established a wks in Millwall, Poplar, London, in partnership with Andrew Murray, a former pupil. But the strain of running two wks was too great and he had to abandon the Millwall wks where about 2000 men were employed. In 1837 he invented and built a rivetting machine. In 1839 he began the building of R locos, the first being Bury type 0–4–0s for the Manchester & Bolton R, and from then until 1862 about 400 were built. As the wks had no rail access these all had to be despatched by road. In the 1840s many Bury type engines were built, with bar frames. The firm built goods engines for the E India R and the GWR. The most famous engines were McConnell's 'Large Bloomers', 2–2–2s for the S div of the LNWR, 1852–4. During 1845–9 F. carried out extensive experiments on the system of wrought iron tubular bridges subsequently erected by Robert Stephenson at Conway, Menai Strait and Montreal. In 10.1846 he and R. Stephenson took out a patent for tubular wrought iron bridge girders and by 1870 F. had built nearly 1000 bridges. In 1859–60 the firm reconstructed in iron the large timber span vdts at Dinting and Etherow on the Manchester–Sheffield R without interrupting traffic. F. and his wife had 7 sons and 2 drs. In 1840 he bought a house, the Polygon, at Ardwick, Manchester, where he lived until his d. He served as a juror at the London exhibitions in 1861 and 1862 and at the Paris exhibition of 1855 when he was made a member of the Legion of Honour. He was also a foreign member of the Institute of France. He received the Gold Medal of the Royal Society in 1860 and was president of the British Association in 1861. He declined a knighthood in 1861 but accepted a baronetage in 1869. In 1860 he was made Hon LLD of Edinburgh and in 1862 of Cambridge. He was president of the IME in 1854 and of the Manchester Literary & Philosophical Soc 1855–60. He was a staunch member of the Cross Street Unitarian Chapel, Manchester, where he was a close friend of the Rev

W. Gaskell whose wife was the famous novelist. He presented numerous papers to various societies, and a full list of his published work is given in the 'Life' by William Pole.

Pole, William (ed), *The Life of William Fairbairn* 1877, 1970; Smiles, Samuel, *Industrial Biography* 1863, 1967; Dempsey, G. Drysdale, *Tubular Bridges* 1864, 1970; Marshall, John, *The Lancashire & Yorkshire R* V 3 1972; Min Proc ICE V 39 1874–5 p 251; Proc IME 1875 p 22; *Engg* V 18, 21.8.1874 pp 147–8; *The Eng* V 38 8.1874 p 154; V 44 1877/2 pp 19, 95, 163, 253, 291; V 129 20.2.1920 p 184

FAIRBURN, Charles Edward, MA

b Bradford 5.9.1887; d London 12.10.1945 aged 58

Elec and mech eng. Ed Bradford Gr Sch. In 1905 he gained an open scholarship in mathematics to Brasenose Coll, Oxford. Gained first class in Moderations and Final Schools, taking BA in 1908. That year Brasenose Coll awarded him a senior Hulme Exhibition and until 1910 he read engg at Oxford, obtaining a first class. He was the first to take the Engg School at Oxford. In his last vacation he worked in a small Bradford engg shop on repairs to textile machinery to gain experience of machine shop and millwright work. In 1910 he became a pupil under H. Fowler (qv) at the MR wks at Derby, also studying metallurgy under Prof Arnold at Sheffield Univ and machine drawing at Derby Tech Sch. In 1912 he gained his MA. In 12.1912 he joined the R dept of the Siemens Dynamo Wks Ltd, Stafford, under F. Lydall whom he assisted on R patents and the layout of R work. From 1913 to 1916 F. was asst to the res eng on the NER Newport–Shildon electrification. He was responsible for the design, administration and erection of the 1500 V dc overhead line, for putting the locos into service and for maintenance for a year. In 1914 he m Eleanor Cadman of Bradford. They had 1 son and 1 dr. In 1916 F. joined the Royal Flying Corps, later RAF, as an experimental officer. He developed formation flying. In 1919 he joined the tech staff of English Electric Co Ltd and was entrusted with the building up of a heavy

traction dept for R electrification. Served EEC on R work in Britain and Europe until 1926. For the next 2 yrs he was g mgr of Dick, Kerr Wks of EEC at Preston. In 1928 he was made g mgr of the Stafford wks in addition. During this period he retained charge of all traction work done by EEC. 1929–31 he was member of the executive committee. In 1931 he became chief eng and mgr of the traction dept of EEC and by 1934 had undertaken electrification schemes on 49 different Rs. In 1934 he was invited by the LMS to become chief electrical eng. In 1938 he was app dep CME under Stanier (qv) in addition to remaining chief elec eng. 1942 became acting CME and on ret of Stanier in 1944 he became CME. The only new loco design to appear under his superintendency was the 2–6–4T of which 277 were built 1945–51. He was the first eng on the LMS to break away from the long-established MR standard coupled wheel spacing of 8ft + 8ft 6in, producing a more compact engine than the Fowler and Stanier 2–6–4Ts and one on which the BR standard 2–6–4T was based. Following his sudden d, he was succeeded by H. G. Ivatt (qv). F. was MICE (8.1.1935), MIEE, MIME (1944), a vice president of the ILE and a member of the Institute of Welding. He held office as a Lieut Col of the Eng and R Staff Corps of the REs (TA). He was a member of numerous other technical bodies. During WW2 he was responsible for mfr of munitions.

The Eng V 180 19.10.1945 p 307 (portrait); *Engg* V 160 19.10.1945 p 315 (portrait); *Journal* ICE V 25 11.1945 p 232; *Journal* ILE V 35 1945 p 388 (portrait); Proc IME V 154 1946 p 354.

FAIRLIE, Robert Francis

b (?) Scotland (?).3.1831; d Clapham, London, 31.7.1885 aged 54.

Inventor of the F. articulated loco. Son of a civil eng. Trained at Crewe, LNWR, and Swindon, GWR. 1853 became loco supt and g mgr of the wks of the Londonderry & Coleraine R, Ireland, and later held a position of importance on the Bombay & Baroda R, India. He then started as a consulting eng in London and on 12.5.1863 (England) and 23.11.1864 (France) he patented his

double-bogie engine (see *The Eng* 2.12.1864). By the time of his d it was in use on 52 Rs on gauges from 1ft 10in (559mm) upwards. Two F. locos are still at work, on the Festiniog R in Wales. In 1873 he went to Venezuela where he contracted sunstroke, fever and blood poisoning and he never fully recovered.
Engg V 40 7.8.1885 p 133; *The Eng* V 60 7.8.1885 p 109; Abbott, R. A. S., *The Fairlie Locomotive* 1970; Wiener, L., *Articulated Loco*s 1930, 1970

FALSHAW, Sir James, JP, DL, FRSE

b Leeds 21.3.1810; d Edinburgh 14.6.1889 aged 79.
Civil eng and contractor. In 1824 articled for 7 yrs to Joseph Cusworth, architect and surveyor at Leeds. 1831 engaged by Hamar & Pratt, contractors on the Leeds & Selby R, and was later employed by them on const of the Whitby & Pickering R, completed in 1836. In 1836 he became principal asst to George Leather of Leeds, eng of the Aire & Calder Nav, Goole docks, etc, mostly on water works. In spring 1843 began business on his own account in Leeds. At this time John Stephenson (qv) of Stephenson, Mackenzie & Brassey, engaged F. to take charge of the const of the Lancaster & Carlisle R and in 6.1844 he moved to Kendall. In 7.1845 he moved to Stirling to take charge of const of the Scottish Central and Scottish Midland Jn Rs, including the 1200yd (1097m) Moncrieff tunnel. The SC was opened on 1.3.1848 between Greenhill Jn and Stirling and to Perth on 23.5.1848. On 2.8.1848 the SM Jn was opened from Perth to Forfar. In 10.1853 he undertook with Brassey the contract for the Inverness & Nairn R, opened 6.11.1855, and later the extn to Elgin, 37 miles (59.5km), opened throughout on 25.3.1858. 1859–60 he carried out the Denny branch of the Scottish Central, and the Portpatrick, Stranraer & Glenluce R. He took up residence in Edinburgh and in 10.1861 was app a dir of the Scottish Central R. In 1862, in partnership with Morkill & Prodham, former assts, he contracted for the const of the Berwickshire R and in 1864 for the Blaydon & Consett branch of the NER including 3 major stone vdts. Completion of this in 12.1867 (freight

traffic began on 18.6.1867) closed his career as a R contractor. In 1876 when Queen Victoria visited Edinburgh he was created a baronet. In 1881 he was dep chairman of the NBR and in 1882–7 chairman.
Min Proc ICE V 99 1889–90 pp 382–90; *Engg* V 47 21.6.1889 p 606

FARMER, John Stinson

b (?) (?).(?).1827; d nr Billingshurst, Sussex, 12.12.1892 aged c 65.
R signal eng. At an early age he entered the service of the LBSCR. In 1849 app asst traffic mgr under George Hawkins. 1862 entered partnership with John Saxby and together they founded the firm of Saxby & Farmer for mfr of signalling equipment and safety devices. They erected wks at Kilburn by the LNWR nr London. Their first apparatus was installed at Bricklayers' Arms, LSWR, London, and consisted of 8 semaphore signals and 6 points, all interlocked. In 1875 S & F brought out a mechanical continuous brake.
Min Proc ICE V 112 1892–3 p 374

FARNAM, Henry

b Scipio, New York State, 9.11.1803; d New Haven, Conn, 4.10.1883 aged c 80.
Surveyor and civil eng, Rock Island RR. No formal ed. 1821 obtained employment with David Thomas, surveyor of the Erie canal. 1826 transferred to the Farmington canal, New Haven to Northampton, Mass, becoming chief eng 1824 until completion in 1835. The canal co failed and F. lost all his money in it, but about this time he was becoming interested in Rs and was taken up by Joseph E. Sheffield who took up F's suggestion to convert the canal to a R, beginning in 1847. In 1849 they sold this to the New York & New Haven RR and moved to the middle west where they began what developed into the 7700 mile (12 400km) Rock Island system. He soon became president of the Chicago & Rock Island RR, but resigned in 1863. He was largely responsible for the first RR bridge across the Mississippi, at Rock Island, opened in 1855.
Trains 12.1948 pp 42–51; DAB V 6 p 281

FAVIELL, William Frederick

b Kirkby Overblow, nr Wetherby, Yorks,

26.7.1822; d Tunbridge Wells, Kent, 3.7.1902 aged 80.
R contractor. Fourth son of Mark F., contractor on canals, bridges and public works. Ed at Lincoln. At age 17 was engaged by his bros to assist on const of part of the Manchester & Leeds R near Wakefield. On completion of this in 1840 he worked on the Dearne & Dove canal. 1841 worked with his bro on the Eastern Counties R nr Colchester. In 10.1846 Mark F. & Son were awarded the contract for the section of the Leeds & Thirsk R between Harrogate and Ripon, completed in 1849. In 1.1847 he m the eldest dr of John Carr of Colchester. In 1850, in partnership with his bro in law John Maxfield, he contracted for the extension of the Leeds & Thirsk R to Northallerton. Later in 1850 F. joined Henry Fowler (bro of Sir John Fowler qv) and undertook const of the R from Bombay to Thana, the first R in India. Fowler left for Bombay in 12.1850 and F. followed in 2.1851. The R was opened on 16.4.1853. The first loco was introduced on 23.2.1852. In 11.1855 F. again went to India as contractor on the GIPR line up the Bhor Ghat, 15 miles (24km), and the extn to Poona, 40 miles (64km). The lines included many heavy engg works. Difficulties arising from the Mutiny in 5.1857 forced him to surrender the contract. In 2.1863 he went to Ceylon to const 73 miles (117.5km) of difficult R from Colombo to Kandy, completed and opened in 8.1867. In 1877 he carried out works in S Africa. He ret in 1882. Became AICE 4.2.1868.
Min Proc ICE V 150, 1901–2 p 463

FAVRE, Louis

b Chène-Thonex, Canton Geneva, Switzerland, 26.1.1826; d in St Gotthard tunnel 19.7.1879 aged 53.
Builder of St Gotthard tunnel. Began life as a common workman. Moved to Paris where he undertook public works with success. When tenders were invited for the St Gotthard tunnel F. obtained the contract. He based his calculations on the use of dynamite instead of gunpowder and of the compressed-air drill invented by his friend Prof Colladon. Although he undertook his part of the contract with efficiency and promptness

he was badly let down by the company and the Federal govt which caused anxieties which led to his breakdown and death from apoplexy inside the tunnel. A week earlier he had been in Paris negotiating with the French govt for const of the Simplon tunnel. Despite his d, the St Gotthard tunnel was completed before the approach lines.
The Eng V 48 1.8.1879 p 82; *Engg* V 28 26.9.1879 p 256

FAY, Sir Sam

b Southampton 30.12.1856; d Awbridge, Romsey, Hants, 30.5.1953 aged 97.
G mgr, GCR. Ed Plenheim House, Fareham. Began R career as a junior clerk in the LSWR traffic dept, 1872. 1884 entered traffic supt's office, Waterloo, London as second clerk. 10 months later app chief clerk to supt of the line. 1891 app asst storekeeper. 1892 left LSWR to become g mgr of M & SW Jn R. By his enterprise and initiative he transformed this into flourishing R. In 4.1900 returned to the LSWR as supt of the line. In 3.1902 became g mgr of the GCR which had shortly before opened its main line to London. Again, by his energy, he developed it into an efficient system, introducing through services via neighbouring Rs. In 1911 he was elected chairman of the G Mgrs' Conference of the RCH. At the opening of Immingham Dock on the Humber on 22.7.1912 he was knighted by King Edward VII. In 3.1918, during WW1, he was made dir gen of movements & Rs with a seat on the Army Council. He was a member of the R Executive Committee.
Dow, George, *Great Central* V 3 1965

FELL, John Barraclough

b London, (?).(?).1815; d Southport, 18.10.1902 aged 87.
Civil and mech eng, inventor of the 'Fell centre rail'. In 1835 moved with his parents to the Lake District. During the 1840s he carried out his first R contract on the Furness & Whitehaven R. In 1852 went to Italy where for several years he was associated with the firm of Brassey, Jackson, Fell & Jopling in the const of several early Italian Rs, including the Central of Italy, Maremma, and Genoa & Voltre lines. After

travelling over the Mont Cenis road several times he thought out the idea of his centre rail. He was reputed to have carried out experiments with it in 1864–5 on the 'Gothland incline' (sic) on the Cromford & High Peak R in Derbyshire, thought to be the Bunsall incline, but it may have been the Goathland incline on the Whitby & Pickering R. This resulted in its adoption for the R over the Mont Cenis Pass, opened in 1868 and operated until the opening of the Mont Cenis tunnel in 1871. He also experimented with a mono-rail system and with narrow-gauge light Rs. Elected AICE 3.3.1863.
Min Proc ICE V 151 1902–3 p 436

FENTON, James

b Dunkenny, Forfarshire, 29.8.1815; d Leamington 22.4.1863 aged 47.
Loco eng. On leaving school he was apprenticed to James Cook & Co, Glasgow, as a mech eng, also receiving training as a civil eng under William Blackadder (1789–1860). In 6.1837 he worked as asst eng under I. K. Brunel on the GWR. At about the same time he became a partner in the Leeds firm of loco builders, Fenton, Murray & Jackson (established 1795, see Murray). On 3.8.1840 he was app loco supt on the Manchester & Leeds R. On 9.11.1842 John Chester Craven (qv) was app loco foreman under F. Fenton, Murray & Jackson closed down in 1843. On 20.1.1843 F. resigned to become acting eng on the Leeds & Thirsk R but after only 18 months he took up a new appointment as mgr of the wks of E. B. Wilson & Co at the R Foundry, Leeds. Here he worked with David Joy (qv) on the design and const of the famous 'Jenny Lind' class 2–2–2 loco. He also built and launched one of the largest landing stages in Britain, at New Holland on the Humber. In 1851 he left the R Foundry to become a consulting eng at the Low Moor Co nr Bradford where he remained until his untimely death. Became MIME 1847, the year the Institution was founded, and MICE in 1849.
Min Proc ICE V 23 1863–4 p 487; Proc IME 1864 p 14; *The Eng* V 15 8.5.1863 p 266; Marshall, John, *The Lancashire & Yorkshire R* V 2 1970

FINDLAY, Sir George

b Rainhill, Lancs, 18.5.1829; d Edgware, Middlesex, 26.3.1893 aged 63.
R contractor, and civil eng. At the time of his birth his f was engaged on const of the skew bridge at Rainhill on the Liverpool & Manchester R. Ed Halifax Gr Sch. His f was then employed on the Halifax branch of the Manchester & Leeds R. In 1845 he went as asst to his bro James on const of part of the Trent Valley R under Brassey (qv). 1847 went to London where he was employed by Bransome & Gwyther, contractors, on const of Camden engine shed, LNWR, and of the 'Round House' at Chalk Farm, intended as an engine shed but converted to a grain store, and now used as a theatre. He was next employed under Brassey's agent Thomas Jones on the const of Harecastle tunnel on the NSR, 1847–9, later building the tunnel entrances, and then on bridges on the NSR Churnet Valley line between Froghall and Alton. In 1849 Brassey put him in charge of the Walton (Sutton) tunnel on the Birkenhead, Lancashire & Cheshire Jn R. In 1850 F. was put in charge of const of the first section of the Shrewsbury & Hereford R, Shrewsbury–Ludlow. On its completion in 4.1852 Brassey app F. as mgr. The extn to Hereford was completed in 1853, forming a through route to Newport. F. was app mgr of all the traffic. In 1862 the LNWR and GWR took a jt lease of the Shrewsbury & Hereford R and F. became an LNWR employee. On its purchase of the Merthyr, Tredegar & Abergavenny R the LNWR app F. as dist mgr for Shropshire & S Wales. He was also app mgr of the Oswestry, Newtown & Llanidloes R and of various adjoining lines. In 1864 he gave these up and transferred to Euston where he became g gds mgr of the LNWR. F. was active as writer and lecturer. Became AICE 1.12.1874. Knighted 5.1892.
Min Proc ICE V 113 1892–3 p 362

FINK, Albert

b Lauterbach, Germany, 27.10.1827; d Kentucky, USA, 3.4.1897 aged 69.
Civil eng and RR operator, and inventor of the Fink truss. Ed at Darmstadt, graduating in engg and architecture in

1848. Having no sympathy with German affairs at that time he emigrated to USA in 1849 and became a draughtsman on the B & O under Benjamin H. Latrobe (qv), chief eng. Soon he had charge of design and erection of bridges, stations and shops from Grafton to Moundsville, W Va. During this period he invented the Fink bridge truss, first used to cross the Monongahela River at Fairmont, W Va, in 1852, with 3 spans of 305ft (92m), then the longest iron R bridge in the USA. He became section eng, then div eng, and in 1857 left the B & O to become const eng on the Louisville & Nashville R. Here he built the bridge over the Green River about 74 miles (120km) S of Louisville, one of the largest iron bridges in N America and second only to the Victoria Bridge, Montreal. In 1859 F. took charge of machinery of the L & N in addition to buildings and bridges and in 1860 became chief eng. After the civil war he had to repair the extensive damage on the L & N. In 1865 he became g supt. During the following 10 yrs he rehabilitated the line and completed his greatest work, the bridge over the Ohio at Louisville, about a mile long with a span of 400ft (122m) over the Indiana Channel, then the longest truss span in the world. After the d of the president of the L & N in 1869 F. was app vice president and g supt. He now began to develop the accounting methods into a science of R economics. The *Fink Report on cost of Transportation* of 1874 became a foundation stone of R economics. He was active in extending the L & N beyond Nashville to Montgomery, Alabama. Thanks to his methods, during the financial panic of 1873 the L & N was one of the few RRs to continue to pay interest and to escape bankruptcy. In 1875 he resigned to take up literary work but was persuaded to reorganise the Southern R & Steamship Association. In 2 yrs he brought order out of chaos and in 1877 again decided to retire but was asked to organise the Trunk Lines Association out of the 4 trunk Rs entering New York City. The Interstate Commerce Act of 1887 made it possible for him to retire at last in 1889. After the d of his first w he m Sarah Hunt of Louisville on 14.4.1869.

DAB V 6 pp 387–8

FITZ-GIBBON, Abraham Coates

b Lilworth, Co Cork, Ireland, 23.1.1823; d Bushey Heath, Herts, 4.4.1887 aged 64. Civil eng, responsible for establishing the 3ft 6in (1.067m) gauge in Queensland, Australia. Ed Royal Naval School, London. Apprenticed 1837–43 to Sir Charles Lanyon who employed him as asst eng on the Londonderry & Coleraine, Belfast & Ballymena, Londonderry & Enniskillen, and other lines. In 1847 he entered the service of William Dargan, contractor and for 5 yrs was one of his principal agents and managers, completing 10 miles (16km) of the Dundalk & Enniskillen, 60 miles (96.5km) of the Dublin & Cork R, and all of the Newry & Portadown R. In 3.1852 he was engaged by Fox Henderson & Co to report on the 704 mile (1133km) route of the proposed Illinois Central R and to estimate the cost of building and equipping it. Following his detailed report he remained 4 yrs in USA and Canada, concerning himself with R, harbour and river works. In 10.1857 he was engaged as principal asst on the R from Colombo to Kandy in Ceylon, about 80 miles (129km). On the suspension of this in 1860 he was engaged by the Dun Mountain Copper Mining Co to select a route for a R in New Zealand. In 1863 he was invited to visit Queensland where he prepared a report with estimates for the 174 miles (280km) of R from Ipswich to Toowoomba and Dalby and Toowoomba to Warwick. In his report he recommended a gauge of 3ft 6in to keep down costs. The R was authorised on 4.9.1863. F-G. was now app chief eng to Queensland Rs. In 1868 he returned to England where he lived in retirement until his d. Became MICE 9.1.1866.
Min Proc ICE V 89 1886–7 p 466

FLANAGAN, Terence Woulfe

b Leixlip, Ireland, 19.2.1819; d London 13.12.1859 aged 40.
Civil eng and R mgr. Ed Paris and Brussels and in 1836 at Dublin Univ. 1837 articled to Charles Vignoles (qv) until 1842. 1843 app res eng on the Blackburn & Preston R under Joseph Locke (qv) and John Collister. Elected

MICE in 1843. On 14.4.1846 he was app res eng on the Blackburn, Darwen & Bolton R under Vignoles. This was a heavy project involving large vdts and Sough tunnel, 1 mile 255yd (1.842km) long, and vast cuttings. Also in 1846 F. was app res eng of the Blackburn, Clitheroe & North Western R, continuing the line northwards, with more heavy works. On 31.8.1848 F. was app g mgr of the Blackburn R, as the whole line from Bolton to Chatburn became known. The line was opened from Blackburn to Bolton on 12.6.1848 and to Chatburn on 21.6.1850. The R co had a long battle with the LYR and ELR, both of which diverted traffic from it, and in the end it was forced into jt amalg with both companies on 1.1.1858. F. resigned before the amalg and worked on the Antwerp–Rotterdam R and on a R in Portugal. Returned to England in 1857 and was app eng on the Southampton–Fareham line. The wet conditions and exposure wrecked his health and led to his early d, robbing Britain of one of its most brilliant and promising R engs. Min Proc ICE V 20 1859–60 p 137; Marshall, John, *The Lancashire & Yorkshire R* V 1 1969

FLEMING, Sir Sandford

b Kirkcaldy, Fife, 7.1.1827; d Halifax, Nova Scotia, 22.7.1915 aged 88.
Canadian eng. Second son of Andrew Craig F. and Elizabeth Sandford Arnott. Studied surveying at Kirkcaldy. In 1845 went to Canada where he met Casimir Gzowski, one of the first great civil engs of Canada, with whom he gained R experience, particularly on the Ontario, Simcoe & Huron R (Northern R, later CNR) including notable engg work around Toronto, of which he was chief eng from 1855–63. In 1864 he was app chief R eng by the govt of Nova Scotia, responsible for building the line from Truro to Pictou which he completed (as contractor from 1866) on 31.5.1867. Also in 1864 he was app to survey a R from Montreal to Halifax, on which he submitted a report in 1865 and of which he was app chief eng in 1867. This, the Intercolonial R, he completed in 1876. 1871 app chief eng of the transcontinental R which was a condition of the entry of British Columbia into the Con-

federation on 20.7.1871. On 16.7.1872 he began his great expedition across Canada, locating the route through the Yellowhead Pass and down the Thompson and Fraser River valleys into Vancouver. However, in 1880 the govt handed over the const to the Canadian Pacific R Co and the R was taken through the mountains by a more southerly route. F's route through the Yellowhead Pass and down into Vancouver was later used by the GTP and Canadian Northern R. Also in 1871 F. was app chief eng of the Newfoundland R on which he worked at the same time as on the Pacific R. By 1880 over 600 miles (966km) of the CPR had been completed, but F. resigned as chief eng, although he became a dir of the CPR, and in 1883 he assisted in the survey through the Kicking Horse Pass. F. and his party were the first white men to cross the Rockies by this route. From 1879 F. had urged the Canadian, Australian and British govts to lay a Pacific cable. Its completion between Vancouver and Australia in 1902 was F's crowning success. From 1876 he took an active part in forcing the adoption of the four standard time zones in North America, which came into use in 1883. F. designed the first Canadian postage stamp and founded the Royal Canadian Institute, one of Canada's oldest scientific bodies. In 1880 he was app Chancellor of Queen's University, Kingston, Ontario. In 1855 he m Ann Jean Hall (d 1888) of Ontario and they were survived by 4 sons and 2 drs. His pub works include: *The Intercolonial: A History 1832–76* 1876; *England and Canada* 1884; *The New Time Reckoning* 1889.
Burpee, L. J., *Sandford Fleming, Empire Builder* 1915; Legget, Robert F., *Rs of Canada* 1973; DNB 1912–21 vol; Lavallée, Omer, *Van Horne's Road* Montreal 1974

FLETCHER, Edward

b Reedwater nr Otterburn 26.4.1807; d West Jesmond, Newcastle upon Tyne, 21.12.1899 aged 82.
Loco eng, NER. In 1825 apprenticed to Robert Stephenson & Co, Newcastle, where he made a considerable part of the machinery of the *Rocket*. He was sent with it to the Killingworth wagon-

way for trials. He then went as eng to the Canterbury & Whitsable R where he drove the first loco, *Invicta*, on the opening day, 3.5.1830. While at Whitstable, in 1836, he m Miss Fedarb. They had 1 son and 2 drs. In 1837 F. went to the York & North Midland R where he worked under T. Cabry on the const of the line. 1845 app loco supt on the Newcastle & Darlington Jn R (which became successively the York & Newcastle, York Newcastle & Berwick, and in 1854 the North Eastern R). Became MIME in 1847, the year the Institution was formed, under George Stephenson as first president. When the Newcastle High Level bridge was formally opened, on 28.9.1849, F. had charge of the royal train. On the formation of the NER on 31.7.1854 F. became loco supt of the entire system, with works at Gateshead. F. made no attempt to standardise loco policy, but gave complete freedom to his local supts at Darlington, Leeds and York. William Bouch (qv) remained in charge on the Stockton & Darlington section from amalg in 1863 until 1866. This avoidance of interference made F. popular with the men under him. F's engines were simple and robust. His best known were the '450' class 2–2–2s of 1861, various outside-framed 2–4–0s and 0–6–0s, and the 'Whitby Bogie' 4–4–0s of 1864 for traffic on the difficult Pickering–Whitby section. In 1872 he introduced the '398' class 0–6–0, an inside-frame version of the '708' class 0–6–0. Among his tank engines were the highly successful 0–4–4s of 1874. Perhaps his most famous design was the '901' class 2–4–0 express engine of 1872. No 910 of this class, built in 1875 and rebuilt in 1886, took part in the Stockton & Darlington Jubilee celebrations in 1875, the Centenary in 1925 and the 150th anniversary cavalcade in 1975. It is now in the NRM, York. F. ret in 1882 after 47 yrs service.

Proc IME 10.1889 pp 748–9; *The Eng* V 69, 3.1.1890 p 18; *Engg* V 49 3.1.1890 p 11; Maclean, J. S. *The Locos of the NER* c 1923; Nock, O. S. *The Locos of the NER* 1954

FORBES, James Staats

b Aberdeen 7.3.1823; d London 5.4.1904 aged 81.

Civil eng, and chairman of the LC & DR and Metropolitan District R. Ed at Woolwich and then trained as eng, in 1840 entering the office of I. K. Brunel (qv) who was then building the GWR. He then joined the GWR and rose to be chief goods mgr at Paddington. He next joined the Dutch Rhenish R, then under English mgt, and rose to be mgr, transforming the line from near bankruptcy to success. In 1861 he became mgr of the LC & DR after twice refusing to be mgr of the GWR. The LC & DR was then in the hands of a receiver and was at war with the SER and LBSCR. In 1871 he joined the bd of dirs and in 1873 became chairman in which position, and that of mgr, he remained until the SER and LC & DR came under joint managing committee on 1.1.1899. On 6.10.1870 he joined the bd of the Metropolitan District R and was chairman from 28.11.1872 to 5.9.1901. For 25 yrs the rivalry between F. of the LC & DR and MDR and Sir Edward Watkin (qv) of the MS & L (GCR), SER and Metropolitan R caused numerous expensive troubles to all the companies and profit only to lawyers. F. was for a time a dir and dep chairman of the Hull & Barnsley R, itself at war with the NER, and financial advisor to the Didcot, Newbury & Southampton R which again was in conflict with the GWR and LSWR. His personal charm and suavity of temper enabled him to hold out against his formidable rival, Watkin.

Barker, T. C. and Robbins, Michael, *A History of London Transport* V 1 1963, V 2 1974; *The Eng* V 97 8.4.1904 p 364

FORMAN, Charles de Neuville

b Glasgow, 10.8.1852; d Davos Platz, Switzerland, 8.2.1901 aged 48.

Civil eng on Scottish Rs. Ed Glasgow High Sch; at private schs in St Andrews, London and Edinburgh; and at Glasgow Univ. 1867–72 apprenticed to Forman & McCall, Glasgow. 1873 emp under James Deas, eng of the Clyde Trust, then engaged on const of Queen's Dock. 1874 returned to Forman & McCall and became a partner 1875. F. had keen commercial instincts. His first R work was the Kelvin Valley R, op 1.6.1878. He then worked on the Strathendrick & Aberfoyle R, op 1.8.1882. F's first parliamentary contest was the promotion of the Clyde, Ardrishaig & Crinan R in 1887. Powers were obtained but were allowed to lapse. One of his most important tasks was the const of the West Highland R from Helensburgh to Fort William, nearly 100 miles (160km). He was instrumental in carrying the Bill through parliament, and the line was op 7.8.1894. Another major understanding was the Glasgow Central R from Lanarkshire coalfield to Queen's Dock, Glasgow, forming an underground and suburban line for the city and opening the way for the extn of the CR in Dumbartonshire. Powers for this were obtained in 1888 after a long struggle, the CR having in the meantime taken over the Glasgow Central. Work began in 1890 and the line was op 1896. The line traversed the busiest thoroughfares in the city in a covered way involving much interception of sewers, drains, water, gas, electricity and other services. In 1890 F. was also engaged on the promotion of the Lanarkshire & Dumbartonshire R forming an extension of the Glasgow Central along the north bank of the Clyde, invading NBR territory and involving tunnelling and city work. At the time of his death F. was engaged on const of extns of the Lanarkshire & Ayrshire R, the Paisley & Barrhead District Rs, the Ballachulish branch, and the Invergarry & Fort Augustus R, this last being part of an attempt to reach Inverness from the West Highland R, forming a more direct route from Glasgow than the HR via Perth. Overwork led to a collapse of his health and his early death. Became MICE 6.12.1887.

Min Proc ICE V 146 1900–01 pp 282–5; Thomas, John, *The West Highland R* 1965

FORNEY, Matthias Nace

b Hanover, Pa, USA, 28.3.1835;
d New York City, 14.1.1908 aged 72.

Eng, editor, inventor. Ed Hanover public schools and in Baltimore. At 17 apprenticed to Ross Winans (qv), loco builder of Baltimore, spending 3 yrs in the shops and 1 yr in the drg office. He then became a draughtsman on the B & O in Baltimore, 1855–8. 1858 went into business in Baltimore. 1861–4 worked as draughtsman on the Illinois Central RR

in Chicago. Here he designed, and in 1866 obtained a patent for, an 'improved tank loco', an 0–4–4 type which afterwards became known as the Forney engine. It was designed specially for suburban and city train services and large numbers were used on the elevated Rs in New York, Brooklyn and Chicago until superseded by electric traction. About 1865 F. went to Boston to superintend building of locos for the Illinois Central by the Hinkley & Williams wks. Late in 1870 he became associate editor of the *Railroad Gazette* pub in Chicago until a fire in 1871 when it was moved to New York. In 1872 F. purchased a half interest in the journal and served as editor until 1883 when he was forced by ill health temporarily to give it up. In 1886 he purchased the *American Railroad Journal* and *Van Nostrand's Engineering Magazine* which he combined, edited and pub under the name of *Railroad & Engineering Journal* until 1893 and as *American Engineer & Railroad Journal* until he sold it in 1896. Altogether he obtained 33 patents for R inventions, including improved car seats, an interlocking switch and signal apparatus, firebox doors, boilers and feed-water heaters. His last was for a fluid pressure engine in 1903. In 1875 he pub his *Catechism of the Locomotive* in the *Railroad Gazette* and in 1875 in book form in which it went into many editions and provided the education for thousands of RR men. He was also the author of *The Car Builder's Dictionary* 1879, and *Political Reform by the Representation of Minorities* 1894. As secretary of the Master Car Builders' Association 1882–9 he reorganised it to achieve closer contact with RR affairs. He was elected a life member in 1890. In 1907, at the age of 72, he m Annie Virginia Spear of Baltimore who survived him.

Sinclair, Angus, *Development of the Locomotive Engine* 1907, 1970; *Cassier's Magazine* 3.1908; *The Eng* V 105 7.2. 1908 p 145; DAB V 6 p 527; White, John H. Jr, *American Locos, an engg history 1830–80* 1968

FORSTER (or FOSTER), Jonathan

b South Tyne Valley, Northumb, (?).(?).1775; d Wylam (?).(?).1860 aged 85.

One of the earliest steam loco engs. In 1801 he was m at Tynemouth. 1809 app enginewright at Wylam colliery. In 1814 he assisted, with Timothy Hackworth and William Hedley (qqv), in the const of the first loco built at Wylam and was later responsible for maintenance of the Wylam locos. Two more of these 'Grasshopper' type engines were built at Wylam in 1814–15, *Puffing Billy* and *Wylam Dilly*. In 1828 F. and J. U. Rastrick (qv) built two more at Stourbridge, Worcestershire. *Agenoria* worked on the Sutt End R, Staffs (it is now in the NRM, York) and the other *Stourbridge Lion* was sent to USA where it was tried on the Carbondale–Honesdale RR on 8.10.1829 (see J. B. Jervis). F. ret in 1853 at the age of 78.
Wylam Parish Council, *Wylam and its R Pioneers* 1975; Young, Robert, *Timothy Hackworth and the Locomotive* 1923, 1975

FORSYTH, John Curphey

b Pembrokeshire, 14.7.1815;
d Newcastle-under-Lyme, Staffs, 15.2.1879 aged 63.
Eng and mgr, NSR. His f later worked on the Liverpool & Manchester R until he was killed in 1844. F. was ed under the supervision of John Dixon (qv) and in 1834 became sub res eng on the Newton–Manchester section of the L & M. In 1837, under T. L. Gooch (qv) he prepared contract drawings for the Manchester & Leeds R. Later became res eng on const of 7–8 miles (11–13km) of the M & L near Huddersfield until the line opened in 1841. 1841–3 res eng under Gooch in Manchester on Victoria stn extn and then on the L & M extn into Victoria stn. F. then worked on plans for various branches of the Manchester & Leeds R. In 1.1845 he became asst to Gooch in London and prepared plans of the Trent Valley R; Leeds & Bradford R extn to Colne; Blackburn, Burnley, Accrington & Colne Extn (ELR) and the abortive Southport–Euxton (Chorley) project. In autumn 1845 he was engaged by G. P. Bidder (qv) on plans for the North Staffordshire R for which Robert Stephenson, Bidder and T. L. Gooch were jt engs. On the passing of the NSR Act in 1846 F. became res eng on a large portion of the line until 1848, remaining as res eng to the co until 1853. In that year the mgr, S. P. Bidder, resigned to go to Canada and F. reluctantly accepted app as mgr in addition to his position as eng until he resigned both in 1864. He then became consulting eng and eng for the const of new NSR lines until his death. During this period he was partly responsible for the Leek branch op. 1.11.1867; Marple–Macclesfield (NSR/MS & L Jt) op 2.8.1869; Silverdale–Madeley–Market Drayton, op 1.2.1870; Audley, Newcastle and Silverdale widening, and the Potteries Loop line, finally op 15.11.1875. When his health began to fail he was assisted by his bro Joseph whom he took as a pupil in 1857. Became MICE 1853; also MIME.
Min Proc ICE V 58 1878–9 pp 343–5

FOSTER, Jonathan (see FORSTER)

FOTHERGILL-COOKE, Sir William

b nr Ealing, Middlesex, (?).(?).1806;
d Farnham, Surrey, 25.6.1879 aged 73.
Developer of the electric telegraph. Began career in the Indian army. On leave in 1835–6 he studied medicine and anatomy at Paris and Heidelberg. Here he was shown a model demonstrating the principle of electric telegraph by movement of a magnetic needle. He then resigned his commission, went to England in 1836 and developed his ideas. His pamphlet on the subject in 6.1836 led to negotiations for an experimental application of the system in a tunnel on the Liverpool & Manchester R. F-C. then became acquainted with Prof Charles Wheatstone (qv) who had also worked on electric transmission of messages. In 5.1837 F-C. and Wheatstone took out a joint English patent. F-C. then persuaded the London & Birmingham R to experiment with the telegraph between Euston, London, and Camden Town. The success of this led to F-C. laying down a telegraph between Paddington and Slough on the GWR. In 1845 this was instrumental in the arrest of a murderer at Paddington, whereupon the future of the telegraph was assured. It was next used on the Blackwall R, then worked by fixed engines and ropes. In 1842 F-C. pub *Telegraphic Rs or the Single Way* which was translated into German, French and

Italian, and led to the introduction of the block system. On 10.4.1843 Wheatstone's royalty on licences was converted to a mileage charge. F-C. sold exclusive telegraph rights in Kent to the SER for £10 000. By 30.9.1845 F-C. had orders for 800 miles (1288km) of telegraph. With John Lewis Ricardo, Sampson Ricardo, G. P. Bidder (qv) and 2 others, F-C. formed the first electric telegraph company. By Act of 1846 the company acquired important privileges and limited liability. The Central Telegraph Co began in 1847 with daily receipts of a few pounds and by the end of 1869 daily receipts exceeded £1000. It was F-C. who first proposed the Great Exhibition of 1851. Elected AICE 5.1867. Knighted 11.10.1869.

Min Proc ICE V 58 1878–9 pp 358–64

FOWLER, Sir Henry, KBE, DSc

b Evesham, Worcestershire, 29.7.1870;
d Spondon Hall, Derby, 16.10.1938
aged 68.
Gas eng, and CME of MR and LMS. Ed Evesham Gr Sch 1879–85, then Mason Science Coll, Birmingham, later part of Birmingham Univ, 1885–7. From 1887–91 he was apprenticed under Aspinall (qv) at the Horwich wks of the LYR. In 1891 he gained the first Whitworth Exhibition awarded to a member of the Horwich Mechanics Institute, later becoming a teacher in the Institute. At the end of his apprenticeship he became asst to George Hughes (qv) in the testing dept of which he later became chief. In 1895 he was app gas eng, LYR. At this time he became interested in automobile engg and in 1920–1 he was elected president of the Inst Automobile Engs. In 1900 F. left Horwich to become MR gas eng at Derby. 1905 app asst wks mgr under Deeley (qv), and in 1907 wks mgr. In 1909 he succeeded Deeley as CME of the MR. He continued the 'small engine' policy established by his predecessors. Among the few new designs to appear while he was in charge were a 2–8–0 type for the Somerset & Dorset Jt R and the 4-cyl 0–10–0 banking engine for the Lickey incline, the only big engine on the MR. During WW1 F. was app dir of production to the Ministry of Munitions in 1915 and asst dir general

of aircraft production in 1917 when he was awarded the CBE. Awarded KBE 1918. On the formation of the LMS on 1.1.1923 he became dep CME under George Hughes (qv) and in 1925, following Hughes' resignation, he succeeded as CME, transferring the headquarters from Horwich to Derby. In this position he perpetuated the MR 'small engine' policy, building out-dated 4–4–0s and 0–6–0s. F's chief abilities as an engineer were in organising production. At Derby he reorganised the repair shops in a way that led to marked economies. His reputation as a loco eng was of a low order and it is doubtful if he contributed anything to loco design. Locos built under his supervision were designed by his subordinates. The most successful design to appear under his supervision was the 2–6–4T of 1927 which, with its long-travel valves and adequate bearings, was directly influenced by the work of George Hughes and his team at Horwich in the design of the LMS standard 2–6–0. The 'Royal Scot' 4–6–0 was produced in a great hurry in 1927 to satisfy urgent traffic demands, following rejection of a compound 'Pacific' design worked out at Derby. The 'Royal Scot' was designed at the North British Loco Co, Glasgow, to a general arrangement based on the SR 'Lord Nelson' 4–6–0, with some Derby fittings. The undersized bearings fitted to so many 'Fowler' locos survived largely because of the inefficient front-end arrangements with small, short-travel valves. One of the feeblest designs was the 2–6–2T. It was F's insistence on small bearing surfaces and use of the out-dated valve gear of the S & D 2–8–0s which ruined the performance of the LMS Garratts built in 1927–30. When a powerful modern front end was fitted, as on the 0–8–0 of 1929, the bearings could not withstand the hammering. F's experimental high-pressure compound 4–6–0 *Fury* of 1930 was an expensive failure and never went into traffic. In 1931, under Lord Stamp, he was app asst to the vice president (Sir Harold Hartley) for research and development and in this work he was able to follow his true bent. He carried out extensive research in metallurgy and in 1932 was elected president of the Inst of Metals. F. had wide interests in engg and took an active interest in the ed of young engs, being a member of the governing body of the Midland Institute at Derby. From 1912–14 he was president of the Univ of Birmingham Engg Soc. He was awarded an hon LLD by Birmingham Univ and a DSc by Manchester, and numerous prizes for papers on various subjects. He was elected president of the ILE in 1912, of the IME in 1927 and was a member of council of the ICE 1928–34. In 1895 he m Emie Needham, dr of Philip Smith. She d 1934 leaving 2 sons and 1 dr.

Journal ILE V 28 1938 pp 606–8 (portrait); Proc IME V 140 1938 p 600; *Journal* ICE V 11 1938–9 p 618; *The Eng* V 166 21.10.1938 p 446 (portrait); *Engg* V 146 21.10.1938 p 484 (portrait); Haresnape, Brian, *Fowler Locos* 1972

FOWLER, Sir John

b Sheffield, 15.7.1817; d Bournemouth, 20.11.1898 aged 81.

Eng of the Metropolitan R and Forth Bridge. Ed privately. Trained under J. T. Leather (qv), eng of Sheffield waterworks; then under J. U. Rastrick (qv) on the London–Brighton R. In 1839, under Leather, he became res eng on the Stockton & Hartlepool R, on the completion of which in 1841 he was app eng, g mgr and loco supt. In 1844 he set up for himself as consulting eng in London and was engaged on lines east of Sheffield which became part of the MS & L. During the 'R Mania' F. took an active part with the numerous bills then before Parliament. He designed the Pimlico bridge, completed in 1860, the first R bridge over the Thames in London. In 1860 he became eng of the Metropolitan R, an exceedingly difficult project involving the underpinning of buildings, diversion of sewers and other services. For this he designed a fireless 2–4–0T, known as 'Fowler's Ghost', but it was not a success. The first section of the Met R was opened 9.1.1863. Of the 13 mile (21km) Inner Circle line F. was responsible for the const of over 11 miles (18km) and also 4½ miles (7.24km) of branches. In 1869 he advised on Rs in Egypt, and in 1870 in India. In 1875 F. took into partnership Benjamin Baker (qv) and together they

designed the Forth Bridge, the greatest R bridge in the world. (See also W. Arrol) It was begun in 1883 and opened on 4.3.1890. F. and Baker were consulting engs for the first London tube R, the City & S London op 1890, and with J. H. Greathead (qv) they were jt engs for the Central London tube R op 1900. On 17.4.1890 F. received a baronetcy. Shortly after this he retired. He became MIME in 1847, the year the Institution was founded, and MICE in 1849 and was president in 1866–7. On 2.7.1850 he m Elizabeth Broadbent of Manchester and they had 4 sons.

DNB V 22 Supplement pp 658–60; Mackay, T., *Life of Sir John Fowler* 1900; Proc IME 1899 pp 128–9; Min Proc ICE V 135 1898–9 pp 328–37; *The Eng* V 86 25.11.1898 p 513; *Engg* V 66 25.11.1898 pp 688–90 (portrait); Westhofen, *The Forth Bridge* 1890; *Engg* 'The Forth Bridge' 28.2.1890

FOX, Sir Charles

b Derby 11.3.1810; d Blackheath, Kent, 14.6.1874 aged 64.

Civil eng and contractor. Youngest of 4 sons of Francis Fox, MD. Abandoned a medical training for engg and at age 19 was articled to John Ericsson (qv) of Liverpool, working with him and J. Braithwaite (qv) on the *Novelty* loco, entered in the Rainhill trials on the Liverpool & Manchester R. His abilities attracted Robert Stephenson who, in 1837, app him as one of the engs on the London & Birmingham R. F. was responsible for Watford tunnel and the incline down from Camden Town to Euston. He presented an important paper on the correct principles of skew arches before the Royal Institution. He then entered into partnership with the contractor Bramah upon whose retirement the firm became Fox, Henderson & Co, specialising in R equipment, wheels, bridges, roofs, cranes, tanks and p w material. The firm was responsible for many important station roofs including Liverpool Tithebarn Street, 1849–50, and Bradford Exchange, 1850, Paddington and Birmingham New Street. In 1850–1 the firm erected the Crystal Palace in Hyde Park, London, for the Great Exhibition, and later dismantled it and reerected it on Sydenham Hill.

For this F. was knighted (together with Joseph Paxton and William Cubitt qv) on 22.10.1851. From 1857 F. practised in London as a civil and consulting eng, and in 1860 took his two sons Charles and Francis into partnership, the firm being known as Sir Charles Fox & Sons. He made a special study of narrow-gauge Rs and in conjunction with G. Berkley he built the first narrow-gauge R in India. He later built narrow-gauge Rs in various other parts of the world. But he was opposed to breaks of gauge where avoidable, and recommended first reduced axle loads, second reduced weight of structures and third reduced speeds, in that order, to achieve economies. His works included the Medway bridge at Rochester, 3 bridges over the Thames, a swing bridge over the Shannon in Ireland, a bridge over the Saône at Lyons and many bridges on the GWR. Rs upon which he was engaged included the Cork & Bandon, Thames & Medway, Portadown & Dungannon, East Kent, Lyons & Geneva (eastern section), Mâcon & Geneva (eastern section) and the Wiesbaden and Zealand lines in Denmark. He was eng to the Queensland Rs, Cape Town Rs, Wynberg R (Cape of Good Hope) and the Toronto 3ft 6in (1.067m) gauge lines. Fox & Sons carried out the complex scheme of bridges at Battersea for the LBSCR, LC & DR and LSWR and the approach to Victoria Station, London, including the widening of the bridge over the Thames. F. was MICE and for many years a member of the council of the IME. He was an original life member of the British Assoc, member of the RSA and a fellow of the Royal Asiatic and Royal Geographical Societies. In 1830 F. m Mary, second dr of Joseph Brookhouse, by whom he had 3 sons and a dr. He was noted for his urbanity and generosity.

The Eng V 37 1874 p 404; *Engg* V 18 17.7.1874 p 53; Min Proc ICE V 39 1874–5 pp 264–6.

FOX, Sir (Charles) Douglas

b Smethwick, Staffs, 14.5.1840; d Kensington, London, 13.11.1921 aged 81.

Oldest surviving son of Sir Charles Fox (qv). Civil eng and contractor. Ed Cholmondeley Sch, Highgate, London, King's Coll Sch and King's Coll, London, (of which he was a Fellow). 1858 articled to his f, then practising in Westminster. 1860 F. and his bro (later Sir Francis F.) were taken into partnership and the firm continued as Sir Charles Fox & Sons until the death of Sir Charles Fox in 1874. During this period the firm carried out various R works (see Sir Charles F.). In 1874 F. became senior partner, the firm becoming Sir Douglas Fox & Partners, the partners later including G. A. Hobson (Min Proc ICE V 203 p 420), F. Douglas Fox, Ralph Freeman and Bertram Douglas Fox. The firm acted as consulting engs to many R projects including the Mersey tunnel (in conjunction with Sir James Brunlees qv), the Hawarden swing bridge over the Dee on the Chester–Connah's Quay R; the West Lancashire R; Liverpool, Southport & Preston Jn R; Liverpool Overhead R; Snowdon Mountain R; Cardiff R; Neath, Pontardawe & Brynamman R; GCR Rugby–Marylebone; Charing Cross, Euston & Hampstead tube R (Northern Line) in conjunction with W. R. Galbraith (qv), and the Great Northern & City tube. Abroad the firm acted as consulting engs to the Central Argentine R (jointly with Livesey Son & Henderson); the Shire Highlands (Nyasaland) R; Rhodesia, Mashonaland & Beira R Co; Benguella R; Trans Zambezia R; British South African Chartered Co (jointly with Sir Charles Metcalfe, qv); Cape Govt Rs (jointly with Gregory, Eyles & Waring); S Indian R Co (jointly with Sir George Bruce and Robert White); Southern San Paulo R; and Dorado (United States of Columbia) R Co. F. was elected MICE 6.2.1866; president 1899. Knighted 1886 with Brunlees in recognition of work on Mersey tunnel. Contributed three papers to ICE: 'Light Rs in Norway, India and Queensland' (Min Proc V 26 p 49), 'Widening Victoria Bridge and approaches to Victoria Station' (Min Proc V 27 p 68), and 'Description of excavating machine on the West Lancashire R (Min Proc V 52 p 250); and with his bro 'The Pennsylvania RR' (Min Proc V 39 p 62). In 1863 F. m Mary, dr of Francis Beresford Wright of Derby, and they had 1 son and 4 drs. F. was very interested in church matters and the YMCA.

Min Proc ICE V 213 1921–2 p 416;
Proc IME 3.1922 p 359

FOX, Francis

b Plymouth, 12.9.1818; d Teignmouth,
13.3.1914 aged 95.
Second son of Robert Were Fox. Ed
Friends' Schools at Croydon and Sidcot.
In 10.1835 became pupil of Edwin O.
Tregelles and was later taken into
partnership until the ret of Tregelles in
1842. In 1839 F. was associated with
the Cornwall Central R project. In 1846
joined the staff of I. K. Brunel as asst
eng on the S Wales R. Later he acted
as contractor's agent for const of a
length of the R in Carmarthenshire. In
1854, after its completion, he acted in
a similar capacity on the Falmouth
branch. At the end of 1854 app eng of
the Bristol & Exeter R, holding this
position until its amalg with the GWR
on 1.1.1876 when he resigned. He also
built the Chard and Cheddar Valley
branches. On his recommendation the
B & E adopted the block system. When
he left the B & E the GWR entrusted
him with the design and const of the
Weston Super Mare loop and new
station, opened 1.3.1883, and the Exe
Valley (op 1.5.1885) and Tiverton & N
Devon (op 1.8.1884) branches. Ret at
end of 1893.
Min Proc ICE V 197 1914 pp 332–4

FRASER, Henry John

b Pudsey, nr Leeds, 20.3.1848;
d nr York 13.10.1889 aged 41.
Civil eng. Eldest son of John F. (qv) of
Leeds, eng of GNR. Articled to his f
1866–70, and was then put in charge of
the works on the Bradford, Eccleshill &
Idle and the Idle & Shipley lines of the
GNR, completed 1874, and from then
until their completion in 1879 the GNR
Bradford–Thornton line which included
immense works. He also had charge of
the Halifax section of the GNR Halifax–
Thornton–Keighley line including
Queensbury tunnel 1 mile 741yd
(2.253km) completed 1879. From 7.1878–
1880 he was engaged on the extension
of this line from Thornton to Keighley,
involving the Lees Moor tunnel, 1533yd
(1.382km) and Hewenden vdt. During
this time he became a partner with his
f. F. also assisted in the preliminary

work and const of the GNR Newark–
Bottesford and the GNR/LNWR jt lines
from Bottesford to Melton 1879 and
the GNR Tilton–Leicester line and preliminary work on the Tilton–Market
Harborough line. On the death of his f
in 1881 he was joined by his bro in law,
W. Beswick Myers, and under the name
of John Fraser & Sons they completed
the Marefield Jns–Leicester (op 15.8.
1882) and Thornton–Keighley (1884) lines.
They also carried out preliminary work
and const of several other GNR lines in
Yorkshire, the Crofton link, Dewsbury
line, Beeston–Batley; and Halifax High
Level; also the Harrow–Stanmore
LNWR. In conjunction with Sir Douglas
Fox (qv) the Driffield–Market Weighton
section of the Scarborough, Bridlington
& W Riding Jn R, op 18.4.1890. F. and
Myers were also engaged on the GNR
Low Moor–Dudley Hill (op 1.12.1893)
and extension of the Pudsey line
(1.11.1893). He became MICE 2.3.1880.
He died after a long illness.
Min Proc ICE V 100 1889–90 pp 383–4

FRASER, John

b Linlithgow, Scotland, 28.7.1819;
d Leeds 24.9.1881 aged 62.
Civil eng, GNR. Eldest son of James F.,
architect of Manchester. Articled to
G. W. Buck. In 1842 app by Edward
Woods (qv) as res eng on the const of
the Liverpool & Manchester R link to
Manchester Victoria station, op 5.5.1844.
F. prepared designs for all the bridges
and vdts. In 1846 app res eng on the
West Riding Jn and Huddersfield &
Sheffield Jn Rs (LYR) under John
Hawkshaw (qv). In 1851–2, again under
Hawkshaw, F. became res eng on the
Leeds, Bradford & Halifax Jn R (GNR),
op 1.8.1854, and on the Leeds–Wakefield
line, op 5.10.1857, and the Gildersome,
op 1.1.1857, and Ardsley, op 10.10.1857,
branches. Later, as chief eng, he carried
out the Methley branch, 6 miles (9.6km),
op 11.6.1866; Ossett branch, 1862–4;
Ossett–Batley and extn to Adwalton,
9 miles (14km), 1863–4. In 1862, in conjunction with John Fowler (qv), he
undertook the West Riding & Grimsby
R, Wakefield–Doncaster, 28½ miles
(46km), op 1.1.1866. When these local
lines became part of the GNR F.
became dist eng and in that capacity

built the connection to the LYR at Bradford, 1864; the Halifax & Ovenden (GNR/LYR) 1865–6; Bradford, Eccleshill & Idle and extns, 1866; Idle & Shipley 1867; Ossett & Dewsbury and Batley & Dewsbury, 1871–2; Pudsey R, 1871; Bradford & Thornton R, 1871; Halifax, Thornton & Keighley, 1873. Of the last the section from Thornton to Keighley was completed by his son Henry John F. (qv) after his death. In 1870–1 he designed and built the North Bridge at Halifax, an iron structure of 2 160ft spans (48.77m), 60ft (18m) wide. F. was also eng with his son of the GNR/LNWR jt lines in Leicestershire and the GNR lines from Newark to Bottesford, 1877–9, and Marefield–Leicester, completed 1882. Became MIME 1859 and MICE in 3.1863.
Min Proc ICE V 70 1881–2 pp 417–19; *The Eng* V 52 30.9.1881 p 247; Proc IME 1882 p 6

FULTON, Hamilton Henry

b London, (?).(?).1813; d Chiswick, nr London, 10.8.1886 aged 73.
Civil eng. Son of Hamilton F., state eng to S Carolina and Georgia. Ed Athens Univ, Georgia. Returned to England 1829 and became pupil to his f who d in 1834. He then worked for John Rennie Jr. In 1839 he was engaged on the Newcastle & Carlisle R for 3 yrs. On 6.5.1845 he became MICE and in 1846 began a practice in London. Among R works to which F. was eng were the W London & Crystal Palace and branches to the Brighton R at Norwood and Battersea, op 1854–7, with heavy works including Penge tunnel 1 mile 381yd (1.957km) long. In 1855 he completed the Stokes Bay branch of the LSWR and the Ryde–Ventnor line in the Isle of Wight; in 1856 the extn of the S Wales R to Milford Haven; in 1860 Salisbury & Dorset Jn R; 1859–63 surveys and parliamentary plans for the Manchester & Milford Haven R. He also designed a huge bridge across the Severn (the Severn tunnel was built instead) and another across the Mersey (made unnecessary by the Mersey R in 1886). F's greatest project was the Manchester Ship Canal which he mooted in 1876. F's scheme was, however, for a tidal canal. In 1882, when a lock system was

adopted, F. severed his connection with it.
Min Proc ICE V 87 1886–7 pp 418–22

GAIRNS, John Francis

b London, (?).(?).1876; d London, 10.12.1930 aged 54.
Writer on locos and editor. At age 18 joined the firm of Wheatley & MacKenzie, patent agents. 1907 pub his first book, *Loco compounding and superheating*. After contributing to *The Railway Magazine* for several years he became its editor in 1910. About the same time he became associated with *Railway News* to which he contributed articles on locos. In 1918, when this journal combined with the *Railway Gazette*, his services were transferred to this, of which he rose to become asst mg editor. He also edited the *Railway Year Book*. In 1923 he pub his most popular book, *Railways for all*, and in 1926 *Loco superheating and feed-water heating*. G. was one of the original members of the Inst of Transport and also of the ILE.
The Locomotive 1.1931 p 34; *The Eng* V 150 19.12.1930 p 667.

GALBRAITH, William Robert

b Stirling, (?).(?).1829; d London, 5.10.1914 aged c 85.
Civil eng, LSWR. Ed Stirling Academy and Glasgow Coll. 1846 articled to John Errington (qv) and was engaged in the London office and on Rs in England and Scotland, including the Aberdeen R (as dist eng); Scottish Central R; LNWR Crewe–Shrewsbury; ELR and LSWR. From 1855 G. was mainly employed on LSWR extns W of Yeovil. 1856 app res eng to the Yeovil & Exeter R and then to Exeter & Exmouth R. On the death of Errington in 1862 he was app eng for new works on the LSWR with supervision of parliamentary business. He built most new LSWR lines during the next 40 yrs in Middlesex, Surrey, Hampshire, Dorset, Devon and Cornwall and, with his partner and former pupil R. F. Church, branches promoted independently and later acquired by the LSWR, to Swanage, Chard, Seaton, Sidmouth, Ifracombe and the extns from Exeter to Okehampton, Plymouth and Devonport,

Holsworthy and the N Cornwall R to Bodmin and Padstow. In 1892 the LSWR became owners of Southampton docks which were greatly extended under G's supervision. From 1880–90 he was consulting eng to the NBR in charge of parliamentary work. He also laid out and built the NBR Inverkeithing & Burntisland and Glenfarg lines in continuation northwards from the Forth Bridge, and he prepared and carried'out parliamentary plans for the alteration and enlargement of Waverley station at Edinburgh. From 1892 he was eng with Greathead (qv) and later Alexander Kennedy on the Waterloo & City R, London, and with Benjamin Baker (qv) and R. F. Church on the Bakerloo line, and with Douglas Fox on the Charing Cross, Euston & Hampstead R (Northern Line), altogether 14 miles (22.5km) of tube Rs. He ret 1907. Elected MICE 7.3.1865.
Min Proc ICE V 197 1914 p 328

GALTON, Sir Douglas Strutt

b Droitwich, Worcestershire, 2.7.1822; d London, 11.3.1899 aged 77.
Inspector of Rs for the BOT. At age 15 entered the Royal Military Academy, Woolwich. 1840 commissioned in REs. 1840 became secretary to the newly formed R Commission. He was also app secretary to the Royal Commission on the use of iron in R structures, set up after the collapse of Robert Stephenson's Dee bridge at Chester in 1847. In 1854 he was app Insp of Rs and secretary of the R Dept of the BOT. From 1860–70 he returned to military duties as asst insp gen of fortifications. In 1858 began his lifelong friendship with Florence Nightingale, becoming one of her leading collaborators in the reform of the army hospital system, and she was instrumental in his app as asst under secretary at the War Office in charge of the health and sanitary administration of the army. He was interested in submarine telegraphy and was app to investigate this subject following the breakage of the Atlantic and Red Sea cables. Between 1.12.1859 and 4.9.1860 his commission held 22 sittings and issued a public report in 1861. He was a member of the consultative committee on Atlantic cables in 1865. From 1866 he served on the Royal Commission on Rs, strongly opposing state purchase. 1869–75 Dir of Public Works and Buildings at the Office of Works. About 1876 he took part in important experiments with automatic continuous brakes on the LBSCR, NER and other lines. In 1878 he conducted experiments on the LBSCR to determine the merits or otherwise of skidding when applying R brakes. In 1880 he supervised the LYR brake experiments at Gisburn. His findings contributed greatly to the development and use of R brakes. He was general secretary of the British Assoc from 1870–95, becoming president in 1895. MIME 1862. Elected FRS in 1863, KCB 1887, hon MICE 1894.
RM 10.1961 p 722; The Eng V 87 3.1899 p 257; Proc IME 1899 pp 129–34

GARBE, Dr Robert

b (?) (?).(?).1847; d Berlin, 23.5.1932 aged 85.
CME of the Berlin div of Prussian State Rs, 1895–1917. One of the greatest European authorities on steam locos. Worked with Schmidt (qv) on development of the high-degree superheater and was largely responsible for its rapid introduction. The success of his standard loco designs is reflected in the large numbers built for Germany and elsewhere; 3850 P8 Class 4–6–0s; 5260 G8 class 0–8–0s, 3000 G10 class 0–10–0s. Pub: The application of highly superheated steam to locomotives 1908; Die Dampflokomotiven der Gegenwart 1920; Die zeitgemässe Heissdampflokomotive 1924.

GARRATT, Herbert William

b London, 8.6.1864; d Richmond, Surrey, 25.9.1913 aged 49.
Inventor of the Garratt articulated loco. Apprenticed at Bow wks, NLR, 1879–82 under J. C. Park (qv). He then moved to Doxford's marine engg wks, Sunderland. After acting as inspector for Sir Douglas Fox (qv) and Sir Alexander Rendel he went to the Central Argentine R in 1889, becoming loco supt in 1892. From 1900 he worked on the Cuban Central, Lagos Govt, Lima (Peru), and New South Wales Govt Rs, returning to England in 1906. After inspecting rail-mounted artillery for the NSW Govt

he visited Beyer, Peacock & Co, Manchester, to discuss a method of mounting heavy artillery on R bogies. The discussion led to the design of the Garratt articulated loco which he patented in 1907. The patent specification drawing shows a 2–4–0 + 0–4–2 with h p cyls at the outer ends of the bogies. However, the first 2 engines, built by Beyer, Peacock for Tasmania in 1909, were 2ft (610mm) gauge compound 0–4–0 + 0–4–0s with cyls at the inner ends of the bogies. The third was a 0–4–0 + 0–4–0 simple for the 2ft gauge Darjeeling Himalayan R with cyls at the other ends of the bogies. Other orders followed, for all gauges in many countries, the biggest user being South Africa. The only conditions in which the Garratt loco was not a success were those where there were abrupt reverse changes of gradient as on the switchbacks on the Central of Peru, where they were also rather long for the reversing necks. G. was elected MIME 1902.

Engg V 96 3.10.1913 p 461; Proc IME 12.1913 p 1334; Durrant, A. E., *The Garratt Loco* 1969; Wiener, Lionel, *Articulated Locos* 1930, 1970

GASS, Edward Mellor

b Manchester, (?).(?).1861;
d (?) 2.5.1942 aged 81.
Chief loco draughtsman, LYR. Apprenticed at Beyer, Peacock & Co, Manchester, 1877–82, remaining as draughtsman until 1884. 1884–8 with Sharp, Stewart, Manchester and Glasgow, as leading loco draughtsman. 1888 app leading loco draughtsman at the new wks at Horwich, LYR, where he remained until he ret in 1926. He was largely responsible for detail design work of all the locos of Aspinall, Hoy and Hughes (qqv). MILE 1919; AIME 1909.
Journal ILE V 32 1942 p 93; Proc IME V 149 1943 p 166

GEOGHEGAN, Samuel

b Dublin (?).(?).1845; d Dublin, 4.9.1928 aged 83.
Loco eng in India, and at Guinness, Dublin. Served 3 yr apprenticeship with Walter May & Co, Birmingham. Later he was draughtsman with P. & W. MacLelland & Howden & Co, Glasgow;

then fitter with Fawcett, Preston & Co, Liverpool. 1869 went to Smyrna as mechanic and draughtsman on the Ottoman R. 1871 moved to Doncaster to become fitter in the GNR wks. 1871 to India where he was engaged on const of a 2 mile (3.2km) long bridge over the River Chenab in Punjab, first as asst eng then as executive eng in charge of half of the bridge. Later served 1 yr as dist loco supt on the line, nr Delhi. In 1874 he was app chief eng to Arthur Guinness & Son, the brewers at Dublin, becoming consulting eng from 1901 until he ret in 1904. He was renowned for his design of an unusual 0–4–0 loco for the 1ft 10in (559mm) gauge internal R system at the Guinness brewery. 19 'Geoghegan Patent' engines were built from 1882–1921. Mounted in a 'haulage truck' one of these could be used as a loco on the 5ft 3in (1.600m) gauge. G. became MIME in 1880.
Proc IME 12.1928 p 1042

GERSTNER, Franz Anton von

b Prague, 11.5.1793; d Philadelphia, Pa, USA, 12.4.1840 aged nearly 47.
Son of Franz Josef von G., founder of the Prague Polytechnic Inst (where G. was ed) and promoter of the R from Danube to the Moldau. In 1818 G. was app prof of practical geometry at Vienna Polytechnic Inst. In 1822 he decided to study R const and visited England. Returning to Vienna he built a 2km long R, a third with wooden rails, a third with CI rails and a third with WI rails. He surveyed the Danube–Moldau R and on 7.9.1824 obtained a concession for the R from Budweis on the Moldau to the Danube near Linz, using wooden and iron rails. In 1826 he again visited England to examine loco haulage on Rs. On 7.9.1827 the Budweis–Trojern section was opened. This had steeper gradients and sharper curves. Still not convinced of the merits of steam power, G. visited England again in 1829. The Budweis–Linz R opened throughout on 1.8.1832. In 1834 he visited Russia intending to lay out a R network and in 1835 presented a memorandum to Tsar Nicholas suggesting that he should be allowed to build a R between Moscow and St Petersburg, Nizhnii Novgorod and Kazan. He asked for a 20 yr mono-

poly of R const in Russia. On 30.10.1837 only the 23km (14 miles) section from St Petersburg to Tsarskoye Selo was opened, extended to Pavlovsk the following summer. In 1838 G. went to America to study Rs there but d in Philadelphia.
Röll V 4 pp 1803–4

GERWIG, Robert

b Karlsruhe, 2.5.1820; d Karlsruhe, 6.12.1885 aged 65.
Eng on St Gotthard R. Ed tech high sch, Karlsruhe. 1840 eng of water and street works in Baden. 1868–71 supervised const of the Black Forest R. 1871 app eng on St Gotthard R, being placed in charge of the Ticino section with its four great spiral tunnels, opened on 1.6.1882.
Röll V 4 p 1806

GHEGA, Karl Ritter von

b Venice, 10.1.1802; d Vienna, 14.3.1860 aged 58.
Eng of the Semmering R, Austria. Son of an Austrian marine officer. Studied at Padua Univ and grad Dr of Maths 1819. For 17 yrs was engaged on street tramways and water supply works at Venice. 1836 app eng on Kaiser Ferdinand's Nordbahn, the first steam R in Austria. 1836–7 visited Belgium and England to study Rs. He then planned the Rabensburg–Brünen, and Lundenburg–Olmütz Rs. In 1842 he visited USA on a study tour. His greatest work was the laying out and const of the Semmering R, Wiener Neustadt–Murzzuschlag, Europe's first 'mountain' R, begun after much delay on 8.8.1848 and opened to freight on 15.5. and passengers 17.7.1854. A large memorial to G. was erected at Semmering station.
Röll; Schneider, A., *Rs through the mountains of Europe* 1967

GIBB, Alexander

b Larbert, Stirlingshire, 21.9.1804; d Aberdeen, 8.8.1867 aged 63.
Civil eng, GN of S. Ed Aberdeen Gr Sch and Marischal Coll, Aberdeen. He then entered the office of T. Telford. Returning to Aberdeen he was engaged on lighthouse const by Robert Stevenson. From 1827 he and his f carried out various bridge and harbour works at Aberdeen, Edinburgh and Glasgow. In

1836 G. and his f built the Victoria bridge over the Wear on the Durham Jn R, under T. E. Harrison (qv), the chief eng. They then contracted for a portion of the Edinburgh & Glasgow R at Almond Valley. In 1842 he returned to Aberdeen as civil eng and planned and carried out many Rs in the north of Scotland. After the d of his f he was eng to the Aberdeen R and the Great N of Scotland R. He remained eng to the GNS until his d. Became MICE 9.2.1830.
Min Proc ICE V 27 1867–8 pp 587–9

GIBB, Sir Alexander, KBE, CB

b Broughty Ferry nr Dundee, 12.2.1872; d Hartley Wintney, Hants, 21.1.1958 aged 85.
Dir gen, civil engg dept, MOT. 5th civil eng in line from William G. b 1736, his great-great grand f; John G. (1776–1850), his great grand f; Alexander G. (qv), his grand f; and Easton, G., his f. Ed Rugby Sch and Univ Coll, London. 1890 became pupil of Sir John Wolfe Barry and H. M. Brunel (qqv). After 4 yrs including one as outdoor insp on the Lanarkshire & Dumbartonshire R he continued another 5 yrs on Wolfe Barry's staff. During this period he was res eng on R widenings and extensions including widening the Metropolitan R (Harrow–Finchley Road) and the Bow–Whitechapel R. In 1900 joined his f's firm Easton Gibb & Son, then building Kew bridge over the Thames. As mg dir of E. G & Son he carried out many important dock works. 1916 app chief eng, const, to British armies in France. Next became civil eng in chief to the Admiralty. 1919 app dir gen civil engg to the Min of Transport. 1921 set up as consulting eng.
The Eng V 205 31.1.1958 p 178 (portrait); *Engg* V 185 31.1.1958 p 132 (portrait)

GIBB, Sir George Stegmann

b Aberdeen, (?).(?).1850; d Wimbledon, Surrey, 17.12.1925 aged 75.
G mgr, NER. Son of Alexander G. (qv). Ed Aberdeen Gr Sch and Univ. Grad LLB London. Articled to a solicitor. 1877 to staff of GWR as asst to solicitor. 1880 into private practice in London. 1882 solicitor to NER. 1891 became g

mgr NER. Given seat on bd of dirs 1906. He was responsible for many varied improvements on the NER, introducing ton-mileage statistics in 1902. Knighted 1904. On 3.1.1906 app dep chairman and mg dir Underground Electric R Co, London, having, in 1903, served on the Royal Commission on London Traffic. 1910 became chairman of the Road Board. In WW1 served on the Army Council responsible for army contracts.

Engg V 120 25.12.1925 p 802

GIFFARD, Henri

b Paris, 8.2.1825; d Paris, 14.4.1882 aged 57.

Inventor of the injector. Son of a poor family. Studied at Bourbon Coll. 1841 began in the wks offices of the Paris–St Germain R. Shortly afterwards he began to study ballooning to which he devoted a great part of his life. 1851 pub *Application de la Vapeur à la Navigation Aérienne*. The following year he made his first ascent in a balloon of elongated form which was intended to be guided by steam power, but it was not a success. 1854 pub *Du Travail depense pour obtenir un Point d'Appui dans l'Air*. At the Paris exhibition of 1867 and again in 1878 he established captive balloons, the last of enormous size. G. is best known in R circles for his invention of the injector in 1859 for which he received the prize for mechanics from the Academie des Sciences. In 1863 he was created a Knight of the Legion of Honour.

Engg V 33 21.4.1882; *The Eng* V 53 28.4.1882 p 309.

GLEHN, Alfred George de
See DE GLEHN

GLOVER, Col George Tertius

b London, (?).(c ?).1870; d Brampton, Cumbria, 24.6.1953 aged 83.

Loco eng, GNR Ireland. Ed Lancing Coll and Royal School of Mines. Apprenticed with James Simpson & Co, London, and Neilson & Co, Glasgow. 1894 entered NER wks at Gateshead as draughtsman. Later in testing dept and boiler insp dept. Then with D. Bain (qv) at York C & W wks. 1901 app mgr of the C & W wks at Walker Gate.

1903, under V. Raven (qv), he was given charge of all electric carriage stock on the Tynemouth electrification, mech and elec running and maintenance. Later app mgr of Shildon wagon wks. 1909 became loco wks mgr, Gateshead. In 1912 he was app loco C & W eng on the GNR, Ireland as successor to Charles Clifford. Elected MIME 1914. At the end of 1916 he was commissioned in the REs and active in France as CME to the transportation scheme inaugurated by Sir E. Geddes, retiring as hon col in 1918. G. introduced the use of the Schmidt superheater on GNR locos, his first engines being the 5 class S 4-4-0s, 5 class SG 0-6-0s and 5 class T 4-4-2Ts, all built by Beyer, Peacock in 1913. His class U mixed traffic 4-4-0s of 1915 were the first engines in Ireland to have the Robinson superheater. His finest engines were the 5 class V 3-cyl compound 4-4-0s of 1932 for the Belfast–Dublin expresses. Ret 1933 and went to live at Park Barn, Brampton, Cumberland, now Cumbria.

Engg V 176 17.7.1953 p 76; *Cumberland News* 4.7.1953 p 3

GOBEY, Francis Edward, OBE

b Cirencester, Glos, 4.11.1873; d Manchester, 2.10.1924 aged 51

C & W eng. Ed Sir Thomas Rich's Sch, Gloucester. In 8.1889 entered service of the Gloucester R C & W Co Ltd. 1897 app draughtsman at the LYR carriage wks, Newton Heath, Manchester. 1901–3 acted as asst in the wks and in 1903 was app chief draughtsman. In 6.1909 became wks mgr and in 1910 asst C & W supt. He visited France, Belgium, USA and Canada to study R wks methods. G. was an outstanding scholar. He was awarded the Queen's prize in maths, 1889; City & Guilds hons silver medal in R C & W building 1899. Lectured on C & W building at Manchester Municipal Coll of Tech, 1900–6, and in R economics at Manchester Univ 1912–18. Awarded Webb prize for his paper on 'All-metal cars for British Rs' to the ICE in 1919. On the formation of the LMS in 1923 he became div supt of carriages at Wolverton. Became MIME 1911, MICE 1918.

Proc IME 12.1924 p 1296; *Engg* V 118 10.10.1924

GÖLSDORF, Dr Karl

b Vienna 8.6.1861; d Semmering,
Austria, 18.3.1916 aged 54.
One of Europe's most outstanding loco
engs. Son of Adolf G., CME of Austrian
Southern R, 1885–1907, d 1911. Graduated with 1st class hons in engg at
Vienna in 1884. Entered the workshops
of Austrian State Rs, becoming chief
of the erecting shop in 1889, CME 1891.
Successively rose to eng, chief eng,
inspector, chief of wks dept, and finally
head of mech engg at the Austrian R
Ministry, Vienna. The varied and often
difficult routes of Austria, then a much
larger country than today, such as the
Arlberg, Tauern, Semmering and
Brenner lines, forced him to design
locos of about 60 classes, within a maximum axle load of 14 tons. He was an
early advocate of superheating, 4-cyl
compounds for express and other duties,
and greater numbers of coupled axles,
allowing side-play to negotiate curves
(eg the 0–10–0 of 1900). He was the first
to use the Brotan boiler with water-
tube firebox and separate steam drum.
For express passenger work he produced
4–4–0s (1898), 4–4–2s (1901), 2–6–2s
(1905), and the famous 4-cyl compound
2–6–4s (1908), using the Krauss–
Helmholz leading truck arrangement.
For the Tauern he produced the first
2–12–0s (1911) and for the Erzberg R
a mixed rack and adhesion 0–12–0
(1912). In 20 yrs he provided the Austrian
State Rs with a stud of engines of simple
design capable of handling every kind of
traffic on all kinds of route. He had a
genius for packing the maximum power
into the minimum weight. He adopted
the first scientific system of loco numbering, later widely adopted. He contributed
numerous articles to the technical press.
He received many honours including a
doctorate from the School of Technology, Hanover.
*Zeitschrift des Vereines deutscher
Ingenieure* V 60 6.5.1916 p 397; Cox,
E. S., *World Steam in the twentieth
century* 1969

GOOCH, Sir Daniel

b Bedlington, Northumberland,
24.8.1816; d Clewer Park, Berkshire,
15.10.1889 aged 73.

First loco supt, and later chairman,
GWR, and layer of the first trans-
Atlantic cable. Ed locally. In 1831 went
with his family to Monmouthshire where
his f had obtained employment at
Tredegar Iron Works, where G. found
his first employment in the foundry and
pattern shop. On 28.8.1833 his f died. In
1.1834 G. left Tredegar to work at the
Vulcan Foundry, Newton le Willows,
Lancashire, which had just been established by Robert Stephenson and Charles
Tayleur. However, in 9.1834 his health
forced him to leave and for a time he
worked under his bro T.L.G. (qv) on the
survey for the London & Birmingham R.
In 1.1835 he obtained employment for
a year at the Dundee Foundry where he
gained experience in marine engines. On
1.1.1836 he left Dundee for Newcastle
where, at the age of 20, he began at the
works of Robert Stephenson & Co, but
left them on 8.10 to work with Sir
Robert Hawks in a new works at Gateshead where they were building 2 locos
for the Newcastle & Carlisle R. However, following a dispute within the firm,
it shut down the following year and G.
was left without work. For a time he
found employment with his bro T.L.G.
on the Manchester & Leeds R at Rochdale. In 7.1837, hearing that Brunel
required a loco supt on the GWR, G.
applied and was appointed. At first he
had great trouble with the 7ft (2.134m)
gauge engines ordered by Brunel, which
led to some brushes with his chief.
However, once he was given a free hand,
he ordered engines of a sound design
from Robert Stephenson & Co, the first
of which, the 2–2–2 *North Star*, established a series of reliable loco types
which served the GWR to the end of
the broad gauge in 1892. The first engine
of G's design to be delivered, in 1840,
was the *Firefly*, based on the Robert
Stephenson design. In 9.1840 G. made
the important decision to site the GWR
loco wks at Swindon at the summit of
the main line and at the junction of
the branch to Gloucester and later to
South Wales. In the following years G.
guided the development of the works
and the new town of Swindon which
grew at the same time. The first engine
built entirely at Swindon was the 2–2–2
Great Western, in 4.1846. In 1843 G.

produced his stationary link motion, replacing the earlier gab motion and allowing for expansive working. It differed from the Howe/Stephenson link motion in that the die block was moved up and down instead of the curved link. In 1864 G. resigned his position as loco supt, to be succeeded by Joseph Armstrong (qv), and he joined the Telegraph Construction Co, formed in 4.1864, and which chartered Brunel's great iron ship *Great Eastern* for the purpose of laying the first Atlantic cable. This was successfully accomplished in 1866 and on 15.11. 1866 G. was made a baronet in honour of his work. In 1865 the affairs of the GWR were in a low state and G. was asked to become chairman. This he did and from then on guided the company to success. He took great interest in the Severn tunnel which he saw through to completion in 1887. He remained chairman until his death in 1889. In 1873 he was back on the *Great Eastern* for the laying of a second Atlantic cable which was successfully landed on 18.7.1873. He was chairman of the Telegraph Construction & Maintenance Co until his death. G. was elected MICE on 18.4.1848. In 1865 he was elected MP for Cricklade, Wiltshire, but he made little impression in Parliament. He was a prominent freemason, and a JP for Berkshire during his later years. On 22.3.1838 he m Margaret, dr of Henry Tanner, by who he had 4 sons and 2 drs. She d on 22.5.1868. On 17.9.1870 he m Emily, dr of John Burder, who survived him until 5.1901. Besides his bro Thomas Longbridge already mentioned, his bros John Viret and William (qqv) were both loco engs.

Ellis, Hamilton, *Twenty Locomotive Men* 1958; Gooch, Daniel, *Memoirs and Diary* 1972; MacDermot, E. T., *History of the Great Western R* 1927; RCTS, *The Locos of the GWR* parts 1 and 2; *The Eng* V 68 18.10.1899 p 335; *Engg* V 48 18.10.1889 p 466; Nock, O. S., *The R Engs* 1955; Parris, Henry, 'Sir Daniel Gooch. A biographical sketch', *Journal of Transport History* 2.1976 pp 203–16

GOOCH, John Viret

b Bedlington, Northumberland, 29.6.1812; d Bracknell, Berks, 8.6.1900 aged 88.

Loco eng, LSWR and Eastern Counties R. Served as pupil under Joseph Locke (qv) during const of the Grand Jn R, opened 1837, subsequently becoming res eng in which position he was responsible for rebuilding the inside-cyl locos with outside cyls. For a brief period in 1840 he was a loco fireman on the Manchester & Leeds R of which his elder bro Thomas (qv) was chief eng. In the same year he m Hannah Frances Handcock, who d 1874. On 1.1.1841 he was app loco supt of the LSWR at Nine Elms, London, where he was the first eng to build locos in the shops instead of ordering them outside. In 11.1843 the first of his o/c 2–2–2s, named *Eagle*, appeared. G. favoured fairly light locos with outside cyls inclined above and in front of the leading wheels. This arrangement influenced the designs of his successor Joseph Beattie (qv). Other features of the 'Eagle' class were boiler feed pumps driven by eccentrics forged solid on the driving axle, firebox fitted with a mid feather made of corrugated plates, and a combined pressure gauge and safety valve. With their 6ft 6in (1.98m) wheels they were among the first standard gauge engines in Britain to have wheels over 6ft (1.83m) diameter. For goods trains he produced the 'Bison' class i/c 0–6–0 with double frames. On 16.5.1850 he was app loco supt of the Eastern Counties R at Stratford, London. His first engines were obtained in 1853 from Longridge near Newcastle (his mother was a dr of Thomas Longridge, the founder of the firm) and were o/c 2–2–2Ts with 6ft 6in (1.98m) wheels. For working expresses he produced an o/c 2–2–2, also with 6ft 6in wheels. 6 were built, 4 of them being completed by his successor Robert Sinclair (qv). His o/c 0–4–2 goods engines, known as the 'Butterflies', had 5ft 6in (1.76m) coupled wheels. Under G. 5 of the old ECR 'Cramptons' were rebuilt as 0–6–0 double-framed goods engines. In 9.1856 G. ret, at the early age of 48, and spent the remaining 40 yrs of his life quietly at his country home, Cooper's Hill in Berkshire.

Engg V 69 15.6.1900 p 789; *Locomotives and Rs* 7.1900 p 82; Bradley, D. L. *The Locos of the LSWR* Part 1 RCTS 1966; Min Proc ICE V 141 1900 p 344

GOOCH, Thomas Longridge

b London, 1.11.1808;
d Newcastle upon Tyne, 23.11.1882
aged 74.

Civil eng, Manchester & Leeds R. First son and second child of John G. and Anna, dr of Thomas Longridge of Newcastle, and bro of John Viret, Daniel and William (qqv), loco engs. About 1815 the family moved to Crowhall, Northumberland, when G's f was app cashier at the Bedlington ironworks. G. was ed at the village school. On 6.10.1823 he was apprenticed to George Stephenson for 6 yrs and entered the wks of Robert Stephenson & Co then in course of erection at South Street, Newcastle. After 2 yrs in the shops he went into the drg office, and also assisted Joseph Locke (qv) in taking levels and making drawings for the projected Newcastle & Carlisle R. With the passing of the Liverpool & Manchester R Act of 1826 G. went with George Stephenson to Liverpool and for $2\frac{1}{2}$ yrs acted as his secretary and draughtsman. He prepared nearly all the working drawings and plans for the L & MR, working from Stephenson's rough sketches. In 1828 he was employed by G. Stephenson as res eng on the Bolton & Leigh R. He then drew up parliamentary plans and sections for the projected Warrington & Newton R, after which he returned to Liverpool where, on 1.1.1829 he was app res eng of the Liverpool end of the L & M R. His succes led to his app, again under G. Stephenson, as res eng of the entire Manchester & Leeds R. He worked intensively by night and day to get the plans and sections ready in time for the 1831 session of Parliament. The Bill was defeated, despite G's excellent performance as parliamentary witness. In 10.1831 he was asked to assist Robert Stephenson in the preparation of plans and sections for the London & Birmingham R. Following the passing of the L & B Act in 4.1833 G. was app res eng of about 36 miles (58km) of the N end of the line. When the Manchester & Leeds R at last got its Act, in 1836, G. was app chief eng and he carried the work through to completion in 1841 despite unusually heavy works. He remained chief eng of the M & L until

1844 while concerned with branches to Heywood, Oldham and Halifax. He then laid out the line of the Manchester, Bury & Rossendale R, later ELR. During the 'R Mania' period which followed G. was fully occupied with numerous schemes, the principal being the Trent Valley line (Stafford–Rugby) on which he was jt eng with Robert Stephenson and G. P. Bidder (qqv). His health now began to suffer from overwork. In 20 yrs his only break had been a 3-day honeymoon, but he found it impossible to get away from work. In 8.1847 he was suddenly taken ill in his office at 24 Great George Street, Westminster, and was ordered by his doctor to have a complete rest. After 8 months he resumed work but was unable to continue and in 1851, at the early age of 42, he was compelled to retire. G. was a man of unpretending manners and kindly disposition and he devoted many years to charitable work. He was elected MICE on 3.6.1845, but took no active part in the proceedings. He lived in retirement until his 75th year.

Min Proc ICE V 72 1883 pp 300–8; Gooch, Daniel, *Memoirs and Diary* 1972

GOOCH, William Frederick

b Bedlington, Northumberland, 19.4.1825; d Newton le Willows, Lancs, (?).(?).(?). aged (?).

Loco eng. 5th son and 10th and youngest child of John G. and younger bro of Thomas, John Viret and Daniel (qqv). Worked for a time on the S Devon R. Became wks mgr at Swindon, GWR, in 1857, under his bro Daniel who hoped W.F.G. would succeed him as loco supt. However, Joseph Armstrong (qv) was appointed and so, in 1864, G. left Swindon to become mg dir of the Vulcan Foundry at Newton le Willows. Ret 1892.

Gooch, Daniel, *Memoirs and Diary* 1972

GRAHAM, George

b Hallhills, Dumfriesshire, (?).(?).1822; d Kelvinside, Glasgow, 30.6.1899 aged 76.

Civil eng, Caledonian R. Apprenticed to Robert Napier, Glasgow, on marine engines. Forced by poor health to adopt an outdoor life, he was engaged in 1845 on the survey for the CR under Locke (qv), and on 10.9.1847 he rode on the engine of the first passenger train from Beattock to Carlisle. In 1853 he succeeded Locke and Errington as chief eng and was responsible for the expansion of the system from 195 miles (314km) to 1116 miles (1796km), bridging the Clyde 7 times. In 1880 he was relieved of the responsibility for p w and works when 2 div engs were app under him and he became responsible only for new works. The system then totalled 775 miles (1247km). His numerous large works included the Greenock tunnel, 1 mile 340yd (1.92km), the longest in Scotland. He joined the Institution of Engineers and Shipbuilders in 1858. Became MICE 1889. He m in 1857, but his wife d 1871, and he was survived by 2 drs and 1 son.

The Eng V 88 7.7.1899 p 7; *Engg* V 68 7.7.1899 p 24; Min Proc ICE V 137 1898–9 p 424.

GRAINGER, Thomas

b Ratho, Midlothian, 12.11.1894;
d Stockton-on-Tees 25.7.1852 aged 57.
Civil eng on Rs in Scotland and Yorkshire. At 16 entered office of John Leslie, Edinburgh, to learn surveying. In 1816 set up on his own account as civil eng and surveyor on road works. In 1823 he surveyed the Monkland & Kirkintilloch R and, following the Act of 1824, carried out its const. In 1834 G. built the Arbroath & Forfar R and in 1836 laid out the Glasgow & Greenock. He then laid out and built the Edinburgh, Leith & Newhaven. After 1845 G. was connected with the Edinburgh & Bathgate and Edinburgh, Perth & Dundee Rs, and harbours at Broughty Ferry and Ferryport-on-Craig on the Tay. He also designed a steam barge to carry R wagons across the Tay. In England G. was engaged on the Leeds, Dewsbury & Manchester R (op 1849), East & West Yorkshire Jn, and Leeds Northern Rs. Works included the Morley tunnel, 1 mile 590yd (2.149km), Bramhope tunnel, 2 miles 234yd (3.433km), and the Wharfe vdt of 21 arches of 60ft (18.288m) span. G. d as a result of a collision on the Leeds Northern R. Became MICE 1829.

Min Proc ICE V 12 1852–3 pp 159–61

GRANTHAM, Richard Boxall

b Croydon, Surrey, 13.12.1805;
d London, 5.12.1891 aged 86.
Civil eng. Eldest son of John G., civil eng. Ed Edenbridge, Kent. At 16 began in drg office of Augustus Pugin (1762–1832), the famous architect, working a 12hr day from 06.00. 1823 went to Ireland to assist his f under John Rennie on a survey of the Shannon for the govt, then on rebuilding bridges over the Shannon at Limerick, Killaloe and Portuma. Later, with his bro John and his f, he was engaged by John and George Rennie in surveying a R from London to Birmingham for the GWR. In 1834, after the death of his f, G. was app surveyor to King's County and Clare and in 1836 to County Limerick. Returned to England at end of 1836 and was engaged by I. K. Brunel (qv) on const of GWR, superintending Brent vdt. Later res eng on Swindon–Gloucester–Cheltenham line, op to Gloucester 1845. 1844 to London where he established an office and was employed under Sir John Rennie on R surveys between London and Manchester, the Direct Northern, Direct Norwich, Birmingham & Gloucester, and other lines. His next R works were in 1852 when he surveyed part of the Portsmouth Direct R under Errington (qv). 1854–7 assisted John Clutton on drainage works in Essex. 1856 began const of Forest of Dean Central R which he had previously surveyed. Later he surveyed other Rs in the Forest of Dean. 1860, with his bro John, app eng to the Northern R of Buenos Aires. For several years he was eng to the Quebrada R Co, Venezuela, originally surveyed by Sir John Hawkshaw. He also carried out R and harbour works on the Isle of Wight, 1879–80. Eected MICE 25.6.1844.

Min Proc ICE V 108 1891–2 pp 399–403

GRAY, John

b (?) (?).(?).(?);
d (?) (?).(?).(?) aged (?).
Loco eng. He appears to have originated at Newcastle. In 1838 he was the first eng to use the balanced slide valve on locos, on the Liverpool & Manchester R. In 1839 he applied a form of expansion gear to the *Cyclops* engine on the

L & M, claiming a 12 per cent fuel economy. This 'horse-leg' motion was used on engines on the York & N Midland R in 1840 and in 1842 on the Hull & Selby R on which, in 1840, he was app loco supt. He was the first eng to use a long-travel valve motion, of about 6in (152mm), on the H & S in 1840. He was one of the first engs to discard the idea of a low centre of gravity as necessary for the safe running of locos. On 27.3.1845 he was app loco supt of the Croydon, Dover & Brighton Jt Committee, and on the formation of the LBSCR on 27.7.1846 he retained the post of loco supt at Brighton. In 9.1845 he ordered 14 2-2-2s of his design from T. Hackworth (qv) at Shildon, but late delivery because of G's constant alterations to the design resulted in his dismissal from Brighton in 1847. Became MIME in 1847, the year the Institution was founded but allowed his membership to lapse in 1852. No other information has been discovered.
Holcroft, H., *The Armstrongs of the Great Western* 1953 pp 28–9; Bradley, D. L., *Locos of the LBSCR* Part 1 (RCTS) 1969

GREATHEAD, James Henry

b Grahamstown, Cape Colony, 6.8.1844; d Streatham, London, 21.10.1896 aged 52.
Civil eng; inventor of the G. tunnelling shield. 1859 went to England to complete his ed and in 1864 began a 3yr pupilage under Peter W. Barlow (qv), followed in 1867 by a year as asst eng on the MR extn from Bedford to London under W. H. Barlow (qv) and C. B. Baker (qv). About this time his former master Peter W. Barlow was proposing a system of underground Rs in London in 'tubes' lined with cast iron segments. In 1869–70 G. worked with Barlow on the pioneer scheme, the Tower Subway under the Thames. The difficulties encountered by Marc Brunel (qv) in building the Thames tunnel at Wapping were such that 26 yrs later no contractor was willing to undertake the Tower Subway. G., then only 24, tendered for the const of the shafts and tunnel for £9400, devising a cylindrical wrought iron shield forced forward by 6 powerful screws as the material was excavated in front of it. In 1870 G.

began to practice on his own account and in 1873 he returned to R const. 1873–7 he was res eng on the Hammersmith extn R and the Richmond extn of the Metropolitan District R. About this time he devised plant for tunnelling under the Thames at Woolwich in water-bearing strata, incorporating an air lock in the front of the shield to act as a trap to prevent loss of air in the event of a blow in the strata. It was insufficiently tried and the tunnelling attempt, at a lower level without its use, was abandoned in 1876. He assisted in the preparation of several projects: Regents Canal R, 1880; Dagenham Dock, and Metropolitan Outer Circle R, 1881; a new London–Eastbourne line, 1883; and various light Rs in Ireland in 1884. Also in 1884 G. was engaged as eng on the London (City) & Southwark Subway, later called the City & S London R, begun in 1886 and op 18.12.1890, the world's first electrical underground R. In 1884 he patented further improvements in his shield. In 1888 he became jt eng with Sir Douglas Fox (qv) on the const of the Liverpool Overhead R, op 1893. With W. R. Galbraith (qv) he carried out the Waterloo & City R, op 1898, and began the Central London R in conjunction with Sir John Fowler (qv) and Sir Benjamin Baker (qv) shortly before his death. Elected MICE 1881.
Min Proc ICE V 127 1896 pp 365–8; *The Eng* V 82 30.10.1896 p 448 (portrait); Jackson, A. A., & Groome, D. F., *Rails through the Clay* 1962

GREENLY, Henry

b Birkenhead 3.6.1876; d Heaton, Middlesex, 4.3.1947 aged 70.
Pioneer of miniature passenger-carrying Rs. In 1887 the family moved to London where G. was ed at Beethoven Street Sch which he left at 14. After a period in a Bayswater jewellers he attended Kenmont Gardens Science Sch on a scholarship, 9.1894–2.1897. On 22.2.1897 he began his engg career as a draughtsman at Neasden wks of the Metropolitan R under James Hunter, the chief draughtsman. He left in 1901 to become asst editor of *The Model Engineer*. In 1906 he became a consulting eng in model subjects and for many years worked with W. J. Bassett Lowke (qv)

designing locos for miniature Rs in Britain and abroad. About this time he started a monthly magazine devoted to models, Rs and locos which ended in 1916. G. then took up an app at the Royal Aircraft Establishment at Farnborough and was responsible for the invention of a flash eliminator for aircraft machine guns. From 1919 he was associated with several firms in the production of model locos and Rs. In 1922 he became eng to the Ravenglass & Eskdale R which, under his guidance, was converted to 15in (381mm) gauge. G. was also associated with the Romney, Hythe & Dymchurch 15in gauge R in Kent from its inception in 1926 until its completion in 1930. He was responsible for all civil engg, design of locos and rolling stock. In 1930 returned to consulting work but still contributed to model engg journals. His books *Model steam locos* 1922, *Model electric locos and Rs* 1922 and *Model Rs* 1924 did much to establish model Rs in Britain. Steel, E. A. and E. H. *The Miniature World of Henry Greenly* 1973; *The. Eng* V 183 14.3.1947 p 209; *Engg* V 163 14.3.1947 p 197

GREGORY, Sir Charles Hutton, KCMG

b Woolwich 14.10.1917; d London 10.1.1898 aged 80.
Civil eng. Apprenticed to Timothy Bramah, millwright and eng. Later became asst eng under Robert Stephenson on the Manchester & Birmingham R; then under James Walker on a graving dock at Woolwich. In 1840 he was engaged as res eng on the London & Croydon R. In 1841 he designed and erected at New Cross the first R semaphore signal. He also const the Croydon & Epsom R (LBSCR) op 10.5.1847. In 1846 he succeeded Brunel as chief eng of the Bristol & Exeter R, building several Rs in the W of England. After various govt appointments he became eng on the Somerset Central and Dorset Central Rs, and later consulting eng on lines in Brazil and Ceylon. 1871 app consulting eng for Rs to the govt of Trinidad and for the Cape Govt Rs.
Min Proc ICE V 132 1897–8 p 377; *The Times* 11.1.1898 p 4

GRESHAM, James

b Newark, Nottinghamshire, 28.12.1836; d Ashton on Mersey 13.1.1914 aged 77.
Ed Newark Gr Sch. Inventor of improvements to steam locos. During training as an artist at S Kensington he was advised by W. P. Frith (1819–1909, famous artist of *The R Station*, 1862) to take up mechanical drawing. This brought him into contact with engg and gave scope for his inventive talent. From 1857 he worked as draughtsman for Sharp, Stewart & Co, Manchester on loco design, also working on improvements to R brakes. G. also applied his inventive genius to textile machinery. In 1864 he began improving the Giffard injector by making the combining cone adjustable relative to the steam cone. This was patented in conjunction with John Robinson who was a partner in the firm. In 1865 G. left Sharp, Stewart and after a period in London started a wks in Manchester in 1866 for the mfr of sewing machines and injectors. He was joined by Thomas Craven and J. S. Heron, but in 1880 when Heron d the title of the firm became Gresham & Craven. In 1877 G. took out his first patent for improvements in the vacuum brake injector. This was followed by numerous other patents concerning the vacuum brake. In 1885 G. patented a steam sanding apparatus which, by overcoming the driving wheel slip on locos, made possible a new lease of life for the single driver type engine. In 1889 he took out his first patent for R passenger communication, consisting of a glass disc, breakage of which admitted air to the train pipe. Elected MIME 1880, MICE 1.12.1885. He was also JP, an art collector, and he presented a statue of King Edward VII to Manchester Corporation.
Min Proc ICE V 196 1914 p 360; Proc IME 2.1914 p 212; *The Eng* V 117 16.1.1914 p 75; *Engg* V 97 16.1.1914 p 78

GRESLEY, Sir Herbert Nigel

b Edinburgh 19.6.1876; d Hertford 5.4.1941 aged 64.
CME on GNR and LNER. 4th son of Rev Nigel G., rector of Netherscale, Leicestershire, and grandson of Sir

William Nigel G. of Drakelow, Derbyshire, 9th holder of a baronetcy created in 1611. Ed Marlborough. 1893–7 apprenticed to F. W. Webb (qv) at Crewe. After a further year there as fitter moved to the LYR wks at Horwich to serve a 2 yr pupilage under Aspinall (qv). In 1899 he was app test room asst, and later running shed foreman at Blackpool, and then one of the outdoor assts in the C & W dept. 1900 transferred to Newton Heath C & W wks of the LYR as asst wks mgr, becoming wks mgr in 1902 and in 1904 asst supt. He m during this period at Newton Heath. They had 2 sons and 2 drs. In 1905 he was app C & W supt at Doncaster, GNR, under Aspinall's great friend H. A. Ivatt (qv). When Ivatt ret in 1911 G. was app his successor as CME. His first locos were developments of Ivatt's designs, with superheaters and piston valves. His first original designs were the 2-cyl 2–6–0 in 1912 and the 2-cyl 2–8–0 in 1913. In 1918 he introduced his 3-cyl 2–8–0 incorporating derived gear for the middle valve (see *Engg* 25.4.1924). Later he developed this gear into a simpler form as established by H. Holcroft (qv) and used on all his later 3-cyl engines. His first design using the new gear was the 2–6–0 N 1000 (later LNER K3 class). The first of his famous Pacifics, No 1470, later named *Great Northern*, appeared in 1922 just before the GNR became part of the LNER. The post of CME of the LNER was first offered to J. G. Robinson (qv) of the GCR, but he suggested that G., then aged 46, should hold the office. Numerous accounts of G's LNER locos make it unnecessary to give details here. They did good work, but unfortunately some designs suffered from structural or mechanical defects which became prominent as maintenance standards declined during WW2. Much of his work was concerned with the modification or rebuilding of locos of the constituent groups, notably the NER, GER and GCR. Among these may be mentioned the B12 4–6–0 of the GER, the B16 4–6–0 of the NER and the B3 4–6–0 of the GCR, and his superheating of the Ivatt Atlantics of the GNR. G. was a bold experimenter, and despite the constant poverty of the LNER he showed great spirit in his efforts to keep

a progressive image of the LNER before the public. His experimental high pressure 4-cyl compound 4–6–4 with a water-tube boiler, No 10 000, attracted wide notice, thought it never achieved complete success. His famous streamlined trains, notably the *Silver Jubilee* and *Coronation*, set a new standard in steam loco performance. On 3.7.1938 his A4 class 4–6–2 No 4468 *Mallard* achieved a world record speed for steam of 126mph which has never been exceeded. G's work in the C & W dept was no less outstanding and although his carriage bogie with its springs inside the frames was criticised from a maintenance aspect, his bow-ended teak carriages were among the smoothest riding ever built. Following the death of his wife in 1929 G. became a victim of alcoholism which seriously underminded his health and undoubtedly hastened his untimely end. Became MIME 1907; also MICE. In 1920 he was awarded the CBE in recognition of work at Doncaster during WW1. He was knighted in 1936; in the same year Manchester Univ conferred upon him an hon DSc, and he was elected president of the IME. (See Wedgwood)

The Eng V 171 11.4.1941 p 22 (portrait); *Engg* V 151 18.4.1941 p 314 (portrait); *Journal and Proc IME* V 147 1942 p 91; *Journal ILE* 1941 p 161; *R Eng* V 1 No 4 7/8.1976 p 40 (IME); Brown, F. A. S., *Nigel Gresley, Loco Eng* 1961; *From Stirling to Gresley* 1975; Nock, O. S., *The Locos of Sir Nigel Gresley* 1945; Bellwood, John and Jenkinson, David, *Gresley and Stanier* 1976; RCTS *Locos of the LNER*, 10 parts from 1963

GREW, Frederick

b Norwich, 26.12.1819; d Lee, Kent, 19.3.1905 aged 85.

Mech eng. Trained under W. Bridges Adams (qv) at Fairfield wks, Bow, London. 1860 was res eng on the Tudela & Bilbao R. Then loco supt on Madrid & Alicante R; next on the Cadiz & Jerez R. 1856–9 chief draughtsman at Brown, Marshall & Co, Birmingham. Then to Belgium for 4 yrs as inspecting eng for rolling stock being built for the Varna R, Turkey. With his bro Nathaniel (qv) he desgined an 'ice loco' which worked in 1861 between St

Petersburg and Cronstadt in Russia. A model of this is in the Science Museum, London. 1867 app asst eng on the Irish R Commission to standardise gauges and details of mgt. Became MIME 1883. Proc IME 5.1905 p 377

GREW, Nathaniel

b Norwich 6.10.1829; d London 11.7.1897 aged 67.

Civil and mech eng. 1846–9 pupil of W. Bridges Adams (qv) at the Fairfield wks, Bow, London. 1849–51 worked on SER in London and Ashford. 1851–3 worked on survey and setting out of part of Madrid & Valencia R from Albacete to Almansa. 1854–9 chief asst to Sir William Siemens on engines, furnaces and iron and steel mfr. 1860 began on his own as a civil eng in London. With his bro Frederick (qv) he designed an 'ice loco'. Became MIME 1874. He was connected with R work in Argentina, Central America, Peru and Brazil.
Proc IME 4.1897 pp 233–4

GRIERSON, William Wylie, CBE

b London 9.12.1863; d San Remo, Italy, 14.3.1935 aged 72.

Chief eng, GWR, Ed Rugby Sch. Pupil under William Dean (qv) at Swindon and later articled to W. G. Owen, then chief eng. In 1.1887 entered eng dept of the GWR and became res eng on the Kemble–Tetbury branch, op 2. 12.1889, and later on the Pangbourne–Didcot widening, extn of Carmarthen–Cardigan line, and the S Wales & Bristol direct R which took 7 yrs to build at a cost of £1 m. It included Sodbury tunnel, 2 miles 913yd (4.054km). 1903 app div eng Wolverhampton, but did not take up the position. 1904 became eng at Paddington, and on ret of W. Y. Armstrong in 6.1916 the office of New Works Eng was abolished and G. was app chief eng in 7.1916, and also jt eng of the W London Extn R. Awarded CBE 1918. Ret 1918 at age 60, but continued to serve on numerous committees. Became MICE 1897 and was president 1929–30. In 9.1927 he m Aleen Bell of Tipperary.
The Eng V 159 22.3.1935 p 297 (portrait); Min Proc ICE V 240 1934–5 p 791

GRIGGS, George S

b (?) New England (?).(?).1805; d (?) (?).?).1870 aged c 65.

American loco eng of wide influence. Trained as machinist in the Locks & Canals Co machine shop, Lowell, Mass. In 1834 app master mechanic of Boston & Providence RR on which he remained. In 1839 he patented a continuous train brake for cars, one of the first such brake systems to be used in USA. His first loco, the 4–4–0 *Norfolk*, was built at the B & P Roxbury shops in 1845. It had inside cyls, and rivetted frame. Over 20 similar 4–4–0s were built in the next 10 yrs. He also patented wooden cushion driving wheels, and a firebrick arch (1857) (see Baird) which G. was the first to use in USA, making possible the burning of coal instead of wood. He also experimented with steam brakes. Sinclair credits him with the invention of the 'diamond stack' (chimney). Building of his inside-cyl engines continued at Roxbury until 3 yrs after G's death by which time they were long out-dated.
White, John H. Jr *American Locos, an engg history 1830–80* 1968; Sinclair, Angus, *Development of the Loco Engine* 1907, 1970

GRISSELL, Thomas

b London 4.10.1801; d nr Dorking 26.5.1874 aged 72.

R contractor. 1815 articled to his uncle, Henry Peto, becoming his partner in 1825. On the death of Peto in 1830 G. was joined by S. Morton Peto (qv) until Peto became MP for Norwich in 1847. S. M. Peto was cousin of G. and m G's sister Mary in 1831. Theirs was one of the largest building and contractors' businesses in Britain. Works included Severn navigation improvements, the GWR including Hanwell vdt, much of the SER under Joseph Cubitt (qv) and many public buildings including the Nelson column and Houses of Parliament. Became AICE 7.3.1843. High Sheriff of Surrey 1854–5.
Min Proc ICE V 39 1874–5 pp 289–90

GROVE, Sir George

b Clapham, London, 13.8.1820; d London 28.5.1900 aged 79.

Civil eng. Ed Clapham Gr Sch. In 1.1836

articled to Alexander Gordon, civil eng,
London. Admitted as graduate ICE 1839.
In 2.1840 went to Glasgow to gain
experience with Robert Napier. 1841 app
res eng on const of Morant Point lighthouse, Jamaica. Returned 1846 and
worked under Robert Stephenson, supervising erection of Chester General
station. Later he moved to Bangor under
Edwin Clark (qv), res eng on the
Britannia bridge. After completion of
the bridge, in the depression following
the 'R Mania' when employment in R
work was difficult, G., always a keen
musician, became secretary of the Society
of Arts. His subsequent career was
almost entirely devoted to music. He
founded the Royal College of Music and
was its first director; but he is chiefly
remembered for his *Dictionary of Music
and Musicians*.
Graves, C. L. *Life of Sir George Grove*
1903

GZOWSKI, Sir Casimir Stanislaus

b St Petersburg 5.3.1813;
d Toronto 24.8.1898 aged 85.
Civil eng and R contractor in Canada.
Son of Stanislaus, Count Gzowski, a
Polish officer in the Imperial Russian
Guard. Studied military engg in Russia
and entered the Russian army. In 11.
1830 he joined the Poles in the expulsion
of Constantine from Warsaw, but was
wounded, captured, imprisoned and
exiled. In 1833 arrived in New York.
1839 m Maria Beebe, dr of an American
physician, and they had 5 sons and 3 drs.
Lived in USA until 1841 when he moved
to Toronto and was employed in the
Canadian dept of public works. Left
govt service in 1848. 1853 established
the firm of Gzowski & Co and obtained
the contract for const of the Grand
Trunk R from Toronto to Sarnia, 172
miles (277km), completed in 1859. In
1871–3 he built the international bridge
at Niagara. Created KCMG 1890. G.
was the first president of the Canadian
Soc of Civil Engs.
Canadian Who was Who V 2; *Dict of
Canadian Biog*; Kos–Rabcewicz–Zubhow-
ski, L., and Greening, W. E., *Sir Casimir
Stanislaus Gzowski: a biography* Toronto
1959

HACKWORTH, John Wesley

b Walbottle, Co Durham, 8.5.1820;
d Sunderland 13.7.1891 aged 71.
Loco eng. Eldest son of Timothy H. (qv).
Trained as mech eng under his f. In
11.1836, when still only 16, he went to
Russia with a 2–2–2 loco built by his f
and at Tsarskoe Selo was introduced to
Tsar Nicholas. At age 20 he m and
settled at Shildon where he became wks
mgr at his f's Soho wks. In 1849 worked
with his f on the 2–2–2 *Sanspareil* (No
2), the last H. loco. Shortly after the
death of his f in 1850 he moved to
Darlington where he took premises in
Priestgate and began making stationary
engines and machinery. In 1854 he
patented a hoisting machine. 1857
patented an improvement to blast furnaces. In 10.1859 he patented his variable expansion radial valve gear for
locos, deriving its motion from a single
eccentric or crank. At the great exhibition in 1862 he exhibited a high pressure
horizontal engine incorporating the new
radial valve gear and the 'pass-over'
slide valve patented with his f in 1849
and used on *Sanspareil*. This led to
orders from Egypt, and H. began the
mfr of cotton machinery for Egypt.
From the proceeds H. built a new wks
at Bank Top, Darlington, but the
Egyptian business collapsed and he was
left in financial difficulties. Like his f
he also built colliery winding machines.
He gave up the Darlington wks about
1871 and visited USA and Canada to
introduce his valve gear. The only record
of its use, however, was on a loco of
the Hudson River RR in 1873. In 1874,
while still in USA, he obtained a patent
for metallic packing. Returned to
England in 1875 and began practice as
a consulting eng in Darlington, later
moving to Sunderland and then to
London. He devised a scheme for better
ventilation of mines. His patent for the
radial valve gear was amended in 1876,
1882 and 1886. Unfortunately H. lacked
business acumen and never achieved a
position merited by his abilities. Also
he was not helped by his impatience and
bad temper. In his later years he devoted
much time to lecturing and writing on
loco history and in trying to establish
his f's merits.

Young, Robert, *Timothy Tackworth and the Locomotive* 1923, 1975; *The Eng* V 4 14.8.1857

HACKWORTH, Timothy

b Wylam, Northumberland, 22.12.1886; d Shildon, Co Durham, 7.7.1850 aged 63. Pioneer of steam locos. Eldest son of John H. who, from 1782 until he d in 1802, was foreman blacksmith at Wylam colliery. Ed at Wylam village school and at age 14 began training under his f. From 1802 his training was supervised by Christopher Blackett (proprietor of the colliery) and in 1807 he became foreman smith, remaining at Wylam until 1816. During this period he was concerned in the design and const of the early locos built at Wylam (see Jonathan Foster and William Hedley). In 1813 he m Jane Golightly at Ovingham. Both were ardent Methodists, H. becoming a lay preacher. In 1816 he moved to Walbottle colliery nr Newcastle as foreman smith. On the opening of the Forth Street wks of Robert Stephenson & Co at Newcastle in 1824 H. was asked to supervise the wks during the absence of George Stephenson on the Liverpool & Manchester R and of Robert in S America. Reluctantly H. agreed, and so he came to supervise the const of the first locos at the wks. Thus it was H. who suggested coupling the wheels of S & D locos No 1 *Locomotion* and its 3 successors with outside rods and return cranks instead of chains. He declined to take a share in the wks, and in 1825 he was app to the S & DR to take charge of locos and machinery. He established his hq at New Shildon. He first built the stationary winding engines for the Brusselton and Etherley inclines. In 1827 he built the first 6-coupled loco, *Royal George*, at Shildon. It was also the first loco on which the cyls drove directly onto the wheels, and it was the first completely reliable loco on the S & DR. Learning of the forthcoming Rainhill trials on the Liverpool & Manchester R in 1829 he designed and built a light 0-4-0 named *Sanspareil*, again with vertical cyls driving directly onto the rear wheels, and with a return-flue boiler. It had to be withdrawn from the competition because of a cracked cyl casting (the cyls had been cast at Robert Stephenson & Co.), but when repaired the engine worked on the Bolton & Leigh R until 1844. It was then used at Coppull colliery nr Chorley (see Daglish) for driving a pump, and for light winding, until 1863. After overhaul and restoration it was presented to the Science Museum, London, by John Hick (qv) of Bolton. In 1829 H. designed coal staithes on the Tees at the new town of Middlesbrough. To carry the S & D Middlesbrough extn across the Tees H. designed a plate-girder bridge, then a completely new idea. Despite thorough testing in model form the design was rejected by the dirs who adopted a suspension bridge designed by Capt Samuel Brown RN (1776–1852), erected in 1830. As H. predicted, it was a failure, and its replacement by Robert Stephenson's cast iron bridge in 1842 was also unsatisfactory (see J. Harris). H's next loco was the 'Wilberforce' class 0-6-0 of which 6 were built in 1831-2. They had vertical cyls at the rear driving cranks on a fixed shaft connected to the wheels by coupling rods, so allowing all axles to be sprung. They had 'return multitubular fire-tube' boilers with a heating surface of about 500sq ft (46.45m²), compared with a c 50sq ft (4.65m²) on *Locomotion*. In 1833 he entered into a new contract with the S & D in which he became responsible for the working of the locos and workshops but remained free to operate his own business as a builder of locos and stationary engines. He opened new workshops, foundry and built houses for workers, and put his bro Thomas in charge of the new wks. Thomas remained there until 1840. Throughout this period from 1827 H. was studying the use of steam expansively, providing lap on all his slide valves. In 1835 he built a new engine for the Black Boy incline, with a cylinder 40in (1016mm) diam x 30in (762mm) stroke, using a 'double trunk' principle in which the connecting rod was pivoted at the piston and worked inside a large tubular piston rod. It was in use until 1874. In 1836 he built a 2-2-2 loco for the Russian govt using the same 'double trunk' principle. It was taken to Russia by H's son John (qv). In 1838 he introduced an improved type of 0-6-0 in which inclined cylinders at the rear drove the front coupled wheels by long connecting rods. One of these type, the *Derwent* built by Kitching of Darlington in 1845, is preserved at Darlington. However, 3 0–6–0s built by H. in 1838 for the Albion Coal Mining Co in Nova Scotia, reverted to the earlier design with vertical cylinders over the rear wheels. One of these, *Samson*, is preserved at New Glasgow, Nova Scotia. In 1840 H. gave up the S & D contract and concentrated on his own Soho engg wks at Shildon where he built locos, stationary engines and boilers. His son John became wks mgr. His last engines for the S & D were 2 0–6–0s, similar to *Derwent*, built in 1842. In 1846 he began an order for 12 2–2–2s for the London & Brighton R (later LBSCR) to a design by John Gray (qv) who, however, made so many alterations to the design that the final delivery time passed before the order could be completed. As a result Gray was dismissed. H's last loco was the 2–2–2 *Sanspareil* (No 2) to his own design embodying all his experience. It was purchased by the York, Newcastle & Berwick R in 1854, becoming No 135, and gave excellent service, running at speeds up to 75mph with trains heavy for the period. It was broken up in 1881. H. has an assured place in loco history as the first to establish the steam loco as a thoroughly reliable machine. Throughout his 25 yrs at Shildon H. took an active interest in the welfare of his employees and their families. Through his efforts a Methodist chapel was built at Shildon in 1829. His wife survived him by 2 yrs, dying in 1852. In 1975, as part of the S & D 250th anniversary celebrations, H's house at Shildon was restored and made into a museum.

Young, Robert, *Timothy Hackworth and the Locomotive* 1923, 1975

HARGREAVES, John

b Bolton 22.10.1800; d Sunning Hill, Berks, 18.12.1874 aged 74.
Earl R operator and mfr. Son of John H. (1780–1860), carrier of Bolton. In 1831 took over the working of the Bolton & Leigh and Leigh & Kenyon Jn Rs, operating locos and rolling stock. On 19.2.1841 became carrier on the Bolton & Preston R and about the same time took charge of traffic on the Lancashire & Preston Jn R. Continued his carrying trade until 31.12.1845 by which time the Bolton–Kenyon R had been absorbed, with the Liverpool & Manchester, into the Grand Junction R. From 1840–3 he was chairman of the Bolton & Preston R. In 1845 he joined his younger bro William (qv) and John Hick (qv) in the firm of Hick Hargreaves, Bolton, mfrs of locos and R equipment. He also operated some collieries and cotton mills.
Local records at Bolton.

HARGREAVES, William

b Westhoughton nr Bolton, 27.11.1821; d Bolton 1.10.1889 aged 67
Mfr of locos and equipment. Youngest son of John H. (1780–1860) and bro of John H. (qv). In 1845 he joined John Hick (qv) to form the firm of Hick Hargreaves, Bolton, where he was in charge until 1889. For the activities of the first see Hick. He m Catherine Withington Mallet who d 1873 aged 52. He was a JP for Bolton.
Local records at Bolton.

HARRIS, John

b in Cumberland 16.7.1812; d Kendal 20.7.1869 aged 57.
Civil eng, Stockton & Darlington R. After completing pupilage with Thomas Storey, a civil and mining eng at St Helens Auckland, Durham, he became eng to the Stockton & Darlington R on p w and works, including Middlesbrough dock, staithes and R approaches; a bridge over the Tees to replace Hackworth's suspension bridge; the Middlesbrough–Redcar R, op 4.6.1846 and the extn of the Wear Valley R from Crook to Waskerley, op 16.5.1845. H. was one of the first to recommend adoption of wooden sleepers in place of stone blocks, in 1839. In 1844 H. became contractor for p w maintenance on the S & D. Was res eng on Wakefield, Pontefract & Goole R (LYR) op 29.3.1848 and branches; and on the Kendal & Windermere R op 22.9.1846. He was also contractor for const of the Middlesbrough & Guisborough R, op 11.11.1853, the S & D Stanley branch; and a large bridge over the Wear near Witton for the S & D. Became MICE 6.4.1841.
Min Proc ICE V 31 1870–1 pp 219–20

HARRISON, Charles Augustus

b Vizianagram, Madras, 27.3.1848;
d Hexham, Northumberland 28.10.1916
aged 68.
Chief eng, N div, NER. Ed Marlborough
Coll. 1867 became pupil of Robert
Hodgson on the NER. He was then app
res eng in charge of dock works at
Hartlepool, and later on R works. In
1888, on the death of his uncle T. E.
Harrison (qv) he was app eng to the N
div of the NER, continuing in that
position until 1914. From 1908 to his
death he was consulting eng to the
NER. During his period on the N div he
carried out extensive works to provide
and to extend R and shipping facilities
for mineral traffic in Northumberland
and Durham, including Dunston and
North Blyth staithes and the Annfield–
Pelton branch, op 13.11.1893, the
Seaham–Hartlepool line, op 1.4.1905 and
the Ponteland branch, op 1.3.1905. His
most notable works were the King
Edward VII bridge at Newcastle (1902–
6) and the Queen Alexandra bridge
over the Wear near Sunderland, completed 1909. He was also responsible for
the alterations and 3rd rail equipment
for the Tyneside electrification in 1904.
In 1906 he received an hon DSc from
Durham Univ. Elected MICE 10.4.1877.
Min Proc ICE V 203 1916–17 p 419

HARRISON, George

b Liverpool 4.6.1815; d London 2.6.1875
aged 60.
Apprenticed at Mather, Dixon & Co,
Liverpool, and Jones at Newton le
Willows. On the opening of the Paris &
Rouen R in 1843 he was app loco supt.
Later he was app loco C & W supt on
the Orleans & Bordeaux R until the
revolution of 1848 compelled him to
return to England. He became loco supt
of the Scottish Central R and of associated lines in Scotland. In 1853 he was
consulted by Peto, Brassey & Betts
concerning const of locos for the Grand
Trunk R in Canada. Following his report
on a visit to Canada it was decided to
establish works in England for building
locos and wrought iron bridges. So H.
established the Canada Works at
Birkenhead and remained connected
with it until his death. The works built

Robert Stephenson's tubular bridge over
the St Lawrence at Montreal and, following completion of the GTR, the works
supplied material for Rs in Britain,
France, Spain, Italy, Portugal, USA,
India, Australia and other parts of the
world. For a period H. was mgr of the
Millwall Ironworks of William Fairbairn
(qv) nr London, and of the Humber
Ironworks at Hull. Elected MICE
18.5.1852; MIME 1856.
Min Proc ICE V 43 1875–6 p 303; Proc
IME 1876 p 21

HARRISON, John Atkinson

b Gateshead 10.10.1816; d Wylam,
Northumberland, 14.2.1880 aged 63.
Ed Morpeth Gr Sch. Articled to R & W
Hawthorn of Newcastle, serving apprenticeship in the shops and drg office. 1845
entered the office of Robert Nicholson
until the death of the latter in 1855. He
then worked on parliamentary surveys in Northumberland, Durham and
Yorkshire for the Border Counties and
the Blyth & Tyne Rs, and was app res
eng of the Morpeth branch of the Blyth
& Tyne R in 1856. From 1858 H. was
constantly involved in parliamentary
battles between the CR and NBR which
ended in the building of the Border
Union and Border Counties extns of the
NBR. In 1859 he was app res eng on the
3 heaviest contracts of the Border Union
R, from Hawick up to and including
Whitrope tunnel, completed in 1863.
In 1870, after taking up private practice
in Newcastle, he became chief eng of
the Scotswood & Newburn R, taking
personal charge of the works for about
a year.
Min Proc ICE V 60 1879–80 pp 407–8

HARRISON, Joseph Jr

b Philadelphia Pa 20.9.1810;
d Philadelphia 27.3.1874 aged 63.
Mech eng. After little formal ed apprenticed 1825 to Frederick D. Sanno, builder
of steam engines. Sanno failed, and H.
was then apprenticed to James Flint. His
loco work began in 1834 when he
obtained employment with William
Norris (qv), then engaged with Stephen
H. Long (qv) in building locos of Long's
design. 1835 became foreman at Garrett
& Eastwick, Philadelphia, who had just
begun mfr of locos. He was entrusted

with the design of the *Samuel D. Ingham* loco, the success of which led to the const of others of the same design. In 1837 H. became a partner in the firm of Garrett, Eastwick & Co. In 1839 G. retired and the firm became Eastwick & Harrison. In 1838 they were the first to establish the standard American 4–4–0 with 'three-point suspension', patented by Harrison in 1839. Locos of this type rapidly became universal throughout America. In 1839 they built the 4–4–0 *Gowan & Marx*, weighing just over 11 tons, which pulled 101 loaded coal cars on the Philadelphia & Reading RR. This achievement attracted the notice of the engs of the St Petersburg & Moscow R and resulted in H. going to St Petersburg in 1843 where, in connection with Thomas Winans (qv) of Baltimore, he carried out a contract for 162 locos and for iron bogies for 2500 freight cars. In 1844 E & H closed their Philadelphia plant and removed some of their equipment to St Petersburg where the firm of Harrison, Winans & Eastwick completed the contract in 1851. Eastwick and Winans remained in Russia to carry out further contracts, but H. returned to Philadelphia. In 1859 he patented a new boiler and in 1862 set up a wks for its mfr. On 15.12.1836 he m Sarah Poulterer of New York. They had 7 children.
Engg V 17 15.5.1874 p 349; DAB V 8 pp 345–6; Reed, Brian, *Loco Profile No 4, The American 4–4–0*; White, John H. Jr, *American locos, an engg history 1830–80* 1968

HARRISON, Thomas Elliott

b Fulham, London, 4.4.1808;
d Whitburn nr Sunderland 20.3.1888
aged nearly 80.
Chief eng, NER. Son of William H. of Somerset House, London. The family soon moved to Sunderland where William H. began a business as ship builder and also promoted several local Rs for coal and lime. T.E.H. was ed at Houghton-le-Spring Gr Sch, Co Durham. At 16 he began an apprenticeship with William Chapman, civil eng, gaining experience in dock construction. After a disappointing introduction to Telford in 1829 he became acquainted with Robert Stephenson with whom, in 1830 and 1831, he was employed in preparing

plans and sections of the Wolverton–Rugby section of the London & Birmingham R. He next became eng of the Stanhope & Tyne R of which he supervised the entire const, with its many inclined planes. It was completed in 1834. He was then engaged on the const of the R between Penshaw and Usworth, including the great Victoria bridge over the Wear in masonry with a central arch span of 160ft (48.77m) at a height of 170ft (51.82m) above foundations, opened in 1838. He continued the line from Darlington to Penshaw forming the last link between London and Newcastle. In 1845–9 he built the Newcastle–Berwick line in association with Robert Stephenson. On the opening to Berwick in 1849 H. was app chief eng of the York, Newcastle & Berwick R. During this period he built the Berwick–Kelso and Durham–Bishop Auckland Rs. In 1852 H. took a leading part in negotiations for bringing about a union between the York, Newcastle & Berwick, York & N Midland and Leeds Northern Rs which resulted in the formation of the NER in 1854, H. becoming chief eng. In 1855–9 he built the Tyne dock at South Shields. He then engineered the line from Doncaster to Hull including the swing bridge over the Ouse at Goole, completed in 1869. In 1870–1 he built a similar bridge over the Ouse at Naburn near York on the line from Selby to York, and at the time of his death he was designing a third swing bridge to be built at Selby. One of his most outstanding achievements was York station, completed in 1877, with its magnificent curving roof. He was responsible for many other NER lines, his last being the Alnwick–Coldstream, 34 miles (54.7km) op 1887. In addition to these Rs he built docks at Hartlepool and Middlesbrough and prepared a report on deepening and improving the entrance to Tyne dock. Became MICE 1834 and president 1873; MIME 1858.
Proc IME 5.1888 p 261; Min Proc ICE V 94 1887–9 pp 301–13; Tomlinson, W. W., *The North Eastern R* 1914, 1967

HARTLEY, Jesse

b nr Pontefract, Yorkshire, (?).(?).1780;
d Bootlemarsh, Liverpool, 24.8.1860
aged 80.

Civil eng, bridge and dock builder excelling in massive masonry. Son of Hugh H., bridge master in the Pontefract district. After apprenticeship to a mason he succeeded his f as bridge master and soon displayed a natural bent towards engg. 1811–12 went to Ireland for the Duke of Devonshire to complete the bridge at Dungarvon. Later became bridge master to Salford Hundred. In 1824 app surveyor to Liverpool dock trustees. H. was responsible for const of docks and warehouses from Princes to Canada in the north and Canning, Wapping, Coburg and Brunswick docks to the south. In 2.1882 he was app to succeed Alexander Nimmo as eng of the Manchester & Bolton R, completed in 1838. H. was one of the old school of practical engs, largely self taught, of simple life and manners, tremendously strong and fit and devoted to his work.

Min Proc ICE V 33 1871–2 p 219; *Liverpool Daily Post* 25.8.1860; *Liverpool Mercury* 25.8.1860; *Times* 25.8.1860

HASLETT, Charles Aaron

b Hallowell, Maine, USA (?).(?).1822; d San Francisco (?).6.1872 aged 50.
Studied engg at Cambridge, Mass, about 1848, took up R surveying, and compiled *The Engineer's Pocket Field Book*, much used by R engs in USA and Canada. H. established the American system of laying out curves. After this his services were widely sought. He worked on the Intercolonial in Canada; the São Paulo R in Brazil where he was employed under James Brunlees (qv) on the famous inclines; the Mugi vdt (Brunlees); Virginian Central; Union Pacific and Western Pacific RRs. In 1872 H. became chief of surveying staff on the Southern Pacific in California where he suddenly d. Became AICE 1865.

Min Proc ICE V 36 1872–3 pp 293–4

HASWELL, John

b Lancefield nr Glasgow (?).(?).1812; d Vienna 8.6.1897 aged 85.
Loco eng. Mgr of the first loco wks in Austria. After graduating at Andersonian Univ, Glasgow, in 1834 he was employed at William Fairbairn & Co, Manchester. Went to Vienna to erect locos for one of the first Rs in Austria

and, on their completion, the chairman of the company asked him to remain in Vienna. 1837 planned and equipped a loco repairing wks on the Vienna Glognitzer R. On completion of the wks he was asked to remain as chief eng. He soon began loco mfr, building some of the first locos on the European continent. He remained head of the wks until 1882. He set up the first iron foundry in Vienna and built a hydraulic forging press used in making loco wheels etc. In 1851 he produced the *Vindebona* for the Semmering trials, the first 8-coupled engine in Europe. He introduced the Stephenson link motion and many ideas of his own, including rudimentary form of the Belpaire firebox, thermic syphons and counter-pressure braking. The *Wien Raab* of 1855, a large long-boiler 0–8–0 with all parts accessible, was the pattern for European heavy freight locos for many years. The *Duplex* of 1861 was one of the first 4-cyl locos. H. was the first inventor of the corrugated firebox used in 1870 on the Austrian State Rs. His wks also produced the first R carriages and post office carriages in Austria. He also took responsibility for the ed of the whole of his staff. He received two orders of knighthood from the Emperor of Austria.

The Eng V 84 9.7.1897 pp 31–2 (portrait)

HAUPT, Herman

b Philadelphia, Pa, 26.3.1817; d Jersey City, NJ 14.12.1905 aged 88.
Civil eng, inventor. Graduated at US Military Academy 1.7.1835 but resigned commission after 3 months to become asst eng on survey of a R from Norristown to Allentown, Pa. 1836 app principal asst eng in Pennsylvania state service and continued in R surveys. In 1840 while on the const of the York & Wrightsville RR he began the study of bridge const and pub a pamphlet on the subject. 1845–7 prof of maths at Pennsylvania Coll, Gettysburg, and wrote his *General Theory of Bridge Construction* pub 1851. 1847 app principal asst eng on const of the Pennsylvania RR and on 1.9.1849 became supt of transportation and evolved a system of organisation for the PRR. From 31.12.1850–1.11.1852 he was gen supt of the road,

then becoming chief eng until the opening of the whole line to Pittsburgh including the section through the Allegheny Mountain tunnel. In 1855 he was asked to examine the Hoosac tunnel project on the Troy & Greenfield RR, Mass, and his favourable report led to his app to supervise const. In 1856 he left the PRR to carry out the tunnel which, after immense difficulties, was opened on 9.2.1875. In 1858 he developed a pneumatic drill better than any other in use. During the civil war in 1862–3 he was app chief of const and transportation on USA military RRs. In 1867 he visited Europe to explain his system of tunnelling machinery. 1870 app chief eng of the Shenandoah Valley RR. 1872–6 he was g mgr of the Richmond & Danville RR. 1876 app by Pennsylvania Transportation Co to const a pipeline to convey crude petroleum from the Allegheny Valley to the tidewater. 1881–4 he was g mgr of the Northern Pacific RR when he saw its completion to the Pacific. 1886–8 he was president of the Dakota & Great Southern RR. 1892–1905 president of Compressed Air & Power Co. His published works include: *Military Bridges* 1864; *Tunelling by Machinery* 1876; *Street Railway Motors* 1893. In 1838 he m Ann Cecilia Keller of Gettysburg, Pa. They had 11 children. He d of heart failure in a train while travelling to his home in Washington DC.
DAB V 8 p 400; *RR Gazette* 22.12.1905

HAWKSHAW, Sir John

b nr Leeds (?).(?).1811; d London 2.6.1891 aged 80.
Civil eng on LYR, E. London R, Severn Tunnel and many other bridges, viaducts and tunnels. Son of Henry H., farmer. Ed Leeds Gr Sch but left early to train with Charles Fowler, road builder, working on the Leeds–Whitehall, Leeds–Heckmondwike, and Dewsbury–Batley roads. Before he was 20 H. had become asst to Alexander Nimmo (qv), then engaged on piers, harbours and other public works in Ireland. In 1830–2 he and Nimmo surveyed the Manchester, Bolton & Bury canal with a view to converting it to a R. After the death of Nimmo in 7.1832 H. took charge of the works of the Bolivar Mining Association

in Venezuela, about 200 miles (322km) from Caracas, remaining there nearly 3 years. Life was hard and unhealthy and many of the men died. Ill health compelled H. to return to England in 1834. (See Hawkshaw, J., *Reminiscences of South America* 1838.) For a period he was engaged by Jesse Hartley (qv) on the Liverpool docks. He then worked with James Walker (qv) laying out the Leipzig & Dresden R. During this period he m the dr of Rev James Jackson of Green Hammerton, Yorks. In 1836 H. took charge, as res eng under Jesse Hartley, of the const of the Manchester & Bolton R which he completed in 5.1838. Also in 1838 H. was engaged with Nicholas Wood (qv) to examine the gauge question in Britain, deciding against Brunel's 7ft (2.134m) gauge on the grounds of inconvenience. He strongly opposed breaks of gauge. In 1845 H. was app chief eng of the Manchester & Leeds R (Lancashire & Yorkshire R from 1847) in succession to Thomas Gooch (qv) and was responsible for the const of many miles of R in Yorkshire in 1850–2, chiefly the West Riding Union lines to Halifax and Bradford, the Leeds, Bradford & Halifax Jn (GNR) and the Huddersfield–Penistone lines. The last included immense viaducts at Lockwood and Penistone and a huge timber trestle at Denby Dale, as well as 6 tunnels totalling 3427yd (3134m). He erected another timber trestle on the Holmfirth branch. Other lines included the Wakefield–Barnsley (1850), Liverpool Exchange station extn (1850), Miles Platting–Stalybridge (1846) and Fleetwood dock (1873–7). H. was one of the first engs to lay out lines for locomotives with gradients as steep as 1 in 50. In 1850 H. moved to Westminster and set up in private practice, at first alone and from 1870 in partnership with his son J.C.H. and his former chief asst Harrison Hayter (qv), but he retained his connection with the LYR as consulting eng until 1888. 1861–81 also consulting eng to the SER, responsible for the bridge over the Thames ino Charing Cross station. In 1865 app eng to the E London R, opened in 1869 to Wapping and in 1876 to the GER, adapting Marc Brunel's tunnel for R use and extending the tunnel beneath the Shadwell basin,

London docks and the Blackwall R vdt. In 1879–84, in conjunction with J. Wolfe Barry (qv) he was eng to the Jt Committee of the Inner Circle Completion R, London, connecting the District R at Mansion House with the Metropolitan R at Aldgate. 1853–7 H. was eng of the Staines–Wokingham (LSWR) line, op 9.7.1856, including the Thames bridge at Staines. 1872–86 jt eng with Sir James Brunlees (qv) on the original Channel Tunnel project. H. was the first to establish the practicability of a tunnel between England and France and all subsequent projects have been based on his pioneering work. However, he decided to withdraw from the scheme following a change of opinion concerning its desirability on grounds of defence. H. was responsible for the const of many bridges including the opening South Bridge at Hull, Londonderry bridge (1862–4), and the Nerbudda bridge in India nearly 1 mile long. With W. H. Barlow (qv) H. completed Brunel's Clifton suspension bridge at Bristol using suspension chains from Brunel's Hungerford bridge over the Thames when that was demolished to make way for the Charing Cross R bridge. His greatest work was the Severn tunnel which H. took over in 1879 and carried through to completion in 1887 in the face of tremendous difficulties in conjunction with the contractor T. A. Walker (qv). In India H. was consulting eng to the Madras R from 1857–88, and E Bengal R until it was taken over by the Indian govt. Among canal projects, H. reported on the proposed Suez Canal in 1863 and on the Panama Canal. 1862 app eng to the Amsterdam Ship Canal, op 1.11.1876. He also completed Holyhead harbour after the death of Rendel (qv) in 1856, and on its completion he was knighted in 1873. H. was also connected with the Mauritius R; Albert Dock, Hull; East & West India Docks, London; foundations of forts at Spithead; the São Paulo R, Brazil; and Dublin water supply. His last job for the LYR was Fleetwood dock, op 8.10.1877. Elected MICE 7.8.1838 and was president 1862–3. Also FRGS and FRS. 1875 president of the British Assoc. About 1880 he began to relax his exertions and on 31.12.1888 he definitely ret, leaving his business to his partners. H. was remarkable in being responsible for not only some of the most difficult engg works but also for a greater number of major projects than any other 19th century eng.
Min Proc ICE V 106 1891 pp 321–35; *Engg* 5.6.1891 p 679; Walker, T. A., *The Severn Tunnel, its construction and difficulties* 1891, 1969

HAWKSWORTH, Frederick William

b Swindon 10.2.1884; d Swindon 13.7.1976 aged 92.
GWR loco eng. Joined GWR as apprentice in 1898. App draughtsman 1905 in the period when Churchward (qv) was developing his range of standard locos. H. made the drawings of *The Great Bear*, Britain's first 'Pacific', built in 1908. In 6.1925 H. became chief draughtsman, and co-ordinated work on the 'King' class introduced in 1927. 1932 app asst to CME, C. B. Collett (qv), and later principal asst. He was instrumental in the modernising of the stationary loco testing plant at Swindon in the late 1930s and he established principles of loco testing which were adopted as BR standard from 1948. Became CME in 1941 following the ret of Collett. WW2 prevented const of the large 'Pacific' he had designed. He was much occupied in adapting pre-war GWR practice to wartime conditions, including modified frame const for 2-cyl locos and the introduction of high-degree superheating. He brought out a modified 'Hall' class 4-6-0 in 1944, with frames continued to the front and cyls bolted on. In 1945 he introduced the 'County' class 4-6-0 using a boiler similar to the Stanier 2-8-0s, many of which had been built at Swindon during the war. In other ways the 'Counties' were non-standard, expensive and unnecessary. He also introduced 3 new pannier tank designs, the 9400 class, a development of the 5700 class but with standard No 10 coned boiler in 1947 and of which No 3409 was the last engine to be built to a GWR design, in 1956; the 1500 class in 1949, an entirely new design with short wheelbase, outside cyls and Walschaert valve gear; and the 1600 class in 1949 to replace the earlier 2021 class. In 1946 he introduced the gas-turbine electric loco on the GWR for express

passenger trains, but work on these was stopped after nationalisation. From 1.1. 1948 he was CME of the Western Region of BR. He ret 12.1949 after over 50 yrs on the GWR. 1951–9 was chairman of Swindon Borough Magistrates, and in 1960 was made a freeman of the borough. He m in 1972.

RG 23.12.1949 pp 723, 739 (portrait); *The Times* 14.7.1976 p 16; *Daily Telegraph* 14.7.1976; SLS *Journal* 11.1976 pp 327–36; Cook, K. J., *Swindon Steam 1921–51* 1974; *The Locos of the GWR* (RCTS) Parts 5 1958 and 8 1953

HAWTHORN, Robert

b Dewley Burn, Walbottle, nr Newcastle upon Tyne 13.6.1796; d Newburn-on-Tyne 26.6.1867 aged 71. Founder of R & W Hawthorn, engine builders, Newcastle. Eldest son of Robert H., eng of Walbottle colliery for over 50 yrs. Ed local schools, and apprenticed at Walbottle colliery. In 1816, after constructing a small condensing engine at the colliery, H. erected a pumping engine at Brinkburn colliery. 1817 began mfr of steam engines and machinery at Newcastle. In 1818 his bro William (1799–1875) joined as asst foreman and in 1819 the wks were extended. In 1820 William H. became partner and the firm became R & W Hawthorn. Began loco building 1831. In 1832 h. invented a new slide rule for the use of engs. In 1834 they built the first Cornish pumping engine made in the district. In 1835 they applied fixed eccentrics on the *Comet* loco for the Newcastle & Carlisle R and used at the opening of the line. The invention soon became universal. Became MICE 13.2.1839; MIME 1848.

Proc IME 1868 p 15; Min Proc ICE V 27 1867–8 pp 590–2; *The Eng* V 134 14.7.1922 p 29

HAWTHORN, Thomas

b Newcastle upon Tyne 19.4.1838; d nr Lucerne, Switzerland, 18.8.1880 aged 42. Loco mfr. Son of Dr H. Ed Dr Bruce's Academy, Newcastle. Apprenticed as mech eng with Robert Stephenson & Co, Newcastle. 1861 became asst eng of docks and warehouses at Marseilles. 1865 returned to Newcastle and in conjunction with William Black (qv) estab-

lished a loco, marine and stationary engine wks at Gateshead under the title of Black, Hawthorn & Co. In 1867 they introduced an axle with lateral play for 6 or 8-coupled locos to ease passage of curves. H. became MIME 1880. At his d he was engaged on a street tramway loco. He was killed by a fall from the Stüsberg between Seilisberg and Beckenried on the Lake of Lucerne.

Proc IME 1.1881 p 4; *The Eng* V 50 1880 p 164.

HAY, David

b (?) 10.4.1859; d Hawkhurst, Kent, 30.10.1938 aged 79. Civil eng. 1877 became pupil of his f. Later became contractor's eng on const of GNR/LNWR jt Rs from Newark to Tilton (1878–9) and Leicester (1882), a total of 44 miles (71km). 1884–5 worked on a new dock at Silloth, Cumberland, after which he spent 3 yrs on the widening of the NER lines around Newcastle upon Tyne. 1888 went to London to become contractor's eng on the completion of the City & S London tube R from Elephant & Castle to King William Street in the City and the extn to Stockwell, op 18.12.1890. Later responsible for widening GNR nr Grantham, 1892 became senior res eng on const of Blackwall tunnel for the London County Council. H. then entered into partnership with Sir Benjamin Baker (qv) and Mr (later Sir) Basil Mott, the firm later becoming Mott, Hay & Anderson. Among other works carried out by Hay were reconstruction of the City & S London R, 1920–4, and its extn from Clapham Common to Morden, 1924–6; improvement of the Central London tube R; and const of 13 bridges on the Liverpool–East Lancashire Road. *Journal* ICE V 11 1938–9 p 620

HAYTER, Harrison

b nr Falmouth 10.4.1825; d Kensington, London 5.5.1898 aged 73. Civil eng. Ed eng dept, King's Coll, London 1839–41; then served under John Harris (qv), eng of Stockton & Darlington R, working on the Middlesbrough–Redcar extn, op 4.6.1846. He then worked for 4 yrs on the GNR under Joseph Cubbitt (qv); later on Dover harbour works under James Walker (qv).

He next worked under Rendel (qv) at Inverness and Holyhead where he remained 3½ yrs as asst eng on the harbour works. On the death of Rendel in 1856 Hawshaw (qv) was app eng of the harbour works and invited H. to become his chief asst at Westminster. From then on H. was associated with Hawkshaw and his son John Clarke Hawkshaw, first as chief asst and from 1870 as partner until Sir John ret in 1888. H. then continued in partnership with J. C. Hawkshaw. During these years H. took an active part in designs, estimates, specifications and parliamentary work carried out under Hawkshaw or partners, including much of the LYR, E London R, S Dock and warehouses for the E & W India Docks Co, Millwall Extn R; Penarth docks; Granville dock, Dover; Maryport docks; Inner Circle line of the Metropolitan and District Rs between Mansion House and Aldgate, op 1884, in conj with Sir John Wolfe Barry (qv); bridges and Rs into Charing Cross and Canon Street, London; Severn tunnel; Staines & Wokingham R, op 1856, and various other dock and bridge works. Abroad he built the West of India Portuguese Guaranteed R; Nerbudda bridge on the Bombay, Baroda & Central India R; Amsterdam Ship Canal; Riga & Dünaburg and Dünaburg & Witepsk Rs in Russia, and Rs in Spain, Australia, Mauritius and Jamaica. He visited many countries to report on Rs and harbours. He was app consulting eng to the Madras R after the ret of Hawkshaw and he designed several bridges for the R. Elected MICE 5.1862 and president 1892-3.
Min Proc ICE V 134 1897-8 pp 391-4; *Engg* V 65 13.5.1898 p 604; *The Eng* V 85 13.5.1898

HEDLEY, William

b Newburn-on-Tyne 13.7.1779; d nr Lanchester, Co Durham, 9.1.1843 aged 63.
Inventor & mech eng. Ed at Wylam. When only 21 app viewer at Walbottle colliery nr Newcastle, and later at Wylam colliery where, in 1811, he assisted T. Hackworth (qv) and Jonathan Foster (qv) in the const of the first loco to be built entirely at Wylam. Two more were built in 1814-15: *Puffing*

Billy now preserved at the Science Museum, London, and *Wylam Dilly* now in Edinburgh Museum. H. was one of the first to argue that a loco with smooth wheels would obtain sufficient adhesion and that the rack used by Blenkinsop (qv) was unnecessary. On 13.3.1813 took out a patent for a smooth wheel and rail system, although the principle had been used by R. Trevithick (qv) in 1804. H. was one of several engs credited with the first use of the 'steam blast'. In 1824 he took over Crow Tees colliery nr Durham and later Callerton colliery nr Wylam. 1828 moved to Shield Row where he rented the South Moor colliery. Warren, J. G. H., *A Century of locomotive building* 1923, 1970; Jeans, J. S., *Jubilee Memorial of the R System* 1875, 1975

HELLWAG, Wilhelm Konrad

b Eutin, Grossherzogtum Oldenburg, 18.9.1827; d Vienna 5.1.1882 aged 54.
Eng on the S Gotthard R. Studied at Kiel Univ. In 1848 was officer in war against Denmark. 1851 continued studies at Kiel and then Munich Polytechnic. His first R work was on the Swiss Central R. In 1857 he was app under Etzel (qv) on the Franz Josef Orient R in Hungary as div eng. He then moved to Vienna with Etzel and in 1861 to Innsbruck to supervise const of the Brenner R, op 24.8.1867. On its completion he moved to Vienna as chief eng of the Nordwestbahn. In 1875 he was app an eng on the St Gotthard R. During location of the ramps to the main tunnel he was in conflict with the management and resigned. He then became a R contractor in Austria. He was very active in literary work and pub several technical books and papers.
Röll V 4 p 1998

HELMHOLTZ, Dr Richard von

b Königsberg, Prussia, 28.9.1852; d Munich 10.9.1934 aged 82
German loco eng. Apprenticed at Borsig Loco Wks, Berlin, and completed his studies at the tech high schools at Stuttgart and Munich. 1881 entered Krauss wks (later Krauss-Maffei Loco Wks) at Munich, and in 1884 was made chief of the drg office until his ret in 1917. 1884 const the straight-link modi-

fication of the Walschaert valve gear. 1888 pub a paper on const of non-articulated locos with 8 or more coupled wheels, which became the standard theoretical work on the subject. Also in 1888 the first loco was built using the Krauss-Helmholtz combination truck composed of a pony axle and a coupled axle. At the Nuremburg Exposition in 1894 his class AA1 single-wheeler loco of the Bavarian State R was displayed, incorporating his auxiliary booster. H. was also responsible for the design of many other locos built at the Krauss wks. In 1930, with Staby, he pub a history of the German steam loco, 1835–80, which became a standard work, and one of the greatest loco histories.
The Locomotive 10.1934 p 328

HENDERSON, Sir Brodie Haldine, KCMG, CB

b (?) 6.3.1869; d Braughing, Herts, 28.9.1936 aged 67.
Ed in Germany; at Owen's Coll, Manchester, and at King's Coll, London. At age 16 became pupil at Beyer Peacock & Co, Manchester, and later of James Livesey, during which time he acted as asst eng on const of the Bobadilla–Algerciras (Gibraltar) R, through hilly terrain, Later emp in the civil eng's dept of the LYR at Manchester. On 6.3.1891 entered into partnership with James Livesey and H. Livesey, forming the firm of Livesey, Son & Henderson, later Livesey & Henderson. Responsible for many R, dock and harbour works including the lower Zambesi bridge, one of the world's longest, and the summit tunnel on the Transandine R. In 1901 m Ella, dr of James Jones of Lechlade, Glos, and had 3 sons and 1 dr.
Journal ICE V 5 1936–7 p 239

HENNINGS, Dr Fritz

b Kiel, Germany, 15.12.1838; d Zurich 2.2.1922 aged 83.
One of Europe's most outstanding R civil engs. Ed 1851–6 at a local school. Studied engg 1856–9 at Hanover Polytechnic and from 1859 at the Zurich Tech High School where he received his diploma in 1861. His first R work was on the Zurich–Zug–Lucerne line. Experience gained here was valuable in

1864–5 when he worked on the preliminary survey of the St Gotthard R. He next worked on the Württemburg Schwarzwald R before going to Austria in 1870 where he worked until 1878 on the Kaschau–Oderberger, Salzburg–Tyrol and Rakonitz–Protiviner lines and the narrow-gauge Salzkammergut R. His competence resulted in his app as section eng at Faido on the S ramp of the St Gotthard R, 1879–83, responsible for surveying the spiral tunnels. Other work on Swiss Rs followed and in 1890 H. moved to N Germany where he worked with Robert Moser (qv), then chief eng of the Nordostbahn, on the Emmersberg tunnel at Schaffhausen. His greatest triumph was his laying out and building of the Albula section of the metre-gauge Rhaetian R between Thusis and St Moritz in Switzerland. Few Rs in Europe contain so many outstanding engg feats in such a distance. He was app chief eng in 1898, and in 1904 the R was completed to St Moritz. He also worked out the general project and estimates for the Inn Valley line of the Rhaetian R from Bever to Schuls, completed in 1905. From 1903–21 H. was prof of R bdg in the Federal Polytechnic at Zurich.
S Bz V 79 18.2.1922 pp 87–8; Marshall, John, *Metre Gauge Rs in S & E Switzerland* 1974

HICK, Benjamin

b Leeds (?).(?).1790; d Bolton 9.9.1842 aged 52.
Mech eng and mfr. Apprenticed at Fenton, Murray & Jackson, engine mfrs, Leeds. At early age he was entrusted with const of several large engines and was later offered a partnership which he declined. He left in 1810 to join the Rothwells (qv) at the Union Foundry, Bolton, which became Rothwell, Hick & Rothwell and later, after the death of Peter Rothwell senior in 1824, Rothwell, Hick & Co. In 12.1830 the firm completed its first loco, the *Union*, a vertical-boiler 2–2–0 for the Bolton & Leigh R (op 1828) of which H. was one of the promoters and original shareholders. (For further details of locos built by Rothwell see Rothwell.) In 1833 H. left to establish his own wks at the Soho Foundry, Bolton, with his sons John (qv) and Benjamin, as B. Hick & Sons.

Benjamin Jr left early to become a partner in a Liverpool firm and d shortly afterwards. About 1814 H. m Elizabeth Routledge. Following H's death John H. carried on the firm, as described under his name.

The Eng V 129 11.6.1920 p 598; various local records; Min Proc ICE V 2 1843 p 12

HICK, John

b Bolton 2.7.1815; d Bolton 2.2.1894 aged 78.

Loco mfr, later dir of LNWR. Eldest son of Benjamin H. (qv). Ed Bolton Gr Sch. On leaving sch joined his f and bro to form the firm of B. Hick & Sons, Soho Foundry, Bolton, in 1833. Their first loco, named *Soho*, was a 0-4-2 goods type built in 1834 for the Bolton, Leigh & Kenyon R. Engines were built for several Rs in England and Europe, including the Eastern Counties, London & Birmingham, Paris & Versailles, Midland Counties, Taff Vale, Edinburgh & Glasgow; and some Norris type 4-2-0s for the Birmingham & Gloucester R. Benjamin H. d in 1842 and John took over sole mgt of the firm. In 1844 he became a member of Bolton town council. In 1845 he took into partnership William Hargreaves (qv) and the firm became Hick, Hargreaves & Co. It still operates under the same title. Loco building ended in 1855. In 1846 H. m Margaret Bashall of Deane, Bolton. She d 1872. H. left the firm in 1868 when elected MP for Bolton. In 1874 he m the dr of Edmund Ashworth. About this time he became a dir of the LNWR. One of Webb's compounds (his worst design), 2-2-2-2 No 20 of 1894, was named John Hick. Became MICE 11.3.1845.

The Eng V 77 9.2.1894 p 120 (portrait); Min Proc ICE V 117 1893-4 p 379; *Bolton Chronicle* 3.2.1894 p 8; Proc IME 1894 p 161

HIGGINBOTHAM, Thomas

b Dublin (?).(?).1820; d Victoria, Australia, 5.9.1880 aged c 60

Left Ireland 1840 and entered office of Sir William Cubitt. Later became asst eng on the Ashford-Canterbury branch of the SER. He was next app res eng on the Huntingdon section of the GNR of which Cubitt was chief eng. After practising in London H. emigrated to Victoria in 1857 and at Melbourne was app chief eng of roads and bridges of the colony. In 1860 he was app chief eng of the Victorian Rs where he remained until 1.1878. 1879-80 worked in S Australia, Tasmania and New Zealand. In 3.1880 he returned to Victoria as chief R eng, remaining in this position until his sudden death, by which time the Rs of Victoria totalled 1182 miles, mostly built under H. to the Irish standard gauge of 5ft 3in (1.600m). H., however, was not responsible for introducing the 5ft 3in gauge to Victoria. The Melbourne & Hobson's Bay R, the first steam R in Australia, was opened to this gauge on 12.9.1854. H. was elected MICE 7.2.1854.

Min Proc ICE V 63 1880-1 pp 314-16

HILL, Alfred John

b Peterborough (?).(?).1862; d Bexhill, Sussex, 14.3.1927 aged 64.

CME of GER. Ed Waternewton Rectory, Northamptonshire. 1877 appreticed at the GER loco C & W wks at Stratford, London, first under William Adams (qv) and later Massey Bromley (qv). In 1882, in the year T. W. Worsdell (qv) became loco supt, GER, H. was transferred to the drg office. Obtained a Whitworth scholarship at the GER mechanics inst at Stratford. At the beginning of 1890 H. became asst wks mgr and in 1899 wks mgr. Following the abrupt resignation of S. D. Holden (qv) in 10.1912 H. was app loco C & W supt, his title becoming CME in 1915. After 35 yrs on the GER it was to be expected that H. would continue the traditions established by James Holden. At the same time he greatly increased the size and power of the locos. His first design was a large 0-4-0T shunter (LNER class Y4), 1913-21. In 1915 came the efficient 0-6-2T class L77 (LNER class N7) of which 22 were built, the last 10 after grouping in 1923. Next were 25 0-6-0s class T77 (LNER class J19) in 1916-20; 25 0-6-0s class D81 (LNER J20), 1920-2, on which he used the same boiler as on the 1500 class 4-6-0, producing the largest 0-6-0 in Britain. In 1922 came the splendid 'Super Claud' 4-4-0, the ultimate GER development of the 'Claud

Hamilton' type with large superheated Belpaire boiler. With their blue livery and shining brasswork they were regarded by many as the most handsome British 4-4-0s. In WW1 H. was active in various national services. 1917 visited USA on behalf of the British govt in connection with the supply of R materials. When the R workshops became involved in munition production H. became chairman of the southern group and later, when on the priority branch of the Ministry of Munitions, he represented the whole of British Rs. For these services he was awarded the CBE. Under H's supervision the Stratford wks were greatly extended. Bogie rolling stock, both for main line and surburban traffic, was standardised. Hill was president of the ILE in 1914–15, and from 1920 until his retirement acted as chairman of the C & W supts meetings at the RCH. Became MIME 1901, MICE 1910. At the ICE in 1895 he read a paper on 'Repairs and renewals of R rolling stock' which was awarded a Watt medal, a Crampton prize and a Telford premium. Another on 'The use of cast steel in locos' in 1887 was awarded the Miller prize. In 1892 he m Margaretta, dr of John Bressey of Bournemouth. H. was keenly interested in ambulance work and for many years was hon sec for the organisation of the many GER ambulance corps. He was also JP for West Ham, London. At the grouping on 1.1.1923. H. ret at the age of 60 and lived at Bexhill, Sussex where he was again made a JP. H. d suddenly on Bexhill golf links. His wife survived him. *Engg* V 123 18.3.1927 p 329; *The Eng* V 143 18.3.1927 p 302; *Proc IME* 5.1927 p 582; *Journal* ILE V 17 1927 p 283

HILL, James Jerome

b Rockwood, Ontario, 16.9.1838;
d St Paul, USA, 29.5.1916 aged 77.
Railroad promoter and financier. Ed Rockwood Academy. His f d in 1852 and H. began as a clerk in the village store. In 1856 he settled in St Paul, beginning as a clerk to a shipping line on the Mississippi. In 1865 he set up his own forwarding and transportation business and became agent of the St Paul & Pacific RR. Foreseeing that coal would replace wood as fuel for locos

he bought up local coal supplies and formed the North Western Fuel Co. In 1878, with 3 partners, H. bought the St Paul & Pacific RR which he rebuilt and extended, to the Canadian border (1878), and through Dakota and Montana to Great Falls (1887), and over the Cascades to the Pacific at Everett (1893), and Seattle. In 1879 the St P & P was reorganised as the St Paul, Minneapolis & Manitoba R. The need for further financing and extensions led to the creation of the Great Northern R Co in 1890. During 1891–1906 an average of 1 mile (1.6km) of R was built and equipped each working day. He was successively g mgr 1879–81, vice president 1881–2, president 1882–1907, and chairman of the bd 1907–12. His lines had no land grants, unlike other USA Rs of the period and thus were free of the ruinous concessions forced from other Rs. He built his Rs where he knew there would be traffic. He was instrumental in rescuing the Northern Pacific RR from receivership. With J. P. Morgan he bought about 97 per cent of the stock of the Chicago, Burlington & Quincy RR to ensure the entry of the GN and NP into Chicago and St Louis, and to thwart the efforts of E. H. Harriman (qv) who had been trying to gain control of the Burlington and with it an entrance to the North West. In 1905 the GN/NP interests were expanded by the const by them of the Portland & Seattle R (later Spokane, Portland & Seattle). In 1907 H. resigned the presidency of the GN and became chairman of the bd until 1912. H. also had great influence in the establishment of the CPR. He resigned from the CPR bd in 1883. His lifelong love of books led him to establish the Hill Reference Library in St Paul in 1912. On 19.8.1867 he m Mary Theresa Mehegan (d 22.11.1921) They had 7 sons and 3 drs.
DAB V 9 pp 36–41

HINKLEY, Holmes

b Hallowell, Maine, (?).(?).1793;
d (?) (?).(?).1866 aged c 73
Loco mfr. Worked as a carpenter until 1823, then began as a machinist in Boston. In 1831 opened a small machine shop in partnership with Gardner P. Drury and Daniel F. Child. Produced

his first loco in 1840, a 4–2–0. His wks soon became the largest loco mfrs in New England. During the mid 1850s H. was one of the major loco builders in USA, but production later fell rapidly and the wks closed in 1889. H. delegated design work to John Souther (qv), but the firm was never in the van with design because they favoured inside cylinders and other out-dated practices. White, John H. Jr *American locos, an engg history 1830–80* 1968

HOGG, Alexander Lauder

b Inverness 17.12.1845;
d Birmingham 17.10.1906 aged 60.
Civil eng, CPR. Ed Inverness Academy. Apprenticed to William Paterson, Inverness. After a brief spell on the CR he left for USA where he was res eng and chief eng on several R surveys and construction works in various states. In 1876 he took charge of the survey and const of the Midland Grand Trunk R of Canada. Later he was in charge of the Rocky Mountain and Eastern divs of the CPR on which he carried out the final location in the Mountain Div. He designed the snow sheds in the Selkirks. On completion of the CPR H. returned to England and became eng of the Birmingham Tramways Co. In 1885 he m the youngest dr of George Rhind, an Inverness architect. He became MICE on 6.4.1866.
Min Proc ICE V 167 1906–7 p 371

HOLCROFT, Harold

b Wolverhampton (?).(?).1882;
d Tadworth, Surrey, 15.2.1973 aged 91.
Loco eng, GWR and SE & CR. Apprenticed at the GWR wks at Wolverhampton 10.1898–1906. Transferred to drg office at Swindon under G. J. Churchward (qv), arriving in the midst of a period of very interesting design work. H. was responsible for the curved shaping at the ends of the footplating of the standard GWR locos and, in 1910, for the general design of the standard GWR 2–6–0, following a visit to USA in 1909. Also in 1910 he produced a design for the 1361 class 0–6–0 saddle tanks. In 1914 he was app chief loco draughtsman on the SE & CR at Ashford, Kent, under R. E. L. Maunsell (qv), taking up his new work on 1.5.1914.

While still at Swindon he devised a conjugated valve gear for 3-cyl engines which H. N. Gresley (qv) adopted, first on the GNR 3-cyl 2–6–0 class in 1920. Holcroft's arrangement was applied on the SE & CR N1 class 2–6–0 in 1922 and on the K1 class 2–6–4T in 1925. He was concerned in the rebuilding of the Wainwright D and E class 4–4–0s into the brilliantly successful D1 and E1 classes. In 1924 the CME's hq were transferred to Waterloo station, London, to where H. was moved in 8.1924. Here he was responsible for the adoption of the 135° crank setting on the 'Lord Nelson' class 4-cyl 4–6–0s introduced in 1926. He remained in the drg office after Maunsell's ret in 1937 and worked under Bulleid (qv) through WW2, retiring in 1945. He then became an author and pub *The Armstrongs of the Great Western* 1953; *An outline of Great Western Loco Practice* 1957. His autobiography *Locomotive Adventure* 1962 was followed by a second volume. He was survived by his 2 sons and 3 of his 4 drs. Was FIME.
SLS *Journal* 4.1973 p 102

HOLDEN, James

b Whitstable, Kent, 26.7.1837;
d Bath 29.5.1925 aged 87.
Loco eng, GER. His mother's sister, nee Fedarb, m Edward Fletcher (qv) while Fletcher was loco eng on the Canterbury & Whitstable R. Because of this relationship, on leaving school H. was apprenticed to Fletcher at the Gateshead wks of the York, Newcastle & Berwick R, later part of the NER. On leaving there he was mgr of an engg wks in Sunderland until 1865 when he began his R service in the C & W dept of the GWR, becoming successively supt of the wks at Shrewsbury and Chester. Later he was app mgr of the extensive C & W wks at Swindon and chief asst to William Dean (qv), the loco supt. While on the GWR H. was intimately concerned in the transformation from broad gauge to standard. When T. W. Worsdell left the GER to become loco supt of the NER at Gateshead in 1885 H. was app his successor as loco C & W supt at Stratford, London. There, despite the good work done in 3 years by Worsdell, H. found plenty of scope for his technical and organising

abilities. He probed into every detail of the department. He had the registers of locos and rolling stock overhauled until he was satisfied that they were absolutely dependable. He set about reducing the large number of different types of locos and effected interchangeability of parts among the survivors. By way of opposing an electrification scheme by a rival company in 1902 (because the GER could not afford electrification) he designed and built a huge 0–10–0T, the first 10-coupled engine in Britain, which could accelerate a train to 30mph (48km/h) in 30secs, Having established this ability, and defeated the electrification scheme, the engine was rebuilt into a 0–8–0 tender engine. He increased the seating capacity of the GER surburban coaches (but not the comfort of the passengers), making possible the famous 'jazz' service from Liverpool Street, London. He showed a sporting spirit, as well as organising ability when, on 10.12.1891, Stratford wks assembled 0–6–0 No 930 in 9hr 47min, a world record which was never beaten. The engine was painted and steamed immediately and, as LNER 7930, ran until 1.1935. For utilising the waste from the GER oil gas plant H. designed a liquid fuel ejector in 1887 making it possible to burn the oil in locos, and about 80 engines and tenders were adapted for oil fuel from 1893. His first GER locos, in 1886, were the 7ft (2.134m) 2–4–0 express engines, class T19, of which 110 were built. Later 21 were rebuilt with large belpaire boilers and in 1905–8 a further 60 were given this boiler and a leading bogie. His next was the T18 0–6–0T of which 50 were built from 1886–8 for freight and shunting. In 1888 his first 0–6–0 appeared, class N31, of which 82 were built until 1898. Other engines were: 20 0–6–0T passenger class E22, 1889–93; 21 2–2–2 7ft (2.134m) express, D27, 1889–93; 100 5ft 8in (1.727m) 2–4–0s class T26, the 'Intermediates', 1891–1902; 50 2–4–2Ts class C32, 1893–1902; 10 7ft 4–2–2s class P43 similar to Dean's on the GWR, 1898; 40 0–4–4Ts, S44, 1898–1901; 90 G58 0–6–0s, 1900–11. These last were later all built or rebuilt with Belpaire boilers, No 1189 being the first GER engine with a Belpaire boiler, in 1901. All had side-window cabs, which H. introduced on the GER. His last and most famous design was the 'Claud Hamilton' type 4–4–0 introduced in 1900, the first numbered 1900. They were later enlarged and improved, being fitted with Belpaire boilers from 12.1903, and superheaters from 1911, becoming some of the finest i/c 4–4–0s in Britain. All H's engines worked well and economically. Most of the design work was carried out by Frederick V Russell, chief draughtsman at Stratford. Under H. the GER built the extensive wagon shops at Temple Mills and the Chemical laboratory at Stratford wks. He built a dormitory at Stratford for GER enginemen which was a model of comfort and convenience. There was only one rule: occupants had to wear slippers provided to avoid disturbing those asleep. He was MIME and MICE; also a JP for Essex and for 3 yrs was a member of West Ham Education Committee. He was a member of the Society of Friends (Quakers), and for many years conducted an adult Sunday school in a poor district of Stratford. He resigned from the GER on 31.12.1907 and was succeeded by his son S. D. Holden (qv).

Proc IME 1.1926 p 57; *The Eng* V 139 12.6.1925 p 656

HOLDEN, Stephen Dewar

b Saltney, Cheshire, 23.8.1870;
d Rochester, Kent, 7.2.1918 aged 47.
Loco supt, GER, 1908–12. Third son of James H. (qv), then supt of the GWR wks at Chester. Ed privately, afterwards at University Coll Sch, London. On leaving school at 16 H. began a 4 yr pupilage at Stratford GER wks under his f. After 18 months in the drg office and 6 months as an inspector in the running dept, in 10.1892 he was app suburban dist loco supt, being transferred to the Ipswich dist 2 yrs later. In 7.1897 he was app London div loco supt. Further promotion followed, to chief of running dept and then asst loco supt. Following his f's resignation in 12.1907 H. was app loco supt in 1.1908 at the age of 37. Unfortunately he had not his f's qualities as eng and administrator, though he was fortunate in having a very capable chief draughtsman, E. S. Tiddeman, who ensured that GER loco

development continued uninterrupted. In 1909 there appeared the 12 2–4–2Ts class Y65, known as the 'Crystal Palace tanks' because of their disproportionately large cabs on such small engines. Building of the 'Claud Hamilton' 4–4–0s continued, superheated boilers being introduced in 1911. In the same year the 1500 class 4–6–0 appeared, and the G69 class 2–4–2Ts with side-window cabs, of which 22 were built. In 1912 there appeared the largest of the GER 0–6–0Ts, C72 class, of which 30 were built. However, in 10.1912 H. suddenly resigned, possibly feeling inadequate for his position. He was elected MIME in 1910.
Proc IME 5.1918 p 382

HOLMES, Matthew

b Paisley, Renfrewshire, (?).(?).1844;
d Lenzie nr Glasgow 3.7.1903 aged 59.
NBR loco eng. Early in his life the family moved to E Scotland where his f was app foreman of the Edinburgh & Glasgow R wks at Haymarket, Edinburgh, where H. was ed. At 15 apprenticed to Hawthorn & Co, engs at Leith. 1859 followed his f onto the E & G where he soon displayed mechanical skill, grasp of business details and command of men. At age 29 he became foreman at Haymarket. During this time, in 1865 the E & G was absorbed into the North British R and in 1875 H. was app chief inspector, also acting as asst to Dugald Drummond (qv) at Cowlairs wks, Glasgow. In 1882 H. succeeded Drummond as loco supt, becoming responsible for 7000 men, 835 engines, 3128 carriages and 63 495 wagons. His most notable engines were the 0–6–0 (1888–1900) which became LNER J36; the 4–4–0 (1890–9) D31; 0–4–0 saddle tank (1882–99) Y9; and the 0–6–0Ts (1900–1, 1904–19) J83 and J88. As a result of heart trouble H. ret in 5.1903, giving his place to W. P. Reid (qv). He was a lovable man, greatly respected by all who worked with him. He was a member of the Inst of Engs & Shipbuilders in Scotland. He was survived by a widow and a young dr.
The Eng V96 10.7.1903 p 45; Engg V 76 10.7.1903 p 58

HOOKHAM, John Albert

b London 9.11.1863;

d Exmouth 24.1.1934 aged 70.
Loco supt NSR. Ed Durham House Sch, Clapham Common, London. 1879 entered on a 5 yr pupilage under William Kirtley (qv) at Longhedge wks of the LC & DR at Battersea, London, serving 4 yrs in the shops and 1 yr in the drg office. 1884–7 remained as asst draughtsman in the loco C & W dept. 1887–91 worked in drg office of Pulsometer Engg Co, Nine Elms Ironworks, Lambeth, on hydraulic and pumping machinery, and in the Glengall Ironworks, Millwall, on marine engines, dredgers and barges. 1891 he returned to the LC & DR as asst draughtsman in the loco C & W dept. In 1899 when the LC & DR and SER came under the Jt Management Committee H. was transferred to Ashford, Kent. In 6.1900 he was app loco C & W supt of the Dona Teresa Cristina R at Santa Catherina, Brazil. After 2 yrs the R was taken over by the Brazilian govt and H. resigned. In 10.1902 he was app loco wks mgr at the Stoke on Trent wks of the NSR, and chief asst to John H. Adams (qv). After the death of Adams in 1915 H. succeeded as loco C & W supt. He introduced soft iron packing for glands, oil fuel and feed-water heating. He also built a 4-cyl 0–6–0T, in 1922, with the cranks set at 90° and 135°, to give an even torque with an 8-beat exhaust. In 1917 he designed and built a 4-wheeled battery loco which worked until 1964. It is now preserved near Stafford. At the grouping of Rs on 1.1.1923 H. became mech eng, Stoke on Trent. When he ret he went to live in Devon. Became MIME in 1.1904 and MICE in 2.1918, MILE 1920.
Journal ILE V 24 1934 p 611; Engg V 137 23.2.1934 p 218; Christiansen, R., and Miller, R. W., The North Staffordshire R 1971; 'Manifold', The North Staffordshire R 1952

HOPKINS, Rice

b Swansea (?).(?).1807;
d (?) 18.12.1857 aged 50.
Civil eng. Son of Roger H. and grandson of Evan H., both engs in S Wales. 1822 became pupil of his f, then engaged on const of Plymouth & Dartmoor Tramroad. Later became partner with his f and then his bro, Thomas (qv). Carried

out works in Devon, S Wales and Dorset. At his death he was eng to the Llanidloes & Newtown R, W Somerset Mineral R and Watchet Harbour Commissioners. MICE 1837.

Min Proc ICE V 18 1858–9 p 192

HOPKINS, Thomas

b Swansea (?).(?).1810; d Rome 8.2.1848 aged 38.

Civil eng. Bro of Rice H. (qv). His f built the tramroad nr Merthyr Tydfil where Trevithick's second steam loco was tried out; also eng of numerous Rs, canals, tramroads, bridges and other public works in England and Wales. Thomas H. learned engg from his f and later became partner with is bro Rice. Besides Rs in Devon, S Wales and Dorset, they built the Victoria Ironworks in Monmouthshire and for several yrs were dirs of it. 1845–6 engaged with his bro in preparing plans, sections and estimates for several proposed Rs but in 1847, in failing health, on medical advice he travelled to Rome, but he d there.

Min Proc ICE V 8 1849 p 11

HOWE, William

b Spencer, Mass, USA, 12.5.1803; d Springfield, Mass, 19.9.1852 aged 42.

Designer of the Howe truss bridge. Began in farming. In 1838 he was commissioned to build a timber bridge at Warren, Mass, for the Boston & Albany RR. Its design incorporated several new features which he developed and patented in 1840. He then used his truss in a bridge he built across the Connecticut River at Springfield for the Western RR, later part of the New York Central. Its success led to many similar jobs, and numerous Howe truss timber bridges were built until the iron bridge was developed. In 1842 he designed and built a roof for the Boston & Worcester RR station at Boston using his truss. In 1846 H. patented an improved truss with a curved member from each buttress to the centre of the span. On 12.3.1828 he m Azubah Towne Stone of Charlton, Mass.

DAB V 9 p 298

HOWE, William

b West Auckland, Co Durham, 3.3.1814; d Clay Cross nr Chesterfield 16.1.1879

aged 64.

Designer of the valve gear known as 'Stephenson's Link Motion'. After little formal ed H. worked as a carpenter at various collieries until, in 1835, he worked under Timothy Hackworth (qv) at Shildon as millwright and pattern maker. After 9 months he went to Lancashire as pattern maker for Jones of Newton-le-Willows, then at Vulcan Foundry nearby, and finally at Mather & Dixon, Liverpool. In 12.1835 he m and had 2 sons while in Lancashire. 1840 moved to Gateshead where, after 6 months at Hawks, Crawshay & Co's wks he joined Robert Stephenson & Co at Newcastle upon Tyne. Here a 'gentleman apprentice' named William Williams showed him a sketch of an idea of his for a reversing gear for steam engines using 2 eccentrics mounted on the crankshaft. Williams' idea was, however, unpractical, but H. took it up and made a wooden model using a radial link connected at the ends to the 2 eccentric rods. This model is preserved in the Science Museum, South Kensington, London. H. showed his invention to William Hutchinson, the wks mgr, who sent the model and sketch to Robert Stephenson who was then in London. Stephenson sent instructions through Hutchinson for Howe to construct a gear in metal, actual size, and to fit one to the second of 2 2–4–0 locos (RS No 359) being built for the N Midland R in 1842. The dispute as to whether to attribute the invention to Williams or Howe was never satisfactorily resolved, and the gear has always been known as the 'Stephenson's Link Motion' after the firm which first applied it. Robert Stephenson always acknowledged the contribution made by Howe to its success. In 1846 H. was app chief eng at George Stephenson's collieries at Clay Cross nr Chesterfield, Derbyshire. The link motion was first fitted to a colliery winding engine designed by H. in 1847 H. became MIME in 1860. A short biography was pub by William L. Howe, the great grandson of H., in 1963.

Proc IME 1880 pp 6–8; Warren, J. G. H., *A Century of Locomotive Building by Robert Stephenson & Co 1823–1923* 1923, 1970

HOY, Henry Albert

b London 13.1.1855; d Fallowfield, Manchester, 24.5.1910 aged 55.
Loco and elec eng; inventor and experimentor. Ed King Edward VI Gr Sch, St Albans, and St John's Coll, Liverpool. 1872 began apprenticeship under Webb at Crewe, LNWR. 1877, after an accident at Wigan, he made a model of the trackwork for the inquiry, and he also made other models for Webb including an interlocking device for points and signals. 1878 transferred to the drg office where he spent much time on designs for continuous brakes. In 1884 he was app outdoor asst in the LYR loco dept under Barton Wright (qv) at Miles Platting, Manchester. 1885 became wks mgr, and in 1886 under Aspinall (qv) he became wks mgr at the new wks at Horwich, then still under const. H. was responsible for the decision to mfr the entire electrical apparatus for the LYR at Horwich. High-speed direct-coupled steam dynamos, electrical cranes and capstans, all of his design, were built under his supervision. While wks mgr he produced several inventions in R electrical apparatus including electric signalling and interlocking. In 5.1899 J. H. Stafford, g mgr LYR, ret and Aspinall was app his successor. In turn H. became CME. His principal work was the design of all apparatus for the electrification of the Liverpool–Southport section, including the motor bogies. Only one new steam loco design was produced under H's supervision, the barely successful 2–6–2T. The first appeared in 10.1903 and 20 were built in 1903–4. They were powerful but troublesome engines and were not popular. (See Mason, Eric *The Lancashire & Yorkshire R in the 20th century* 1961 pp 130–3; Marshall, John, *The Lancashire & Yorkshire R V 3* 1972 pp 147–57.) H. also experimented with boilers with corrugated steel stayless fireboxes, fitted to 21 0–8–0s in 1902–3, following 2 boiler explosions resulting from stay fractures. The boilers were poor steamers, and the fireboxes became distorted. Another experiment was the fitting of the Druitt–Halpin thermal storage apparatus to 6 Aspinall 2–4–2Ts. Economies were overruled by sedimentation troubles and the apparatus

was soon removed. Early in 1904 H. resigned from the LYR to become g mgr of Beyer Peacock & Co, Manchester, where he reorganised the wks, but he d after only 6 yrs. Elected MIME 1891 and AICE also in 1891, MICE 1907. Also a member of the Iron & Steel Institute and president of the Manchester & District Engineering Employers Federation.
Min Proc ICE V 182 1909–10 p 327; Proc IME 5.1910 p 778; *The Eng* V 109 25.5.1910

HUBER-STOCKAR, Emil

b Zurich-Reisbach, Switzerland, 15.7.1865; d (?) 9.5.1939 aged 73.
Mech & elec eng, Swiss Federal Rs (SSB). Trained in mech engg at Federal Polytechnic, Zurich. Later entered Maschinenfabrik Oerlikon (MFO). He visited N America with his friend Sulzer, returning in 1892. 1892–1911 he progressed through MFO, reaching the position of general director. During this period he initiated the experimental single-phase electrification of the Seebach–Wettingen line, so becoming a pioneer in single-phase traction on Rs. In 1903 app to a commission to study R electrification. When the SBB decided upon electrification in 1912 H. was placed in charge of the programme, and was responsible for the decision to use 15 000 V, 16 2/3 Hz. Received hon doctorate at Zurich 1925. In 1855 he m Helene Stockar and they had 2 drs.
S Bz V 114 22.7.1939 pp 48–9

HUDSON, George

b Howsham, nr York, 10.3.1800; d London 14.12.1871 aged 71.
R promoter and financier. Apprenticed to a draper in York, later taking a share in the business. In 1827 he received a bequest of £30 000 of which he eventually invested much in the York & N Midland R Co which was formed in 1833. In the same year he established the York Banking Co and was head of the Conservative party in York. In 1835 he became a town councillor and in 1837 Lord Mayor. In 1837 he was app chairman of the Y & NM in which he owned 500 shares. He next assisted the Great N of England R and the Newcastle & Darlington to complete the line from

York to Newcastle. In 6.1842 he was elected chairman of the Newcastle & Berwick R, subscribing 5 times as much as any other dir. H. instituted the R. Clearing House, in 1.1842. In 1844 he manipulated the amalgamation of the Birmingham & Derby Jn, N Midland and Midland Counties Rs to form the Midland R with a capital of £5 million, of which he was chairman. By now he was in control of 1016 miles (1635km) of R, and he became known as the 'Railway King'. The aristocracy sought his acquaintance, even the Prince Consort, despite H's rough north country speech and uncultivated manners. In 1845 he was elected Conservative MP for Sunderland which he represented until 1859. With his rising power his financial dealings became questionable, and on the amalg of the Newcastle & Berwick and Newcastle & North Shields Rs he increased the authorised share issue from 42 000 to 56 000 and made no entry of this in the accounts, appropriating 9956 shares for himself by which he profited by about £145 000. Other dishonest transactions followed by which he enriched his personal friends. On the advice of George Stephenson in 1845 he caused the Newcastle & Darlington Co, of which he was chairman, to purchase the GN of E (York–Darlington) and the price of shares jumped from £200 to £255. Also in 1845 he became chairman of the Eastern Counties R and paid dividends out of capital, charging £294 000 to capital account after 3 yrs. Once his methods were revealed he was forced to resign from the ECR, MR, York Newcastle & Berwick and Y & NM Cos, and he was forced to repay immense debts. From 1849 he spent much of his time abroad but was unable to recover his earlier success and he d in comparative poverty.
Lambert, Richard S., *The Railway King* 1934, 1964; DNB V 10 pp 145–7; Williams, F. S. *The Midland R* 1877 pp 99–124, 132; ILN 6.9.1845 p 157 (portrait); 14.4.1849 p 233; 23.12.1871 p 619; *The Times* 16.12.1871 p 9 and 22.12.1871 p 3; Peacock, A. J., and Joy, D., *George Hudson of York* 1971

HUDSON, William Smith

b Smalley, nr Derby, 13.3.1810;

d Paterson, NJ, USA, 20.7.1881 aged 71. Mech and loco eng and inventor. Ed Friends' Sch, Ackworth, Yorks. Worked in Robert Stephenson & Co's wks at Newcastle. 1835 emigrated to New York and became loco eng on the Troy & Saratoga RR, NY; then to Buffalo as eng on the Rochester & Auburn RR for several yrs. He then became eng to the state prison at Auburn for 11 yrs, building 2 locos during this time. 1849 became master mechanic of the Attica & Buffalo RR. 1852 supt of loco wks of Rogers, Ketchum, Grosvenor & Co, Paterson, NJ, in succession to John Cooke (qv). In 1856 these wks were incorporated as Rogers Loco & Machine Wks of which H. became mech eng and supt until his death. He devised many improvements in locos; before 1860 designed and patented a feed-water heater, improved rocking grate and a new method of rivetting boiler plates; in 1861 patented the application of cast iron thimbles to the ends of boiler tubes to prevent leaking. His inventions 1860–70 included improved valve gear, link motion, spark arrester, safety valves and levers, a tank loco, and an equalising lever or radius bar to aid a loco in curves. After 1870 he patented 7 more tank engines and a compound. In his *Locos & Loco Building*, pub 1876 and 1886, he outlined improvements in loco const. H. became a US citizen on 22.10.1841. On 6.10.1836 he m Ann Elizabeth Cairns of Jedburgh, Scotland, at Kingston, NY. She survived him, with 1 dr.
DAB V 9 p 342; *RR Gazette* 29.7.1881; White, John H. Jr. *American Locos, an engg history 1830–80* 1968

HUGHES, George

b Norfolk 9.10.1865; d Stamford, Lincs, 27.10.1845 aged 80.
Loco eng, CME of LYR and LMS 1904–25. Ed Norfolk County Sch 1880–2. 1882 became a premium apprentice under F. W. Webb (qv) at Crewe, LNWR. In 5.1887 moved to the new LYR wks at Horwich and was engaged in fitting, millwright and erecting work. 1888 placed in charge of testing shop which he developed into a physical laboratory for testing all purchased materials. In 5.1894 he became asst in the outdoor

loco running dept and later that yr took charge of Horwich gas wks and general gas lighting system. In 10.1895 promoted to chief asst in C & W dept, Newton Heath, Manchester. Returned to Horwich in 1899 to become principal asst to CME, H. A. Hoy (qv), and wks mgr. When Hoy left in 1904 H. succeeded him as CME of the LYR, from 12.3.1904. The first new loco design to appear under his supervision was the 2–4–2T with saturated Belpaire boiler, in 4.1905. In April–July 1905 he visited the Altoona wks of the Pennsylvania RR to study American loco practice. To effect economies in local passenger operation because of losses resulting from street tramway competition he introduced two rail-motors, built by Kerr Stuart of Stoke on Trent to a Taff Vale R design, in 6.1905. Their success led to a design prepared at Horwich and introduced in 5.1906. H. made a study of loco compounding and to prove his theories he rebuilt an Aspinall 0–8–0 as a 4-cyl compound in 2.1906 and built 10 similar ones in 1907. At the same time he introduced the Schmidt high degree superheater on 2 0–6–0s and proved that superheating gave greater economies than compounding, with less complication. In 1909 20 further superheated 0–6–0s were built. In 3.1908 the first of 6 0–8–2T banking engines appeared, followed in 1907 by 15 4-cyl 4–6–0s. These had saturated boilers and Joy valve gear and were generally unsatisfactory. In 1909 he rebuilt 4 Aspinall 4–4–0s with Schmidt superheaters, Walschaert valve gear and inside admission piston valves with 6in (152mm) travel and 1½in (38mm) lap. They were the first engines outside the GWR to have such then modern valve events, and their performance was revolutionised. Had the 4–6–0s been built a little later (they had been urgently needed by the operating dept), they might have benefited from this experiment. In 1910 came the first of his large-boilered 0–8–0s. In 1911 the 2–4–2Ts and 0–6–0s with superheated Belpaire boilers and in 1912 the 0–8–0s with large superheated boilers appeared. A visit to Belgium in 1911 resulted in const of a dynamometer car of advanced design, and after study of the Flamme

2–10–0 design a similar machine was designed for the LYR in 1913 but the war prevented further development. In 1919 he redesigned his 4–6–0 with superheater, Walschaert valve gear and long travel valves, and 70 were built, including 10 rebuilt from the original 4–6–0s. H. also designed a 4–6–4T version of the engine and 10 were built in 1924. At the LYR/LNWR amalgamation on 1.1.1922 H. remained CME of the entire system, responsible for work at Crewe and Horwich. On 1.1.1923, on the formation of the LMS, H. became CME of the new group, retaining his headquarters at Horwich. Here he supervised design of the standard 2–6–0, the LMS 'Crab', but arguments with Henry Fowler (qv) at Derby and with E. F. Trench (qv) chief civil eng, led to H's resignation in 1925, to be succeeded by Fowler. He moved to Cromer where he advised on coastal defence work, and later to Stamford, Lincs, where he d. H. was a man of great warmth and friendliness, simple and approachable, and an enthusiastic horticulturist, and always interested in the well being of the workers at Horwich. Author of *The const of the modern loco* 1894. Became MIME in 1889 and served as a member of the council of the IME from 1911–20. Also MICE and member of the Iron & Steel Inst; also M Inst of Metals.

RG 14.8.1925 p 233; 12.12.1925 p 814; *The Eng* V 180 2.11.1945 p 349; Proc IME V 154 1946 p 355; Marshall, John, *The Lancashire & Yorkshire R* V 2 1970, V 3 1972

HUISH, Capt Mark

b Nottingham (?).(?).1808;
d Bonchurch, Isle of Wight 18.1.1867 aged 58.

G mgr LNWR. His f was 40 yrs Dep lieutenant of Notts. At early age entered E India Co and was rapidly promoted. In 1839, on return from India, he became sec & g mgr of the Glasgow, Paisley & Greenock R, op 3.1841. 1841–5 was sec & g mgr of the GJR. In 1845 the GJR was amalg with the Liverpool & Manchester and Bolton & Leigh Rs and H. was app mgr of the united companies. He took an active part in the gauge contest in 1845–6 and at the same time sought an independent GJR line to London which led, in 1846, to its amalg with the London & Birmingham and Manchester & Birmingham Cos to form the LNWR of which H. became g mgr. He enforced high standards of discipline throughout the system, and under him the LNWR achieved great efficiency. He resigned in 9.1858 because he disagreed with traffic arrangements made with competing lines. Under his guidance the LNWR expanded, capital growing from £16 mil in 1846 to £25 mil in 1858, and revenue increasing from £2 mil to £3 mil. H. was also chairman of the Clifton Suspension Bridge Co, dep chairman of the Electric & International Telegraph Co and a dir of the Isle of Wight R Co. After his resig he lived nr Bonchurch, IW. Elected AICE 6.4.1852. He d after a short illness.

Min Proc ICE V 27 1867–8 pp 600–2; *ILN* V 33 4.12.1858 pp 517–19 (portrait)

HUNT, William

b Banbury, Oxfordshire, 8.1.1843;
d Manchester 29.3.1897 aged 54.
Civil eng, LYR. Ed Bedford Commercial Sch. In 11.1858 articled to H. D. Martin, chief eng of E & W India Docks, London. 1861 entered the loco wks of the N London R at Bow, first in the shops and later in the drg office under William Robinson. 1862–5 engaged on const of Rs in the Isle of Wight. 5.1868–9.1869 asst res eng under Benjamin Burleigh (qv) on the E London R S of the Thames, then res eng under Hawkshaw on the E London R works N of the Thames including the difficult section under the eastern basin of London docks. H. then became chief asst to John Smith Burke on the Dublin Trunk connecting line and other Rs, and also on preparation of parliamentary plans and estimates. In 6.1876 he was app chief asst eng on the LYR under Sturges Meek (qv) and was engaged on the completion of the R from Chatburn to Hellifield, Manchester Loop, Manchester–Radcliffe, Ripponden branch, Clayton West branch, Thorpes Bridge Jn–Oldham and Brighouse–Wyke lines. In 9.1882 he succeeded Meek as chief eng. Under H. the LYR carried out works involving expenditure of £8 million, including rebuilding Liverpool Exchange station, new goods and passenger stations at

Bradford and extensive widening works around Manchester and the rebuilding of Manchester Victoria station. At the time of his death he was superintending the passage of a large LYR Bill through Parliament. Became MICE 1.1876.

Engg V 83 2.4.1897 p 449; Min Proc ICE V 129 1896–7 pp 372–4; Marshall, John, *The Lancashire & Yorkshire Railway* V 1 1969, V 2 1970

HUNTINGTON, Collis Potter

b Harwinton, Conn, 22.10.1821;
d nr Raquette Lake, NY, 13.8.1900 aged 78.
RR promoter and capitalist. 5th of 9 children of Elizabeth Vincent and William H., farmer and small mfr, of English descent. Left sch at 14 and, already 6ft (1.829m) tall, in 9.1836 went to New York and peddled merchandise, mainly watches, throughout the southern states. 1842 opened a store at Oneonta, NY. In 1849, with his wife, he set out for California with other 'fortyniners'. In a 3 month wait in Panama he traded with success. In Sacramento he dealt in miners' supplies. In 1860 his opportunity came when he met T. D. Judah (qv) who proposed to build a R over the Sierra Nevada mountains as part of a transcontinental route, and H. put his savings into the enterprise. In 1861 the Central Pacific RR Co was formed. Once govt grants were secured H. and his associates Charles Crocker (16.9.1822–14.8.1888), Mark Hopkins (1.9.1813–29.3.1878) and Leland Stanford (9.3.1824–21.6.1893), known as the 'Big Four' pushed the work through. Judah d 1863 and H's party assumed control and the RR was completed to a jn with the Union Pacific RR on 10.5.1869. H. and his associates next interested themselves in a line from San Francisco via El Paso to New Orleans, in the name of the Southern Pacific RR which subsequently leased the Central Pacific and California RRs. The line to New Orleans was completed on 12.1.1883. Until 4.1890 Stanford remained president of the Central Pacific and then of the SP. H. was agent and attorney for the SP and on the bds of dirs of the SP and Central Pacific. Outside the SP his principal interest was in the Chesapeake & Ohio RR which he acquired in 1869, becoming president,

and extending it to Memphis, Tenn, and founding the town of Newport News, Va, as a deep sea terminal. He was also president of the Pacific Mail Steamship Co and of the Mexican International R Co, and had many other connections. He was twice m: on 16.9.1844 to Elizabeth T. Stoddard of Litchfield County, Conn (d 1884); then on 12.7.1884 to Mrs Arabella Duval Worsham of Alabama. He had no children. He was a crafty, ruthless and amoral dealer, using bribes or any other methods to secure his own ends, but unlike Cornelius Vanderbilt (1) (qv) he was concerned for the public which his RRs served.

DAB V 9 pp 408–12; Kraus, George, *High Road to Promontory* California 1969

HURST, William

b Markinch, Fife, Scotland, 5.1.1810; d Liverpool 22.10.1890 aged 80.

Loco eng, NBR, LYR. Began training as eng under Jesse Hartley (qv) at Liverpool docks before 1835 where, on 8.6.1838, he m Ann Calder. In 1845 went to Salford as loco supt on the Manchester & Bolton R (which had been built by Hartley), remaining in charge at Salford after the M & B was absorbed in 1846 by the Manchester & Leeds R which, in 7.1847, became the Lancashire & Yorkshire R. On 3.10.1849 the two loco depts were combined and H. moved to Miles Platting wks, Manchester. On 20.12.1854 he resigned and on 26.1.1855 became loco supt on the NBR at St Margarets, Edinburgh, responsible for locos and rolling stock, steamers on the Solway, Forth, Tay and Clyde, the rail steeling plant at Baileyfield and various R co gas wks. However, as a result of some underhand dealings with the 'Scottish Wagon Co', a finance house of which he was a dir, at the expense of the NBR and to his own advantage, he was given 6 months notice of dismissal on 16.8.1866 and he left on 31.1.1867. On 18.9.1867 he returned to the LYR as 'indoor loco supt' at the former ELR wks at Bury. After the death of the loco supt, William Jenkins (qv) later that year, H. moved to Miles Platting as outdoor loco supt, with William Yates as indoor supt responsible for loco design. He remained until 1875 when, because of reorganisation of the LYR loco dept under one head, he was asked to resign, at the age of 65. On the app of Barton Wright (qv) he ret to Liverpool. He was buried at Edinburgh in the same grave as his son who d in 1866 at the age of 19 before H. was dismissed from the NBR.

Marshall, John, *The Lancashire & Yorkshire R* V 2 1970; Thomas, John, *The North British R* V 1 1969

HUTCHINSON, Major-General Charles Scrope, RE, CB

b Hythe, Kent, 8.8.1826; d Blackheath 29.2.1912 aged 85.

H. was one of the best known BOT inspectors of Rs during the latter half of the 19th century. Obtained his commission 1843, becoming substantive colonel 1876 when he ret with hon rank of major general. App Inspector of Rs to BOT 1867 until he ret 1895. Among the most important works he inspected were the Tay and Forth bridges.

Min Proc ICE V 189 1911–12 p 352

HYDE, Mark

b Sheffield 13.3.1823; d Manchester 10.5.1893 aged 70.

Civil eng MS & LR. 1844–50 engaged on surveying and preparing parliamentary drawings for several R schemes in Yorkshire, Lincolnshire and Nottinghamshire. He then joined staff of John Fowler (qv) under whom he worked on the east section of the MS & LR between Sheffield, Grimsby and New Holland. On its completion he moved to Manchester, the headquarters of the company, where he remained as chief engg asst until 6.1886 when ill health forced him to retire. His most important works were the Grimsby–Cleethorpes, Godley–Woodley, Tinsley–Rotherham, Rotherham–Masborough lines and the doubling of the Barnsley branch. He also assisted in the const of the CLC Manchester–Warrington–Liverpool line, opened 1873. Elected MICE 5.12.1871.

Min Proc ICE V 117 1893–4 p 380

INGLIS, Sir James Charles

b Aberdeen 9.9.1851; d Rottingdean, Sussex, 19.12.1911 aged 60.

Chief eng, GWR. Ed Aberdeen Gr Sch,

and Aberdeen Univ 1867–70. Entered wks of Norman Copeland & Co, millwrights and engs, Glasgow. After 2 yrs became pupil of James Abernethy, London, with whom, 1871–4, he was engaged on dock harbour const, mainly at Newport, Mon. In 1.1885 he became asst to P. J. Margary (qv), chief eng of the S Devon and Cornwall Rs, later GWR. Under Margary Inglis was engaged on const of Plymouth stn, and the harbour R there, and widening the Newton Abbot–Torquay line. 1887 joined the GWR staff and became res eng of dock wks at Millbay. He then took up private practice, mainly on harbours, but also built the GWR Princetown branch, 1881–3, and Bodmin branch 1887. In 6.1892 he became GWR asst eng and in 10.1892 chief eng. He was much occupied with replacement of Brunel's timber viaducts. 1903 app g mgr and consulting eng of GWR. In this position he was responsible for the const of Fishguard harbour and the establishment of the fast steamer service to Rosslare. He was also concerned with the S Wales direct line and Chipping Sodbury tunnel, and the GCR/GWR jt line. Elected MICE 18.3.1884 and was president 1908–10.
Min Proc ICE V 187 1911–12 pp 319–22; *Engg* V 92 22.12.1911 pp 835–7 (portrait); *The Eng* V 112 22.12.1911 p 635

INGLIS, Sir Robert John Mathison, CIE, TD, DL, FRSE

b (?) 5.5.1881; d Helensburgh, Dumbartonshire, 23.6.1962 aged 81.
Civil eng, NBR and LNER. Ed Bennington Park and Edinburgh Univ. Joined NBR as pupil in 1900 and during next few yrs spent much time as res eng on various works including Edinburgh–Portobello widening. 1909 became chief asst in charge of works dept. 1911 app dist eng, N div, Thornton. 1916 dist eng, W div, Glasgow. In 1919 app to Min of Transport as dep chief eng, Rs, later becoming chief eng, Rs. In 1921 resumed work as dist eng, Glasgow. 1929 app asst eng of p w, S area, LNER; 1931 asst eng, const; 1934 asst eng under C. J. Brown (qv) whom he succeeded as eng S area in 1936. 1943 app div g mgr, Scottish area, Edinburgh. Later that year he spent 4 months in India investigating

the Indian Rs for the govt. 1945–9 in Germany as chief transport officer, British zone, and later in the combined British and American zones. 1948 spent 2 months in S Africa advising on the location of a new station in Durban. 1949 app chairman of Glasgow & District Transport Committee (set up by BTC) which, among other things, recommended electrification of Rs in Glasgow and the Clyde valley (Inglis Rept 1951). 1954–5 chairman of the investigating committee on Rhodesia Rs. Knighted 1947 and app a deputy Lieutenant for Dumbartonshire in 1957.
Proc ICE V 27 1963 p 428; *The Times* 25.6.1962 p 12

IVATT, Henry Alfred

b Cambridgeshire 16.9.1851;
d Haywards Heath, Sussex, 25.10.1923 aged 72.
Loco eng GS & WR and CME of GNR. Son of Rev. A. W. Ivatt, Ed Upper Sch, Liverpool Coll. At age 17 apprenticed at Crewe, LNWR, under Ramsbottom and Webb (qqv). After 6 months in the traffic dept under G. P. Neale he became asst foreman at Stafford loco shed. In 9.1874 took charge of loco dept at Holyhead and early in 1877 moved to the Chester district. In 10.1877 app dist supt S div GS & WR, Ireland, with headquarters at Cork. 1882 became asst loco eng and wks mgr under John Aspinall (qv). The two were lifelong friends from apprentice days. In 1886, when Aspinall became CME of the LYR, Ivatt succeeded as loco eng at Inchicore, Dublin. In 1895 he was offered the position of loco eng, GNR, and in, 3.1896 took up his new duties at Doncaster, in succession to Patrick Stirling (qv). At that time train weights were increasing. He began by introducing the first GNR 4–4–0, in 1896, followed in 1898 by Britain's first 'Atlantic' engine, 4–4–2 No 990. Later he improved the type by fitting a much larger boiler with the first wide firebox in Britain, spread over the trailing wheels. The performance of the 'Atlantics', however, was not outstanding until they were superheated. For mineral traffic and fast goods work he introduced various classes of 0–6–0s of increasing size, and a large i/c 0–8–0 in 1901. For short-distance goods and

passenger work he produced tank engines of 4-4-2, 0-6-2 and 0-8-2 types. Only his 4-2-2 express engine had a short life. He was one of the first British loco engs to use the Walschaert valve gear with success and to apply super-heating. His last loco design, a power-ful superheated 0-6-0, which became LNER class J6, appeared in 1911. He ret 2.12.1911 and was succeeded by H. N. Gresley (qv). His son H. G. Ivatt (qv) became CME of the LMS. His dr Marjorie m O. V. S. Bulleid (qv), CME of the SR.
The Eng V 136 2.11.1923 p 481 (por-trait); *Engg* V 116 2.11.1923 p 567 (portrait); Proc IME 12.1923 p 1174; Brown, F. A. S., *From Stirling to Gresley 1882-1922* 1974

IVATT, Henry George

b Dublin (?).5.1886; d Melbourne, Derbyshire, 4.10.1972 aged 86.
Son of H. A. Ivatt (qv); CME of LMS. Ed Uppingham. Began apprenticeship at Crewe, LNWR, 3.10.1904 at age 18, and in 1907 entered the drg office. On 21.1.1909 app asst foreman at Crewe N shed and on 1.5.1910 asst outdoor mach-inery supt, Crewe. On 23.1.1913 m Dorothy Harrison. During WW1 he served in France with a mobile work-shop. On 8.9.1919 moved to Stoke on Trent as dep loco C & W supt under J. A. Hookham (qv) on the NSR. He continued at Stoke after the grouping until the wks were closed down in 1927. He was then app special asst to Fowler at Derby until 1928 when he became wks supt. On 1.11.1932 he moved to St Rollox, Glasgow, as mech eng, LMS, Scotland for 5 yrs until 1.10.1937 when R. A. Riddles (qv) took his place and Ivatt moved to London as chief asst to Stanier (qv) at Euston. When C. E. Fairburn (qv) took over as CME in 1945 Ivatt remained as chief asst. How-ever, Fairburn d on 12.10.1945 and on 1.2.1946 Ivatt succeeded to the position of CME of the LMS. In this position he is chiefly remembered for his 'Class 2' 2-6-0 and 2-6-2T designs and his 'Class 4' 2-6-0, all three adopted as standard BR designs with little alteration. He also designed Britain's first main-line diesel-electric loco, LMS CoCo No 10000, which appeared in 1947. He also fitted a Stanier

Class 5 4-6-0, No 4767, with outside Stephenson link motion and 20 others with Caprotti valve gear. He made other modifications to the Class 5, fitting roller-bearing axleboxes, and built the two final LMS Pacifics with altered rear ends. With nationalisation on 1.1.1948 Ivatt became chief mech & elec eng, London Midland Region of BR, but he disagreed with the standard steam loco policy arguing, rightly, that existing designs were adequate and so, at the end of 6.1951 he resigned and became for a time engaged in the mfr of diesel locos.
Bulleid, H. A. V. *Master builders of steam* 1963

JAMES, William

b Henley-in-Arden 13.6.1771; d Bodmin, Cornwall, 11.3.1837 aged 66.
Early R surveyor and projector. Ed Warwick and Winson Green schools. Trained in law in London. At age 25 m Miss Tarleton of Henley-in-Arden and soon began business as land agent and surveyor. Connected with several drainage schemes. Dissatisfied with the oppressive conduct of canal companies in connection with mines in Staffordshire he became interested in Rs and surveyed a line from Wolverhampton to Birming-ham. 1802 made surveys for Rs around Bolton, Wigan, Leigh and Ashton-under-Lyne. In 1803 he made his first survey for a R from Liverpool to Manchester. In 1809 he engineered the short plate-way from Gloucester to Cheltenham. His most important line was the Strat-ford-on-Avon & Moreton-in-Marsh R surveyed in 1821, which he saw as part of a line from Birmingham to London via Oxford. On this he recommended wrought iron rails in chairs. It was built by J. U. Rastrick (qv) and opened in 1826. In 1822 J. formed a Liverpool & Manchester R Co to const an 'engine railroad' and surveys were completed that year. J. at that time was financially embarrassed and he recommended George Stephenson as eng. In the sub-sequent progress of the work the pioneer-ing carried out by J. was forgotten. Other lines surveyed by J. included; Birmingham–Manchester; Canterbury–Whitstable; Bishop's Stortford, Cam-bridge & Newmarket; London–Brighton;

London–Portsmouth; London–Chatham; Bristol–Bath–Bradford-on-Avon; Bristol–Salisbury–Southampton; Padstow–Bodmin–Fowey; Truro–St Agnes. J. had intelligence, skill and foresight but lacked the business acumen to carry out his projects successfully. He never gave sufficient attention to any one scheme and had too many in progress at once. It was his more patient single-minded successors like the Stephensons who brought the schemes into effect and won the fame.

Paine, E. M. S. *The two James's and the two Stephensons* 1861, 1961; Baxter, Bertram, *Stone blocks and iron rails* 1966

JAMES, William Henry

b Henley-in-Arden (?).3.1796; d Dulwich College Almshouses 16.12.1873 aged 77.
Civil and mech eng, eldest son of William J. (qv). Assisted his f in the survey of the Liverpool & Manchester R. Practised as an eng in Birmingham. Took out patents for locos, steam engines, R carriages, diving apparatus, etc, and was credited with the invention of the firetube boiler as used on the *Rocket* loco of G. and R. Stephenson. He did patent a steam carriage water-tube boiler in 9.1821, but not a fire-tube boiler.

Boase *Modern English Biography* 1897; Paine, E. M. S. *The two James's and the two Stephensons* 1861, 1961

JANNEY, Eli Hamilton

b Loudoun County, Virginia, USA 12.11.1831; d Alexandria, Va, 16.6.1912 aged 80.
Inventor of the standard automatic coupler used throughout North America. Ed in native village and at Oneida Conference Seminary, Cazenovia, NY, 1852–4. Spent several years in farming with his f. In 1857 he m Cornelia Hamilton of Loudoun County. Served in Confederate army throughout Civil War. In 1865 he became interested in the problem of coupling railroad cars automatically to end the numerous accidents with link and pin couplers. Despite his lack of mechanical training he obtained his first patent for an automatic coupler on 21.4.1868. He improved this and obtained a second patent on 29.4.1873, this forming the basis of the present standard coupler. With financial help from friends he had some couplers made in Alexandria, Va, and these were fitted to two cars on what is now the Southern RR. Their success led to the formation of the Janney Car Coupling Co which J. controlled until the last patent expired. The Pennsylvania RR adopted the coupler after exhaustive tests in 1874–6, but it was only in 1888, following J's patents of 1874, 1879 and 1882, that the Master Car Builders Association made the J. coupler the standard for American RRs which, however, did not adopt it generally until J. had waived patent rights on the contour lines of the coupler.

DAB V9 p 610

JEE, Alfred Stanistreet

b Liverpool 2.8.1816; d Santander, Spain, 30.8.1858 aged 42.
Civil eng. Son of Matthew J., a merchant of Liverpool. Love of mathematics and observations of work on the Liverpool & Manchester R led him to take up engg. 1831 became pupil of Locke (qv), working on the Grand Jn R. 1838 res eng on Lancaster & Preston Jn R, completed 1840. Then to Sheffield & Manchester and Huddersfield & Manchester, and the Huddersfield–Penistone lines. On the Sheffield–Manchester he was responsible for erection of Dinting and Etherow viaducts and Woodhead tunnel, 3 miles 22yd (4.848km), opened on 23.12.1845. On the Huddersfield & Manchester he was responsible for the first Standedge R tunnel, 3 miles 66yd (4.888km), opened 1.8.1849. He was elected MICE 1844. In 1851 his advice was sought in Spain where he built the line from Alardel-Rey to Reynosa, 35 miles (56.327km), opened 3.1857. On 30.8.1858, with his bro Morland Jee, he was driving an engine along an embankment which suddenly sank. The engine was thrown down and he was killed instantly. His bro d 10 days later.

Min Proc ICE V 18 1858–9 pp 193–6

JEFFREYS, Edward Alexander

b Shrewsbury 20.8.1828;
d Leeds 3.4.1889 aged 64.
Loco eng. At age 14 apprenticed to Bury, Curtis & Kennedy, Liverpool, where he later worked on designs of

locos and marine engines, afterwards superintending the working of them. In 1845 app loco supt on the Shrewsbury & Chester R on which, for the first 14 months, he supervised const of rolling stock. On amalg with the GWR in 1853 he obtained employment with Thomas Brassey (qv) on const of rolling stock for the GTR of Canada. On the opening of the Shrewsbury & Hereford R Brassey app J. as res eng and loco supt until 1862. In 1863 J. became g mgr of the South Eastern R of Portugal but after a few months he resigned to become consulting eng to Low Moor Ironworks nr Bradford. In 7.1879 he became a partner of James Kitson (qv) in the Monkbridge Ironworks, Leeds. J. became a dir of the co until his death. Became MICE 1.12.1863.
Min Proc ICE V 96 1888-9 p 319

JENKINS, William

b Llanddewi Brefi, Cardiganshire, (?).12.1803; d Manchester 20.11.1867 aged 63.
Loco eng, LYR. Son of a millwright with whom he served part of an apprenticeship; later with Hughes & Wren in Manchester. From 1826-35 he was engaged under Jesse Hartley (qv) on Liverpool Docks in charge of engines and machinery. In 1830 he superintended the construction of canals and tramroads in the Scottish quarry from which the granite was obtained. In 1835 he joined Hartley on the Manchester & Bolton R on which Hartley had been app eng in 1832. Here he supervised const and also took charge of the canal. On opening of the R on 29.5.1838 J. became supt and mgr responsible for locos at the Salford wks. In 1845 he was app loco supt on the Manchester & Leeds R, being succeeded on the Bolton R by W. Hurst (qv). J. was responsible to John Hawkshaw (qv) for the erection and fitting out of the workshops at Miles Platting, Manchester, which were opened in 1846. At the works, under J., the M & L became the first R company in the world to build its locos in its own wks as routine practice. J's first engines were o/c 2-2-2s and i/c 0-4-2s for passenger and goods trains. On 3.10.1849 the Bolton and Manchester divs were amalgamated under J. with

Hurst as outdoor supt until 1854 when Hurst left for the NBR and J. was given sole command at Miles Platting. In that year the first of 12 5ft (1.524mm) 0-6-0s appeared followed by 149 4ft 10in (1.767m) 0-6-0s in 1855-7. J. introduced a 5ft 9in (2.103m) 2-4-0 in 1861 and various 0-6-0 saddle tanks and 2-4-0 well tanks. Because of a severely restricted budget J. was required to keep engines in service for too long and LYR operation suffered accordingly. In 1867 he became too ill to continue and on 28.8 he was granted leave, but he d shortly afterwards. Became MIME 1857.
Proc IME 1868 p 16; Marshall, John, *The Lancashire & Yorkshire R* Vs 1-3 1969, 1970, 1972

JERVIS, John Bloomfield

b Huntington, NY, USA, 14.12.1795; d Rome, NY, 12.1.1885 aged 89.
Pioneer of Rs in USA. His family moved to New York in 1788 and later J. worked in his f's lumber business. Served under Benjamin Wright on the survey of the Erie Canal and in 1819 was made res eng of 17 miles of the canal. 1823 became supt of 50 miles and responsible for traffic. 1825 principal asst to Wright on Delaware & Hudson Canal & R. On resignation of Wright in 1827 J. became chief eng concerned with the R. from Honesdale to mines at Carbondale, Pa, 16 miles (25.75km). He recommended inclined planes with stationary engines and level sections worked by locos. He trained other men, including Horatio Allen (qv) and prepared a specification for the *Stourbridge Lion*, one of the first locos in USA. (See Foster and Rastrick.) J. left the D & H in 5.1830 to become chief eng of the Mohawk & Hudson R. For this he surveyed a route which could be worked by locos throughout. In 1832 the West Point Foundry Co built the 4-2-0 *Experiment* loco to his plans, the first engine with a bogie. In its day it was the fastest loco in the world. On completion of the M & H and the Schenectady & Saratoga R of which J. was also chief eng, he became chief eng to the Chenango (NY) Canal in 4.1833, and of the enlargement of the Erie Canal in 1836. After a period on municipal water supplies he became chief eng of the Hudson River RR in 1847. In 1850

he spent 4 months in Europe, after which he built the Michigan Southern & Northern Indiana RR and the Chicago & Rock Island R. In 1861 became gen supt of the Pittsburgh, Fort Wayne & Chicago R. Resigned in 1864 but remained as consultant until 1866 when he retired. In 1834 J. m Cynthia Brayton of Western, NY. She d 1839, and he later m Elizabeth R. Coates. At his death his home and library at Rome became the Jervis Library by his bequest. Port Jervis, NY, is named after him, and in 1927 the Delaware & Hudson named their finest loco, No 1401, after him. Author of several political and engg works.

Proc Am Soc Civil Engs V 11 (1885); DAB V 10 pp 58–60

JESSOP, Josias

b Fairburn, Yorkshire, 24.10.1781; d Derbyshire (?).(?).1826 aged 45.

Second son of William J. (qv). Eng of canals and early Rs. In 1782 the family moved to Newark and in 1790 to Butterley, Derbyshire, where William J. established the Butterley wks. J. was trained under his f, partly on the Croydon, Merstham & Godstone R, 1803–5. For a short period he was eng of the Severn & Wye R. In 1811–16 he surveyed and built the Wey & Arun Jn Canal. He surveyed the Montgomeryshire Canal in 1814, and in 1825–6 surveyed an extension to his f's Ashby Canal Tramroad at Gresley. He is chiefly remembered for his work as eng of the Cromford & High Peak R in Derbyshire, begun in 1825 and completed in 1831 after his death. He is commemorated by plaques on the Newhaven tunnel beneath the Buxton–Ashbourne road. (See T. J. Woodhouse.)

JESSOP, William

b Devonport 12.1.1745 old style (23.1.1745 new style); d Butterley Hall, Derbyshire, 18.11.1814 aged 69.

Builder of canals and early Rs. Son of Josias J., a foreman shipwright in the naval dockyard (d 1761). At 16 he became a pupil of John Smeaton, working with him on the Calder & Hebble and Aire & Calder navigations in Yorkshire. J's first major work was the Grand Canal across Ireland, begun in 1853 but

not completed until 1805. He was also engaged in the improvement of navigation on the Trent and Severn, Sussex Ouse, and upper Thames. One of J's principal works was the Cromford Canal, to link Arkwright's mills at Cromford with the Derbyshire coalfield and Nottingham, to which he became chief eng in 1789. It included the 2966yd (2.840km) Butterley tunnel, and it was the work on this which led J., with Benjamin Outram (qv), John Wright and Francis Beresford, to found the Butterley Co in 1790. This co was later responsible for many iron R bridges. It was to connect the Cromford Canal with the Peak Forest Canal at Whaley Bridge that the Cromford & High Peak R was built, engineered by J's son Josias (qv), 1825. In 1793 J. was app chief eng to the Grand Jn Canal which included the 3056yd (2.794km) Blisworth tunnel. While this was being completed J. built a R over the hill to enable traffic to operate on the canal, in 1799. It was the first R in Northamptonshire. Similar Rs were built by J. and Outram at Ashby and Loughborough in Leicestershire, and to connect with the Cromford Canal. In conjunction with John Rennie (qv) J. laid out the Surrey Iron R, incorporated by Act of 21.5.1801, and J. was app chief eng. The R was opened in 1802. Next J. was app eng, with his son Josias as asst, for the Croydon, Merstham & Godstone R Co, incorporated by Act of 17 May 1803 and opened on 24 July 1805.

Rolt, L. T. C., *Great Engineers* 1962

JOHNSON, Lacey Robert

b Abingdon, Berkshire, 22.6.1855; d Montreal 17.4.1915 aged 59.

Loco and marine eng. Apprenticed at Swindon, GWR, 6.1870–12.1875, afterwards spending 6 months in drg office. Became foreman of mechanics at Woolwich Arsenal, and later fitter and erector. 1878 app mgr of G. Davis & Sons engine wks, London, and later at their new wks in Abingdon. In 9.1879 went as draughtsman to the Scinde, Punjab & Delhi R and later became foreman of the machine and erecting shops. His health suffered and in 3.1882 he was app draughtsman on the GTR at Montreal. 6 months later he became

foreman of the CPR shops at Carleton Jn, Ontario, until 12.1885 when he became asst master mech of the Lake Superior div. 1886 app master mech of the Pacific div, Vancouver, and on the inauguration of the trans-Pacific service his jurisdiction was extended over the engg dept of the steamships, during which period he spent three winters at Hong Kong superintending alterations and repairs to CPR ships. Following purchase of the CP Nav Co by the CPR, from 4.–9.1901 he acted as superintending eng of the combined fleets which was detached from the loco dept. In 9.1901 app asst supt of motive power of CPR at Montreal, and in 7.1912 became gen supt of Angus shops dist, Montreal. In 3.1915 app gen welfare agent of CPR in Montreal, but he d a few weeks later. Became MIME 1891. Also M Canadian Soc Civil Engs.
Proc IME 5.1916 p 456

JOHNSON, Richard

b Spalding, Lincs, (?).(?).1827;
d Hitchin 9.9.1924 aged 96.
Chief eng GNR. In 1840 at age 13 apprenticed to a builder and contractor at Spalding and for 5 yrs worked as a carpenter. In 10.1847 app to Brydone & Evans, engs, on const of GNR loop line (Peterborough–Boston–Lincoln). 1855 app dist eng of the loop (op 17.10.1848) with an office at Boston. 1859 app dist eng on the 'Towns Line', Peterborough–Grantham–Newark–Doncaster, op 15.7.1852. On 25.6.1861 app chief eng in succession to Walter Marr Brydone. J. was responsible for the planning and const of the GNR 'Derbyshire extensions', op 1875–8, and the Leen Valley line in Nottinghamshire, op 18.10.1881. He also reconstructed the Newark Dyke bridge, one of the largest on the GNR, with a span of 262ft (79.86m), in 1889–90, and built the new Copenhagen and Maiden Lane tunnels nr King's Cross, London, 1892. He also reconstructed the bridges carrying the GNR over the MR at Peterborough and the Don at Doncaster. He ret at end of 12.1896 at age 69 after a working life of 57yrs, 49yrs on the GNR.
RM 7.1897 pp 11–19 (portrait); RG 12.9.1924 p 354; 19.9.1924 p 387 (portrait); 31.10.1924 p 587

JOHNSON, Samuel Waite

b Bramley, Leeds, 14.10.1831;
d Nottingham 14.1.1912 aged 80.
Loco eng, MR. Son of James J., later an eng on the GNR. Ed Leeds Gr Sch. Entered pupilage under James Fenton at E. B. Wilson & Co, Leeds, where he asssisted David Joy (qv) in the drawings for the Jenny Lind loco, and in the const of some of McConnell's 'Bloomers' for the LNWR. His first app was under Sturrock on the GNR where he became wks mgr in the shops at Peterborough. 1859 became acting loco supt on MS & L at Gorton, Manchester, and in 1864 loco supt of the Edinburgh & Glasgow R at Cowlairs, Glasgow. In 1865 the E & G was amalg with the NBR. 1866 J. moved to Stratford, London, to become loco supt of the GER in succession to Robert Sinclair. Here he designed a successful 2-4-0 of which 40 were built 1867–72, one (the first) of which ran until 12.1913. 1872 introduced the first of the 30 0-4-4Ts. Following the death of Matthew Kirtley (qv) on 2.7.1873 J. was app loco supt on the MR at Derby where he remained for over 30 yrs. His first MR engines, in 1876, were 2-4-0s based on Kirtley's engines, but with inside frames. In the same year the first of his famous MR 4-4-0s appeared, followed in 1877 by a new 2-4-0. The first of his numerous 0-6-0 goods engines appeared in 1878. The basic design, with wheel spacings of 8ft+8ft 6in (2.438+2.591m), was repeated by his successors at Derby until the MR had more 0-6-0s than any other R in Britain and possibly in the world. This wheel spacing in fact became standard for almost all 6-coupled engines designed at Derby until Stanier's designs of the 1930s. Other notable designs were the 0-6-0T which also became standard, and the 0-4-4T. His most famous engines were the graceful 4-2-2s, introduced in 1887, and of which 60 were built until 1893. They were the result of the introduction of steam sanding in 1886 which enabled the single driver loco to pull heavier loads without slipping. Some ran until 1927, and one, withdrawn in 1928, is preserved near Ripley, Derbyshire, in the MR Musuem. All J's engines so far had two safety

valves, a lock-up in a brass casing over the firebox and a double Salter type on the dome. His last designs were totally different, incorporating much larger boilers and Belpaire fireboxes. First were the 700 class 4–4–0s of 1900, and the 3-cyl Smith type compound 4–4–0 of 1901. J. was responsible for changing the loco livery on the MR. Until 1881 engines were dark green which, however, J. lightened in 1876. In 9.1881 the first engines appeared in the new red livery which, with some variation, remained standard until WW2 and was even adopted by BR for some of the Stanier Pacifics. J. ret on 31.12.1903 and from then until his death in 1912 lived in Nottingham where he was a JP and a supporter of St Peter's church. He was succeeded on the MR by R. M. Deeley (qv). Became MIME 1861, MICE 1867 and in 1898 was president of IME.
Radford, J. B. *Derby Works and Midland Locos* 1971; Ellis, Hamilton, *Twenty Locomotive Men* 1958; Proc IME 3.1912 pp 302–4; Min Proc ICE V 188 1911–12 p 430; *The Eng* V 113 1912 p 63

JOHNSTONE, William

b Glasgow 1.7.1811; d Glasgow 27.4.1877 aged 65.
Chief eng, G & SWR. 1826 articled to David Smith, civil eng, and remained with him 10 yrs. 1837 joined staff of Grainger & Miller and worked on plans of Glasgow & Ayr R, later becoming a res eng on the line. On its opening in 1840 J. was app eng & g mgr. He carried out extensions of what became the G & SWR with over 300 miles (483km) of route. He also built the St Enoch station, Glasgow. Resigned 31.12.1874. 1861 was president Inst of Engs & Shipbuilders of Scotland. MICE 4.12.1866.
Min Proc ICE V 49 1876–7 p 261

JONES, David

b Manchester 25.10.1834; d Hampstead 2.12.1906 aged 72.
Loco eng, Highland R. Son of David Jones, eng. Left school 1847 and apprenticed at Longsight, Manchester, and at Crewe, LNWR, under Ramsbottom (qv) until 31.10.1855. On 15.11.1855 he went to Inverness to work on the Inverness & Nairn R. On 17.4.1858 William Barclay,

loco supt, app J. as his principal asst. On 16.9.1858 J. m Mary Ann Snowie of Inverness. Barclay resigned on 31.5.1865 and J. became acting loco supt of what was by then the Highland R. The directors, however, engaged William Stroudley (qv) as permanent loco supt and until the end of 1869 J. was loco running supt. Among his colleagues was Dugald Drummond (qv), then wks mgr. Stroudley went to Brighton in 1870 and for a short time Drummond was loco supt until J. was app to the permanent post in 2.1870, holding it for 27 yrs. J. began by rebuilding old Aberdeen & Inverness Jn R engines (for details of locos see HR books listed below). HR engines were painted yellow until 1885 after which J. adopted green. His first 4–6–0 came out in 1894, the famous 'big goods' and the first 4–6–0 to operate on a British R. 15 were built. His last locos were the 'Loch' class 4–4–0s, 1896. In these and the 4–6–0s J. abandoned the 'Crewe' type framing. A notable feature of J's engines was the ventilated outer casing to the chimney. On 7.9.1894, during trials of the 4–6–0 he met with a scalding accident which almost involved loss of his left leg. But he had to retire at the end of 10.1896 and a passenger version of the 4–6–0 which he designed was produced by his successor Peter Drummond (qv) as the 'Castle' class. After a motor accident in which his other leg was damaged, J. never fully recovered and he d at Hampstead, London. The first 4–6–0, No 103, wrongly painted yellow, is preserved in the Glasgow Transport Museum.
Ellis, Hamilton, *Twenty Locomotive Men* 1958; *The Locomotive* 8.1937 pp 253–6; Vallance, H. A. *The Highland R* 1938, 1963; *The Highland R 1855–1955* SLS 1955; Allchin, M. C. V. *A History of Highland Locomotives* 1947

JOY, David

b Leeds 3.3.1825; d Hampstead 14.3.1903 aged 78.
Marine and loco eng, inventor of the Joy radial valve gear. In 1840 he spent a yr at Wesley Coll, Sheffield, learning mech drawing. 1841 entered his f's oil mills. From here to the loco wks of Fenton, Murray & Jackson until they closed in 1843 when he transferred to

Shepherd & Todd, then engaged on Gray's patent engine with expansion gear. J. later brought out his own design of expansion and reversing gear. Todd (qv) left the firm in summer 1844 and in the autumn was succeeded by E. B. Wilson. In 1845 J. became acting chief draughtsman and was later joined by John Fenton (qv) from his former employer. Together they designed the famous 'Jenny Lind' type 2–2–2 in 1846–7, the first appearing in 5.1847, becoming LBSCR No 60. After a dispute in 6.1850 J. left E. B. Wilson, but shortly afterwards undertook management of the Nottingham & Grantham R, then being worked by Wilson at 2s (10p) per train mile. Late in 1851 J. left the N & G and in 1852 became supt of the Oxford, Worcester & Wolverhampton R until 1855 when he returned to the Railway Foundry, Leeds. Here he const Willis's 'Farmer's Engine', one of the first road locos, and he shared in the design of a compound marine engine and a steam rivetting machine. After a short period with De Bergue (qv), bridge builders, he set up a wks in Middlesbrough, 1860–71, to mfr his steam hammers and organ blowers and other objects. In 1874 he went to the Barrow Shipbuilding Co as mgr of their water-tube boiler dept, becoming sec of the co in 1876. In 1865 he had begun the design of a radial valve gear and in 1875 he took this up again, constructing a large model in 1878–9. The Joy valve gear was patented in 1879. It was first tried with success on a marine engine and its first application to a loco was on an old Bury 0–4–0 on the Furness R. In 1880 it was fitted new to a Webb 'Cauliflower' 0–6–0 built at Crewe. From then on it was adopted for hundreds of locos built at Crewe and was introduced to the LYR by Aspinall (qv) in 1886. Aspinall adopted it as standard on the LYR and its use was continued at Horwich until 1920. Abroad it achieved success in India, South Africa and USA, and it found use in marine engines by Maudslay. Its main practical defect was the boring of the connecting, or main rod. While not serious in small engines, it resulted in several fractures in large machines. The last locos to be fitted with Joy gear were Beames' 0–8–4T built at Crewe in 1923.

Joy left Barrow in 1881 and took up private practice as a consulting eng in Westminster. He was a MICE, MIME from 1853–67 and from 1880, and M of the Marine Engs and the Naval Architects. He m in 1867 and was survived by 3 sons and 2 drs.

The Locomotive 4.1903 p 218; 6.1940 pp 153–7; *The Eng* 20.3.1903 p 290; Proc IME 5.1903 pp 357–60

JUDAH, Theodore Dehone

b Bridgeport, Conn, 4.3.1826;
d New York 2.11.1863 aged 37.

Eng of the Central Pacific RR through the Sierra Nevada. Ed Rennselaer Polytechnic Inst, Troy, NY. On 10.5.1847 he m Anna Ferona Pierce. He was first employed on the New Haven, Hertford & Springfield RR and the Erie Canal. Also erected a large bridge at Vergennes, Vt, planned and built the Niagara Gorge RR and was in charge for some time on the const of the Buffalo & New York R, later part of the Erie system. In 1854 called to Pacific coast as chief eng of the Sacramento Valley RR, completed in 1856 to Folsom. While in the California mountains on other projects he conceived the idea of a R from California to link with those in the Mississippi states. For this he fought tirelessly in Washington and the Eastern states and in 1860 he announced that he had discovered a practical R route across the Sierras. In 1861 he persuaded Collis P. Huntington to join him in forming the Central Pacific RR Co, and to contribute to the cost of a survey over the mountains. This proved satisfactory and another visit to Washington secured the Federal Act of 1.7.1862 for the first transcontinental R. He then returned to California to direct construction. Unfortunately, friction between J. and the Huntington group led to them buying him out in 1863. Judah sailed for the east and contracted typhoid while crossing the Isthmus and d in New York 6 yrs before his great transcontinental line was completed.

Kraus, George, *High Road to Promontory* California 1969; Griswold, Wesley S., *A work of Giants* 1963; DAB V 10 p 229

KEELING, George William

b (?) (?).(?).1839; d Cheltenham
21.6.1913 aged 74.
Eng of Severn & Wye R and GWR.
Son of George Baker K., secretary and
mgr of the S & W. Trained under
Thomas Blackwell whom he succeeded in
1860 as eng of the S & WR which he
extended and converted to a passenger
carrying R in 1875, so opening up the
Forest of Dean. In 1879, in conjunction
with George Wells Owen, he completed
the great Severn bridge, giving the S &
W access to Sharpness docks. On the
absorption of the S & W by the GWR
and MR jointly in 1894 K. became eng
of the Gloucester & Hereford div of
the GWR in succession to J. W. Armstrong. Ret 1904 and engaged in private
consulting practice, and for several yrs
was consulting eng to Sharpness docks
and the Gloucester & Birmingham Nav
Co. Elected MICE 20.5.1873.
Min Proc ICE V 196 1914 p 362; *Engg*
V 95 27.6.1913 p 874; Paar, H. W., *The
Severn & Wye R* 1963 pp 141–3

KELLEY, Howard George

b Philadelphia, Pa 12.1.1858;
d San Diego, Cal, 15.5.1928 aged 70.
Eng on American Rs. Ed Polytechnic
Coll of Pennsylvania, graduating 1877.
From then to 1880 he was asst eng on
works on the Pacific coast of USA.
In 1881 he was app asst eng on location
and const of the Western and Pacific
divs of the Northern Pacific RR between
the Rockies and the Pacific coast. Later
in charge of design and const of timber
vdts and Howe truss bridges on Clarke
Forks div, Montana. He then took
charge of the field work of Tacoma
harbour. 1884–7 worked on mines in
Montana. He then became res eng for
maintenance of way and supt of bridges
on the St Louis South Western RR, of
which he was app chief eng in 1890.
During 1887–98 this R was extended
from 720 miles to 1228 miles, and steel
bridges over the entire line were rebuilt.
In 1897 he was retained as consulting
eng to the Gray's Point Terminal RR.
In 1898 he was app chief eng of the
Minneapolis & St Louis RR. In 1899 he
was made chief eng of the Iowa Central
RR in addition to the above positions.

In 1907 app chief eng of the Grand
Trunk R, Canada, and under his direction 10 000 miles of track were built,
largely in unexplored country. In Oct
1911 he became vice president in charge
of operation, maintenance and const,
and in Sept 1917 became president of
the GT and Grand Trunk Pacific Rs.
In 1922 when the Dominion of Canada
took over control of the consolidated
GT and Canadian Northern systems he
ret and returned to USA. Elected MICE
1920, M American Soc of Civil Engs
1889. M Engg Institute of Canada 1907.
In 1899 he m Cora Lingo of Denison,
Texas.
Min Proc ICE V 228 1928–9 p 351

KENNEDY, James

b Liberton, nr Edinburgh 13.1.1797;
d Liverpool 25.9.1886 aged 89.
Early loco eng and mfr. Left school at
13 and was apprenticed for 5 yrs to a
millwright near Dalkeith. After a period
at Sir John Hope's Collieries at Lasswade
in charge of winding and pumping
engines he worked as millwright in some
cotton mills at Blantyre near Glasgow.
He next worked for John Stevenson in
fitting water wheels at Monkland steel
works. He then spent 2 yrs erecting
pumping and winding engines of his
design at Lavenoch Hall nr Hamilton.
Next, in Edinburgh, he built an engine
for the Lochrin distillery and built
direct-acting marine engines. One of
these was for the *Emerald Isle* of the
St George's Steam Packet Co, Liverpool.
While superintending its erection at
Liverpool he was introduced to George
Stephenson who was then establishing
the works of Robert Stephenson & Co in
Newcastle to which, in 1824, K. was app
mgr, remaining there for 18 months.
While there he designed and built
engines for a tug on the Tees, and two
pairs of winding engines with vertical
drums for hauling loaded wagons up
inclines on the Stockton & Darlington R.
He also planned the first 3 locos by
which the S & D was opened in 1825.
At the end of 1825 he returned to
Liverpool and undertook mgt of the
wks of Mater & Dixon. Later he became
a partner in the firm of Bury, Curtis &
Kennedy, builders of locos, marine and
stationary engines. The first loco built

by K. was the *Dreadnought* for the
Liverpool & Manchester R in 1829.
It had horizontal cylinders working on
a crankshaft connected to the driving
axle by a chain drive. In 1830 his second
loco, the *Liverpool*, was placed in
service. This was the first British loco
with horizontal inside cyls driving direct
onto the driving axle. The success of an
engine for the Leicester & Swannington
R resulted in the firm receiving the
contract for locos for the London &
Birmingham R, in 1838. From 1832–4
the firm sent a number of locos and
parts for wagons and carriages to USA.
In 1844 he joined the firm of Thomas
Vernon & Sons, Liverpool, builders of
iron ships. K. introduced iron deck
beams. He was founder M of the IME,
from 1847, and president in 1860.
Proc IME 10.1886 pp 542–3; *The Eng*
1.10.1886 p 268; *Engg* 1.10.1886 p 351

KERR, James

b Glasgow 14.4.1851;
d Glasgow 4.12.1884 aged 33.
R equipment mfr. Studied arts at Glasgow Univ, then spent 3 yrs with Snell,
Stuart & Co, Glasgow, rolling stock
mfrs, designing and inspecting rolling
stock. He then carried on in business on
his own for 10 yrs as designer and
contractor of rolling stock, and latterly
as mgr and senior partner in the firm
of Kerr, Stuart & Co, London and
Glasgow, makers of portable and narrow
gauge R plant. Designed and completed
7 miles (11.265km) of light R with
rolling stock for the Prince of Morvi.
MIME 1884.
Proc IME 1.1885

KETTERING, Charles Franklin

b nr Loudonville, Ohio, 29.8.1876;
d Dayton, Ohio, 25.11.1958 aged 82.
Pioneer of R diesel traction in USA.
Graduated in mech engg at Ohio State
Univ 1904. Began with Star Telephone
Co, Ashland; later with National Cash
Register Co, Dayton, Ohio. Served 27
yrs as vice president of General Motors
Corpn and as g mgr of research labs
div. Responsible for GM diesel engines.
Developed high-speed 2-stroke types up
to 3000bhp. His engines were specially
developed for rail traction and in 1935
he predicted that in 20 yrs no more

steam locos would be built in USA.
In 1927 he formed the Charles F.
Kettering Foundation for research into
diseases including cancer.

KIRTLEY, Matthew

b Tanfield, Co Durham, 6.2.1813;
d Derby 24.5.1873 aged 60.
Loco supt MR. Son of a colliery owner
who had worked on the Stockton &
Darlington and London & Birmingham
Rs. Pupil of G. and R. Stephenson on
Stockton & Darlington R at age 13.
Later fired locos on Liverpool & Manchester and Warrington & Newton Rs,
becoming a driver on the Hull & Selby
and then London & Birmingham Rs.
K. drove the first loco to enter London
on the London & Birmingham R. When
the Birmingham & Derby Jn R was
opened in 1839 K. was app by the
Stephensons as loco foreman under
Birkenshaw at Hampton. In 1841 at age
28 he became loco supt at Birmingham.
On the formation of the MR in 5.1844
he was app loco supt. There were then
about 100 locos. By the time of his
death the stock had been increased to
1050. Some of his engines were still
running after the formation of British
Railways in 1948. One, 2–4–0 No 158A,
is preserved at the MR Museum near
Ripley, Derbyshire. In 1859 K. was the
first loco eng to combine the firebox
brick arch and the firehole deflector
plate. For details of his locos see *Derby
Works and Midland Locos* by J. B.
Radford, 1971, and also Ellis (below).
In 1847 K. became one of the founder
members of the IME.
Ellis, Hamilton, *The Midland Railway*
1954, 1966; Barnes, E. G., *The Rise of
the Midland R 1844–74* 1966

KIRTLEY, Thomas

b Tanfield, Co Durham, (?).(?).1810;
d Brighton 16.11.1847 aged 37.
Loco supt, N Midland R and LBSCR.
Began career as engine driver on Liverpool & Manchester R, with his bro
Matthew (qv). He then founded the firm
of Thomas Kirtley & Co, Warrington,
building locos between 1837 and 1841.
The firm failed during a slump in 1841.
After working with his bro Matthew
on the Warrington & Newton R he was
app supt of the loco dept, N Midland R,

on 4.4.1843, until 5.1844 when he was succeeded by Matthew on the formation of the Midland R. He remained on the MR as inspector until 5.1845 when he left to work on the Trent Valley R under Thomas Brassey (qv). On 1.2.1847 he was appointed to succeed John Gray (qv) as loco supt of the LBSCR, but his career was cut short in Nov by a brain tumor. He was a highly efficient and well liked loco eng.
Brighton Gazette 25.11.1847; Bradley, D. L., *The locos of the LBSCR* Part 1 (RCTS) 1969

KIRTLEY, William

b Warrington (?).(?).1840;
d Clapham, London, 7.10.1919 aged 78.
Loco supt LC & DR. Son of Thomas K. (qv) and nephew of Matthew K. (qv), loco supt of the MR, under whom, from 24.4.1854 to 1860, he served as a pupil at the Derby MR wks. He then spent 9 months as asst to Charles Markham, supt of outdoor operation, MR. From 11.1861 to 2.1864 K. was running foreman in the loco dept of the MR in the London dist. In 1.1864 he was app supt of the loco wks at Derby and of various repair shops where he continued until 1874. On 12.3.1874 he was app loco C & W supt on the LC & DR at the Longhedge wks, London, to succeed William Martley (qv) who had died. During 1884–5 K. also acted as consulting eng to the H & BR until the app of Matthew Stirling (qv), designing some 0–6–0Ts, 0–6–0s and 2–4–0s for the opening of that line. Full details of the locos of K. are given in *The locos of the London, Chatham & Dover R* by D. L. Bradley (RCTS) 1960. K. ret at the end of 1898 when the LC & DR entered a working arrangement with the SER under the title of South Eastern & Chatham R.
Engg V 88 17.10.1909 p 521

KITCHING, Alfred

b Darlington 19.6.1808;
d Darlington 13.2.1882 aged 74.
Loco mfr. With his elder bro William (qv) he established Hope Town Foundry, Darlington, in 1832. After the death of William in 1850 the business was carried on by Alfred until 1860 when the loco wks was closed to allow extn to the Stockton & Darlington R. The wks and machines were transferred to Whessoe Foundry where wagons, turntables, weighing machines and general castings were made. M of Soc of Friends (Quakers).
The Eng 29.10.1920 p 419; Quaker records at Friends' House, London

KITCHING, William

b Darlington 1.6.1794;
d Darlington 4.9.1850 aged 56.
Loco mfr. First child of William K., hardwareman, later ironmaster, and Hanah, and bro of Alfred (qv). One of the original directors of the Stockton & Darlington R from 1823. With Alfred he established Hope Town Foundry, beside the S & D at Darlington, in 1832. Their first engine, 0–6–0 *Enterprise*, was built in 1833. They also built the first S & D passenger engine, 0–4–0 *Queen*, in 1837. One of their engines, the Hackworth 0–6–0 *Derwent*, built for the S & D in 1845, is preserved at Darlington. K. was a M of the Soc of Friends.
The Eng 29.10.1920 p 419; Quaker records at Friends' House, London

KITSON, Frederick William

b Leeds 29.6.1829;
d Leeds 25.11.1877 aged 48.
Loco designer and mfr. Eldest son of James K. (qv). Qualified as eng at the wks of K. at Airedale Foundry, Leeds, becoming head of the drg office and principal designer of locos. About 1854 he joined his f and bro James K. (qv) in founding the Monk Bridge Iron & Steel Wks for mfr of R materials such as boiler plates, tyres and axles. Invented solid weldless iron tyres and improvements in mfr of R wheels. K. was a vice president of the Iron & Steel Inst. MIME 1859; MICE 12.1.1869.
Proc IME 1.1878 pp 11–12; Min Proc ICE V 52 1877–8 p 277

KITSON, James (senior)

b Leeds 27.10.1807;
d Leeds 30.6.1885 aged 77.
Founder of the firm of Kitson's, Leeds, loco builders, of Airedale Foundry, and a dir of the NER. Ed at local schools, Mechanics Inst, and Leeds Literary Soc. Though not trained as eng, K. had great business ability and towards the end of

1837, seeing a great future in Rs, he went into partnership and formed the firm of Todd, Kitson & Laird which began making R machinery and locos in 1838. This was the origin of the R Foundry, later well known as E. B. Wilson & Co. The first engines to be built, in 1838, were the 0-4-2s *Lion* and *Tiger* for the Liverpool & Manchester R. (*Lion* is preserved at Liverpool Museum). In 1839 Kitson and Laird withdrew from the partnership. Charles Todd continued with John Shepherd as Shepherd & Todd of the R Foundry. Laird, Kitson & Co established the Airedale Foundry in 5.1839. Their first locos were built for the N Midland R in 1840 and began a long association between K. and the Midland R (formed in 1844 and incorporating the N Midland). Other early engines were built for the Manchester & Leeds R and the York & N Midland R. All these were 2-2-2s with outside sandwich frames. In 1842 David Laird withdrew and the firm was reconstituted as Kitson, Thompson & Hewitson. The first locos built for overseas were for the Altona–Kiel R, Germany, in 1844, and they were followed by many hundreds built for India, Australia, South Africa, South America and other countries. Thompson ret in 1858 and the firm continued as Kitson & Hewitson until the death of Hewitson in 1863. In 1865 the entire interests were taken over by the Kitson family and the firm became Kitson & Co. K. was later joined by his sons James and John Hawthorn. K. ret in 1876 and the business was transferred to his two sons. K. was on the bd of the NER and was a dir of the Yorkshire Banking Co. He was a magistrate for the borough of Leeds and West Riding. He was twice m and had 6 children by his first wife and 4 by his second. *Engg* 3.7.1885 p 20; *The Eng* 3.7.1885 p 20; 23.11.1923 pp 548–50; reports in Leeds newspapers 7.1885

KITSON, Right Hon James, Baron Airedale of Gledhow, PC

b Leeds 22.9.1835; d Paris 17.3.1911 aged 76.
Loco mfr. Son of James K. (qv), founder of Airedale Foundry. Ed at Wakefield and Univ Coll, London. With his bro F.W.K. (qv) he was placed in charge of the Monk Bridge Ironworks which had been purchased by his f in 1854 to supply the Airedale and other wks with reliable Yorkshire iron. In 1877 F.W.K. d and K. had to assume direction of the ironworks and also help his f at the Hunslet wks. The latter developed to cover 12 acres and to employ 2000 men. It was converted to a limited liability co in 1886, but K. continued to direct affairs assisted by his eldest son A.E.K. and nephew F.J.K. Although building stationary engines and other machinery the wks are best known for locos for use all over the world. K. maintained a happy relationship with all under him, and was a prominent local citizen and member of the Liberal Party. He was president of the Leeds Chamber of Commerce in 1881. Created baronet 28.8.1886; president of the Iron & Steel Institute (of which he was a founder m) 1889–91. In 1891 he entered Parliament as M for the Colne Valley. He was the first Lord Mayor of Leeds, 1896–7. He was awarded the Bessemer Gold Medal 1903. In 1904 the Univ of Leeds conferred on him the hon degree of D.Sc. On 30.6.1906 he was made Privy Councillor, and his career as MP was terminated on 17.7.1907 when he was created Baron Airedale of Gledhow. He was a Unitarian and gave much of his time to the chapel affairs. Elected MIME 1859 and MICE 12.1876.
Proc IME 1911 p 409; Min Proc ICE V 186 1910–11 p 446; DNB Supplement 1.1901–12.1911; *The Times* 17, 23, 29.3. 1911

KITSON, John Hawthorn

b Leeds 17.5.1843; d Leeds 21.5.1899 aged 56.
Loco mfr. Third son of James K. (qv) after whose friend Robert Hawthorn (qv) he received his second name. Ed Univ Coll Sch, London; BA 1863. Entered Airedale Foundry later becoming a partner with his f and then, on his f's ret, with his bro Sir James K., T. P. Reay and E. Kitson Clark (qv). He managed the loco wks for 36 yrs. Became MIME 1868, MICE 1875.
Min Proc ICE V 137 1898–9 p 430; Proc IME 1898 Part 2 p 269

KITSON, William

b Leeds (?).(?).1813;
d London 27.11.1875 aged 62.
Loco supt GER. Employed on ECR
from 1844. In 12.1865 he succeeded
Robert Sinclair (qv) as loco supt but left
in 6.1866 to become London representative of Kitson & Co, Leeds. K. was
bro of James K. (qv), loco mfr, Leeds,
and of Thomas K., loco supt Great
Luxembourg R.
Engg V 20 10.12.1875 p 453

KITSON CLARK, Edwin (see CLARK, Edwin Kitson)

KLOSE, Adolph

b Pirna, Saxony, (?).(?).1844;
d Munich 2.9.1923 aged 80.
Swiss R eng. Went to Switzerland in
1870, after various R experience, to
take up position as machine inspector in
the then Vereinigten Schweizer Bahnen
(Associated Swiss Rs) in St Gallen. 1884
app to Royal Württemburg State Rs in
Stuttgart. In the same year, with
Bissinger, he brought out the rack-rail
system known as Bissinger-Klose, introduced on the Höllental R. In 1888–9 K.
returned to Switzerland where he supervised const of the rack R from St
Gallen to Gais, the later Appenzeller
street R (now SGA). There he established the Klose system rack. In this
connection he supervised const of the
section from Honau to Lichtenstein and
Freudenstadt to Klosterreichenbach. In
between he was a dir of the Württemburg State Rs.
S.Bz V 82 3.11.1923 p 224

KNIGHT Jonathan

b Bucks County, Pa, USA, 22.11.1787;
d East Bethlehem, Pa, 22.11.1858
aged 71.
Civil eng, Baltimore & Ohio RR. Largely
self ed. At 21 began as a school teacher
and surveyor. In 1809 m Ann Heston
who bore him 10 children. 1816 app to
survey and map Washington County,
Pa. Assisted in surveys for the Chesapeake & Ohio canal and the national
road between Cumberland Md and
Wheeling, W Va, which, in 1825 he
extended through Wheeling through
Ohio and Indiana to Illinois. This impor-

tant work brought him into prominence
as an eng and in 1827 he was app by
the Baltimore & Ohio RR Co to survey
part of the route. 1828–9 accompanied
Whistler and McNeill (qqv) to England
to study Rs and locos. On his return to
USA he was app chief eng to the B & O,
responsible for designing structure and
machinery and letting contracts. On
leaving the B & O in 1842 he became a
consulting eng.
DAB V 10 p 467

KRAUSS, Georg von

b Augsburg 25.12.1826;
d (Munich?) 5.11.1906 aged 79.
Founder and gen dir of Kraus Loco
Wks, Munich. Ed Augsburg Polytechnic.
1847 entered wks of J. A. Maffei,
Munich. 1849 moved to Bavarian State
Rs. 1857 app chief loco supt on the
Swiss North Eastern R at Zurich. In
1866 he founded the firm of Krauss &
Co, loco mfrs, Munich. In 1872 a second
wks was established in Munich–Sendling
and in 1880 a third wks in Linz,
Austria. By 1904, of 5220 locos built,
2186 were for export.
ZVDI V 50 15.12.1906 p 2009; *Engg*
V 82 16.11.1906 p 662

LAMBIE, John

b Saltcoats, Ayrshire, (?).(?).1833;
d Hillhead, Glasgow, 1.2.1895 aged 61.
Loco eng, Caledonian R. His family
moved to Motherwell in 1840 when his
f became traffic mgr of the newly
opened Wishaw & Coltness R which
became part of the CR in 1848. Entered
R service 1846, just after the death of
his f. Apprenticed 5 yrs as fitter in wks
at Holytown Bridge. Became asst loco
supt and in 1891 succeeded Hugh Smellie
(qv) as loco supt, CR. He designed the
condensing locos for the Glasgow underground lines and the 4.4.0s of 1895
developed from the Drummond 'Dunalastair' type. He was succeeded by J. F.
McIntosh (qv).
The Eng V 79 8.2.1895 pp 113, 407
(portrait); *Engg* 8.2.1895 p 178

LANE, Francis Lawrence, OBE

b Manchester (?).(?).1856;
d Headingley, Leeds, 12.3.1931 aged 74.
Rolling stock eng. 1871 apprenticed

under S. W. Johnson (qv) at Stratford wks, GER. 1873 transferred with Johnson to the MR at Derby. 1878 app mgr of the tube dept at Kingston Metal Wks of Allen Everitt & Sons, Birmingham. 1882 app under A. M. Rendel and for 5 yrs engaged on insp of R rolling stock during const at wks in Glasgow and Manchester. Then app wks mgr at Ashbury's R C & W Co, Manchester. 1895 app wks mgr Leeds Forge Co, later becoming g mgr and mg dir. During this period he modernised the wks and patented several details in the use of pressed steel in the mfr of R stock. Received OBE for mfr of munitions in WW1. 1919 left Leeds Forge to become advisory dir to Clayton Wagons, Lincoln, when this co began building R carriages and wagons. Again became dir of Leeds Forge Co when it became associated with Cammell Laird & Co. Became MIME 1896.
Proc IME V 120 6.1931 p 747; *The Locomotive* 15.4.1931 p 143; *Engg* V 131 27.3.1931 p 432

LANE, Michael

b London 26.10.1802;
d London 27.2.1868 aged 65.
Chief eng, GWR. Began engg career in the Thames tunnel under Marc Brunel. 1832-4 res eng at Bristol docks under I. K. Brunel, and then at Monkwearmouth dock, Sunderland, until 12.1840. He then became asst to G. E. Frere, res eng on W div GWR. In 1842 became res eng at Hull docks until 8.1845 when he rejoined the GWR as p w supt. On the resignation of T. H. Bertram at the end of 1860 L. became chief eng until his death from Bright's disease. Much of his work was concerned with the installation of locking apparatus for signals and points. Principal lines built under L. were: Berks & Hants extn Hungerford–Devizes op 11.11.1862; Wycombe R, to Thame op 1.8.1862, to Oxford 24.10.1864 and Princes Risborough–Aylesbury op 1.10.1863; Wenlock R, Bildwas–Much Wenlock op 1.2.1862, to Coalbrookdale 1.11.1864, to Presthope 5.12.1864 and to Marsh Farm Jn, (Craven Arms) 16.12.1867; Nantwich–Market Drayton op 20.10.1863; Wellington–Market Drayton 16.10.1867; Marlborough branch 14.4.1864 and Faringdon

branch 1.6.1864. L. became MICE 5.2.1861.
Min Proc ICE V 30 1869–70 p 441

LANGE, Hermann Ludwig

b Plauen, Saxony, 10.5.1837;
d Manchester 14.1.1892 aged 54.
Chief eng, Beyer, Peacock & Co Ltd. Ed in Plauen. In 4.1855 went to Berlin and served a $3\frac{1}{2}$ yr apprenticeship in engg in the wks of F. Egells until 7.1858. He then spent 2 yrs studying civil and mech engg at Karlsruhe Polytechnic School. 1861 moved to England at invitation of Charles Beyer (qv) and entered the wks of Beyer, Peacock, Manchester, on 15.1.1861 spending his first yr in the wks. He then transferred to the drg office, working first on designs for machine tools, then for locos. 1864 became head draughtsman, and on the death of Beyer in 1876 became chief eng and co-mgr. In 1883 the business was converted into a company and in 1888 L. became a dir. His outstanding abilities showed themselves in his designs for steam tramway engines and rack locos. Elected MICE 5.3.1889. In 1865 he m Miss Mayerhöffer, a friend of his student days.
Proc IME 1892 p 406; Min Proc ICE V 109 1891–2 p 407; *Engg* V 53 1.1892; *Beyer Peacock Quarterly Review* 4.1928

LATROBE, Benjamin Henry

b Philadelphia, Pa, USA, 19.12.1806;
d Baltimore 19.10.1878 aged 71.
Civil eng, chief eng Baltimore & Ohio RR. Son of Benjamin Henry L. (1.5.1764 –3.9.1820), architect and civil eng. Ed Georgetown Coll. 1817 moved to Baltimore where he studied mathematics at St Mary's Coll 1821-3. After a short career in law he obtained a position as eng on the B & O in 1831. He was soon chief asst to Jonathan Knight (qv), chief eng. 1832 L. was placed in charge of survey of line from Baltimore to Washington and later built the Thomas viaduct 9 miles (14.5km) SW of Baltimore, the first stone R viaduct in USA. In 1835 he became chief eng of the Baltimore & Port Deposit RR for which he built 34 miles (54.7km) from Baltimore to Havre de Grace, Md. He then returned to the B & O and built the line through the mountains from Harper's Ferry to

Cumberland in 1836–42. Knight resigned as chief eng 30.9.1842 and L. was app his successor. From 1847 he laid out and built the extn to Wheeling, W.Va, on the Ohio River, 200 miles (322km) of R, including 113 bridges and 11 tunnels, in less than 4 yrs. L. next built the NW Virginia RR (1851–2) for the B & O. L. originated the RR unit of work, the 'ton-mile', and established the max gradient of 1 in 45.5. Ret 1875. In 1833 he m his cousin Maria Eleanor Hazelhurst at Salem, NJ. Their son Charles Hazelhurst L. (qv) also achieved distinction as a R eng.
DAB V 11 pp 25–6

LATROBE, Charles Hazlehurst

b Baltimore, Md, USA, 25.12.1834;
d Baltimore 19.9.1902 aged 67.
Son of Benjamin Henry L. (qv). Ed St Mary's Coll, Baltimore, and learned civil engg under his f and then on the B & O. Later he moved to Florida as chief eng on the Pensacola & Georgia RR. After the civil war he returned to Baltimore and from 1866–77 worked with his f and Charles Shaler Smith in the Baltimore Bridge Co. One of his works was the Verrugas Bridge on the Peru Central R, 575ft (175.264m) long and 252ft (76.810m) high.
DAB V11 p 26

LAVALLEY, Alexander

b Moscow (?).11.1821; d Normandy,
France, 20.7.1892 aged 70.
Ed English school, Tours, and in 1840 at the Polytechnic, Paris. Spent 2 yrs with Bury, Curtis & Kennedy, Liverpool. Returning to France, he worked first under Tétard, eng of the Northern R, then with Le Chatelier on the Paris–Lyon line. 1846 became eng and wks mgr of Ernest Gouin & Co, Paris, for the const of locos and machinery. After inspecting the Menai bridge he began building iron bridges, in France where the firm built the first, and in other countries. Besides many bridges in Russia the firm built the only tunnel on the St Petersburg & Warsaw R. In 1862 they completed the Northern R of Spain, across the Pyranees, in 2 yrs. L. then had to resign from the firm because of ill health. He next undertook const of the Suez Canal which was completed

and opened on 17.11.1869. The work included the filling of the Bitter Lakes with water from the Mediterranean. On its completion he was app eng in chief of the canal. He was created a Chevalier of the Legion of Honour in 1853 and an officer in 1868. MIME 1881, also MICE. President ICE 1877. M Inst CE of France.
Proc IME 2.1893 pp 93–5

LAWS, William George

b Tynemouth 18.4.1836; d Newcastle upon Tyne 22.12.1904 aged 68.
Civil eng NER. Ed Durham Univ. 1853 articled to James Burnett of Thompson & Boyd, Newcastle, for 4 yrs, afterwards remaining in his office until 8.1857. He was then with John F. Tee on surveys for the Border Union, Border Counties and NBR Wansbeck Valley lines. In 6.1860 app res eng on the Wansbeck Valley line for 5 yrs, designing and carrying out all the works. 1865–7 worked under Lane (qv) on surveys for the Bristol & N Somerset and Teign Valley lines. 1867 entered into partnership with his bro Herbert and practised in Newcastle until 1874 during which time they built the Scotswood, Newburn & Wylam R for which L. designed the arched iron bridge over the Tyne at Wylam, op 13.5.1876. In 1874 he became chief asst to T. E. Harrison (qv), NER, in which position he carried out alterations and extensions to Hartlepool docks, the Monkwearmouth–Sunderland line including the bridge over the Wear, and the extn of the South Shields branch of the NER, with the new station. In 12.1881 he was app city eng for Newcastle where he remained for 20 yrs. Under his direction the first electric tramway system was installed in Newcastle in 1900–1. MIME 1874; also MICE
Proc IME 2.1905 pp 151–3

LAYCOCK, William Samuel

b Sheffield 20.10.1842;
d Sheffield 2.3.1916 aged 73.
Inventor and mfr of R equipment. Eldest son of W.E.L. of Samuel Laycock & Sons, hair seating mfrs, Sheffield. After working in family business in 1884 he decided to start on his own as a mfr of R equipment. His first works were in

Victoria Street, Sheffield, and after several enlargements new wks were opened beside the MR at Millhouses. He mfrd a large number of fittings such as carriage blinds, ventilators, window lifts, automatic couplers and vestibules, steam heating apparatus, and numerous specialities connected with carriage upholstery. His firm equipped many Pullman cars, including the *Southern Belle*. In 1910 he became chairman of Cravens Ltd, rolling stock builders, of Darnall, Sheffield, and re-equipped the works with modern machine tools to enable them to build Pullman cars and other high-class rolling stock for British and foreign Rs, in addition to wagons. Among his earliest successes were the pull-down blinds with self-balancing roller, and the 'torpedo' ventilator. He introduced a storage heating system for carriages, and the 'Morton' and other types of wagon brakes, and elastic axlebox packing. On his return from a visit to USA he devised a 'buck-eye' coupling by which the American MCB type could be combined with the British drawbar hook so that carriages could be coupled either automatically or with screw couplings. These were used extensively on the LNER later. Elected MIME 1883.
Proc IME 5.1916 p 458; *The Locomotive* 5.1916 p 82

LEATHER, John Towlerton

b Kirkham Gate, Wakefield, 30.8.1804; d Leventhorpe Hall nr Leeds 6.6.1885 aged 80.
Civil eng and contractor. Eldest son of James L., colliery proprietor, Beeston Park, Leeds. Articled to his uncle George L., eng of Aire & Calder Nav, Goole docks, etc, and in 1829 began practice as eng in Sheffield. 1833 eng of Sheffield waterworks, constructing reservoirs at Redmires and Crooke's Moor. In 1838 joined Waring to form a contractors firm. Their first work was a portion of the N Midland R near Chesterfield. 1839–40 they built the Crewe–Chester R (LNWR). After dissolution of the partnership L. undertook on his own the abortive Tadcaster & York R and then, from 1847–50, he built the Erewash Valley line of the MR. After this he was engaged on various non-R works.

Ret 1877. AIME 1859.
Proc IME 5.1886 p 262

LEATHER, John Wignall

b nr Leeds 26.4.1810; d Leeds 31.1.1887 aged 76.
Trained as civil eng under his f, George L. His early work was principally in connection with reservoirs in Yorkshire, at Eccup, Washburne Valley, Hewenden Beck Valley and the Worth Valley, for Leeds and Bradford Corpns. He also carried out drainage works in the Lincolnshire Fens and for Leeds. With his f he was eng for the Aire & Calder Nav including an aqueduct at Wakefield and locks at Goole. His first principal R work was the Stockton & Hartlepool R, 1837–41, including Greetham viaduct of 92 arches, requiring considerable deep piling. He also laid out the Birmingham, Dudley & Wolverhampton R, 1835, and carried out work on the N Midland and Manchester & Leeds Rs. He also built two notable bridges, Victoria and Crown Point, at Leeds. Ret 1877. MICE 6.3.1849.
Min Proc ICE V 89 1886–7 pp 473–9

LEMON, Sir Ernest John Hutchings

b (?) (?).(?).1884; d London 15.12.1954 aged 70.
Loco eng, LMS. Ed Heriot Watt Coll, Edinburgh. Trained at Hyde Park Wks of NB Loco Co, Glasgow. Served for a time with Brown Bros & Co Ltd, Edinburgh. He then joined the staff of the HR at Inverness. Later worked with Hurst, Nelson & Co Ltd, Motherwell. Returned to R work in 1911 when he was app chief wagon insp, MR. 1917, at age 32, became wks mgr at the MR wks, Derby, and at grouping in 1923 was app div C & W supt at Derby with control of wks at Newton Heath and Earlstown. In 1927 he became C & W supt of the whole of the LMS. In 1931 temporarily succeeded Sir Henry Fowler (qv) as CME until 1932 when he succeeded Lieut Col J. H. Follows as vice president. He was active in the modernisation of motive power depots and goods terminals of the LMS and was responsible for introducing continuous production methods in the const of locos, carriages and wagons. He initiated the school of transport at Derby and was

interested in other training courses. In 1938 he was seconded to the Air Ministry where he served as Dir Gen of Aircraft Production. He returned to the R in 1940 and was app chairman of a commission to consider post-war planning and const of Rs. In 1948 he was made chairman of a govt productivity committee. Made OBE 1918. MIME 1929; also M Inst T.

Engg V 178 31.12.1954 p 845

LENTZ, Dr Hugo

b Keiskama-Hoek, S Africa; 21.7.1859; d Bockfliess, Lower Austria, 21.3.1944 aged 84.

Loco eng in Austria and Germany; inventor of the poppet valve gear for steam engines. In 1866, after the death of his f Louis L., a German sea captain, L. went to Hamburg where, later, he received his first practical education and at the same time pursued his technical studies. Military service in the navy gave him the first impetus for his later inventions and in 1887, after several voyages on steamships, he opened a works in Vienna for the building of small steam engines to his designs and patents. From Vienna he moved to Brünn (Brno, Czechoslovakia) where he invented his poppet valve gear and also an ash regulator and a friction packing for piston rod and valve spindle glands. In 1900 a 1000hp engine with L. valve gear was awarded a Grand Prix in Paris. In the same year L. moved to Berlin where he opened another works. His primary interest was in building steam engines and here he introduced a new design of valve gear for both stationary engines and locos. The valve gear which L. invented at Brno was applied with success to stationary engines by Hanomag (Hannoversche Maschienenfabrik, Hanover), proving its efficiency at over 300rpm. This gave L. the idea of applying it to locos and road vehicles and the first loco with L. valve gear was built by Hanomag in 1902. This had 4 vertical valves above the cylinders operated by a longitudinal slotted valve spindle and normal valve gear. It later became standard on the Oldenburg State R. His next design was an oscillating cam type gear with horizontal valves operated by a central camshaft and

normal valve gear. This was first used in Prussia in 1907 and became standard on the Austrian Federal Rs. His third design was a rotary cam type also with horizontal valves and central camshaft operated by a worm drive. The cams were arranged in steps, cut-off variation and reversal being by transverse movement of the camshaft. It was first used on a German industrial engine in 1921 and later became standard on the Malayan R. It was applied by Gresley (qv) to two NER 'Atlantica' and was used on the D49 'Hunt' class 4-4-0s on the LNER. Cast iron valves proved too heavy and in 1922 L. introduced light steel valves. The fourth design using concentric valves with oscillating cams was introduced for use with Walschaert valve gear and existing piston valve cylinders. In 1926 L. introduced a reversing gear using a variable eccentric, normally fitted outside. In the same year he introduced a pressure equalising arrangement using a device for holding the valves open. His last design was a rotary gear giving a freer exhaust and functioning without to and fro moving parts and links, giving a smooth-working gear with little wear. By 1944 there were about 2000 locos with L. valve gear in various countries. The L. valve gear was also used extensively in marine engines and steam road vehicles. Over 600 marine engines were so fitted, and on the occasion of the 100th such installation, in 1927, L. was made hon Dr of Engg at the Tech High School at Danzig. In 1916 he was awarded the title of Baurat (M of Bd of Works). In 1907 Heinrich Lanz of Mannheim took over the L valve gear design which, with the use of superheated steam, resulted in the most significant improvement in steam road vehicle design. In 1910 a steam consumption of only 2.57kg/hp was measured, a record. In his last years L. worked primarily towards increasing the speed of the steam engine. He also devised a coupling between a marine engine and the propellor shaft which reduced weight on bearings.

Die Lokomotive V 41 5.1944 p 95; RCTS *Locomotives of the LNER* Part 4 1968 pp 90-5

LEVESON GOWER, George Granville William, KG, third Duke of Sutherland

b (Trentham, Staffs?) 19.12.1828;
d Dunrobin Castle, Sunderland,
22.9.1892 aged 63.

R promoter in N Scotland. Ed Eton and King's Coll, London. The connection between the Dukes of Sutherland and Rs began when the first Duke gave substantial financial assistance to the Liverpool & Manchester R and was granted the right to nominate 3 dirs. On the formation of the LNWR in 1846 the Dukes were given the right to nominate one dir. The third Duke was nominated by his f in 1852 and served until his death. He spent much time at Wolverton shops and served as a pupil of J. E. McConnell (qv), acquiring skill as a mechanic and becoming a competent engine driver. He was MP for Sutherlandshire 16.7. 1852–28.2.1861. He succeeded to his Sutherland estate in 1861. He was largely responsible for the const of the Sutherland R from Bonar Bridge to Golspie (op 13.4.1868), providing nearly half the capital. The extn Golspie–Helmsdale (op 1.11.1870) was built solely by his enterprise as 'The Duke of Sutherland's R'. He then became the largest shareholder in the Sutherland & Caithness R, Helmsdale–Wick and Thurso, op 28.7. 1874. These lines all became part of the Highland R in 1884. He was also one of the promoters of the Mont Cenis Summit R (see J. B. Fell). Elected MICE 2.5.1865.
Min Proc ICE V 111 1892–3 pp 359–64; *The Times* 24.9.1892 p 7; *ILN* 1.10.1892 p 419 (portrait); *Graphic* 1.10.1892 p 394 (portrait); Boase, *Modern English Biography*; Vallance, H. A., *The Highland R* 1938, 1963

LIVESEY, James

b Preston (?).(?).1831;
d London 3.2.1925 aged 94.

Eng of the Transandine R. Son of Joseph L., editor of the *Preston Guardian*. Trained at Beyer, Peacock & Co Ltd, Manchester, from where he took up an appointment in Spain, later returning to England to establish himself as a consulting eng. He visited Canada and USA to gain knowledge of R requirements abroad. He was then app consulting eng to the Buenos Aires Great Southern R, followed by similar appointments to other important Rs in S America. The Transandean R, one of the greatest engg feats in S America, was begun on the Argentine side in 1887 and on the Chilean side on 5.4.1889 and was completed in the summit tunnel, 3463yd (3.167km) long at an altitude of 10 466ft (3191m) in 1910. During this time, in 1894, he took his son Harry into partnership and in 1900 Brodie H. Henderson. Both the latter were knighted for services during WW1.
Beyer Peacock Quarterly Review 4.1928

LIVESEY, Robert Martyn

b Caernarvon (?).(?).1874; d Perth,
W Australia 28.12.1944 aged 70.

Eng and loco supt, County Donegal Rs Jt Committee. Ed Caernarvon Gr and Collegiate Sch. Began engg training under his f, then eng and g mgr Donegal R, Ireland. Completed pupilage in wks and drg office in Neilson, Reid & Co, Glasgow. Also studied maths and engg at the Royal Tech Coll, Glasgow. On completion of training he rejoined his f on the Donegal R but soon returned to Glasgow and worked as improver at Barclay, Curle & Co, shipbuilders, and as draughtsman in the millwrights' drg office of Neilson, Reid & Co. After work as asst eng with Topham, Jones & Railton on Bute docks and Port Talbot dock and R contracts he became asst to the CME of Gibraltar Naval Harbour contract. After a few months he was app CME of the entire works, at the age of 25. In 1930 he returned to Britain and surveyed, designed and built aerial ropeways in the British Isles and Algeria for J. M. Henderson & Co of Aberdeen. On 1.11.1906 he succeeded his f as eng and loco supt on the County Donegal Rs (3ft, 0.914m gauge), and from 1.1.1907 was app traffic supt also. He was the first eng to introduce superheaters on narrow gauge locos in the British Isles, and probably in the world. His numerous inventions included pressure lubrication of axleboxes, a wagon brake which could be worked from both sides, an exhaust by-pass arrangement, acetylene generator, concrete sleeper (1915 and other items. In 1912 he read a paper to the IME on rolling stock of the Irish narrow-gauge Rs. He resigned in 7.1922 and went to India as eng and mgr of the Bombay municipal water supply scheme involving const of a pipe line 110 miles (177km) long. Its completion in a year under the contract time displayed organising ability of a high order. In 1927 he settled in Australia and spent several years in farming. From 1936 to his death he acted as designer and consultant to the Swan Portland Cement Co of Perth, WA. Became MIME 1903. Also M Inst Engs & Shipbuilders, Scotland. IME records. *R Yr Bk* 1920 etc

LOCHER-FREULER, Eduard

b Zurich 15.1.1840; d Zurich 2.6.1910 aged 70.
Builder of the Pilatus R and inventor of its horizontal double rack rail. Son of Johann Jakob Locher, Zurich city architect. After leaving school in 1857 he spent a year at Yverdon, Switzerland, then entered the wks of J. J. Richter & Co in Töss to learn mech engg. The sudden death of his f in 1861 gave him the opportunity to leave the mfr of textile machinery and to follow his f's career in architecture. A plan to emigrate to USA was thwarted by the civil war there. In 1863 he supervised building of a factory for an established weaving firm at Azmoos, later becoming a dir. In 1871, with his bro, he formed the firm of Locher & Cie in Zurich. In 1873 he studied the theory of bridges and R building with Prof Calmann and his asst, later Prof W. Ritter, at the Federal Polytechnic. By diligent application the two bros built up the firm and were engaged on the const of the St Gotthard R, Flüelen to Göschenen including the Pfaffensprung spiral tunnel. Faced in 1888-9 with the const of a R to the summit of Pilatus near Lucerne with gradients of 480°/oo, the steepest in the world, L. designed a special rack with horizontal teeth on each side. The pairs of rack wheels engaging these teeth could not climb out, and also prevented derailment. After being engaged on various water projects, L. worked on the first Simplon tunnel in collaboration with Brandt, Brandon & Co, and Sulzer Bros, Winterthur. Soon after the tunnel was started Brandt d

and L. took on responsibility for the whole work, working in temperatures of 55°C which ruined his health. In 1905 the two bros handed over the business to their sons. L. became a dir of SLM, Winterthur, and of the Pilatus R. His advice was often sought and freely given almost up to his death from a heart attack.
ZVDI V 54 18.7.1910 p 1035; Hefti, Walter, *Zahnradbahnen der Welt*, Basel 1970 pp 17-18; *The Eng* V 109 6.1910

LOCKE, Joseph

b Attercliffe nr Sheffield 9.8.1805; d Moffat, Dumfriesshire 18.9.1860 aged 55.
Civil eng. Fourth and youngest son of William L., colliery mgr. Ed Barnsley Gr Sch. 1810-20 pupil of William Stobart of Pelaw, Durham, a colliery viewer. 1823 articled to George Stephenson at Newcastle, with whom he remained to assist on the Liverpool & Manchester R. In 1832 he discovered errors in the survey of the tunnel from Edge Hill to Liverpool Lime Street station, and this led to a difference with Stephenson and L's resignation from the L & M. He then set up on his own account and built the Grand Junction R (Birmingham-Warrington) 1835-7; London-Southampton 1836-40; Sheffield-Manchester, taken over from Vignoles (qv), 1838-40; Lancaster & Preston Jn R 1837-40; Paris-Rouen 1841-3; Rouen-Havre 1843; Barcelona-Mattaro, Spain, 1847-8, and the Dutch Rhenish R, completed 1856. In 1840, during const of the continental works L. took J. E. Errington (qv) into partnership and together they const the Lancaster & Carlisle line, 1843-6; parts of the East Lancashire R 1846-7; Scottish Central 1845; Caledonian R (Carlisle-Glasgow and Edinburgh) 1848; Scottish Midland and Aberdeen Rs; Greenock docks; and a line from Mantes to Caen and Cherbourg, 1852. Locke's lines were noted for their economy of const and his avoidance of tunnels, but with summits like Shap and Beattock between Lancaster and Glasgow which were expensive to operate. He became MICE in 1830. In 1847 he was elected Liberal MP for Honiton, Devon. To Barnsley, Yorkshire, he presented Locke Park. In 1834 he m Phoebe McCreery

who d 15.12.1866.

Webster, N., *Joseph Locke, Railway Revolutionary* 1970; Min Proc ICE V 20 1860 pp 141–8; *The Eng* V 10 9.1860 p 194; Walker, Charles, *Thomas Brassey, Railway Builder* 1969; Nock, O. S., *The Railway Engineers* 1955; Williams, R. A., *The London & South Western R* V 1 1968; Rolt, L. T. C., *Great Engineers* 1962; Morgan, Brian, *Railways, Civil Engineering* 1971; Devey, Joseph, *The Life of Joseph Locke* 1862

LOMONOSSOFF, Dr George Vladimir

b (?) Russia 24.4.1876;
d Montreal 19.11.1952 aged 76.
Loco eng. Grad Inst of Transport, St Petersburg, 1898. Spent 2 yrs in loco testing dept, Kharkoff–Nicolauf R. 1901 app lecturer in R eng and later Prof of R eng and economics, Kiev Polytechnic Inst. During his 6 yrs there the Inst conferred on him D.Eng. 1908–10 app CME Tashkent R. 1911–21 prof of R eng and economics St Petersburg Inst of Transport. During this period he was also president of the Loco Research Bureau; CME Nicolas R; asst dir gen Russian Rs; M of Russia's supreme engg council; Under-Sec of Transport, and president of the Russian War R Mission to USA. In this position, in the latter part of WW1, L. was responsible for design and ordering about 2000 locos. 1921 app high commissioner for R orders and at about this time his proposal for the building of some diesel locos was rejected. Later, as high commissioner for diesel locos, L. was authorised to build 3. In 1925 L. visited England and placed an order with Sir W. G. Armstrong Whitworth & Co Ltd for a 1200 bhp diesel loco designed by Schlebest, but it was sent to Russia in 1926 before completion. After research work in Germany, and lecturing in California he pub *Introduction to R Mechanics* OUP 1933. Became MIME 1931.
The Eng V 194 5.12.1952 p 763 (portrait)

LONG, Stephen Harriman

b Hopkinton, NH, USA, 30.12.1784;
d Alton, Ill, 4.9.1863 aged 78.
Civil eng and explorer. Graduated from Dartmouth Coll, 1809. In 1814, after a period of teaching, he entered the army as an eng. Became explorer and in 7.1820 discovered the peak in the Rockies named after him. In 1823 he became interested in RR routes. In 1826 patented a coal-burning loco. 1827 assigned by War Dept as consulting eng for the Baltimore & Ohio RR Co and in assoc with Jonathan Knight (qv) selected the route. Later president of its bd of engs. In 1829 pub his Railroad Manual, the first American work on the subject. In 1832, with William Norris (qv) and several partners, he formed the American Steam Carriage Co. L's unorthodox designs were not a success and after building about 6 engines the partnership was dissolved in 1834. He then surveyed routes for a R in Georgia and Tennesssee. 1837–40 was chief eng of the Atlantic & Great Western RR. He was interested in bridge const, on which he pub pamphlets in 1830 and 1836. On 3.3.1819 he m Martha Hodgkins who survived him. They had 4 sons and a dr.
DAB V 11 p 380; White, John H. Jr *American Locos, an engg history 1830–80* 1968

LONGBOTTOM, Luke

b Wakefield 2.3.1826;
d Stoke on Trent 12.2.1902 aged 76.
Loco C & W supt, NSR. Apprenticed at Fenton, Murray & Jackson, Leeds, and following failure of this firm with E. B. Wilson, Railway Foundry, Leeds. He then joined Kitson, Thompson & Hewitson, Leeds, loco builders, later going as wks mgr to Bray & Waddington, Leeds. 1855 app gen eng to the Kendal & Windermere R Co. On its amalg with the LNWR in 1860 he entered service with the LNWR, becoming dist loco foreman at Tebay and Preston until 12.1882 when he was app loco C & W supt NSR, remaining in this position until his death. Became MIME 1884. His loco designs were mainly tanks, for short distance traffic; the 'D' class 0–6–0T, 1882, and the DX 0–6–2T, 1899. He also introduced the '100' class 0–6–0 in 1896. He adopted a policy of standardisation and built up a stock of spare boilers, cylinders and fittings common to all locos.
Proc IME 1902 p 198; *RM* 1.1903 p 193

LONGRIDGE, James Atkinson

b Bishopwearmouth, Sunderland,

31.5.1817; d Jersey 15.4.1896 aged 78.
Civil eng. Son of Michael L. (qv) of
Bedlington. Ed at Plessey, Northumb,
where he studied with Daniel Gooch
(qv), and then privately. After a period
at Edinburgh Univ in 1833 he was
apprenticed to George Stephenson at
the Newcastle wks, and later on surveys
on Rs of which G.S. was eng. In 1842
he was at Naples and in the following
18 months in Russia, Germany and Italy,
negotiating contracts for Rs and other
work on behalf of the Bedlington Iron
Co. In 1845 he undertook const of the
Whitehaven & Furness R after which
he moved to Newcastle upon Tyne. In
9.1846 he m Hanah Stanley. On
4.10.1856 he left for Calcutta and laid
out the Calcutta & South Eastern R
from Calcutta to the River Mutla with
extensions eastwards to Dacca and the
Burmese provinces, and in 1857 he was
app eng for the const. In 1858 he went
to Mauritius to lay out a R system in
the island. The lines were begun in
1860 and were carried out by Brassey,
Wythes & Co, L. becoming their chief
agent in Mauritius. In 1865 became
co-partner in contracts for lines from
Bucharest to Giurgovo and for iron
bridges in Wallachia and Roumania. In
1869, at Brassey's request, he managed
the Mont Cenis Summit R (see Fell)
until 1870 when he undertook contracts
for Rs in Cornwall, Sweden, Hungary,
Italy, France and Argentina, visiting S
America in connection with the last in
1875. These contracts resulted in heavy
losses because of the Franco-Prussian
war. Poor health forced him to retire
in 1881 and he removed to Jersey.
Elected MICE 5.2.1856.
Min Proc ICE V 127 1896–7 pp 372–9

LONGRIDGE, Michael

b Bishopwearmouth, Sunderland,
(?).(?).1785; d Bedlington, Northumb,
4.10.1858 aged 73.
Early loco mfr. Son of Michael L. who,
in 1785, purchased the Bedlington Ironworks. In 1823 he entered a partnership
with George and Robert Stephenson and
Edward Pease of Darlington (qqv) for
the formation of the firm of Robert
Stephenson & Co of Newcastle upon
Tyne and the following year, on the
withdrawal of George Stephenson, L.

became mgr. At the same time he was
proprietor of the Bedlington Ironworks
where the first malleable iron rails were
rolled in 1820 under the patent of John
Birkinshaw (qv). Between 1834 and 1837
L. began mfr of locos at Bedlington.
The earliest loco which can be dated
was an 0–6–0 for the Stanhope & Tyne
R in 1837. In 1842 L. severed his connection with RS & Co to give his whole
attention to Bedlington. The last main-
line engines, to a design by J. V. Gooch
(qv), were built in 1852. The last locos
were built in 1855.
Warren, J. G. H. *A Century of locomotive building* 1923, 1970; *The Eng*
21.1.1921 p 68

LONGRIDGE, Michael

b (?) (?).(?).1847; d Exeter 18.1.1928
aged 80.
Son of James Atkinson L. (qv) and
grandson of Michael L. (qv) of Bedlington Ironworks. Ed Radley Coll and
Trinity Coll, Cambridge. Mathematical
tripos 1869. Then worked with his f on
location and construction of Rs in
Europe, first on Mount Cenis Fell R
(see Fell), then on survey for a line to
connect Terni and Ceprano, Italy. He
then helped in const of what later
became the Swedish Central R. Returning to England he supervised design and
const of p w material, bridges and rolling
stock for the Oxelösund Fleu R, Sweden.
In 8.1875 he joined his uncle, R. B.
Longridge, eng of the Boiler Insurance
& Steam Power Co of Manchester, to
be concerned with insurance against
breakdown of steam engines. In 1878
became chief eng of the reformed company, the Engine & Boiler Insurance Co,
later British Engine, Boiler & Electrical
Insurance Co, until his death. Became
MICE and MIME 1880.
The Eng V 145 27.1.1928 p 107

LOREE, Leonor Fresnel

b Fulton City, Ill, USA, 23.4.1858;
d West Orange, NJ, 6.9.1940 aged 82.
Civil eng and RR executive. 2nd son
and 3rd of 6 children of William
Mulford L., shipbuilder and millwright.
Ed Rutgers Coll. BSc 1877, MSc 1880,
hon CE 1896, LLD 1897. 1877 became
asst in eng corps of the PRR. 1879–81
worked as transitman in US Army Corps

of Engs. 1881–3 served as leveller, transitman and topographer in the prelim survey of the Mexican National R between the Rio Grande River and Saltillo. Rejoined the PRR in 1883 as asst eng on the Chicago div of Pennsylvania Lines West, the system west of Pittsburgh operated by the PRR Co. In 1884 he became eng of maintenance of way, Indianapolis and Vincennes div, and in 1886 in the Chicago div and in 1888 in the Pittsburgh div which, with its immense traffic in ore and coal, heavy goods and many curves, mostly single track, was considered the most difficult operating problem in Pennsylvania Lines West. L. improved the operating efficiency, introducing the lap sdg, and in 1889 he was made div supt. His continued progress led to his app as g mgr of Penn Lines W in 1896 and as 4th vice president on 1.1.1901. Early in 1901 the PRR acquired a controlling interest in the B & O and on 1.6.1901 L. was elected vice president of the B & O. His numerous innovations and energetic leadership resulted in much improved efficiency and co-operation with other Rs. He introduced Walshaert valve gear on locos and also Mallet locos. Under him the B & O acquired a controlling interest in the Philadelphia & Reading RR and the Central RR of NJ, so gaining entry to New York City and other important parts. For 9 months in 1904 L. served as president of the Rock Island RR Co (NJ) and chairman of the executive committee of the Chicago, Rock Island & Pacific, the St Louis–San Francisco and associated lines. In 1907 he became president, chairman of the executive committee and M of the Bd of mgrs of the Delaware & Hudson RR Co. Although he served as chairman of the executive committee of the Kansas City Southern in 1906–36, and from 1909 as chairman of the bd, it was the D & H to which he gave most attention thereafter. He improved workshops and took a leading role in guiding the course of RR politics in the Eastern States. In 1922 he pub *RR Freight Transportation*, one of the most outstanding analyses of R operation in the English language. He was a M of the National War Labour Bd in WW1. Ret as president of the D & H in 1938 and d of a heart attack at his home 2 yrs later. In 1885 he m Jessie Taber of Logansport, Ind. They had 2 sons and 1 dr.
DAB V 22 pp 291–3; *New York Times* 7.9.1940 p 15 (portrait)

LOTT, Julius

b Vienna 25.3.1836; d Vienna 24.3.1883 aged 47.
Eng of the Arlberg R. Studied in Göttingen and Vienna. 1861 directed const on Brenner R, opened 1867. 1869 worked on Hungarian Rs. 1875 director of const on Austrian State Rs. In 1880 he was appointed eng for const of the Arlberg R, including the Arlberg tunnel, 6 miles 650yd (10.250km) long, and the Trisanna bridge with a span of 394ft (120m) at a height of 287ft (87.4m). During the const of the Arlberg tunnel L. became ill and died before its completion. The Arlberg R was opened throughout on 20.9.1884. A monument to L. and his colleagues stands at the St Anton end of the tunnel.
Röll; Schneider, Ascanio, *Rs through the mountains of Europe* 1967

LOVELL, Thomas

b London 6.1.1827; d Mussoorie, India, 23.8.1878 aged 51.
Eng on Indian Rs. Son of Charles Wells L., solicitor. Ed King's Coll Sch, London. At age 16 articled to William Stamp, civil eng engaged on Admiralty works in Malta. He was next engaged on the SER between Folkestone and Dover, and later for 6 yrs as contractor's eng on the Portland and Holyhead breakwaters. In 3.1855 he was app asst eng on the Madras R, until he resigned in 5.1862. Later he assisted in the const of the Jubbulpore line of the East India R. After a brief visit to England he was engaged as dist eng on the Oudh & Rohilkund R, in 1868, including the first bridge to be built over the Ganges, at Rajghat, and at the same time on the const of the main line to Moradabad, 215 miles. On 1.2.1869 he became dep chief eng and later chief eng of the Rohilkund line. During his term of office a second bridge was built across the Ganges, at Cawnpore, and other important bridges on the Oudh line, the Touse near Akberpore, in Fyzabad, the Gumti and Saie in Jounpor and

the Burna at Benares. In 1876 he drew up a project for a steam ferry at Rajghat, Benares, to enable goods wagons to cross from the Oudh & Rohilkund R to the EIR across the Ganges. In 1878 he lost his wife and he d shortly afterwards. Elected MICE in 1862.

Min Proc ICE V 57 1878–9 p 309

LOWKE, W. J. Bassett
See BASSETT-LOWKE

LUNDIE, Cornelius

b Kelso (?).5.1818; d Cardiff 12.2.1908 aged 89.
Eng and g mgr, Rhymney R. After attending science classes at Glasgow and Edinburgh Univs, and after the death of his f, in 1832 he began in the service of Charles Atherton on the Broomielaw bridge over the Clyde. In 1836 he moved to Durham, in charge of the Clarence R. From 1839–47 he worked in New South Wales, Australia. After this he was employed by Thomas Brassey (qv) on various R works. 1855–61 acted as mgr of the Blyth & Tyne R. In 1861 he began his long connection with the Rhymney R, then just beginning. As mgr and eng he designed and carried out many extensions and widenings, including Caerphilly tunnel, a vdt of 7 spans over the Taff, new loco shops at Caerphilly, and other works. In 1905 he ret as mgr and was app consulting dir. Elected MICE 7.3.1876.

Min Proc ICE V 174 1907–8 p 380

McCLEAN, John Robinson

b Belfast (?).(?).1813; d Stonehouse, Kent, 13.7.1873 aged 60.
Chief eng, Furness R. Studied at Glasgow Univ. 1838 entered office of Walker & Burges and worked on improvement of Birmingham canal. Later he began on his own in London and was engaged as eng on the S Staffordshire R and branches, the Birmingham–Dudley–Wolverhampton line. He was then app chief eng of the Furness R, carrying out the harbour, docks and Rs around Barrow. He was also connected with the iron and steel mfrs of the district. From 1849 he was connected with London

waterworks. Other Rs with which he was connected were the Tottenham & Hampstead Junction (MR); Bristol & Portishead Pier & R (GWR); and Rs in Galicia and Moldavia for which Brassey was contractor. He was also engaged on numerous non R works at home and abroad. MICE 1844 and president 1865.

Min Proc ICE V 38 1873–4 pp 287–91

McCONNELL, James Edward

b Fermoy, Co Cork, 1.1.1815; d Great Missenden, Bucks, 11.6.1883 aged 68.
Loco eng, LNWR. Apprenticed at Girdwood & Co, Glasgow. He then became foreman at Bury, Curtis & Kennedy, Liverpool, where he first became familiar with loco work. Next with Vernon & Co, Liverpool, and later mgr of a machine shop in Manchester. In 1842, at age 27, app loco supt Birmingham & Gloucester R. His principal app came in 1847, as loco supt of the S div of the LNWR at Wolverton. He gave much attention to the introduction of coal as loco fuel, and he designed a double firebox. His most famous engines were the 'Bloomer' class i/c 2–2–2s, of 3 varieties: the 'Large Bloomers' (1851–61), 'Small Bloomers' (1854–61) and the 'Extra-large Bloomers' (1861). They were finished in bright brick red. He also produced some fine 0–6–0s, the 'Wolverton Goods', 1854–63. When Richard Moon (qv) became chairman of the LNWR in 1861 his antagonism towards M. at Wolverton led to McConnell's resignation in 3.1862 after which he practised as a consulting eng. MICE 1851 and also one of the founder members of the IME in 1847. Following his resignation the N and S loco divs of the LNWR were amalgamated under Ramsbottom (qv) at Crewe.

The Eng V 55 15.6.1883 p 455; Min Proc ICE V 74 1882–3 p 285

McDONALD, John Allen

b Bristol 9.7.1847; d Borrowash nr Derby 18.12.1904 aged 57.
Chief eng, MR. Ed Bristol Gr Sch. 1865 became pupil of his bro A. H. McD, then res eng under W. R. Galbraith (qv) on several branches of the LSWR in Surrey and Dorset. On completing his pupilage he was appointed asst to Charles Richardson on the Bristol Har-

bour R. In 1869 he was app eng for Eckersley & Bayliss, contractors on the LNWR/Rhymney jt Rhymney extn and on the MR Yate–Thornbury branch. On this he was brought into contact with J. S. Crossley (qv), chief eng MR. In 8.1871 he was engaged under John Underwood, eng for new works, MR. As res eng he carried out the Trent–Leicester widening, branches at Burton on Trent and Kettering and other MR works. In 1889 McD. was transferred to Derby as chief asst for new works under A. A. Langley, then chief eng. On the ret of Langley in 7.1890 McD. was app chief eng, MR. He carried out much heavy work, including the Saxby–Bourne line, op 1.5.1894, the branch to Higham Ferrers, op 1.9.1893, new lines between Sheffield and Barnsley, op 1893 and 1897, the New Mills–Heaton Mersey line, op 1901, 1902, including Disley tunnel 2 miles 346yd, Heysham branches, op 11.7.1904, swing bridge over the Nene at Sutton Bridge, and rebuilding of stations at Sheffield and Nottingham. At his death he had nearly completed the first 10 miles (16km), op 1905, 1909, of the never finished main line between Royston and Bradford. Widenings carried out by McD. totalled 167 miles (269km) and included London–Kettering, Erewash Valley line, and Masborough–Royston. He also replaced almost all the cast iron and timber bridges on the MR. In 1896 he introduced a heavier bull-head rail of over 100lb/yd (50kg/m), and over 500 miles (805km) of line were relaid with this before his death. His last and greatest work was the const of Heysham harbour in conjunction with G. N. Abernethy. McD. was unmarried. MICE 5.3.1878.
Min Proc ICE V 159 1903–4 p 370

McDONNELL, Alexander

b Dublin 18.12.1829;
d Holyhead 4.12.1904 aged 75.
Irish loco eng; NER loco supt. Grad with hons at Dublin Univ 1851. Became pupil of Charles Liddell in the firm of Liddell & Gordon, remaining with them until 1858 when he became res eng and loco eng on the Newport & Hereford R. This became part of the W Midland R in 1860. M. stayed until the end of 1861. 1862 joined the Danube & Black Sea Co and was sent out to Eastern Europe to organise the loco dept. 1864 app loco, C & W supt, GS & WR, at Inchicore, Dublin. This was then a smaller system than it later became and was beset with rough track resulting in frequent broken springs on locos. Inchicore works had been built in 1846 and had built locos since 1853. McD's loco designs were influenced by Ramsbottom (qv) but had a better cab than Webb's. His first GS & W engines were 0-6-0s in 1866; 99 were built until 1899. In 1869 he brought out his 6ft 7in (2.007m) 2-4-0s for expresses and a 5ft 7½in (1.714m) 2-4-0 for stopping passenger trains. In 1869–70 he introduced an i/c 0-4-4T single Fairlie loco. The rear bogie had outside frames. Later he brought out an ordinary 0-4-4T, continued by Aspinall (qv) until 1887. In 1876 he brought out the first 0-6-4T for any British R, a class of 6 with 4ft 6½in (1.384m) wheels. In 1877 he introduced the swing-link bogie from America, for the first time in Europe, on a class of 5ft 7½in (1.714m) 4-4-0s, originally 2-4-0s. Another 0-6-4T type appeared in 1880, but these were properly 0-6-0s with the bogie supporting the front of a coach to form a railmotor for the Castle Island & Gortatlea line in Kerry. He also experimented with steel fireboxes. In 1882 he left Inchicore to succeed Fletcher (qv) as loco supt on the NER at Gateshead. Here his sweeping changes antagonised the men. His first NER engine was a 0-6-0 with 5ft (1.524m) wheels, 44 being built from 1883–5. His 4-4-0, 1884–5, with 6ft 7in (2.007m) wheels and the first swing-link bogies in Great Britain, were not entirely successful and led to his resignation. He later worked with Sir William Armstrong, and the Maxim–Nordenfelt Co and visited Brazil and Australia on consulting work. He became ill and d at Holyhead while returning to Ireland in 1904. MIME 1865.
Min Proc ICE V 160 1904–5 p 392; *The Locomotive* 9.1939 p 257

McINTOSH, David

b Cheddleton, Staffordshire, 16.5.1799;
d (?) 7.1.1857 aged 56.
R contractor; son of Hugh M., contractor (d 1840). Ed Univ of Glasgow

and trained under his f. Carried out many major R contracts: 1834–8 Dutton vdt, GJR; 1836–40 5 contracts on GWR, 1837–41 3 contracts on London & Southampton R; 1837–41 Belper contracts on N Midland R; 1838–41 Rugby–Leicester, Midland Counties R; 1838–40 a portion of the Northern & Eastern R.

Min Proc ICE V 16 1856–7 p 162

McINTOSH, John Farquharson

b Forfarshire (?).(?).1846;
d Pollockshields, Glasgow, 6.2.1918 aged 72.

Loco eng, CR. In 1860 entered the works of the Scottish North Eastern R at Arbroath. During this period the Dundee & Arbroath R was amalgamated with the SNE. At the end of his apprenticeship in 1867 he was app to Montrose wks where he remained for 10 yrs. In 1866 the CR absorbed the northern lines. In 1876 M. lost his right hand in an accident, and on his return to duty he was app insp of lines between Greenhill and Aberdeen. 1882 dist loco supt, Aberdeen, and in 1884 at Carstairs. 1886 took charge of running shed at Polmadie, Glasgow. 1891 became chief insp of entire CR loco dept, based at St Rollox wks, Glasgow, under Lambie (qv). Lambie d in 1895 and M. succeeded him as loco C & W supt. His first locos were the '709' class small 0–6–0s of 1895–7, of which 83 were built. They were a development of Dugald Drummond's (qv) design of 1883. Next were the 10 '19' class 0–4–4Ts for Glasgow suburban work of 1895, developed into the '92' class of 1897–1900 of which 22 were built and the '439' class of 1900–14 numbering 68. The class was continued by M's successor Pickersgill (qv) from 1915–22. In 1895 he also introduced the '29' class 0–6–0T of which 9 were built, followed in 1898–1913 by the 120 similar engines of the '782' class. From 1895–1908 he added another 14 of the Drummond 0–4–0ST 'pug' engines. The first of his famous 4–4–0 'Dunalastair' class appeared in 1896, No 721, based on the 4–4–0 design of Dugald Drummond; 15 were built, followed in 1897–8 by 15 engines of 'Dunalastair II' class. The 16 4–4–0s of the '900' or 'Dunalastair III' class appeared in 1899–

1900. In 1904–10 the 'Dunalastair IV' class with 5 ft (1.524m) diam boiler was introduced; 19 were built followed in 1910–14 by the 22 engines of the '139' class of redesigned 'Dunalastair IVs' with altered frames, extended smokebox and Schmidt or Robinson superheaters. Two of these fine engines, nos 48 and 121, were involved in the terrible disaster at Quintinshill in 1915. The later Pickersgill 4–4–0s were a direct development of the '139' class. Several engines of the earlier classes were later superheated. For working trains round the 'Cathcart Circle' he introduced the 12 '104' class of 0–4–4Ts with 4ft 6in (1.372m) coupled wheels in 1899. An enlarged 0–6–0, the '812' class appeared in 1899–1900. The 79 engines of this class were followed in 1908–9 by the 17 of the similar '652' class. In 1912 he brought out the '30' class superheated 0–6–0, but after 4 were built he added a pair of leading wheels to carry the extra weight in the front, the engine becoming the '34' class 2–6–0 of which 5 were built in 1912. A heavy 0–8–0 design numbering 8 engines, with odd wheel spacings, came out in 1901–3, and in 1903–4 6 0–8–0Ts. In 1902 his first 4–6–0 design appeared, the '55' class with 5ft (1.524m) coupled wheels, for the Oban line; 5 were built in 1902 and 4 in 1905. They were the first of a series of i/c 4–6–0s of increasing size and power. Next were the 'Sir James Thompson' class, nos 49–50, of 1903 followed in 1906 by the 5 similar engines of the '903' or 'Cardean' class with larger boilers. These were the most famous of M's express engines. Also in 1906 he brought out the 10 mixed traffic 4–6–0s of the '908' class with 5ft 9in (1.753m) coupled wheels, and the '918' class, 5 engines similar to the '55s' but with 5ft 2¼in (1.575m) diam boilers. His last 4–6–0 was the '179' class of 11 engines built in 1913–14 for express goods work, a development of the '908' class with Robinson superheater and side-window cabs. M. ran the St Rollox wks in a methodical and progressive manner and had a sympathetic relationship with the men. He was as much respected by everyone at the wks as by the chairman and dirs of the co. He was M of the Assoc of R Loco Engs and was president 1911. In 1913 King George V made him

MVO. He ret in 5.1914. He was survived by a widow, 3 sons and 4 drs.
Engg 15.2.1918 p 182 (portrait); *The Eng* V 125 2.1918 p 145; MacLeod, A. B. *The McIntosh Locos of the CR 1895–1914* 1944

MACKENZIE, William

b Burnley, Lancashire, 20.3.1794;
d (?) 19.10.1851 aged 57.
Prominent R contractor. Apprenticed to Thomas Clapham, lock carpenter on the Leeds & Liverpool canal, and at Troon Harbour, Scotland. After the death of Clapham M. worked under Cargill on const of Telford's iron bridge at Craigellachie. Later, until 1832, he worked under Telford on the Birmingham canal. At this time he transferred to R work and became contractor for the tunnel under Liverpool from Edge Hill to Lime Street station. Other contracts followed, on the GJR, Glasgow, Paisley & Greenock, North Union and Midland Rs. In 1840 began his connnection with Thomas Brassey (qv) with whom he carried out much work on Rs in France including a large portion of the Paris & Rouen line, the whole of the Rouen & Havre and Rouen–Dieppe, all under Locke (qv). The revolution of 1848 forced a return to England where, with Brassey, he completed the Eastern Union R and, in conjunction with John Stephenson (qv), the whole of the lines from Lancashire to Edinburgh and Glasgow under Locke and Errington (qv), the Scottish Central to Perth, the Scottish Midland to Forfar, part of the Chester & Holyhead under Robert Stephenson, part of the North Staffordshire under Bidder (qv), the whole of the Trent Valley line and the Liverpool, Ormskirk & Preston section of the East Lancashire R, again under Locke and Errington. Altogether the contracts executed by M. alone and in conjunction with Brassey and John Stephenson totalled over £17 million. Overwork and exposure led, in 1848, to an attack of gangrene in his foot and from then his health declined.
Min Proc ICE V 11 1851–2 p 102

MACNEILL, Sir John Benjamin

b County Louth, Ireland (?).(?). c 1793;
d Kensington, London, 2.3.1880

aged c 87.
Civil eng. Trained under Telford, then engaged on roads and bridges in Scotland and England. About the time of Telford's death in 1834 M. set up as a consulting eng in London. Built the Wishaw & Coltness R and other short lines in Scotland and conducted experiments in canal boat traction on the Forth & Clyde canal. For the Irish R Commission M. was entrusted with surveys in the N of Ireland, and he completed the Dublin & Drogheda R, op 26.5.1844. Knighted in 1844 on completion of the first section of the GS & WR. Later became blind and withdrew from professional work.
Min Proc ICE V 73 1882–3 p 361; *The Eng* V 49 19.3.1880 p 215

McNEILL, William Gibbs

b Wilmington, NC, USA, 3.10.1801;
d Brooklyn, NY, 16.2.1853 aged 51.
Pioneer civil eng of USA RRs. Son of Dr Charles Donald McN. His great grandfather, after the battle of Culloden, had emigrated from Scotland with the famous Flora McDonald in 1746. Ed near New York and began his career in the army where he became a friend of George Washington Whistler (qv) who later m his sister. In 1823 transferred to the corps of topographical engs and was employed to ascertain the practicability and cost of building a R or canal between Chesapeake Bay and Ohio River, across the Allegheny mountains. He also surveyed the James River and Kanawha canals and the Baltimore & Ohio RR. In recognition of his work he was made a M of the Bd of Engs and in 1828, with Whistler and Jonathan Knight, he was sent to England to study R const and there met George Stephenson. Convinced of the practicability of Rs he returned to USA where he and Whistler became joint engs on several R projects in Eastern USA. With Whistler, or alone, he was engaged on the Baltimore & Ohio; Baltimore & Susquehanna; Paterson & Hudson River; Boston & Providence; Providence & Stonington; Taunton & New Bedford; Long Island; Boston & Albany; and Charleston, Louisville & Cincinnati. In 1834 he became brevet-major of engg. 1837 resigned from the army and

became eng for the state of Georgia, conducting surveys for a R from Cincinnati to Charleston. In 1842 he became involved in quelling political disturbances. In 1851 he visited Europe in an attempt to recover his declining health, and in London he was the first American to be elected MICE. But his health was severely undermined by overwork and on his return to USA in 1853 he d suddenly. He m Maria Matilda Camman of New York and had 7 children.
Min Proc ICE V 13 1854; DAB V 12 pp 152–3

McQUEEN, Walter

b (?) Scotland (?).(?).1817;
d (?) (?).(?).1893 aged c 76.
Loco eng, supt and vice president, Schenectady Loco Wks. Emigrated with his parents to USA in 1830, settling in New York State. 1840–5 machinist and loco eng on Hudson & Berkshire RR and Utica & Schenectady RR. 1840 built a small 7 ton 4–2–0 at Albany for Ithaca & Oswego RR. 1845 became master mech of Albany & Schenectady RR. Rebuilt several old engines and built a new one named *Mechanic*. His 4–4–0 *Mohawk* was probably the first engine with cast smokebox saddle and cylinder unit. M. also designed high-speed locos for the Hudson River RR in 1850–2. 1852–76 was supt of Schenectady Loco Wks. Ret 1876 but remained vice president of the wks until his death. M. was the first to apply the air dome to boiler feed pumps. He was a tireless advocate of the American 4–4–0.
White, John H. Jr *American Locos, an engg history 1830–80* 1968

MAHONE, William

b Vermont, USA, 1.12.1826;
d Washington 8.10.1895 aged 68.
Civil eng and president of the Norfolk & Western RR. 1851 became eng of the Norfolk & Petersburg RR of which he became president, chief eng and supt in 1861. He served as a confederate soldier in the civil war. Returned to railroading in 1867 and in 1870 created the Atlantic, Mississippi & Ohio RR out of three short lines from Norfolk to Bristol, thus becoming president of what in 1881 became the Norfolk &

Western RR. In 1880 he was elected to the US Senate. In 2.1855 m Ortelia Butler and they had 3 children.
DAB V 12 pp 211–12

MALCOLM, Bowman

b Chester (?).(?).1854;
d Belfast 3.1.1930 aged 76.
Began R career in loco eng's office of the Belfast & N Counties R in 1870. 1876 app loco eng, at age 22. In 1903 the B & NC system was acquired by the Midland R of England which, in 1906, app M. as civil eng as well as head of the loco dept. At the same time M. became civil eng of the County Donegal Rs. He was responsible for the design and const of the large bridge over the River Bann at Coleraine on the Belfast & Londonderry line, though it was not completed until after his retirement. He was an advocate of the 2-cyl compound system which gave good results on his line, no doubt because of the adoption of Walschaert valve gear. He was the first loco eng to use the Ross 'pop' safety valve which he fitted to 2–4–0 No 57 in 1908. He was also the first British eng to use high-capacity wagon stock, some 30 ton bogie wagons being introduced on the NC in 1891. He ret in 9.1922 after 52 yrs on the R. He was MIME, MICE and M of the Assoc of R Loco Engs.
Proc IME V 124 6.1933 pp 778–9; *The Locomotive* 2.1933 p 29; *RM* 9.1971 p 474

MALLET, Anatole

b Carouge nr Geneva (?).(?).1837;
d Nice (?).10.1919 aged 82.
Loco eng; inventor of the Mallet articulated loco. When he was still a child his family moved to Normandy. Ed Central School of Arts & Mfrs, Paris, 1855–8. After a period on French Rs, and the Suez Canal, in 1864 he was eng for the dredging of Italian ports. 1867 turned to machinery and became interested in compound steam engines. The first compound loco to M's designs was a 2-cyl engine for the Bayonne–Biarritz R, 1876. Adopted in Russia 1880, Germany 1883. 1884 patented his 4-cyl compound articulated engine with hp cyls at the front of the fixed rear unit and lp cyls at the front of the swivelling

front unit. First used 1887 on light Rs. Introduced on European main lines 1890. Appeared in USA on the Baltimore & Ohio 1894. In USA it developed to its greatest extent. M. opposed simple expansion types, arguing that the lp steam gave less trouble with swivelling pipe joints, but the simple type developed in the USA to the UP 'Big Boy' 4–8–8–4s, the world's largest steam locos. From 1880–1918 M. wrote technical articles for the bulletin of the Society of Civil Engs of France.

S.Bz V 74 13.12.1919 p 295; Durrant, A. E., *The Mallet Loco 1974*; Reed, Brian, *Loco Profile 6. The Mallets* nd; Wiener, Lionel, *Articulated Locos* 1930, 1970

MANSON, James

b Saltcoats, Ayrshire, (?).(?).1845;
d Kilmarnock 5.6.1935 aged 89.

Loco supt GN of S and later G & SW Rs. Son of Samuel M., dist traffic supt G & SWR, Ayr. Ed Ayr Academy and the Science & Arts Sch, Kilmarnock. In 1861 he began his training under Patrick Stirling (qv) at the G & SW wks at Kilmarnock. When Stirling left to become loco supt of the GNR at Doncaster in 1866 M. continued his training under James Stirling (qv), working in the drg office. In 1869 M. went to Barclay, Curle & Co, Glasgow, and in 1870 obtained a job as third eng with the Bibby Line, sailing between the Mersey and the Mediterranean, soon rising to chief eng. In 1878, when Hugh Smellie (qv) succeeded J. Stirling as loco supt at Kilmarnock, M. was app wks mgr. In 1883 William Cowan (qv) ret and M. was app his successor as loco supt of the GN of S at Kittybrewster, Aberdeen. Here he introduced two new loco types, 9 0–6–0Ts in 1884–5 and 6 i/c 4–4–0s in 1884; 15 more built 1888–90. On 1.9.1890, following the resignation of Smellie from the G & SW, M. was app loco supt at Kilmarnock. For the G & SW he produced a series of handsome and sound engines including 57 4–4–0s class 8, 1892–1904, and 25 more with smaller wheels in 1895–9. In 1897 he built an experimental 4-cyl 4–4–0; 57 goods 0–6–0s followed in 1897–1907 and in 1903 his splendid 4–6–0 design of which 17 were built,

and two more with superheaters in 1911. He also produced 0–6–0 and 0–4–4Ts, and more 0–6–0s and 4–4–0s. He ret at the end of 1911. His most important contribution was his automatic tablet exchanger of 1886 which, to encourage its adoption by other Rs, he refused to patent, thereby ending much physical suffering resulting from hand exchanging. This was typical of his humanitarian outlook. He treated all the hundreds of men under him with the same grave courtesy. His one flaw was a tendency to inflict severe punishments and drastic demotions often on conscientious men who were merely victims of adverse circumstances. Many of these were remitted by his successor P. Drummond (qv). M's long retirement was saddened by seeing many of his engines ruined by rebuilding, and scrapped by the LMS. He was MIME 1891, M of the Assoc of Loco Engs of GB & Ireland, and of the Inst of Shipbuilders & Engs, Scotland.

Proc IME V 131 1935 p 639; Ellis, Hamilton, *Twenty Locomotive Men* 1958; SLS *The Glasgow & South Western R* 1950; Vallance, H. A. *The Great North of Scotland R* 1965; Smith, D. L., *Locos of the G & SWR* 1976

MARGARY, Peter John

b Kensington, London, 2.6.1820;
d London 29.4.1896 aged 75.

GWR civil eng. In 1838 articled to William Gravatt, then chief asst on the Bristol & Exeter R under Brunel. He later assisted Brunel with the atmospheric system on the S Devon R. On the death of Brunel in 1859 M. was app chief eng of the S Devon R. He carried out the extn from Tavistock to Launceston and the branches to Moreton Hampstead, Ashburton and St Ives. In 1868 app chief eng to the Cornwall R. On its amalg with the GWR in 1876 M. became res eng of the Western Div of the GWR, including the GW Docks at Plymouth which he extended in 1878–81. He also reconstructed the St Pinnock and Moorswater vdts on the Cornwall R. He ret at the end of 1891. Became MICE 31.1.1860.

Min Proc ICE V 125 1895–6 p 409

MARINDIN, Col Sir Francis, KCMG

b Weymouth 1.5.1838;
d London 21.4.1900 aged 62.
Senior inspecting officer of Rs for BOT.
Ed Eton and Royal Military Academy,
Woolwich. Entered Royal Engs 1854.
1860-3 was ADC and private sec to Sir
William Stevenson, Govr of Mauritius.
1866-8 Adjutant at Chatham School of
Military Engg. 1869 app Brigade Major.
1872 obtained his majority and after
vacating his staff appointment at
Chatham in 1874 he joined the BOT in
1877 as an inspecting officer of Rs.
In 1897 he ret from the REs as a
major but later renewed his association
with the army as an honorary colonel in
the Eng & R Volunteer Staff Corps. In
1887, after services to Egyptian State Rs,
he was made a CMG. Knighted in 1897.
M. made several able reports on R
accidents. He advocated the engagement
of relief signalmen and upheld the
importance of housing men near their
work.
RE 6.1900 p 161; The Times 24.4.1900
p 6

MARKHAM, Charles

b Northampton 1.3.1823;
d Tapton House, Chesterfield, 30.8.1888
aged 65.
Ed Oundle. Began business as mgr of
Marquise Iron Wks and Rolling Mills
nr Boulogne in partnership with James
Morrison. The industry was wrecked in
the revolution and in 1848 he returned
to England and joined the engg staff
of the GER. 1851 app asst loco supt
MR under Matthew Kirtley (qv) and
came into prominence with the introduction of coal for loco fuel, instead of
coke. After prolonged experiments he
devised a combination of brick arch,
firehole deflecting plate and blast pipe.
In 1860 he presented a paper to the
IME (Proc 1860 p 147) on coal burning
in locos. 1864 became mg dir of Staveley
Ironworks, making his home in Tapton
House nr Chesterfield, formerly the
home of George Stephenson. MIME
1856.
Proc IME 7.1888 pp 439-40

MARRIOTT, William

b Basle (?).(?).1857;
d (?) (?).(?).1944 aged c 87.
Eng and traffic mgr, M & GN Jt R. Ed
in England and at Neuwied and Lausanne.
Became a pupil at Ransome & Rapier,
Ipswich, 1875-9, and with R. H. Hill,
civil eng in London. 1880-1 emp as
draughtsman at Ransome & Rapier.
1881 app eng and contractor's agent on
const of various sections of the Yarmouth & N Norfolk R and the Yarmouth
Union R for Wilkinson & Jarvis. App
eng to Eastern & Midlands R in 1883
and loco supt in 1884. Negotiated parliamentary work, const Lynn loop 1885
and Cromer line 1887. Also worked in
private practice. In 1893 he transferred
to the service of the M & GN Jt Committee on its purchase of the line. On
the death of J. J. Petrie in 1918 M. was
app to the combined position of eng
and traffic mgr, from 1.1.1919. He ret
on 31.12.1924. MIME 1887.
Wrottesley, A. J., The Midland & Great
Northern Jt R 1970; Clark, R. H., A
short history of the M & GN Jt R
1967; The Locomotive 14.2.1925 (portrait)

MARSH, Douglas Earle

b Brighton (?).(?).1862;
d Bath 25.5.1933 aged 71.
Loco supt LBSCR. Ed Brighton Coll.
1879 entered a 3 yr engg course at Univ
Coll, London. Began R career at
Swindon wks, GWR, under William
Dean (qv) and was later emp as draughtsman and insp of materials. In 1888
became asst wks mgr, Swindon. 1896
app chief asst mech eng under H. A.
Ivatt (qv) at Doncaster, GNR. On
1.1.1905 app loco supt LBSCR at
Brighton to succeed R. J. Billinton (qv).
He was an early advocate of feed-water
heating and superheating. He abandoned
the Stroudley yellow livery for passenger
engines and adopted a dark umber brown,
and black for goods engines. His first
design, to supply urgent demands for
powerful express engines, was a 4-4-2
similar to Ivatt's GNR type, class H1, 5
engines built 1905-6 followed by 6
class H2 in 1911-12. For suburban
traffic he designed 4 types of 4-4-2T,
classes I1-I4. Only the I3s were wholly
successful. In 1909 one of the I3s demonstrated the advantages of superheating
during trials on the LNWR. His C3

0–6–0 of 1906 was a big advance in freight power. In 1910 and 1912 he brought out his two fine 4–6–2Ts. The second was the first LBSCR engine to have Walschaert valve gear. He ret towards the end of 1911. Became consulting eng to Rio Tinto Co until 1932. Elected MIME 1896.
Proc IME 3.1934 p 475; *The Locomotive* 15.6.1933 p 194

MARSH, Thomas Edward Milles

b Biddestone, Wiltshire, 3.4.1818; d Bath 19.12.1907 aged 89.
Civil eng. Trained under G. E. Frere on const of the W div of the GWR. Later became res eng on the works at Bath and, on the opening of the line on 30.6.1841 until 12.1841, he was responsible for p w up to and including Box tunnel. After a period on the Caledonian R, River Wye works and a colliery near Newport, Mon, in 1844, he became chief eng of the Monmouthshire Canal Nav Co for the survey and const of the Newport–Pontypool R until work was suspended in 1846. M. then worked under Brunel as res eng on the Wilts, Somerset & Weymouth R. In 1847 Brunel appointed him insp of all p w work and materials. On the death of Brunel in 1859 M. was entrusted with similar work for other engs in England, Canada and S America and for Hawkshaw (qv) in India and Mauritius. In 1860–3 M. was chief eng to the Sittingbourne & Sheerness R (LCDR op 19.7. 1860) and Queensborough pier.
Min Proc ICE V 176 1908–9 p 329

MARSH, Sylvester

b White Mountain Village, NH, USA 30.9.1803; d Concord, NH, 30.12.1884 aged 81.
Builder of the first mountain rack railway. At age 19 he walked 150 miles (241km) to Boston to find employment. In 1833 he moved to Chicago, then a settlement with a pop of only 300, and became prominent in the meat canning industry. In 1855 took up the idea of a cog R to the summit of Mount Washington close to his old home. After many attempts he obtained a concession and the assistance of financiers. Work began in 1866 and on 3.7.1869 the line was opened, one of the roughest and oddest

Rs ever built. The original loco is preserved, and the line still operates today. The ladder type rack formed the prototype of that designed by Riggenbach (qv).
Teague, Ellen, C., *Mount Washington R Co*, Newcomen Soc of N America 1970

MARSHALL, William Prime

b St Albans 28.2.1818; d Edgbaston, Birmingham, 27.3.1906 aged 88.
Ed by his f, Rev William M. and at King's Coll, London. 1835 entered office of Robert Stephenson (qv) and worked on drawings for the London & Birmingham R. In 1839 he designed and built the stations on the N Midland R on the opening of which, in 1840, he was app loco supt, holding this office until the formation of the MR in 1844. In 1843 he carried out experiments in atmospheric propulsion with Geoge Berkeley on the Dalkey extn of the Dublin & Kingstown R. In 9–10.1844 he altered the gauge of the Eastern Counties R from 5ft (1.524m) to standard. In 1845, on the recommendation of R. Stephenson, he was app loco eng on the Norfolk R. In 1848 engaged in consulting practice in Birmingham. On 24.1.1849, on the nomination by R. Stephenson, he was app secretary of the IME, holding office for 29 yrs until the removal of the Inst to London, at the same time continuing in private practice. During this period he was engaged on investigations and in preparing reports on matters including working of locos between London and Rugby for the LNWR, and on the mfr of springs for the E India and Madras Rs. He ret from the secretaryship of the IME in 1877 and, in partnership with his son W. Bagley M., continued his inspection work until 1904. He was a M of various societies in Birmingham. In 1908 he gave a paper to the ICE on *The evolution of the loco engine* (Min Proc ICE V 133 p 241) for which he was awarded the George Stephenson Medal and a Telford premium. Elected MICE 10.4.1866. MIME 10.1847, the year the Inst was founded.
Min Proc ICE V 163 1906–7 p 345; Proc IME 5.1906 pp 335–6

MARTLEY, William

b Ballyfallon, Ireland, 4.1.1824;
d Clapham, London, 6.2.1874 aged 50.
Loco supt, LC & DR. In 1841 articled to Daniel Gooch at Swindon, GWR, and later app dist loco eng at Exeter. 1847 app loco supt of Waterford & Limerick R but left after a few months to become loco supt on the S Devon R. On the opening of the first section of the S Wales R, from Chepstow to Swansea, in 1850 he was app loco supt of that company, with hq at Newport. On 5.4.1860 he was app loco supt of the LC & DR (to which its name had been changed from E Kent R on 1.8.1859) with responsibility also for the cross-Channel steamer service, remaining in this position at Longhedge wks, London, until his death. His first engines were 14 0-6-0 gds ordered from Sharp, Stewart and R. Stephenson in 1861-2 and 6 from J. Fowler & Co in 1866. The 12 'Dawn' class 2-4-0s came from Sharp, Stewart in 1862-3. In 1863 his 6 'Rose' class 2-4-0Ts were delivered from R. & W. Hawthorn, and were followed by 6 more 2-4-0Ts built at Longhedge and 6 2-4-0s by Brassey & Co in 1865. For working over the Metropolitan R in 1866 M. ordered 14 0-4-2WTs from Neilson & Co. All had Scottish names and were known as the 'Scotchmen'. 6 'Large Scotchmen' were delivered from Neilson in 1873. His last engines were 2-4-0s, the 3 'Enigma' class, built at Longhedge in 1869-70 and the 6 'Europa' class, 4 by Sharp, Stewart 1873 and 2 built at Longhedge in 1876 after M's death. All his engines had names only: they were numbered by his successor W. Kirtley (qv). The last M. engines in service were two Large Scotchmen wdn 1914. M. was noted for his happy disposition and sense of humour. Became MICE 2.4.1867.
Min Proc ICE V 41 1874-5 p 221; Bradley, D. L., *Locos of the LC & DR* RCTS 1960

MASKELYNE, John Nevil

b Wandsworth Common, London, 3.1.1892; d London 24.5.1960 aged 68.
Loco historian and model engg consultant. Grandson of the famous stage illusionist. Ed St Paul's Sch, Hammer-

smith, 1905-11. His tech training was at King's Coll, Univ of London, 1911-14. He then joined Waygood Otis Ltd, lift and escalator engs, until 1932 when he set up as a model engg consultant. He gave much of his time to the study of loco engg and history and to the design of model locos. In 1909 began writing for R and model R periodicals. 1919 elected AILocoE. 1926 pub *Locos of the LBSCR 1903-23*, continuing the history by G. F. Burtt (qv). In 1935 he became editor of *Model R News* and tech editor of *Model Engineer* until he ret in 1956. He was president of the SLS from 1925 to 1960. As a musician he was a fine pianist and organist and also composed but had none of his music published.
SLS Journal 7.1960 pp 207-8; 8.1960 pp 240-3; *Journal* ILE V 50 1960-1 p 395

MASON, William

b Mystic, Conn, USA, 2.9.1808;
d Taunton, Mass, 21.5.1883 aged 74.
Inventor, loco mfr. Began in textiles, inventing various improvements in textile machinery. 1835 went to Taunton, Mass, and in 1842 purchased the plant of Leach & Keith, producing textile machinery and general engg. Began building locos 1852, completing his first on 11.10.1853. The 700th was completed a week after his death. He built locos 'for fun' (his statement) and he made no profit on them. His locos were noted for their beauty and symmetry of design and excellence of workmanship, and they influenced N American loco const. He also mfrd car wheels with tubular spokes. On 10.6.1844 he m Harriet Augusta Metcalf of Cambridge, Mass, and was survived by 2 sons and a dr.
DAB V 12 pp 377-8; White, John H. Jr, *American Locos, an engg history 1830-80* 1968

MAUNSELL, Richard Edward Lloyd, MA

b Raheny, Co Dublin, 16.4.1868;
d Ashford, Kent, 7.3.1944 aged 75.
CME of SER, and SR. 7th son of John M. Ed Armagh Royal Sch and grad MA at Trinity Coll, Dublin. Decided to study R engg and became a pupil of H. A. Ivatt (qv), then loco eng GS &

WR at Inchicore wks, Dublin. In 1891 joined the LYR at Horwich under Aspinall (qv) who had been Ivatt's predecessor at Inchicore, gaining experience in the wks and drg office. Later became loco foreman at Blackpool and Fleetwood. 1894 app asst loco supt E Indian R, later supt Asansol loco dist, Bengal, nr the border with Bihar. 1896 app wks mgr Inchicore under Robert Coey (qv), succeeding Coey as CME of the GS & WR in 1911. In 1911 app loco C & W supt SE & CR at Ashford, Kent. His 2-6-0 and 2-6-4T designs were outstanding engines, based on GWR practice. After WW1 M. helped in preparing designs for British standard locos, but the grouping of Rs in 1923 halted progress with these. On 1.1.1923 M. became CME of the new Southern R, in charge of loco wks at Ashford, Brighton and Eastleigh. He adopted the 4-6-0s of Robert Urie (qv) of the LSWR as a basis for a series of SR standard designs. His 'Lord Nelson' class 4-cyl 4-6-0 of 1926 was unusual in having cranks set at 90° and 135°, but it was never an outstanding success. His 'School' class 3-cyl 4-4-0 of 1930, however, was a brilliant performer. He also had some of Wainwright's (qv) 4-4-0s rebuilt into modern machines. His 'Q' class 0-6-0 of 1938 gave good service. He completely reorganised the wks at Ashford and Eastleigh. He was MIME and president ILE 1916, 1928. Ret 10.1937. Proc IME V 152 1954 pp 109–10 (portrait); *Engg* V 157 17.3.1944 p 215; *The Eng* V 177 17.3.1944 pp 212–13; *Journal ILE* V 34 1944 p 63 (portrait); *The Locomotive* 15.8.1923 p 245 (portrait); Bradley, D. L. *The Locos of the SR 1975, 1976* (RCTS); Holcroft, H., *Locomotive Adventure* 1962; Nock O. S. *The Locos of R. E. L. Maunsell 1911–37* 1954

MEARS, Otto

b Kurland, Russia, 3.5.1840; d Pasadena nr Los Angeles 24.6.1931 aged 91.
Famous road and R eng in the Colorado Rockies. One of 10 boys and 2 girls with English f and Russian mother. As a boy travelled to England and at age 10 to New York and on to Califorina. He built his first road, 50 miles (80km) from Saguache to Nathrop over Poncha Pass, Colorado, in 1867. It was followed in 1871 by the 96 mile (154.5km) toll road from Saguache to Lake City over Cochetopa Pass. Eventually M. had built 450 miles (724km) of road in the San Juan County of Colorado and over these, from 1866–73, he operated pack trains. His greatest work was around Silverton where he arrived on 14.7.1875. Other important Colorado roads were: 1877 Lake Fork–Ouray; 1878–9 Marshall Pass; 1882 Ouray–Red Mountain; 1883 Red Mountain–Silverton. His interest now turned to the 3ft (0.914m) gauge Rs then being built in Colorado, many of them on the formation of his roads, to serve the mines. He began the Silverton RR in 1887, the first of his three 3ft gauge 'short lines' at Silverton; short, but magnificently engineered. On the Silverton RR with a summit of 11 235ft (3425m) at Red Mountain Pass and on the Silverton Northern, 1889, he even operated sleeping cars. The impossibilty of extending to Ouray from the south forced him to build the 162 mile (261km) Rio Grande Southern RR from Durango to Ridgway north of Ouray, in 1890-1. From 1907–12 he was engaged in mining activities in Colorado.
Decker, Sarah Platt, *Pioneers of the San Juan Country* 1942; DAB V 12 p 485

MEEK, Sturges

b Staffordshire 9.4.1816; d Kensington, London, 23.2.1888 aged 71.
Civil eng, E Lancs R and LYR. Pupil of George Stephenson. Worked on the London & Birmingham R from age 17 in 1833 and was soon app asst eng. In 1841 on the recommendation of Locke (qv) he was app eng on a section of the Paris–Rouen R. He then worked under Locke on the GNR from 1844. In 1845 he m Josephine Hownam. Following a dispute between Locke and the GNR Co in 1844 M. went with Locke to Holland to work on the Dutch Rhenish R. Also with Locke M. worked on various Rs in S England, and on the Derby–Stoke–Crewe line of the NSR. In 1846 he became eng of the Liverpool, Ormskirk & Preston R, later E Lancs R. 1853 succeeded John Hawkshaw (qv) as chief eng of the LYR which, in 1859, was amalgamated with the ELR of which he was also eng. He was responsible for

many important works: Accrington vdt 1848; North Docks branch, Liverpool 1855; Chatburn–Hellifield line, completed 1879; Meltham branch 1868; doubling Halifax branch 1869; Newton Heath Carriage wks 1877; Cheetham Hill–Radcliffe 1879; Denby Dale new vdt 1880; Brighouse–Wyke line 1881; Rochdale–Bacup 1870, 1881; Bacup branch widening 1857, 1881. He was a man of absolute integrity and enjoyed universal confidence as an arbitrator. Ret after the passing of the LYR 1882 Act and was succeeded by W. Hunt (qv), his chief asst since 1876. MICE; also MIME 1863.
The Eng V 65 2.3.1888 p 181; Proc IME 2.1888 p 155

MEIGGS, Henry

b Catskill, Green County, NY State, 7.7.1811; d nr Lima, Peru, 30.9.1877 aged 66.
Eng and contractor, responsible for possibly the most outstanding piece of R engg in the world, the Peru Central. He had an astute business sense, ability to select the right men to serve under him, and he was a skilled mathematician. Achieved his first success as timber merchant in Boston, moving to New York in 1835. Here he made a large fortune, only to lose it all in the financial panic of 1837. However, in another year he was the owner of a large timber yard in Williamsburg, becoming insolvent again in 1842. He then returned to New York where he took a keen interest in the establishment of musical activities. The discovery of gold in California lured him away from New York for ever. He left with a cargo of timber which he sailed round the cape and, in 7.1849, sold in San Francisco at a profit of $50 000. There followed a period of speculative adventures until another financial crisis in 1854 crippled him once more. His unscrupulous principles now showed themselves, and by means of forgeries he acquired $900 000, immediately sailing to Chile to avoid capture. It was here he began his R activities, constructing the Santiago R at a profit of $1 320 000. After living a princely life in Chile, he removed to Peru in 1867 and began the Oroya R from Lima to

Oroya in the Andes, later the Central of Peru, climbing to 15 688ft (4781m) in little over 100 miles (160km), the highest R in the world. The daring conception of the R and the immensity of the problems in its construction must have imposed a severe strain for in 1875 he suffered a paralytic stroke from which he never fully recovered. He d before the R had achieved its summit, but the rest of the route was fully worked out. Apart from this he completed all his R contracts ahead of time. To the end, however, he was unscrupulous, his speculations even injuring the Peruvian currency. At the same time, possibly for the benefit of his own concience, he showed great generosity towards charitable causes, even anonymously paying gambling debts of men in his employment. He was always considerate of the men under him and was well liked by them, and he was the first big contractor in N or S America to treat the imported Chinese coolies as humans.
Engg 2.11.1877 p 343; Stewart, Watt, *Henry Meiggs, Yankee Pizarro* USA 1946; Fawcett, Brian, *Rs of the Andes* 1963

METCALFE, Sir Charles Herbert Theophilus

b Simla, India, 7.9.1853; d Godalming, Surrey, 29.12.1928 aged 75.
Civil eng. Ed Harrow Sch from age 14; 1874 to Univ Coll, Oxford, where he formed a lifelong friendship with Cecil Rhodes. 1878–81 articled to Sir Charles Fox & Sons. Later engaged as asst eng on Irish lines and on the W Lancs R. In 12.1881 he was app res eng on the Southport & Cheshire Lines Extn R and on the Hesketh Marsh reclamation. 1884–6 res eng on Liverpool, Southport & Preston Jn R and in 1886 jt eng with Sir Douglas Fox (qv) for the Liverpool, St Helens & S Lancs R. In 6.1888, as partner in firm of Sir Douglas Fox & Partners, he became jt eng with Sir Douglas Fox on the Bechuanaland R, his first experience in S Africa where he remained connected until his death. His firm surveyed and supervised the whole of the R from Kimberley to the Congo as well as the Beira & Mashonaland R and they built the great bridge over the Zambesi at Victoria Falls. It

was a result of M's business sense that the route of the R was directed westwards to the Congo instead of northwards to Tanganyika, so gaining enormously in traffic. At the time of his death M. was consulting eng to the Rhodesia R, Mashonaland R, Beira R and others. MICE 1897 and M of Council ICE 1904.
Min Proc ICE V 228 1928–9 pp 352–3; *Beyer, Peacock Quarterly Review* 4.1929

MEYER, Adolphe

b (?) 8.10.1840; d (?) 29.6.1891 aged 50.
son of J.J.M. (qv) and joint inventor of the M. articulated loco.

MEYER, Jean Jacques

b (?) (?).(?).1804;
d Vienna (?).(?).1877 aged c 73.
Inventor of the M. articulated loco. Obtained a diploma in mech engg at the Ecole des Artes et Métiers, Paris. In 1831 he established the Mulhouse wks where he built locos for German and Austrian Rs and built the first bogies to be used in France. Financial trouble forced him to sell the business which later became the Société Alsacienne de Constructions Mécaniques. On 15.3.1861 M. and his son Adolphe took out a French patent for articulated tank engines. The original M. designs were 0–4–4–0 and 0–6–6–0. Both power bogies were pivoted and the cylinders were at the inner ends. He exhibited his drawings at the London exhibition of 1862 and the Paris of 1867 and the first M. loco was built in 1868. The design was taken up by Kitsons of Leeds and extended to give greater space for the firebox. The first Meyer–Kitson engines, 0–6–6–0s with cyls at the rear of each bogie, were built in 1903. A later design with cyls at the outer ends appeared in 1908.
Wiener, Lionel, *Articulated Locos* 1930. 1970

MILLER, George Mackay

b Pentonville, London, 7.12.1813;
d Dublin 4.1.1864 aged 50.
Civil and loco eng. Apprenticed to Lloyd of Southwark, London, mech engs and millwrights. He was then engaged by John Dixon (qv), res eng on the Liverpool & Manchester R, as asst in the drg office. He was later app in the same

work by R. Stephenson on the London & Birmingham R. In 1839 he became res and loco eng of the London & Greenwich R and was in charge for several yrs. In 1844 he was app by Locke (qv) as eng to the Jamaica R for which he prepared the drawings and carried out the const. On his return he was app res eng, loco C & W supt of the GS & WR, Ireland until his sudden death resulting from a chill caught while riding on an engine.
Became MICE 6.1844
Min Proc ICE V 24 1864–5 p 534

MILLER, Dr John

b Tyrone, Ireland, 29.2.1872;
d Woodford Green, Essex, 16.5.1942 aged 70.
Chief civil eng GER. Ed St Wearstown Academy and Belfast Univ (BSc engg 1904). After 5 yrs as lecturer in mathematics at Central Tech Coll of the City & Guilds of London Inst he went to USA in 1909 as asst eng on track const and bridge work, Pennsylvania RR, serving as draughtsman, inspector, then asst eng. Returned to England 2.1916 and entered service of GER. On ret of Horace Wilmer in 1917 the g mgr was additionally app eng in chief. M. became chief assst in civil eng's dept. App chief civil eng in 1919. Following formation of the LNER on 1.1.1923 M. was app chief eng NE Area in 1925 with hq at York. He was in charge of widening main line York–Northallerton and installation of colour-light signalling on that section. He also carried through electrification of the Newcastle–South Shields line. In 1922 Queen's Coll, Belfast, conferred on him hon LLD. Ret 1937. MICE 1923. President P W Inst 1920, 1921.
The Eng V 173 22.5.1942 p 430; *Engg* V 153 22.5.1942 p 414

MILLHOLLAND, James

b Baltimore, (?).(?).1912;
d (?) (?).(?).1875 aged c 63.
Loco eng; pioneer of coal-burning fireboxes. At 18 apprenticed in George W. Johnson's machine shop, assisting in const of Cooper's *Tom Thumb* and another engine built by Johnson in 1831. Later he worked at the Allaire marine engine wks, New York City. 1838 master mech on Baltimore & Susquehanna RR.

Built 2 heavy freight 4–4–0s, and designed a cast iron crank axle for i.c. engines. 1843 patented a 6-wheeled freight car. Built a plate-iron bridge in 1847. 1848 master mech on Philadelphia & Reading RR. 1855 designed a firebox for burning anthracite. The P & R became one of the first all coal burning Rs in USA. 1863 built the first 0–12–0, *Pennsylvania*, at Reading shops. M. was one of the first to use feed-water heaters, superheaters and steel tyres. Ret 1866. White, John H. Jr, *American locos, an engg history 1830–80* 1968

MITCHELL, Alexander

b Nova Scotia (?).(?).1832;
d (?).(?).1908 aged c 76.
Loco eng, and originator of the 2–8–0 type. Began as machinist in the Camden & Amboy RR shops. 1859–61 asst supt of Trenton Loco Wks, NJ; then joined Lehigh Valley RR until his ret in 1901. In 1866 he built the first 2–8–0 named *Consolidation* which gave its name to the type, which became the most numerous in USA. 1867 assisted in design of the first 2–10–0 to be built in USA. White, John H. Jr, *American Locos, an engg history 1830–80* 1968

MITCHELL, Joseph

b Forres, Morayshire, 3.11.1803;
d Inverness 26.11.1883 aged 80.
Civil eng in Scottish Highlands. Son of John M. who worked under Telford on Highland roads and bridges. Ed Inverness Academy and at Aberdeen. Learned practical masonry under Telford on the Caledonian Canal locks at Fort Augustus. Subsequently spent 3 yrs as pupil of Telford. On the death of his f in 1824 M. succeeded to the charge of Highland roads and bridges for 18 yrs. In this capacity he also erected 40 churches in the Highlands and Islands for the Govt as representing the Church of Scotland. 1828 app eng to the Scottish Fishery Bd, designing and maintaining harbours etc all round the Scottish coast. 1837 M. surveyed the R from Edinburgh to Glasgow via Bathgate. 1844 surveyed and laid out the Scottish Central R. 1845 he surveyed the R from Perth to Inverness over the Grampians, with branches, altogether 183 miles, but the Bill was defeated in 1846 on grounds of impracti-

cability. Subsequently, however, the Highland R main line was built along his route. Largely by the exertions of M. a company was formed in 1853 to build a R from Inverness to Nairn. This opened in 1855 and by 1858 was extended to Elgin and Keith to join the GN of S. In 1859 M. surveyed the line into Ross-shire, opened to Invergordon in 1863 and to Bonar Bridge in 1864. In the summer of 1860 M. began the survey of the Highland line from Forres to Dunkeld, 104 miles (167 km), which was opened throughout in 1861. In 1862 M. entered into partnership with his two assts, William and Murdoch Paterson (qv). In 1864 M. surveyed the Skye line which was const by M. Paterson and opened in 1870. M. next surveyed the R to Brora in Sutherland for which the Act was obtained in 1865, but he ret before the R was completed. In 1864 Mitchell & Co were also commissioned to survey a R in Caithness, but because of formidable difficulties the R, built by M. Paterson, was not opened to Wick and Thurso until 1874. M's many viaducts and bridges, soundly built on secure foundations, are notable for their architectural grace. In 1862 M. was struck down by a paralytic disease and after a slow recovery he ret in 1867. Until his death 16 yrs later he took an active interest in many public works in and around Inverness, and his advice was constantly sought and given. Elected MICE 1837. He was the first to establish the minutes of proceedings of the Institution.
Min Proc ICE V 76 1883–4 pp 362–8; Mitchell, Joseph, *Memories of life in the Highlands*

MITCHELL, Thomas Telford

b Inverness (?).(?).1815;
d Perth 31.12.1863 aged c 48.
Youngest son of John M., eng and general inspector for Highland roads and bridges and bro of Joseph M. (qv). Served a pupilage under his bro and was later employed by his bro and Leslie. He then became res eng for 2 yrs on the Newtyle & Coupar R and res eng for 8 yrs on the Slamannan R under Sir John Macneill (qv). Next, on the staff of Stephenson, Mackenzie & Brassey, contractors, he had charge of

the const of the Scottish Central R tunnel at Perth and of the Scottish Midland R from Perth to Forfar. On the death of his brother Alexander M. in 1848 he succeeded to the Perth business as a civil eng. He const the R from Dunblane to Callander, 13 miles (21km) and on his own account contracted for the const of several branch lines in Perthshire and about 30 miles (48km) of R in Galloway. Elected AICE 24.6.1845.
Min Proc ICE V 24 1864–5 pp 542–3

MODJESKI, Ralph

b Cracow, Poland, 27.1.1861;
d Los Angeles 26.6.1940 aged 79.
American bridge eng. Only child of Gustav Sinnmayer Modrzejewski, a theatrical producer. M. decided on an engg career at age 14, but he also studied music and became a fine pianist. With his mother and step f (Charles Bozenta Chlapowski) moved to USA in 1876 and adopted the name Modjeski. By 1878 he had decided definitely on engg and he studied in Paris, grad in civil engg at Ecole des Ponts et Chaussées in 1885. Returning to USA he began engg practice under George S. Morison, a leading bridge eng. He became a naturalised USA citizen in 1887. In 1893 he opened his own office in Chicago and from then onwards was responsible for the design of over 50 bridges. His first major work, in 1894, was a 7-span road and R bridge over the Mississippi at Rock Island, Ill. In 1902–5 with Alfred Noble he built a double-track R bridge over the Mississippi at Thebes, Ill. 1905–15 chief eng of bridges for the Oregon Trunk R Co and in 1911 built the great 340ft (103.63m) steel arch across the Crooked River Canyon at a height of 320ft (97.5m). Other R bridges of this period include the Broadway bridge across the Willamette River, Portland, Oregon (1910–12); the concrete arch Cherry Street bridge, Toledo, Ohio (1912); and the Harahan bridge across the Mississippi at Memphis, Tenn (1914–16). His Metropolis bridge (1917) across the Ohio River, Ill, includes the longest simple truss span on USA Rs of 720ft (219.5m) and 4 other spans of over 555ft (169m). The Delaware River (Benjamin Franklin) bridge between

Philadelphia and Camden (1921–6) is the longest suspended span carrying trains (1750ft, 533m). In 1923 M. took Frank M. Masters into partnership and then Clement E. Chase, both his former pupils. Later works included several large road bridges. His last project was the San Francisco–Oakland Bay bridge, from 1931. It was completed in 1936.
DAB Supplement 2 p 463

MOON, Sir Richard, Bart

b Liverpool 23.2.1815;
d Coventry 17.11.1899 aged 84.
At age 33 became a dir of the LNWR, devoting the remainder of his life to that R. 1862 elected chairman until he ret 1891. A hard worker and stern disciplinarian. Made baronet in 1887 in Q Victoria's Jubilee celebrations.
The Eng V 88 24.11.1899 p 524; *The R Eng* 12.1899 p 361

MONTAGUE, Samuel Skerry

b Keene, NH. USA, 6.7.1830;
d California (?).(?).1883 aged 53.
Civil eng responsible for completion of the first transcontinental R in USA. In 1836 the family moved to Rockford, Ill, where M. was ed. He began training as eng on the Rock Island & Rockford RR in 1852. He was later on the Peoria & Bureau Valley RR and the Burlington & Missouri River RR. 1859 M. and 3 friends travelled to California where M. built the Folsom–Marysville line. On 12.2.1862 he joined the Central Pacific and worked with Judah (qv) on the surveys. On the death of Judah in 11.1863 M. became acting eng on 31.3.1868 chief eng, carrying the R through Nevada and Utah to completion in 1869. He continued as chief eng of the CP, building many lines in California, until his death.
Kraus, George, *High Road to Promontory*, California 1969; Griswold, Wesley S., *A work of giants* 1963

MOORSOM, Capt William Scarth

b nr Whitby, Yorks, (?).(?).1804;
d London 3.6.1863 aged c 59.
Ed Sandhurst 1819–22, learning surveying. After work in Nova Scotia he left the army to reside with his f, Robert M., close to the works of the London & Birmingham R on which he made the

acquaintance of Robert Stephenson. In 1835–6 M. visited almost every R and canal work going on in England. In 1836 app to survey the Birmingham & Gloucester R including the Lickey incline which he proposed should be worked by locos. M. was responsible for the selection and ordering of 4–2–0s from Norris of Philadelphia. His method of using iron caissons at the bridge over the Avon won him the 'Telford Medal' of the ICE. He then went on to lay out the lines from Plymouth to Falmouth and the W Cornwall R from Truro to Penzance. During 1844–5 M. was engaged on laying out lines from Birmingham to Wolverhampton, Shrewsbury and Chester; the Yarmouth Jn R; Naas–Tullamore–Galway in Ireland; London–Tilbury; London–Hammersmith –Staines–Windsor; and several smaller lines. Of these M. carried out const of the Southampton–Dorchester and the Waterford–Kilkenny lines. The latter included a timber span of 200ft (61m), 85ft (26m) high over the River Nore. In 1850 he won first prize out of 61 entries for a design for a multiple bridge over the Rhine at Cologne. In 1856 he reported on a R proposal from Colombo to Kandy in Ceylon. Elected MICE 20.2.1849.
Min Proc ICE V 23 1863–4 pp 498–504

MORGAN, Sir Charles Langbridge, CBE

b Worcester 1.1.1855;
d Hove, Sussex, 9.11.1940 aged 85.
Civil eng, LBSCR. Ed at private schools in Australia and England. Began his engg pupilage in 1870 under Edward Wilson. From 1877–83 he was chief asst eng to E. Wilson & Co on R const contracts in Great Britain. During that period he was res eng on the const of the Banbury–Cheltenham R GWR, op Bourton on the Water–Cheltenham 1.6.1881, King's Sutton–Chipping Norton 6.4.1887. In 1883 he was app asst eng GER and in 1896 chief eng LBSCR and Newhaven Harbour Co. He was responsible for numerous improvements including const of the line from Stoats Nest to Earlswood (op 5.11.1899) providing a route to Brighton independent of the SER, and for complete reconstruction of the LBSCR side of Victoria stn, London.

On his ret in 2.1917 he was elected a dir of the co and later he became a M of the Bd of Dirs on the SR. Knighted 1923. In 1883 he m Mary Watkins and they had 2 sons and 2 drs.
Journal ICE V 15 1941 p 224

MORISON, George Shattuck

b New Bedford, Mass, USA 19.12.1842;
d New York 1.7.1903 aged 60.
Civil eng and bridge designer and builder. Grad from Harvard Coll 1863; later studied law there, receiving LLB 1866, but soon turned to engg. His first appointment was under Octave Chanute on the Kansas City bridge across the Missouri, 1867–71. In 1871–3 he was eng of the Detroit, Eel River & Illinois RR. 1873, again under Chanute, he was asst eng of the Erie RR, being engaged on rebuilding Portage vdt, 850ft (259m) long and 234ft (71.3m) high, carried out in 86 days following destruction of the earlier timber bridge by fire. In 1875 he became a consulting eng engaged principally in bridge design. Between 1880 and 1893 he designed and superintended const of 9 bridges across the Missouri, 3 across the upper Mississippi, 1890–3, and the Memphis bridge over the Lower Mississippi in 1892, with a cantilever span of 790ft (241m) and foundations 96ft (29.36m) below low water. He was president of the American Soc of Civil Engs in 1895. Elected MICE 5.5.1891.
Min Proc ICE V 154 1902–3 p 379; *Engg* 24.7.1903

MORRISON, Gabriel James

b London 1.11.1840; d Kensington, London, 11.2.1905 aged 64.
Civil eng. Studied at Glasgow Univ. Apprenticed 5 yrs with Robson, Forman & McCall, Glasgow. Worked under Daniel Gooch (qv) on the first Atlantic cable. For 1½ yrs he was res eng of the Glasgow & Milngavie R. In 1863 he left Glasgow and joined the staff of James Brunlees (qv) with whom he remained 11 yrs, acting as res eng on the Cleveland R, Lynn dock, and Clifton Extn R, Bristol. Also engaged on various docks, the Central Uruguay, and Honduras Rs, the Solway Jn R, the Lynn & Sutton and Spalding & Bourne lines. On completion of the Clifton Extn R he began

his own practice at Westminster, but soon afterwards he went to China where he laid down the first R there, between Shanghai and Woosung, opened on 1.7. 1876. It aroused suspicions, was bought by the Chinese govt, torn up and dumped on Formosa. He then established himself as a civil eng in Shanghai. In 1885 he entered into partnership with F. M. Cratton, and they carried out important works in China. Returned to London 1902 and was associated with Sir John Wolfe Barry (qv) as consulting eng of the Shanghai–Nanking R. Was MICE; awarded James Watt Medal 1876; also MIME (1900), MIEE and FRGS.
Proc IME 2.1905 pp 154–6

MOSER, Alfred

b Berne, Switzerland, (?).(?).1879; d Basel (?).(?).1953 aged 74.
Swiss loco eng and historian. Author of *Der Dampfbetrieb der schweizerischen Eisenbahnen* (Steam operation of Swiss Railways) (Basel 1938. New edn 1967). Trained in mech engg in an arms factory in Berne 1895–9. Following further tech studies in Berne he took up employment with the Jura–Simplon R in 1902. In 1912 he was app loco supt at Basel where he remained until his death. His famous history of Swiss steam locos first appeared in 1923. A much enlarged edition followed in 1937. A revised and updated edition bringing the history to the end of steam on Swiss Rs appeared in 1967.

MOSER, Dr Robert

b Herzogenbuchsee, Switzerland, 4.4.1838; d Switzerland 20.1.1918 aged 79.
Swiss civil eng. Gained his diploma at the Federal Polytechnic, Zurich, 1859. His first appointment was as a municipal eng at Basel, and from 1860–4 as eng on the Bernese Town R between Schwenden and Zollikoven. After further municipal work at Basel he began his career as a R eng in 1869 on the Kaschau–Oderberger R. In 10.1872 he went to Norway to prepare surveys for narrow-gauge Rs. In the same year he became chief eng of the Swiss North Eastern R (NOB). From 1879–82, in conjunction with Edward Locher (qv), Fischer and Schmaziger, he undertook const of the N ramp of the Gotthard R.

From 1888–95 he returned to the NOB as chief eng and was responsible for several important sections, also the main station at Zurich. He carried out surveys and const of several sections of the Rhaetian R, much of it in conjunction with Hennings (qv), including Chur–Thusis–Bevers; Filisur–Davos; and Reichenau–Ilanz–Disentis. He also surveyed the Ricken line, Wattwill–Rapperswil, the Bodensee–Toggenburg R and the 'East Alpine R'. The length of Rs projected by M. totalled 930 miles (1500km) and under his direction about 267 miles (430km) were built.
S.Bz V 71 2.2.1918 pp 58–9; Marshall, John, *Metre gauge Rs in S and E Switzerland* 1974

MUHLFELD, John Erhardt

b Peru, Ind, USA, 18.9.1872; d New York City 19.6.1941 aged 69.
Loco eng. Trained in mech engg at Perdue Univ. Entered RR service as a young man and was promoted through ranks, becoming supt of motive power of the Baltimore & Ohio RR and later vice president and g mgr of the Kansas City Southern R. He was also master mechanic on the GTR of Canada and supt of machinery on the Canadian Govt R. In 1910 he began in business on his own as consulting eng. He was in frequent communication with European engs in England, France, Germany, Italy, Holland, Belgium and other countries on matters concerning design and development of locos and rolling stock. He was responsible for the adoption of Walschaert valve gear (see W. Mason). In 1904 he designed the first Mallett loco to operate in USA; he developed the use of pulverised fuel for locos and stationary power plants. Between 1924 and 1933 he designed 4 types of high-pressure freight locos for the Delaware & Hudson RR. The first three, all 2-8-0s, had cross-compound cylinders; the last, a 4-8-0, had 4 cyls arranged for triple expansion and a working pressure of 500 psi ($35.154kg/cm^2$). All had water-tube fireboxes, but fire-tube boilers. The shortness and rigidity of the Muhlfeld boiler, however, led to cracks in the header plates at the connections of the two firebox steam drums. He also carried out experimental work on twin-cycle

diesel engines. He made many reports and studies on RR problems including valuations of RR properties, rate making and rebuilding after WW1. He pub: *Pulverised fuel for locos* NY 1916; *Tractive power and hauling capacity of steam locos* NY 1924; *The economics of R motive power and train service* NY 1935; *The Railroad Problem and its solution* NY 1941, and pamphlets for the American Soc of Mech Engs, *Railway Age* and the Engs' Soc of W Pennsylvania, and articles in the 14th and 15th edns of *Enc Brit*. He designed and supervised plant facilities for the Union stn at Washington DC. During his career he was employed by many RRs inc Wabash, Erie, Toledo & Ohio Central, Chicago Southern, Carolina, Clinchfield & Ohio, Minneapolis & St Louis, Boston & Albany, and the Itbira R of Brazil. He left a widow, 1 son and 2 drs.
New York Times 20.6.1941 p 21; Sinclair, Angus, *Development of the loco engine* 1907, 1970

MURRAY, Matthew

b nr Newcastle upon Tyne (?).(?).1765;
d Holbeck, Leeds, 20.2.1826 aged 61.
Inventor, mechanic and builder of the first steam locos in regular use. Apprenticed to a blacksmith. In 1789 began work at Marshall's flax spinning works at Leeds. Took out several patents for improvements in flax spinning machinery. In 1795 started in business in Leeds with James Fenton and David Wood; later the firm became Fenton, Murray & Jackson, at the Round Foundry, mfrs of steam engines and rivals of Boulton & Watt who bought up the adjacent land to the works to prevent its expansion. M. was one of the first to improve the general form of the steam engine, making it more compact and the parts more accessible. M. is generally credited with the invention of the short 'D' slide valve which he patented in 1802. In 1811–13 M. was employed by Blenkinsop (qv) to build locos for his R from Middleton collieries to Leeds. The engines were propelled by a rack wheel engaging in teeth cast onto the side of the rail. Four such engines were built and they ran for 20 yrs. They had 2 double-acting cyls and no flywheel, a great advance on current practice. M.

also built engines for boats from about 1813.
Smiles, Samuel, *Industrial Biography* 1863, 1967, pp 260–4; Proc IME 1882 p 266; Rolt, L. T. C., *Great Engineers* 1962

NASMYTH, James

b Edinburgh 19.8.1808;
d London 5.5.1890 aged 81.
Loco eng and mfr; famous for his steam hammer. Younger son of Alexander N. (1758–1840), Scottish portrait and landscape painter. Ed at Edinburgh. In 1829 went to London to become asst to Henry Maudslay (1771–1831). On the death of Maudslay he returned to Edinburgh where he made tools. With these he established a business in Manchester in 1835, building up the Bridgewater Foundry at Patricroft, covering 12 acres (4.85ha). He built his first steam hammer in 1839 and patented it in 1842. (The steam hammer had been invented and patented by James Watt but never built.) He was joined about this time by Holbrook Gaskell and the firm became Nasmyth Gaskell & Co. Gaskell left the firm in 1850 and it became James Nasmyth & Co. In 1857 N. ret leaving Henry Garnett as proprietor. Robert Wilson (1803–82) became a partner and the firm became Nasmyth Wilson & Co Ltd. They built some of the early Norris type 4–2–0s for the Birmingham & Gloucester R, 16 of Daniel Gooch's 'North Star' type 2–2–2s for the GWR in 1840–2 and some Gooch 0–6–0s in 1842. They also built engines for India, New Zealand, and other countries and, during WW1, a large number of Robinson GCR 2–8–0s for the ROD. On his ret N. lived at Penshurst, Kent, where he took up astronomy.
Engg V 49 9.5.1890 p 569; *The Eng* V 69 19.5.1890 p 383; V 129 19.3.1920 p 287; V 171 23.5.1941 p 337; Smiles, Samuel, *Industrial Biography* 1863, 1967

NEACHELL, Edward John

b nr Kidderminster (?).(?).1873;
d Waterloo, Liverpool, 5.12.1934 aged 61.
Eng and g mgr Liverpool Overhead R. 1890 apprenticed with Electric Construction Co, Wolverhampton, and after 4½ yrs in the shops was engaged on con-

tracts around the country including, in 1900, the new generating stn of the City & S London R. 1901–3 elec & mech eng at Dick, Kerr & Co, Preston, responsible for the equipment of the Grimsby & Cleethorpes and Portsmouth Corporation tramways, also Portsdown & Horndean Lt R and other installations. 1903 app chief eng, LOR, becoming eng & g mgr 1908. MIME 1908, also MIEE (resig 1933). Ret 1926.
Proc IME 1933 p 542; Box, C. E., *The Liverpool Overhead R* 1959

NEGRELLI, Alois Ritter von Moldelbe

b Primiero, S Tyrol, 23.1.1799;
d Vienna 1.10.1858 aged 59.
Went to Switzerland in 1832, becoming one of the first R engs in Switzerland. He laid out and built the Zurich–Baden R, the first Swiss R. In 1840 he returned to Austria and entered the service of the Ferdinands Nordbahn and became gen insp of the Vienna–Olmütz section. In 1842–8 he directed const of lines Olmütz–Prague; Prague–Bodenbach; Brünn (Brno)–Böhmisch Trübau. In 1848 he entered the Austrian Ministry for Public Works in Vienna.
Röll V 5 p 2442

NEILSON, Walter Montgomerie

b Glasgow (?).(?).1819; d Florence, Italy, 8.7.1889 aged 69.
Scottish loco mfr. Son of James Beaumont N. (1792–1865), inventor of the hot blast for iron mfr. Trained as mech eng in the wks of his uncle, John N., of the Oakbank Foundry, builders of the first iron ship on the Clyde. He then entered into partnership with Stewart Kerr and founded the Hyde Park Loco Wks, Glasgow, first building stationary and marine engines. They soon began building locos. On the ret of Kerr, N. was next associated with James Mitchell and subsequently with Henry Dübs (qv) who later founded his own wks. Later N. took James Reid (qv) as his partner who became principal of the firm after N's death. The firm undertook many overseas orders for locos for India, Europe and the colonies. In 1861–2 the wks were moved to Springburn, retaining the name Hyde Park Wks. In 1865 N. succeeded to the Queenshill Estate to which he ret in

1878. He was associated with the founding of the Clyde Loco Co, later amalgamated with Sharp, Stewart & Co, earlier of Manchester. He was survived by a son and a dr. Became MICE on 3.4.1860. In 1903 the Hyde Park Wks became part of the North British Loco Co. Sixty yrs later, in 1963, the wks closed.
Engg V 48 12.7.1889 p 54; *The Eng* V 68 12.7.1889 p 33; Min Proc ICE V 100 1889–90 p 400; Thomas, John, *The Springburn Story* 1964.

NELSON, Thomas

b Browhouses nr Annan, Dumfriesshire, c 1807; d (?), Dumfriesshire, 19.9.1890 aged 83.
R contractor. Began his career as a mason, later employed under George Stephenson. He built many NER lines under T. E. Harrison (qv) and Robert Hodgson, and many Scottish lines. His works included: Elizabeth dock, Maryport; Silloth R and dock; Loch Ken vdt; Portpatrick & Stranraer R; Arnside–Furness; NER Castleton–Grosmont; Whitby–Pickering rebuilding; York–Doncaster; Selby new lines and station; Leeds–Wetherby; Knaresborough–Boroughbridge; Castle Eden–Stockton; 3rd Standedge tunnel. With his sons T.B.N. and John N., carried out large LNWR contracts including Bletchley–Roade and the new Birmingham station. Also built the new Cardiff docks. N. was mayor of Carlisle 1851–2.
Engg V 50 3.10.1890 p 404

NEWLANDS, Alexander, CBE

b Elginshire, Scotland, 11.1.1870;
d Glasgow 28.8.1938 aged 68.
Chief eng, HR and LMS. Ed West End Sch, Elgin. Apprenticed with Gordon & MacBey of Elgin, engs and surveyors. 1892 entered service of HR, at first attached to head office staff, Inverness. Having been engaged on parliamentary work on the Kyle of Lochalsh Extn R (10 miles) including the deep water pier at Kyle of Lochalsh, he was app in 1893 res eng on the wks which he completed in 1897. He also assisted in preparation of various R schemes in the Highlands and Isle of Skye and the Lewis which were not built. 1897 app res eng on widening HR main line, later extended to 24 miles (38.6km). In 1899,

as chief engg asst, he returned to hq at Inverness. In 1900 he m Bessie Hamilton and they had 3 drs. 1902 app asst eng. Supervised location and const of the Dornoch Lt R, 7 miles (11km); Wick & Lybster Lt R, 14 miles (22.5km); and the Cromarty & Dingwall Lt R which was not completed. He completed widening of the HR main line N of Inverness, Clachnaharry–Clunes, in 1914. In 1.1914 app chief eng of the HR. On the formation of the LMS on 1.1.1923 he was app W div eng at Crewe and in 1927 succeeded E. F. C. Trench (qv) as chief civil eng until he ret in 1933. In 1936 he pub *The British Railways.* MICE 9.1.1912. CBE 1920.
The Eng V 166 2.9.1938 p 257; *Engg* V 146 2.9.1938 p 272; *Modern Transport* 17.12.1927; File of correspondence etc at Public Records Office, London.

NICCA, Richard La

b (?) 16.8.1794; d (?) 27.8.1883 aged 89.
Prominent Swiss civil eng and pioneer of Alpine Rs; Canton road and waterworks eng, Graubünden. In 1838 began surveys for a R through the Rhaetian Alps via the Splügen Pass, then in 1845 via the Lukmanier Pass, and worked towards these objectives for 30 yrs. In 1845 he obtained concessions for Rs in Graubünden and formed a company in Turin to build a R from Lake Maggiore to the Bodensee. In 1850 he finalised his Lukmanier project, with a summit tunnel of 10 miles 1429yd (17.4km) at a ht of 3668ft (1118m), or of 1 mile 208yd (1.8km) at a ht of 6135ft (1870m). He then prepared plans for a R through the Cristallina valley and through a tunnel 3 miles 406yd (5.2km). In 1852 the St Gotthard tunnel project was begun. The struggle between these two projects lasted until 1869, ending with a decision to build the St Gotthard R. La N. then unsuccessfully proposed a combination of the 2 projects, leaving the Reuss valley at Silenen. A 4 mile 724yd (7.1km) tunnel would have emerged in the Vorder Rhine valley to unite at Disentis with the Lukmanier project. But the St Gotthard project was eventually carried through and La N's work came to nothing.
Röll V 5 p 2450

NICHOLSON, Sir John Rumney, CMG

b Langwathby, Cumb, 25.3.1866; d Keswick, Cumb, 22.11.1939 aged 73.
Ed St Bees Sch and trained with Black, Hawthorn & Co Gateshead. 1888–9 in charge of erection of Pangdon Dene power stn, Newcastle. 1889 app asst eng of the Quebrada R and copper mines, Venezuela; 1891 became CME and also CME of the South Western R of Venezuela. 1895–9 designed the locos and rolling stock for the Port Talbot R & Docks and was res eng of the graving docks at Port Talbot. After work on docks at Singapore he returned to England in 1919, having been awarded the CMG in 1913 and KB in 1919. He was then chief eng for docks on the NER and following the same grouping on 1.1.1923 he held the same position on the LNER until he ret in 1927. In 1902 he m Sybil Helen Croft (OBE) and they had 1 son and 1 dr.
Journal ICE V 14 1940 p 249

NIMMO, Alexander

b Kirkcaldy, Fife, Scotland, (?).(?).1783; d Dublin 20.1.1832 aged 48.
Son of a watchmaker. Ed Kirkcaldy Gr Sch and St Andrews and Edinburgh Univs, achieving distinction in Latin, Greek and maths. At 19 he began a career as a school teacher, but on the recommendation of Telford he was app to the parliamentary commission to fix the boundaries of the Scottish counties. Following this he took up surveying and was app to survey and report on reclamation of Irish bog land. Next he prepared an accurate chart of the coast of Ireland and surveyed and built harbours and piers in over 30 places in Ireland and at Porthcawl in S Wales. In 1830–2 he prepared surveys for a R from Liverpool to Leeds and the Humber but it was not built, and the Manchester & Bolton R. He also acted as consulting eng for the Mersey & Irwell Nav; St Helens & Runcorn Gap R; Preston & Wigan R and the Birkenhead & Chester R. Besides his abilities as eng he was proficient in modern languages, chemistry, geology, astronomy and mathematics. For *Brewster's Cyclopaedia* he wrote the article on inland navigation and with Telford the one on bridges.

Conolly *Eminent Men of Fife*; Chambers
Eminent Scotsmen; DNB

NORRIS, Richard

b Baltimore, Md, (?).(?).1807;
d Philadelphia (?).(?).1874 aged c 67.
Loco mfr; bro of Septimus and William
(qqv). Became active in the Norris Loco
Wks 1839 and partner with William N.
in 1841. He forced William's resignation
in 1844. By mid 1850 the wks were the
largest loco builders in USA. Between
1834 and 1867 they built over 1000
engines.
White, John H. Jr *American locos, an
engg history 1830–80* 1968

NORRIS, Septimus

b (?) (?).(?).1818; d Philadelphia
(?).(?).1862 aged c 44.
Loco mfr; bro of Richard and William
(qqv). He was active in the development
of coal-burning locos and was the first to
use a long-wheelbase leading bogie truck
(spread truck, USA). Patented boilers
and, with Jonathan Knight, a loco valve
gear.
White, ibid

NORRIS, William

b Baltimore, Md, 2.7.1802;
d Philadelphia 5.1.1867 aged 64.
Loco mfr; bro of Richard and Septimus
(qqv). After graduating from St Mary's
Coll, Baltimore, began business in a dry
goods store. In 1832, with Stephen H.
Long (qv) he founded the American
Steam Carriage Co and began building
a loco designed by Long. A second, built
in 1833, named *Black Hawk*, was used
first on the Philadelphia & Columbia RR
and later on the Philadelphia & Germantown RR. They then built 3 anthracite
burning locos in 1834 for a RR in New
England. About this time N. bought up
Long's interest, and he completed the
loco *Star* for the Philadelphia & Germantown RR. In 1835 he moved his wks
from Kensington, Pa, to Philadelphia
and in conjunction with Joseph Harrison
(qv) and 6 employees completed the
George Washington loco in 1836 for the
Philadelphia & Columbia RR. This was
the first of the famous 4–2–0s which
brought Norris world-wide fame. In 1837
he received an order for 17 similar
engines for the Birmingham & Gloucester

R in England (see Moorsom, W. S.) and
by 1855 the Norris wks had exported
100 engines to France, Austria, Prussia,
Italy, Belgium, S America and Cuba
besides many for USA. In 1841 N.
formed a partnership with his bro
Richard (qv) who, in 1844, forced N's
resignation because of his inefficient
business methods. N. then took charge
of the Austrian govt loco shops nr
Vienna. Returned to USA in 1846 and
became eng of the Eastern Div of the
little Panama RR. In 1855 he tried to
organise const of a fast Atlantic steamship, but failed. N. was, in fact, a poor
eng in addition to being a none too
successful business man. In 1825 he m
May Ann Heide. He was survived by a
son. He was a keen musician, composed
sacred music and, in 1841, produced
Mozart's *The Magic Flute* at his own
expense.
DAB V 13 pp 555–6; Reed, Brian, *Loco
Profile No 11: The Norris Locos* 1971;
White, ibid

O'BRIEN, H. Eoghan

b (?) (?).8.1876; d nr Dublin (?).10.1967
aged 91.
Elec & mech eng, LYR and LMS. Ed
Eton and Leeds Univ. Trained in engg
at Kitson & Co, Leeds; on the Dublin &
South Eastern R, and at Horwich wks,
LYR, under Aspinall (qv). 1903 app elec
eng in charge of the LYR Liverpool–
Southport electrification. In 1909 succeeded J. P. Crouch as wks mgr at
Newton Heath C & W wks, Manchester.
1910 app wks mgr, Horwich, LYR, and
chief asst to George Hughes (qv), the
CME. In WW1 served with the REs
abroad. On 1.1.1922 became chief elec
eng LNWR, following the amalg with
the LYR, and on 1.1.1923 of the LMS.
On 27.3.1924 he read a paper to the
IEE on R electrification which led to
friction with the LMS management, and
he resigned. He moved to Dublin where
for 20 yrs he lectured on transport at
Trinity Coll.
Marshall, John, *The Lancashire & Yorkshire R* V 2 1970

O'DONNELL, John Patrick

b Dublin 1.7.1859; d Banstead 2.12.1919
aged 60.

R signal eng. In 1875 articled with Stephens & Sons, R signalling engs of London and Glasgow. 1882 app asst signal supt, LYR. 1885-9 in service of LSWR under Jacomb, the chief eng, when he designed and carried out extensive alterations to the signalling at Waterloo station and elsewhere. Later joined Dutton in establishing the firm of Dutton & Co, signalling engs, at London and Worcester. Left in 1894 and in conjunction with A. G. Evans founded the firm of Evans, O'Donnell & Co, R Signal Wks, Chippenham and London. This firm later amalgamated with Saxby & Farmer Ltd, and O'D. held the position of jt mg dir for many yrs. In 1901 formed the British Pneumatic R Signal Co and started the first wks for mfr of pneumatic tools on a considerable scale in Britain. He installed the first automatic signals on passenger lines. Extensive contracts were carried out under his direction on the GCR, LSWR, Central Argentine and other Rs. At Victoria Station, London, SE & CR, he installed the first 3-position all-electric interlocking system. He was a prolific inventor and M of many technical societies. He was mg dir of the Superheater Corporation Ltd and British Power Signalling Co Ltd. MIME 1888; also MICE and M American Soc of Civil Engs and M Canadian Soc of Civil Engs. Proc IME 4.1920 pp 553-4

OGILVIE, Alexander

b Clocksbriggs, Forfarshire, 15.2.1812; d (?) 15.2.1886 aged 74.
Ed Edinburgh High Sch and Univ. Studied engg under S. Fowls, eng to the trustees of the River Weaver and Bridge Master of Cheshire. Here he became acquainted with Thomas Brassey (qv) with whom he became partner. With Brassey and other contractors O. was engaged on lines forming the GER, chiefly Colchester–Ipswich; Ipswich–Bury St Edmunds; Haughley–Norwich; Sudbury–Bury St Edmunds–Cambridge; Epping–Dunmow; North Devon R; Portsmouth Direct and Salisbury–Yeovil lines of the LSWR. He also built the LNWR Weaver Jn–Widnes line with its great bridge over the Mersey; and many foreign contracts, chiefly in Argentina. Became AICE 7.5.1850.

Min Proc ICE V 86 1885-6 p 373

ONDERDONK, Andrew

b New York City 30.8.1848; d Oscawana-on-the-Hudson, NY, 21.6.1905 aged 56.
Eng and contractor, famous for his work on the CPR in British Columbia. Descended from Dutch family of Adrian van der Donk who settled on the Hudson River in 1672. Ed Troy Inst of Tech, NY, obtaining degree in engg. Worked on New Jersey Central RR, built roads and laid out several towns in NJ. After building a sea wall at San Francisco he arrived in Ottawa in 1879 as tenders were being opened for the CPR contracts through British Columbia. O's tenders were not successful but with overwhelming financial backing from bankers he purchased the contracts from the lowest bidders for $215 000. On 22.4.1880 he arrived at Yale, BC, where he made his hq and from where he built the difficult 127 miles (204km) of line through the Thompson and Fraser canyons from Savona to Port Moody. He was the first to employ Chinese coolies on the CPR. He enforced a high standard of discipline on his contracts. For rapid ballasting he devised the 'wing plough' which unloaded gravel from a train of flat cars at high speed. He established a nitro-glycerine factory at Yale, and rebuilt it after it blew up and nearly wrecked the town. On relays of horses he would inspect up to 100 miles (160km) of works in a day, twice in a month. In 1882 he built the 250 ton steamer *Skuzzy* and manoeuvred and winched it through the Hells Gate Canyon in 9.1882; the only steamer ever to 'navigate' this section of the Fraser River. It was used to transport materials. By 1885 the line was completed to Port Moody, but O., a modest and retiring man, was not in the famous 'last spike' photograph. He went straight off to Argentina where, in 1886, he built the Entre Rios R N of Buenos Aires. After this he built 9 miles (14.5km) of drainage tunnels in Chicago, and the Chicago Northwestern Elevated R. Returning to Canada in 1895 he built the Trent Valley and Soulanges canals, including one of the largest rock cuttings in N America, and the double-track tunnel at

Hamilton on the Toronto, Hamilton & Buffalo R, and carried out part of the rebuilding of the Victoria bridge over the St Lawrence at Montreal. In 1905 he was g mgr of the New York Tunnel Co, building a tunnel under the east branch of the Hudson River, then considered the most difficult piece of work ever undertaken by a contractor. He died from overwork.

Enc Canadiana V 8 p 20; Berton, Pierre, *The Last Spike; the great R 1881–5* 1971; Lavallee, Omer, *Van Horne's Road* 1974

OUTRAM, Benjamin

b Alfreton, Derbyshire, 1.4.1764;
d London 22.5.1805 aged 41.
Builder of early Rs and tramways. Son of Joseph O. (1732–1810). Named after Benjamin Franklin who was a friend of his f. Trained as a civil eng on canals and roads. Achieved fame in the laying of iron rails for tramways and Rs. In 1790, in conjunction with William Jessop (qv), John Wright and Francis Beresford, he founded the Butterley Co near Ripley, Derbyshire. On 4.6.1800 he m Margaret Anderson. They had 5 children of whom Sir James O. (1803–63) achieved fame in Indian campaigns.
DNB; Baxter, Bertram, *Stone Blocks and Iron Rails* 1966

OWEN, William Lancaster

b Bath 8.11.1843; d London 28.11.1911 aged 68.
Civil eng, GWR Trained under his f who, in 3.1868, became chief eng, GWR, and also in the Swindon loco wks. In 1865 entered service of the GWR as asst eng and, except for 3 yrs 1872–5 when he was eng to the Monmouthshire R & Canal Co, remained on the GWR until his retirement in 1891. He was successively dist eng, eng for new works and, following the death of his f, chief eng for const. He was concerned with many important works, including conversion from broad to standard gauge.
Elected MICE 28.3.1882.
Min Proc ICE V 187 1911–12 p 329

PALMER, Sir Frederick, KCMG, CIE

b Llandovery, Wales, 31.1.1862;
d Lingfield, Surrey, 7.4.1934 aged 72.

Apprenticed on the GWR 1877–9 and continued as asst eng until 11.1883. He was then selected by Alexander Rendel as asst eng on the East Indian R and in 1889 he became res eng on the Ghat section. Was personal asst to the chief eng, F. E. Robertson from 1891 until 1893 when he was promoted to dist eng on surveys and construction. Responsible for const of the Moghalserai–Gaya line, begun in 1896 and completed in 1900, including the Sone bridge of 96 spans of 100ft (30.48m), the longest bridge in India at 10 054ft (3064m), opened on 27.2.1900. Returned to England on leave and while there was app chief eng to the port of Calcutta. Here he was responsible for many improvements. Retired from India in 1909 to become chief eng to the new Port of London Authority where he was responsible for the King George V dock and the new lock, docks and passenger landing stage at Tilbury. The plan was evolved in 4 yrs after which he resigned to enter into partnership with Sir Alexander Rendel, while retaining connection with the PLA as consulting eng. He was connected with the designing of the new Hooghly Bridge, Calcutta, completed 1942, and other important works abroad. MICE 1896; president 1926–7 and on council from 1915 to his death.
Min Proc ICE V 238 1933–4 p 539

PARK, James Crawford

b Liverpool 1.7.1838; d Dundalk, Ireland, 27.5.1895 aged 56.
Loco supt, GNR Ireland. In 1856 apprenticed at the LNWR loco wks at Crewe, later moving to the drg office until 1866 when he was app head of the drg office at the GNR wks at Doncaster, first under Sturrock (qv) and from 12.1866 under P. Stirling (qv). In 1873 transferred to Peterborough wks as asst shop mgr. In 1.1881 he was app loco supt of GNR Ireland in charge of locos and rolling stock. In 1887 he established the wks at Dundalk, but he continued the relationship already established with Beyer, Peacock & Co, ordering locos from Manchester to his specification. First were the Class A 0-6-0s, 1882–90; then came the BT 4-4-0Ts, first delivered in 1883. One of this class was the first engine built at Dundalk wks, in

1887. There followed the P5/6 4–4–0s in 1892 and the AL 0–6–0s in 1895. P. became MICE 3.5.1887.

Min Proc ICE V 122 1894–5 p 382

PARK, John Carter

b Aberdeen 2.1.1822;
d Bournemouth 28.10.1896 aged 74.
Loco eng, N London R. Eldest son of Charles P. who, in 1832, took his family to Leghorn, Italy, and started in business there as a mech eng. The revolution of 1848 forced him to move to Genoa. P. then completed his training at the wks at Sanpierdarena, Italy, which were erected by the Italian govt. On completion of his pupilage P. went to sea as an eng. In 1853 he was app loco supt of the Lucca, Pisa & Pistoja R, Central Italy, but he resigned in 1854 to join the Sardinian navy to serve in the Crimean war. After this he went to England where he obtained employment under John Ramsbottom (qv) at the Longsight wks of the LNWR at Manchester. In 1859 he became loco supt of the Buffalo & Lake Huron R, Canada, until the line was taken over by the Grand Trunk R in 1864. In 1865 he became wks mgr at the Inchicore wks of the GS & WR, Ireland, until 1873 when he succeeded William Adams as loco supt at the Bow wks of the N London R on which he remained for nearly 20 yrs until he ret in 1893. He produced a class of o/c 4–4–0T for passenger work and o/c 0–6–0T for goods. Some of the 0–6–0Ts later found employment on the Cromford & High Peak R and one is preserved.
Elected MICE 6.2.1877.

Min Proc ICE V 127 1896–7 p 383

PARKER, Thomas

b Ayrshire 11.7.1829; d Gorton,
Manchester, 25.11.1903 aged 74.
Loco supt, MS & LR. 1847 apprenticed at the Greenock wks of the CR under Robert Sinclair (qv). 1851 served for a year on the LSWR under J. Beattie (qv), then returning to the CR where he was engaged on inspection of materials and rolling stock supplied to the company on contract. 1858 app C & W supt on the MS & L and he supervised const of the entire C & W shops at Manchester. He introduced 6-wheeled bogie coaches on the R, and his 12-wheeled dining

car, built in 1885, was regarded as the finest in the country. In 1886, on the resignation of C. R. Sacré (qv) he was app loco C & W supt on 28.5. His new 4–4–0 No 561 (11.1887) was exhibited at the Manchester Jubilee exhibition. His 0–6–2T No 7 (9.1891) was the first loco on any British R to have a Belpaire firebox. In 1892 he remodelled the Gorton loco shops and built a large new erecting shop. He ret in 1893. During his career with the MS & L the wagon stock was increased from 4182 to 17 933 and the carriage stock from 338 to 1106. MIME 1872; MICE 1889.

Proc IME 12.1903 p 924; Min Proc ICE V 155 1903–4 p 435; Dow, George, *Great Central* V 2 1962; V 3 1965

PARKER, Thomas

b Tettenhall, Wolverhampton,
22.12.1843; d Ironbridge, Shropshire,
5.12.1915 aged 72.
Electrical eng. Ed Quakers' Sch, Coalbrookdale; afterwards entered wks of the Coalbrookdale Co. At age 23 went to Manchester to complete his tech studies, then returned to the Coalbrookdale Co as foreman. He was later given charge of the chemical and electro-depositing depts; and he finally became mgr of the engg portion of the wks. While on electro-depositing he made discoveries concerning storage batteries which led to his setting up in Wolverhampton with P. B. Elwell as Elwell, Parker & Co Ltd, constituted in 1882, to make accumulators. He soon began mfr of dynamos and then everything electrical. P. had great interest in electric traction from its beginning and he was responsible for the design of electric plant for the tramway along the front at Blackpool, the first electric line to use a slotted system. P. remained eng to the tramway until 1893 when it was taken over by the corporation. He also designed an electric loco used on the Birmingham & Bournbrook tramway. Later his firm built electric equipment for the Liverpool Overhead R. His biggest contract was for electric equipment for the Metropolitan R, London, completed 1905, including Neasden power stn. He invented the Parker & Weston steam pump and also the first slow-combustion stoves to be made. The

business of Elwell, Parker was sold in 1888 to the Electric Construction Corporation of Wolverhampton of which P. was eng and mgr for 5 yrs, and he planned and erected the Bushbury wks. Besides the LOR he designed the electric lighting installations at Oxford and Burnley and a traction system in S Staffordshire. On the termination of his agreement with the corporation he and others founded Thomas Parker Ltd, Wolverhampton, later Rees Roturbo Mfg Co Ltd. P. was JP for Shropshire and for Wolverhampton. MIME, MICE, MIEE. Awarded Stephenson Medal and Telford Premium 1893–4. FRS of Edinburgh and a govr of Birmingham Univ. *The Eng* V 120 10.12.1915 p 549

PARRY, Edward

b Hendy Mold, Flintshire, 8.11.1844; d Leamington 11.8.1920 aged 75.
Civil eng. Ed at a private sch in Chester. Began civil engg career on MR 1869–79, being asst eng on the Nottingham–Melton Mowbray line. In 1879–89 he was county surveyor of Nottinghamshire and at the same time was responsible for the const of the Nottingham Suburban R, opened 1889. With J. S. Story of Derby he was jt eng of the MR Dore & Chinley line, opened 1893. He later was res eng on the Great Central main line from Annesley to Rugby, including the tremendous earthworks through Nottingham, and Nottingham Victoria station, 1898–1900. In 1905–9 he was eng of the South Yorkshire Jt R. Most of his bridges, viaducts and tunnels were faced in blue vitrified bricks, and it is unfortunate that R politics have resulted in the abandonment of many of the lines he built. His works were outstanding for their fine durable construction which made their dismantling the more difficult and expensive. In addition to his civil engg practice he was chairman of the R & General Engg Co of Nottingham, and dir of Digby Collieries, Nottinghamshire, and of Nottingham Patent Brick Co, two of whose wks were in direct connection with his Nottingham Suburban R, close to which he lived, at Woodthorpe Grange, until his ret.
Nottinghamshire and Derbyshire at the opening of the 20th C 1901; Mellors, Robert, *Men of Nottingham and Notts*

1924; *RM* 6.1961; Dow, George, *Great Central* V 2 1962; *Nottingham Guardian* 14.8.1920

PATERSON, Murdoch

b Inverness (?).9.1826; d Culloden Moor, Inverness, 9.8.1898 aged nearly 72.
Civil eng, HR. Ed Calcabock parish school and Royal Academy, Inverness. Spent 2 yrs with a banker. 1846 apprenticed to Joseph Mitchell (qv), then govt eng of roads, bridges, harbours and buildings in the Highlands. Left Mitchell in 1851 to work with a firm of contractors enlarging harbour accommodation at Inverness which P. completed on his own. In 1854 he returned to work with Mitchell on const of the HR. P. was in charge of const from Inverness to Keith and Bonar Bridge, and from Forres to Dunkeld on the Perth main line. In 1862 Mitchell took P. and his bro William P. into partnership, the firm being known as Joseph Mitchell & Co. Mitchell ret in 1867 and the Sutherland line came under the full command of P. who also laid out and built the Dingwall–Kyle of Lochalsh line, completed to Strome Ferry in 1870. The Sutherland line was completed to Helmsdale in 1871 and P. then went on to build the Caithness lines to Wick and Thurso, completed in 1874 when they were taken over by the HR of which P. then became chief eng. He laid out and built lines to Buckie, Black Isle and Strathpeffer and surveyed several proposed lines which were not built. The direct line from Inverness to Aviemore which he laid out was almost finished when he d. It included the Findhorn vdt, 445yd (407m) long, with 9 spans of 130ft (39.624m), 141ft (43m) high, and the Nairn vdt on Culloden Moor where he d, 600yd (549m) long with a main arch of 100ft (30.48m), 130ft (40m) high. P. also designed the Inverness water supply, the new Ness bridge, and many other works. Became MICE 3.2.1874.
Min Proc ICE V 135 1898–9 pp 351–3

PEACOCK, Richard

b Swaledale, Yorkshire, 9.4.1820; d Gorton, Manchester, 3.3.1889 aged 68.
Loco eng. Seventh son of Ralph P., mine overseer who, about 1830, was app asst supt on const of the Leeds & Selby

R. He then removed to Leeds where P. was ed at the Gr Sch which he left at age 14 to be apprenticed to Fenton, Murray & Jackson, then building locos for the Liverpool & Manchester R and Leeds & Selby R. P. was placed under Jackson, mg partner in the firm. He remained there, engaged chiefly on loco work, until 1838 when he became loco supt on the Leeds & Selby R at the age of only 18. When the L & S was amalg with the York & N Midland in 1840 P. removed to London and presented himself to Daniel Gooch on the GWR. He served on the GWR until 1841 when, at the age of 21, he was app loco supt of the Sheffield, Ashton & Manchester R, then nearing completion. He remained here for 14 yrs and was responsible for selection of the site at Gorton for the R wks. In 1854 P. resolved to start in business on his own account and entered into partnership with Charles Beyer (qv) who had been for several yrs mechanical head of Sharp Bros & Co at Gorton. Here they purchased 12 acres (4.85ha) of land and the firm of Beyer, Peacock & Co Ltd began operations in 5.1854. Within 12 months the first engine was delivered, for the GWR. The wks were well planned to cover the entire land. Beyer d in 1876. P. did valuable work in the early development of the steam loco, particularly in experiments with the blast pipe. He was active in affairs in the Gorton district and was president of the local mechanics institute until his death. In 1885, when the parliamentary div of Gorton was created P. was elected its first representative, which he remained until his death. In 1847 he became a founder M of the IME.

Min Proc ICE V 97 1888–9 pp 404–7; Proc IME 1.1889 pp 197–9; *Engg* V 47 29.3.1889 pp 311–12; *The Eng* V 67 29.3.1889 p 207; Smith, W. *Old Yorkshire* 1890 (portrait); *Figaro* 9.3.1889 p 9 (portrait)

PEARCE, Robert Webb

b Macclesfield, Cheshire, 11.11.1831; d London 26.7.1889 aged nearly 58. C & W supt, E Indian R. Ed Macclesfield Gr Sch. Apprenticed at Brown Marshalls & Co, Birmingham, R carriage mfrs, becoming chief draughtsman. 1855 app C & W supt EIR. He designed and built the Howrah shops nr Calcutta where the whole of the EIR stock was built for the 5ft 6in (1.676m) and metre gauge. He was the first to introduce iron instead of wood for panels and framing of carriages and wagons, and to change from grease to oil lubrication. His design of axlebox for oil lubrication was universally adopted in India. He nearly doubled the carrying capacity of the Indian wagon stock. His prolonged application to work in the Indian climate ruined his health and in 4.1888 he returned to England on leave, but was unable to recover. Became MIME 1867

Proc IME 5.1890 pp 291–3

PEASE, Edward (and Joseph and Henry)

b Darlington 31.5.1767; d Darlington 31.7.1858 aged 91. Known as the 'father of Rs'; supporter of George Stephenson, and promoter of the Stockton & Darlington R. Ed at Leeds. Began in the woollen industry with his f at Darlington. In 1796 he m Rachael Whitwell; they had 5 sons and 3 drs. About 1817 he left the woollen industry and became interested in establishing a tramroad from collieries in S Durham to Stockton. The Stockton & Darlington R Act was passed in 1821. Pease, who had by then become acquainted with George Stephenson, was instrumental in his appointment as eng. In 1823 P., together with Thomas Richardson and George Stephenson, established the firm of Robert Stephenson & Co at Newcastle, with Robert Stephenson as mgr, to mfr locos for the S & D. The R was op on 27.9.1825, but it was a sad day for P. whose son Isaac had d that morning. The first locos were not a complete success and the wks did not prosper. P. wished to retire from the company, but George Stephenson was unable to buy him out. It was only after Hackworth (qv) had established the steam loco as a reliable machine that the company prospered. P. retained an interest in the S & D up to his death. He was a M of a staunch Quaker family and active opponent of slavery.

His son Joseph (1799–8.2.1872) was treasurer of the S & D and founder of the town of Middlesbrough. He was a partner in Robert Stephenson & Co from 28.10.1846. He became the largest colliery owner in S Durham. Another son, Henry (1807–30.5.1881), promoted the line from Redcar to Saltburn (which town he established) and the S Durham & Lancashire Union R. He became the first Quaker to enter Parliament, as M for S Durham, in 1832, until 1841.

Jeans, J. S., *Jubilee Memorial of the R System* 1875; Warren, J. G. H., *A Century of Locomotive Building* 1923, 1970; Tomlinson, W. W., *The North Eastern R* 1914, 1967; Smiles, S., *Life of George and Robert Stephenson* 1879; Skeat, W. O., *George Stephenson, the engineer and his letters* 1973

PEPPERCORN, Arthur Henry, OBE

b Leominster, Herefordshire, 29.1.1889; d Doncaster 3.3.1951 aged 62.
Loco eng, LNER. Ed Hereford Cathedral Sch. In 1905 he began a premium apprenticeship under H. A. Ivatt (qv) at Doncaster GNR wks. Gained further experience at the GNR shed at Colwick nr Nottingham, and later as asst dist loco supt, Ardsley and Peterborough. During WW1 P. served in the CME's dept of the REs in France. Returned to the GNR as dist loco supt, Retford, then to Doncaster as asst in charge of the wagon shops. 1921 app asst C & W supt, Doncaster; 1923 wks mgr, C & W dept, York. In 1933 P. went to London as asst mech eng at Stratford wks. 1937 became loco running supt, LNER S Area. 1938 mech eng, NE Area, Darlington. 1941 to Doncaster again as asst CME and mech eng. In 1945 became asst to Edward Thompson (qv) and took charge of the dept in Thompson's absence. When Thompson ret in 1946 P. succeeded as CME of the LNER. On nationalisation he became CME of the E and NE Regions. Ret at end of 1949 after 44 yrs service. P. was MIME and MILE (1946). Awarded OBE in the Birthday Honours 1945. He is best remembered for his two series of 4–6–2s, the A1 class with 6ft 8½in (2.043m) driving wheels and the A2 class with 6ft 2in (1.878m) wheels, both excellent machines, powerful and free-running, and among the finest examples of their type in Great Britain.
Journal ILE V 40 1950 p 711; *The Eng*

V 191 9.3.1951 p 322

PERRING, John Shae

b Boston, Lincs, 24.1.1813; d Manchester 16.1.1869 aged nearly 56.
Chief eng, E Lancs R. Ed Donington Gr Sch. On 28.3.1826 articled to Robert Reynolds, surveyor of the port of Boston, and worked on Fen drainage schemes. In 1833–6 he worked on various engg works in London. In 3.1836 he went to Egypt as asst eng to Galloway Bey to carry out public works, and later he became a M of the Bd of Public Works. His careful measurements of the pyramids resulted in the pub of *The Pyramids of Egypt* in 1839–42, the first authentic account of this subject. Returned to England 1840 and on 1.3.1841 became engg supt of the Llanelly R, docks and harbour. In 1844 he became res eng on the E Lancs R, at first under C. E. Cawley (qv) and later S. Meek (qv). He continued as ELR eng until after its amalg with the LYR in 1859. On 4.7.1860, when the engg dept was concentrated under Meek, P. retired. Later he surveyed the Chorley–Blackburn section of the Lancashire Union Rs. Became MIME 1856; also MICE.
Proc IME 1870 p 15; Min Proc ICE V 30 1869–70 pp 455–6; Marshall, John, *The Lancashire & Yorkshire R* V 1 1969

PETO, Sir Samuel Morton

b Woking, Surrey, 4.8.1809; d Tunbridge Wells, Kent. 13.11.1889 aged 80.
R contractor and civil eng. At 14 apprenticed to his uncle as a builder and with his cousin, Thomas Grissell, eventually succeeded to the business. The partnership lasted 16 yrs during which they carried out many important works including const of part of the GWR and erection of the new Houses of Parliament. The partnership was dissolved in 1846. P. then entered into another partnership with his bro in law E. L. Betts (qv) and with him built the GNR loop line from Peterborough to Doncaster via Boston and Lincoln, 1847–8, the Oxford, Worcester & Wolverhampton R, op 1850–4, and the GWR Oxford–Birmingham line op 1850–2, including one of the largest cuttings in England, 1 500 000 cu yd (1 146 000m³) of excavation. In connection with Thomas Brassey (qv)

the firm did much work abroad including Rs in Australia and the Canadian Grand Trunk line with the Victoria tubular bridge over the St Lawrence at Montreal. In England they built the Victoria and Thames graving docks. With T. R. Crampton (qv) P. took up the contract for the London, Chatham & Dover R and the suspension of payment caused failure of the firm. He founded the guarantee fund for the Great Exhibition of 1851, with £50 000. He built the first military R, from Balaclava to Sebastopol during the Crimean war, without profit or remuneration, which earned him a baronetcy in 12.1854. He was chairman of the Chester & Holyhead R from 1851 until its amalg with the LNWR in 1859. He was twice m; in 1831 to Mary, dr of Thomas de la Garde Grissell, (d 1842), and in 1843 to Sarah Ainsworth, dr of Henry Kelsall of Rochdale. He was deputy lieutenant for Suffolk and a JP for Middlesex. He was Liberal MP for Norwich 1847–55, for Finsbury 1859–65 and Bristol 1865–8. He was succeeded by his son Henry, b 1840.

The Eng V 68 22.11.1889 p 438; *Engg* V 48 29.11.1889 p 634; Min Proc ICE V 99 1889–90 pp 400–3; Baughan, Peter, *The Chester & Holyhead R* 1972

PETTIGREW, William Frank

b Glasgow 24.1.1858; d Redhill, Surrey, 22.1.1942 aged 84.

Loco eng on the Furness R. Son of John P. of Greenock. Ed Wolvesey Palace Sch, Winchester, later at Finsbury Tech Coll and Univ Coll, London. 1874 began a 5 yr pupilage under W. Adams (qv) at the Stratford wks of GER. When Adams left to become loco supt of the LSWR in 1.1878 P. completed his training under Massey Bromley (qv). In 4.1879 he worked at Millwall, London, on hydraulic cranes and at various times assisted his f in the const of steamers and marine engines on the Clyde. In 12.1879 P. returned to Stratford as draughtsman and later as asst in the wks mgr's office under Bromley. In 3.1883 he was app asst wks mgr at Stratford, first under T. W. Worsdell (qv) and later under James Holden (qv). In 3.1886 P. was app mgr of the LSWR wks at Nine Elms, London, under his former chief W. Adams. He had full

charge of the wks and the installation of machinery, engines and boilers at the new wks at Eastleigh in Hampshire. In 1896 P. was app loco C & W supt on the Furness R at Barrow, his title later becoming CME. P. was the first eng to design locos specially for the FR, first producing 3 4ft 8in (1.422m) 0–6–2Ts for the Cleator dist in 1898. Next came some new 0–6–0s of similar design to the tanks and in 1900 some 6ft (1.828m) 4–4–0 passenger engines. In 1904 another batch of 0–6–2T and 0–6–0 tender engines appeared standard with the previous engines but with 5ft 1in (1.549m) wheels for mixed traffic. These basic classes were improved and enlarged from 1913 to handle ever increasing traffic. P. introduced electric lighting as standard equipment in passenger stock. He also had charge of the mechanical appliances at Barrow docks, owned by the FR. He pub *A Manual of Loco Engg* 1899 which reached a third edition. Ret 1918 and was succeeded by D. L. Rutherford (qv). MIME 1898.

Proc IME V 148 1942 p 219; *Engg* V 153 30.1.1942 p 94; *The Eng* V 173 6.2. 1942 p 109; *The Locomotive* 2.1942 p 23

PICKERSGILL, William, CBE

b Crewe (?).(?).1861; d Bournemouth 2.5.1928 aged 67.

Loco supt GN of SR and CR. Entered service of GER at Stratford, London, 1876. 1883 app loco insp and remained in running dept until 1891 when he was app dist loco supt, Norwich. 1894 succeeded James Johnson (qv) as loco C & W supt GN of SR. During his term of office on the GN of S the wks were removed from Kittybrewster, Aberdeen, to Inverurie. P. continued the const of i/c 4–4–0s to handle most traffic. In 3.1914 he succeeded J. F. McIntosh (qv) as loco C & W supt on the CR. He was awarded CBE for services in WW1. Besides 0–6–0s and 4–4–0s, enlargements of existing designs, he introduced the '60' class 4–6–0s in 1916 and the 4–6–2Ts in 1917. In 1921 his disappointing 3-cyl 4–6–0 class appeared. At grouping on 1.1.1923 he was app mech eng, N Div, LMS, with hq at St Rollox, Glasgow, until he ret in 1925. Became MIME 1923. President ILE 1919–20.

Proc IME 5.1928 p 515; *Journal* ILE V

18 1928 p 308 (portrait)

PIERCY, Benjamin

b Trefeglwys, Montgomeryshire,
16.3.1827; d Assam, India, 24.3.1888
aged 61.
Eng of Cambrian and other mid-Wales
Rs. 3rd son of Robert P., valuer and
surveyor. Trained in his f's office and
about 1847 became chief asst to Charles
Mickleburgh of Montgomery. During
this period P. spent all his spare time
studying Rs and civil engg. His first R
work was under Henry Robertson in
making the parliamentary surveys for the
Shrewsbury & Chester R and later for a
R from Oswestry to Newtown. In 1852 he
was app eng of the Red Valley R project
from Shrewsbury to Minsterley and Newtown and for the Shrewsbury–Welshpool
line. Other Rs on which P. was eng
were: Oswestry, Ellesmere & Whitchurch
R, op 1863–4; Llanidloes & Newtown
R op 1859; Newtown & Machynlleth
R op 3.1.1863; the Welsh coastal
lines from Aberystwyth to Pwllheli,
op 1863–7; the Vale of Clwyd R, (Rhyl–
Denbigh) op 5.10.1858; Caernarvonshire
R, (Menai Bridge–Caernarvon) op 2.9.
1867; Denbigh, Ruthin & Corwen R,
op Ruthin 1862, Corwen 1864; Bishops
Castle R, op 24.10.1865; Mid Wales R,
(Moat Lane Jn–Talyllyn) op Llanidloes
1859, Talyllyn 1864; Hereford, Hay &
Brecon R, op 1862–4; Kington &
Eardisley R (Kington–New Radnor) op
25.9.1875; Hoylake R (Birkenhead–
Hoylake) op 2.7.1866; and Wrexham,
Mold & Connahs Quay, op 1.1.1866, with
extns and branches. These lines included
extensive works such as Oswestry and
Welshpool stations, Talerddig cutting,
120ft (37m) deep and many bridges
including the great Barmouth bridge.
In 1862 he was asked to resurvey the
proposed Sardinian R system which he
did, reducing the tunnelling and producing an acceptable project which was
adopted. Because of war and political
troubles the lines were not completed
until 1881. During 25 yrs in Sardinia he
carried out many improvements in agriculture. In France he was chief eng of
the Napoléon–Vendée R, about 160 miles
(257km), from Tours via Bressuire to
Sables d'Olonne. In India he was eng of
about 90 miles (145km) of the line of

the Assam Rs & Trading Co and it
was while out there that he died. Elected
MICE 8.1.1860.
Min Proc ICE V 96 1888–9 pp 333–9

POLLITT, Harry

b Ashton-under-Lyne nr Manchester
26.12.1864; d (?) (?).(?).(?) aged (?)
Loco supt, Manchester, Sheffield &
Lincolnshire/Great Central R. Son of
Sir William P. (b Ashton-u-L 24.2.1842;
d Bowdon, Ches, 13.10.1908), g mgr of
the MS & L 1886–99. Ed Reading, and
Owens Coll, Manchester. Trained under
Thomas Parker (qv) at the MS & L wks
at Gorton, Manchester, becoming wks
mgr. Following the resig of Parker,
12.1903, P. was app loco eng from
1.1894. In 6.1894 'Marine Eng' was
added to his title, and in the same
yr he was elected MIME. He was also
MICE and F of the Iron & Steel Inst.
At first he continued to add to the loco
classes introduced by Parker, except that
Pollitt used the Stephenson link motion
instead of Joy valve gear. His first
engines were the class 5 o c 0–6–0Ts,
and the 11A i/c 4–4–0s designed for the
opening of the London extn. These were
a development of the Parker 4–4–0, with
Belpaire firebox. Early in 1900 he introduced a 7ft 9in (2.362m) 4–2–2 with a
much larger Belpaire firebox. These
worked the London extn until 1904 when
they were transferred to the CLC. P.
resigned in 6.1900 at the early age of 39,
the reason is obscure, and he seems to
have vanished from engg records. He m
an Australian woman in the same year.
Records in Manchester Library; *RM*
3.1939 pp 182–9; 4.1939 pp 273–81;
Dow, George, *Grant Central* V 2 1962

POTTER, James

b Lichfield, Staffs, 10.3.1801;
d (Sheffield?) 23.8.1857 aged 56.
Chief eng, MS & L. Trained under his
f, Joseph P., architect, from age 16.
Afterwards articled to William Brunton
(qv) at the Eagle Foundry, Birmingham.
1822 worked with his f on bridges and
was app res eng under Telford on const
of the 2nd Harecastle canal tunnel,
2926yd (2675m), completed in 3 yrs.
In 1830 he rebuilt the Oxford canal.
1835–6 undertook mgt of the Croydon
div of the SER and in 1837 was emp

by J. U. Rastrick (qv). In 1845 app asst eng on the London–Brighton R under Rastrick, carrying out const of all tunnels. He also superintended const of part of Brighton–Chichester R. He was then app res eng on the Sheffield–Grimsby line (MS & L) and in 1852 was app chief eng, remaining so until his death. Elected MICE 1.6.1824.
Min Proc ICE V 17 1857–8 pp 94–6

POTTS, Arthur

b Glan-yr-Afon, Denbighshire, 23.6.1814; d Hoole Hall, Cheshire, 4.4.1888 aged 75.
Loco mfr. Apprenticed to Mather, Dixon & Co, Liverpool, where he was a contemporary of W. B. Buddicom (qv). At Liverpool he became closely acquainted with R. Stephenson, Locke and Errington (qqv). After completing his apprenticeship P. joined John Jones at the Viaduct Foundry nr Newton le Willows, Lancashire. Here Jones & Potts employed about 800 men and for several yrs were fully employed making locos for various Rs, chiefly the Caledonian, at the rate of about one a week. The firm also built stationary and marine engines. In 1852 the LNWR offered to buy the Viaduct wks without the machinery, and upon its sale P. ret. Elected MICE 6.12.1870.
Min Proc ICE V 96 1888–9 p 339

PRICE, Edward

b Callow Hill nr Minsterley, Shropshire, (?).(?).1805; d Highgate, London, 31.3.1871 aged 64.
Civil eng and contractor. As a boy he was engaged by Mackenzie (qv) on the Worcester & Birmingham canal as time-keeper. Soon afterwards he found employment on sewers in London. When the London & Birmingham R was being built he obtained employment in Primrose Hill tunnel, under the contractor Thomas Jackson, later under R. Stephenson, who gave him more responsibility in Kilsby tunnel. 1838–9 executed a contract on the GWR at Chippenham. 1844, on recommendation of R. Stephenson, he went to France where he built the tunnel at La Nerthe on the Marseilles–Lyons line. 1846–9 contracted for part of the NSR in England under G. P. Bidder. 1851–4 he built the Benha

and Kaffre Azayat bridges over the Nile for R. Stephenson, and part of the Alexandria–Cairo R. The bridges involved sinking caissons 90ft (27m) into the river bed. He then contracted for the Dom Pedro Segundo R, Brazil, from Rio de Janeiro to the foot of the Serra S. Anna, 40 miles (64km). Further foreign contracts followed, in Portugal and Asia Minor, but the financial stress of the latter broke his health. AICE 2.12.1856.
Min Proc ICE V 33 1871–2 pp 267–9

PRICE, James

b Monkstown, Co Dublin, 18.1.1831; d Dublin 4.4.1895 aged 64.
Chief eng, MGWR. Ed Trinity Coll, Dublin, obtaining Dip Eng 1850, BA 1851. 1855–7 res eng on Banbridge Jn R under James Barton. 1859–60 res eng on Cootehill–Ballybay line and 1860–2 in charge of pw and works on Dublin & Belfast Jn R (later GNR). At end of 1862 P. was app eng in chief of the MGWR and of the Royal Canal, until 5.1877 after which he practised on his own account in Dublin. MICE 1.3.1870.
Min Proc ICE V 121 1894–5 p 327

PRYCE, Henry J.

b Hereford (?).(?).1852; d Hampstead, London, 13.8.1918 aged 66.
Loco eng, N London R. When his f occupied a senior position at the Inchicore, Dublin, wks of the GS & WR P. joined that co and served his time in the shops and drg office. Returned to England 1878 with J. C. Park (qv) who was then app loco supt NLR. P. became signal supt in 1878 and signal & telegraph supt in 1884. Park ret in 1893 and P. succeeded him as loco supt, retaining the position of signal & telegraph supt. P. was MICE. He ret when the LNWR took over the NLR in 1909. In 1891 P. was one of the two founders of the Confederance of R Cos' Signal Supts & Engs and its first sec. He invented the Park & Pryce train protection bar, extensively used before adoption of electrical bars and track circuits, and was joint inventor of the Pryce–Ferreira block instrument. He was survived by a widow, 1 son and 1 dr.
RG 23.8.1918 p 215; The Eng V 126 23.8.1918 p 157 (portrait)

PULLMAN, George Mortimer

b Brocton, NY, USA, 3.3.1831;
d Chicago 19.10.1897 aged 66.
Founder of the Pullman Car Co. Left
school at 14 and worked in a store in
Westfield. In 1848 joined his bro, a
cabinet maker in Albion, NY. 1835
removed to Chicago where he soon began
to consider improvements in sleeping
accommodation on R trains. By 1858 he
had developed his ideas sufficiently to
remodel two day coaches on the Chicago
& Alton RR into sleeping cars, making
upper berths hinged to the side of the
car. He built a third car in 1859.
Because other Rs would not take up his
cars, he moved to Colorado where he ran
a store from 1859–63, at the same time
designing his first Pullman car. On
returning to Chicago he and Ben Field
of Albion carried out the design, also
patenting the folding upper berth on
5.4.1864. They then built their first
Pullman car, *Pioneer*, completed in 1865,
for which they obtained a patent for
the lower berth adapted from the seats.
The same principle is still in use. The
car was well received and in 1867 the
partners organised the Pullman Palace
Car Co which grew to be the largest
car-building firm in the world. P. established his first mfg plant at Palmyra,
NY, but soon removed it to Detroit,
Mich. As the business grew more plants
were opened at St Louis (1880), Elmira,
NY, (1873–83), Wilmington, Del, (1886),
San Francisco, and at Pullman (1880),
now part of Chicago. Here P. built the
entire town, completing it in 1881. It
was judged the healthiest city in the
world. In addition to the sleeping car,
P. introduced the combined sleeping
and dining car in 1867, the dining car
in 1868, the chair car in 1875 and the
vestibule car in 1887. P. was also the
owner of the Eagleton Wire Wks, NY,
and president of the Metropolitan
Elevated RR in NY City. On 13.6.1867
he m Hattie Sanger of Chicago who
survived him with 4 children. The
Pullman Car Co stopped operating
sleeping cars in USA on 31.12.1968.
DAB V 15 pp 263–4; *Trains* 11.1969
pp 20–31; *The Eng* V 84 22.10.1897
p 405

RAMSBOTTOM, John

b Todmorden 11.9.1814; d Alderley Edge,
Cheshire, 20.5.1897 aged 82.
LNWR loco eng. Began work with his
f, later joining Sharp, Roberts & Co,
Manchester. In 5.1842, at age 28, he was
app loco supt on the Manchester &
Birmingham R with wks at Longsight,
Manchester. On 16.7.1846 the M & B
was amalgamated with the London &
Birmingham and Grand Junction Rs to
form the LNWR of which Ramsbottom
became dist supt of the NE div, remaining at Longsight. About 1850 he introduced his double-beat regulator valve.
His next important invention, in 1852,
was the split piston ring. In 1856 he
invented his famous safety valve and
the dipslacement lubricator. On 1.8.1857
F. Trevithick (qv) retired as N div loco
supt at Crewe. The N and and NW divs
were then united under the name of the
N div and Ramsbottom became loco
supt at Crewe. The first of his locos to
be built at Crewe was the DX class
0–6–0 No 355 *Hardman* in 9.1858.
Altogether 942 of this class were built,
an all-time record for a British loco
class. In 11.1859 there followed the first
of his 2–2–2 express engines, No 184
Problem. In 1860 he took out a patent
for a water trough and water pick-up
apparatus and the first ones were
installed the same year at Mochdre on
the Chester–Holyhead section. Finding
that engines picked up most water at
40mph (64km/h) he invented a speed
indicator. In 1861 F. W. Webb (qv)
(who completed his apprenticeship at
Crewe the day Trevithick ret) became
wks mgr and in 3.1862 McConnell (qv)
retired from Wolverton where he was
loco supt of the S div. All loco work
was then concentrated at Crewe and
the S div was abolished, and by 1873
engine building at Wolverton had
finished. Ramsbottom now introduced
standardisation of parts. He introduced
an 18in (457.2mm) gauge tramway at
Crewe wks in 1862 and designed a loco
to work on it, named *Tiny*. In 1863
the first of his 4ft (1.219m) ST shunters,
No 835, appeared. In 5.1863 the first of
his 2–4–0 mixed traffic engines, 633
Samson, appeared. The first of his 6ft 6in
(1.981m) 2–4–0s, 1480 *Newton*, appeared

in 4.1866. In 1868 he installed a Siemens-Martin steel furnace at Crewe. His last engine was the 4ft 3in (1.295m) 0–6–0ST 1750 built in 1870. At the age of 57 his health began to decline, so on 1.10.1871 he resigned and was succeeded by Webb. However, his health recovered and he began another period of usefulness as a consulting eng and a dir of the LYR, and was largely responsible for the planning of Horwich wks. He was also a dir of Beyer, Peacock & Co, Manchester, in which firm his two sons John and George held important positions. In 1890 he received an hon degree of Master of Engg from Dublin Univ. He was an early MIME and was president in 1870.

Hambleton, F. C., in *The Locomotive* 7.1941 pp 143–7 and. 8.1941 pp 178–82; Min Proc ICE V 129 1896–7 p 382; Proc IME 4.1897 pp 236–41; *The Eng* V 83 1897 pp 549, 568; *Engg* V 63 1897 pp 722, 751

RANDOLPH, Epes

b Lunenburg, Virginia, 16.8.1856;
d Tucson, Arizona, 22.8.1921 aged 65.
RR president and civil eng. Son of William Eston and Sarah Lavina (Epes) Randolph. Began his career in 1876 as const eng, surveying 6 RRs in Kentucky, Alabama, Tennessee, Mississippi, Georgia and Texas. His drive and efficiency brought him to the notice of C. P. Huntington (qv) who entrusted him with const of a bridge to carry the Chesapeake & Ohio RR across the Ohio River from Covington, Ky, into Cincinnati. In 1894 he had to retire to recover from tuberculosis, but at the same time supervised const of another bridge across the Ohio from Louisville to Jeffersonville, acquired by the C & O. In 1901 he was transferred to Los Angeles to build and operate the Pacific Electric R. After 2 yrs as vice president and g mgr he was forced by ill health to return to Arizona, establishing his hq at Tuscon. In 1895 he joined the Southern Pacific RR as supt of line in Arizona. In 1905 he became responsible for preventing destruction of the Imperial Valley when the Colorado River broke through irrigation works into the Salton Sink in California. By 4.1906 it was flowing in at the rate of 4000 million cut ft of water a day, flood-

ing the SP main line. After several attempts, by dumping rock faster than it could be washed away, he succeeded finally on 10.2.1907 and so saved the SP main line and the Imperial Valley for irrigation and agricultural development. It was one of the greatest works of its kind ever accomplished. In 1886 he m Eleanor Taylor of Winchester, Va, who survived him. They had no children.

Trains 7.1950 pp 44–9; DAB V 15 pp 357–8

RAPIER, Richard Christopher

b Morpeth, Northumb, 7.6.1836;
d Folkestone 28.5.1897 aged 61.
Ed Christ's Hospital, London. Apprenticed 7 yrs at R. Stephenson & Co, Newcastle. 1862 entered service of Ransomes, Ipswich, and for 6 yrs was in charge of the R dept at the Orwell wks. In 1868 the agricultural implement and R sides of the business were divided and Rapier became the engg partner in the R business as Ransomes & Rapier at Waterside Ironworks. In 1896 the firm became a limited company and Rapier became mg dir. In 1874 they contracted for the first R in China, a narrow gauge line from Shanghai to Woosung (see J. Dixon), for which they built all the equipment. They also supplied much of the material for the n g Rs in the Welsh slate quarries during the 1870s. Rapier took a leading part in the change from wròught iron to steel structures at this time and bridges, turntables and steam cranes (from 1875) were built in great numbers. Some of the largest R breakdown cranes were built by the firm. Rapier also promoted the Southwold R, using some of the equipment recovered from China in 1879 and became its first chairman. In 1878 he pub *Remunerative Rs for New Countries,* advocating n g lt Rs. Became MICE 17.4.1877.

Min Proc ICE V 129 1876–7 p 389; Brownlie, John S., *R Steam Cranes* 1973

RASTRICK, John Urpeth

b Morpeth, Northumb, 26.1.1780;
d Chertsey, Surrey, 1.11.1856 aged 76.
Civil and mech eng. The family originated in Rastrick, Yorks. Son of John Rastrick (1738–1826) who m Mary Urpeth of Rothbury in 1774 and estab-

lished himself in London in 1798. J. U. Rastrick was articled to his f also in 1798. In 1801 he entered Ketley Ironworks, Shropshire, to gain experience in the use of cast iron for machinery. Shortly afterwards he entered into partnership with John Hazeldine of Bridgnorth, taking charge of the iron foundry. In 1808–9 he was associated with Richard Trevithick (qv) in the unsuccessful Thames tunnel attempt. In 1814 he patented a steam engine and he experimented in steam R traction. In 1815 he designed and built the cast iron bridge over the Wye at Chepstow, opened on 24.7.1816. About 1817, after the death of Hazeldine, he became mg partner of Bradley, Foster, Rastrick & Co, ironfounders and mfrs of machinery, at Stourbridge, Worcestershire, designing and building rolling mills, steam engines, etc. At this period he also designed ironworks at Chillington nr Wolverhampton and at Shutt End nr Stourbridge. In 1822 he was eng of the Stratford & Moreton R, the first to use Birkinshaw's wrought iron rails, opened 5.9.1826 (see William James). In 1.1825 he and George Stephenson, on behalf of the Liverpool & Manchester R promoters, visited collieries in the N of England to report on their tramroads and engines, and in 4.1826 he was the first witness, before the parliamentary committee, in support of the L & M Bill. His evidence on the use of locos encouraged a favourable report. As a result he was engaged to give support to a large number of R Bills. On 2.6.1829 he completed and opened the Shutt End colliery R, Staffs, working it with a loco of his design having 3 boiler flues, the *Agenoria*, now in the NRM, York. A similar engine, the *Stourbridge Lion*, was built to the order of Horatio Allen (qv) for the Delaware & Hudson RR, becoming the first loco to run in N America. (See also J. B. Jervis.) In 10.1829 he and Nicholas Wood (qv) and John Kennedy (qv) were appointed judges at the Rainhill trials on the Liverpool & Manchester R. In 1830, with George Stephenson, he made preliminary surveys for the Grand Junction R (Warrington–Birmingham) and later marked out the Manchester & Birmingham R. In 1835 he was eng to the Manchester & Cheshire Jn R which

became part of the NSR system, and the Trent Valley line. In 1836 he undertook his greatest work, the London & Brighton R including the great Ouse vdt of 37 arches of 30ft (9.144m) span, 92ft (28.042m) high, Clayton tunnel 1 mile 506yd (2.072km), Merstham tunnel, 1 mile 71yd (1.674km), and Balcombe tunnel 1141yd (1.043km). The R was op in 1841. He also engineered the Brigton–Lewes–Hastings line with the huge London Road vdt at Brighton; Brighton–Portsmouth; and branches to Horsham, Newhaven, East Grinstead and Epsom. In 1840–1 he was chief eng to the Bolton–Preston R; in 1845 Gravesend–Rochester and in 1846 Nottingham–Grantham. He ret 1847 and settled at Chertsey, Surrey, where he d. He was buried at Brighton. Became MICE 1827; M Soc Arts 1833; FRS 19.1.1837. He was m and left a son, Henry, who d on 1.11.1893.
Min Proc ICE V 16 1857 pp 128–33; *The Eng* V 2 1856 p 627; *Transactions of the Newcomen Soc* V 4 1923 p 48; V 26 1947–9; DNB

RATTRAY, David Campbell

b Dundee (?).(?).1858; d Southport, Lancs, 11.1.1927 aged 69.
Chief civil eng, LYR. Ed High Schools, Dundee. Apprenticed in mech eng at Pearse Bros, Dundee. Later became a pupil and then asst on the CR and G & SWR Jt Rs. Attended classes in civil engg at Glasgow Univ and obtained BSc Engg. He then joined the LYR, first as chief asst, E Div eng's office, and later as asst in pw dept in Manchester. In 1890 moved to the MS & L as chief of the drg office at Manchester where he prepared parliamentary plans and estimates. In 1893 became dist eng for the entire MS & L west of Penistone. In 1897 returned to the LYR as asst eng under W. B. Worthington (qv) and in 4.1905 succeeded to the position of chief eng. Ret at the grouping of the Rs at the end of 1922 and lived in Southport. He left a widow, Agnes Mary.
R Yr Bk 1921; RM 5.1905 p 403; Marshall, John, *The Lancashire & Yorkshire R* V 2 1970

RAVEN, Sir Vincent Litchfield

b Great Fransham, Norfolk, (?).(?).1858; d Felixstowe 14.2.1934 aged 75.

NER loco eng. Son of Rev Vincent Raven. Ed Aldenham Sch, Herts. From 1877–80 he served an apprenticeship under Edward Fletcher (qv) at Gateshead, NER. He then spent 2 yrs in the drg office and 5 yrs firing locos and on inspection duties. 1888 became asst div loco supt; 1894 div supt; and 1903 chief asst mech eng. On 1.6.1910 he succeeded William Worsdell (qv) as CME, remaining in that position until he ret in 1923. He was a strong advocate of 3-cyl locos, among which were the 4–4–2, 4–6–0, 4–6–2 and 0–8–0 tender engines and the 4–4–4 and 4–8–0 tanks. He also fitted a 4–6–0 and a 4–4–2 with Stumpff (qv) uniflow cyls. He took a great interest in electrification and on 16.6.1913 opened the electrified mineral line from Shildon to Newport on Tees, the first in Britain to use 1500 V dc. In 1922 he built a 2-Co-2 express loco with the intention of electrifying the York–Newcastle line on the same system, but the project was abandoned at the grouping in 1923. In 1915 he was made chief supt of the Royal Arsenal, Woolwich, and in 1917 controller of armament production for the Admiralty. After the war he returned to the NER. He was made KBE in 1917. Following his ret, in 1924 he and Sir Sam Fay (qv) visited New South Wales and New Zealand to report on Rs, and in 1925 he was app chairman of a committee reporting on R workshops in India. Became MIME 1895, and president 1925, MICE 1911, MIEE and M of the Soc of Civil Engs of France.
The Locomotive 3.1934 p 70; *The Eng* V 157 23.2.1934 p 206; *Engg* V 137 23.2.1934 p 217; Proc IME 3 1934 p 478; Nock, O. S. *The Locos of the NER* 1954

RAYNAR WILSON, Henry

b Derby (?).(?).1863; d London 19.4.1936 aged 73.
R signal eng. Ed Derby Sch. Joined the MR as examining clerk in the staff office of the supt of the line, in which he gained a detailed knowledge of the standard R rule book. 1881 transferred to the signal dept and shortly before he was 21 was app chief indoor asst to the signal supt. 1889, when only 27, app signal supt on the LYR where he was able to initiate several economical signalling arrangements and to standardise

signalling over the whole line. In 1898 he became interested in automatic signalling and after a visit to USA he resigned from the LYR in 1901 to become representative in Britain of the Hall Signalling Co, to develop track circuit and automatic signalling. The NER was the only R to respond to his efforts, with the Alne–Thirsk installation, completed in 1905. RW was instrumental in introducing long-burning oil lamps for signal lighting in Britain in 1903. He visited USA 5 times early in the 20th century, but his business enterprises failed. RW is best known for his writings, in the *R Eng* from 1893. Pub his first book *R Signalling* in 1900. From 1905 he contributed to *The Eng* and from 1912 to the *RG*. Pub *The Safety of British Rs* 1909; *R Accidents* 1925. Compiled comprehensive records of R accidents. In 1917 the Foreign Office commissioned RW to compile a record of the R communications built by the British Army in France in WW1. His connection with the International R Congress began in 1895.
RG V 64 24.4.1936 pp 803–4 (portrait)

REAY, Thomas Purvis

b South Shields, Co Durham, 13.10.1844; d Leeds 22.2.1912 aged 67.
Mech eng. Pupil for 6 yrs at Kitsons, Leeds, afterwards entering drg office, becoming a skilled draughtsman. Engaged in design of locos, tramway and waterworks engines, forge and blast furnace machinery, winding and hauling engines and hydraulic cranes. 1875 app wks mgr, subsequently becoming a partner in the firm and later mg dir. On the death of Lord Airedale (qv under Kitson, James) in 3.1911 he became chairman of Kitson & Co Ltd. He had an intimate knowledge of all aspects of loco engg and of the design and mfr of rolling mill and blowing engines. He was also interested in steam tramway traction. He was a man of indomitable energy and great technical ability with a keen eye for the detection of incongruities in design. M of Engg Standards Comm; MIME; MICE from 24.5.1867.
Min Proc ICE V 188 1911–12 p 432

REID, Andrew Thomson

b Glasgow 17.7.1863;

d Glasgow 16.9.1940 aged 77.
Chief mg dir, NB Loco Co. Son of
James Reid (qv). Ed Glasgow Academy,
Loretto Sch, Musselburgh, and Glasgow
Univ. 1883–8 apprenticed at Neilson,
Reid & Co, Glasgow. After a share in
the mgt of that firm he became a partner
in 1893 and in 1903 was app mg dir of
the Hyde Park Wks on the amalgama-
tion of Neilson, Sharp Stewart and
Dübs to form the North British Loco
Co. In this position he was responsible
for design and mfr of locos. MIME 1897;
also MICE.
Proc IME V 145 1941 p 238; *Engg* V
150 27.9.1940 p 255

REID, Sir Hugh, Bart, CBE, LLD

b Manchester 9.2.1860; d Springburn,
Glasgow, 7.7.1935 aged 75.
Loco mfr. Son of James Reid of
Auchterarder, Perthshire. From 1876–
81 apprenticed at Hyde Park Loco Wks
of Neilson & Co, Glasgow, later studying at Glasgow. Univ. Spent his whole
working life with Neilson Reid & Co
and the North British Loco Co Ltd,
becoming a partner in the former with
his 3 bros in 1893. On the death of his f
in 1894 he became senior partner in
the firm which, in 1903, became part of
NB Loco Co with Reid as dep chairman
and chief mg dir. In 1910 he was joint
inventor of the Reid–Ramsey steam-
turbine electric loco. A second turbine
loco with direct drive was exhibited at
the Wembley Exhibition in 1924. During
WW1 he was a M of the Mgt Bd for the
supply of munitions in Glasgow and W
Scotland, and was also closely associated
with Red Cross work in the area. He
received the CBE and in 1922 was
created a baronet. In 1917 he received
the freedom of the city of Glasgow. In
1929 Glasgow Univ conferred on him
the hon LLD. In 1888 he m Marion,
youngest dr of John Bell of Prestwick,
Ayrshire.
Proc IME V 130 1935 p 543; *Journal*
ILE 1935 p 561; *Journal* ICE V 1 1935–
6 p 539; *The Eng* V 160 7.1935 p 42

REID, James

b Kilmaurs, Ayrshire, 8.9.1823;
d St Andrews 23.6.1894 aged 71.
Loco mfr. Apprenticed to James Liddell,
millwright and eng at Airdrie, and at

the Kilmarnock Foundry Co. From
1847–51 he was with Scott, Sinclair &
Co, Greenock. In 1851 he became chief
draughtsman with Caird & Co, Glasgow,
and in 1852 mgr of the Hyde Park Street
Wks of Neilson & Co. In 1858 he went
to Manchester to join Sharp Stewart &
Co until 1863 when he returned to
Glasgow as mgr at Neilson & Co, Springburn Wks. Neilson withdrew from active
mgt of Hyde Park Wks in 1872 and left
the firm in 1876. Reid remained as sole
partner until 1893 when he was joined by
4 of his sons, Hugh (qv), Andrew (qv),
John (qv) and Walter. In 1877 Reid
became a M of Glasgow town council.
He was president of the Inst of Engs &
Shipbuilders 1882–4 and Lord Dean of
Guild 1893. He d on St Andrews golf
course during a game.
Proc IME 1894 p 278; Min Proc ICE V
117 1893–4 pp 385–7; *The Eng* V 77
29.6.1894 p 570

REID, Sir John, KBE

b Manchester 28.10.1861; d Glasgow
25.1.1933 aged 71.
Loco mfr; dir of NB Loco Co. Son of
James Reid (qv). Ed Glasgow Academy,
Herbertshire Castle Sch, Stirlingshire and
Glasgow Mechs Inst which became the
Coll of Sc & Arts 1879. In 1880 Reid
began a 5 yr apprenticeship in his f's
firm Neilson Reid & Co (founded 1837)
at Hyde Park Loco Wks, Glasgow, and
afterwards served as draughtsman for
about 3 yrs. From 1888 he was given
increasing responsibility and in 1.1893
was taken into partnership. The NB
Loco Co was formed in 1903, absorbing
Neilson Reid & Co and in 1908 became
a dir until his death. He had many
interests outside engg, was a M of the
Inst of Engs & Shipbuilders in Scotland
from 1894 and MIME from 1897.
Knighted 1918; KBE 1925.
Engg V 135 1.1933 p 137; Proc IME V
124 6.1933 p 784; *Journal* ILE V 23 1933
p 158; Thomas, John, *The Springburn
Story* 1964

REID, Sir Robert Gillespie

b Coupar Angus, Perthshire, (?).(?).1842;
d Montreal 3.6.1908 aged 66.
R builder in Canada and USA. 1865
went to Australia where he was successful in the gold fields. 1871 went to

America where he undertook the building of the international bridge across the Niagara near Buffalo. In 1872 he built the bridges between Montreal and Ottawa on the Montreal, Ottawa & Quebec R, now CPR. He built the bridge over the Colorado River at Austin, Texas; all iron and masonry bridges west from San Antonio on the Southern Pacific; the international bridge across the Rio Grande between Texas and Mexico in 1882, and the R bridge across the Delaware River at Water Gap, Pa. During const of the CPR Reid undertook the building of the heaviest section N of Lake Superior. He erected permanent and temporary bridges on 250 miles of line E of Port Arthur, and built the Lachine bridge over the St Lawrence. In 1887 he built the Soo bridge, and then 86 miles (138.4km) of the CPR Sudbury branch. He then moved to Newfoundland where he built a bridge across the Great Narrows at Cape Breton, and in 1889 he contracted with the Newfoundland Govt to build the Hall's Bay R, 260 miles (418.4km), completed in 1893. He then undertook the Western R from Port au Basque on the W coast, 250 miles (402km), completed in 1897. In 1898 he contracted with the govt to operate all trunk and branch lines in the island for 50 yrs, paying $1 mil for the reversion of the whole lines at the end of that period, and receiving additional land concessions, amounting to about 4½ million acres, thus becoming one of the largest land proprietors in the world. He also contracted to build 8 steamers for passengers and freight. He took over the dry dock in St John's harbour and the whole of the land telegraph lines throughout the island. These interests combined to form the Reid Newfoundland Co of which Reid was first president. Created Knight Bachelor 1907. 1865 m Harriet Duff; 3 sons, 1 dr.

The Eng V 105 26.6.1908 p 671; *Macmillan Dict of Canadian Biog*; DAB 2nd Suppl 1 V 3 pp 176–8

REID, Robert Whyte, CBE

b Glasgow (?).(?).1884; d Duffield nr Derby 28.3.1929 aged 45.

Latterly vice president for works and ancillary undertakings, LMS. Son of W. P. Reid (qv) of the NBR. Ed Royal High Sch, Dundee, and Royal Tech Coll, Glasgow. Received engg training at Glasgow, London, Loughborough and Wolverton before joining the MR staff at Derby as wks asst in 1909. In 4.1916 he became wks mgr; 10.1916 asst C & W supt; 1.5.1919 C & W supt, until 31.12.1922. From formation of the LMS on 1.1.1923 until 31.12.1926 Reid was C & W supt of the LMS. He then became vice president for works and ancillary undertakings. In 8.1919, at the request of the MR dirs, he visited USA to study methods of construction, repair and administration in C & W shops. Later he applied mass production methods to the building of rolling stock in the various LMS wks. In 1920 he received the CBE for services during WW1 in the mfr of ambulance trains. MIME 1921, MILE 1921.

The Eng V 147 5.4.1929 p 384 (portrait); *The Locomotive* 9.1916 p 189; Proc IME 5.1929 p 580; *Journal* ILE 3–4.1929 p 142; *Beyer Peacock Quarterly Review* 7.1929 p 70; Radford, J. B., *A century of progress* 1976

REID, William Paton, CBE

b Glasgow (?).(?).1854; d Glasgow 2.2.1932 aged 77.

Loco supt, NBR. Son of Robert Reid who was C & W supt of the Edinburgh & Glasgow R and who introduced the centre cradle continuous drawgear for wagons originating from trouble on Cowlairs incline with loaded brake wagons fitted with draw hooks on the headstocks. The centre cradle with long drawbars took the stress off the body. Stroudley (qv) took the idea with him when he left the E & G to join the HR and thereafter the design became standard practice on British Rs. In 1879 W. P. Reid entered Cowlairs Wks, NBR, under M. Holmes (qv). In 1883 he was selected to take charge of the loco dept at Balloch. In 1889 he moved to Dunfermline and in 1891 to Dundee. On 1.5.1900 he became supt at St Margarets, Edinburgh. On the creation of the post of outdoor asst loco supt he was app to this position until, following the ret and death of Holmes, he was finally app loco supt on 2.6.1904. Unlike the CMEs of some other Rs, Reid's position was one of servility under the mgt, and at times he had to endure humiliation such as some of his contemporaries would not have tolerated. He developed the 0-6-0 and 4-4-0 designs of Holmes into the massive B, and S class 0-6-0s of 1914 (LNER J37), and the 'Scott' and 'Glen' 4-4-0s. Also, in 1906, he introduced the famous NBR 'Atlantics'. His 0-6-2T (1909) and 4-4-2Ts (1911, 1915) also did good work. Many of his engines lasted well into BR days. He ret 31.12.1919 on reaching the age limit. In 1920 he received the CBE.

The Eng V 153 12.2.1932 p 185; *Engg* 12.2.1932 p 184; *The Locomotive* 2.1932 p 63; *RM* 8.1904 p 172; Thomas, John, *The North British Atlantics* 1972; *The North British R* V 2 1975; RCTS *Locos of the LNER*

RENDEL, James Meadows

b nr Okehampton, Devon (?).(?).1799; d London 21.11.1856 aged 56.
Civil eng, mainly of docks and bridges. Learned surveying under Thomas Telford and c 1822 settled at Plymouth and worked on roads in N Devon. For his iron bridge at Lara, Plymouth, in 1827 he received a Telford Medal from the ICE. In partnership with Nathaniel Beardmore he built various bridges and chain ferries, or 'floating bridges', in 1832-4. In 1829 he began his work on harbours, carrying out works at Par, Cornwall, 1829; Bude 1835; Brixham 1836; and in 1836-7 he designed the Millbay terminus of the S Devon R and Millbay docks later built by Brunel (qv). About 1838 the partnership with Beardmore was dissolved. Various other dock works followed: Grimsby 1844-53; Leith 1848-53; Garston LNWR 1850-3; and London. In 1845 he planned and later built the packet and refuge harbour at Holyhead. His actual R work was limited; in England he built the Birkenhead, Lancashire & Cheshire Jn R, op Chester–Warrington 18.12.1850, and in India he directed const of the East Indian and Madras Rs. MICE 1824 and president 1852-3; FRS 23.2.1843.
Min Proc ICE V 16 1857 pp 133-42; Proc Royal Soc of London V 8 1857 pp 279-83; *Times* 22.11.1856 p 12; *Gent Mag* V 1 1857 pp 114-15; Baughan,

Peter E., *The Chester & Holyhead R* 1972

RENNIE, Sir John

b London 30.8.1794; d Hertford 3.9.1874 aged 80.
Civil eng; 2nd son of John Rennie, civil eng, 1761-1821. Trained under his f. After early work on bridges, piers and breakwaters, he surveyed the Liverpool & Manchester R 1825-6, later relinquishing this to George Stephenson. In 1831 he was knighted, following the completion of London Bridge. His acceptance of this established a precedent for the knighting of engs. In 1852 he laid out lines in Sweden and in 1855 in Portugal. MICE 25.6.1844; president 1845-8.
Min Proc ICE V 39 1874-5 p 273; *Engg* V 21 16.6.1876 p 505

RICHARDSON, Charles

b nr Chester 14.8.1814; d Bristol 10.2.1896 aged 81.
Civil eng, GWR lines and Severn tunnel. At age 19 apprenticed to I. K. Brunel. His first practical experience was under Marc Brunel on const of the Thames tunnel, and then on Clifton suspension bridge. As pupil he did much work on the GWR around Gloucester. He was then app res eng on the Hereford, Ross & Gloucester R, 1853-5. 1858 app res eng on the Bristol & S Wales Union R and on the death of Brunel, in 1859, he became chief eng in conj with R. P. Brereton. This led to his app as chief eng of the Severn tunnel. In 3.1873 the first shaft was sunk on the W side. In 1879 an influx of water under the Shoots led the GWR to app Sir John Hawkshaw (qv) as chief eng in conjunction with Richardson. He was also eng of the Bristol Harbour R. As a result of work on the Bristol & S Wales Union line, he established extensive brick works near Patchway tunnel. MICE 6.4.1875.
Min Proc ICE V 124 1895-6 p 409

RICHES, Tom Hurry

b Cardiff 24.11.1846; d Cardiff 4.9.1911 aged 64.
Loco supt, Taff Vale R. In 1863 entered wks of the TVR as apprentice

under Joseph Tomlinson and spent 5 yrs in the shops and drg office. 1868 awarded a scholarship at the Royal School of Mines. After a period at sea, gaining experience as second eng on SS *Camilla* he returned to Cardiff to continue his studies. He later became mgr of Bute Iron Wks and of Bute Old Wks under John McConnochie, engaged on const of bridges, roofs, boilers, engines and gen engg. 1872 returned to the TVR as chief loco foreman. On 1.10.1873 he was app loco supt in succession to B. S. Fisher; at barely 27 he was then the youngest loco supt in Great Britain. He retained the position until his death. During his career he was president of the Assoc of Loco C & W Supts of UK; elected MICE 10.1.1882; M of the Iron & Steel Inst; British Assoc; S Wales Inst of Engs, and other bodies. Also MIME 1874 and president 1907–8. He contributed several important papers. In Cardiff he was active in local affairs and education. His principal engines were the standard 0–6–0s of classes K and L, 85 engines 1874–89. It is interesting that the K class was adopted by Barton Wright (qv) as a standard engine on the LYR. Riches was also responsible for the introduction of the 0–6–2T into S Wales, in 1885, a type which had been introduced on the LYR by Barton Wright. It became the most popular type in S Wales. For full details of TVR locos see *The Locos of the GWR* (RCTS) Part 10 1966.

The Eng V 112 8.9.1911 p 256; *Engg* V 92 8.9.1911 pp 325–7 (portrait); Min Proc ICE V 187 1911–12 p 330; Proc IME 1911 pp 1054–6; *The Locomotive* 15.9.1911 p 192; Barrie, D. S. M., *The Taff Vale R* 1939, 1969

RIGGENBACH, Nikolaus

b Basle, Switzerland, 21.5.1817;
d Olten 7.7.1899 aged 82.
Eldest of 8 children of a prominent sugar refiner. Displayed an interest in Rs from childhood. 1840–2 and 1844–53 worked in Emil Kessler'schen loco wks, Karlsruhe, where, during these years, 150 steam locos were built, including the first 4 locos for the Zurich–Baden R, opened in 1847, Switzerland's first

R. He drove the first loco on the line, and the first train from Zurich to Baden. Soon after this he took charge of the machine shop of the Swiss Central R, first in Basle then, from 1855, in Olten, in that year taking full charge. Under him 53 locos were built, including 7 for other countries. His acquaintance with the old Hauenstein line (Basle–Olten) with its gradients of 26°/oo (about 1 in 40) led him to consider arrangements for making locos independent of their adhesion with the rails. From Blenkinsop (qv), Cathcart, and Marsh (qv) he developed the idea of a rack R. With the firm of André Köchlin & Co, Mülhausen, he evolved a system which was patented on 12.8. 1863 for 15 yrs. The patent included a rack loco and a machine with coupled rack and adhesion drive. Originally he had thought of grade limits of 50–55°/ oo (1 in 18–20) and in 1863 he looked for a R on which to experiment. After 6 months in N America, in the spring of 1866 his idea began to achieve notice. Also the General Assembly of Swiss Engs in Glarus discussed his ideas in 1866 with enthusiasm, but financing was a problem. In 1867 the then General Counsel Hitz head of the Mount Washington R then under const and eng Otto Grüninger went to USA to see it. In the meantime Riggenbach joined with Oliver Zschokke of Aarrau and Adolf Näff of St Gallen. At the suggestion of Hitz they explored the idea of a R up the Rigi, obtaining a concession on 18.4.1869. Early in June Grüninger reported on the feasibility of the project. On 6.6.1869 Canton Lucerne took a share of the concession for a rack R from Vitznau to Kaltbad–Staffelhöhe on which a limited company was founded. Const was rapid and was only delayed by the war in France from where the rails were obtained. On his birthday, on 21.5.1871, Riggenbach opened the R. Also in 1871 the quarry R in Ostermundigen was opened giving R. an opportunity to build a mixed rack and adhesion R. After the Rigi R an 'International Company for Mountain Rs' was formed with hq in Basle with Riggenbach as dir, but it collapsed after a few yrs. Riggenbach then rejoined the firm of Kessler which meanwhile had opened a second factory in Esslingen. So in 1879 he became established with his patent in Esslingen. In 1881 he set up as a civil eng in Olten, visiting Germany, Italy, Portugal, Brazil, Hungary and other countries, only giving up his work when very old.

S Bz V 34 2.8.1899 p 45; Hefti, Walter, *Zahnradbahnen der Welt* Basle 1971 pp 15–16

RIHOSEK, Dr Johann

b in Polish part of Austro–Hungarian Empire (?).(?).1869; d Vienna (?).(?).1957 aged 88.
CME Austrian State Rs. Studied at Tech Univ, Vienna, and trained at Floridsdorf Loco Wks. 1897 entered service of Austrian State Rs and worked in the design office under Gölsdorf (qv), finally as his asst. In 1916, following the death of Gölsdorf, Rihosek succeeded him as CME and continued to design locos for the different lines of Central Europe. He played an important part in developing the vacuum brake and later the air brake. Among his best known designs were the '81' class 2.10.0 (1920) for heavy gds and passenger work on the Semmering, Tauern and Arlberg lines. One of these is preserved at the Vienna R Museum. When he ret in 1924 he was app lecturer (later professor) of loco engg at Vienna Univ. When he ret from the chair in 1939 he continued to write on loco subjects.
The Locomotive 2–3.1957 p 37

RINECKER, Franz

b Würzburg, Germany, 16.12.1843; d Würzburg 10.4.1899 aged 55.
Eng of Abt rack Rs. Studied maths and engg at Polytechnic Sch, Karlsruhe, and at Zurich. Began practical work in 11.1864 as asst eng on Bavarian State Rs, laying out and building part of the Munich–Ingolstadt R until 11.1867. From 5.1869 to 6.1873 he was employed on the Pittsburgh, Fort Wayne & Chicago RR and then on the Pennsylvania RR, laying out and building new lines. Returned to Europe and from 1.1874 to 5.1876 was div eng on the Swiss Central R for surveys and const of the Liestal–Waldenburg (n g) and Liestal–Oensingen lines. 1876–83 occupied with technical studies concerning devel-

opment of the Abt rack system. In 8.1883, he established the firm of Rinecker, Abt & Co at Würzburg and was engaged on many Abt rack Rs including Harzbahn, Germany; Usui Toge R, Japan; Transandine R; Nilgiri R, India; Snowdon R, Wales; Mount Lyell R, Tasmania and Mount Morgan R, Queensland. MICE 3.12.1889.
Min Proc ICE V 137 1898–9 p 433

ROBERTS, Richard

b Carreghova, Llanymynech, Wales, 22.4.1789; d Manchester 11.3.1864 aged 75.
Inventor of the self-acting spinning mule; one of the partners in Sharp Roberts & Co, loco mfrs. Son of a shoemaker. He had almost no ed, but soon showed mechanical abilities. After working at a quarry he found employment as pattern maker at Bradley ironworks nr Bilston under John Wilkinson, the first ironmaster that James Watt could find capable of boring a cylinder truly. He then went to Birmingham where he gained further experience in various shops. After a short spell at Horsley Ironworks at Tipton he went to Liverpool where he became a cabinet maker, then to London where he spent a period with Henry Maudslay. In 1816 he went to Manchester where he established a business in Water Street, helped by his first wife, and made parts for machines. He soon had to move to larger premises. Roberts was an active promoter of the first mechanics institution in Manchester. He became one of the first members of the corporation and with John Dalton and others was an active member of the Literary & Philosophical Society. He invented an improved screw lathe and the first practical gas metre. In 1817 he invented and built the first planing machine, now in the Science Museum, London. A screw-cutting lathe followed in 1820; this is now in the North West Museum of Science & Industry, Manchester. In 1825 he invented the self-acting spinning mule. In 1828 he was taken into partnership by Sharp Bros (Thomas, Robert Chapman and John qqv) who had founded the firm in Manchester in 1806. It then became Sharp, Roberts & Co. Loco mfr began in 1833. R's first loco, *Experiment*, with

vertical cylinders, was built for the Liverpool & Manchester R. Three similar engines were built for the Dublin & Kingstown R. They had cylindrical slide valves which he patented in 1832, at the same time as a variable expansion gear for steam engines and a differential gear for road locos. He also invented a steam brake. His locos were distinguished by superior workmanship and finish, stronger framing and larger bearing surfaces than were customary at the time. He was probably the first among British engs to apply weights to the driving wheels to balance revolving masses. Loco const was resumed in 1837 with the const of 2-2-2s of the Stephenson 'Patentee' type which developed into the famous 'Sharp singles' of the 'Atlas' class of 1838. Thomas Sharp d in 1841, and in 1843 Roberts ret from the Partnership but retained the old factory. (For the continuance of the loco wks see Sharp Bros.) Roberts carried on in business until 1852 when he gave it up and started as a consulting eng in Salford. His plate punching machine made possible the rapid const of the Conway and Britannia tubular bridges in Wales in 1846-50, despite strikes of workmen. Roberts' many other inventions related to machines not connected with Rs. He became MICE 20.3.1838.

Beyer Peacock Quartely Review 4.1929 pp 31-56; Min Proc ICE V 24 1864-5 pp 536-9; *The Eng* V 17 25.3.1864 p 183; V 183 14.2.1947 pp 176-8; 7.3.1947 pp 189-90; Smiles, Samuel, *Industrial Biography* 1863, 1967 Ch 14

ROBERTSON, Henry

b Banff, Scotland, 16.1.1816; d Pale Hall, Llandderfel, nr Bala, N Wales, 22.3.1888 aged 72.
Civil eng. Ed Banff and Aberdeen Univ where he grad MA. Began career as R contractor, carrying out contracts at Port Glasgow under Locke (qv). Later he did much to develop the N Wales mineral district. In 1842 he was asked to advise on the revival of the Brymbo Ironworks. He recommended a R to the River Dee at Connah's Quay. He projected the N Wales Mineral R, Wrexham -Chester with a branch to Brymbo (op 11.1847), afterwards extended to Ruabon and Shrewsbury. It later became part of

the GWR. Robertson was responsible for carrying out all the GWR extensions in N Wales. He projected and carried out the GWR Shrewsbury-Hereford line, op 1852-3, and the LNWR Central Wales line from Craven Arms to Llandovery, op 1861-8. About. 1850 he became eng of the Shrewsbury & Birmingham line, then worked in conjunction with the Shrewsbury & Chester. He also projected and built the branch to Coalbrookdale, Horsehays, and other parts of that district. Carried out the Ruabon-Dolgelly line, op 1861-8, and the branch to Bala and Blaenau Ffestiniog, op 1.11.1882. Robertson designed and carried out the fine vdts carrying the GWR over the Cefn and Chirk valleys and the Kingsland bridge over the Severn at Shrewsbury, then one of the largest single-span iron bridges in Britain. His last major work was the projection and carrying out of the Dee extn and the Wirral Rs to connect with the Wrexham, Mold & Connah's Quay R over the Hawarden bridge. As proprietor of the Brymbo ironworks, in 1883 he transferred it into the largest steelworks in N Wales. He also owned and operated several collieries in N Wales. He was one of the original partners in the Manchester firm of Beyer, Peacock & Co, loco builders, and took an active part in its running until his death. Also partner in firm of Robertson & Mackintosh, civil engs, London. He was chairman of the Llangollen & Corwen R, Corwen & Bala R, Vale of Llangollen R, Minera Lime Co, Broughton & Plas Power Coal Co, Wirrall Rs Co, Brymbo Steel Co and Brymbo Water Co, and was a dir of the Wrexham, Mold & Connah's Quay R. As politician Robertson was Liberal MP for Shrewsbury 1862-5, and from 1874 and 1880. He was JP for Merionethshire and Denbighshire, MIME 1848, MICE 5.6.1849.

Min Proc ICE V 93 1887-8 pp 489-92; Proc IME 1888 pp 264-5; *The Eng* V 65 6.4.1888 p 283

ROBINSON, John Frederick

b Manchester 27.5.1853;
d Inverness 12.7.1918 aged 65.
Mg dir, Atlas Wks, Glasgow and dir of NB Loco Co. Studied civil and mech engg at Owen's Coll, Manchester, 1869-

72. 1872–5 apprenticed at Sharp, Stewart & Co, Manchester, loco mfrs, of which his f, John, was a partner. 10.1875–12.1876 at LNWR wks, Crewe. 2.1877–3.1878 at Baldwin Loco Wks, Philadelphia. 1881 became one of the mg dirs of Sharp, Stewart & Co, Manchester (see Sharp Bros), and on the removal of the wks to Glasgow where it became Atlas Wks in 1.1888 he became sole mg dir. Later he became dir of the NB Loco Co into which Sharp, Stewart was amalg in 1903, remaining in this position until his death. MIME 1878; MICE 1896. *Engg* 19.7.1918 p 64

ROBINSON, John George

b Bristol 30.7.1856; d Bournemouth 7.12.1943 aged 87.
CME of GCR 1902–23. Son of Matthew R., div loco C & W supt, GWR, Bristol. Ed Chester Gr Sch. In 1872 at age 16 he began a 6 yr pupilage under Joseph Armstrong (qv) and later William Dean (qv) at Swindon, GWR, and also at Chester and Bristol. In 1878 he was app to the running dept at Bristol as asst to his f. In 4.1884 app asst loco C & W supt on the Waterford, Limerick & Western R, Ireland, and in 1889 became supt, in succession to Henry Appleby. He changed the loco livery from green to red, with black panels, and chimneys with polished copper caps—from his GWR days. He designed some highly attractive engines: 2–4–0s (1889), 2–4–2Ts (1891), 0–4–4Ts (1895), 4–4–2Ts similar to his later GCR type (1896), 6ft (1.828m) 4–4–0s (1896–7) and 0–6–0s (1893–9). Most of his carriages were 6-wheeled, but latterly he introduced 8-wheeled bogie coaches. His work clearly impressed the mgt of the GCR for in 6.1900 he was app loco and marine eng at Gorton, Manchester, in succession to Harry Pollitt (qv). In 1902, following the retirement of J. Parker, Robinson was made CME with charge of the C & W dept also. His loco designs were noted for their handsome lines. They have been frequently described and illustrated (see below). His finest designs were the 2–8–0 freight engine, adopted by the War Office during WW1 and built in large numbers for use at home and abroad, the 'Atlantics', 'Immingham' and 'Director' class express

engines, the 0–6-0 (LNER class J11) and 4–4–2 and 4–6–2 tank classes. For many years Robinson devoted himself to the development of the loco superheater and in 1911 he originated the equipment which bore his name. He then developed superheaters for marine boilers and several of his design were fitted to Atlantic and other lines. He also designed a force-feed lubricator, the 'Intensifor', fitted to numerous GCR locos. His other inventions included apparatus for preparing and burning pulverised coal, oil and colloidal fuel in stationary, loco and marine boilers, and anti-collision buffers on coaches. For his services in WW1 he was awarded the CBE in 1920. At the grouping of British Rs on 1.1.1923 he was offered the post of CME of the LNER but he decided to ret, and he recommended the app of H. N. Gresley (qv). MIME 1891; MICE 1902.
Proc IME V 151 1944 p 353; *Engg* V 156 17.12.1943 p 494; *The Eng* V 176 17.12.1943 p 477; Dow, George, *Great Central* V 3 1965; Tuplin, W. A., *Great Central Steam* 1967; RCTS *Locos of the LNER*, most parts; *RM* 3 and 4.1939; Ahrons, E. L., *Loco and train working* etc V 6 1954

ROBINSON, Moncure

b Richmond, Va, USA, 2.2.1802; d Philadelphia, Pa, 10.11.1891 aged 89.
Civil eng. Ed Gerardine Academy, and in 1816–17 at the Coll of William & Mary. 1818 began with a corps of surveyors and in 1822 worked on the James River canal, Va. He then became interested in Rs and in 1825–8 visited Europe to study public works. On his return to USA he made surveys for the Pottsville & Danville R and the Allegheny Portage RR. In the next 3 yrs he was engaged in building the Petersburg & Roanoke and Richmond & Petersburg lines. For the latter he built a bridge over the St James River 2844ft (867m) long with 19 spans of 140–153ft (42.7–46.6m). In 1834 he began his major work, the Philadelphia & Reading RR, including a 644yd (589m) tunnel at Phoenixville and a stone vdt of 4 spans of 72ft (22m). In 1836 he went to England to raise funds to complete the R. In 1840, on the invitation of the Czar

of Russia, he advised on const of Rs there. Ret 1847. On 2.2.1835 he m Charlotte Randolph Taylor and they had 5 sons and 5 drs. Although a self-taught eng he was elected hon M of the American Soc of Civil Engs.
DAB V 16 p 48

ROEBLING, John Augustus

b Mülhausen, Thuringia, Germany, 12.6.1806; d Brooklyn, New York, 22.7.1869 aged 63.
Bridge builder and mfr; pioneer of the wire-rope suspension bridge. Ed Mülhausen schools and Royal Polytechnic Inst, Berlin, where he was a pupil of Hegel, and also learned engg, obtaining degree of civil engg in 1826. After a frustrated start he and his bro Karl emigrated to USA in 1831 and bought 7000 acres (2833ha) of land in Butler County near Pittsburgh. In 5.1836 he m Johanna Herting and the following year he gave up farming and became a state eng at Harrisburg. Observation of the hemp ropes on the inclines of the Allegheny Portage RR led him to develop a wire rope and in 1841 he mfd the first wire rope made in America, in a small factory at Saxonburg. In 1848-9 he transferred his factory to Trenton, NJ. At the same time he developed his interest in bridge building and in 1846 completed his first suspension bridge, at Pittsburgh. In 1848-50 he built 4 suspension aqueducts for the Delaware & Hudson Canal. One of his most important bridges was the double deck suspension bridge carrying the Great Western R of Canada over the Niagara gorge, completed in 1855 and replaced in 1897. In the course of surveys for the Brooklyn bridge his foot was injured on a jetty in a ferry collision and he contracted tetanus from which he d. His son Washington Augustus (1837-1926) who was associated with him from 1857 carried on the construction of the bridge to completion in 1883. Roebling was a vigorous opponent of slavery and a strict self-disciplinarian. His book *Long and short span R bridges* 1869 was in the press when he d. He was a keen musician and played both the flute and piano.
DAB V 16 pp 86-9

ROGERS, Thomas

b Groton, Conn, USA, 16.3.1792; d New York 19.4.1856 aged 64.
Loco mfr, responsible for some of the greatest advances in American loco design. At 16 apprenticed to a carpenter and later learned blacksmithing from an uncle. 1812 settled in Paterson, NJ, and after serving in the war that year he worked in a shop making wooden looms. He also learned pattern making. In 1819 bought the mfg rights of a newly imported power loom. With John Clark he formed the firm of Clark & Rogers to make looms and to spin cotton. In 1820 a second partner, Abraham Godwin, joined. In 1829 Rogers withdrew with $38 000 as his share of the profits. In 1832, having built up a wks, he organised the Rogers, Ketchum & Grosvenor Machine Wks, of which he was president. They began making RR car wheels and were soon asked for locos. On 6.10.1837 his first loco made its first trip and was bought by the Mad River & Lake Erie RR and named *Sandusky*. Three similar ones were completed in 1838. His standard American 4-4-0 appeared in 1844 and was developed into the 2-6-0 built in large numbers and which became the most familiar Rogers type. Rogers engines were noted for efficiency, safety and durability and were used all over USA, in Cuba, and S America, on many gauges. Designs were largely by William S. Hudson and William Swinburn (qqv). Rogers m Marie Small of Paterson, NY, and was survived by 5 drs.
DAB V 16 p 112; White, John H. Jr, *American Locos, an engg history 1830-80* 1968; Sinclair, Angus, *Development of the Loco Engine* 1907, 1970; Bruce, A. W. *The Steam Loco in America* 1952

ROSS, Alexander

b Laggan, Inverness-shire, 20.4.1845; d Hampstead, London, 3.2.1923 aged 77. Ed at Aberdeen and at Owens Coll, Manchester. Began R career as eng on the Great N of Scotland R under A. Fraser (qv) for 5 yrs, becoming principal asst eng, GN of S, for a further 5 yrs. 1871 joined staff of LNWR, but in 1873 left to take charge of the NER Leyburn-Hawes extn. In 10.1874 he

rejoined the LNWR as dist eng at Liverpool under W. B. Worthington (qv), chief eng of the N div. In 1884 he became asst eng on the LYR and in 1890 chief eng MS & L. On 4.12.1896 he was app chief eng, GNR, until he resigned on 30.9.1911 to engage in private practice as consulting eng in Westminster. Rs for which Ross was responsible included the Leen Valley extn, connecting line to GCR at Nottingham, widenings N of London and the southern section of the Enfield–Stevenage loop on the GNR; the Piccadilly tube from Finsbury Park to Strand, and the steel vdt across Breydon Water, Yarmouth. In 1878 he m Annie Stephens who survived him, with 3 sons and 1 dr. Two sons were lost in WW1. His eldest son. A. P. Ross, became eng on the CLC. Ross was president of the ICE 1915–16.
Min Proc ICE V 215 1923 p 342; *The Eng* V 135 9.2.1923 p 150

ROTHERHAM, Thomas Forth

b York 28.6.1850; d Perth, W Australia, 11.9.1903 aged 53.
CME to W Australian Govt Rs Dept. Trained on MS & L at Gorton, Manchester, and NBR at Cowlairs, Glasgow. After some marine experience he returned to the NBR and took charge of erecting indoor and outdoor machinery and plant. Later worked on R equipment for Ransomes & Rapier. 1875 entered service of New Zealand Govt Rs as g mgr of Picton & Blenheim R (1875–8); g mgr Wanganui, Foxton & New Plymouth R (1878–85); Loco supt Herunui–Bluff R (1885–8); loco supt NZ Rs 1888–4.1890. 1891 app by NSW R Commissioners to enquire into merits of Westinghouse and vacuum brakes on goods trains. App CME of W Australia Govt Rs 1891. MICE 12.1.1886.
Min Proc ICE V 155 1903–4 p 437

ROTHWELL, Peter

b Bolton (?).(?).1792; d Glasgow 27.2.1849 aged 56.
Early loco eng and mfr. His f, Peter (b Bolton 1755; d Bolton 2.8.1824 aged 69), was a timber merchant who also founded the Union Foundry at Bolton. Rothwell decided to join the foundry, of which he became mgr. In 1810 he was joined by Benjamin Hick (qv) and the firm became Rothwell, Hick & Rothwell; later, on the death of Rothwell senior in 1824, it became Rothwell, Hick & Co. Rothwell was one of the original promoters and shareholders of the Bolton & Leigh R, op 1828. It was for this line that the firm built its first loco, the *Union*, in 12.1830, a vertical boiler 2–2–0. Further locos followed for overseas. In 1833 Hick left to set up on his own at the Soho Foundry, and the firm became Rothwell & Co. In 1839 Rothwell introduced the variable blast pipe, in the form of a hollow cone which could be raised or lowered inside the blast pipe orifice from a lever on the footplate. The most famous engines built by the firm were the 8 4–2–4Ts with 9ft (2.743m) driving wheels for the 7ft (2.134m) gauge Bristol & Exeter R in 1853–4. The last 2 engines were GWR 7ft gauge 0–6–0s built in 1860. Altogether they built about 200 engines. The wks then became part of the Bolton Iron & Steel Co (see F. W. Webb) until 1906 when it was absorbed by Henry Bessemer & Co Ltd. It was dismantled in 1926. In 1843 Rothwell was chairman of the Bolton & Preston R, until it was absorbed by the North Union R on 10.5.1844.
Min Proc ICE V 9 1849–50 p 100; *The Eng* V 129 11.6.1920 p 598; local records at Bolton.

ROUS-MARTEN, Charles

b London (?).(?).1844; d London 20.4.1908 aged 64.
Writer of reports on Rs and loco performance. At age 15 he went to New Zealand where he acquired a position in the S Island of some political importance. 1887 returned to England to prepare a report on the Rs, in the course of which he travelled 40 000 miles (64 400km). The report, pub autumn 1877, at once brought his name before the R world. On his return to Wellington he prepared reports on Rs of New Zealand, New South Wales, Victoria, South Australia and Italy, and less complete ones on Ceylon and Switzerland. In 1893 he returned to England where he represented the NZ press. In 1897 he became interested in the French Rs and 'discovered' the French compounds

and brought their outstanding work to wider notice. From 1895 he was a regular contributor to *The Eng* on matters relating to loco design and performance, and later he also contributed to the *RM* (founded 1897). He was responsible for timing the record breaking GWR run on 9.4.1904 when *City of Truro* reached about 100mph (160km/h). His figure of 102.3 has since been disproved. Besides his interest in Rs he was an accomplished musician and possessed the largest music library in the S hemisphere. He was also a competent astronomer and established, and for 10 yrs conducted, the most southerly observatory in the world, near Foveaux, NZ. He recorded the total eclipse of the sun in 1885. He d from a heart attack following influenza.

The Eng V 105 24.4.1908 p 431; *RM* 6.1908 pp 455–7

RUTTAN, Henry Norlande, CMG

b Cobourg, Ontario, 21.5.1848; d Winnipeg 13.10.1925 aged 77. Canadian civil eng. Ed locally. In 1867 he was app to the engg staff of the GTR and a yr later asst on the engg staff of the Intercolonial R, later emp as res eng on const. 1874 engaged on prelim surveys on N shore of L Superior for the CPR. 1875–7 responsible for survey of 400 miles (644km) and location of 200 miles (322km) of the CPR E of the Yellowhead Pass in the Rockies. He acted as res eng from 1877–80 for the contractors on const of the line from Lake of the Woods, Ontario, to Winnipeg. In 1880 he began private practice. He designed and built the swing bridge over the Red River at Emerson and over the Assiniboine River at Winnipeg. He was eng and contractor for the first 40 miles (64km) of the Manitoba North Western R and contractor for the const of the first 50 miles (80km) of the Manitoba South Western R. In 1885 he left R work and became city eng of Winnipeg, until 1914. In 1871 he m Andrina Barberie who survived him, with 4 sons and 1 dr.

Min Proc ICE V 223 1926–7 p 315

SACRÉ, Alfred Louis

b London 6.4.1841; d London 25.7.1897

aged 56. Loco eng and mfr. Younger bro of C. R. Sacré (qv) Ed Marylebone Gr Sch. In 1857 he was articled to Archibald Sturrock (qv) at the GNR wks at Peterborough where his bro was asst loco supt, and where S. later became foreman of the C & W dept and then chief loco mgr of the Peterborough dist. In 1865, on the formation of the Yorkshire Engine Co at Sheffield upon a suggestion of Sturrock, Sacré, probably again on Sturrock's recommendation, was engaged as wks mgr, later becoming mgr and mg dir. In 1871 he transferred to the Avonside Engine Wks at Bristol as mgr. In 1877, after visiting Russia on the company's behalf, he began on his own as a consulting eng in London. In 1882 he also became mgr of the Vacuum Brake Co and later mg dir. MIME 1866; AICE 2.2.1869.

Proc IME 2.1897 pp 141–2; Min Proc ICE V 130 1896–7 p 319; *The Eng* V 134 18.8.1922 p 160

SACRÉ, Charles Reboul

b London 4.9.1831; d Manchester 3.8.1889 aged 57. Loco supt, MS & L. One of 13 children of a Huguenot refugee, John Joseph Berlot de Sacré. In 1846 he was articled to Archibald Sturrock (qv) at the GNR wks at Boston. On completion of his apprenticeship he became asst loco supt at Peterborough, the main wks having been established at Doncaster in 1853. In 1858 he was app chief eng and loco eng of the MS & L at Gorton, Manchester, and began there on 1.4.1859. He produced an outstanding series of double-framed 0–6–0 goods engines, the largest being the 60 built in 1880–5. For the fastest expresses, chiefly on the CLC, he designed a massive o/c 2–2–2 with 7ft 6in (2.286m) wheels. He also produced a powerful i/c 4–4–0 with double frames. Several of the 0–6–0s and 4–4–0s lasted until LNER days, into the 1920s. S. was interested in extending the MS & L by a tunnel under the Humber into Hull, but in this matter and concerning the proposed London extension he came into conflict with the chairman, Sir Edward Watkin (qv). S. was deeply distressed by the accident near Penistone on 16.7.1884 when the crank-axle of

4–4–0 No 434 broke and caused a disastrous derailment in which 19 were killed including Massey Bromley (qv), formerly loco supt of the GER. Though no blame was attached to S. he felt responsible, partly because he had yielded to pressure from Watkin to adopt the Smith non-automatic vacuum brake. He was a friendly and approachable man, and well liked by the men under him. However, early in 1885, at the early age of 53, he resigned, accepting a position as consultant to the MS & L. But he had lost the will to live and on 3.8.1889 he shot himself. MIME 1859, MICE 8.1.1867.
Proc IME 5.1889 p 339; Min Proc ICE V 98 1888–9 p 399; Ellis, Hamilton, *Twenty Loco Men* 1958

SALUZ, Peter Otto

b Lavin, Graubünden, Switzerland, 6.4.1847; d Chur 8.9.1914 aged 67.
Civil eng, Rhaetian R. Ed at Chur and Tech High Sch, Zurich, where he gained a diploma in civil engg in 3.1870. After 2 yrs on road and water schemes, in 1873 he was app eng on the Swiss North Eastern R. In 1879 he worked on the St Gotthard R. From 1885–8 he was municipal eng at Chur. Early in 1889 he went to the Govt R Dept, Bern. His work on the Rhaetian R (RhB) began in 1898 when he was app eng on the Reichenau–Ilanz section. From 1905 he was chief eng on the difficult Davos–Filisur, Bever–Schuls and Ilanz–Disentis sections. On 1.1.1914 he was app chief eng of RhB, but his term of office was soon cut short by his death.
S Bz V 64 26.9.1914

SAMUEL, James

b Glasgow 21.3.1824; d London 25.5.1874 aged 50.
Civil eng. Ed Glasgow High Sch and Glasgow Univ. In 4.1839 articled to Daniel Mackain at Glasgow waterworks. 1.1846 app res eng Eastern Counties R. Patented a fish joint for rails. 1851–8 built the Morayshire; Newmarket; Llanelly extn, and Vale of Towy Rs. 1858, with John Pitt Kennedy, made plans and estimates for a R from Smyrna to Cassaba and then to Ushak in Asia Minor. In 1861 went to USA to report on the estimate for completion of the Grand Rapids & Indiana R. Afterwards he was continuously employed in reporting on various projects. At beginning of 1864, with Col Talcott, app joint eng in chief on the Mexican R from Vera Cruz to Puebla and Mexico. 1871–2 S. carried out a 3ft (0.914m) gauge R in Cape Breton for coal mines. In 1869 became consulting eng of Mexican Rs. He was a great advocate of light rolling stock. MICE 5.6.1849.
Min Proc ICE V 39 1874–5 pp 280–2; *The Eng* V 37 29.5.1874 p 364; *Engg* V 17 19.6.1874 p 454

SAXBY, John

b Brighton 17.8.1821; d Hastings nr Haywards Heath, Sussex, 22.4.1913 aged 91.
Inventor of signal interlocking. At 13 began as a carpenter's apprentice. Later emp on LBSCR as a carpenter. S. became interested in problems of safety on Rs following several accidents, particularly one at Bricklayers' Arms, London, resulting from irregular working. He patented his system of interlocking of points and signals in 1856 and it was first applied in that year at Bricklayers' Arms. The first interlocking frame of the type which became universal was installed on the LBSCR near Haywards Heath. S. was emp by the LBSCR for 22 yrs. He introduced important improvements in the original 1856 patent in 1860 and 1867. The success of the system was such that in 1861 S. began business on his own account at Haywards Heath for the mfr of signalling apparatus. In 1862 he formed with J. S. Farmer (qv) the firm of Saxby & Farmer, on the LNWR at Kilburn. They were sole signalling contractors to the LNWR and LBSCR. In 1871 they introduced the 'rocker & grid' interlocking frame. In 1878 wks were established at Creil nr Paris, managed by S's son James. His partnership with Farmer ended in 1888, Farmer remaining at Kilburn until his death. In 1889 the French wks became part of John Saxby Ltd and in 1893, with the Kilburn wks, Saxby & Farmer Ltd. In 1902 Evans O'Donnell & Co of Chippenham was leased to Saxby & Farmer and in 1903 mfr was transferred there. S. became MIME 1880.
Engg V 95 25.4.1913 p 576; *The Eng*

V 115 25.4.1913 p 445; Proc IME 4.1913
p 637

SCHMIDT, Wilhelm

b Wegeleben nr Halberstadt, Saxony,
18.2.1858; d Bethel nr Bielfeld,
Westphalia, 16.2.1924 aged 66.
Responsible for design and introduction
of high-degree fire-tube superheaters for
steam locos. Son of a simple countryman.
Ed Dresden Tech High Sch. In Brunswick, where he had spent 20 yrs as asst
to a locksmith, he established wks in
1883 and built an engine to run on hot
air and steam at a temperature of 350°C
at a pressure of 80atm (1138psi). This led
to development of ideas for using superheated steam. In 1891 S. moved to
Kassel. He built an engine to work on
superheated steam at 350°C and a compound engine which used only 4.5kg/hp
hr. In 1898 the first loco superheater was
used on the Prussian State Rs, a large
central flue with horizontal elements. In
1899 the second type was introduced on
the Prussian Rs, a smokebox apparatus.
In 1901 he introduced the fire-tube type,
first used in Belgium. Within 10 yrs it
was fitted to most large locos all over
the world.
ZVDI V 68 15.3.1924 pp 249-50; S Bz
V 83 12.4.1924 pp 177-8; The Eng V 137
7.3.1924 p 259

SCHÖNERER, Matthias Ritter von

b Vienna 10.1.1807; d Vienna 31.10.1881
aged 74.
Austrian civil eng. Studied in Prague
and Vienna and in 1824 worked on the
Linz–Budweis R (the first on the European continent—see Gerstner). 1829–32
he assisted with const of the horse
operated Linz–Gmunden R. He then
travelled extensively in Britain and USA.
From 1839 he was employed on the
loco-worked Vienna–Gloggnitz R, becoming supt in 1842, dir of const 1846–53,
in 1850 working on several sections of
the Semmering R (see Ghega). 1854–6 he
built the Bruck an der Leitha–Raab and
Neu Szöny line. From 1856 to his death
he was in the mgt of the Kaiserin
Elisabeth–Bahn as tech consultant.
Röll V 6 p 2953

SCHUCAN, Achilles

b Avignon, France, 1.3.1844; d Chur,

Switzerland, 18.7.1927 aged 83.
Eng and mg dir, Rhaetian R, Switzerland. When still a child his family moved
to their native Engadin and S. was ed
at the Canton school and the Federal
Polytechnic, Zurich, where he gained
a diploma in engg in 1844. He began his
engg career on roads, later turning to Rs
and eventually becoming leading eng in
the Swiss R Dept at Bern. 1879 transferred to the Federal R Inspectorate. To
gain experience in R mgt, in 1855 he
took over the poverty-stricken Seetal R
which he brought to a position of
security in 3 yrs. 1888 app chief eng of
the metre gauge Landquart–Davos R,
the nucleus of the Rhaetian system. On
its completion in 1889 he continued the
line through Chur to Thusis, transferred
his hq to Chur and as mg dir of what,
in 1896, became the Rhaetian R, he
guided the affairs of the company to the
completion of the 172 mile (277km)
network, supervising also the preliminary
electrification work on the Engadin
section. Ret 1.10.1918.
S Bz V 90 30.7.1927 p 66

SCHUCAN, Paul

b (Bern ?) 10.12.1879; d Salta,
Argentina, 5.9.1930 aged 49.
Swiss civil eng. Son of Achilles S. (qv).
Ed at Davos and Chur, and Federal
Polytechnic, Zurich, qualifying as eng in
1902. After a year on the Rhaetian R he
worked on the Bodensee–Toggenburg R
1904–6. 1906 asst eng on RhB Davos–
Filisur section. 1909–12 res eng on
Engadin section at Zernez. 1913 section
eng on Furka R Andermatt–Disentis
section. 1919 became chief eng RhB but
in 1923 he went out to Argentina as
chief eng on a survey for a R across the
Andes. While there he contracted acute
dysentery which caused his early death.
S Bz V 96 18.10.1930 p 198

SCOTT, James

b Keighley, Yorks, 20.10.1846;
d (?) 27.11.1903 aged 57.
Contractor's agent and eng. 1862–6 pupil
of his f, Thomas S., engaged on const
of Met R Euston–Paddington; and MS &
L Marple–New Mills–Hayfield line. 1866–
8 emp as contractor's eng on contract
No 1 of MR London extn from the N
London R to St Pancras gds yard. 1868–

73 contractor's eng on contract No 1 of MR Settle–Carlisle line; 1873–8 on widening LNWR main line King's Langley–Bletchley; and on the Clydach–Bryn Mawr section of the LNWR Abergavenny–Merthyr line. 1878–83 on Weymouth–Abbotsbury R; widening CLC at Liverpool; 1883–8 on Baltinglass extn of GS & WR, Ireland, and on the Heanor–Ripley extn of the MR and Nottingham Suburban R (see E. Parry). 1888–95 contractor's agent on MR Dore & Chinley contract No 2 including Cowburn tunnel 2 miles 182yd (3.385km). 1895–9 contractor's chief agent on GCR London extn contract No 4 Rugby–Woodford including Catesby tunnel 1 mile 1237yd (2.74km). From 1899 he was engaged on MR Thackley tunnel and widening between Keighley and Bradford; GCR Northolt–Neasden; and MR widening Finchley Road–Welsh Harp. Elected MICE 1.5.1894.
Min Proc ICE V 155 1903–4 p 441

SCOTT, Sir Walter, Bart

b Abbey Town, W Cumberland, 17.8.1826; d Mentone, France, 8.4.1910 aged 83.
Civil eng and publisher. Began work as a mason, and was later emp on R const in N England. 1846 acted as foreman on the Gretna section of the Caledonian R. 1848 went to Newcastle upon Tyne and was emp on const of Central station and on const of Newcastle–Berwick line. Here he set up on his own account as a contractor. 1867 began his R work on the NER Newcastle quayside branch and from then on was actively engaged on many NER works. In 1882 the firm became Walter Scott & Co on admission of his son John and J. T. Middleton, his eng and agent. They carried out work on Rs in Essex and on the City & S London R. Scott's other activity, his publishing wks at Felling, Co Durham, became famous for its editions of standard classics. He was knighted in 1907. AIME 1887.
Proc IME 1911 p 204

SEGUIN, Marc

b Annonay, Ardèche, France, 20.4.1786; d Annonay 24.2.1875 aged 88.
Pioneer of the multi-tubular boiler. Trained under Joseph Montgolfier, one of the brothers who invented the hot-air balloon. Seguin's first major work was an iron suspension bridge in 1820. In 1825 he built a steamship with a fire-tube boiler for service on the Rhone. He patented a multi-tubular boiler in 1827 and used this type of boiler in a loco in 1828. It used a forced draught provided by a fan driven by the tender wheels. (A model can be seen in the Science Museum, London.) In 1826, in conjunction with E. Biot & Co. he obtained a concession for a R between Lyons and St Etienne which he surveyed. His loco was the first to be used on it when it was opened in 1829. With other French scientists he visited England from 9.12.1827 to 3.2.1828 and he met George Stephenson. S. pub the first French study of R engg.
Grimal, Pierre, *Dictionnaire des Biographies* 1958; Warren, J. G. H., *A century of loco building* 1923, 1970

SÉJOURNÉ, Paul

b Orleans, France, 21.12.1851; d Paris 15.1.1939 aged 87.
French civil eng. 1871 began training at Polytechnic Sch, Mende, and qualified as bridge and road eng in 1877. His first R work was on the Montauban à Castres line on which he built the bridges at Castalet, Lavaur and Antoinette. 1899–1902 built the great bridge on the Pétrusse in Luxembourg with a span of 279ft (85m). In 1900 he entered the PLM as chief of const and remained on that R until 1928. He built some of the most difficult mountain lines in France: the Tarentaise line; Moutiers–Bourg St Maurice, op 20.11.1913; Frasne–Lausanne including Mont d'or tunnel 3 miles 1388yd (6.097km); and, with Andre Martinet (1878–1947), the Nice–Breil sur Roya line, op 1914. He also began the Le Puy Lalevade and Chorges–Barcelonette lines. From 1901–22 he was prof at the National Sch of Bridges and Roads. In 1913–16 he pub his book *Grandes voûtes* (Large arches) in 6 vols. From 1910 he served on the editorial panel of *Le Genie Civil*. In 1924 he was made M of the Académie des Sciences and in 1918 was awarded the Prix Caméré. His widow survived him by only 4 days.
Le Genie Civil V 114 28.1.1939 p 94;

Schneider, Ascanio, *Rs through the Mountains of Europe* 1967

SHARP Bros

Thomas, b Manchester c 1780; d Cheltenham 20.4.1841 aged 61. John, b Manchester (?).(?).1786; d Manchester 16.9.1856 aged 70.
Loco mfrs and gen engs; descendents of a family of joiners and builders. In 1806 Thomas started a workshop in Manchester. In 1811 it was Sharp, Greenleaves & Co. Thomas's bro Robert Chapman Sharp joined the firm, and in 1823 his other bro John, when it became Sharp Bros. Richard Roberts (qv) became a partner in 1828, the firm then becoming Sharp, Roberts & Co. They built their first loco, *Experiment*, in 1833 for the Liverpool & Manchester R. It was a 2–2–0 with vertical cylinders. Three similar engines were built for the Dublin & Kingstown R in 1834. In 1837–8 10 2–2–2s of the 'Atlas' class were built for the GJR, a design which developed into the famous 'Sharp singles', of which about 600 were built for numerous Rs at home and abroad. In 1841 Thomas S. d and in 1843 Roberts ret from the partnership, but retained the wks. The loco building firm moved to Atlas wks and was continued by John S., with Thomas Beatt Sharp (son of Thomas) and John Robinson, the elder son of a Skipton banker, under the title of Sharp Bros & Co. In 1845 they introduced another type of 2–2–2 with outside cylinders and inside bearings; most went to German Rs. In 1846–9 they built some 0–6–0s, the most powerful of their time, for the Manchester & Birmingham; Sheffield & Manchester; and LNWR. John S. ret in 1852 and his place was taken by Charles Patrick Stewart (qv), the firm becoming Sharp, Stewart & Co. Thomas Beatt S. ret shortly afterwards and was succeeded by Stephen Robinson, bro of John. In 1854–65 they built outside-frame 0–6–0s for the MR, Egypt and many other Rs. Many of these engines ran for 40–60 yrs. The firm became a limited liability company in 1864 with Stewart as chairman until his death in 1882. In 1881 John Frederick Robinson (qv), son of John, became mg dir. In 1888 Sharp Stewart & Co transferred their business

from Manchester to Glasgow where they took over the Clyde Loco Wks from Neilson (qv), retaining the name 'Atlas Wks'. John Robinson ret from the firm on completion of the transfer, John Frederick continuing on the executive bd as sole mg dir. The mg directorship of the wks later passed to John Hutchinson Sharp, son of Rev John Prior Sharp and grandson and great nephew of the founders. In 1903 the firm became part of the North British Loco Co, by amalg with Neilson, Reid & Co, and Dübs & Co.
Local records in Manchester Public Library; *The Eng* V 136 24.8.1923 pp 194–6; *Manchester City News* 28.3.1903

SHAY, Ephraim

b Ohio, USA, 17.7.1839; d Harbor Springs, Mich, 20.4.1916 aged 76.
Mech eng, inventor of the 'Shay' geared loco, first built in 1880 and produced in large numbers by the Lima Loco Wks at Lima, Ohio, mainly for logging lines in USA and Canada. Most Shays had 2 trucks, but 3 and 4 truck machines were built. Most had a 3-cylinder vertical engine on the RH side driving a longitudinal shaft connected to the axles by bevel gearing. Some 2-cyl Shays were also built. The boiler was mounted to the L of centre. The last Shay was built for Western Maryland in 1945.
Trains 11.1954 p 66; Wiener, Lionel, *Articulated Locos* 1930, 1970, p 30

SIEMENS, Dr Ernst Werner von

b Lenthe nr Hanover 13.12.1816; d Berlin 6.12.1892 aged 75.
Pioneer of electric traction. Eldest bro of Sir William S. (qv). Ed at the Gymnasium, Lübeck. 1834 entered the Prussian artillery as volunteer, receiving a commission in 1839 after which he devoted himself to the study of chemistry and physics. During an experiment an explosion damaged his right ear. In 1840 he was sentenced to 5 yrs in prison for acting as second in a duel. However, he continued his experiments in prison and was released after a month. In 1841 he devised a method of electro plating. In 1842 he and his bro invented a differential governor. In 1845 he invented the dial and printing telegraph instruments. While still a military officer

he founded a wks in Berlin in 1847 for the production of telegraph apparatus. In 1846 he adopted gutta-percha for insulating wires laid underground. In 1848 he laid the first great underground telegraph line from Berlin to Frankfurt-am-Main, and others in 1849 from Berlin to Cologne, Aix-la-Chapelle and Verviers. In 1856 he brought out a system of duplex telegraphy by which two messages could be sent simultaneously along a single wire. He introduced the mercury standard of electrical resistance, and the pneumatic system of despatching messages. His crowning achievement was his work on the dynamo on which he pub an account in 1866. This was followed in 1867 by a proposal for electric Rs. He is best remembered for having built the first practical electric R, for the Berlin Trades Exhib, operated from 31.5–30.9.1879 on a 600yd (549m) stretch of n g track. In 1860 he received an hon doctorate from Berlin Univ. He was raised to the rank of nobility in 1888 in the same year as he became MIME.

Proc IME 1892 p 570

SIEMENS, Sir William, DCL, LLD, FRS

b Lenthe nr Hanover 4.4.1823; d London 19.11.1883 aged 60.

Ed at the Gymnasium, Lübeck, Polytechnic Sch at Magdeburg, and Göttingen Univ where he studied in 1841–2 under Wöhlar and Himly. 1842 went to the engine wks of Count Stolberg. 1843 to England to introduce a joint invention by himself and his elder bro Werner (qv) in electro plating which was taken up by Elkington & Mason, Birmingham. 1844 returned to England with another joint invention, the chromatic governor which was applied by the Astronomer Royal for regulating the great transit and touch-recording instrument at Greenwich observatory. Remained in England and in 1846 invented a double-cylinder air pump. In 1847 at the Bolton wks of John Hick (qv) he built a 4hp engine using superheated steam and having a condenser provided with regeneration. In 1858 he established the firm of Siemens Bros for the mfr and laying of submarine cables and land lines and for const of electrical instruments and machines. About the same time he was engaged

with the youngest bro Frederick in the invention of the regenerative gas furnace of which the first practical application was made in 1861. Experimental wks were erected in Birmingham in 1866 where the process of producing steel on the open hearth of a regenerative gas furnace was developed, in conjunction with Pierre Emile Martin (1824–1915) of Sireuil, France, into the Siemens-Martin process. He took a prominent part in the development of electrical power for lighting, and of transmitting power. One of his last works was the Portrush–Giants Causeway Tramway in Ireland, one of the pioneer electric Rs in the British Isles, op 28.9.1883. His death was the result of a fall while walking.

Proc IME 1884 pp 69–71; *The Eng* V 74 1884 p 507

SIGL, Georg

b Breitenfurth, Lower Austria, 13.1.1811; d Vienna 9.5.1887 aged 76.

Austrian industrialist and loco eng. In 1840 he founded a wks in Berlin for the mfr of power printing presses. In 1846 he moved to Vienna where he combined the mfr of presses with machine mfr. In 1851–2 he built the first power lithograph press in Europe and installed the first pneumatic post installations in Berlin, Munich and Vienna. In 1857 he established workshops at Vienna and Wiener Neustadt where many types of locos were built for Austria and other countries. One of his locos, 0-6-0 No 106 *Fusch*, built for the Vienna–Linz R in 1868, is preserved outside Linz station.

Brockhaus Enzyklopädie V 17; *Schweizer Lexikon* V 6; Engel, F. R., *Beiträge zur Geschichte der Technik* (8) 1918

SINCLAIR, Robert

b London 1.7.1817; d Florence, Italy, 20.10.1898 aged 81.

Loco eng in France, and latterly on the GER in England. Son of Alexander S., founder of the firm of Sinclair, Hamilton & Co. Ed at Charterhouse where, under Dr Russell, he decided upon a career in engg. Served apprenticeship with Scott, Sinclair & Co, Greenock, of which the Sinclair was his uncle Robert. He then obtained employment on the

Liverpool & Manchester R at Edgehill, Liverpool, under W. B. Buddicom (qv). In 1841 Buddicom left to establish the wks of Allcard, Buddicom & Co at Sotteville in France to provide locos for the Paris & Rouen R. While the wks was being built S. was app mgr of the smaller wks at Les Chartereux, nr Rouen. In 1844, following the death of Ilbery, loco supt of the Glasgow, Paisley & Greenock R, the engs Locke and Errington (qqv) app S. to succeed him. In 1847 the line became part of the Caledonian R and S. was app loco supt of the entire system. In 1851 he was made res eng in addition. His work contributed notably to the financial improvement of the CR. In 1856 he succeeded J. V. Gooch (qv) as loco supt of the Eastern Counties R which, in 1862, became a part of the Great Eastern R, S. once more becoming loco supt of the entire system. In 1857, on the ret of Peter Schuyler Bruff (qv) he succeeded to the additional position of chief eng. He held this dual office until his resignation in 1866. During this period he acted as eng to various new lines on the GER and also as consulting eng to the East Indian R and the Luxembourg R of Belgium for both of which he designed engines and rolling stock. One of a large class of o/c locos designed by S. for the EIR and built by W. G. Armstrong & Co, together with another of his engines built by Robert Stephenson & Co for the GER was displayed at the London Exhibition of 1862. Following his early training at Crewe, S's loco designs showed the influence of Buddicom, with a preference for outside cylinders. But his designs were not without originality; eg for the Luxembourg R in 1860 he designed a class of 2-4-2s of which the first was built by Robert Stephenson & Co, with a leading Bissell truck, probably the first use of this type of leading truck in Europe (see Bissell). In 1864 he adopted the same arrangement for 20 2-4-2Ts on the GER. He advocated large bearing surfaces and structural rigidity, years before these became general practice. S. took a leading part in the development of the loco cab from the primitive weatherboard. He was one of the pioneers in the use of steel for loco parts, and was probably the first to use steel regularly for axles and tyres. He was also one of the first engs to make regular use of injectors on locos and to dispense with feed pumps. He was an early advocate of standardisation, and interchangeability of parts. The use of roller bearings received his special attention, and during the early 1860s the up morning express from Ipswich to London and back in the afternoon had roller bearings to nearly all axles. Trouble with various materials, insufficiently developed at the time, ended the experiment. S. was a good leader of men, straightforward in his affairs, with geat firmness and kindness, and he was greatly respected. He was one of the founder members of the IME, joining in 10.1847, the year of its formation. Became MICE 1858. He m the dr of John Campbell of HM Customs, Greenock, and they had 2 sons and 2 drs of whom the drs and the elder son survived him.

Proc IME 1898 part 3 pp 707-9; Min Proc ICE V 135 1898-9 p 353; *Engg* 11.11.1898 p 623; *The Eng* V 86 11.11. 1898 p 471; Ellis, Hamilton, *Twenty Locomotive Men* 1958

SMELLIE, Hugh

b Ayr 3.3.1840; d Bridge of Allan 19.4.1891 aged 51.

Loco supt, G & SWR and CR. At 16 apprenticed to Patrick Stirling (qv), then loco supt G & SWR. Spent 1 yr in running sheds at Ayr, then at Kilmarnock. After about 2 yrs as journeyman fitter he entered the service of Young & Co. Ayr, as engine fitter. About 1864 returned to the G & SWR shops and after 1 yr took charge of the drg office. 1866, when P. Stirling went to the GNR, S. was app wks mgr at Kilmarnock under his successor, Stirling's bro James (qv). In 2.1870 app loco eng and C & W supt, Maryport & Carlisle R. He also acted for Maryport Town and Harbour Trustees on harbour and water works. On 30.6.1878, after James Stirling had moved to the SER at Ashford, S. was app loco supt of the G & SWR. He was immediately concerned with the adoption of continuous brakes. He also fitted carriages with gas lighting. His loco designs on the G & SWR were noted for free steaming boilers, sound front-end design, and good workmanship resulting in low maintenance costs, simplicity of layout and ease of handling, coupled with graceful appearance following the Stirling tradition. He designed the first Scottish 0-4-4Ts in 1885 for the Glasgow–Johnstone and Potterhill services. He was the first G & SWR loco supt to introduce steam brakes on goods engines and vacuum brakes on passenger engines, 4-4-0s 139, 140. His first engines were the 6ft 9in (2.057m) 2-4-0s in 1879–80. Next were the 0-6-0s of 1881 and the 4-4-0 'Wee Bogies' in 1882-5. His 4-4-0 express engines of 1886-9 were outstanding, working the Glasgow–Carlisle Pullmans in conjunction with the MR. He enlarged the Kilmarnock wks, introducing labour-saving tools, and lowered production costs. In autumn 1890 app loco supt on the Caledonian R, succeeding Dugald Drummond (qv), but after only a few months his health declined severely. During the R strike at the beginning of 1891 he was overworked. A chill developed into pleurisy and, after appearing to recover, he suddenly d at Bridge of Allen. Became MICE 5.3.1889.

Min Proc ICE V 107 pp 412–14; *RM* 1.1942 p 28; Smith, D. L., *Locos of the G & SWR* 1976

SMELLIE, John Hugh, DSO, OBE, Lieut Col RE

b Kilmarnock 15.2.1874; d St Annes on Sea 17.7.1931 aged 57.

Apprenticed at the G & SWR wks at Kilmarnock while his f, Hugh S. (qv), was loco C & W supt there. On completion of his apprenticeship he spent 2 yrs in the drg office and was then app asst foreman in the turning shop. 1900 app asst loco supt Rohilkund & Kumaon R, India. 1905 app loco C & W supt on the 2ft 6in (0.762m) gauge Kalka–Simla R, and dist loco supt, NWR, India, in 1908. By 1914 he had become dep loco supt and C & W supt. He was then app CME to the E African Forces, receiving DSO. After WW1 returned to the NWR, India. In 1927 he returned to Scotland and became g mgr of R. Y. Pickering & Co, rolling stock builders, Whishaw.

Journal ILE V 21 1931 p 624; *RG* 31.7.1931 p 151; *The Locomotive* 15.8. 1931 p 265

SMITH, Frederick George

b Newcastle upon Tyne 20.4.1872; d Newcastle upon Tyne 25.2.1956 aged 83.

Mech eng; loco supt HR. Son of Godfrey S., dist passenger supt NER. Ed at Newcastle. 1888 began 5 yr apprenticeship at the NER Gateshead wks under T. W. Worsdell (qv) who, in 1890, was succeeded by his bro Wilson Worsdell (qv). In 1892-3 S. spent 18 months in the drg office. He also received tech ed at Rutherford Coll, Newcastle, and at the Durham Coll of Science. From 1893 he remained on the NER, working at running sheds at Gateshead, Middlesbrough, Shildon and Blaydon. After a short spell as eng with a tramcar mfr in Shropshire, in 1900 S. became a partner in the Crown Iron Foundry in Birmingham. He then moved to Essex, becoming mech insp to Crampton & Co, Chelmsford. In 12.1903 S. returned to R work as wks mgr at the HR Lochgorm wks, Inverness, under Peter Drummond (qv). When, in 1906, Drummond's status was raised from loco C & W supt to CME S. became asst CME. In 2.1912 he succeeded Drummond, but with the title of loco C & W supt. One of his first duties was to order 4 more 'Castle' class 4-6-0s. In ordering a larger turntable for Inverness shed S. came into conflict with Alexander Newlands (qv) who had been app chief civil eng on 1.1.1914. During the winter of 1913–14 S. worked on a design for a large and powerful 2-cyl 4-6-0. The actual drawings were carried out in the NBR drg office at Cowlairs, Glasgow, because at Inverness the HR employed only one draughtsman. Six engines were ordered from Hawthorn Leslie & Co, Newcastle upon Tyne. They were the first HR engines to have smoke-tube superheaters and Walschaert valve gear. When the first, named *River Ness*, arrived at Perth in 8.1915, Newlands pronounced it too heavy for the HR routes. S. was called before the HR bd on 24.9.1915 when his immediate resignation was demanded. It seems likely that had S. had the persuasive power of Churchward he might have survived in his position. As it was, the 6 engines were sold to the CR, at a profit. At the time a 4-4-0 design was being prepared and this also was awarded to Hawthorn Leslie who developed it and built the two engines named *Durn* and *Snaigow*. S. and his wife and son returned to Newcastle where he was emp by the Ministry of Munitions. He became MIME but made no contributions to the proceedings. His subsequent activities are obscure and he had no further connection with Rs.

Atkins, C. P. Biography in *RW* 1.1977 p 14 (portrait); Atkins, C. P., *The Scottish 4-6-0 classes* 1976

SMITH, Marcus

b Ford, Northumb, 16.7.1815; d Ottawa 14.8.1904 aged 89.

Eng on CPR. Began engg career in 1844 on the Oxford, Worcester & Wolverhampton R under I. K. Brunel (qv). In 1845 he engaged in independent practice and completed a total of 230 miles (370km) of lines. In 3.1849 he went to New York and was emp on the Hudson River R. In 1850 he moved to Canada and was engaged on the Great Western R, then under const. On completing this engagement he was app chief eng of the Hamilton & Toronto R. From 1860-4 he was engaged in S Africa, becoming chief eng of the Cape Town & Wynberg R. He again went to the USA and obtained employment on the Detroit & Milwaukee R in 1868, but later took up an appointment on the Intercolonial R of Canada under Sandford Fleming (qv). In 1872 Fleming was app chief eng of the CPR, then about to be begun, and S. became his chief asst as eng in charge of surveys for the Western div, about 1000 miles (1600km) from the Rocky Mountains to the Pacific. 1876-8 he was app acting chief eng during Fleming's absence in England. On completion of the R he moved to Ottawa. His last work for the CPR was a large wharf at Port Moody, completed in 12.1886. S. retired in 1893. Elected MICE 5.5.1874.

Min Proc ICE V 161 1904-5 p 358; Berton, Pierre, *The National Dream, the Great Railway* Toronto 1970

SMITH, Walter Mackenzie

b Ferry-Port-on-Craig, Scotland, 25.12.1842; d Newcastle upon Tyne 25.10.1906 aged 63.

Mech eng, NER. Ed Dundee High Sch. 1858 apprenticed to William Norman &

Sons, engs, and Todd & McGregor, Clyde Foundry, both in Glasgow. After this he entered Neilson & Co, loco mfrs, for 1½ yrs. He then joined Samuel Johnson (qv) on the Edinburgh & Glasgow R. He invented an auxiliary regulator valve. 1866 went with Johnson to the GER wks at Stratford, London, and designed rolling stock. 1874 app loco, C & W supt, Imperial Govt Rs, Japan, the first British loco eng there. In 1876 erected workshops to enable rolling stock to be built in Japan. In 1883 returned to England and was app to the NER under McDonnell (qv) who had become loco supt at Gateshead in 1882. S. was placed in charge of workshops and machinery. Following McDonnell's forced resignation in 1844 S. continued through the interregnum and through the reign of T. W. Worsdell (qv) and, from 9.1890, under Wilson Worsdell (qv) who gave him complete freedom to experiment with his loco designs and even to have engines constructed. S. designed the first successful British compound loco, NER 4-4-0 No 1619, in 1898. This was the engine upon which S. Johnson based his famous MR compounds and J. G. Robinson (qv) his GCR 4-4-2 compounds. Smith's finest engines were the two 4-cyl compound 4-4-2s, NER 730/1, of 1906. He also designed a cross watertube firebox.

Proc IME 12.1906 pp 953-5; *The Eng* V 102 2.11.1906 p 454; *Engg* V 82 2.11.1906 p 592; *RM* 11.1906 p 508

SOUTHER, John

b Boston, Mass (?).(?).1814; d Newton, Boston, 12.9.1911 aged 97.

Loco mfr. Began as a ship's carpenter. 1840 engaged by Holmes Hinkley (qv) as a pattern maker and was probably responsible for the design of Hinkley's first loco. 1846 started his own machine shop in Boston, building locos, sugar mill machinery and steam excavators. For a period Zerah Colburn (qv) worked with him as chief draughtsman. In 1852 he established a precedent by reducing working time from 12 to 10 hrs a day. Strikes followed which forced other firms to do the same. Also, in 1852 S. went to Richmond, Va, to manage the loco shop of Tredegar Iron Wks. Returned to Boston in 1854 and began at the new

Globe Wks where he built locos until 1864. Built i/c locos until 1853, but was then forced to adopt more progressive designs.

White, John H. Jr, *American Locos, an engg history 1830–80* 1968; NYT 13.9. 1911 p 7

SPECK, Thomas Samuel

b London (?).(?).1836; d London 3.11.1883 aged c 47.

Loco, C & W supt, Met Dist R. Pupil of F. H. Trevithick with whom he went to the GTR, Canada, where he prepared drgs of the first loco built by the company. Later engaged on const of C & W stock and on supervision and working of the W section of the R. Returned to England 1860 and became asst to W. Martley (qv), loco C & W supt LC & DR. In 1868 app loco C & W Supt Scinde R, India, and on its amalg with Punjab R he declined app as asst loco supt of the Bombay, Baroda & Central India R. Returned to England early 1871 and app res eng and loco C & W supt of the Met Dist R, London, until 6.1881. Became MICE 11.5.1875.

Min Proc ICE V 76 1883–4 p 370

SPOONER, Charles Easton

b Maentwrog, Wales, (?).(?).1818; d Portmadoc 18.11.1889 aged 71.

Eng of Festiniog R, Wales. Son of James S. (qv). After leaving school he was engaged with his f from 1832–6 in const of the 1ft 11½in (600mm) gauge Festiniog R which his f had originated. The line, with its even falling grade, was a marvel of engg skill in mountainous country. On the death of his f in 1856 S. became mgr and eng of the R and from then until shortly before his death he devoted his whole time to its success. In 1863 he introduced steam locos, the first on this gauge, and in 1865 the line opened for passenger traffic. The R attracted attention from engs throughout the world, by its cheapness of const and its engg. S. pub *Narrow Gauge Rs* 1870.

The Eng V 68 29.11.1889 p 451; *Engg* V 48 29.11.1889 p 638; Boyd, J. I. C., *The Festiniog R* Vs 1 & 2 1960, 1976

SPOONER, George Percival

b Beddgelert, Wales, 13.6.1850; d London 21.1.1917 aged 66.

Son of C.E.S. (qv), mgr and eng Festiniog R. Ed Harrow, and at Karlsruhe Polytechnic, Germany. Articled to his f in the shops and drg office of the Festiniog R, during which time he was engaged on surveying, levelling, draining and the design and const of reservoirs, dams, locos, rolling stock, stations and general R equipment. From 1872–9 he was chief eng to the Festiniog R. 1879 to India as asst dist & loco supt on Indian State Rs. On his ret in 1894 returned to England and was occupied with scientific instruments and organ building. MIME 1885.

Proc IME 5.1917 p 444; Boyd, J. I. C., *The Festiniog R* 1960, 1976

SPOONER, James

b (?) (?).(?).1789; d Portmadoc, Wales, 18.8.1856 aged 66.

Eng of Festiniog R. Son of Thomas S. and Elizabeth Daffy Swinton. He m Elizabeth Easton and they had 5 sons, the 2nd, James Swinton and the 3rd, Charles Easton (qv). In 1825 he went to Maentwrog from Birmingham. Pioneering work in the area had been carried out by William Alexander Madocks (1773–1828) who had built the embankment known as the Cob across the Traeth Mawr estuary, completed in 1811, and established the town of Portmadoc. In 10.1825 S. was employed by Nathan Meyer Rothschild, the London banker (1777–1836) to survey a tramway from Portmadoc to slate quarries in the Moelwyn area. The original survey was not carried out, but in 1830 he carried out a new survey for Samuel Holland (1803–92), one of the pioneers of the N Wales slate industry, from quarries at Blaenau Ffestiniog on an even gradient down to the Cob and across to Portmadoc. The Act for the Festiniog R (with one F) was passed on 25.5.1832, and S. directed const of the 1ft 11½in (600mm) gauge R, assisted by his son Charles Easton, then only 14. The R was opened on 20.4.1836. Loaded trains ran down by gravity and empties were drawn back by horses. In 1845 S. became sec of the FR.

Dictionary of Welsh Biography 1959; Boyd, J. I. C., *The Festiniog R* 1960, 1976; Lewis, M. J. T., *How Festiniog got its R* 1968

SPRAGUE, Frank Julian

b Milford, Conn, 25.7.1857; d New York 25.10.1934 aged 77.
Pioneer of electric traction in USA. In 1878 he graduated in the US Naval Academy, Annapolis. 1878–80 served on the *Richmond* flagship. 1882 visited the Crystal Palace exhibition at Sydenham, London, serving on the jury for gas engines, dynamos and lamps. 1883 resigned from the navy to join Edison, but after a year started the Sprague Electric R & Motor Co. He then adapted his motor for street R use after experiments on the New York Elevated R. In 1887 he equipped the Richmond, Va, Union Passenger R, the success of which led to over 100 contracts for Sprague Rs in USA and abroad. In 1890 his company was absorbed by the Edison General Electric Co, and in 1892 he formed the Sprague Electric Elevator Co, building about 600 elevators before the business was absorbed by the Otis Co. Experience with elevator control led to a system of multiple-unit control for trains without locos, which he perfected in 1895, ensuring quick acceleration and turn-round. It was first used on the Chicago South Side Elevated R in 1897, and was later adopted for subway, elevated and suburban Rs. Its development led to the establishment of the Sprague Electric Co which was absorbed by the GEC in 1902. S. developed an automatic train control system. He served on the commission for electrification of the Grand Central Terminal, New York City, 1903–8, and shared in the design of the projected 3rd rail conductor used on NYC lines. In 1885 he m Mary A. Keatinge by whom he had a son. On 11.10.1899 he remarried, Harriet Chapman Jones of New Hartford, Conn. They had 3 children. During WW1 he served as chairman of the committees on electricity and ship const of the Naval Consulting Bd.
DAB V 21 p 670

STAMER, Arthur Cowie, CBE

b Shrewsbury 7.3.1869; d Darlington 14.2.1944 aged 75.
Loco eng, NER and LNER. 5th son of Rt Rev Sir Lovelace T. Stamer, Bart, DD, Suffragan Bishop of Shrewsbury. Ed Rugby Sch. Pupil at Beyer, Peacock, Manchester, 1886–90. 1891 joined NER as improver. 1892 app asst shed foreman at York. 1900 m Everilda Mary, dr of G. A. Thompson of Terrington Hall, Yks. They had 1 dr. After much running shed experience at various depots he was app div loco supt at York in 1902. 1906 joined CME's staff and in 1910 became chief asst mech eng NER under Vincent Raven (qv). During WW1 he took over all the duties of CME of the NER and was responsible for munition production. Awarded CBE. From grouping on 1.1.1923 S. continued as asst CME, LNER, Darlington, under Gresley (qv) until his ret in 1933. MIME; MILE (1918); president 1923–4.
The Eng V 177 25.2.1944 p 153; *Journal ILE* V 34 1944 p 62 (portrait); *LNER Magazine* V 23 1933 p 662; *Darlington & Stockton Times* 19.2.1944

STAMP, Sir Josiah Charles

b Kilburn, London, 21.6.1880;
d London 16–17.4.1941 aged 60.
Chairman, LMS, statistician, administrator. 3rd of 7 children of Charles S. who had managed a R bookstall at Wigan, then owned a provision shop in London. Left sch at age 15. 1896 entered civil service by examination and began as a boy clerk in the Inland Revenue dept. His progress was swift and at 23 he was asst insp of taxes in Hereford: at 29 1st class insp in London and at 36 asst sec to the Bd of Inland Revenue. In 1903 he m Olive Jessie, dr of Alfred Marsh, builder, of Twickenham. He rapidly developed as one of Britain's leading economists, working with inexhaustible energy. When nearly 39 S. left the civil service for business and began in 3.1919 as sec and dir of Nobel Industries Ltd from which Imperial Chemical Industries later developed. In 1.1926 he became the first president of the executive of the LMS. On the ret of H. G. Burgess on 31.3.1927 the position of g mgr was abolished and executive control was vested in the president. On the ret of Sir Guy Granet as chairman in 10.1927 S. was app to succeed him. The economic crisis of 1931 made him decide to make the LMS his main concern, and so it remained until his death. He united it into a closely integrated organisation.

In 1924 S. was the British rep on the Dawes Committee on whose recommendation the German State R was formed on 11.10.1924 to unite all the separate state systems. Gen Dawes considered the 'Dawes Plan' should have been called the 'Stamp Plan'. S. played a major part in furthering Anglo-German relationships in finance and transport spheres, and it was by an ironic twist of events that he was killed by a German bomb, with his wife and eldest son, while sheltering from an air raid at his home at Shortlands. Made CBE 1918; KBE 1920; GBE 1924 and GCB 1935; in 1938 he was raised to the peerage as Baron Stamp of Shortlands. He received a total of 23 hon degrees from universities.

RG 25.4.1941 pp 479–82; DNB 1941–50 p 817

STANIER, Sir William Arthur, FRS

b Swindon, Wiltshire, 27.5.1876;
d London 27.9.1965 aged 89
CME of LMS. His f was stores supt at the GWR Swindon wks. S. began apprenticeship there under Dean (qv) in 1.1892. 1897 transferred to drg office, when Churchward (qv) was introducing his new boilers. 1900 app insp of materials; next assisted in erection of Old Oak Common running sheds, London. 1906 became asst to loco wks mgr. After further promotions became wks mgr 1920. When C. B. Collett (qv) succeeded Churchward in 1922 S. became his principal asst and was chosen to accompany the 4–6–0 No 6000 *King George V* to the B & O centenary celebrations at Baltimore in 1927. It was unfortunate that S. was fated to be always one step behind Collett, 5 yrs his senior, throughout his career at Swindon, for there is little doubt that S. would have made a more progressive and successful CME. His chance came at last in 1932 when he was app CME of the LMS in succession to Sir Henry Fowler (qv). Here loco affairs were in a mess because of the continuance of Midland 'small engine' policies and the friction between the former MR at Derby and the LNWR at Crewe. S. with no interest in either faction, immediately began to restock the LMS with a succession of fine modern locos combining

GWR practice with the best features of existing LMS designs, beginning with a 2–6–0 in 1933. His 4–6–2 express engine was closely modelled on the GWR *Great Bear* 4–6–2 and the *King* 4–6–0 and appeared in 1933. In 1934 came the Class 5 and 'Jubilee' class 4–6–0s, in 1935 the 2–8–0s and 2–6–4Ts and 2–6–2Ts. In 1937 he brought out an improved 4–6–2, the 'Coronation' class, at first in streamlined form and, in 1938, in orthodox form. All had tapered boilers, Belpaire fireboxes, modern steam distribution and adequate bearing surfaces. There were initial steaming difficulties, but once these were overcome they all gave many years of excellent service. His rebuild of the 'Royal Scot' class produced probably the finest British 4–6–0. The 2–8–0s and 'Class 5' 4–6–0s were among the last steam locos on BR in 1968. S. was an active MIME and was president in 1941. Later he received their highest award, the James Watt International Medal. As MILE he was president in 1938 and received their gold medal in 1957. He was knighted in 1943 and in 1944 was elected FRS. In 1942 his R work came to an end when he was made scientific advisor to the Ministry of Production. Later he was app a dir of Power Jets Ltd, and served on the Aeronautical Research Council.

SLS Journal 11.1965 p 309; *The Eng* V 220 1.10.1965 p 555 (portrait); *The Times* 28.9.1965 p 15 (portrait); 7.10.1965 p 14; Bellwood, John, and Jenkinson, David, *Gresley & Stanier* 1976

STEPHENS, Lieut Col Holman Frederick

b London (?).(?).1869;
d Dover 23.10.1931 aged 65
Eng and mgr of various lt Rs. Son of F.G.S, art critic of the *Athenaeum*. Ed Univ Coll Sch, London, and at Karlsruhe (Baden) and Vitre (et Villaine). At Univ Coll, London, he was a pupil of Sir Alexander W. B. Kennedy. From here he went to the loco & carriage shops of the Metropolitan R at Neasden, and the running sheds. He then became res eng of the Cranbrook & Paddock Wood R, op 1892–3. He was eng of the Sheppy R,

op 1901; reconstructed the Burry Port & Gwendreath Valleys R as a passenger line and rebuilt the E Cornwall R for the Plymouth, Devon & SW Jn R. Later he became associated with 11 lt R undertakings of which the Shropshire & Montgomeryshire; West Sussex (Chichester–Selsey); Kent & E Sussex; N Devon & Cornwall Jn; E Kent; Weston, Cleveland & Portishead, totalling 112 miles (180km) were standard gauge, and the Festiniog; Welsh Highland; and Ashover, 49 miles (79km) were 1ft 11½in (600mm) gauge; the Rye & Camber, 3ft (914mm) gauge and the Snailbeach, 2ft 4in (711mm) gauge. At the time of his death he was chairman, mg dir, eng & loco supt of the Shropshire & Montgomeryshire; W Sussex and Festiniog Rs; mg dir, eng & loco supt of the Kent & E Sussex; dir, eng & loco supt of the Rye & Camber; mg dir & eng of the N Devon & Cornwall Jn; g mgr, eng & loco supt of the E Kent and Weston, Clevedon & Portishead; g mgr & eng of the Welsh Highland; eng of the Ashover Lt R. He was also Chairman of the Assoc of Rs of Local Interest (later the Assoc of Minor Rs) being an official in 11 of its 23 members. *RM* 11.1971 p 630; *The Locomotive* 11.1931 p 400

STEPHENSON, George

b Wylam, Northumberland, 9.6.1781; d Tapton House nr Chesterfield 12.8. 1848 aged 67
Mech eng and inventor, and founder of the modern R. Son of Robert S. (qv), fireman at Wylam colliery where S. worked as a boy. By 1798 he had become 'plugman' at Wylam colliery and was taking lessons in reading and writing. In 1801 he became brakesman at Black Callerton colliery. Having by now achieved some substance, on 28.11.1802 he m Frances Henderson, and at about the same time became engineman at Willington Ballast Hill. Here, in his spare time, he became skilled in repairing watches and clocks. William Fairbairn (qv), an apprentice in the neighbourhood, became his close friend at this time. On 16.10.1803 his only son Robert (qv) was born. In 1804 he moved to Killingworth where his wife d of tuberculosis on 14.5.1806. During

1807 he managed a Boulton & Watt engine at Montrose, Scotland. On his return he and two other men continued to manage the engines at Killingworth colliery. His f became incapable of further work and S. had to support his parents. He also had to find money to avoid conscription. His skill as eng led to his app as enginewright at Killingworth in 1812. He then devoted his scientific knowledge to the invention of a miners' safety lamp which he tested on 21.10. 1815. On 30.11.1815 he tested an improved lamp himself in the most dangerous part of the mine. His invention was independent of Sir Humphrey Davy (1778–1829), the famous chemist, who also invented a miners' safety lamp on the same principles in 1815. S., already familiar with the steam locos working on the Wylam wagonway and elsewhere, now became interested in its development, and on 25.7.1814 his first engine, named *Blutcher*, successfully pulled 30 tons up 1 in 450 at 4 mph (6.5km/h). It had 2 cyls and gear drive. In 2.1815 he patented an improved engine in which he used the steam blast to draw the fire. The wheels were directly driven, without gears. He now had to design an improved rail to carry the locos. In 1819 S. supervised the laying of an 8 mile (12.9km) R at Hetton colliery, op 18.11.1822. Traction was by stationary engines and locos. On 29.3. 1820 he m Elizabeth Hindmarsh. They had no children. On 19.4.1821 the Stockton & Darlington R Act was passed. S. was app eng by Edward Pease (qv), the promoter. He re-surveyed the route and in 1823 began const. He recommended malleable iron rails instead of cast iron. This caused trouble with one of the directors, a mfr of cast iron rails, so that part of the line had to be laid with these. He also advised the use of locos. To mfr these he induced Edward Pease and his cousin Thomas Richardson (1771–1853) to join him in establishing a works in Newcastle to be known as Robert Stephenson & Co. The wks began operation in 8.1823. The S & D opened on 27.9.1825, but the first locos, *Locomotion, Hope, Black Diamond* and *Diligence,* were barely successful, and it was only after Hackworth (qv) had established the

reliability of the steam loco in 1827 that the wks began to prosper. S's work on the S & D led the promoters of the Liverpool & Manchester and Manchester & Leeds Rs to app him as eng in 1825, but because the steam loco was still not an established success, a competition was held at Rainhill in 1829 for locos to prove themselves. It was won by the *Rocket* designed and built by George and Robert S. S. was also eng to the Birmingham & Derby, N Midland, York & N Midland, Leicester & Swannington, and other lines. After living for a period close to collieries nr Ashby de la Zouch, in 1843 he moved during const of the N Midland R to Tapton House nr Chesterfield to be near the collieries and the Ambergate lime wks which he had opened up close to the NMR. He made several visits to Belgium to advise on Rs, and in 1845 visited Spain to examine the course of a proposed R. In that year his second wife d and early in 1848 he m Miss Gregory who nursed him in his final illness. In 1847 he founded the IME of which he was the first president. At Tapton House he indulged his favourite recreation of horticulture, with notable success. GS has been described as having bestowed more benefits on civilisation than any other man. His name is certainly the most famous in the history of Rs, despite frequent attempts to belittle his achievements.
Proc IME 25.10.1848; Min Proc ICE V 8 1848 p 29; Rolt, L. T. C., *George and Robert Stephenson* (with full bibliography) 1960; Skeat. W. O., *George Stephenson; the Engineer and his letters* 1973; Smiles, Samuel, *Life of George Stephenson* 1864, 1904; Warren, J. G. H., *A century of loco building* 1923, 1971; *The Eng* V 3 1857 p 501; V 4 1857 p. 73, 224

STEPHENSON, George Robert

b Newcastle upon Tyne 20.10.1819;
d Cheltenham 26.10.1905 aged 86
Civil eng. Only son of the elder Robert Stephenson (qv), bro of George S. (qv). Began by assisting with the underground surveys and working in the shops of the Pendleton colliery where his f was chief eng. At 15 he entered King William's Coll, Isle of Man, for 2 yrs. On the death of his f in 1837 his uncle George S.

placed him in the drg office of the Manchester & Leeds R under Thomas Gooch (qv). In 1843 he was app to superintend engg at Tapton collieries nr Chesterfield, but soon he was invited by his cousin Robert S. (qv) to take charge of the new lines of the SER. In 1848 he was eng on the Liverpool, Crosby & Southport R; in 1849–50 on the Nottingham–Grantham R; and the Northampton–Market Harborough line, LNWR. He was then app with Bidder (qv) as jt chief eng, Danish Govt Rs, and was consulting eng to the province of Canterbury, New Zealand, and he built the first R there, from the port of Littleton to Christchurch. In 1864 he was associated with Hawkshaw (qv) on const of the E London R including utilisation of Marc Brunel's Thames tunnel. He also built many bridges of which one of the first was the Sutton swing bridge over the River Nene in 1851. In conjunction with Robert S. he designed the great tubular bridge over the St Lawrence at Montreal. On the death of Robert S. in 1859 S. succeeded to the mgt of the collieries at Snibston in Leicestershire and at Tapton and the mgt of Robert Stephenson & Co, Newcastle. MIME 1868; also MICE of which he was president 1876. Also a keen yatchtsman.
Proc IME 12.1905 pp 1057–8; Min Proc ICE V 163 1905–6 p 386; *The Eng* V 100 11.1905 p. 439

STEPHENSON, John

b (?) (?).(?).1794;
d Rotherham 8.7.1848 aged 54
Civil eng and contractor, friend and adviser of George Stephenson. Began his career on the Stockton & Darlington R in 1924. He was responsible for completing the Summit tunnel on the Manchester & Leeds R, 1839–40; Chorley cutting and tunnel, Bolton & Preston R, 1841. He d shortly after completing part of the Blackburn–Preston R, while on a visit to the N Midland R. He was a M of the firm of Stephenson Mackenzie & Brassey.

STEPHENSON, Robert (the elder)

b Wylam, Northumb, 10.3.1788;
d Pendleton, Lancs, 15.1.1837 aged 48
Bro of George S. (qv), 4th child and 3rd

son of Robert (1) S. and Mabel (Carr). In 1806 he m his bro George's housekeeper and on 20.10.1819 they had a son, George Robert (qv). In 1819 George S. was invited to build a new colliery R between Hetton colliery and Bishop Wearmouth, c 8 miles (12.9km). The sinking of the colliery was begun 19.12. 1820. S. was app res eng for const of R and sinking of pits. The R was op 18.11.1822. In 1825–8 S. was emp under Robert Daglish (qv) on const of the Bolton & Leigh R. He was also engaged about the same time on const of the Nantlle R in N Wales, c 9¼ miles (15km), op 1828 with a gauge of 3ft 6in (1.067m). At the opening of the Liverpool & Manchester R S. drove the loco *North Star*. Shortly after this he was app chief eng of the Pendleton collieries nr Manchester where he spent the rest of his career.

Lee, Charles E., *Transactions of the Lancs & Ches Antiquarian Soc* V 77 1967 pp 128–36

STEPHENSON, Robert

b Willington Quay, nr Newcastle upon Tyne 16.10.1803;
d London 12.10.1859 aged nearly 56
Son of George S. (qv). His mother d 14.5.1806. Ed Bruce's Academy, Newcastle, 1814–19. 1819 apprenticed to Nicholas Wood (qv) at Killingworth colliery. In 1821 he assisted his f in the survey of the Stockton & Darlington R. In 1822 he spent 6 months studying at Edinburgh univ where he met George Parker Bidder (qv) who became a lifelong friend and with whom he carried on much of his professional work. On leaving Edinburgh in 1823 he took up mgt of the newly established firm of Robert Stephenson & Co. Bad health forced him to leave England, and in 6.1824 he sailed to S America to superintend the working of some gold and silver mines in Colombia. There he met Richard Trevithick (qv), then without money, whom he helped to repatriate. S. returned in 1827 and at once became involved in the dispute over the form of traction for the Liverpool & Manchester R, resulting in the building of the *Rocket* in 1829 (see George S.). On 16.6.1829 he m Frances Sanderson of London. He was elected MICE 1830 and

was president 1856–7. In 1833, with the passing of the Act for the London & Birmingham R, S. was app eng. There were huge works: Kilsby tunnel through running sand, 1 mile 666yd (2.218km), Tring and Blisworth cuttings; and it was the first main line into London, op 1838. S. was active in the 'battle of the gauges', upholding the standard gauge against the 7ft (2.134m) gauge of Brunel (qv). Despite this, S. and Brunel were close personal friends to the end of their lives. On 4.10.1842 his wife d, aged only 39, without children. S. is best known for his bridges. His career could have been ruined by the collapse of the bridge over the Dee at Chester on 24.5.1847. The accident led to a scrutiny of all cast iron spans. He survived this, however, and went on to build the High Level Bridge at Newcastle, 1846–9, and the Royal Border Bridge, Berwick, a stone vdt of 28 spans 61ft 6in (18.745m), 1850. With his f's friend William Fairbairn (qv) he evolved the wrought iron tubular girder which he used successfully in the Conway (1847–9) and Menai (1847–50) bridges on the Chester & Holyhead R and the Victoria Bridge (1854–9) over the St Lawrence at Montreal, then the world's longest bridge. Two more were erected in Egypt. During the erection of the tubes of the Menai bridge, in his most anxious moments he was supported by the presence of Brunel. S. returned this support during the erection of Brunel's Saltash bridge in 1859. On 30.6.1847 S. was elected conservative MP for Whitby, remaining its rep until his death, but he rarely spoke in Parliament except on engg matters. He opposed the Suez Canal scheme. Early in 1859 his health gave way and he was forced to give up work. A yachting cruise to Norway failed to restore him. He was buried in Westminster Abbey beside Telford.

Rolt, L.T.C., *George & Robert Stephenson* 1960; Jeaffreson, J.C., with Pole, William, *The Life of Robert Stephenson* (2 vols) 1864; Smiles, Samuel, *Life of George Stephenson* 1864, 1904; Baughan, Peter, *The Chester & Holyhead R* 1973; Min Proc ICE V 19 1859–60 pp 176–82; *The Eng* V 8 10.1859 p 309; V 10 1860 p 107;

V 208 1959 p 512

STEVENS, John

b New York City (?).(?).1749;
d Hoboken, NJ, 6.3.1838 aged 89
Pioneer of mechanical transport in America. Son of John S. whose f, also John, had gone to America in 1699 at the age of 16 as an indentured law clerk, and of Elizabeth, dr of James Alexander. After leaving sch in 1872 S. joined his family in New York and 4 yrs later graduated at King's coll (now Columbia Univ) and then studied law for the next 3 yrs. In the Revolutionary War he served under Gen Washington as capt, later col. 1782-3 he was surveyor gen for the E div of NJ. On 17.10.1782 he m Rachael Cox. In 1784 he bought a large tract of land in NJ on W side of Hudson River, including most of what is now Hoboken. About 1788 he became interested in the work of John Fitch and James Ramsey in the development of the steamboat, and from then until his death S. gave himself and his fortune to the advance of mech transport on land and water. He turned his attention to boiler design and in 8.1791 he was among the first dozen American citizens to receive US patents, for an improved vertical boiler and an improved Savery type steam engine for steamboats, and a steam bellows. On the death of his f in 1792 he had to administer a vast estate, but continued with his steam engine experiments. About 1797 he met Nicholas J. Roosevelt who operated a foundry in NJ, and with Robert R. Livingston, bro in law of S., they formed a partnership and built experimental steamboats. On 11.4.1803 S. patented a multi-tubular boiler and in 1804 built a steamboat with two screw propellors. Other vessels followed and in 6.1809 his *Phoenix* became the first sea-going steamship in the world. In 1810 he turned to the adaption of steam power to Rs. On 6.2. 1815 the NJ Assembly created a company, chartered by S., 'to erect a rail road from the river Delaware near Trenton to the river at Rariton at or near New Brunswick'. This was the first American RR Act. After 8 yrs struggle, on 31.3.1823 an iron RR worked out by S. from Philadelphia to Columbia Pa was authorised by the Pennsylvania legislature. Another Act had to be obtained in 1828, and in 1834 the R was opened, and was called the Pennsylvania RR. It later became part of the PRR system. In 1825, at age 76, S. designed and built a steam loco, and ran it on a circular track on his estate in Hoboken. This was the first American-built steam loco. It was, however, an experimental machine, not a load hauler as was *Tom Thumb* of 1830, built by Peter Cooper (qv). With this S. ended his engg work and devoted the rest of his life to study, writing essays on metaphysical subjects, political economy and education. He was survived by a widow and 7 children.
DAB V 17 pp 614–16

STEVENS, Robert Livingston

b Hoboken, NJ, USA, 18.10.1787;
d Hoboken 20.4.1856 aged 69
Mech eng, naval architect, inventor; son of John S. (qv). Ed privately; later assisted his f in his experimental engg on steamboats including the *Juliana* which began operation between New York and Hoboken on 11.10.1811, so establishing the world's first steam ferry system. He was now wholly occupied in naval architecture, and in the next 25 yrs designed and had built over 20 steamboats and ferries incorporating numerous inventions and improvements. In 1830, on the establishment of the Camden & Amboy RR & Transportation Co, he was elected president & chief eng. Also in 1830, as did Allen, Whistler and McNeill (qqv), he went to England to study locos, and to purchase one and to order iron rails. On the way he designed the flat-bottomed rail (commonly attributed to Vignoles, qv), and after difficulties he had this rolled in England. At the same time he designed the rail spike and the fish plate and the necessary bolts and nuts. He bought the Stephenson 'Planet' type loco *John Bull* which, on its trial trip driven by S. at Bordentown, NJ, on 12.11.1831, inaugurated the first steam R service in NJ. During the next 15 yrs he divided his time between RRs and steam navigation. In the RR shops at Hoboken he devised a double-slide cut-off for locos, designed and built locos of several types,

improved boilers, and was successful in burning anthracite in locos. During the war in 1812 he designed arms and ammunition for naval vessels. S. never m. He was prominent in musical circles in New York and Hoboken.
DAB V 17 pp 619–20

STEVENSON, Francis

b (?), Scotland, 27.8.1827;
d London 1.2.1902 aged 74
Chief eng, LNWR. Ed Edinburgh Academy. At 13 articled to R. B. Dockray, then an eng on the London & Birmingham R. 1843 became M of engg staff. Engaged on const of Northampton–Peterborough line, op 1845, also res eng on Coventry & Nuneaton R, completed 1850. Later transferred to Euston. 1855 became asst to William Baker whom he succeeded as chief eng in charge of all new works and parliamentary business in 1.1879. His extensive knowledge of the history of the LNWR induced the dirs to appoint him in 1886 to take charge of the maintenance of the whole system. S. was a lover of nature and of old buildings and always strove to blend his works into the landscape. Became MICE 5.2.1867.
Min Proc ICE V 149 1901–2 p 353; RM 3.1902 p 281

STEVENSON, Robert

b Glasgow 8.6.1772;
d Edinburgh 12.7.1850 aged 78
Ed privately by his mother. Trained in engg by Thomas Smith of Edinburgh, the lighthouse eng. In 1797 S. made his first inspection as eng to the Bd of Northern Lighthouses, a position he held until 1842 during which period he erected 23 lighthouses, including Bell Rock. S. was also engaged in many works in England, Ireland and Scotland, and also reported on many early R projects. He is credited with first suggesting the use of malleable iron instead of cast iron for rails and tramplates. His sons Alan (b Edinburgh 1807; d Portobello 23.12.1865), David (b Edinburgh 11.1.1815; d N Berwick 17.7.1886) and Thomas (b Edinburgh 22.7.1818; d Edinburgh 8.5.1887) were all outstanding civil engs. Thomas's only son, Robert Louis, (1850–94), intended as an eng, became the famous writer of essays and

novels
Min Proc ICE V 10 1850–1 p 94; DNB V 18

STEWART, Alexander Forrester

b Black River, Richmond, Nova Scotia, 8.1.1864; d Halifax, NS, 30.10.1937 aged 73
Civil eng on CPR and CNR. Ed Pictou Academy, NS, and Dalhousie Univ, and received scientific training at McGill Univ. Entered service of CPR 1887 and worked on pioneer R const in the west. 1895 went to S Africa until 1906, working on surveys and const in Natal, Transvaal, Zululand and Cape Colony. During the Boer War he worked on the Imperial Military Rs in the Transvaal. From 1903–6 he worked on surveys and maintenance for the Cape Govt Rs. Returned to Canada 1906 to work with the Canadian Northern R until its incorporation in the CNR system. In 1920 he was app chief eng of the CNR Atlantic Division. Ret 1932.
Journal ICE V 9 1937–8 p 592

STEWART, Allan Duncan

b (?) 7.3.1831; d Inverhadden nr Pitlochry, Perthshire, 31.10.1894 aged 63
Grad in maths at Cambridge 1853. 1855–8 articled to Benjamin Hall Blyth (qv). 1859–60 acted as res eng on const of Banffshire R and section of Portpatrick R. 1861 began practice as civil eng in Edinburgh. During next 20 yrs he prepared parliamentary plans for, and laid out, various Rs including Ascot–Aldershot, and Chapel-en-le-Frith–Buxton. S. was extensively emp as asst to Thomas Bouch (qv) in the design and const of several iron and steel bridges, his mathematical ability being particularly valuable. For Bouch he prepared the working drawings for the Redheugh Bridge, Newcastle; the whole of the girders of the first Tay bridge (many still in use on the present bridge); roofs of Edinburgh Waverley and Dundee stations, and for the steel piers, chains and girders for the proposed Forth Bridge. In 1880 he gave important evidence before the Royal Commissioners on the Tay Bridge disaster. From 1881–90 S. acted as chief asst eng for Sir John Fowler and Sir Benjamin Baker (qqv) on the design and const of the

Forth Bridge. He then practised in Westminster and obtained, in conj with J. M. Maclaren and W. Dunn, the first prize of 500 guineas (£525) in the competition for designs for the Wembley Tower (see Watkin). While engaged with Baker on this he became ill and died. MICE 7.2.1882.

Min Proc ICE V 119 1894–5 p 399

STEWART, Charles Patrick

b Dublin (?).(?).1823;
d Sunninghill, Berks, 6.7.1882 aged 58
Loco eng and mfr. Apprenticed in London. Joined firm of Sharp Bros & Co, Manchester, 1852, the firm then becoming Sharp, Stewart & Co. It became a limited liability company in 1864 with S. as chairman until his death. He was influential in introducing the Giffard injector in England. Sharp Stewart & Co moved to Glasgow in 1888 and in 1903 became part of the NB Loco Co (see Sharp Bros).

Proc IME 1883 p 27; *The Eng* V 54 14.7.1882 p 26

STEWART, Hugh Percy

b (?) (?).(?).1870; d (?) 2.10.1933 aged 63
Eng and loco supt, NCC, Ireland. Began R career on Belfast & N Counties R, and on completing apprenticeship entered the Belfast wks of Harland & Wolff Ltd. Later became chief eng of one of E. Bates & Sons' steamers. 1910 returned to N Counties R as wks mgr and in 1915 became asst loco eng. 1930 became eng & loco supt, NCC. While in office he supervised const of the Greenisland loop lines to avoid Greenisland junction and to give a direct run from Belfast to Portrush, 1934. He converted compound locos to simples and introduced the 2–6–0 type and petrol railcars. Ret 30.6.1933. MILE 1932.

Journal ILE V 24 1934 p 142; *RG* 22.9.1933 p 422 (portrait); *The Locomotive* 15.11.1933 p 345

STILEMAN, Francis Croughton

b Winchelsea 25.5.1824;
d London 18.5.1889 aged 64
Chief eng, Furness R. Ed Coll of Civil Engs, Putney, 1840–4. Then articled to J. R. McClean (qv) and acted as res eng on the S Staffs R; the Birmingham–

Dudley–Wolverhampton R, Staffordshire & Worcestershire Canal reservoirs and the S Staffs waterworks. 1849 entered partnership with McClean and shortly afterwards left Staffs for the Furness district where he lived 1850–3. In 1853 he moved to London, being associated with McClean as eng to the FR; FR & MR jt line; Tottenham & Hampstead R; Eastbourne water & sewage wks; Ryde Pier & Tramways; Bristol & Portishead R; Portishead docks, and for the system of Rs in Galicia and Moldavia known as the Lemberg & Czernovitz. One of his tasks on the FR was the enlargement of Lindal tunnel from single to double line. The tunnel remains unlined and without portals today. (See Min Proc ICE V 19 1859–60 p 229.) On ret of McClean in 1868 S. became chief eng of Furness Rs, harbours & docks. MICE 5.3.1855.

Min Proc ICE V 98 1888–9 p 401

STIRLING, James

b Methven, Perthshire, 20.7.1800;
d Edinburgh 10.1.1876 aged 75
Son of a farmer. Originally studied for the church but changed to mech engg. Apprenticed to Claude Girdwood & Co, Glasgow, and was later eng at Deanston wks. Became eng and then mgr of the Dundee Foundry where he built a steamer for the Swedish govt. Besides other general engg work, from 1833 S. built several locos for the Dundee & Newtyle, Coupar Angus and the Arbroath & Forfar Rs. One of these he drove up the 1 in 25 Balbuchlay incline on the Dundee & Newtylw R. He designed a loco reversing gear. 1846 left Dundee and settled in Edinburgh where he continued to practice as eng. MICE 10.6.1834. He m 1857.

Min Proc ICE V 44 1875–6 pp 221–4

STIRLING, James

b Galston, Ayrshire, 2.10.1835;
d Ashford, Kent, 12.1.1917 aged 81.
Loco eng, G & SWR and SER. Ed privately, then spent 2 yrs with the village millwright. Apprenticed under his bro Patrick S. (qv), then loco supt G & SWR at Glasgow, and after a year was sent to Kilmarnock where he passed through all the loco depts. He was then made a chargeman, and later worked in the

drg office. To gain experience he then
moved to Sharp Stewart & Co, Manchester, as a fitter for a year, then
returned to the drg office at Kilmarnock,
later becoming wks mgr until 1866.
When Patrick S. left to become loco supt
of the GNR in 1866, James was app his
successor on the G & SWR. He introduced a more powerful passenger engine
with 6ft 6in (1.981m) wheels then, for
the through trains in connection with the
MR, an even larger type with 7ft
(2.134m) wheels. In 1874 he introduced
a steam reversing gear for locos, and
in his coaches he was the first supt to
provide cushioned seats for the 3rd class.
1878 moved to Ashford, Kent, where on
28.3. he was app loco supt of the SER.
Introduced many improvements in locos,
among them his design of bogie and the
steam reversing gear. He was the first
eng to use 19in (483mm) inside cylinders
with the valves between them. He continued the Stirling tradition of domeless
boilers, but carried the policy of standardisation to the point where the introduction of larger locos for increased
loads was delayed too long, and at his ret
the SER was under-powered. His first
SER locos were based on his G & SWR
designs: the 'O' class 0-6-0s of 1878-
97; 'A' class 4-4-0s with 6ft 0½in
(1.841m) wheels, 1880; 'Q' class 0-4-4T,
1881-97; and the 'F' class 7ft (2.134m)
4-4-0s of 1883-98. In 1888 he introd the
'R' class 0-6-0T and in 1897 the 'B'
class 4-4-0 with 7ft wheels, his last
design. All the engines gave good service, and in rebuilt form some survived
to become BR stock. In Scotland S. was
hon sec to the Scottish Loco R Engs
Assoc. At Ashford he was hon sec of
the Assoc of Loco Engs of GB & Ireland
until his ret in 1898. MIME 1880; also
MICE, and JP for Kent. After his ret
he remained at Ashford.
Engg V 41 14.1.1876 p 29; *Proc IME*
5.1917 pp 445-6; *Min Proc ICE* V 204
1916-17 p 431; SLS *The Glasgow &
South Western R* 1950; Smith, D. L.,
The Locos of the G & SWR 1976;
Bradley, D. L., *The Locos of the SER*
(RCTS) 1963

STIRLING, Matthew

b Kilmarnock 27.11.1856;
d Hull 5.10.1931 aged 74.

Loco supt, Hull & Barnsley R. Second
child of Patrick S. (qv) in a family of
5 sons and 4 drs, and nephew of James
S. (qv) of the G & SWR and SER. Ed
Kilmarnock, Doncaster and Ayr. Apprenticed at Doncaster GNR wks. 1880 went
to Nottingham as asst to dist sup, GNR.
1883 transferred to Peterborough as asst
to the dist supt. In 5.1885 app loco supt
of the H & BR, remaining in that position until 1922 when the H & B was
amalg with NER, when he ret, at age
65. In the Stirling tradition his engines
had domeless boilers. His principal types
were the 0-8-0 mineral engine of 1907,
the 4-4-0 of 1910 and the 0-6-2T of
1913-14. All his loco designs had inside
cylinders. Became MIME 1885.
The Locomotive 15.10.1931 p 344; RCTS
Locos of the LNER

STIRLING, Patrick

b Kilmarnock 29.6.1820; d Doncaster
11.11.1895 aged 75.
GNR loco eng. Son of Rev R. S., a
Scottish minister with a flair for mechanical invention. 1837-43 apprenticed
under his uncle James S. (qv) at Dundee
Foundry where some engines were built
for the Arbroath & Forfar R in 1839-
40. He then worked for 3 yrs on marine
engines on the Clyde under Robert
Napier. In 1846 he went to the Hyde
Park wks of Neilson & Co, Glasgow,
where he became a shop foreman. In
1851 he became loco supt of the Caledonian & Dumbartonshire Jn R (a short
branch from Bowling to Balloch on
Loch Lomond, 8 miles, 12.9km). He
then returned to marine work with
Lawrence Hill of Port Glasgow from
where he went to R. & W. Hawthorn
of Newcastle upon Tyne. Hawthorns
supplied most of the locos for the G &
SWR. In 1853 this R needed a new loco
supt and S. was app. He took up his
duties at the Crook Street wks, Glasgow,
on 3.5.1853. One of his first tasks, in
8.1853, was to select a site for a new
loco wks at Kilmarnock. His first loco
designs were all o/c types, 0-4-2, 0-6-0
and 2-2-2s. The first engine to be built
at the new Kilmarnock wks was the first
of his '2' class 2-2-2 o/c express engines
in 1857, the forerunner of his famous
8ft (2.438m) single on the GNR. From
1860 he adopted the domeless boiler

which became a prominent feature of his designs and subsequently those of his bro James and his son Matthew (qqv). He considered that a dome weakened a boiler; his boilers had plenty of steam space and did not prime. In 1864 he produced a 0-4-2 i c goods type and in 1865 an o/c 2-2-2, an interesting feature of both being a 'wrap-over' cab which was to become standard GNR practice until 1923, and a circular side window. In 1.1866 S. was app asst loco supt on the GNR at Doncaster and he left the G & SWR on 1.3.1866. On 1.10.1866 he was made chief loco supt in succession to his cousin Archibald Sturrock (qv) who resigned on 31.12.1866. His first GNR engines were 6ft 7in (2.007m) 2-4-0s. In 1868 his first i/c singles appeared, the 7ft 1in (2.159m) 2-2-2s. For goods traffic he designed an 0-6-0 type which, with variations and enlargements, continued to be built well into the regime of H. A. Ivatt (qv). He also produced a 0-4-2 tender and tank engines, 0-6-0ST and 0-4-4Ts. In 1870 his most famous design appeared, his o/c 8ft single, 4-2-2 No 1, now preserved at the National R Museum, York. This type continued to be built, with improvements, until 1895. They achieved amazing feats of speed and haulage. His 7f 7½in (2.171m) 2-2-2s were also an outstanding success. S. was one of the earliest Ms of the Inst of Engs & Shipbuilders in Scotland. MIME 1867 and MICE 1878. Unfortunately, S. remained in office too long, and instead of retiring at the height of his glory he stayed until poor health prevented him from fulfilling demands for more powerful locos to handle the increasing traffic. In the end H. A. Ivatt (qv) was app his successor and on 1.11.1895 S. was asked to resign. He d only 11 days later.

Min Proc ICE V 124 1895-6 pp 421-4; Proc IME 1895 p 542; *Engg* V 60 11.1895 p 612; *The Eng* V 80 11.1895 p 485; Ellis, Hamilton, *Twenty Locomotive Men* 1958; Smith, D. L., *Locos of the G & SWR* 1976; Brown, F. A. S., *Great Northern Locomotive Engs 1846–81* 1966; and *From Stirling to Gresley 1822–1922* 1974; Leech, K. H., and Boddy, M. G., *The Stirling Singles* 1965; Bird, G. F., *The Locos of the GNR* 1910; Tuplin, W. A., *Great Northern Steam* 1971

STRACHAN, John

b Aberdeen 14.3.1848; d Sydenham, Kent, 2.4.1909 aged 61.
R contractor. Ed Gordon's Coll, Aberdeen. Apprenticed with John Gibb, eng of the GN of S. Later engaged on const of Callander & Oban R, having joined the service of Easton Gibb in 1873. He also had charge of the Leyburn & Hawes R, Yorks, and of the Rhymney R into Cardiff and of LNWR lines in Staffordshire. Later emp by Thomas Nelson & Co. Afterwards, on his own account, S. carried out large works for the LNWR, GWR, LYR, GCR, Cardiff R, Barry R, TVR, Rhymney R, Cambrian Rs. His last works were the Red Wharf Bay line in Anglesey and the Welshpool & Llanfair R and the Oswestry–Llangynog line. After the death of his wife in 1908 he moved to Sydenham. MIME 1885.
Proc IME 5.1909 p 534

STROBRIDGE, James Harvey

b Albany, Vt, USA, 23.4.1827; d Hayward, Cal, 27.7.1921 aged 94.
Civil eng and contractor. At 16 he obtained employment as a tracklayer on the Boston & Fitchburg RR, Mass, and later built 2 miles (3.291km) of line on the Naughatuck RR, Conn. 1849 went to California, with the 'forty-niners', and worked in agriculture, freighting and mining. 1863 worked on the San Francisco & San Jose RR. 1964 joined the Central Pacific on which he was soon in charge of the entire const. Determined to drive the line through the Sierra Nevada in the shortest possible time, he organised supply routes and bases and drove the summit tunnel through in 1 year, a third of the time estimated. As a result of his efforts the CP drove right into Utah, 7 yrs ahead of schedule, to meet, and pass, the Union Pacific graders who went on constructing 225 miles (362km) of parallel grading because no point of junction had been established and each company was receiving $48 000 a mile in Federal loans. After completion of the line in 1869 he settled on a farm near Hayward, using this as a base from which he directed his contracts. About 1877 he took over the work on the SP Los Angeles–New

Orleans route which he completed in 1883. He also built the line from Mojave to Needles and, in 1883, began the line up the Sacramento River Canyon towards Oregon. In 1889 he ret to his farm.

Kraus, George, *High Road to Promontory* California 1969; Griswold, Wesley S., *A work of Giants* 1963

STROUDLEY, William

b Sandford, Oxford, 6.3.1833;
d Paris 20.12.1889 aged 56.
Loco eng, LBSCR. After a brief schooling S. began work in an Oxford paper mill; later in various engine wks in Birmingham. In May 1853 he began his training as loco eng under Daniel Gooch (qv) at Swindon, GWR. 1854 moved to Peterborough to continue training under Charles Sacré (qv), becoming running foreman. In 1857, for 1 year, S. took charge of the Edenham & Little Bytham R, op 8.12.1856 and owned by Lord Willoughby d'Eresby, afterwards returning to Peterborough. 1861 app mgr of Edinburgh & Glasgow R Cowlairs Wks, coming briefly under the influence of S. W. Johnson (qv). On 19.6.1865 app loco supt of HR at £500 p a, in succession to Barclay, at Inverness. Began by rebuilding the 2–2–2s into 2–4–0s. 1869 designed a small 0–6–0T, a forerunner of the LBSCR 'Terrier'. S. also introduced the yellow loco livery on the HR. 1870 app loco supt LBSCR at Brighton following resig of J. C. Craven (qv). At Brighton he designed new workshops and sheds and adopted the practice of painting the driver's name inside the cab. S's first LBSCR engines were 2 0–4–2Ts, using old boilers. There followed 2 gds engines, then a 6ft 6in (1.981m) 2–4–0 express engine with domeless boiler and double frames, 1872, of which 6 were built. The first S. single, 326 (orig 151) *Grosvenor* with 6ft 9in (2.057m) wheels of 1874, was the forerunner of a series of 2–2–2s. S. firmly advocated the Westinghouse brake. He favoured large boilers for the period, and did not over-cylinder engines. He used Gresham & Craven's steam sanding gear. He avoided compounding and bogies. Except the 2 'C' classes of 0–6–0s and the 2 0–4–2Ts of 1871, all his engines were named, mostly after places con-

nected with the LBSCR. He devised a speed indicator using a fan and a column of water. His 36 6ft 6in (1.981m) 'Gladstone' class express engines were unique. The pioneer, No 214 *Gladstone* was withdrawn in 4.1927 with a mileage of 1 346 918 and is preserved today in the NRM at York. S. would not use injectors, but relied on a feed pump. He adopted a standardisation policy, sweeping away the numerous Craven classes. He designed 3 main tank classes: 0–6–0 'Terrier', 1872 (of several preserved one is in NRM, York); 0–4–2 'D', 1873; and 0–6–0 'E', 1874. The first of the 0–6–2 radial tanks was under const when S. d. For freight and mixed traffic he brought out his 'C' class 0–6–0 in 1871 and 'D' class 0–4–2 in 1876. The well designed S. cab with broad side sheets and domed roof derived from a design by Barclay on the old Inverness & Aberdeen Jn R and improved by S. It was developed further by the Drummonds and D. Jones (qqv). S. was one of the few British loco engs to favour inside bearings for tender wheels to make use of worn loco wheels, and this again was copied by the Drummonds, though they used them only for bogie tenders. S. also designed all the LBSCR carriages, finished in polished mahogany, and he fitted up one of the LBSCR Pullmans with electric light in 1881. In addition to all this he designed engines for the LBSCR cross-channel steamers. At the Paris Exhib 1889 where S. exhibited 0–4–2 *Edward Blount* he developed acute bronchitis and d there.

MIME 1865; MICE 6.2.1877.
Min Proc ICE V 99 1889–90 p 355; Proc IME 10.1889 pp 751–2; *The Locomotive* 5.1937 pp 149–52 (Ellis); Ellis, Hamilton, *Twenty Loco Men* 1958; Cornwell, H. G. Campbell, *William Stroudley, Craftsman of steam* 1968; *The Eng* V 68 27.12.1889 p 539; *Engg* V 48 27.12.1889 p 745

STRUB, Emil Viktor

b Trimbach nr Olten, Switzerland, 13.7.1858; d Zurich 12.12.1909 aged 51.
Swiss mountain R eng. On leaving sch went to Aarau to study mech eng where, as was Abt (qv), he was influenced by Riggenbach (qv) who interested him in mountain Rs. After further tech studies at Mitweida, and at the engg wks of

Hohenzollern and Esslingen, in 1888 he was app to the Federal R Dept as a leading eng in a new office concerned with mountain Rs. 1891 app insp on the newly opened Bernese Oberland R. 1897–8 was dir of the Jungfrau R, then under const, having come to this through the prize competition organised by the erectors Guyer-Zeller to celebrate their 90th year. He won the first prize for the formation work. On the Jungfrau R his rack rail system was used for the first time. (It was replaced by the Lamelle system rack in 1955.) It was a combination of the Riggenbach and Abt systems. The mfr of the Strub rack was undertaken from the start by L. vo Rollischen Ironworks, Gerlafingen, with which S. worked for the remainder of his life. By 1909 it was in use in Switzerland, France, Germany and Italy. From 1898 S. established his own engg office, in Montreaux until 1901 and then in Zurich, where from 1905, he worked with H. H. Peter. His work led to a succession of Swiss mountain Rs in 1889–1909. In 1902 his book *Die Bergbahnen der Schweiz bis 1900* was pub. He d from heart failure in the midst of work.

Hefti, Walter, *Zahnradbahnen der Welt* Basle 1971

STUART, Herbert Akroyd

b Yorkshire 28.1.1864; d Claremont, W Australia, 19.2.1927 aged 63.

Inventor of the compression-ignition oil engine later developed by Diesel (qv). Ed Newbury Gr Sch, Berks, and City & Guilds of London Tech Coll, Finsbury. Received early practical training in the engg wks of his f, Charles S., at Fenny Stratford. On the death of his f S. became mgr of the wks. Began experimental work on oil engines in 1886 at Bletchley Iron Wks which led to his discovery of automatic ignition by hot compressed air, or compression ignition. This was patented (7146) on 8.5.1890 and (15994) on 8.10.1890. On 26.6.1891 the sole right to mfr and develop Akroyd Stuart oil engines was acquired by Richard Hornsby & Sons, Grantham. With the introduction of the engine in Germany the idea was taken up by Diesel who came to an agreement with Maschinenfabrik Augsburg, Nürnberg

(MAN) in 1893 for Germany and with Krupp, Essen, for outside Germany. The diesel engine as evolved by MAN in 1897 differed from the AS engine in using highly compressed air to inject and spray the charge of fuel oil while the AS engine had a fuel oil pump and spraying nozzle. The engine is now universally known as the diesel although it was not invented by Diesel but was evolved by MAN and promoted by Diesel.

Robinson, William, *Heavy oil engines of Akroyd type* 1931; Proc IME 5.1927 p 577

STUBBS, William Henry

b Spalding (?).10.1847; d Blackpool 21.6.1890 aged 42.

Civil eng, GNR, NSR, MS & L. 1862 articled to his uncle Richard Johnson (qv), eng of the GNR. 1869–70 engaged as asst eng on the Wood Green–Enfield branch and in 1870 app res eng on the Bourne–Sleaford line. 1871–2 on prelim surveys for GNR Derbyshire and Staffordshire extns and was app res eng under Johnson on the first 20 miles (32km) from Colwick nr Nottingham to Pinxton including Mapperley tunnel, Watnall tunnel and the immense cutting and the Nutbrook vdt. In 7.1877 app eng of the NSR until 11.6.1886 when he became eng of the MS & L on the ret of Charles Sacré (qv). In 1889 he became ill and never fully recovered his health. Elected MICE 3.12.1878.

Min Proc ICE V 102 1889–90 p 331; Dow, George, *Great Central* V 2 1962

STUMPF, Johannes

b Mülheim, Germany, 4.4.1862; d Berlin 18.11.1936 aged 74.

Mech eng, developer of the Stumpf 'Uniflow' steam loco. Studied under Riedler at the Tech H Sch, Aachen. In 1888 when Riedler moved to the Tech H Sch at Charlottenburg he chose S. as his asst. With Riedler S. greatly improved pumping machinery. 1893 went to Chicago with Riedler and became chief eng of Allis Chalmers where he supervised building of pumps, compressors and Corliss steam engines. 1896 app prof of steam engines at the Tech H Sch at Charlottenburg where he designed his

Uniflow steam engine. The principle had been first applied in England in 1845 on a 2–2–2 engine built under J. I. Cudworth (qv) for the SER and was further developed by T. J. Todd in 1885. In this system the steam is exhausted through ports in the middle of the cylinder. To achieve this the piston has to be nearly half the length of the cylinder. The idea is to maintain a uniform direction of steam flow, avoiding reversal at each piston stroke. The Stumpf system was applied in England by Vincent Raven (qv) on the NER, first on S2 class 2-cyl 4–6–0 825 in 1913 (rbt to normal arrangement 1924), and on Z1 class 3-cyl 4–4–2 2212 in 1918 (rbt with Lentz poppet valves 1934). Both showed coal economy, but the use of the Stumpf arrangement was not extended. In 1920 S. was awarded a D Eng at Aachen Tech H Sch.

ZVDI V 80 26.12.1936 p 1554

STURROCK, Archibald

b Petruchie, Angus, 30.9.1816;
d London 1.1.1909 aged 92.
GNR loco eng. In 1832 apprenticed under James Stirling (qv) at East Foundry, Dundee, where he assisted in erection of the Carmichaels' bogie engine *Trotter*, the 3rd engine built for the 4ft 6in (1.372m) g Dundee & Newtyle R, 1833. It had vertical cylinders and bell crank drive to the leading wheels. It was probably the first loco S. saw. At East Foundry Daniel Gooch (qv) worked as draugtsman. After his apprenticeship S. worked in Fairbairn's wks, Manchester, for 6 months. In 1840 he moved to the GWR to work with his former colleague D. Gooch, first at Paddington running shed, London, and from 1843 at Swindon where he became the first wks mgr at the new wks set up there by Gooch. In 1850 S. applied successfully for the post of loco supt at GNR wks at Boston, at a salary of £500 p a, at the same time recommending himself as C & W supt for an additional £250 p a. In autumn 1852 he and his staff moved to the new wks at Doncaster. S. advocated greater heating surface and higher pressure than most of his contemporaries used. He retained many GWR features, including sandwich frames and domeless boilers. In 1853 he brought out his famous 4–2–2 215 with 7ft 6in (2.286m) wheels, cyls 17½ x 26in (445 x 660mm) and a domeless boiler with a working pressure of 150psi (10.55kg/cm²) and a total heating surface of 1718sq ft (159.6m²). It was built by R & W Hawthorn, Newcastle. His standard express engine built from 1859 was a 2–2–2 with 7ft (2.134m) wheels. In 1866 he brought out his 7ft 2–4–0 express engines which, however, were not so successful and were later rbt as 2–2–0s by P. Stirling (qv). In 1863 S. introduced his 0–6–0 with steam tender (see *The Eng* 17.1. and 9.5.1919) which could pull 450 tons up 1 in 178. The men disliked the engines and complained of excessive heat on the footplate, and of having to drive two engines while getting paid for only one. For the traffic through to the underground lines in London he designed a 0–4–2T, and for through coal trains by the Met R tunnels to the LC & DR S. ordered 2 o/c 0–8–0Ts with inside frames in 1866. In the same year, on 31.12. he decided to ret, aged 50; and he spent his remaining 42 yrs hunting, shooting and fishing. He was succeeded by P. Stirling.

Engg V 87 8.1.1909 p 44; *The Locomotive* 1.1909 p 3; 3.1938 pp 93–6 (Ellis); Ellis, Hamilton, *Twenty Locomotive Men* 1958; Brown, F. A. S., *Great Northern Loco Engs* 1966; Bird, G. F., *The Locos of the GNR* 1910; Tuplin, W. A., *Great Northern Steam* 1971

SUMMERSON, Thomas

b South Shields (?).4.1810;
d Houghton-le-Skerne, Co Durham, 6.12.1898 aged 88.
Mfr of R ironwork. From a delicate boy he became strong enough to walk 50 miles in a day. Began at age 14 drilling stone block sleepers for the Stockton & Darlington R. Later emp on const of Stanhope & Tyne R and was present at its opening in 1834. In 1836 was emp on the survey of the Great North of England R with Storey. 1839 became pw insp on the S & D. Later worked with Harris (qv) on const of the Middlesbrough & Guisborough R, the work being done with such expedition that S. was awarded an honorarium of £1000 which enabled him to become a partner

in the patent brick works at Bank Top, Darlington. The enterprise failed and he lost the £1000. 1853 app mgr of Hope Town Foundry, Darlington, and in conj with Harris patented a rail chair with a wooden cushion under the rail; also a special form of chilled cast iron wheel for chaldron wagons. Large numbers of these wheels were made at Hope Town. The Albert Hill Foundry at Darlington was built as a branch, and on the death of Harris in 1869 it was acquired by S. and it became Thomas Summerson & Sons. S. designed the first wrought iron crossing and made a speciality of its mfr. *The Eng* V 86 16.12.1898 p 587; *The R Eng* 1.1899 p 1

SUTHERLAND, Third Duke of, see Leveson Gower

SWANWICK, Frederick

b Chester 1.10.1810; d Bournemouth 15.11.1885 aged 75.
Ed at Leeds and Univ of Edinburgh. 1829 articled to George Stephenson, becoming also his sec in succession to T. L. Gooch (qv). At the opening of the Liverpool & Manchester R in 1830 S. drove *Arrow*. From 1832–6 he assisted George Stephenson on the Whitby & Pickering R and from 7.1834 he was given supervision of the work. From 1836–40 S. was engaged on the N Midland R from Derby to Leeds. He also surveyed the York & N Midland and Sheffield & Rotherham Rs. Also in 1836 S. gave evidence before the Commons committees on all these lines and on the Derby & Birmingham. During the autumn of 1845 S. worked almost continuously, hardly sleeping. On the formation of the Midland R in 1844 he took charge of all newly projected lines under W. H. Barlow. These included the Nottingham–Mansfield, 1848; Nottingham–Lincoln; Erewash Valley; Pinxton–Mansfield; and the junction line between the MS & L and the MR at Sheffield (Wicker) in 1846–7. In addition S. was engaged in preparing several bills for lines which were not built immediately. Throughout his working life he worked long hours, often twice round the clock.
Min Proc ICE V 85 1885–6 pp 401–7; Williams, F. S. *The Midland R* 1878 edn pp 42–5

SWINBURNE, Thomas

b nr Newcastle upon Tyne 31.1.1813; d Houghton, Lancs, 8.1.1881 aged c 68.
Pw eng, ELR and LYR. His f Robert S., was emp for 50 yrs on a coal wagonway, under Lord Ravensworth. Left sch 1825, and in 1829, at the request of George Stephenson, went to work on the Bolton & Leigh R where his bro Ralph had contracted to lay rails from Hulton colliery to Leigh. S. remained in charge of the B & L pw until 1838 when he was engaged by Peter Sinclair, sec of both the B & L and the Preston & Walton tramway, to take charge of the latter. When it closed in 1842 he was transferred to the Bolton & Preston R of which Sinclair was also sec. In 1843 this was transferred to the North Union R. In 1846, when the NUR was absorbed by the LNWR and Manchester & Leeds R, S. transferred to the Blackburn & Preston R of which Sinclair was sec & mgr. This became part of the ELR in 1846. S. remained as pw eng on the ELR until 1859 when it was amalg with the LYR on which he remained a pw eng until his death. In 1849–50 he was an eng on the Huddersfield–Penistone line. A stone carving of his head was installed at Berry Brow stn nr Huddersfield; it is now in the NRM, York. S. was responsible for many improvements in pw, signalling and point operation which became widely applied, but he never patented anything.
Marshall, John, *The Lancashire & Yorkshire R* V 1 1969

SWINBURNE, William

b Brooklyn, NY, (?).(?).1805; d Paterson, NJ, (?).(?).1883 aged c 78.
Loco eng. Settled in Paterson 1833, and c 1835 was emp by Thomas Rogers (qv) as pattern maker and asst in const of Rogers' first loco, *Sandusky*, 1837. 1848 joined Samuel Smith of Paterson to form the loco wks of Swinburne, Smith & Co. 1851 became independent. Built some of the first long-bogie, level-cylinder 4–4–0s, establishing a standard American design. 1855 built some 4–4–0s for the Chicago & Alton RR, with cyls behind the bogie. In the commercial panic of 1857 the wks closed and the plant was sold to the

New York & Erie RR in 1858 for use as a repair shop. S. then ret and took up civic work in Paterson.

White, John H. Jr, *American Locos, an engg history 1830-80* 1968; Sinclair, Angus, *Development of the Loco Engine* 1907, 1970, pp 243-6 (portrait)

SYKES, Joseph Charles

b London (?).(?).1871; d London 5.1.1931 aged 59.
Signalling eng. Son of W.R.S. (qv), inventor of the lock & block signalling system. Ed King's Coll, London. Pupil of William Kirtley (qv) at Battersea loco wks, London. LC & DR. After experience in drg office and running dept took charge of Margate dist loco C & W dept. 1896 joined his f in mgt of W. R. Sykes signal wks, London and Glasgow, and took charge of electrical signalling on the LC & DR. Later the firm was converted into a limited liability company under the title of W. R. Sykes Interlocking Signal Co. S. became successively asst wks mgr, asst g mgr and, on the death of his bro, W.R.S. Jr, in 1908, became dir & mgr. Among numerous works carried out under S. were the electrical signalling of the G & SWR at St Enoch, Glasgow, and Dalry stns, and of Victoria stn, LBSCR, London. Latterly S. was hon sec ILE. MIME 1905.
Proc IME V 120 6.1931 p 757; *Engg* V 131 16.1.1931 p 87

SYKES, William

b Cortworth nr Wentworth, Yorks, 27.9.1815; d (?) Canada 3.4.1872 aged 56.
Trained on colliery and building works. When just over 20 he took a contract on the Midland R and in 1839 built a stn, engine house and workshops at Bromsgrove on the Birmingham & Gloucester R. 1846, with Wardrop, built a large portion of the R between Dumfries and Glasgow. In 1853 he went to Nova Scotia to survey a R and later returned to Canada as one of the firm of Sykes, De Bergue & Co, as contractors of the Brockville & Ottawa, and Montreal & Bytown (Ottawa) Rs, of which S. supervised the whole of the preliminary works. S. then moved to Upper Canada where he worked out a new system of tunnelling under rivers. While working on the Canada Southern

R he became ill and d. AICE 7.4.1868.
Min Proc ICE V 36 1872-3 p 305

SYKES, William Robert

b London (?).4.1840; d Bickley, Kent, 2.10.1917 aged 77.
Inventor of lock & block signalling system. 1863 entered service of LC & DR and within 2 yrs he had designed and installed an electrical repeater for indicating the position of signals out of sight of signalmen, an automatic recorder for showing what block signals the signalman had sent and received and, most important, had installed at Brixton in 1864 a short length of track circuiting. S. thereby preceded USA with this and also with automatic signals. In 1872 he devised a scheme whereby trains on the Met Dist R protected themselves automatically, similar to that installed later on the Paris Metropolitaine. The signals had red and white lights which were changed by the rise and fall of a red lens actuated electrically when a train passed over a contact. In 1874 he went to J. Staats Forbes (qv) with a scheme whereby the instruments at 3 successive signal boxes—Shepherds Lane, Brixton and Canterbury Jn—were to be controlled by the movement of the trains, and the instruments were to control the levers working the signals. The result was the original Sykes patent, No 662, of 23.2.1875, known as the 'lock and block'. Following an accident on 19.11.1875 the BOT reported favourably on the invention, and similarly in 24 subsequent reports in the next 10 yrs. Eventually the whole of the LC & DR, Hull & Barnsley, Met Dist, Mersey and Wirrall Rs were equipped with the apparatus. Other lines followed. In 1882 it was first installed in USA where, under the name 'controlled manual block system' it was extensively used on the NY, New Haven & Hartford RR, NYC, and other lines. It was also introduced in Russia and Japan. S. also devised the 'electro-mechanical' method of working points and signals in which signals were worked electrically and points by rods. This originated in 1875 when S. installed electrically worked signals at the ends of Penge tunnel. But the electro-mechanical system was not fully developed until 1900. On the formation of the SE & CR

in 1899 S. left the R and formed the W. R. Sykes Interlocking Signal Co. He was, however, retained by the SE & CR Jt Mg Comm as consultant electrical eng.
The Eng V 124 12.10.1917 p 319; *RM* V 41 11.1917 pp 349–50; *RG* 12.10.1917 p 410

SZLUMPER, Alfred Weeks

b Milford, Pembrokeshire, 24.5.1858; d Richmond, Surrey, 11.11.1934 aged 76. Chief civil eng, LSWR. Ed Aberystwyth Gr Sch and Univ of Wales. 1873 articled to his elder bro James (later Sir) S., then on R work in Wales, and was engaged as res eng and chief asst on Cardiff, Ogmore and other Welsh Rs. 1879 joined SER as asst to Francis Brady, chief eng. 1881 app res eng on a section of the GIPR with extensive bridge, vdt and improvement works. On his return to GB he was engaged with his bro on preparation of parl schemes for const of Rs in Wales and of Barry dock. 1884 app engg asst on staff of LSWR with which co he remained. At first he was engaged as res eng on extensive widening works between Waterloo, London, and Barnes, then with Thames bridges at Barnes and Richmond. Also widening Hampton Court Jn–Woking, Winchfield–Basingstoke and Worting Jn. 1897 app div eng London dist and was concerned with prelim work for rbg Waterloo stn, const of Bentley–Bordon Lt R; fly-over at Hampton Court Jn; Feltham gravity yard; and civil engg works for electrification in the London area from 1913. 1914 app chief eng. Major works included rbg Waterloo stn 1900–22, and Southampton docks. Ret 1927. During WW1 S. was lieut col in the Eng & R Staff Corps. MICE 1890 to which he presented many valuable papers.
Engg V 138 23.11.1934 p 570; *The Eng* V 158 16.11.1934 p 489 (portrait)

TEMPEST, Sir Percy Crosland

b Leeds 24.2.1860; d London 2.11.1924 aged 64.
G mgr and chief eng, SE & CR. Ed City of Leeds Gr Sch and Leeds Univ. Articled to Leeds borough eng. Began R career on LNWR extn into Leeds.

In 1881 joined the SER. 1895 app pw eng. Became chief eng when the SER and LC & DR came under jt mgt in 1899. In WW1 he was responsible for important govt work. On ret of Sir Francis Dent in 1920 T. was app g mgr and chief eng. 1923 became jt g mgr with Sir Herbert Walker (qv) of the SR, retiring when Walker was made sole g mgr. T. was an ardent supporter of the Channel tunnel project and was eng to the British Channel Tunnel Co from 1916. During WW1 T. acted as agent for the N R of France and for Belgian State Rs, and purchased large quantities of materials. For his war service he was made CBE in 1918, KBE 1923. Elected MICE 1897.
The Eng V 138 7.11.1924 p 520; *Engg* V 118 7.11.1924 p 649; *RG* 7.11.1924 p 616 (portrait)

TENNANT, Henry

b Countersett, Wensleydale, Yorks, (?).(?).1823; d York 25.5.1910 aged 86.
G mgr and chairman, NER. Ed Friends' sch, Ackworth nr Pontefract. Entered service of Brandling Jn R 21.2.1844. Became mgr of the Leeds & Thirsk (later Leeds Northern) R to which post he was app at age 25. He was the leading spirit on the Leeds Northern R when negotiations were entered into between that co and the York, Newcastle & Berwick and the Y & NM which in 1854 resulted in the formation of the NER. With the amalg he left Leeds and went to Newcastle where for c 18 yrs he was accountant and shared largely in the forming of the policy of the NER. 1871 app g mgr and took up residence at York. In addition to other duties he took charge of the loco dept during the interregnum of nearly a year in 1884–5 between the resignation of McDonnell (qv) and app of T. W. Worsdell (qv). During this period a series of 2-4-0s was built, known as the 'Tennant' class. (One is preserved at Darlington.) T. continued as g mgr until 1891 when he was app a NER dir. In 1892 the shareholders presented him with £10 000. In 1905–6 he was chairman jointly with Rt Hon John Lloyd Wharton and 1906–10 with Rt Hon Lord Knaresborough. He declined a knighthood because of his age.

The Eng V 109 27.5.1910 p 540; *The Locomotive* 6.1910 p 112; *Yorkshire Gazette* 28.5.1910; *Yorkshire Evening Press* 25.5.1910

THOM, Robert Absolom, OBE

b Aberdeen 14.6.1873; d Ilkley, Yorkshire, 2.11.1955 aged 82.
Loco C & W supt, Lancashire, Derbyshire & East Coast R; mech eng GCR and LNER. Received tech ed at Robert Gordon's Coll, Aberdeen. Apprenticed 1888–93 at loco C & W wks, GNSR, Kittybrewster. 1893–8 insp and dep wks foreman, GNSR. 1898 app foreman at the Met R wks, Neasden. Later wks foreman with Thomas Beeley & Sons, Hyde Jn, Manchester. In 10.1902 app loco C & W supt, LD & ECR, at the Tuxford wks in Nottinghamshire. In 5.1904 he brought out the large 0–6–4T which became class M1 on the LNER. On the absorption of the LD & ECR by the GCR in 1907 he transferred to Gorton, Manchester, under J. G. Robinson (qv), CME of the GCR. On the formation of the LNER on 1.1.1923 T. was app dist mech eng, GC section. In 1924 he became mech eng, Scottish area, and in 1927 mech eng at Doncaster. On 1.1.1934 he was app mech eng, southern area, LNER. Ret 1938.
Locos of the LNER (RCTS) pt 1 1963, pt 9; *RG* 18.11.1955 pp 600–1 (portrait); *Journal* ILE V 47 1955 p 450

THOMPSON, Edward, OBE

b Marlborough, Wilts, 25.6.1881; d Brymbo, Wrexham, 15.7.1954 aged 73.
Loco eng, NER, GNR, CME LNER. Only son of F.E.T., a master at Marlborough Coll where T. was ed. In 1902 grad in Mech Sciences Tripos at Pembroke Coll, Cambridge. Began training at Beyer, Peacock, Manchester, and later moved to the MR. 1905 joined staff of Royal Arsenal, Woolwich, for 1 yr. 1906 app to NER running dept, leading to his app as asst div loco supt, Gateshead, in 3.1909. While on the NER he visited USA. Early in 1912 he was app C & W supt on the GNR at Doncaster. In 3.1916 he returned to the Royal Arsenal at Woolwich on war service and in 12.1916 he went to France where he was attached to the hq staff of the Dir Gen of Transportation.

Became lieut col. In 3.1918 was twice mentioned in despatches and was awarded the OBE. In 3.1919 he returned to the GNR and in 1923 was app C & W workshops mgr, NE area, LNER. In 6.1927 he became asst mech eng at Stratford, London, and in 3.1930 he succeeded C. W. L. Glaze as mech eng, Stratford. He was responsible for the highly successful rbg of the 1500 class 4–6–0s and 'Claud Hamilton' 4–4–0s. On the death of Gresley (qv) in 1941 T. succeeded to the position of CME of the LNER, taking over at a period of great difficulty. His greatest success was the B1 class 4–6–0 of 1942; other types were the K1 class 2–6–0; and L1 2–6–4T of 1945. They were built in large numbers and gave good service. His 3-cyl A2/3 class 4–6–2s of 1946 were developed from rebuilt or redesigned Gresley engines. Unlike Gresley's 3-cyl engines, they had divided drive and 3 independent sets of Walschaert valve gear. By rebuilding the first Gresley 'Pacific', No 4470 *Great Northern*, to form a prototype A1 class, T. brought upon himself the wrath of hosts of loco enthusiasts. The A1 was redesigned and produced by his successor A. H. Peppercorn (qv). T. ret, at age 65, on 30.6.1946. He was a man of great warmth and kindness, greatly loved by those who knew him well.
The Eng V 198 23.7.1954 p 128; *Engg* V 178 23.7.1954 p 100; *RG* 21.6.1946 p 671; 23.7.1954 p 103; RCTS *Locos of the LNER* pts 1, 2A, 2B, 6, 9

THOMSON, John Edgar

b Springfield Township, Delaware Co, Pa, USA, 10.2.1808; d Philadelphia, Pa, 27.5.1874 aged 66.
Civil eng, and 3rd president of the Pennsylvania RR. Descended from a Quaker family. His f was a civil eng and was engaged on const of the Delaware & Chesapeake canal. After little formal ed he worked with his f on engg projects and became M of a team surveying a R from Philadelphia to Columbia on which he became asst eng. In 1830 he was given charge of a div of the Camden & Amboy RR, NJ. On its completion he visited Europe to study R transport and British civil and mech engg practice. Returned to USA 1832

and was app chief eng of the Georgia RR for a line from Augusta to Atlanta. He remained with this company for 15 yrs, becoming famous as an engg authority. In 1849 the PRR was incorporated to build a R from Harrisburg to Pittsburgh to by-pass the old Portage RR and canals. T. was app chief eng and located the line through the Alleghenies with the famous Horseshoe Curve and with practicable gradients. It was op in 2.1854. Meanwhile, in 1852, T. had been made president. Through his dealings the PRR came into possession of the entire 'State Works', 278 miles (447km) of canals and 117 miles (188km) of R and all equipment for $7 500 000. His determination to expand the system led in 1856 to the amalg of various western lines into the Pittsburgh, Fort Wayne & Chicago R which was leased to the PRR in 1869. In 1870-1 the Pennsylvania Co was formed to take over the property W of Pittsburgh. Through T's negotiations in 1871 the PRR reached New York by the lease of the United Cos of NJ, 456 miles (734km) of R and 65 miles (105km) of canal. In 1869 he decided upon an independent line from Baltimore to Washington, and in 1873 he effected a connection with the southern States by a one sixth interest in the Southern R Security Co. In 1870 T. was instrumental in establishing the American Steamship Co under the patronage of the PRR, thereby making Philadelphia a trans-Atlantic port. Late in life he m Lavinia Smith. They had no children.
DAB V 18 pp 486-7; Burgess, G. H., and Kennedy, M. C., *Centennial History of the Pennsylvania RR Co* 1949

THOMSON, Peter

b Forgue nr Hurley, Aberdeenshire, c 1815; d Liverpool 13.5.1876 aged c 61.
R contractor. Son of a builder. At age 22 he joined his elder bro George, by then a noted R contractor, and after a few yrs became a partner. He also joined the firm of Rennie, Logan & Co of Newport, Monmouthshire. In 1847-9 he went to Heywood nr Rochdale and had charge of const of part of the Liverpool & Bury R (part of LYR), and of extn of LYR Oldham branch. In 1849 he returned to Liverpool where he established hq. He also worked on the Tithebarn

Street extn and stn of the LYR at Liverpool; part of the Liverpool–Southport Line and N Docks branch; and LNWR works at Liverpool. Other works included the Leeds, Bradford & Halifax Jn R (GNR); LNWR and MR works in Leeds, 1848-9; the MR between Whitacre and Nuneaton; Newport, Abergavenny & Hereford R; a part of the S Wales R between Newport and Swansea; docks at Newport and Penarth; LNWR Edgehill–Bootle and Canada Dock branch; LYR North Mersey branch; LNWR Huyton–St Helens; most of the MR Chesterfield–Sheffield line; Leeds New Station and its connection to the NER; part of the MR (Leeds & Bradford R) Shipley–Bingley; part of the MR through Darley Dale and Rowsley–Buxton with its difficult engg works through the Wye valley. With his bro T. became proprietor of the ironworks at Normanton. After the death of George T. at Cheltenham in 1867 he had to carry the whole of the responsibility for the works. His great practical knowledge led to his being frequently consulted by principal engs. On ret from business he became a dir of the LYR. In 11.1875 he was elected chief magistrate of Liverpool; and was also a JP for Lancashire.
Min Proc ICE V 44 1875-6 pp 235-7

THORNTON, Sir Henry Worth

b Logansport, Indiana, USA, 6.11.1871; d New York 14.3.1933 aged 61.
Chairman, CNR. Son of Henry Clay and Millamenta Comegys (Worth) T. Grad St Paul's Sch, Concord, NH, 1890; B Sc Univ of Pa 1894; D Sc 1923. On 20.6. 1901 m Virginia Dike Blair of Newcastle, Pa. They had 1 dr and 1 son. On 11.9.1926 m Martha Watriss of New York. 1894 began as a draughtsman in the office of the chief eng of the SW System of Pennsylvania Lines West of Pittsburgh. 1895-6 asst eng of const, Cleveland & Marietta RR (sibsid of PRR). Later emp in field work of the SW System; supervisor of yards at Columbus, Ohio; asst eng Cincinnati div, and asst eng in special work; 1899-1901 eng of maintenance of way, Erie & Ashtabula div of NW System of PRR; 1901-2 supt Cleveland, Akron & Columbus RR and of the Erie & Ashtabula div in 1902-11. The Long Island RR was

acquired by the PRR in 1911 and in Feb he was app asst g supt; in Nov g supt until 1914. He was largely responsible for the opening of the PRR terminal in New York City and the organisation of the company's electric services on Long Island. In 1914 he was app g mgr of the GER, England, when the chairman, Lord Claud Hamilton, declared that a suitable man could not be found in England. He served on the executive comm of g mgrs which, under the direction of the govt, controlled and worked the British Rs in WW1. 1916 app dep dir of inland water transportation with rank of Col in the REs. 1917 asst dir gen of movements of Rs in France. 12.1917 dir gen of same with rank of Brig Gen. 1918 insp gen of transportation with rank of Maj Gen. 1919 became naturalised British subject and made KCBE. Served on comm to investigate operations and financial condition of Metropolitan Water Bd, London, 1920. In 1922 he resigned from the GER and in 10.1922 was app chairman and president, CNR. He completely reorganised the system, welding the GT, GTP, Canadian Northern and Intercolonial Rs into one efficient entity. He took over mgt of Canadian National Steamships and the Central Vermont R as well as the lines of the GT in USA. After being a political liability, under T. the CNR with its 22 000 miles (35 400km) of route and many subsidiaries became divorced from political interference and was brought to a high standard of efficiency and financial success. T. was the first Canadian R executive to install radio communication in passenger trains. It was first tried on the Montreal–Toronto and Montreal–Quebec lines in 1924 and proved highly successful. He also inaugurated telephone communication between a running train and distant points, in 4.1930, on a train running at 60 mph (96.5km/h) between Toronto and Montreal, and conversations were made with Washington and London. He resigned on 19.7.1932, after criticism of expenditure and of his taking time off in 1927 to survey the Mexican R situation. He also declared that the govt had not maintained its policy of non-interference. He was MICE, M Inst T and M American Soc of Mech Engs.

NYT 15.3.1933 p 17 (portrait); *The Eng* V 155 17.3.1933 p 263

TOLMÉ, Julian Horn

b Havana, Cuba, 28.1.1836; d Lindfield, Sussex, 25.12.1878 aged 42.
Civil eng. 1855–60 articled to Locke & Errington (qqv), being emp largely under the latter, then chief eng LSWR. On the death of Errington in 1862 T. joined with W. R. Galbraith (qv), one of the partners, to continue the work of the firm. Galbraith was app eng of the LSWR and T. was left to carry on the firm. The partnership was dissolved in 1869. Among works carried out by T. were the Thames Valley R 1863; Mid Hants R (Winchester–Alton) op 1865; Garstang & Knott End R 1864–70; completion of Shrewsbury & N Wales R; Newport Pagnell R; Harborne R; Wigtownshire R, 1872–5; and, in conj with A. S. Hamand, T. was eng for Birmingham Dist Tramways; Halesowen R; and Whitby, Redcar & Middlesbrough Union R. With F. S. Gilbert he was eng of the Met Dist Extn to Hammersmith. One of his last works was laying out the Devils Dyke branch nr Brighton, not, however, opened until 1887. MICE 13.3.1866.
Min Proc ICE V 55 1878–9 pp 319–20

TOMLINSON, Joseph

b London 11.11.1823; d West Hampstead, London, 22.4.1894 aged 70.
Loco supt, Taff Vale R, Wales; res eng and loco supt Met R. Ed at private sch 1831–6; London and Darlington 1836–7. Trained at Shildon wks, Stockton & Darlington R, under T. Hackworth (qv) 1837–9; and Miles Plating wks, Manchester & Leeds R, 1839–42. Returned to the S & DR until 7.1846 when he became outdoor foreman at Nine Elms, LSWR London, under J. V. Gooch (qv), and had charge of engines and their work in the London dist until 30.6.1852, from 1850 under Joseph Beattie (qv). 1852 joined LNWR at Crewe as draughtsman under F. Trevithick and Alexander Allan (qqv). On the app of Allan to the Scottish Central R in 1853 T. was app his asst. 1854 app asst to M. Kirtley (qv) on the MR in charge of the outdoor dept. In 1.1858 app loco supt Taff Vale R, Cardiff. 1869 resigned

from TVR to become consulting eng in marine and civil engg until 1872 when he was invited to join the Met R as res eng and loco supt until he resigned on 8.4.1885 to become a consulting eng and a dir of the TVR. T. was MICE and MIME.

The Eng V 77 4.5.1894 pp 378, 402 (portrait); Min Proc ICE V 117 1893–4 pp 388–90; Proc IME 1894 p 163

TRAILL, William Acheson

b Bushmills, Ireland, (?).(?).1844; d Portstewart, Ireland 6.7.1933 aged 89. Eng of Giant's Causeway electric tramway, the first to use hydro-electric power. Ed at private schools and Trinity Coll, Dublin. Grad 1865 and M Eng 1873. 1868 joined geological survey of Ireland. Resigned 1881. T. conceived the idea for the Giant's Causeway tramway between Portrush and Bushmills with the support of William Siemens (qv). Two Acts had to be obtained, against strong opposition. It was op 1883. The original side collectors were replaced by trolley arms in 1900. In 1884 T. patented an underground conduit current collection system later used on London tramways in a modified form.

Engg V 136 14.7.1933 p 47; *The Eng* V 156 14.7.1933 p 25; *The Locomotive* 7.1933 p 213

TRENCH, Ernest F. Crosbie, CBE

b Ardfert Abbey, Co Kerry, Ireland, 6.8.1869; d nr Marlborough, Wilts, 15.9.1960 aged 91.
Chief eng LNWR. Cousin of Louis T. (qv). Ed Monkton Combe Sch, Bath, and at Lausanne, Switzerland. 1888–92 Univ of Dublin; grad BA and BAI in Engg; MA 1903. 1893 began as a pupil under E. B. Thornhill, then chief eng LNWR. Spent part of time in drg office at Euston, London, and as asst on various works. 1895 worked on the Spen Valley line between Huddersfield and Leeds, first as pupil, then as asst eng. 1899 app res eng on MR and supervised several important widening works including the Alfreton second tunnel on which he read a paper to the ICE in 1905. In 1.1903 app chief eng N London R on which he carried out strengthening works. 1.3.1906 returned to LNWR, first as asst eng and, on 1.3.1909, as chief

asst eng until ret of Thornhill in 9.1909. T. succeeded him as chief eng from 1.10.1909. Remained in this position until grouping in 1923 when he became chief eng, LMS. His obstructiveness towards designs for LMS standard locos soon after grouping led to the resignation of George Hughes (qv) and the transfer of LMS loco design from Horwich to Derby. From 1.2.1927 adopted the position of consulting eng, LMS, until he ret on 31.3.1930. T. was president ICE 1927–8. Also M Inst T. His last public act was the unveiling of the centenary plaque on Robert Stephenson's tubular bridge on 3.11.1950.

RM 11.1909 p 417; 10.1915 p 251; 3.1927 p 241; *Modern Transport* 11.3.1922; 5.2.1927; 17.9.1927; *RG* 4.2.1927; 5.10. 1960 p 409; 7.10.1960 p 428 (portrait)

TRENCH, Louis

b (?), Ireland, (?).(?).1846; d (?) 30.1.1940 aged 93.
First chief eng of the GWR; later eng on LNWR. Cousin of E.F.C.T. (qv). After graduating at Cambridge he served as a pupil of James Barton, an eng in private practice in Ireland, and was engaged on the const of the Dundalk, Newry & Greenore R. When this was taken over by the LNWR T. went to England and worked for the LNWR on several important works. Became a div eng in charge of maintenance of the S Wales div and later of the Birmingham div. In 2.1891 he was app first chief eng, GWR, and was responsible for the fine organisation which governed the final abolition of the broad gauge without interruption of traffic. A disagreement led to his resignation from the GWR in 10.1892 and his return to the LNWR. In 1894 he supervised const of the Spen Valley line between Huddersfield and Leeds with his cousin E.F.C.T. as asst. Later he went to Euston, London, as asst for new works to E. B. Thornhill. When Thornhill ret in 1909 T. was 63 and was considered too near ret for app as chief eng, so E.F.C.T., 23 yrs his junior, was app. T. assisted his cousin for 2 yrs until he ret in 1911. T. was a strong, upright man, with an uncompromising outlook, and no patience with fools. But he gained the confidence, esteem and affection of many.

The Eng V 169 23.2.1940 p 188

TREVITHICK, Francis

b Cornwall (?).(?).1812; d Penzance
27.10.1877 aged 65.
Loco eng LNWR. Eldest son of Richard
T. (qv). 1840 became res eng on the
GJR between Birmingham and Crewe.
1841 app loco supt, GJR, at Edge Hill,
Liverpool, in succession to Buddicom
(qv). In 1843 he was transferred to the
new wks at Crewe as loco supt, N Div.
(McConnell, qv, was in charge of the
S Div at Wolverton.) In 1857 the N and
NE Divs were combined; T. was forced
to resign and was succeeded by John
Ramsbottom (qv) who had been NE Div
loco supt at Longsight, Manchester, since
1842. In 1872 T. pub his *Life of Richard
Trevithick*.
The Eng V 44 10.1877 p 314

TREVITHICK, Frederick Harvey

b Crewe (?).(?).1852; d Avignon, France,
9.12.1931 aged 79.
CME of Egyptian State Rs. Son of
Francis T. (qv), loco supt LNWR, and
grandson of Richard T. (qv). Ed at
Cheltenham Coll. Apprenticed with
Harvey & Co, Hayle, Cornwall, afterwards working in the GWR shops at
Swindon. In 1880 he became C & W
supt of the GWR, London dist, at Westbourne Park. 1883 app chief traction
eng (later CME) of the Egyptian State
R, taking part in the reorganising
scheme of Sir Evelyn Baring. At the
time the Egyptian Rs were in a deplor-
able condition. No loco was less than
20 yrs old, and nearly all rolling stock
was at least 12 and mostly about 30 yrs
old. The average no of engines per class
was less than 2. T. set about building up
a stock of sound locos and rolling stock.
After 20 yrs the number of loco types
was reduced from 54 to 22 and the
average no of engines per class was 20.
Latterly T. conducted trials on feed
water heating and superheating. In 1884
he was sent to Russia to report on the
petroleum industry; in 1896 to India to
report on Rs; in 1900 to Canada and
USA. He became MICE 1891, MILE
and MIME in 1913. He had ret to
Richmond, Surrey, and was on a journey
to revisit Egypt when he d.
Engg V 132 18.12.1931 pp 769–70; *The*

Locomotive 2.1932 p 36; Proc IME V
121 12.1931 p 618; *Journal* ILE V 22
1932 p 157

TREVITHICK, Frederick Henry

b (?) 6.11.1843; d Exeter 19.9.1893
aged 49.
Son of F.H.T., loco supt of the GTR,
Canada, Nephew of Francis T., loco supt
LNWR, Crewe, and grandson of Richard
T. At age 18 began as a pupil at the
works at Hayle, Cornwall, founded by
his great grandfather John Harvey. In
1862 he entered the drg office of the
LNWR at Crewe. In 1864 he was app
to take charge of the R between Frank-
furt and Homburg, 12 miles (19.3km).
1866 became mgr of the Danish Rs
until they were taken over by the state
in 1868. 1869–71 T. was in the loco
dept of the Central Pacific RR at
Sacramento, California. 1871 returned to
England and was engaged on const work
at Cardiff. 1874 app eng and mgr of the
Isle of Man R. 1876 went to India to
succeed W. Barton Wright (qv) as loco
supt of the Madras R. In 4.1891 ill
health forced his resignation. MICE
19.5.1885.
Min Proc ICE V 115 1893–4 p 396

TREVITHICK, Richard

b Illogan, Cornwall, 13.4.1771;
d Dartford, Kent, 22.4.1833 aged 62.
Inventor of the high pressure steam
engine. Son of Richard T. (1735–1.8.
1797), Cornish mines mgr. T. displayed
mathematical and mechanical ability at
an early age and was renowned for his
feats of strength. He began by improving the Boulton & Watt 1p engines. On
the expiry of Watt's patent in 1800 T.
built a double-acting hp engine. From
1796 he built working model locos using
hp steam. 1800–1 built a steam carriage
which, on 24.12.1801, was the first
vehicle to convey passengers by the force
of steam. On 24.3.1802 he obtained a
patent for which the specification was
drawn up by Peter Nicholson. In this use
of hp steam he was only just in advance
of Oliver Evans (qv) of Philadelphia. T.
built a second steam carriage in 1803
and exhibited it in London. In the same
year he built a loco which worked on a
3ft (0.914m) g plateway at Coalbrookdale
in Shropshire. This was the first loco to

run on rails. It was built at the Coalbrookdale ironworks. This is the engine whose drawing is well known and of which a model can be seen at the NRM, York. He built his second loco while employed as eng at the Penydarren ironworks nr Merthyr Tydfil, Wales. Drawings of this can be seen at the Science Museum, London. On 22.2.1804 it pulled 10 tons of iron, 70 men and 5 extra wagons for $9\frac{1}{2}$ miles (15.3km) at nearly 5mph (8km/h) excluding stops. Like the Coalbrookdale loco it had a single horizontal cylinder and flywheel. It was the first loco to have a return flue boiler, steam blast in the chimney and all four wheels driving, by gearing. A third engine was built at Gateshead by John Whinfield, to a design by T., in 1805, but at 5 tons it proved too heavy for the rails. It was the first loco to have flanged wheels. Drawings of it can be seen at the Science Museum, London. In 1808 T. built his fourth and last loco, named *Catch me who can*, for demonstration on a circular track in London. Nothing seems to be known of the actual form of this loco. Having failed to interest industrialists in the steam loco for use on rails T. abandoned his interest in it. From 1803–7 he was engaged in improving a steam dredger in the Thames estuary. In 8.1807 he began a tunnel under the Thames at Rotherhithe, which was abandoned when the driftway was three quarters finished. The project was taken up again in 1825 by Marc Brunel (qv) who completed it in 1843. In 1811 T. built a steam threshing machine at Hayle foundry in Cornwall. It is now in the Science Museum, London. In 1814 he built 9 engines for mines in Peru and in 1816 went out there to supervise their installation and operation, arriving in Lima in 2.1817. He remained as eng for 10 yrs, but was ruined in the war of independence and his return to England had to be assisted by Robert Stephenson (qv). He arrived on 9.10.1827. His last patent, for the use of superheated steam, was dated 22.9.1832. He d in dept while working at John Hall's workshop at Dartford, Kent. He was given a proper funeral by the workmen. On 7.11.1797 he m Jane Harvey (1772–1868) of Hayle. They had 4 sons and 2 drs. Francis T. (qv) became loco supt of the LNWR,

and wrote a biography of T.
Trevithick, F. *Life* 1872; Warren, J. G. H., *A century of loco building 1823–1923* 1923, 1970; *The Eng* 4.3.1921 pp 242–4; 28.4.1933 pp 416–19; 5.5.1933 pp 442–4; *Engg* 21.4.1933 pp 439–41; 30.6.1933 pp 693–5

TREVITHICK, Richard Francis

b Cornwall 11.12.1845; d Southampton 13.12.1913 aged 67.
Grandson of Richard T. Apprenticed to Harvey & Co, Hayle, Cornwall. 1867 entered Crewe loco wks, LNWR. 1871 app CME on the Rosario–Cordova R, Argentina. Later he was app CME on Ceylon Govt Rs, and then on the W Div of the Imperial Govt Rs, Japan. Responsible for the first loco built in Japan. At his ret in 1904 he was the last foreign R official to leave the country. Elected MICE 5.5.1885.
Min Proc ICE V 192 1913 p 322; *Engg* V 95 28.2.1913 p 303

TREVITHICK, Robert Lowthian

b Cornwall 31.8.1848; d Clifton, Bristol, 3.2.1933 aged 84.
Loco, C & W eng, MR and GIPR. Grandson of Richard T. (qv). In 10.1866 he entered the fitting and erecting shops of Harvey & Co, engs, of Hayle, Cornwall. From 4.1870 he continued his training in the erecting shops of the GWR at Swindon, and remained there until 9.1872. After a year in Portugal on various engg works he returned to England to take up an appointment in the drg office of the GWR. In 1.1876 he was app to the MR at Derby where he took charge of the machine shop of the C & W wks. In 9.1876 he became dist loco supt on the GIPR until, in 4.1891, he was promoted to loco C & W supt of the R where he remained until he ret in 1901. MICE 12.12.1897.
Engg 17.2.1933 p 197

TURNER, Frederick Thomas

b Hereford 4.8.1812; d London 21.8.1877 aged 65.
Civil eng, LC & DR. Ed Margate. Articled to John Fawcetts, surveyor, London. Later becoming asst to J. U. Rastrick (qv) on London–Brighton R. 1845–6 worked under Frank Giles on Rs in Sussex, Staffordshire and Shropshire.

1847–9 eng to John Tredwell on N Kent R. 1852 went to Spain on R surveys then, in 1853, to Russia to lay out a R from St Petersburg to Peterhoff. From 1854 to his ret T. was continuously engaged on Rs in Kent. 1857–61 Faversham–Herne Bay, then extns to Margate and Ramsgate, 1863. 1858 laid out extn of the E Kent R from jn with SER at Strood to Bickley, op 1860. T. then projected the London extns of the LC & DR to Victoria and Farringdon Street, op 1866, and the semi-circular R from Victoria to Ludgate Hill, London, via Brixton, including several heavy engg works. His last major work was the line to Crystal Palace High Level, op 1.8. 1865. MICE 6.2.1866.

Min Proc ICE V 50 1876–7 pp 181–4

TWINBERROW, James Denis

b (?) 9.10.1866; d Bickley, Kent, 10.2.1932 aged 65.

Designer of locos and rolling stock. Ed Bedford, and Armstrong Coll, Newcastle upon Tyne. Apprenticed under T. W. Worsdell (qv) at Stratford, GER, London, moving to Gateshead in 4.1885 when Worsdell was app loco supt, NER. For 2 yrs he was inspector on testing materials for the NER. 1891 took charge of a copper smelting wks in Wales. 1892 joined staff of Chester Hydraulic Engg Co in design of Pelton wheels and Hydraulic gear. 1894 was with Elliott Metal Co, Birmingham. Later engg mgr at Saltley wks of Patent Axlebox & Foundry Co Ltd. 1897–1905 joined G. H. Sheffield to form the firm of Sheffield & Twinberrow at Newcastle, designing power station structures, self-acting R inclines, steelwork for buildings, and steam engines; also all-steel high-capacity R wagons. 1905–10 chief draughtsman of NER C & W dept. 1910–12 travelled in Canada, USA and Europe. 1913–30 on staff of Merz & Maclellan, consulting engs, Newcastle, then London. Worked on mechanical sections of electric locos and rolling stock. Early 1931 began as consulting eng in Westminster, specialising in electric locos and rolling stock; also took special interest in development of diesel-electric locos, in the future of which he believed strongly. T. was MICE 1893, MIME 1902, MILE. He had wide interests, was a fair classical scholar,

mastered 4 languages and was a student of literature. On 29.1.1932 he read a paper to the IME on the mechanism of electric locos.

The Eng V 153 19.2.1932 p 215; *The Locomotive* 3.1932 p 97; *Engg* V 133 10.2.1932 p 215; *Journal* ILE V 22 1932 p 265; *RG* V 56 19.2.1932 p 257; Proc IME V 122 1932 p 736

TYE, William Francis

b Haysville, Ontario, Canada, 5.3.1861; d Paris 9.1.1932 aged 70.

Eng on Rs in N America. Ed at Ottawa Coll, and Sch of Practical Science, Toronto, 1878–81. 1882 entered service of CPR and until 1885 was engaged as rodman, transitman and asst eng on const of the line from Winnipeg to British Columbia, and in 1886–7 on the St Paul, Minneapolis & Manitoba R, Montana extn. In 1887 he was in Mexico, first as track and bridge eng on the Mexican Central R, and then as mining eng. For the next 2 yrs he was successively div eng on the Great Falls & Canada R in Montana, and on the Great Northern R in charge of const W of the Cascade Range in Washington. In 1895 he was chief eng of the Kaslo & Slocan R, BC, and of the Columbia & Western R, Columbia, from 1896–9. In 1900 he became chief eng of const, in 1903 asst chief eng, and in 1904 chief eng of the CPR. In 1906 he ret from that office and practised as consulting eng. He was at one time president of the Sterling Coal Co. In 1920 he left Canada and travelled extensively throughout Europe. In the course of one of his train journeys he was seized with sudden illness and he d in Paris. T. became M Eng Inst of Canada 1896, served on its council 1905–10 and was president in 1912. He became MICE 11.1.1910. In 1898 he m Mabel S. Moloney who survived him.

Min Proc ICE V 235 1932–3 p 512

TYER, Edward

b Kennington, London, 6.2.1830; d Tunbridge Wells 25.12.1912 aged 82.

Developer of R signalling and telegraph. Ed City of London Sch. After a short period in his uncle's city office he decided to devote himself to the development of electrical appliances. In 1852 he took out a patent for an electrical signalling device operating on the engine, and this became the first of a long series of inventions which did much to bring R signalling to a high state of efficiency. Among his more important inventions were his ingenious instruments used in his system of block signalling, and especially the tablet system introduced in England in 1878 (following the Thorpe accident on the GER in which 25 were killed) and later used all over the world. T. first used a single-wire system and later developed the three-wire system. He was also a pioneer in telegraphic communication, originating what became the postal telegraph service of London. He was the founder of the firm of Tyer & Co Ltd and undertook much work at home and abroad. He took a keen interest in scientific progress and was a Fellow of the Royal Astronomical, Geographical, and Microscopical Societies, and a MIEE 1883. AICE 1861. His last patent was granted in 1910, when he was 80.

Min Proc ICE V 195 1914 p 379; *Engg* V 95 3.1.1913 p 24; *The Eng* V 115 3.1.1913 p 22

UNDERWOOD, John

b (?) (?).1.1814; d (?) 15.8.1893 aged 79. Civil eng, MR. Began with J. U. Rastrick (qv) preparing plans and sections for part of the London–Brighton R, and later becoming res eng for the section including Merstham tunnel. In 1845 Rastrick, then too busy, handed over to U. the completion of the Nottingham & Grantham R, opened 15.7.1850, the only section built under the Ambergate, Nottingham, Boston & Eastern Jn R Act. Curiously, nearly 25 yrs later, U. built the Ambergate–Codner Park line of the MR, op 1.5.1875, following nearly the same course as the western part of the original Ambergate line. U. took into partnership Andrew Johnston, and for several years they practised as engs in Nottingham. On his app as chief eng of the MR in 1858 J. S. Crossley (qv) induced U. to become a M of his staff. At this time the MR was extending in many directions and U. was kept busy. Under Crossley he carried out the Mansfield–Worksop, op 1.6.1875; Cudworth–Barnsley including the great iron vdt nr

Barnsley, op 28.6.1869; Chesterfield–Sheffield, op 1.2.1870; Mangotsfield–Bath, op 4.8.1869; and branches in Derbyshire and West Riding. The greatest project was the Settle & Carlisle line, begun in 1869 and op 1.5.1876. Following Crossley's ret in 1875 U. was app eng in charge of new const. Among the lines he carried out were Nottingham–Melton Mowbray, op 1.11.1879; Skipton–Ilkley, op 1888, the new approach into Birmingham from the west, op 1.10.1885, which placed Birmingham stn on the route from Derby to Bristol. He also carried out const of several MR lines around Manchester and Liverpool and he was responsible for works in London such as Poplar dock and its rail connections, the depots in Whitecross Street, the vast extns of Somers Town gds stn on Euston Road and at St Pancras where he covered an area of above 10 acres (4.047ha) with iron girders on columns to support one goods yard about another, using 20 000 tons of iron. He ret in 1889 because of failing sight. He was a man of genial and unassuming manners and was highly regarded by all his staff. His work was always thorough; he detested 'cheese paring' designs often carried out by engs on speculative lines. U. was one of the few important engs who never became MICE. When often asked to do so he replied 'I did not in my early days and now I am too old'.

The Eng V 76 25.8.1893 p 199

URIE, Robert Wallace

b Ardeer 22.10.1854; d Largs, Ayrshire, 6.1.1937 aged 82.
Last CME of the LSWR. Ed Glasgow High Sch. 1869 began a 6 yr apprenticeship in Glasgow at Gauldie, Marshall & Co; Dübs & Co, and William King & Co. He then worked as draughtsman at various loco builders. Joined the CR as draughtsman under D. Drummond (qv). 1890 became chief draughtsman at St Rollox wks, CR, Glasgow. 1896 wks mgr. 1897 moved with Drummond to the LSWR as wks mgr at Nine Elms, London. 1909 transferred to the new wks at Eastleigh, nr Southampton. 1912 succeeded Drummond as CME, holding the post until the LSWR was absorbed into the SR on 1.1.1923 when he ret. During WW1 served on comm of loco

engs for designs of standard locos during the war and organised Eastleigh wks for munition mfr. His loco designs were simple and robust, all with 2 o/c. They were 3 classes of 4-6-0, one of which formed the pattern for the 'King Arthur' class; 4-8-0T and 4-6-2T. He rebuilt the Drummond 'paddlebox' 4-6-0 into a better machine. Designed the 'Eastleigh' superheater. MIME 1898. Proc IME V 135 1937 p 565; *The Locomotive* 2.1937 p 53

URIE, William M.

b Glasgow (?).(?).1850; d Bishopbriggs, Scotland, 9.12.1917 aged 67.
Wks mgr, St Rollox, CR, Glasgow. Ed St Enoch's Sch and Training Coll, Glasgow. Served a 6 yr apprenticeship in Hyde Park Loco Wks and Glasgow Loco Wks. From 1870 he worked in the Fairfield Wks of John Elder & Co; Bowershall Wks, Leith; Palmers Wks, Jarrow; and Beyer Peacock, Manchester. He then went to the Belgian Loco Wks, Brussels, as draughtsman, and Gouin's Loco Wks, Paris, returning to Brussels as draughtsman. For 8 yrs from 1875 he was draughtsman of the NBR wks at Cowlairs, Glasgow, and afterwards occupied a senior position in the CR wks. 1883-7 he was eng and mgr of the Steam Tramway Co, Singapore. Returning to Glasgow he served as asst to John Strain. 1889 went as draughtsman, then chief draughtsman, at the CR St Rollox wks. Later became wks mgr and close personal friend of J. F. McIntosh (qv). He ret about the same time as McIntosh, in 1914. MIME 1899.
Engg V 104 14.12.1917 p 626

VANDERBILT, Cornelius

b Port Richmond, Staten Island, NY, 27.5.1794; d New York 4.1.1877 aged 83.
American steamship and RR promoter and financier. His paternal ancestors, van der Bilt, were Dutch and settled in Long Island in 1670-1700. His f was a farmer and boat operator of poor means. V. had little formal ed. At about 16 he bought a small sailing boat and began a freight and passenger ferry between Staten Island and New York City. On 19.12.1813 he m his cousin Sophia Johnson. In the war of 1812 his business grew and he soon had several boats and was trading up the Hudson River and along the coast from New England to Charleston. 1818 entered a shipping business on the New York-Philadelphia route. In 1829 V. and his wife, having amassed a good fortune by their considerable exertions, and with a large family, moved to New York where he established a shipping line on the Hudson River, eliminating competitors by rate cutting. He greatly improved the size and comfort of the river vessels, and in 1846 launched the finest boat on the Hudson up to that time. By now he was a millionaire. In the gold rush of 1849 he developed a new shorter route to California via Nicaragua and captured most of the traffic. His career as RR promotor began in 1862 and he became president of the NY & Harlem RR. He next gained control of the Hudson River RR and in 1867 of the NYC. He spent $2 mil on improvements, and in 1869 united the two RRs as the NYC & Hudson River RR. In 1872 he leased the Harlem RR to it. In 1873 he gained control of the Lake Shore & Michigan Southern R and in 1875 the Michigan Central RR and Canada Southern R, so creating one of the greatest American RR systems. In his last years he had a stabilising influence on American finance, and in the panic of 1873 he built the Grand Central Terminal in New York City, with 4-track approaches, giving employment to thousands of men. His first wife d 1868. On 21.8.1869 he m Frank(?) Armstrong Crawford. He left a fortune of over $100 mil. His great-grandson Cornelius (qv) became a loco eng on the NYC. V. regarded RRs as a source of financial gain and was unconcerned for their function as a public service.
NY Tribune, NYT, 5.1.1877; DAB V 19 pp 169-73

VANDERBILT, Brig Gen Cornelius

b New York 5.9.1873; d Miami Beach, Fl, 1.3.1942 aged 68.
Loco eng. One of 7 children of Cornelius V. and Alice Claypoole (Gwynne) and great-grandson of Commodore Cornelius V. (qv), RR financier. Ed privately and at St Paul's Sch, Concord, NH; and Yale Univ. BA 1895; B Phil 1898; Mech Engg

degree 1899. While at coll he frequented the NYC shops and design dept to study loco engg. Disregarding family opposition V. m Grace Wilson on 3.8.1896 and so forfeited his V. inheritance on the d of his f in 1899. Partial reconciliation was achieved by his sister Gertrude, but not until 1926 was the family breach healed. His mother left him an interest in her residuary estate on her death in 1934. The Vs led a brilliant social life. In Germany he befriended Kaiser Wilhelm, and they entertained Prince Henry of Russia when he visited New York in 1902. They also entertained King Edward VII and George V of England on their yacht during frequent visits before WW1. In 1919 they were hosts to King Albert and Queen Elizabeth of Belgium. Meanwhile V. was devoting ever more time to loco and mech engg. He patented over 30 devices for improving locos and freight cars including several which brought him large royalties. One of the most important was a circular corrugated firebox for locos, resembling that introduced by Lentz (qv) in Germany in 1888, dispensing with stays. (See also H. A. Hoy.) He patented this, with a tapered boiler, in 1899. It was adopted by the Missouri Pacific and Baltimore & Ohio RRs before the NYC took it up. About 10 or 12 such boilers were made and were fitted to 2-6-0, 4-6-0 and 2-8-0 types. Grate area was too small to sustain high enough steaming rates and the boilers were soon discarded. He also invented a cylindrical tank car for oil and a cylindrical loco tender, and made many improvements and refinements of detail in other types of equipment. On his frequent visits abroad V's keen interest led him to study closely the London and Paris underground R systems. He realised that New York would soon need subways and on his return he associated with August Belmont in organising the Interborough Rapid Transit Co for the const of the first New York subway. His business activities were constantly broadening and by the early 20th century he was a M of bds of dirs of many important corporations, including RRs, banks and insurance companies. He made himself familiar with every aspect of the businesses. His expanding activities lessened the time available for R engg, but he maintained his interest. Besides all these interests he also became a soldier. On 20.9.1901 he became 2nd lieut of the 12th Infantry Regt, NY National Guard, and remained in its service 33 yrs. After the Villa raids on the Mexican frontier in 1916 V. served at the border and was made Col in command of the 22nd Engs. In WW1 he served overseas and on 26.6.1918 was commissioned Brig Gen in command of the 25th infantry brigade. He continued to serve in reserves until 1.1935 when he asked to be relieved because of his business interests. He received the DSM of USA and many other military distinctions. His favourite recreation was yachting and he owned several vessels. In his schooner yacht *Atlantic* bought in 1922 he won a trans-Atlantic race for a cup from the Kaiser. V. had 1 son, Cornelius, b 1898 and 1 dr, Grace, b 1900. The son became a journalist and writer and in 1923 founded the Vanderbilt Newspapers Inc. Late in 3.1940 V. suffered a severe illness aboard his yacht *Sabiha III* at Miami Beach and it was there, on his yacht *Ambassadress* that he d of a cerebral hemorrhage.

NYT 2.3.1942 pp 21, 24 (portrait); *The Eng* V 173 22.5.1942 p 438

VAN HORNE, Sir William Cornelius

b Will County, Ill, USA, 3.2.1843; d Montreal 11.9.1915 aged 72.

RR executive and the driving force behind the const of the CPR. First of 5 children of Cornelius Covenhoven VH. and his 2nd wife Mary Minier (Richards), of Dutch ancestors on the f's side. Ed by his mother and at school in Joliet, Ill. His f d in 1854. At age 14 he was employed as a telegraph operator with the Illinois Central RR, later with the Michigan Central. Enlisted in Civil War but was released for RR work. In 1862 VH. transferred to the Chicago & Alton RR as ticket agent and operator in Joliet; in 1864 train despatcher on the C & A at Bloomington; 1868 supt of telegraph; 1870 supt of transportation. In 1872 became g supt of a subsidiary line, the St Louis, Kansas City & Northern R. His success led to his app as g mgr and later president of the Southern Minnesota RR with offices at

La Crosse, Wis. Under his leadership the RR was brought out of receivership in 1877. In 1879 he returned to the Chicago & Alton as g supt, soon moving to the Chicago, Milwaukee & St Paul as g supt. On the recommendation of James J. Hill (qv) of the Great Northern VH. was app to take charge of the const of the CPR, moving to Winnipeg on 31.12.1881. He carried the project through to completion in 1886, serving from 1881–4 as g mgr and from 1884–8 as vice president, becoming president in 1888. Until his resignation, because of ill health, on 12.6.1899, he controlled the expansion of the CPR. Following a return to health he visited Cuba in 1900 where, with G. M. Dodge (qv), he initiated const of the Cuba RR, 350 miles (563km) long through the eastern provinces of the island. It was op 1.12. 1902. He next moved to Guatemala where, in 1903, he undertook to direct const of the last 65 miles (105km) of a RR from Puerto Barrios to Guatemala. After delays it was completed in 1.1908. He was also connected with many other industrial enterprises. Returning from his last trip to Cuba in 6.1915 he was stricken with fever and d in Montreal. He m Lucy Adaline Hurd in 3.1867; they had 2 sons and 1 dr, but one son d aged 5.

DAB; Vaughan, Walter, *The life and work of Sir William Van Horne*, 1920; Skelton, O. D., *The Railway Builders* 1916; Gibbon, J. M., *Steel of Empire* 1935; Innis, H. A., *A history of the CPR* 1923, 1972; Lavallée, Omer, *Van Horne's Road* 1973

VAUCLAIN, Samuel Matthews

b Philadelphia, Pa, USA, 18.5.1856; d Rosemont, Pa, 4.2.1940 aged 83.
Chairman of Baldwin Loco Wks and inventor of the system of loco compounding named after him. Shortly after his birth his f, Andrew V., formerly emp by M. W. Baldwin (qv), founder of the Baldwin Loco Wks, entered the service of the PRR and removed to Altoona. There the son was brought up in R surroundings, and at age 16 entered the Altoona shops of the PRR as apprentice. At age 21 he was app foreman in the frame shop. In 1882 he was sent to the Baldwin Wks to inspect some locos

then being built for the PRR and as a direct outcome was offered a position in those wks. In 7.1883 he entered the company's service as supt of the Seventeenth Street Shops. Three yrs later at age 30 he was app g supt of the plant. 1896 became M of Burnham Williams & Co, at that time proprietors of the wks. In 1911, the company having been incorporated in the Baldwin Loco Wks, V. was made a vice president, becoming a senior vice president 2 yrs later. In 1929 he relinquished the presidency to G. H. Houston and was elected chairman of the bd. During his 57 yrs association with Baldwin Wks V. was responsible for many technical developments in design and const of locos. In 1889 he produced his famous 4-cyl compound design in which the high and low pressure piston rods on both sides of the engine were connected to common crossheads, driving 2 cranks. It was first tested in 1891. Later 4-crank arrangements were produced. Up to 1907 over 2000 V. compounds were built. In 1905 he designed a smokebox superheater. Other developments for which he was largely responsible were the first 10-coupled heavy goods engine, a 2–10–0 weighing 195 000 lb, supplied in 1886 to the Dom Pedro II RR of Brazil; the first 'wagon-top' boiler, for the Denver & Rio Grande RR, and the first 2–8–2, supplied to the Japanese Rs in 1897, hence the name 'Mikado'. In 1892 he built his first engine to burn lignite fuel, for SW USA. Besides loco design, V. also introduced new methods connected with their const and sale. Shortly after becoming g supt of the Baldwin Wks he introduced the hydraulic forge for the production of driving wheel centres. A few yrs later he decided to reduce the idle time of machines by introducing the then novel principle of double-shift working. He also fitted machines for individual motor driving, so much in advance of the time as to arouse the ridicule of his friend George Westinghouse (qv). He was an outstanding salesman. Once he sold $15 mil worth of locos and machinery to the Roumanian govt, payment being made in 60 monthly instalments in cash or oil. He sold the oil to the British govt at a good profit. At the time of his death he was M of the bds of several banks and insurance companies and a dir of 7 engg and allied works, subsidiaries of the Baldwin Co. Also M of the bds of Westinghouse Electric & Mfr Co and the Westinghouse Electric International Co.

The Eng V 169 8.3.1940 p 234; DAB Supplement 2 p 680; Vauclain, S. M., *Steaming up* (autobiography) 1930; Baldwin Loco Wks, *The History of Baldwin Loco Wks* 1924

VIGNOLES, Charles Blacker

b Woodbrook, Co Wexford, Ireland, 31.5.1793; d Hythe, Hampshire, 17.11.1875 aged 82.
Civil eng. Began his career in the army; went onto half pay in 1816, but did not leave the army until 1833. From 1816 he was engaged on a survey of S Carolina and adjoining states, returning to England in 5.1823. In 1825 he worked for the Rennies (qv) on the projected R to Brighton, and he also carried out surveys on the Liverpool & Manchester R. On 7.9.1830 in conjunction with John Ericsson (qv) he patented a new method of ascending steep inclines by a centre rail gripped by two horizontal wheels operated by a lever (No 5995). This was the forerunner of the Fell (qv) centre-rail system. In 1831 he was occupied on what became in 1834 the North Union R, Parkside–Wigan–Preston. 1832 chief eng Dublin & Kingstown R, the first R in Ireland, op 17.12.1834; 1835–8 chief eng Sheffield, Ashton & Manchester R including Woodhead tunnel, 3 miles 22yd (4.848km), which was later taken over by Locke (qv). About this time he was consulted on some of the earliest continental lines, chiefly Paris & Versailles, German Union, and others in Germany. In 1837 he introduced the flat-bottomed rail named after him, similar in section to that invented by R. L. Stevens (qv) of USA in 1830. In 1841 he was elected the first prof of civil engg at Univ Coll. London. In 1843–4 he advised on Rs in Württemburg. During the 'R Mania' in 1846–8 V. was engaged on many lines including the E Kent (later LC & DR); North Western (later MR); Blackburn R (later LYR); Waterford & Limerick. In 1847 he visited St Petersburg and during the next 5 yrs paid many visits to Russia where he had a large professional staff.

His main work was the suspension bridge over the Dnieper at Kiev, then the longest in the world. In 1853–5 he built the first R in western Switzerland, and in 1854 surveyed the Balica & San Francisco R in Brazil, built 1857–61. In 1857–8 with Thomas Brassey (qv) he carried out a line through the Basque provinces in Spain. His last important undertaking was the Warsaw–Terespol line, 1865. He then ret from active work, but continued to advise engs on many important schemes. He took a keen interest in scientific matters; was elected fellow of the Royal Astronomical Society on 9.1.1829; MICE 10.4.1827, and president 1869–70; FRS 7.6.1855. On an expedition in the *Psyche* to observe the eclipse of 22.12.1870 he was wrecked on Sicily. On 13.7.1817 he m Mary Griffiths who d 17.12.1834; in 1849 he m Elizabeth (?) who d 30.3.1880. He was survived by 4 sons.

Min Proc ICE V 43 1875–6 p 306; *The Eng* V 40 19.11.1875 p 359; *Engg* V 20 19.11.1875 pp 400–2

VOGT, Axel S.

b (?), Sweden, (?).(?).1849; d (?), USA, 11.11.1921 aged 72.
Mech eng, Pennsylvania RR. He began his career with the PRR in 1874 and was app mech eng at Altoona on 1.3.1887, succeeding John W. Cloud who had served since the death of John B. Collin, mech eng from 1866 until his death on 20.3.1886. V. experimented with oil fuel on a loco in the Pittsburgh div in 1887 and established with Dr Charles B. Dudley that 1 lb of oil was the equivalent in heating value to $1\frac{3}{4}$ lb of coal, but the costs at that time made the use of oil unacceptable, though the experiment was a success. In 1888 V. obtained a 3-cyl LNWR Webb compound 2-2-2-0 engine, No 1320 *Pennsylvania*, from Beyer, Peacock & Co, Manchester. It was similar to the 'Dreadnought' class, with 6ft 3in (1.905m) driving wheels, uncoupled. It was reported to be 'of very superior workmanship' but starting troubles led to its withdrawal in 1897, having by then had an American cab fitted. V. early adopted the Belpaire firebox which thereafter became standard on the PRR. In 1892 the PRR completed the Juniata shops just E of

Altoona, with a capacity for building 150 locos per year. Two experimental 4-4-0s and two 4-6-0s were obtained, one of each, from Baldwin and ALCO in the same year, to establish the ability of larger and heavier designs to meet growing traffic conditions. Progressively larger engines continued to emerge from the shops, all of handsome appearance. In 1898-9 the large H5 and H6 2-8-0 classes were built, weighing 186 500lb (84 600kg). The first of his famous 4-4-2s, the E1 class, were built in 1899. They had driving cabs mounted halfway along the boiler, and broad fireboxes. The larger E2 class, of more conventional appearance, followed in 1901 and the E3a in 1902. Following the example of the GWR in England, in 1904 the PRR obtained a de Glahn 4-cyl compound 4-4-2 from Societe Alsacienne de Constructions Mecaniques, Belfort, France. It was thoroughly tested on the new loco testing plant designed and installed in 1904 under V. and the results led to the design of the large E28 class, 4 balanced compounds built by ALCO and Baldwin in 1905. The success of the wide firebox led to its application to freight engines of the H6a class of 1902 and H6b of 1905, built by Baldwin and the PRR. The H6b was the first PRR type to have the Walschaert valve gear which thereafter became standard. To handle the ever heavier passenger trains an experimental 4-6-2 was obtained from ALCO in 1906. Its success led to the design at Fort Wayne in 1910 of the K2 class 4-6-2. In 1913 it was redesigned with superheater, becoming class K3s. The superheater now became standard on all new PRR designs. V's final designs were large, powerful engines which became the basis of standard designs used until the end of steam power on the PRR. The remarkable E6s 4-4-2s were among the largest 'Atlantics' ever built, and the famous K4s 'Pacific' of 1914 based on the E6s became the standard PRR express engine. V. ret on 1.2.1919 at the age of 70 after a career as mech eng of 32 yrs; and, as if this were not enough, he continued in an advisory capacity in the Baldwin Loco Wks, Philadelphia, until his death 2 yrs later. His work had a profound influence on the development of American steam loco design.

Warner, Paul T., *Locos of the Pennsylvania RR 1834-1924* 1959

VOLK, Magnus

b Brighton 19.10.1851; d Brighton 20.5.1937 aged 85.

Builder of the first electric R in GB. Son of a German clock maker. Began in his f's workshop, continuing it himself when his f d in 1865 when he was only 14. In 1881 he was awarded a gold medal for a street fire alarm and in 1882 he equipped his house with the first telephone and first electric light in Brighton. In 1883 he installed electric light in the Brighton Pavilion and built a 2ft (610mm) g electric R along the beach using a Siemens dynamo and a 2hp Crossley gas engine. The first section opened on 4.8.1883, 8 weeks before the Portrush-Giant's Causeway Tramway in Ireland. In 1884 the g was changed to 2ft 9in (838mm) and the line was extended and reopened 4.4.1884. His most extraordinary venture was the Brighton & Rottingdean Seashore Electric Tramroad with a car like a ship on long legs which ran through the sea at high water. The line was about 2¾ miles (4.4km) long and ran from 28.11.1896 to 1.1901. An attempt to extend the Brighton Electric R to Rottingdean in 1902 failed for lack of capital.

Jackson, Alan A., *Volk's Railway, Brighton, 1883-1964* 1964; *The Eng* V 163 5.1937 p 627

VON BORRIES, August

b Niederbecksen, nr Bad Oeynhausen, Westphalia, Germany, 27.1.1852; d Meran, Austria (now Italy) 14.2.1906 aged 54.

Loco eng. Studied in the Berliner Gewerbeakademie 1870-3, and from there went to the Prussian State Rs. 1875-1902 loco supt Prussian State Rs. During this period he worked out his patent system of compounding for locos in association with T. W. Worsdell (qv) of the NER in England. His first 2-cyl compound was built in 1880 and his first 4-cyl in 1899. Among his numerous innovations in German locos was the use of nickel steel for boilers in 1891. In 1902 he became prof of transport machinery in the Charlottenberg Tech

Sch, Berlin, and remained in that position, in spite of failing health, until his death. He wrote extensively on loco matters.

S Bz 3.1906; *ZVDI* V 50 10.3.1906 pp 353–4 (portrait); *The Locomotive* 3.1906 p 43; *Neue Deutscher Biographie* V 2 pp 474–5

VON HELMHOLZ See Helmholz, Von

WADDELL, John

b Gain, nr Airdrie, Scotland, (?).(?). 1828; d Edinburgh 17.1.1888 aged 59.
R contractor. Began work as a contractor at an early age and for several yrs carried out minor works. His more important works included: Leadburn & Dolphinton; Carstairs & Dolphinton; Cleland & Mid Calder; Camps & Addiewell; Glasgow & Coatbridge; Sighthill branch; Hawthornden & Penicuik; Millerhill, Loanhead & Glencorse; Byker, Walker & Percy Main; Sunderland & Monkwearmouth including iron bridge over the Wear; Leuchars & Tay Bridge R; Dundee Tay Bridge Stn and Dock Street tunnel; E Norfolk R; Montrose & Arbroath; Ely & Newmarket R; Downham & Stoke Ferry; Tweedmouth R; Burndall & Yarmouth; Lofthouse & Whitby; Whitby & Scarborough; Llanelly & Mynydd Mawr; new Putney bridge over Thames; Mersey R and tunnel works; Edinburgh & South Side Suburban R. W. was also chairman of Burntisland Oil Co; Northern Cable Tramways Co, and Rosewell Gas Co. MIME 1887.

Proc IME 2.1888 pp 156–7; Moore, R. F. *Paddy Waddell's R* 1973

WAGNER, Dr R. P.

b Berlin 25.8.1882;
d Vellberg, Wurttemberg, 14.2.1953 aged 73.
German loco eng. Ed in Berlin. Studied mech engg at Charlottenburg Tech Coll. While studying he spent a year on the R and passed the engine driver's test on 17.11.1905. During training as govt const supt with the R administration of Berlin and Magdeburg he made several educational visits to England. He passed the constructional admin exam with distinction and was awarded an educational tour to USA. His civil service began with the Maschineninspektion, Wittenberge. Worked in the Dortmund loco dept and in inspection. 1920 was commissioned to establish a new loco research dept. 1922 called to R central office and for 20 yrs was head of loco const section. The establishment of the German Reichsbahn on 11.10.1924 made necessary a reduction in the number of loco types taken over from the various state Rs. W. established a standard loco design in cooperation with German loco builders. He was responsible for numerous developments in loco design including the use of high and super pressure, turbine drive, and coal-dust fuel. He collaborated on the design of light shunting locos. In 1924 he was nominated Oberregierungsbaurat (chief of const dept). In 1929 he became hon MILE. 1931 awarded hon doctorate by Aachen Tech Coll. 1938 nominated departmental president. Ret 1942. W. was the only German to be made a M of the Royal Soc of Arts. After WW2 he gave further service to aid the restoration of the German Rs. 1946–8 acted as administrative dir for supply, planning and buying section, first at the General Reichsbahn admin at Bielfeld and lastly at the head admin of the German Bundesbahn (DB) in Offenbach. Following his final ret W. remained active as presiding M of the German Standards Inst, as president of the Tech Standards Comm steam locos and as collaborator in the tech comm on locos in the DB. He was active up to his death.

Journal ILE No 231 1953 pp 150–1

WAINWRIGHT, Harry Smith

b Worcester 16.11.1864;
d Bexhill 19.9.1925 aged 60.
Loco eng, SE & CR. Son of William W. (qv). Ed Worcester Gr Sch; St Andrews, Derby; Central Tech Coll, London. At age 14 began on MR in the carriage shops under T. G. Clayton. 1882 joined the SER where he worked under his f who was then C & W supt. Later became draughtsman under Thomas Whitelegg (qv) in the loco dept of the London, Tilbury & Southend R. 1899 returned to SER as inspector. 1890 became wks mgr, C & W dept. 1895 app C & W supt. 1899 became chief loco eng and C & W

supt, on the formation of the SE & CR. He was best remembered for his 'D', 'E', and 'L' class 4–4–0s, 'C' class 0–6–0s and 'H' class 0–4–4Ts. W. delegated almost all design work to his chief draughtsman, Robert Surtees, a former LC & DR man, and his team. He considerably extended Ashford Wks. He was responsible for one of the most elaborate colour schemes ever applied to British locos, which can be seen on the 'D' class 4–4–0 in the NRM, York. W. was MICE, M Royal Soc of Arts. For several years he was hon sec to the Assoc of R Loco Engs of GB of which he was president in 1913. Also JP for Kent. He was forced to ret because of ill health in 1913.
The Eng V 140 25.9.1925 p 324; *Engg* V 120 25.9.1925 p 394; Bradley, D. L., *The Locos of the SE & CR* RCTS 1961

WAINWRIGHT, William

b Leeds 2.8.1833;
d Ashford, Kent, 21.5.1895 aged 61.
1847–54 apprenticed at E. B. Wilson & Co, Leeds. 1854 began on Oxford, Worcester & Wolverhampton R where he rapidly rose to the position of foreman and in 1860 became loco & Carriage supt. Upon amalg with GWR in 1863 he was app supt of loco & carr dept of Worcester div. 1873 left GWR and for 5 yrs was mgr of Worcester C & W Co. In 1.1877 he was app chief outdoor asst of C & W dept of MR at Derby, where he had charge of about 1500 men. In 4.1882 he was app chief C & W supt of the SER at Ashford, Kent, and during the next 13 yrs he revolutionised SER coach design. MICE 24.5.1887.
Min Proc ICE V 122 1894–5 p 388

WALKER, Sir Herbert Ashcombe

b Paddington, London, 16.5.1868;
d London 29.9.1949 aged 81
G mgr, Southern R. Son of George Stephen W., a doctor of medicine. Ed N London Collegiate Sch and Bruges, but abandoned medical training early and at 17 began his R career in the office of the supt of the line, LNWR. In 1.1889 became outdoor asst to supt of the line, covering the whole of the LNWR. 1893 was made dist supt, N Wales Div, Chester. 1894 asst dist supt, S Div, until 1902 when he became dist supt, Euston. Visited USA in 1902 to report on R

matters. In 1895, while at Chester, he m Ethel Walker. She d in 1909, and in 1910 he m Lorina Shilds. On 1.1.1912 W. succeeded Sir Charles Owens as g mgr, LSWR. W. was responsible for the app of R. Urie (qv) as loco supt on 6.12. 1912, and also for the rebuilding of Waterloo stn, London, 1913. He reorganised the operating dept, and set in motion the LSWR electrification programme, using the 600V dc 3rd rail system. He was knighted on 1.1.1915. Soon after grouping, on 1.1.1924, he became g mgr of the entire Southern R. His biggest project was Southampton docks and the establishment of Southampton as the major trans-Atlantic port. Another important development carried out under W. was the hump yard at Feltham, 1920–1. He continued the extension of electrification until the network covered the SR lines in the London Suburban area, the main lines to Brighton and Portsmouth, and several routes in Sussex and Hampshire. He also developed the cross-Channel shipping services. Ret 10.1937, and served as dir of SR until end of 1947. He was a strong advocate of the Channel tunnel scheme, and was chairman of the Channel Tunnel Co Ltd.
RG 7.10.1949 p 427 (portrait); *The Times* 30.9.1949 p 7; *NYT* 30.9.1949 p 24; Klapper, C. F. *Sir Herbert Walker's Southern R* 1972; Moody, G. T. *Southern Electric* 1968; *The Eng* V 188 7.10.1949 p 406

WALKER, James, LLD, FRS

b Falkirk (?).(?).1781;
d Edinburgh 8.10.1862 aged c81.
Civil eng. At age 19 articled to his uncle, Ralph W., eng in London, and was emp on E & W India docks, London. App eng to Commercial docks 1806. Following the death of Thomas Telford in 1834 many important works were entrusted to W., including Vauxhall bridge, London, and Victoria bridge over the Clyde; repairs to Caledonian Canal; coffer dam and river wall at new Houses of Parliament; Birmingham Canal; Tame Valley Canal; Betley Canal and Netherton tunnel; and various lighthouses including Bishop Rock off the Scilly Isles. Early in the history of Rs W. was app with J. U. Rastrick (qv) to report on

the system of traction on the Liverpool & Manchester R. He built the Leeds & Selby R, op 1834, and the Hull & Selby R, op 1840. Became MICE 1823, and succeeded Telford as president 1834–5. Min Proc ICE V 22 1862 pp 630–2

WALKER, Thomas Andrew

b (?) (?).(?).1828; d nr Chepstow, Monmouthshire, 25.11.1889 aged 61.
Civil eng and contractor. After a brief course of engg training at King's Coll, London, at 17 he was engaged on various R surveys, later finding employment under Brassey (qv) on the NSR. He remained with Brassey until 1854, on the Royston & Hitchin (GNR), NSR Ashbourne branch and, from 1852, on the Grand Trunk R of Canada. He then began contracting on his own and remained in Canada for a further 7 yrs building Rs for the govt of the lower provinces. He returned to England in 1861 and then went to Russia to survey the Orel & Vitepsk R, and to Egypt in 1864–5 where, and in Sudan, he made extensive R surveys as far south as Metammen, 100 miles N of Khartoum. On his return to England W. contracted for the extn of the Met R and the Met Dist R, London, in Assoc with Peto, Betts (qqv), Kelk and Waring Bros, and completed the works by 1.7.1871. From then until his death he worked on contracts on his own account. For John Hawkshaw (qv) until 1876 he undertook the E London R from the N end of Marc Brunel's Thames tunnel to its jn with the GER at Shoreditch, carrying the line beneath London docks. In 1879 he was app by Hawkshaw to complete the Severn tunnel which became his greatest and most difficult work, completed in 1887. Other works undertaken by W. were Barry dock and Rs, 1889, Preston dock, 1892, the govt docks at Buenos Aires and lastly the Manchester Ship Canal which was in progress when he d. He became ill when on a visit to Buenos Aires and d of Bright's disease. AICE 2.4.1867.
Min Proc ICE V 100 1889–90 pp 416–19; *The Eng* V 68 29.11.1889 p 450; *Engg* V 48 29.11.1889 pp 635–6; Walker, T. A., *The Severn Tunnel 1872–87* 1888

WALSCHAERT, Egide

b Mechlin, nr Malines, Belgium, 20.1.1820; d St Lilles, Brussels, 18.2.1901 aged 81.
Loco eng; designer of the Walschaert steam loco valve gear. The family name was originally Walschaerts (a Dutch name pronounced Vahlshairtz) but when Belgium revolted against Holland in 1830 and became independent the name was changed to Walschaert (and pronounced Volshair). W. started work as a mechanic on Belgian State Rs at Malines. 1844 app foreman of the Brussels Midi Stn and shops which had just been started. In the same year he invented his famous valve gear, but as a foreman was prohibited from advertising and deriving royalties from a patent, by a rule of Belgian State Rs, it was patented by M. Fischer, eng of Belgian State Rs, on 30.11.1844, but in the name of Walschaert as inventor. Claims were made in Germany for Prof Heusinger von Waldegg as inventor but, in a letter dated 3.4.1875, he recognised the right of W. to priority. In 1848 W. was permitted to fit his valve gear on an i/c 2–2–2 at Brussels, with excellent results. In France the Crampton engines 165–70 of the Nord built by J. F. Cail, Paris, in 1859, were fitted with the W. valve gear and in Belgium it was applied to all o/c locos, but the Stephenson gear was preferred for i/c locos. W. invented several other improvements to locos, among which was a steam governor with superimposed slide valves, but no information as to its adoption can be found. He also invented a valve gear for stationary engines, similar to the Corliss or Sulzer principle and built a shop at Brussels for the mfr of such engines. It was managed by his son. He was awarded a gold medal for his engine at the Paris exposition of 1878, and in 1883 he received a diploma at the Antwerp exposition for his loco valve gear. He ret in 1885. His great merits as an eng and inventor were never fully recognised and his death at the age of 81 passed almost unnoticed; yet his valve gear became used on locos throughout the world.
RM 10.1904 pp 298–301; *The Locomotive* 15.9.1932 pp 313–4; Wiener, Lionel, *Articulated locos* 1930, 1970, p 27

WARDLE, Charles Wetherell

b Rothwell nr Leeds 21.1.1821;
d Wetherby, Yorkshire, 3.7.1888 aged 67.

Senior partner in firm of Manning, Wardle & Co, Leeds, loco mfrs. Son of former vicar of Beeston nr Leeds. Trained under Matthew Murray (qv); then went to Milton Ironworks, and later to E. B. Wilson & Co, R Foundry, Leeds, as g mgr, becoming chief eng and outdoor rep. On the closure of the R Foundry in 1858 he entered into partnership with Alexander Campbell and others who had held important positions there and established the Boyne Engine Wks on a portion of the same site at Hunslet, Leeds. Later he was joined by John Manning and the firm became Manning, Wardle & Co Ltd. In about 15 yrs, following withdrawal or death of the other partners, the business devolved wholly upon himself and his son. In 1868 he was engaged by the govt in valuing the Rs in Ireland. MIME 1856. Manning, Wardle & Co Ltd closed down in 1927.

Proc IME 7.1888 p 442

WARREN, James Graeme Hepburn

b Bawdrip, Somerset, 30.8.1875;
d Bath (?).3.1935 aged 59.

Loco draughtsman and historian. At 16 apprenticed at Neilson, Reid & Co, Glasgow, 1893–8. In 1899 he joined Kerr, Stewart & Co as loco draughtsman until 1904 when he became chief draughtsman at Robert Stephenson & Co under J. M. Galt. W. undertook the drawings for the full-size replica of *North Star* built at Swindon for the R Centenary of 1925 (now in Swindon GWR Museum), and for the reconstruction of the Liverpool & Manchester R *Lion* (now in Liverpool Museum) for the L & M centenary, 1930. He ret because of acute eye trouble in 1923. He is best known for his monumental book *A Century of Loco Building* 1923, 1970. He was interested also in music, heraldry, wood carving, architecture and gardening. MIME 1907.

Journal ILE V 25 1935 p 443; Proc IME V 129 1935 p 560; *The Eng* V 159 5.4. 1935 p 350

WATKIN, Sir Edward William

b Salford 26.9.1819; d Northenden, Cheshire, 13.4.1901 aged 81

R promoter and mgr. Son of Absolom W., cotton merchant and prominent Manchester citizen. After working with his f, W. entered R work in 1845 when he became sec of the Trent Valley R, which was later sold at a profit to the LNWR whose services W. then joined. In 1853 he became g mgr of the MS & L and entered into negotiations with the GNR, LNWR and MR to ensure the survival of his company. At the request of the Sec of State for the Colonies he visited Canada in 1861 to investigate means of confederating the 5 British provinces into a dominion of Canada, and of transferring the Hudson Bay territory to the control of the govt. He was also engaged in planning Rs to Quebec. On his return he resigned from the MS & L because in his absence the dirs had come to terms with the MR, and he became president of the GTR of Canada. However, in 1863 he resumed his connection with the MS & L, becoming chairman in 1.1864. He remained in that position until 5.1894. With this office he combined chairmanship of the SᴱR from 1866–94 and of the Met R 1872–94. For a short time in 1866 he was a dir of the GWR and in 1867 of the GER. He negotiated the new line of the CLC, op 1877, by way of gaining access to Liverpool for the MS & L. He also negotiated links in Cheshire and Wales in connection with the MS & L. His rivalry with J. S. Forbes (qv) of the LC & DR led to the const of numerous duplicate lines in SE England. His connection with the Met and SER led him to work towards the building of a Channel tunnel and a new main line from Sheffield via Nottingham and Leicester to join the Met R, with a connection to the SER, to connect Manchester and London with Paris. A Channel Tunnel Co was formed in 1872 under W's direction and excavation began in 1881 under John Hawkshaw (qv). By the time the main line to London was completed in 1898-9, however, the relationship with the southern companies had changed and the vast scheme remained incomplete. In 1897

the MS & L changed its name to Great Central, but the line became a success only through the efforts of Sir Sam Fay (qv). In 1889 W. became chairman of a company to erect a tower at Wembley Park to rival that of Eiffel (qv) at Paris, but it rose to only the first stage in 1896 and was demolished in 1907. (See A. D. Stewart) In 1857 W. was MP for Great Yarmouth; 1864–8 MP for Stockport, and for Hythe 1874–95. He was a M of Manchester City Council 1859–62 and High Sherriff of Cheshire 1874. He was Knighted in 1868 and created a baronet in 1880. In 1845 he m Maray Briggs (d 8.3.1887). In 1893 he m Ann, then aged 81, widow of Herbert Ingram, founder of the *Illustrated London News*. She d 26.5.1896. W's ambition resulted in vast expenditure on unnecessary schemes, and his unbending, inconsiderate manner led to the resignation of J. I. Cudworth (qv) of the SER and the resignation and possibly even suicide of C. R. Sacré (qv) of the MS & L.
R Eng 5.1901 p 129; *Manchester Guardian* 5.4.1901; Dow, George, *Great Central* V 2 1962

WATSON, Allan Griffiths

b Hopetown, Cape Province, (?).(?). 1876; d Cape Town 13.11.1945 aged 69. CME S African Rs & Harbours. Ed S Africa Coll (now Cape Town Univ). Began an apprenticeship at the Beaufort W Wks in 1894, but in 1895 went to Glasgow where he spent 5 yrs at the Hyde Park Loco Wks (later NB Loco Co) and at Glasgow Tech Coll where he studied mech eng. Returned to S Africa in 4.1900 and rejoined the Cape Govt Rs at Springfontein as loco rep. In 1901 he was app temporary acting dist loco supt at Naauwpoort. 1902–10 chief draughtsman at Uitenhage. In 1910, when the various Rs were united to form S African Rs & Harbours Admin, W. was app asst supt (mech) at Kimberley. In 1914–15 he was on active service in SW Africa in the S African Engg Corps, returning to Kimberley until 1922 when he was app mech eng at Uitenhage wks. In 1926 he was app to the same position at Durban wks where he designed and built some low-cost double-engined railcars for branch line work.

On 1.4.1928 he was app asst CME at Pretoria and on 1.4.1929 succeeded Lt Col F. L. Colins as CME of the entire S African Rs & Harbours. He introduced water softening plants for the Karoo Cape Midlands and SW African systems, modernised works with improved layouts, machinery and SW African systems, modernised works with improved layouts, machinery and buildings, and established the construction of rolling stock in the admin's own wks. He introduced 3 standard loco boilers and developed several large loco types including the 15E class 4–8–2 and 16E class 4–6–2 for main line work, and the 19B and 19C class 4–8–2s, 20 class 2–8–2 and 21 class 2–10–4 for branch line service on 45 and 60 lb/yd (22.322 and 29.763 kg/m) rails. In 1935 elevated to asst g mgr (tech) and CME, but he ret in 1936 on reaching the age limit. Elected MICE 1926; MIME 1930; MILE.
Proc IME V 154 1946 p 360; *Journal ILE* V 26 1946 p 96; *Beyer, Peacock Quarterly Review* 10.1929 p 24; Holland, D. F., *Steam Locos of the S African Rs 1910–55* 1972

WATSON, Sir Arthur

b Manchester 18.9.1873; d Exeter 13.4.1954 aged 80.
Civil eng, and g mgr, LYR, LNWR, LMS and Buenos Aires & Pacific R. Ed Manchester Gr Sch and Victoria Univ, Manchester. 1890 articled to William Hunt (qv), chief eng LYR, and from 1893–7 acted as asst to J. S. Chorlton, res eng. 1898 app central div eng, LYR, becoming a res eng in 1899, responsible for the reconstruction of Bolton stn, completed in 1904. 1905 became asst eng. On 1.1.1911 he succeeded J. P. Crouch as passenger supt which office, in 9.1911, was extended to include the office of supt of the line. 1914 elected M of the R Executive Comm. In 4.1918 he was app asst g mgr. LYR, in addition to his duties as supt of the line, and in 1.1919, on the ret of J. A. F. Aspinall (qv) he became g mgr. On the amalg with the LNWR on 1.1.1922 he continued as g mgr of the combined undertaking and a year later as g mgr of the LMS. He was knighted on 1.1.1924. Later that year resigned because of ill health. In 10.1925 he was app g mgr of the Buenos Aires & Pacific

R and took up his duties on 1.2.1926. Finally ret 19.3.1928 and returned to England. Lady W. d 21.5.1946. He was survived by 2 drs. MICE 1911; and was a founder M of the Inst T.
Proc ICE 1954 p 625; *RG* 22.10.1926 p 495; 20.4.1928 p 559; 23.4.1954 p 471; Marshall, John, *The Lancashire & Yorkshire R* V 2 1970

WATSON, Edward Augustus

b Clones, Ireland, 23.8.1881;
d Mobberley, Cheshire, 25.8.1922 aged 41.
Loco C & W supt, GS & WR, Ireland; g mgr and chief eng, Beyer, Peacock & Co Ltd. Ed privately. Began his career in USA, first with ALCO at Schenectady, later with PRR at Altoona. Returning to England he joined the GWR at Swindon wks as asst wks mgr for 4 yrs. In 1911 he joined the GS & WR as wks mgr at Inchicore wks, Dublin. 1913 succeeded R. E. L. Maunsell (qv) as loco C & W supt. In 11.1921 became g mgr and eng in chief, Beyer, Peacock & Co Ltd, Manchester. MICE 1915.
The Eng V 134 8.9.1922 p 250

WEBB, Francis William

b Tixall Rectory, Staffordshire, 21.5.1836; d Bournemouth 4.6.1906 aged 70.
Loco eng, LNWR. Second son of Rev William W. In 1851 he entered Crewe wks, LNWR, as a pupil of Francis Trevithick (qv) until 1.8.1857 when T. resigned. In 1859 he was made chief draughtsman and in 1861 chief asst to John Ramsbottom (qv). In 6.1866 he left Crewe to become mgr of Bolton Iron & Steel Co. On the ret of Ramsbottom on 1.10.1871 W. was app CME at Crewe. His career was distinguished by his persistent devotion to compounding with 3 or 4 cylinders. Altogether several hundreds were built, none absolutely reliable and some, like the 8 'Greater Britain' class of 1891–4, positively bad. After W's ret his successor George Whale (qv) withdrew or rbt all but a few of the compounds within 3 yrs. By contrast W's simple designs were excellent and gave long and reliable service. Some of his engines were still running in the 1950s. During his career over 4000 locos were built at Crewe. He developed and expanded the

wks into one of the largest and most efficient in the world. Under W. the working force increased from 13 000 to 18 000. He was twice mayor of Crewe whose population during his time there was increased from 18 000 to 40 000. W. was a severe, autocratic and intolerant man. He would listen to no complaints. He never married and made few friends. He made a large amount of money, most of which he gave or bequeathed to charities. His erratic temper and manner eventually led to his enforced resignation in 1904. Became MICE 1872.
Min Proc ICE V 167 1906–7 p 373; *The Eng* V 101 8.6.1906 p 579; *Engg* V 81 8.6.1906 p 764; Ellis, Hamilton, *Twenty Loco Men* 1958

WEBER, Baron Christian Philipp Max Maria von

b Dresden 25.4.1822;
d Berlin 18.4.1881 aged 59.
Civil eng in Germany and Austria. Son of the famous composer Carl Maria von W. who d in London on 5.6.1826. Ed privately by his mother and by Lichstenstein, a friend of his f, and at Dresden Polytechnic where he studied engg. In 1840 he began training in mech engg in the Borsig Loco Wks, Berlin, at the same time attending lectures at Berlin Univ. In 1842 he was emp in const of the Saxo–Bavaro–Rhenish and Saxo–Austrian Rs, with many major bridges and other engg works. For a year he worked as an engine driver. In 1844 he travelled over Europe studying Rs in Germany, Belgium and France, and then went to England where he worked for a year under Robert Stephenson and Brunel. In 1845 the French govt commissioned him to report on conditions for emigration in North Africa. This resulted in two publications on Africa and French N Africa, and an award of Knight of the Legion of Honour. In 1850 he returned to Germany as tech officer in the Saxon Ministry for Public Works, and in 1852 he took control of the Saxon State Telegraphs. He was made a Royal Saxon Director of State Rs and a M of the R Bd in 1853. In 1868 when the R admin was changed he left to become consulting eng to the Austrian Ministry of Trade and Public Works, Vienna. However, following the

economic crash of 1873, he became dissatisfied with this work and in 1875, at the end of his 5 yr contract, he resigned. While at the head of Austrian R affairs he advised on the choice of gauge in Norway and Sweden and also inspected the Rs of European and Asiatic Turkey. He also wrote extensively on Rs. In 1878 he was asked by the German Bd of Trade & Industry and the Ministry for Public Works to report on the canals and Rs of Sweden, England, France, and N America. He never agreed with the policy of R nationalisation and this caused some differences, leading to his development of his literary activities. He had just finished his report on the Rs and canals of N America when he d suddenly of a heart disease in 1881. He left a son and a dr. He was a man of wide interests and could give information on a great range of subjects. His writing on Rs raised the subject from dull prose into lively, readable literature. In addition he wrote a biography of his f which has been a valuable source book for later writers. He was MICE from 14.1.1873 and M of many European learned societies. A list of his works appears in *The Eng* V 51 22.4.1881 p 298 (qv).
Min Proc ICE V 65 1880-1 pp 371-4

WEDGWOOD, Sir Ralph Lewis, CB, CMG, TD

b Barlaston Lea, Stoke on Trent, 2.3.1874; d Leith Hill, nr Dorking, Surrey, 5.9.1956 aged 82.
Chief g mgr, LNER. Third son of Clement Francis W. and great grandson of Josiah W., founder of the W. pottery firm. His great uncle by marriage was Charles Darwin, the great naturalist. Ed at Clifton Coll, Bristol, and Trinity Coll, Cambridge, where he obtained a first in the Moral Philosophy Tripos. In 1896, at age 22, he entered service of the NER on the invitation of Sir George Gibb, thereby fulfilling an early love of trains and Rs, and began on Tees-side. In 1898 he was transferred to W Hartlepool where he served in the dock supt's office, latterly as asst dock supt. 1902 became dist supt at Middlesbrough, but in 1904 was app sec to the NER. In 1905, however, at his own request, he was transferred to the traffic dept and was app

N Div gds mgr at Newcastle. On 1.10.1911 he became asst gds mgr, York. Shortly afterwards he was app chief gds mgr in succession to Eric Geddes who was app dep gds mgr. On the ret of Philip Burtt, passenger mgr, in 1914 W. added this office to his own. On the outbreak of WW1 he volunteered for service abroad and served in the transport establishment in France. In 7.1915 he was transferred to the new Ministry of Munitions until 10.1916 when he was app dir of docks under dir gen of transportation (Sir Eric Geddes). Awarded CMG 4.6.1917 and CB in 6.1918; also decoration of Officer of the Legion of Honour, France, and Commander of the Belgian Order of the Crown. Returned to the NER in 6.1919 as chief gds mgr and passenger mgr. In 8.1919 he added the office of dep gds mgr. He was chairman of the Gds Mgrs' Conference of the RCH in 1920 and frequently gave evidence on behalf of the R companies before the Rates Advisory Committee. On 1.1.1922 he succeeded Sir Alexander Butterworth (qv) as g mgr, becoming g mgr of the LNER on its formation on 1.1.1923. Knighted 1924. Under the LNER divisional system of mgt W. became the only R officer in GB with the title of chief g mgr. The LNER was constantly on the borderline of solvency, and W. seized every opportunity to present a favourable public image and to add to the prestige of the company. He was responsible for the introduction, in 1935, of the *Silver Jubilee,* Britain's first high-speed streamlined train. He ret on 3.3.1939, but in 9.1939, on the outbreak of WW2, he was app chairman of the R Executive Comm, retiring from this in 8.1941. In 1942 he was created a baronet. He was a man of keen intelligence, and his advice was often sought and acted upon. He was prominent in the passing of the Rs Act in 1921 and appeared before Parliamentary committees and Royal Commissions. As a witness he could be a formidable opponent. He was a M of the Weir Comm and M of the Electricity Bd, and of the Chinese Govt Purchasing Commission. In 1936 he visited India as chairman of the Committee of Inquiry into the Indian Rs. He was a M of the Sulter Conference of

1932 on the recommendations of which the Rail Traffic Act of 1933 was based, and he took a leading role in the proceedings of the Transport Advisory Council. He inaugurated the 'Give the Rs a Square Deal' campaign in the 1930s, and he gave it its name. He was a deeply cultured man and a close friend of his cousin, the composer Ralph Vaughan Williams, who dedicated to W. two of the best of his early works: *In the Fen Country* (1907) and *A Sea Symphony* (1910). In 1906 he m Iris Veronica, dr of Albert H. Pawson of Farnley, Leeds. She was author (Iris Veronica W.) of *The Livelong Day*, 1925; *The Iron Age*, 1927; *Perilous Seas*, 1928; *The Fairway*, 1929; *Northumberland and Durham*, 1932; *Fenland Rivers*, 1936. They had one son, Major J. H. W., b 1907, on whom the baronetcy devolved, and 1 dr, the well known English historian and biographer Dame (Cecily) Veronica W., b 20.7.1910.
RG 14.9.1956 pp 311, 327–8 (portrait); *The Times* 6.9.1956 p 15; Allen, Cecil J., *The London & North Eastern R* 1966; Kennedy, Michael, *The Works of Ralph Vaughan Williams* 1971 edn.

WESTINGHOUSE, George

b Central Bridge, Schoharie County, New York, 6.10.1846;
d New York 12.3.1914 aged 67.
Inventor and designer of the W. air brake. In 1856 the family moved to Schenectady where W. attended the High Sch. Left at 13 and entered his f's engg wks at Schenectady. From 6.1863 to 11.1865 he served first in the army then the navy. After a short time in college he returned to work with his f. His first invention, in 1865, was a device for re-railing rolling stock. In 1866 he began working out his air-brake system and the first patent was taken out in 1868 for the non-automatic 'straight air' brake. The automatic brake (which applied itself if the train broke apart) was developed in 1872–3. Still further improvements were made in 1886–7 by which the brake could be applied much more rapidly. From the beginning W. insisted upon a rigorous standardisation policy, so that W. fitted stock from any Rs can be coupled. W. also invented improvements in buffing and drawgear.

In 1886 the W. Electric Co was formed, becoming in 1891, after absorption of other companies, the W. Electric & Mfg Co, at Pittsburgh, Pa. W. was one of the pioneers of alternating current machinery. He went on taking out patents for new inventions almost to the end of his life. In addition to his inventive skill W. was also an able financier and was well equipped to turn his inventions to good account. He d from a heart disease. Besides several wks in N America, W. founded numerous others in Europe, those of the British W Electric & Mfg Co at Trafford Park, Manchester, being largely a reproduction of the original Pittsburgh wks. In GB the principal Rs using the W. brake were the CR, GER, NBR and NER and, in S England, the LBSCR.
Prout, Henry G., *A Life of George W.* 1922; DAB V 20 pp 16–18; *The Eng* V 117 20.3.1914 pp 315–16

WHALE, George

b Bocking, Essex, 7.12.1842;
d Hove 7.3.1910 aged 67.
CME of LNWR. Ed at a private sch at Lewisham. At age 16 entered the LNWR loco wks at Wolverton under J. E. McConnell (qv) and from 1862 under J. Ramsbottom (qv), passing through the shops, running dept and drg office. In 1865 moved to the drg office at Crewe and in 1867 app asst to J. Rigg, then supt of running dept. In 9.1877 he succeeded Rigg as supt of N Div running dept. 1899 became supt of running depts of the entire LNWR. On the ret of F. W. Webb (qv) in 1903 W. was app CME. He energetically replaced the troublesome Webb compounds with simple, reliable engines; from 1904 130 'Precursor' 4–4–0s, and from 1905 45 'Experiment' 4–6–0s; also 130 mixed traffic 4–6–0s and 40 4–4–2Ts. He also rbt many Webb engines into more reliable machines. He ret in ill health in 6.1909 and was succeeded by C. J. Bowen Cooke (qv). MIME 1900; MICE 22.12.1903. Also a magistrate, Alderman of Crewe, and once railway mayor of Crewe. Survived by a widow and 2 sons.
The Locomotive 1.1901 p 2; *The Eng* V 109 11.3.1910 p 246; Min Proc ICE V 182 1909–10 p 330; Proc IME 5.1910 p 785

WHEATLEY, Thomas

b Micklefield nr Leeds (?).(?).1821;
d (?) Wigtownshire 13.3.1883 aged 62.
Apprenticed on the Leeds and Selby R,
beside which he was b, for 7 yrs. After
several yrs on the MR he worked for
17 yrs on the MS & L. He next had
charge of the loco dept of the LNWR
S div for 5 yrs. On 1.2.1867 he was app
loco supt of the NBR at Edinburgh.
Here he introduced the first i/c 4-4-0
on a British R. The first, 224, went down
with the first Tay bridge on the night
of 28.12.1879. As a result of dishonest
conduct (which was a common feature
of the NBR hierarchy) he was dismissed
in 10.1874 and on 31.7.1875 he was app
to the Wigtownshire R, a little branch
from Newton Stewart to Whithorn and
Garliestown, as gen eng, for a period
of 5 yrs. The contract was renewed in
1880, and he d in office.
Thomas, John, *The North British R* V 1
1969; Smith, D. L., *The Little Rs of
SW Scotland* 1969; Proc IME 1884 p
74; *Engg* V 35 30.3.1883 pp 299–300

WHEATSTONE, Sir Charles

b Gloucester (?).2.1802; d Paris 19.10.
1875 aged 73.
Collaborator with Fothergill-Cooke (qv)
in development of the electric telegraph.
Son of a music seller in Gloucester. At
age 21 began as a musical instrument
maker in London, and in 1829 invented
the concertina. After experiments in
sound and light he turned his attention
to the electric telegraph and conducted
experiments to discover the speed of
transmission of electricity. In conjunction
with Fothergill-Cooke he elaborated the
5-needle telegraph, and then the 2-needle
telegraph in 1837, a letter-showing dial
telegraph in 1840 and a type-printing
telegraph in 1841. In 1845 he patented
a single-needle apparatus. He also made
improvements in the dynamo. From 1837
he devoted much of his work to submarine telegraphy. He devised the application of 'Wheatstone's Bridge' to electrical measurement. Elected FRS 1836, a
Chevalier of the Legion of Honour 1855,
and foreign associate of the Académie
des Sciences 1873. Created DCL, Oxford,
2.7.1862, and LLD, Cambridge, 1864.
Knighted 30.1.1868. On 12.2.1847 he m

Emma West, and they had 5 children.
Proc Royal Soc of London V 24 1876
pp 16–27; *Telegraphic Journal* 15.11.1875
p 252

WHEELWRIGHT, William

b Newburyport, Mass, USA, 18.3.1798;
d London 26.9.1873 aged 75.
Promoter of Rs in S America. After a
varied career at sea he became US
consul at Guayaquil, Ecuador, for 5 yrs.
In 1829 he m Martha Gerrish Bartlet
of Newburyport. On 17.2.1840 he secured
a British charter for the Pacific Steam
Navigation Co. In 1844 he urged the
building of a R across the Isthmus of
Panama. In 1849–52 he built the 51
miles (82km) of standard g R from
Caldera, Chile, to Copiapó, and
soon extended it to Tres Puntas, 6600ft
(2011.7m) above sea level. In 1850 he
opened up the first telegraph line in
Chile. He projected a trans-Andean R,
nearly 1000 miles (1600km) from Caldera
in Chile to Rosario in Argentina, crossing the San Francisco Pass at 16 000ft
(4876m). He began it at the Argentine
end and the Grand Central Argentine R
from Rosario to Cordoba was op 16.5.
1870. W. created the port of La Plata
and on 31.12.1872 completed a R from
there to Buenos Aires.
DAB V 20 pp 63–4; Wardle, Arthur C.,
Steam conquers the Pacific 1940

WHISHAW, Francis

b London 13.7.1804; d London 6.10.1856
aged 52.
Civil eng, and author of *The Rs of GB
and Ireland*. Third son of John W.,
solicitor. Articled to James Walker (qv).
In 1832 he prepared drawings for the
Holborn Viaduct, London. 1835 acted as
asst eng under T. L. Gooch (qv) in preparing estimates for the Manchester &
Leeds R. In 1837 he pub his *Analysis of
(projected) Rs*, followed in 1840 by his
Rs of GB and Ireland for which he
travelled 7000 miles (11 265km) to collect
information. In 1837–40 he conducted
experiments on the working of trains on
gradients. In 1837 he invented a
hydraulic telegraph, but the introduction
of electric telegraph made it unnecessary.
MICE 1834.
Min Proc ICE V 16 1856-7 pp 143–50

WHISTLER, George Washington

b Fort Wayne, Indiana, USA, 19.5.1800; d St Petersburg, Russia, 7.4.1849 aged 48.

Pioneer of R engg in USA and Russia. Ed at West Point, NY. At an early age showed skill in drawing. Began in the army, employed in topographical work, establishing the boundary between Canada and USA between Lake Superior and Lake of the Woods. 1821 m Mary Swift, but she d in 1827, leaving one dr and 2 sons, one of whom became an eng and R mgr and who d in Russia 1869. W. later spent much time as eng 'on loan' by the govt to civilian projects. In connection with the survey of the Baltimore & Ohio RR W. was sent to England in 11.1828 with his friend W. G. McNeill (qv) to study R const, and in 5.1829 they returned to begin work on the B & O. His next major work was the Paterson & Hudson River RR, later part of the Erie system. During this period he m McNeill's sister, Ann Matilda, and in 1834 a son, James Abbot McNeill W., was b at Lowell, Mass, later to become the famous American artist (d 1903). 1834–7 supt of the Locks & Canals Machine Shop, Lowell, building locos of Stephenson's 'Planet' type. He then surveyed the Concord RR (later part of Boston & Maine) and moved on to the New York, Providence & Boston, then the Western RR which, as chief eng, he carried across the Berkshire mountains from Worcester to Albany, 156 miles (251km), completed in 1841. For this line he adopted the unsuccessful 0–8–0 'Crabs' of Ross Winans (qv). He was responsbile for the introduction of the loco whistle in USA. In 1842 he was invited by Czar Nicholas I to survey and build the R from Moscow to St Petersburg. For this he adopted a g of 5ft (1.524m), then standard for many early lines in USA, and thus he established the 5ft gauge as the standard throughout Russia, while in USA the 5ft g lines were all rebuilt to standard g. Construction of the 420 mile (676km) R began in 1844. It was one of the straightest lines of its length ever built. It proved to be his undoing, however. The work became protracted and late in 1848 he succumbed to an epidemic of cholera, dying the following April, a year before the R was completed. In 1847 he was awarded the Order of St Anne by the Emperor.

DAB V 20 p 72; *Trains* 4.1948 pp 14–18; White, John H.Jr, *American Locos, an engg history 1830–80* 1968

WHITELEGG, Robert Harben

b Garston, Liverpool, (?).10.1871; d Chelsea, London, 9.3.1957 aged 85. Loco supt, LT & SR; CME G & SWR. Trained under his f Thomas W. (qv) at the Plaistow wks, LT & SR. In 1891 he was app insp of new rolling stock and materials. He then went to Spain where he was in charge of inspection of some British built locos. Returning to England in 1905 he became wks mgr at Plaistow and succeeded his f as loco supt in 6.1910. Following an enlarged 4–4–2T in 1912 he produced his fine 4–6–4T and some splendid coaches for the Ealing and Southend services. Before delivery of the 4–6–4Ts the LT & S was amalgamated with the MR, in 1912. W., unable to accept a subordinate position, left the R. He applied unsuccessfully for the post of CME on the GER, but A. J. Hill (qv) was app. So W. sought what employment he could find, becoming partner in a small agricultural engg firm at Towcester. In 1915 he became consulting eng in London for the Canadian Loco Co, then supplying locos for the forces in France. In 1917, at the invitation of the dep controller of merchant shipbuilding he joined the Admiralty where he was chiefly engaged on standardisation of shipyard machinery and inspection of shipbuilding material for const of standard ships. On 6.8.1918 he returned to R work as loco supt of the G & SWR at Kilmarnock, and on 1.1.1919 his title became CME. He found the entire loco stock and the wks terribly run down after WW1. W. had to order 10 Drummond 0–6–2Ts from North British Loco Co, built in 1919. He also had to send out boilers for overhaul. He rebuilt several existing locos and, in 1922, brought out his impressive 4–6–4T for fast passenger trains between Glasgow and the coast. He also prepared designs for a 4–4–4T and a 4–6–6T, but on 1.1.1923 the G & SWR became part of the LMS and further

developments were stopped. So again W. left the R and was app g mgr of Beyer, Peacock & Co, Manchester. In 1929 he left to tour Rs in Canada and USA. In 1930 he turned to consulting work in partnership with J. D. Rogers, former asst supt of motive power, Virginian Rs. He ret 1941. Became MILE 1918, president 1922–3. Vice president of SLS.
Engg V 183 5.4.1957 p 421; *The Locomotive* 15.8.1910 p 158 (portrait); *RG* 15.3.1957; 22.3.1957 (portrait); Smith, D. L., *Locos of the G & SWR* 1976; *Journal* ILE V 46 1956 p 592

WHITELEGG, Thomas

b (Manchester ?) 1836–7;
d Highgate, London, 30.3.1911 aged 74.
Loco, C & W and marine supt, LT & SR. Began career as engg pupil at Sharp, Stewart & Co, Manchester, later becoming a leading erector in that firm, erecting a loco exhibited at the Manchester Exhib of 1862. He worked for Neilson Reid & Co, Glasgow; Hamilton Windsor Ironworks Co, Garston, Liverpool (where his son R. H. W. (qv) was born) and where he gained experience in marine engg and design of pontoons and piers; and Ruston Proctor & Co, Lincoln. While there he worked on designs of locos being built for the GER. He then obtained employment in the drg office of the GER wks at Stratford, London, where he remained until 9.1879 when he was app loco C & W and marine supt, LT & SR, at Plaistow wks. He was the first LT & SR loco supt, because from its opening in 1854 until 1875 the line was worked by the contractors Peto, Brassey & Betts (qqv), and from 1875 until W's app rolling stock was hired from the GER. He introduced the highly successful o/c 4–4–2T type which became the mainstay of the LT & S passenger services. Ret 7.1910.
The Locomotive 15.8.1910 p 158 (portrait); *RG* 7.4.1911 p 354 (portrait); *The Times* 1.4.1911 p 1 col 1

WHITTON, John

b Foulby, nr Wakefield, (?).(?).1819;
d Mittagong, nr Sydney, NSW, 20.2.1898 aged 79.
Civil eng, NSW Rs. 1835 articled to William Billington, eng of Wakefield waterworks and of early Rs. W. helped him on surveys for parliamentary plans for Rs and for a ship canal from Liverpool to Manchester. About 1846 W. was engaged under Hawkshaw (qv) on parliamentary surveys and R work in Lancashire. 1848–9 acted as asst eng on const of E Lincolnshire R under John Fowler (qv) and was later engaged under Fowler on completing the Oxford, Worcester & Wolverhampton R and in 1851–6 on R const in Yorkshire and elsewhere. On 27.3.1856, on recommendation of president of the BOT, app chief eng of NSW Govt Rs, Australia, being given sole charge of surveys and const of Rs there, and also of loco and pw depts for 16 yrs. He insisted on the adoption of standard gauge throughout NSW. On his arrival in Sydney there were only 22 miles (35.4 km) of Rs in NSW. On his ret in 1890 there were over 2000 miles (3220 km) open. His greatest work was the carrying of the Great Western line over the Blue Mountains by the Lapstone zig-zag (1867) and the great Lithgow zig-zag (1869), including the Knapsack vdt, at 126ft (38.4m) the highest in NSW. The Lapstone zig-zag was by-passed in 1913 and the Lithgow in 1910, but the works remain as monuments to W's ability. Elected MICE 2.5.1854.
Min Proc ICE V 132 1897–8 pp 393–4; Bayley, William A., *Lapstone Zig Zag R NSW* 1972, and *Lithgow Zig Zag R NSW* 1973

WHITTY, Irwine John

b Kilrush, Co Clare, 18.6.1839;
d Bristol 22.2.1913 aged 73.
Eng of Darjeeling Himalayan R. Ed Queen's Coll, Cork. Served pupilage with P. R. Roddy on const of Cork & Limerick lines. 1863 joined staff of E India R and served for 16 yrs in its development. 1879 app chief eng for const of the Darjeeling Himalayan R, on completion of which he joined the staff of the Bengal-Nagpur R. Ret 1889 as executive eng. MICE 30.10.1877.
Min Proc ICE V 196 1914 p 369

WHYTE, Frederic A.

b (?) (?).(?).1865; d Tarrytown, NY,

(?).(?).1941 aged 75.
Inventor of the 'wheel-arrangement' system of classifying steam locos. Graduated at Franklin Academy 1884; Silbey Coll 1889. Worked as a draughtsman or mech eng for the Lake Shore & Michigan Southern, Baltimore & Ohio, Mexican Central, New York Central, and other RRs until 1910. About 1911 he became vice president of the Car Roof Co. He ret about 1936. He invented his wheel arrangement system in 1900.

WILKINSON, John Sheldon

b Spalding 22.5.1837;
d Manchester 23.6.1880 aged 43.
Eng of Cheshire Lines Rs. Ed St Alban's Gr Sch, and from 1854 King's Coll, London. In 12.1856 articled to W. M. Brydone, chief eng GNR. After pupilage continued on GNR, being engaged for 20 months on rebuilding the bridge over the Witham at Bardney on the loop line. W. then became a contractor's eng, in charge of const on the Aylesbury & Buckingham R. He was later asst eng on the GNR for 2 yrs; afterwards res eng on the Cheshire Lines. He then took up business in Manchester and built the W Cheshire R, completed in 1869, from Northwich to Helsby. In Spring 1870 he was app eng for the Chester & W Cheshire Jn R, opened 5.1875, including the terminus at Chester. In autumn 1871 he took charge of the works of the Ashburys, Stockport & Romiley lines, completed 1875. His last major work was the Manchester South District R, opened 1880. MICE 3.12.1867.
Min Proc ICE V 63 1880–1 p 320

WILLET, Archibald William

b Aberdeen 29.1.1858;
d Aberdeen 11.10.1942 aged 84.
Son of John W. Ed Aberdeen Gr Sch and Univs of Aberdeen and Edinburgh. Pupil of his f. 1881 joined LNWR under Francis Stevenson (qv) and was res eng on numerous LNWR works. 1912 succeeded G. R. Jebb as chief eng to Birmingham Canal Nav.
Journal ICE V 19 1942 p 203

WILLET, John

b Aitkenhead, Ayrshire, 6.2.1815;
d Aberdeen 15.8.1891 aged 76.

Civil eng on Scottish Rs. Ed Ayr Academy and Sch of Arts, Edinburgh. At 22 apprenticed to James Thomson, civil eng, Glasgow. Then entered office of Andrew Thomson, Glasgow, concerned with const of Rs. Engaged on Pollock & Govan R and other parts of later CR system. Assisted Thom of Greenock on const of town's waterworks. 1843 to Liverpool as asst to Locke and Errington (qqv), on Grand Junction R, Lancaster & Carlisle R, Harrogate R, LNWR Runcorn line to Liverpool, Birkenhead & Manchester, and Aberdeen R. 1845 app res eng on const of CR northwards from Carlisle. 1849 to Aberdeen as res eng, Aberdeen R, later amalg with Scottish Midland as the Scottish North Eastern which, in 1866, became part of the CR. Acted as chief eng and was retained by CR as eng on the completion of Denburn Valley R including the present jt stn at Aberdeen, on Dundee & Forfar and Newtyle branches, and other works. 1849–69 engaged on Deeside R and extns and on other lines in Aberdeenshire. After severing his connection with the CR he carried out several R works including the Brechin–Edzell line in Forfarshire. He m in 1854 and was survived by widow, 4 sons and 3 drs. MICE 7.12. 1852.
Min Proc ICE V 107 1891–2 p 414

WILSON, Lt Col George Robert Stewart, CBE

b Devizes, Wilts, 17.4.1896;
d London 20.3.1958 aged nearly 62.
Chief inspecting officer of Rs 1949–58. Ed Marlborough Coll, and Royal Military Academy, Woolwich. Served with REs in France and Macedonia in WW1. Later became instructor at the R Training Centre, Longmoor, Hants. Joined R Inspectorate at MoT 1935. Recalled to military service in WW2. 1940 resumed work with R Inspectorate and was app inspecting officer 1941. Became chief inspecting officer 1949. He investigated and reported on the double collision at Harrow, 8.10.1952. At the time of his death he was working on the report on the Lewisham accident, 4.12.1957. Visited USA and France to study safety methods in R operation. He advised the MoT on the system of automatic train

control adopted by BR, now known as Automatic Warning System. Awarded CBE 1953.
The Eng V 205 28.3.1958 p 467 (portrait)

WILSON, Henry Raynar

b (?) (?).(?).1862;
d London 19.4.1936 aged 73.
Signalling eng. Ed Derby. Began R career 1876 on MR in office of supt of the line. 1881 transferred to signal dept and became chief indoor asst to signal supt. 1889 app signal supt LYR. 1901 took up the British agency of the Hall Signal Co, USA. This system of automatic signalling was installed between Alne and Thirsk on the NER main line. He also introduced long-burning oil lamps for signals in 1903. As the business was not a success W. took up journalism and, though a special contributor on signalling and other R matters, he was recognised as an authority on various subjects. His books include: *R Signalling* (1900); *Mechanical Signalling; Power R Signalling; The Safety of British Rs* (1909); and *R Accidents from 1825 to 1924.*
Engg V 141 1.5.1936 p 477; *The Locomotive* 5.1936 p 165

WILSON, Robert

b Dunbar, E. Lothian, (?).(?).1803;
d Matlock 28.7.1882 aged 79.
Partner in firm of Nasmyth, Wilson & Co, Patricroft. Began as a marine eng. In 1832 he established a business in Edinburgh, but later moved to Manchester and in 1838 became mgr of the Bridgewater Foundry at Patricroft where Nasmyth (qv) gave birth to the steam hammer. The first of these was delivered to Low Moor Ironworks, Bradford, in 8.1843. In 1853 W., then eng at Low Moor, fitted it with a 'circular balanced valve'. In 1856, on the ret of James Nasmyth, W. returned to Patricroft and became a partner in the firm of Nasmyth, Wilson & Co, successors to Nasmyth, Gaskell & Co, mfrs of locos since 1839. (See Ahrons in *The Eng* V 129 19.3.1920 p 289). W. claimed to be the inventor of the screw propellor. MIME 1857.
Proc IME 1883 p 29

WILSON, William

b Alnwick, Northumb, 20.1.1822;
d W Kensington, London, 20.9.1898 aged 76.
Civil eng on various British Rs. Youngest son of George W., a proprietor of mail coaches between London and Edinburgh. At age 16 articled to John Bourne of Newcastle upon Tyne and became acquainted with George Stephenson. From Newcastle he went to London to work for Fox, Henderson & Co on the roof of Dover stn. Next, under John Fowler (qv), he worked on the MS & L and Oxford, Worcester & Wolverhampton R and Wolverhampton stn. W. then became associated with Fowler on const of the Victoria Stn–Pimlico R in London including the bridge over the Thames, 1859–60, also on Millwall docks, Hammersmith & City R, and W London Extn to Addison Road stn. He then acted for Sir Charles Fox (qv) and the contractors Peto & Betts on enlargement of Victoria Stn and widening of the Thames bridge, 1865–6. He also acted for Peto & Betts, Sir John Kelk and Waring on the Met R extn to Notting Hill and Brompton, the Met District R, and the Met R extn to Tower Hill, and for Kelk on the widening of the Met R from King's Cross to Farringdon Street. Among other works by W. were: Aylesbury & Buckingham R; Banbury & Cheltenham Direct R; Jerez R; Algeciras R, and Folkstone pier. He was twice m, first to Hannah Kirkby of Sheffield, second in 2.1857 to Flora M. E. Dawson of Cambridge. Elected MICE 1.5.1849.
Min Proc ICE V 135 1898–9 pp 361–2; *Engg* V 66 30.9.1898 p 440

WINANS, Ross

b Sussex County, NJ, USA, 17.10.1796;
d Baltimore, Md, 11.4.1877 aged 80.
Inventor and loco mfr. Became interested in Rs in 1828 while in Baltimore. 1829 went to England with Whistler, Knight and McNeill (qqv) to study Rs and locos. On his return he became eng on the Baltimore & Ohio RR (1829–30), assisting Peter Cooper (qv) with his *Tom Thumb* loco. As M of the firm of Gillingham & Winans, 1834, he took charge of Mount Clare shops of the B & O and devoted the next 25 yrs to

improving R machinery. He designed the first 8-wheeled passenger car in the world and is credited with the innovation of mounting a car on two bogies. In 1842–4 he built the 0–8–0 'Mud Digger' loco, and in 1848 the first of his 0–8–0 'camels' with wide fireboxes designed to burn anthracite, of which he built over 100 for the B & O. After criticism of his 'camel' design and loss of sales he retired from loco building in 1860. He built about 300 locos. In 1843 he declined to join Whistler in Russia to build rolling stock for the Moscow–St Petersburg R, but sent his sons Thomas De Kay W. (qv) and William. He was twice m, on 22.1.1820 to Julia De Kay of NJ (d 1850) and in 1854 to Elizabeth K. West of Baltimore. He had 4 sons and a dr.

DAB V 20 p 371; Reed, Brian, *Loco Profile* No 9 'Camels and Camelbacks' 1971; White, John H. Jr, *American Locos, an engg history 1830–80* 1968; *Engg* V 23 27.4.1877 p 334

WINANS, Thomas De Kay W.

b Vernon, NJ, (?).(?).1820;
d (?) (?).(?).1878 aged c 58.
Loco eng. Eldest son of Ross W. (qv). Partner with Joseph Harrison (qv) and Eastwick in const of rolling stock for Moscow–St Petersburg R, his designs following those of Ross W. On return from Russia W. assisted in design and const of two experimental passenger locos, *Centipede* 1855, the first 4–8–0, and *Celeste* c 1854, a high-speed 4–4–0, tested on the Reading RR.

White, John H. Jr, *op cit* above

WOLFE-BARRY, Kenneth Alfred, OBE

b London 16.3.1879;
d London 1.7.1936 aged 57.
Son of Sir John WB. (qv). Ed Winchester from 1892, and 1897–9 at Trinity Coll, Cambridge, where he studied engg. 1899–1903 articled to his f's firm, gaining experience in civil engg on various works including the GNR, Piccadilly & Brompton, and Whitechapel & Bow Rs. He then became a partner in his f's firm. He was consulting eng to the Bombay Port Trust, Aden Port Trust, Southern Punjab R, Darjeeling Himalayan R, Bengal–Nagpur R, Kowloon-Canton R, and the Tower Bridge, London; also many other works including docks. He devoted much time to the progress of Westminster Hospital. MICE; MIME 1920. In 1902 he m Helen Mary, dr of John Strain MICE, and they had 3 sons and 1 dr.

Journal ICE V 3 1935–6 p 610; Proc IME V 133 1936 p 543

WOLFE-BARRY, Sir John, KCB, LLD, FRS

b (?) Scotland, 7.12.1836;
d Chelsea, London, 22.1.1918 aged 81.
R civil eng and contractor. Son of Sir Charles Barry RA, architect of the Houses of Parliament. Ed Glenalmond Sch, Perthshire, and King's Coll, London. Trained as eng in shops of Lucas Bros. Then became pupil of John Hawkshaw (qv) on Charing Cross and Cannon Street stns, London, and the bridges over the Thames. 1867 started on his own. MICE 1868. As consulting eng he was associated with the Met Dist R, Ealing-Fulham; Lewes-East Grinstead; the 'Inner Circle', Mansion House–Aldgate and Whitechapel, and other London lines; Barry R; CR underground lines in Glasgow and the Central stn; Ballachulish branch of CR and the cantilever bridge over Loch Etive; Lanarkshire & Ayreshire extns. Besides R bridges over the Thames he was also responsible for the Tower Bridge, finished 1894, and the King Edward VII bridge, Kew, 1903. About middle 1880s the firm took up dock const. Built Barry and Tyne docks, Grangemouth dock extn, Surrey Commerical dock extn, Middlesbrough dock extn, Alexandra dock at Newport, and Immingham dock. Among foreign Rs and works were the Shanghai–Nanking; Bombay Port Trust; Durban harbour (with Charles Hartley). He presented a paper to the ICE on Charing Cross stn in 1868, and with Sir Benjamin Baker (qv) on the Met R, 1905. Pub *R Appliances* 1874–92; *Lectures on Rs and Locos* 1882; *The Tower Bridge* 1894. 1901–2 founded the Engg Standards Comm, later British Engg Standards Assoc. Under this, for example, the number of patterns of tramway rail were reduced from 70 to 9. WB. was interested in tech and scientific education; was chairman of the City & Guilds

of London Inst; and was associated with many other educational bodies. In 1874 m Rosalind Grace Rowsell. They had 4 sons and 3 drs. One son, Kenneth Alfred (qv) became senior partner in the firm.

Min Proc ICE V 206 1917–18 pp 350–7; *DNB* Supplement 1912–21 p 585; *The Eng* V 125 25.1.1918 pp 68–9 (portrait); *Engg* V 105 25.1.1918 pp 95–8 (portrait)

WOOD, Nicholas

b Ryton, Co Durham, 24.4.1795; d London 19.12.1865 aged 70.

Mining and civil eng, and early advocate of steam locos, and Rs. Trained as a colliery viewer (mgr) at Killingwirth colliery nr Newcastle where he met George Stephenson (qv) with whom he was associated in experiments with the safety lamp for mines and with locos. In 1822 he became involved in the controversy concerning stationary *v* loco engines, and in 1825 he pub *A practical treatise on Railroads and interior communication in general* (also 1831, 1838). In 1829 was app one of the judges at the Rainhill trials on the Liverpool & Manchester R. As a mining eng he was mineral adviser to the Durham Bishopric Estates, and to Lord Ravensworth, and was mgr of Hetton colliery and others and was consulted on mining matters by the govt. MIME 1858.

The Eng V 20 22.12.1865 p 415; V 21 12.1.1866 p 37; Proc IME 1866 p 15

WOODARD, William E.

b Utica, NY, 18.11.1873; d Forest Hills, NJ, 24.3.1942 aged 68.

Loco eng. Vice president of engg, Lima Loco Wks. Trained at Dickson Mfg Co, Scranton, Pa (merged with ALCO 1901). From 1915, together with Samuel G. Allen, chairman, and W. L. Reid, vice president of mfg, he reorganised the Lima Wks, transforming it from a small mfr of Shay Geared locos and light machinery into a great industrial works. His main contribution towards the development of 'Lima Super Power' locos was increased boiler capacity and higher steam pressure. His first high-horse-power 2–8–2 incorporating his principles was delivered to the NYC in 1922. It weighed barely 2 per cent more than the conventional NYC 2–8–2, but

gave 17 per cent more power. In the next 2 yrs 300 more similar engines were built. In 1925 he developed the first of what became known as the 'Super Power' locos. This was the first 2–8–4 to be built. The trailing truck, fitted with booster, carried a huge firebox with a grate area of 100 sq ft (9.29m²). Its success led to its acceptance as a new standard of high power loco design and it was followed in 1925 by the 2–10–4, in 1926 by the 4–8–4 and in 1927 by the 4–6–4 express passenger type. In 1925–9 70 'Super Power' 2–10–4s were built for the Texas & Pacific RR. The last of the 'Super Power' 2–8–4s was built for the Nickel Plate Road in 1949 and was the last Lima steam loco.

Atkins, C. P., and Reed, Brian, *Loco Profile* 31, 'Lima Super Power' 1973; Sinclair, Angus, *Development of the loco engine*, 1907, 1970; Bruce, Alfred W., *The steam loco in America* 1952

WOODHOUSE, Thomas Jackson

b Bedworth, Warwickshire, 9.12.1793; d Turin, Italy, 26.9.1855 aged 61.

Eng on Cromford & High Peak, Dublin & Kingstown Rs etc. Son of John W., civil eng, whose f was also a civil eng. Ed Towcester, Northants. After a period at sea he was trained as civil eng under his f, being engaged on the Grand Junction Canal, including Blisworth tunnel, then on the Worcester & Birmingham canal including Tardebigge tunnel (568yd), and the Gloucester & Berkeley canal. In 1825, with Josias Jessop (qv) he surveyed the R from Birmingham to Bristol. In 1826 he was app res eng under Jessop on the Cromford & High Peak R, opened 1830–1. In 1832 he was app eng of the Dublin & Kingstown R, the first R in Ireland. He was later app eng for Belfast Harbour Trust and for the R from Belfast to Lisburn. 1836 app res eng to the Midland Counties R for lines connecting Nottingham, Derby, Leicester and Rugby, completing the works in 1841. His bridge over the Trent, of 3 iron spans of 100ft (30.5m) was remarkable for its lightness and strength. In 1842 he surveyed the LNWR line from Leamington to Coventry. He then went to France with Brassey and Mackenzie (qqv) to build the Rhone-Marne canal. In 1843 he was app eng for a R linking Orleans, Tours and Bordeaux. Returned to England 1848 but was soon engaged by Brassey for the Prato–Pistoja and Turin–Novara Rs in Italy. In 9.1855 he suddenly became ill and d. MICE 1838.

Min Proc ICE V 16 1856–7 pp 150–4

WOODS, Edward

b London 28.4.1814;
d London 14.6.1903 aged 89.

Civil eng on Liverpool & Manchester R and in S America. After some training at Bristol he became asst to John Dixon (qv) on the Liverpool & Manchester R, being placed in charge of the section from Liverpool to Newton le Willows, including the tunnel from Edge Hill down to Liverpool Lime Street. In 1836 he succeeded Dixon as chief eng. After the L & M was amalgamated with the Grand Junction R in 1845 and LNWR in 1846 W. remained in charge of the L & M section until the end of 1852, including the const of Victoria and Waterloo tunnels, over 2 miles long, from Edge Hill down to the docks, and a large goods station at Waterloo dock. He also engineered the Patricroft–Clifton line, including Clifton Hall tunnel (op 1850) which collapsed in 1953. During his 18 yrs on the L & M, W. carried out important experiments on the wastage of steam at the Edge Hill winding engines, and in fuel consumption in locos. In 1853, in conjunction with W. P. Marshall, he carried out some experiments on LNWR locos, leading to a report on the use of coal instead of coke. In 1853 he set up as a consulting eng in London, and from 1854 he was connected with Rs in S America, including the Central Argentine; Copiapo extn, Santiago & Valparaiso and Coquimbo Rs in Chile; and the Mollendo–Arequipa and Peru Central. He also carried out, in 1851, a wrought iron pier 2400ft (731m) long, built on screw piles, at Pisco, Peru. MICE 7.4.1846 and president 1886–7. In 1840 he m Mary Goodman of Birmingham. They had 3 sons and 2 drs.

Min Proc ICE V 153 1902–3 p 342; *The Eng* V 95 19.6.1903 p 625; *The Times* 16.6.1903

WOOTTEN, John E.

b Philadelphia (?).(?).1822;
d (?) (?).(?).1898 aged c 76.

Loco eng, originator of the wide firebox. Apprenticed to Baldwin (qv) 1837. Worked there until 1845 when he joined the Reading RR to become chief asst to James Millholland (qv). Succeeded Millholland 1866 and was supt of motive power until 1871. After further promotions he became g mgr 1877 until he ret 1886. A prolific inventor; patented smoke stacks, steam gauge, car heater, and in 1877 the wide firebox to burn culm, or anthracite waste, a development of earlier designs by Dripps, Winans, Millholland and Colburn (qqv), to provide a large grate for the slow combustion. Its success led to its use on well over 3000 engines.

White, John H. Jr, *American locos, an engg history, 1830–80* 1968

WORSDELL, George

b Preston 21.5.1821;
d Lancaster (?).12.1912 aged 91.

Mech eng and mfr of R plant. Son of Thomas Clarke W. and bro of Nathaniel (qqv). In 1836–8 he accompanied his f to Germany to help with const of carriages for the Leipzig & Dresden R. After his return he worked for successive short periods at Euston (London & Birmingham R), New Cross (London & Croydon R) and Swindon (GWR). While in London he studied for a time under a civil eng. In 1841 he joined his f at the wks of the Hull & Selby R at Hull and while there, in addition to R work, he repaired the engines of the *Syrius,* the first steamship to cross the Atlantic. In 1845 he started on his own at the Dallam Forge at Warrington. Here he produced the first rolled bar iron in Lancashire. At the 1851 Exhibition he won a gold medal for the excellence of his iron and R plant. On 27.3.1851 he m Jane Bolton. Later he took a partner and this brought trouble to the wks which was forced to close in 1858. It later became Pearson & Knowles, associated with the Wigan Coal & Iron Co. Following a breakdown in health, in 1858 he went to Workington for a 2 year rest and on 25.5.1860 took up an app at Ashburys Carriage & Plant

Wks, Manchester, where he became g mgr. His health broke down again in 1863 and he went to join his elder bro Thomas at Birmingham until 1866 when he took over mgt of the Lancaster Wagon Co. Ret 1872, and spent his last 30 yrs in Lancaster.
Family records; *Railway News* 7.12.1912 p 1302

WORSDELL, Nathaniel

b London 10.10.1809;
d Birkenhead 24.7.1886 aged 76.
Inventor; carriage builder. First child of Thomas Clarke W. and bro of George (qqv). 1823 apprenticed with Jonathan Dunn, coach builder of Lancaster, with whom his f was working. In 1827 he and his f moved to Liverpool and established a coach building business, Worsdell & Son. They built the first carriages for the Liverpool & Manchester R and also, in 1829. the tender for the Stephensons' *Rocket*, and tenders for other locos. In 1836 he succeeded his f as supt of the carriage dept of the L & M at Edge Hill, Liverpool. In 1837 he invented an apparatus for picking up and depositing mail bags which was patented in 1838, but he never received any remuneration from it. He also designed a screw coupling (first invented by Henry Booth qv), but with a single right hand thread only. In 1838, shortly after his son Thomas William (qv) was born, he built the *Enterprise* coach for the L & M, consisting of three horse carriage bodies on a R truck, thereby establishing the form of the compartment coach which became universal in Britain and much of Europe. Also in 1838 he was app, in a consultative capacity, inspector of carriages on the Manchester & Leeds R. In 1843 he moved to the new Grand Junction wks at Crewe where he was in charge of the C & W dept. He played an important part in the development of the new town. After 37 yrs at Crewe he ret in 1880 and moved to Birkenhead where he d 6 yrs later. Like his f, W. was a Quaker, and was renowned for his integrity. It was said of him that he would speak the truth if he had to die for it (Mins of Hardshaw West Monthly Mtg, Soc of Friends, 30.3.1887). Of his 5 sons Thomas William and Wilson (qqv) became loco engs on the NER, Henry

worked on Indian Rs and Robert was also an eng on the NER. His dr Emily (b 23.5.1843) was the mother of Arthur Collinson (qv) of the NER.
From family records.

WORSDELL, Thomas Clarke

b Hayes, nr Bromley, Kent, 3.12.1788;
d Nantwich, Ches, 22.4.1862 aged 73.
Coach builder. Apprenticed with Howe & Shanks, Long Acre, London. In 1807, before the end of his apprenticeship, he m Elizabeth Taylor and they had 6 children of whom the first was Nathaniel (qv). In 1811 he moved to Preston, largely to recover his health, and there he joined the Soc of Friends, or Quakers. In 1813 he set up his own business in Blackhorse Street, Bolton, but after 10 yrs, as a result of a partnership, the business failed and in 1823 he returned to Preston where he became a partner of Edward Leese. There followed a period with Jonathan Dunn at Lancaster. In 1827 he and his son Nathaniel established a business, Worsdell & Son, coachbuilders, in Pontack Lane, Liverpool. Here he was introduced by James Cropper to George Stephenson for whom he built the tender for the *Rocket*, and tenders for other engines as well as carriages for the L & M from 1828. Stephenson stated that W. was 'the best coach builder he ever knew'. In 1836 he was app carriage builder to the Leipzig & Dresden R which opened on 7.4.1839. He then moved to Manchester to become carriage inspector on the Manchester & Leeds R. In 1840 he took up a similar app on the London & Birmingham R at Euston, London, and in 1841 on the Hull & Selby R at Hull, to be joined there by his son George (qv). Ret 1847 and went to live at Nantwich, Cheshire.
From family records; *RM* 10.1938 pp 235–6

WORSDELL, Thomas William

b Liverpool 14.1.1838; d Arnside, Westmorland, 28.6.1916 aged 78.
Loco eng, GER and NER. Son of Nathaniel W. (qv) and bro of Wilson (qv). Ed at the Quaker sch at Ackworth nr Pontefract from 1848, and at Queenwood Coll, Hampshire, from 1853. After leaving he spent a period in the LNWR

wks at Crewe, but left to serve an apprenticeship under his uncle Thomas W. at Birmingham. In 1858 he returned to Crewe and worked in the drg office under Ramsbottom (qv). In 1860 he became mgr of an engg wks in Birmingham, but left in 1865 to join the staff of the Pennsylvania RR. He soon became master mech at the Altoona loco shops where, in 7.1867, he was joined by his younger bro Wilson. They both returned to England in 1871, and T.W.W. was app mgr of Crewe wks, LNWR, under Webb (qv) who had just succeeded Ramsbottom as loco supt. In 1882 he was app loco supt of the GER at Stratford, London. While there he patented his 2-cyl compound loco in conjunction with A. von Borries (qv) of the Hanover State Rs. In 1884–5 11 compound 4–4–0s were built, with 7ft (2.134m) coupled wheels. They were similar in many details to his 2–4–0s of 1882–3. Neither of these types was a great success. His famous 0–6–0 type, of which 289 were built from 1883–1913, became LNER class J15. Forty 2–4–2Ts, known as the 'gobblers' because of their heavy coal consumption, were built from 1884–7. On 17 April 1885 he was app loco supt of the NER at Gateshead, taking up his duties on 1.9.1885. Here he continued to produce 2-cyl compound designs which this time functioned much better. He first produced a simple expansion 2–4–2T in 3.1886 of which 60 were built; many worked for over 50 yrs. He introduced a new system of loco classification under which these were class A. His first NER compound design was the C class 0–6–0 of 1886, on which he introduced the spacious side-window cab which was to become a standard feature of NER locos, probably influenced by his work in USA. At the same time he produced a similar, simple, 0–6–0, class C1. Similarly he built 51 compound 0–6–2Ts class B and 11 simples class B1. His compound 2–4–0 express engine was followed by the F class 4–4–0 of 1887, 10 compounds and 10 simples. In 1888 he produced his compound 4–2–2 express engine, class I, with 7ft (2.134m) wheels. His J class 4–2–2 of 1890 was a larger engine with 7ft 6in (2.286m) wheels, designed for the traffic following the opening of the Forth Bridge. For shunt-

ing he produced the E class 0–6–0T in 1886 which became LNER J71. An example of his compounding, NER 2–2–4T *Aerolite*, is preserved at the NRM, York. W. established a tradition of handsome loco designs which continued until the end of the NER. A prominent feature was the brass casing enclosing the Ramsbottom safety valves. In 9.1890 he resigned and was succeeded by his bro Wilson. He continued to act as consulting eng for the NER until 1893 when he ret and moved to Arnside in the southern Lake District where he spent his final years. MIME 1874; MICE 1884.

The Eng V 122 7.7.1916 p 15 (portrait); Proc IME 10.1916 pp 569–70

WORSDELL, Wilson

b Crewe 7.9.1850; d Ascot 14.4.1920 aged 70.

NER loco eng. Son of Nathaniel W. (qv) and bro of T.W.W. (qv). Ed at the Quaker sch at Ackworth nr Pontefract. At age 16 returned to Crewe and spent 6 months in the drg office of the LNWR. In 7.1867 he joined his bro Thomas William at Altoona, Pa, and became a pupil in the loco shops of the PRR under Dr E. Williams, then supt of motive power and later one of the members of the firm of Burnham, Williams & Co which became part of the Baldwin loco wks. In 1871 W. returned to England with his bro and re-entered the loco dept of the LNWR at Crewe, to work in the erecting shops and drg office. In 1872 he was app asst foreman in the running sheds at Stafford. In 1876 he was promoted to foreman at Bushbury, and in 1877 he was in charge at Chester. In 1883 he was app asst mech eng on the NER at Gateshead under Alexander McDonnell (qv), then loco supt. In 1884 McDonnell was forced to resign and on 17.4.1885 Thos W. Worsdell was app loco supt on the NER and for the next 4 yrs W. served under him. In 9.1890 T.W.W. ret and Wilson W. became loco supt. His 20 yrs in this office covered a most interesting period in NER loco history when train loads were increasing and engines of ever greater power were needed. W. was the first in England to introduce the 4–6–0 for passenger work, in 1899. These engines, class S, with

6ft 1in (1.854m) wheels, were followed in 1900 by class S1 with 6ft 8in (2.032m) wheels. Other notable passenger engines designed under W. were the 4-4-0s of class M in 1892 and class R in 1899, and R1 in 1908; 4-4-2s of class V in 1903 and V1 in 1910. His goods engines included the T and T1 class 0-8-0, first introduced in 1901, and various classes of 0-6-0. These types were the last pre-grouping steam engines to operate on British Railways. Among his tank engines were the O class 0-4-4 for local passenger work, the U class 0-6-2, the W or 'Whitby' class 4-6-2 and the heavy 4-8-0 goods. Most of his engines were of good design, both mechanically and aesthetically, and gave many years of useful service. They were distinguished by the large side-window cab, continued from T.W.W.'s designs. It was during W's career that the old North Road wks at Darlington were considerably developed, gradually gaining ascendancy over Gateshead in the const of new locos. W. was outstanding in his ability to delegate work, to his chief asst Vincent Raven and his chief draughtsman W. M. Smith (qqv), thereby enabling himself to obtain a more comprehensive picture of the loco dept. So strong was Smith's influence that in 1898 he was able to introduce his system of compounding in a 4-4-0 (on which the MR compounds of Johnson and Deeley (qqv) were based) and in 1906 in two 4-cyl 4-4-2s. The freedom W. gave to his assistants was an indication of his strength and confidence. It was under W. that the Tyneside electrification work was undertaken. Electric trains began running on 29.3.1904, a week before the LYR Liverpool–Southport line. W. also took an active part in C & W work on the NER. MIME 1894, and for many yrs M of the Council. Also a JP. He took great interest in the welfare of staff and workers and was well liked. Ret 31.5.1910 after 27 yrs with the NER. His death occurred suddenly at Ascot, Berkshire.

Engg V 109 23.4.1920 p 533 (portrait); *The Eng* V 129 23.4.1920 p 402; Hoole, K., *North Road Loco Wks, Darlington* 1967; MacLean, J. S., *The Locos of the NER* nd; Nock, O. S., *Locos of the NER* 1954

WORTHINGTON, Edgar

b Lancaster (?).(?).1856; d London 23.1.1934 aged 77.
Civil and mech eng. Son of S.B.W. and bro of W.B.W. (qqv). Tech ed at Owen's Coll, Manchester; later grad at Manchester Univ. 1875–8 apprenticed under Webb at Crewe, LNWR. Later emp on erection of machinery at Holyhead docks. 1880 engaged on erection of LNWR engine shed at Colwick, Nottingham. After 1 yr as wks mgr, Crewe, he went to the Altoona Wks of the PRR and later moved to the Rhode Island wks, Providence, as leading draughtsman. He made many valuable contributions to the US tech press. Returned to England 1883 and after a short time as asst mgr, Crewe, in 1885 he was app chief asst eng at Beyer, Peacock & Co Ltd, Manchester. MIME 1888; also MICE. 1898–1920 he was sec of the IME during which period membership increased from 2500 to 7500.
Proc IME V 126 3 1934 p 482; *The Locomotive* 15.2.1934 p 47

WORTHINGTON, Samuel Barton

b Stockport 14.12.1820; d Bowdon, Cheshire, 8.2.1915 aged 94.
LNWR civil eng. In 9.1836 he was articled for 6 yrs to Joseph Locke (qv), first on const of the Grand Jn R. Engaged on surveys for many of the English and Scottish Rs for which Locke was eng, including London–Southampton; Glasgow–Greenock; Lancaster & Preston Jn; Sheffield & Manchester; Shrewsbury & Wolverhampton; Stone & Rugeley, and also on the Preston & Wyre. In 1840–3 went with Locke to France to help in const of the Paris & Rouen R and remained as res eng from the opening on 1.5.1843 until 6.1844 when Locke recalled him to England to be res eng on the S half of the Lancaster & Carlisle R. On its opening in 1846 he became eng to the company, in charge of the line and rolling stock. In 1850 the Lancaster & Preston Jn R was placed under his charge and in 1854 he was app eng to the Carlisle Jt Stn Comm. When the Lancaster & Carlisle was leased to the LNWR in 1859 William Baker (qv) was app eng for new and Parliamentary

works and W. was placed in charge of
the lines from Carlisle to the Liverpool
& Manchester line. In 11.1862 his div
was extended to include all lines N of
Crewe except the Cromford & High
Peak R and his hq was moved from
Lancaster to Manchester where he re-
mained eng of the LNWR N div until
his ret in 6.1886. From then until 1896
he practised as a consulting eng, devot-
ing much of his time to the City of
Manchester. MICE 1861; and MIME.
Min Proc ICE V 200 1915 pp 466–8;
The Eng V 119 12.2.1915 p 170; *Engg*
V 99 12.2.1915

WORTHINGTON, William Barton

b Lancaster 8.7.1854; d Bushey Heath,
Middlesex, 29.12.1939 aged 85.
Civil eng, LNWR, LYR. Ed at Lancaster
and at Owen's Coll, Manchester, and
grad B Sc in Univ of London. 1873
became articled pupil to his f, Samuel
Barton W. (qv) and in 1875 joined the
staff of Blyth & Cunningham, Edinburgh,
with whom he was engaged on works
for the CR and on the reconst of the
jt stn at Carlisle. 1876 app res eng
under William Baker (qv) for new works
on the LNWR in S Lancashire, including widening the Liverpool & Manchester
R from Chat Moss to Manchester and
the const of Manchester Exchange stn,
op 1884. In 1883 he became asst to his
f whom he succeeded in 1886 as dist and
div eng of the N div of the LNWR.
In 1890 he joined the LYR as asst eng
and on 7.4.1897 he succeeded William
Hunt (qv) as chief eng. On the LYR he
was responsible for the Kirkham–Blackpool direct line, extn of Manchester
Victoria stn and new Collyhurst lines,
Bolton stn; and the Crofton–Shafton and
Horbury–Crigglestone lines nr Wakefield.
In 1905 he moved to the MR as chief
eng until his ret in 1915 after which he
practised as a consulting eng in London.
In 1883 he m Lilian Broadfield Hughes
(d 1937). In 1923 his services to civil
engg were recognised by Manchester
Univ by the award of D Sc. He was
MICE; MIME 1897.
Journal ICE V 13.2.1940 p 355; *The
Eng* V 169 5.1.1940 p 17; *Engg* V 149
5.1.1940 p 19; Proc IME V 143 1940
p 144

WRIGHT, Benjamin

b Wetherfield, Conn, USA, 10.10.1770;
d New York City 24.8.1842 aged 71.
Canal and early R eng. Began canal
engg in 1792 and became chief eng of
the Erie canal, begun 1816 and completed 1825–7. Many early American
engs were trained under him, including
John B. Jervis (qv). Also eng for the
Delaware & Hudson canal and, from
1828–31, of the Chesapeake & Ohio,
and of the St Lawrence canal in 1823.
He was consulting eng for surveys for
the New York & Erie RR; Harlem RR,
NY; and RRs in Virginia, Illinois and
Cuba. On 27.9.1798 he m Puilomela
Waterman of Plymouth, Conn. They
had 9 children. His son Benjamin H.
W. became a civil eng and completed
several projects reported on by his f.
DAB V 20 p 543

WRIGHT, Major Frederick George

b (?) (?).(?).1862; d Swindon 7.4.1938
aged 75.
Designer of GWR loco sheds and
equipment. Apprenticed at GWR sheds
at Gloucester, Bristol and Swindon.
Later became loco draughtsman at
Swindon and in 1892 chief draughtsman.
Responsible for much design work on
many locos including Dean 4-2-2s. 1896
became asst loco wks mgr, Swindon.
1903 asst to Churchward (qv). His most
important work was in the standardisation of running sheds including the design
of Old Oak Common shed, London. He
also designed over 20 new loco depots
and devoted much attention to cranes
and hydraulic plant. MIME 1897.
Proc IME V 138 1938 p 350.

WRIGHT, William Barton
See BARTON WRIGHT

WURMB, Carl

b Neumarkt, nr Wels, Austria, 8.9.1850;
d Vienna 31.1.1907 aged 56.
Eng of Austrian Rs. Studied at Zurich
Polytechnic. After experience on the
Südbahn, Salzkammergutlokalbahn, and
Arlberg R he was app general insp of
light Rs to the Min of Trade in 1894.
1901 app section head and Imperial and
Royal Director for const of Rs in the R
Ministry, and was responsible for const

on many Austrian alpine lines including the Tauern, Phyrn, and Karawanken. Following criticism of the high cost of the Tauern R in 1905 W. resigned. Shortly after this the Tech High Sch in Vienna conferred upon him an hon doctorate. After his death a statue of him was erected in Salzburg.
Röll, Schneider, Ascanio, *Rs through the Mountains of Europe* 1967

YATES, Henry

b Walton-le-Dale, Preston, 28.10.1820; d Brantford, Ontario, 22.7.1894 aged 73. Loco eng. Apprenticed at Nasmyth, Gaskell & Co, Patricroft nr Manchester. He then went to France to assist in const of Paris–Rouen R. Returned to England 1846 and was emp in loco wks of LSWR to superintend const of locos and rolling stock. 1853 engaged for 10 yrs as chief loco supt on Great Western R of Canada. In 1857 he completed the Buffalo & Lake Huron R, becoming chief mech supt and eng. 1862 became chief contractor for maintenance of pw and whole of works between Buffalo and Goderich. In 1863, when Sir Edward Watkin (qv) became president of the Grand Trunk R, Y. was app chief eng of the whole R until 1866. He was eng and contractor for works for the GTR again 1880–6. He also surveyed and built the Michigan Air Line R. In 1869 he entered into partnership with John H.

Stratford for supplying R materials. Became MIME 1878. Also M of Canadian Soc CE.
Proc IME 1894 pp 466–7

YOLLAND, Col William, CB, FRS

b (?) (?).(?).1810; d Atherstone, Warwickshire, 3.9.1885 aged 75.
Inspecting officer of Rs in GB. Trained in Royal Academy, Woolwich. Obtained commission in REs 1828. Became Lt Col 1855; Brevet Col 1858. After being emp in Canada, in 1835 he was emp at the Ordnance Survey, and he also made astronomical observations. In 1854 he was app one of the inspectors of Rs for the BOT. In this position he inspected many new R works and prepared numerous reports on R accidents.
The Eng V 60 11.9.1885 p 206

YORKE, Lt Col Sir H. Arthur

b (?) 3.6.1848; d London 10.12.1930 aged 81.
Chief inspecting officer of British Rs. Bro of Earl of Hardwicke. Ed Charterhouse and Sandhurst. Served in Afghan war 1879–80. Nile expedition 1884–5. 1886 to Woolwich and to REs. After service in the East he was app Insp of Rs for the BOT 1891. 1900 Chief Insp Officer. Ret 1913. Was dir of GWR and formerly of GTR of Canada. CB 1904. Kt Cr 1913.
The Locomotive 15.1.1931 p 34

INDEX

America, *See* Canadian; USA; South America

Australian Rs, 50, 64, 73, 80, 113, 187, 237

Austrian Rs, 7, 38, 39, 91, 92, 94, 107, 140, 145, 183, 190

Baltimore & Ohio RR, 136, 137, 138, 143, 145, 240

Belfast & Northern Counties R, 150, 205

Belgian Rs, 25, 229

Birmingham & Gloucester R, 146, 165

Bristol & Exeter R, 9, 187

Caledonian R, 16, 38, 55, 70, 74, 77, 83, 96-7, 136, 148, 149, 159, 173, 194, 207, 221-2, 238

Cambrian Rs, 17, 22, 173

Canadian Pacific R, 25, 81, 114, 115, 129, 180, 188, 196, 204

Canadian Rs, 81, 102, 166, 188, 204, 212, 215-16, 247; *See also* Grand Trunk R

Ceylon Rs, 78, 80

Cheshire Lines Committee, 238

Chinese Rs, 50, 161

County Donegal Rs, 141

Cromford & High Peak R, 128, 241

Darjeeling Himalayan R, 237

Eastern Counties R, 9, 37, 95, 120; *See also* Great Eastern R

East Lancashire R, 49, 155, 171

East London R, 43, 46, 108, 111, 229

Egyptian Rs, 218

Festiniog R, 77, 197

French Rs, 11, 21, 38, 44-5, 50-1, 52, 65, 71, 72, 74, 105, 138, 191, 194, 225

Furness R, 43, 146, 172, 205

German Rs, 90, 112, 136, 140, 226, 227, 232-3

Glasgow & South Western R, 33, 70-1, 130, 151, 194, 205-6, 236-7

Grand Junction R, 11, 44-5, 74, 121, 142, 148

Grand Trunk R, Canada, 38, 102, 127, 132, 229, 247

Great Central R, (*See* MS & L), 20, 78, 169, 173, 185, 190-1, 207, 230-1

Great Eastern R, 8, 39, 41, 113-14, 115-16, 157, 166, 193-4; *See also* Eastern Counties R

Great Northern R, 21, 27, 38, 40, 45, 47, 61, 88-9, 99-100, 110, 124-5, 129, 152, 171, 186-7, 206-7, 209, 210, 238

Great Northern R (Ireland), 93, 167

Great Northern / London & North Western

Jt, 88-9, 110

Great North of Scotland R, 33, 52, 58, 92, 151, 173

Great Southern & Western R, 16, 54, 124, 147, 157, 232

Great Western R, 13-15, 19, 20-1, 27, 39, 42, 51-2, 53, 54-5, 64, 65, 79, 84, 88, 94-5, 97, 101, 108, 109, 115, 123-4, 132, 137, 148, 151, 153, 160, 167, 171, 181, 184, 191, 207, 217, 246

Highland R, 70-1, 130, 141, 158, 163, 169, 195, 208

Hull & Barnsley R, 27, 206

Hull & Selby R, 97-8, 229

Indian Rs, 23, 27, 29, 32, 38, 41, 78, 91, 145-6, 167, 170, 195, 219, 237

Irish Rs (general), 80

Italian Rs, 49

Japanese Rs, 196

Lancashire & Yorkshire R, 9, 16-17, 22-3, 29-30, 32, 43, 59, 63, 79, 80-1, 84, 91, 96, 106-7, 108-9, 119, 120-1, 122, 123, 127, 155-6, 165, 176, 177, 182, 201, 207, 215, 231, 246

Lancashire, Derbyshire & East Coast R, 20, 214

Leeds & Selby R, 169-70, 229

Leek & Manifold Valley Light R, 48

Liverpool & Manchester R, 11, 34, 37, 44, 67, 74, 79, 84, 125-6, 132-3, 142, 181, 200-1, 242, 243

Liverpool Overhead R, 58, 162

London & North Eastern R, 99-100, 125, 164, 170, 198, 214, 233-4

London & Birmingham R, 46-7, 202

London & North Western R and constituents, 11, 16, 19, 24, 37-8, 44-5, 56-7, 58, 59, 79, 97, 113, 121-2, 126, 146, 149, 159, 175, 201, 202, 204, 207, 217, 218, 225, 231, 232, 234, 238, 242, 245-6

London & South Western R, 7, 8, 24, 28, 38, 48, 69-70, 74, 89-90, 95, 166, 213, 221-2

London, Brighton & South Coast R, 20, 21, 30-1, 33, 46, 59, 89, 97-8, 99, 133-4, 152-3, 160, 177, 208

London, Chatham & Dover R, 20, 27, 82, 134, 154, 212, 219-20

London, Midland & Scottish R, 29-30, 76, 85-6, 121, 125, 139-40, 163-4, 165, 180, 198-9, 231

London, Tilbury & Southend R, 39, 236, 237

London Underground Rs, 9-10, 98

Manchester & Birmingham R, 44, 175
Manchester, Sheffield & Lincolnshire R (formerly Sheffield, Ashton & Manchester, *see also* GCR), 13, 39, 86, 123, 126, 168, 169-70, 173, 188-9, 209, 225
Maryport & Carlisle R, 9, 40
Mersey R, 87
Metropolitan and Metropolitan District Rs, 10, 18, 82, 86, 98, 111, 190, 197, 216, 230-1, 239, 240
Midland R, 13, 17-18, 23-4, 39, 41, 60, 65, 85, 119-20, 129-30, 133-4, 146-7, 153, 180, 190-1, 201, 219, 221, 228
Midland & Great Northern Jt R, 41, 152
Midland Great Western R, 174

Netherlands Rs, 56
Newfoundland R, 81, 179-80
New Zealand Rs, 80
Norfolk & Western RR, 150
North British R, 16, 35, 40, 50, 69-70, 82-3, 105, 117, 123, 124, 180-1, 235
North Eastern R, 17-18, 26, 31, 35, 41, 48, 55, 62-3, 77, 81-2, 92-3, 104-5, 106, 115, 119-20, 138, 147, 164, 177-8, 196, 198, 202, 210, 213, 214, 233, 243-5; *See also* Stockton & Darlington R
North London R, 19, 168, 174
North Staffordshire R, 7, 59, 67-8, 79, 84, 117, 143, 209
North Western R (MR), 58

Oldham, Ashton & Guide Bridge R, 32

Pennsylvania RR, 40, 69, 107-8, 144-5, 214, 225

Ravenglass & Eskdale R, 99
Rhymney R, 146
Romney, Hythe & Dymchurch R, 99
Russian Rs, 91, 102, 143, 225

Severn & Wye R, 132
Severn Valley R, 19, 39
Signalling, 77, 84, 119, 189, 212, 220, 239
Solway Jn R, 43
South African Rs, 87, 156, 231
South American Rs, 27, 43, 47, 61, 68, 101, 141, 156, 235, 242
South Carolina RR, 12
South Eastern R, 21-2, 33, 61, 62, 101, 154-5, 205-6, 210, 230
South Eastern & Chatham R, 73, 115, 213, 227-8
Southern Pacific RR (inc Central Pacific), 122, 131, 159
Southern R, 45, 73, 154-5, 160
Spanish Rs, 101, 126
Stockton & Darlington R, 35-6, 62, 67, 103, 104, 170, 200-2; *See also* North Eastern R
Stratford & Midland Jn R, 27
Swedish Rs, 144
Swiss Rs, 7, 25, 26, 33, 34, 36, 38, 40, 57, 74, 78, 92, 119, 136, 142, 161, 163, 164, 182, 183, 189, 190, 208, 225

Taff Vale R, 38, 48, 181-2, 216

USA RRs (general), 40, 49, 54, 63, 68, 71, 77, 79-80, 83, 101, 105-6, 107, 114, 126, 127, 132, 138, 143, 144, 149, 155, 158, 159, 161, 165, 185, 186, 198, 203, 211, 220, 222-4, 236

West Lancashire R, 43